DICTIONARY OF
MENTAL HANDICAP

DICTIONARY OF MENTAL HANDICAP

Mary P Lindsey

London and New York

First published in 1989
Reprinted in 1990
by Routledge
11 New Fetter Lane, London EC4P 4EE
29 West 35th Street, New York NY 10001

Disc conversion by Columns Typesetters of Reading
Printed in Great Britian by T.J. Press (Padstow) Ltd, Cornwall

British Library Cataloguing in Publication Data

Lindsey, Mary P. *1947-*
  Dictionary of mental handicap
  1. Mentally handicapped persons
  I. Title
  362.3

ISBN 0–415–02810–8

PREFACE

The major shift from hospital care to community care for mentally handicapped people has led to the involvement of many new professional and non-professional staff. Each profession and discipline has its own terminology and, although the cause of the mental handicap may be medical, the subsequent interventions may be sociological, paramedical, psychological, educational or psychiatric. This book is an attempt to demystify the terms so that they can be more readily understood by lay people, unqualified staff and staff from the same or other disciplines. The language has been kept as simple as possible but, to prevent lengthy explanations, a system of cross-referencing has been used. Words which are in italics are an entry in their own right and, by looking them up, either a definition or more information will be obtained.

References have been supplied for readers who wish to find out more about a subject. Many of these are from professional journals and it may be necessary to contact someone in that profession in order to obtain the article.

Entries have been selected through the process of reading a broad selection of literature on mental handicap and by selecting those terms which are most commonly used and which are least likely to be understood. The author is in practice in this speciality and is only too well aware of the problems met by many staff and families when they encounter the 'professionals' and the jargon they use.

ACKNOWLEDGEMENTS

This book would not have been possible without the computing skills, tolerance and fortitude of my husband Paul who has so laboriously and painstakingly typed, retyped and rearranged the text on his word processor. We both would like to thank Kim and Shelley who have had to live through their parents' preoccupation.

Our thanks are also due to friends and colleagues who have read the manuscript or helped with the computing and have provided useful comments and ideas. We are particularly grateful to Dr. David James, Keith Garwood and Dr. Paul Robinson.

A

AA
= *Achievement Age.*

AAMD
= *American Association on Mental Deficiency.*

Abasia
Inability to walk due to poor co-ordination.

ABC analysis
A process used in *behaviour modification* to analyse a behaviour which is a target for intervention (*behaviour analysis*). The client is observed and a careful record is kept of the *antecedents* (A), the defined behaviour (B) and the consequences (C). The ABC analysis provides the information needed to develop a programme and monitor its effect.

Abderite
An obsolete term meaning 'stupid person' derived from the town of Abderite in Thrace whose inhabitants, according to Greek legend, were less intelligent than normal.

Abductors / abduction
The abductor muscles of a joint move the limbs away from the mid-line of the body (abduction). They may be tightened by *cerebral palsy* so that the limbs are pulled outward at that point.

Abetalipoproteinaemia
= *Bassen-Kornzweig syndrome.*

Abortion
The separation and expulsion of the contents of the pregnant uterus before the 28th week of pregnancy. One of the causes of spontaneous abortion is an abnormality of the fetus. Examination of spontaneously aborted fetuses has shown that 20–40% have abnormal chromosomes.

Therapeutic abortion is the medical termination of pregnancy. In the U.K. it may be carried out under the Abortion Act 1968 if there is a substantial risk that if the child were born it would suffer from such physical or mental abnormalities as to be seriously handicapped. Two registered medical practitioners must agree that this is the case. The likelihood of a suspected abnormality may be established following *amniocentesis* or *chorion biopsy*. There are other grounds for therapeutic abortion relating to the mental or physical health of the mother or her other children.

The fact that a pregnant woman is mentally handicapped is not considered to be a reason, in itself, for carrying out an abortion. There must be grounds as specified under the Abortion Act.

In the U.S.A. in 1973 the Supreme Court stipulated that the only legal restriction to be imposed on abortions in the first three months of pregnancy was that the procedure must be performed by, or under the direction of, a licensed physician. Different states define the indications for therapeutic abortion using various criteria. The common ones are risk to the physical or mental integrity of the child; risk to the physical or mental health of the mother; effects on the existing family; rape or incest.

ABORTION ACT (1968) London: HMSO.

Absence seizures
A type of *epilepsy* which begins in childhood. The onset is usually abrupt with 20 or more daily attacks. There is no warning of an attack which is characterized by a brief loss of consciousness without the person going limp. There is immobility during the attack but a full and immediate recovery afterwards. These rarely last more than 10

seconds and usually there is no memory of the loss of consciousness. Minor movements such as lip smacking or twitching of the eyelids or face may occur. The person may also have *grand-mal convulsions*. The *electroencephalogram* tracing may be characteristic with spikes and waves at a frequency of 3 cycles per second and this confirms the diagnosis. Certain *anticonvulsant* drugs (*ethosuximide* and *sodium valproate*) are particularly indicated for this type of epilepsy. Absence seizures may also be called petit-mal, but as this term is also often used to describe other types of seizures it is best avoided.

DALBY, M.A. (1969) Epilepsy and 3 per second spike and wave rhythms. Acta Neurol. Scand. Suppl., 40:45
SATO, S. et al (1976) Prognostic factors in absence seizures. Neurology, 26:788–796.

Absence status

A state of continuous *absence seizures* in which the person appears to be confused. Untreated it may last from several hours to several days. It almost always occurs in people with existing brain abnormality, mental handicap and other types of *epilepsy*.

BRETT, E.M. (1966) Minor epileptic status. J. Neurol. Sci., 3:52.
NEIDERMEYER, E. & KHALIFEH, R. (1965) Petit mal status ('spike-wave stupor'). Epilepsia (Amst.), 6:250–262.

Abstract thinking / Abstract operational stage of intellectual development

The ability to form concepts and ideas and to theorize and hypothesize. The abstract operational stage of intellectual development normally begins at about the age of 11 years. Severely and profoundly mentally handicapped people usually have difficulties in abstract thinking and remain at the level of concrete thinking.

Acalculia

An inability to carry out arithmetical oper-

ations when abilities in other areas suggest that this should be possible. It is usually associated with damage to the parietal lobe of the brain. It is sometimes associated with disturbances of speech.

Acathisia

= *akathisia*.

Accessory auricles

= *preauricular skin tags*.

Accreditation Council for Services for Mentally Retarded and other Developmentally Disabled Persons

An organization in the U.S.A. that publishes detailed guidelines for the public accreditation of services. Accreditation involves the completion of a questionnaire by the staff, followed by a site survey to observe whether the facility and its programs are relevant to the needs of the clients. Accreditation may be granted or alternatively a report is supplied which indicates how standards can be improved to a satisfactory level. The Commission on Accreditation of Rehabilitation Facilities has also produced an accreditation manual.

ACCREDITATION COUNCIL FOR SERVICES FOR MENTALLY RETARDED AND OTHER DEVELOPMENTALLY DISABLED PERSONS (1983) Standards for Services for Developmentally Disabled Individuals (2nd edit.). Washington D.C.: ACMRDD.
COMMISSION ON ACCREDITATION OF REHABILITATION FACILITIES (CARF) (1978) Standards Manual for Rehabilitation Facilities. Chicago: CARF.
JOINT COMMISSION ON ACCREDITATION OF HOSPITALS (1973) Standards for Community Agencies Serving Persons with Mental Retardation and other Developmental Disabilities. Chicago. Joint Commission on Accreditation of Hospitals.

Achievement Age

The age of achievement is measured by standardized achievement tests which are educationally based. It can then be compared with the chronological age of the child to give an achievement quotient. The ratio between the achievement quotient and the *intelligence quotient* is used to derive an accomplishment quotient. These measures are used in the U.S.A. but not in the U.K.

JASTAK, J. & BIJOU, S. (1965) Wide Range Achievement Test (2nd edit.). New York: Psychological Corporation.

Achondroplasia
A common cause of restricted growth in which the limbs are short while the trunk and head are of relatively normal proportions. The majority of people with this condition are of normal intelligence and opinions differ as to whether or not there is an increased incidence of mental handicap. *Hydrocephalus* may be caused by an abnormally small opening (foramen magnum) in the skull where the brain joins the spinal cord. Achondroplasia is inherited in a dominant manner (*dominant inheritance*).

COHEN, M.E. et al (1967) Neurological abnormalities in achondroplastic children. J. Pediatr., 71:367.
ROGERS, J.G. et al (1979) IQ measurements in children with skeletal dysplasia. Pediatrics, 63:894.

ACMRDD
= *Accreditation Council for Services for Mentally Retarded and other Developmentally Disabled Persons.*

Aconuresis
= *enuresis.*

Acoustic impedance testing
A screening procedure used to assess suspected hearing problems. An instrument known as an acoustic impedance bridge measures pressure relationships at the eardrum and also the middle ear function. This requires minimal co-operation and is useful where middle ear problems are suspected and require further investigation.

ACPS syndrome
= *Carpenter's syndrome.*

Acquired Immune Deficiency Syndrome
Infants and children with this disease often have signs that the brain is affected. There can be loss of developmental milestones, floppiness of muscles, *epilepsy* and a small head. Sometimes other viral diseases are also found to be present including *cytomegalic inclusion disease* and *toxoplasmosis.*

SHAW, G.M. et al (1985) HTLV-III infection in brains of children and adults with AIDS encephalopathy. Science, 227:177.

Acrocephalopolysyndactyly
= *Carpenter's syndrome.*

Acrocephalosyndactyly
A combination of *acrocephaly* and *syndactyly* as occurs in *Apert's syndrome* (Types I and II), *Chotzen's syndrome* (Type III) and *Pfeiffer's syndrome* (Type VI).

Acrocephaly
An abnormal skull shape. The skull is taller than usual and this is caused by some of the bones of the skull fusing together too early in development (*craniostenosis*). The forehead is high, wide and flat and the back of the head may also be flattened. It is nearly always associated with a malformed face including wide-spaced protruding eyes. Acrocephaly may occur in isolation but is usually one of a number of abnormalities which are evident at birth. It is a feature of *Apert's syndrome, Carpenter's syndrome, Chotzen's syndrome, Pfeiffer's syndrome* and *Crouzon's syndrome* which are usually associated with mental handicap.

Acromicria
A medical term for small extremities (hands and feet). It is a feature of *Down's syndrome* and *Prader-Willi syndrome* both of which are associated with mental handicap.

ACTH
= *adrenocorticotrophic hormone.*

Adaptive behaviour
The effectiveness with which the individual copes with the natural and social demands of his or her environment. The *DSM III* definition of mental retardation includes a deficiency or impairment in adaptive behaviour (taking the person's age into account).

Adaptive Behavior Scale
This scale is designed to provide a quantitative description of the *adaptive behaviour* of a mentally retarded person. This is thought to be a separate dimension from measured intelligence. The scale is in two parts and the first part rates development levels in ten areas including language, independence and socialization. The second part rates maladaptive behaviours such as *hyperactivity*, violence and destructiveness, *stereotypies* and anti-social behaviour. A profile of skills and behaviour problems can then be constructed for each individual but the scoring system is complex and training is needed to use the scale effectively. The scores are translated into percentiles which can be presented as a visual profile showing areas of relative strength and weakness. The scale can be used for assessment, *goal planning* and evaluation and is standardized on American institutionalized mentally retarded people.

FOGELMAN, C.J. (1975) AAMD Adaptive Behavior Scale Manual. Washington D.C.: American Association on Mental Deficiency.
MACDONALD, L. & BARTON, L.E. (1986) Measuring severity of behavior: a revision of Part II of the Adaptive Behavior Scale. Am. J. Ment. Defic., 90: 418–424.
NIHIRA, K. et al (1974) AAMD Adaptive Behavior Scale, Revision. Washington: American Association on Mental Deficiency.

Adaptive Functioning Index
Checklists used with adolescents and young adults who are mentally handicapped. They are used for assessment, target setting and evaluation. There are three checklists: social education test (reading, writing, numeracy, time, money etc.), vocational checklist (work skills and habits etc.) and residential checklist (personal habits, community awareness etc.). The scores are used to fill in a wheel shaped profile and summary sheet for *goal planning.*

MARLETT, N.J. (1971) Adaptive Functioning Index. Alberta, Canada: Vocational & Rehabilitation Research Institute.

Addison-Shilder's disease / Addison's disease with cerebral sclerosis
See *sudanophilic leucodystrophy.*

Additive-free diet
= *Feingold diet.*

Adductors / adduction
The adductor muscles move a joint toward the mid-line of the body (adduction). The adductors at the hip joint are frequently affected by *cerebral palsy* and this may lead to hip dislocation and *scissoring* of the legs with discomfort and hygiene problems.

Adenoma sebaceum
A skin condition characteristically occurring in *tuberose sclerosis*. Adenoma sebaceum becomes evident at about 4 years of age or later. It consists of small lumps just under the skin and these may gradually increase in size. The lumps are benign tumours caused by overgrowth of the sebaceous glands in the skin. The usual distribution of the red rash is on the cheeks spreading out from the nose like the wings of a butterfly. It also occurs on the chin. Similar lumps, sometimes larger, may occur elsewhere on the body.

Adenovirus meningoencephalitis
Adenovirus infection usually causes a common cold with conjunctivitis. A very small number of people also develop infections of

the brain and nervous system with a severe *encephalitis* or *meningoencephalitis*. Death or permanent brain damage may follow in the more severe cases.

KIM, K.S. & GOHD, R.S. (1983) Acute encephalopathy in twins due to adenovirus type 7 infection. Arch. Neurol., 40:58–59.
SIMILA, S. et al (1970) Encephalomeningitis in children associated with an adenovirus type 7 epidemic. Acta Paediatr. Scand., 59:310–316.

Adiposo-hypogenitalism
= *Prader-Willi syndrome.*

Adiposogenital dystrophia
= *Frohlich's syndrome.*

Adjustment disorder / reaction
A maladaptive reaction to a stress or crisis. It is transient and resolves once the stress or crisis is finished or once the person has learnt to cope. Behaviour or symptoms are more than the normal response to the stress and interfere with normal functioning.

Admission to Hospital
See *Mental Health Act 1983* and *compulsory admission to hospital.*

Adolescence
The time of development between *puberty* and physical maturity. There are physical and emotional changes which take place leading to full sexual maturity and also emotional changes relating to the development of an individual identity as an adult member of society. Adolescence is generally regarded as a difficult time and mentally handicapped people are no exception. Problems may be greater when it is harder to achieve independence and self-esteem. Whereas the non-handicapped adolescent can usually achieve emotional independence and sense of personal identity with or without assistance from parents, the mentally handicapped person can rarely do this without encouragement and support from

the family. Many of the problems of behaviour and adjustment at this time may stem from this problem and the very natural fears parents have about letting their mentally handicapped child grow up. The attitudes of parents and professionals toward the mentally handicapped adolescent are important at this difficult time. Sexual development often causes particular anxiety and it is necessary to give information and, if necessary, training in dealing with personal relationships and aspects of sexuality (*sex education*).

ANASTASIOW, N.J. (1986) Development and Disability. Baltimore: Paul H. Brookes.
CHESELDINE, S.E. & JEFFREE, D.M. (1981) Mentally handicapped adolescents: their use of leisure. J. Ment. Defic. Res., 25:45–59.
CHESELDINE, S.E. & JEFFREE, D.M. (1982) Mentally handicapped adolescents: A survey of abilities. Special Education. Forward Trends 9(1):19–22.
JEFFREE, D.M. & CHESELDINE, S.E. (1983) Working with parents of adolescents: the work of the PATH project. In: Parents, Professionals and Mentally Handicapped People – Approaches to Partnership. Mittler, P. & McConachie, H. London: Croom Helm.

Adoption
A legal process whereby parental rights are given to selected adults who are not the natural parents but who undertake the care of the child as if their own. Until a few years ago it was considered impossible to place mentally handicapped children for *fostering* or adoption. One of the first agencies to place severely handicapped children for adoption was 'Spaulding for children' in Michigan in the 1960's. Branches of this organization now exist all over North America. In the U.K. agencies such as Barnardo's, National Children's Homes and Parents for Children became involved with 'hard to place' children. As a result of the success of the many agencies involved, the professional attitudes have gradually changed and it is now very unusual to take

even a profoundly mentally handicapped child into any form of residential care on a permanent basis. Parents are given encouragement and support to keep their mentally handicapped child at home but if they are unable or unwilling to do so it is now the usual practice for the child to be placed for fostering or adoption.

ARGENT, H. (1984) Find Me A Family. London: Souvenir Press.
ARGENT, H. (1986) Adoption and Down's children. Down's Children's Assoc. News, 45:10–12.
MACASKILL, C. (1985) Against the Odds. London: British Agencies for Adoption and Fostering.

Adrenocorticotrophic hormone

A hormone released by the *pituitary gland* to stimulate the adrenal glands usually as a reaction to stress. It may also be given as an injection and is used as a treatment for severe cases of *infantile spasms* and of *hypoglycemosis* which are associated with mental handicap. It is usually given as a course of injections gradually reducing the dosage according to response. It may also be used to reduce inflammation in rheumatic/arthritic conditions.

RIIKONEN, R. & DONNER, M. (1980) ACTH therapy in infantile spasms: Side effects. Arch. Dis. Childh., 55:664–672.
SNEAD, O.C. et al (1983) ACTH and prednisone in childhood seizure disorders. Neurology, 33:966–970.

Adrenoleucodystrophy

= *sudanophilic leucodystrophy*.

Adult education

See *further education*.

Adult Training Centre

These day centres for mentally handicapped people began to develop in the 1950's and the number of such centres in the U.K. has steadily increased. There were approximately 46,000 mentally handicapped people attending adult training centres in 1985 and it has been predicted that by 1991 64,000 places could be required. Centres are run by Local Authority Social Services departments and the staff are usually called instructors. In the 1970's–80's many were renamed Social Education Centres (SEC) and this has reflected the move from an industrial approach to an educational orientation. The early training centres provided repetitive work tasks usually in a simple assembly line but the range and nature of activities has gradually changed. Whereas it was previously necessary for the people attending to have some work skills, most centres nowadays cater for the full range of disability including *special care* provision. Such centres therefore offer the opportunity for day occupation to those adult mentally handicapped people who live in the community. More recently there has been concern that the ATCs are too segregated from the community and lack clarity about the aims of the service. They have also been criticized for a lack of active and well planned programmes of training and *habilitation* to prepare individuals for entry into more ordinary settings. See also *day care*.

DHSS (1980) Adult Training Centres, Circular LAC 80(2). London: HMSO.
GRAY, B. (1985) Social Education Centres and employment. In: Mental Handicap. A multidisciplinary approach. Craft, M. et al. London: Baillière Tindall. pp. 258–270.
NATIONAL DEVELOPMENT GROUP FOR THE MENTALLY HANDICAPPED (1977) Day Services for Mentally Handicapped Adults. NDG Pamphlet 5. London: DHSS.
NATIONAL SOCIETY FOR MENTALLY HANDICAPPED CHILDREN (1977) Minimum Standards for ATCs. London: NSMHC.
PORTERFIELD, J. & GATHERCOLE, C. (1985) The Employment of People with Mental Handicap: Progress towards an ordinary working life. King's Fund Project Paper No 55. London: King's Fund Centre.
WHELAN, E. & SPEAKE, B.R. (1977) Adult Training Centres in England and Wales.

Manchester: National Association of Teachers for the Mentally Handicapped, Hester Adrian Research Centre, University of Manchester.

An Ordinary Working Life – Vocational services for people with mental handicap (1984) King's Fund Project Paper No 50. London: King's Fund Centre.

Living like other People – Next steps in day services for people with Mental Handicap (1985). Independent Development Council for People with Mental Handicap, 126, Albert St., London. NW1 7NF.

Advocacy

An arrangement that provides a supporter to speak and act on behalf of a disabled person. The purpose is to obtain rights and services for that person to meet his or her needs. It is essential for those who cannot plead effectively for themselves. Advocates may be consumers, volunteers or professionals who act independently. Loyalty, confidentiality and zealous promotion of the cause of the person are essential, and independence and separation from service providers is also a necessity.

In the 1950's references to mental handicap as a legal and human rights problem began to appear. The United Nations Declaration on the Rights of Mentally Retarded Persons (1971) included specific articles defining rights to personal advocacy. In Sweden mentally handicapped people have the legal right to the assistance of a paid and independent spokesperson. The Developmentally Disabled Assistance and Bill of Rights Act (1974) requires each American state to establish an independent agency to pursue the individual rights of disabled persons. Most states rely on staff attorneys and staff advocates but a few have primarily used citizen advocacy.

In the U.K. advocacy was discussed and encouraged by the Jay Committee and Advocacy Alliance was started in 1982 as a pioneering project to create a one-to-one scheme of friendship, protection and representation for people in long-stay mental handicap hospitals.

There are several types of advocacy:

1. *Self-advocacy* has existed in the U.S.A. and Sweden since the early 1970's where local self-help groups, composed of and led by handicapped persons, have come together to speak up for their rights.

2. Citizen advocacy (lay advocacy) is one-to-one assistance, usually on a voluntary basis, by people who have been selected, trained, co-ordinated and supported. It may involve expressing the person's worries and hopes (expressive advocacy), seeing that the necessary services are provided (instrumental advocacy) and giving practical and emotional support. Examples are The Georgia Advocacy Office and Advocating Change Together (Minneapolis) in the U.S.A.; and Advocacy Alliance in the U.K.

3. Legal advocacy is a service provided by lawyers or other skilled individuals to help mentally handicapped people exercise or defend their rights. It may also involve more general representation to interpret laws, negotiate settlements, change laws, etc.

HERR, S.S. (1983) Rights and Advocacy for Retarded People. Massachusetts: Lexington Books.

SANG, B. & O'BRIEN, J. (1984) Advocacy. The U.K. and American Experiences. King's Fund Project Paper Number 51. London: King's Fund Centre.

WOLFENSBERGER, W. (1977) A Multi-component Advocacy and Protection Scheme. Toronto: Canadian Association for the Mentally Retarded.

Further information:
Advocacy Alliance, 115 Golden Lane, London EC1Y 0TJ.

Aerophagia

Swallowing of air often to such an extent that the abdomen becomes distended. It is an unusual habit which can occur in people who are mentally handicapped as a symptom of anxiety or as a means of self-stimulation.

Aetiology

The study of the causes of diseases or conditions. Mental handicap has many possible causes which may operate before, during or after birth.

Affective disorder

A type of psychiatric disorder which can occur in people of any intellectual level including severe mental handicap. The mood of the person is disturbed as in depression or elation. See *depression, hypomania, mania* and *manic-depressive psychosis*.

REID, A.H. (1985) Psychiatry and mental handicap. In: Mental Handicap. A multidisciplinary approach. Craft, M. et al. London: Baillière Tindall. pp. 322–324.
RUSSELL, O. (1985) Mental Handicap. Edinburgh: Churchill Livingstone. pp. 138–143.
SOVNER, R. & HURLEY, A.D. (1983) Do the mentally retarded suffer from affective illness? Arch. Gen. Psychiat., 40:61–67.

Affective illness

= *affective disorder*.

AFP

= *alpha-feto protein*.

Aftercare

Continuing *rehabilitation*, treatment or support provided to a person after discharge from an institution. It is most important that this is planned and arranged before discharge and maintained for as long as is necessary.

Age-appropriateness

A concept which has developed as part of the *normalization* principle. The environment, possessions, relationships, activities, etc., of a person who is mentally handicapped should be appropriate for his or her actual age and not related to *mental age*. It is, for example, regarded as demeaning to give children's toys to an adult or to relate to adults with a mental handicap as if they are, and always will be, children. It also creates low expectations.

Ageing

During the last fifty years the life expectancy of mentally handicapped people has increased considerably and in many cases is the same as that of the general population. Whereas elderly people in general have had their medical, psychiatric and social needs well studied, there is comparatively little information on any special characteristics and needs of elderly mentally handicapped people.

DAY, K.A. (1985) Psychiatric disorder in the middle-aged and elderly mentally handicapped. Brit. J. Psychiat., 147:660–667.
JANICKI, M.P. & WISNIEWSKI, H.M. (Eds.) (1985) Ageing and Developmental Disabilities: Issues and Approaches. Baltimore: Paul Brookes.

Agenesis

Failure of development of a structure or part of the body. This may occur in many conditions associated with mental handicap.

Agenesis of corpus callosum

See *corpus callosum*.

Aggression

A term used to describe behaviours which are either menacing or injurious to others or destructive to property. It is generally considered that the majority of mentally handicapped people are no more aggressive than any other members of society. Premeditated acts of aggression are particularly rare. A small number of mentally handicapped people do have problems in self-control and are less able to predict the consequences of their actions. Aggressive behaviour may be precipitated by demands on the individual, crowding, noise, invasion of territory, illness, change and victimization. It may also occur because of inability to use other ways of expressing anger or because it gains attention. There are usually warning signs from the individual indicating tension, confusion or distress. The problems can often be resolved or reduced by restructuring the environment to reduce unnecessary stress, by teaching other ways of behaving and communicating, by improving living conditions and by changing the consequences of aggressive behaviour. This may involve the use of *behaviour modification* techniques such as *time-out, differential reinforcement of other behaviours, response-cost, overcorrection* and brief physical *restraint. Psychotropic drugs* especially *phenothiazines* and *haloperidol* may be prescribed but misuse in the past has drawn attention to the need for careful and close monitoring. They are most likely to be effective when a *psychiatric illness* is present. See also *behaviour disorders.*

BOSTOW, D.E. & BAILEY, J.B. (1969) Modification of severe disruptive and aggressive behavior using brief timeout and reinforcement procedures. J. Appl. Behav. Anal., 2:31–37.
CARR, E.G. et al (1980) Escape as a factor in the aggressive behavior of two retarded children. J. Appl. Behav. Anal., 13:101–117.
CRAFT, M. & BERRY, I. (1985) The role of the professional in aggression and strategies of coping. In: Mental Handicap. A multidisciplinary approach. Craft, M. et al. London: Baillière Tindall. pp. 397–409.
GARDNER, W.I. et al (1986) Reducing aggression in individuals with developmental disabilities: an extended stimulus control, assessment and intervention model. Education and Training of the Mentally Retarded, 21(1):3–12.
MULICK, J.A. & SCHROEDER, S.R. (1980) Research relating to management of antisocial behavior in mentally retarded persons. Psychological Record, 30:397–417.

Agnathia
Total or partial absence of the jaw.

Agnosia
The absence of the ability to recognize the character of objects through the senses. It is usually due to damage to the brain especially the parietal lobe. Tactile agnosia is the inability to recognize objects by touching them. Visual-spatial agnosia is the failure to understand the spatial relationships of objects and to perform simple constructional tasks under visual control. Auditory agnosia is the inability to find noises meaningful.

Agranulocytosis
A condition in which one type of white cell in the blood becomes seriously reduced in number. This may occur as a reaction to certain drugs and makes the person very susceptible to infections. This necessitates regular blood tests when these drugs are used.

Agraphia
The inability to communicate ideas in writing.

Agyria
Absence of folds and convolutions on the surface of the brain (see *lissencephaly*).

Aicardi's syndrome
A very rare condition, apparently confined to females, in which severe mental handicap, *infantile spasms*, abnormality of the lining of the eye and defects of the brain (including agenesis of the *corpus callosum*), spine and ribs occur. The *electroencephalogram* recording is very characteristic in infancy. The cause of the condition is not known.

BERTONI, J.M. et al (1979) The Aicardi syndrome: Report of 4 cases and review of the literature. Ann. Neurol., 5:475–482.
DE JONG, J.D. et al (1976) Agenesia of the corpus callosum, infantile spasms, ocular anomalies (Aicardi's syndrome). Neurology, 26:1152.

AIDS
= *Acquired Immune Deficiency syndrome.*

Air encephalogram

This investigation is becoming obsolete where *CT scans* are available. A lumbar puncture is carried out and a small amount of air introduced to replace some of the fluid which bathes the brain and spinal cord. This air then fills the cavities of the brain and shows up on an X-ray. This investigation is unpleasant and there is a small risk. It has therefore never been widely used. It was used in the diagnosis of suspected abnormalities of the brain including those which might cause mental handicap.

Akathisia

Abnormal restlessness in which the person has great difficulty in sitting still and will pace up and down. This is a side-effect of a number of major tranquillizers including *chlorpromazine, promazine, fluphenazine, haloperidol, benperidol* and others. It may be associated with other symptoms such as *parkinsonism* and *tardive dyskinesia*. It may be reduced by the use of *anti-parkinsonian* drugs but, like tardive dyskinesia, may sometimes be made worse when these drugs are given.

BREUNING, S.E. & POLING, A.D. (Eds.) (1982) Drugs and Mental Retardation. Illinois: Charles C. Thomas.

Akinesia

Absence or impairment of voluntary movement.

Akinetic seizure

A type of *seizure* where the person drops suddenly to the ground but does not convulse. This is associated with a brief but sudden muscular contraction. This type of *epilepsy* is uncommon in the general population but more common in mentally handicapped people.

Akinetic-astatic seizure

= *akinetic seizure*.

Alalia

Partial or total absence of speech.

Albers-Schönberg syndrome

= *osteopetrosis*.

Albright's syndrome / Albright's hereditary osteodystrophy

People with this rare condition are thick set and below average height with a round face. There is a slightly unusual shape to the hands and feet and poor growth of nails. The degree of mental handicap is usually severe and the *electroencephalogram* is often abnormal. There is often a low level of calcium in the body and this may cause cataracts, weak teeth and *seizures*. This may be treated with vitamin D and calcium supplements. It is a genetic condition probably with *sex-linked inheritance*.

HOLMES, L.B. et al (1972) Mental Retardation. New York: Macmillan Publishing. pp. 50–53.
MANN, J.B. et al (1962) Albright's hereditary osteodystrophy comprising pseudo-hypoparathyroidism and pseudo-pseudo hypoparathyroidism. Ann. Intern. Med., 56:315–342.

Alcohol

See *fetal alcohol syndrome*.

Alexander's disease

A very rare condition in which progressive enlargement of the head is usually noted within the first year of life. This is due to an increase in the size of the brain which is microscopically very abnormal. Most infants affected by this condition are severely mentally handicapped, epileptic and spastic, and there is a slowly progressive deterioration in mental and physical abilities resulting in an early death. It may be the same condition as *Canavan's disease*. The cause is possibly genetic with *recessive inheritance*.

RUSSO, L.S. et al (1976) Alexander's disease: A report and reappraisal. Neurology, 26:607–614.

Alexia

Lack of the ability to read.

Allan-Dent Disease

= *argininosuccinic aciduria*.

Allergy

The special sensitiveness of an individual to particular substances. These may be foods, drugs, chemicals, pollens, animals, insect bites, etc. An allergic reaction may be shown as a skin rash, swelling, fever, asthma attack, stomach upset, hayfever or in many other possible ways. A number of *behaviour disorders* in children, including overactivity, have been widely attributed to food allergies especially to some food additives. Avoidance of responsible substances is generally recommended but if impossible then, in the case of skin rashes, sensitivity may sometimes be controlled by the use of antihistamine drugs. The benefits of the *Feingold diet* for *hyperactive* or behaviourally disordered mentally handicapped children has yet to be proven.

Allowances

Mentally handicapped people may be eligible for a number of allowances depending on age and nature and extent of disabilities. In the U.K. these include *attendance allowance, mobility allowance* and *severe disability allowance*. Carers may be entitled to *invalid care allowance*.

Disability Rights Handbook (updated every year) from The Disability Alliance ERA, 25 Denmark St., London WC2H 8NJ.

Alogia

Absence of speech usually due to mental handicap or confusion.

Alopecia

A term for baldness. It occurs prematurely in a few rare conditions which cause mental handicap including Down's syndrome.

Alopecia areata

A disorder in which the hair comes out in patches resulting in bald areas. It occurs in a number of conditions which cause mental handicap including Down's syndrome.

Alper's syndrome

A progressive disorder with deterioration of the mental and physical state from a few weeks of age and with a very early death (between 4 weeks and 5 years). *Spasticity* and *Epilepsy* are present. The head circumference is below normal at birth or within a few months. There is considerable variation in the infants reported to have Alper's syndrome and it is probable that several disorders of different causation have been reported as examples of this syndrome.

LAURENCE, K.M. & CAVANAGH, J.B. (1968) Progressive degeneration of the cerebral cortex in infancy. Brain, 91:261.

Alpha-feto protein (AFP)

This substance can now be estimated in the blood of a pregnant woman to indicate the probability of a child having *meningomyelocoele* or *anencephaly*. The levels of alpha-feto protein are increased in these conditions. Low levels occur more often when a fetus has *Down's syndrome* and 20% of Down's syndrome pregnancies can be detected by this means. AFP can be more reliably estimated in the amniotic fluid surrounding the baby in the womb. This can be obtained by *amniocentesis*. It is an important development in the prevention of these serious abnormalities which may be associated with mental handicap. It offers the possibility of a therapeutic abortion.

CUCKLE, M.S. et al (1984) Maternal serum alpha-feto protein measurement: a screening test for Down's syndrome. Lancet, I:926–9.
HADDOW, J.E. (1985) Identifying fetal disorders by maternal serum alpha-feto protein screening. The Practitioner, 229:721–725.
LORBER, J. & WARD, A.M. (1985) Spina bifida – a vanishing nightmare? Arch. Dis. Childh., 60:1086–1091.
MERKATZ, I.R. et al (1984) An association

between low maternal serum alpha-feto protein and fetal chromosomal abnormalities. Am. J. Obstet. Gynec., 148:886–894.
STANDING, J.S. et al (1981) Maternal alphafetoprotein screening. Two years' experience in a low-risk district. Brit. Med. J., 283:705.

Alzheimer's disease

A condition which occurs in the general population and is a type of *pre-senile dementia*. It is more common than usual in people with *Down's syndrome* and the onset may be as early as 40 years of age. In the early stages there is loss of memory, concentration and skills. Later the person becomes physically less able but is often restless and overactive for some time. In the terminal stages the person is profoundly disabled physically and mentally. The cause is not known and there is no known treatment. It may last from several months to over 10 years but average duration of life once symptoms appear is 6 years.

LOTT, I.T. (1982) Down's syndrome, ageing and Alzheimer's disease: a clinical review. Ann. New York Acad. Sciences, 396:15–27.
MINISZEK, N.A. (1983) Development of Alzheimer's disease in Down's syndrome individuals. Am. J. Ment. Defic., 87:377–385.

Amaurotic familial idiocy

This group of disorders are usually inherited from both parents who are carriers (*recessive inheritance*). Some fats (lipids) are stored abnormally throughout the body causing degeneration of the tissues. There is progressive deterioration in vision and mental abilities. These disorders include the *sphingolipidoses*, the *gangliosidoses* and the *ceroidlipofuscinoses*.

Amblyopia

Defective vision without any abnormality of the structure of the eye or nerves to the eye. An amblyopic eye is commonly called a 'lazy eye'. The most common cause is a squint. It can also be due to a large difference in focusing power between the two eyes. It is fairly common (2% of all children) but especially so in mentally handicapped people. Careful assessment of vision is therefore very important for all mentally handicapped children.

Amelia

Absence of limbs. This is evident at birth and may very rarely be associated with other abnormalities including mental handicap. The commonest cause was thalidomide and this did not cause mental handicap.

Amenorrhoea

Absence of menstruation at any time of life when it would normally occur. This may happen in a number of conditions which cause mental handicap especially those where there is an abnormality of the sex chromosomes as in *Turner's syndrome*. It is also a side-effect of the anticonvulsant drug *sodium valproate*.

Amentia

A term which was used to describe mental handicap. Primary amentia refers to an intellectual disability that is *genetic*, chromosomal or innate. Secondary amentia is caused by damage to the fetus by childbirth or infection in infancy.

Amer-ind

A system of communication using mimed gestures which is generally easy to understand even by untrained observers. There is a limited number of signs which can be combined to express sentences although there are no grammatical rules. It is most useful as a simple *gesture system* for indicating basic needs. It cannot be used to express abstract ideas.

DANILOFF, J.K. et al (1983) Amer-Ind transparency. J. Speech Hear. Dis., 48:103–110.
SKELLY, M. (1979) Amer-ind Gestural

Code Based on Universal American Indian Hand Talk. New York: Elsevier.

American Association on Mental Deficiency

A non-profit making organization estab lished in the U.S.A. as an interdisciplinary association of professionals in the field of mental retardation and developmental disabilities. It aims to promote the welfare of people who are mentally retarded, the individuals who work with them and the field of mental retardation in general. This involves prevention, research, maintenance of high standards, dissemination of knowledge, promotion of community services and the influencing of public policies. The AAMD carries out its aims through the activities of its national and regional governing bodies, its annual meeting and its standing and ad hoc committees. The AAMD is also organized into 19 professional divisions. It publishes the 'American Journal on Mental Deficiency' and 'Mental Retardation' as well as many books.

Further information:
AAMD, 5201 Connecticut Av., N.W, Washington DC 20015.

American Sign Language (ASL or Ameslan)

This is used by deaf people and is a true language with its own grammar which is not the same as that in written or spoken English. It is very similar to *British Sign Language* but tends to have more signs using both hands performing mirrored gestures while BSL has more one-handed signs. It uses single signs for ideas or 'words' but also uses finger spelling, facial expression and limited lip movements and vocalizations. When used with mentally handicapped non-speakers ASL signs have frequently been modified and English grammar is generally used.

FRIEDMAN, L.A. (Ed.) (1977) On the Other Hand. New Perspectives in American Sign Language. New York: Academic Press.

WILBUR, R.B. (1979) American Sign Language and Sign Systems. Baltimore: University Park Press.

Ametropia
Defective vision.

Amino acids
The proteins of living organisms are made up from combinations of amino acids which are often called the building blocks of proteins. Disorders of the chemical processes dealing with amino acids may cause mental handicap and are known as *amino acidurias*.

Amino acidurias
These are disorders in which there are biochemical abnormalities in the body usually caused by the inheritance of the same abnormal recessive gene from both parents. A few are caused by other types of inheritance. The abnormal genes cause a lack of chemicals (*enzymes*), which are involved in important biochemical processes in the body. The abnormal biochemical processes cause particular amino acids to appear in the urine in far greater quantities than usual. Different amino acids appear in each of these disorders and special tests on the urine make it possible to detect these substances and to make the diagnosis. This group of disorders includes *phenylketonuria, homocystinuria, argininosuccinic aciduria, arginaemia, histidinaemia, maple syrup urine disease, Lowe's syndrome, Hartnup's disease* and many other rare conditions. A few of these conditions may be treated by diet or by other means but untreated they are usually associated with severe mental handicap and some with reduced life expectancy.

CHALMERS, R.A. et al (1980) Screening for organic acidurias and aminoacidopathies in newborns and children. J. Inherited Metab. Dis., 3:27–43.
WATTS, R.W.E. et al (1980) Organic acidurias and aminoacidurias in the aetiology of long-term mental handicap. J. Ment. Defic. Res., 24:257–270.

Aminopterin-induced embryopathy
= *camptomelic dwarfism.*

Amitriptyline
A drug used for the treatment of *depression*. It may also be effective in the treatment of *nocturnal enuresis*. Side-effects include dry-mouth, sleepiness (especially at the start of treatment), constipation, blurred vision, nausea and difficulty in passing urine. It should be used with caution in people with heart problems, epilepsy, liver disease and thyroid disease. Common trade names are Tryptizol and Lentizol (a slow release form of the drug). Treatment should generally not be stopped abruptly.

Amniocentesis
A procedure whereby a small amount of *amniotic fluid*, which contains cells shed by the fetus, is drained off from the womb between the 11th and 18th weeks of pregnancy. A special needle is inserted through the abdominal wall using *ultrasound scanning* to give a picture of the position of the baby and the placenta. Chemicals in the fluid may be tested and the cells collected and grown. This is used for detection of abnormal *chromosomes* as occur, for example, in *Down's syndrome*. Many other conditions may be detected including *meningomyelocoele, anencephaly, Tay-Sachs disease, Lesch-Nyhan syndrome, fragile-X syndrome* and over fifty others. It offers the mother the chance of having an *abortion* if an abnormality is detected. There is a slightly increased risk of spontaneous abortion with amniocentesis and it is therefore only recommended where there is known to be an increased risk of having an abnormal baby (e.g. the increased risk of chromosomal abnormalities in the babies of women over 35 years of age or abnormal *alpha-feto protein* levels in the mother). *Chorion biopsy* may be available as an alternative to amniocentesis.

RODECK, C.H. & NICOLAIDES, K.H. (Eds.) (1984) Prenatal Diagnosis. London: Royal College of Obstetricians & Gynaecologists.

Amnioscope
A flexible, fine instrument used to look at the baby in the womb. It is inserted into the womb through the abdominal wall using *ultrasound scanning* to show the position of the baby and the placenta. This makes it possible to detect disorders where there are obvious limb abnormalities such as those which occur in *acrocephalosyndactyly*. The procedure carries a significant risk of *abortion*.

Amniotic fluid
The fluid which surrounds the baby in the womb.

Amphetamines
This group of drugs, which usually stimulate people, have a different effect on some hyperactive children. The level of *hyperactivity* may be reduced by the use of one of these drugs, such as *dextroamphetamine*, although *methylphenidate* is usually regarded as the drug of choice. Caution should be exercised when giving these drugs to mentally handicapped children as the response is very unpredictable.

Amsterdam dwarf
= *de Lange syndrome.*

Amyotonia
Extreme looseness of muscles. This occurs in babies who develop *Prader-Willi syndrome* and may be so severe that sucking is poor and tube feeding is necessary. Babies with *Down's syndrome* are also floppy at birth but this is usually described as *hypotonia* which is less extreme than amyotonia.

Anacusia
Total deafness.

Anaesthesia
The absence of sensation. This may be caused by damage to those areas of the brain involved in the perception of sensation. It can be associated with physical and mental handicaps which are also caused by the brain damage. It usually affects only

part of the body. There are other possible causes apart from brain damage but these are not generally associated with mental handicap.

Anaesthesia may be induced medically by using drugs in order to prevent or treat pain and this is just as important for mentally handicapped people as for anyone else. It may be induced in part of the body (local anaesthetic) or render the person unconscious (general anaesthetic). General anaesthesia may also have to be used for a person who cannot co-operate with a treatment from a doctor or a dentist. There is a difficult ethical problem when an adult is unable to give consent for a general anaesthetic or for treatment (*consent to treatment*).

Analgesia

Absence of the sense of pain. This is not associated with mental handicap except in extremely rare cases of damage occurring to those parts of the brain which deal with the appreciation of pain. Analgesia may be induced medically in order to prevent pain, or to treat pain and this is just as important for mentally handicapped people as for anyone else. Pain killers such as aspirin and paracetamol are called analgesics.

Anarthria

Inability to speak clearly.

Anderson-Fabry disease

= *Fabry's syndrome.*

Androcur

=*cyproterone acetate.*

Anencephaly

A condition in which the baby is born with very little brain tissue and a small abnormal skull. Such children rarely survive more than a few hours after birth.

Anesthesia

= *anaesthesia.*

Angelman's syndrome

= *happy puppet syndrome.*

Angiofibroma

= *adenoma sebaceum.*

Angiogram

An X-ray following an injection into an artery of a substance which is harmless but will show up on an X-ray. It is then possible to see all the blood vessels of the area. It can be used to study the blood vessels of the brain following an injection into the carotid artery or the vertebral artery in the neck. It may be used to investigate the cause of mental handicap if an abnormality of the blood vessels of the brain is suspected.

Angioma

A benign tumour composed of blood vessels. Such tumours may occur anywhere in the body and, if in the skin, are a type of birth mark. Extensive angiomas, usually confined to one side of the body, occur in *Sturge-Weber syndrome*. If the brain is affected mental handicap may be a consequence.

Angiomatosis

= *Sturge-Weber syndrome.*

Aniridia

Absence or partial absence of the *iris* in one or both eyes. Smaller defects of the iris are known as *coloboma*. Abnormalities of the iris occur in a few rare conditions associated with mental handicap including *Goltz's syndrome*.

Aniridia-Wilm's tumour syndrome

A very rare condition in which the iris is absent from both eyes at birth and a tumour of the kidneys (*Wilm's tumour*) develops later. There may be other abnormalities of the eyes and of other parts of the body. Mental handicap has been reported in a few children with this syndrome.

SHANNON, R.S. et al (1982) Wilm's tumour and aniridia: clinical and cytogenetic features. Arch. Dis. Childh., 57:685–690.

Anodontia

Partial or total absence of teeth as may occur in many conditions associated with mental handicap.

Anoesia

An obsolete term for mental handicap.

Anomaly

A deviation from average. This may be used in medical language to describe an under-developed or abnormally developed part of the body.

Anophthalmia

Absence of one or both eyes. It may occur in some rare *syndromes* associated with mental handicap especially *chromosome* abnormalities (*Trisomy* 8 and *Patau's syndrome*).

Anorexia

Loss of appetite. This has many possible physical and emotional causes.

Anosmia

Loss of smell. This is not particularly associated with mental handicap except, very rarely, when brain damage also affects the nerves and the brain areas which deal with the sense of smell.

Anoxia

A state of lack of oxygen in the body. It has a number of possible causes. It may be caused by complications of pregnancy or birth (*fetal anoxia*). The brain tissues are particularly sensitive to lack of oxygen and may be permanently damaged if this state is prolonged. This may result in mental handicap.

CORAH, N.L. et al (1965) Effects of peri-natal anoxia after 7 years. Psychological Monograph, 79:1–34.

Anquil

= *benperidol*.

Anson House Checklist

A set of checklists designed for use with handicapped children. It can be used in sections or as a complete set. It needs to be completed by more than one person over a period of time. It covers motor skills, com-munication and language, cognitive skills, self-help skills, social skills and play. It can be repeated as often as monthly and a summary graph can be drawn. Extra mater-ials, such as toys, are required to carry out the assessment. It can be used as a basis for teaching.

GUNSTONE, C. (1985) Anson House Check-list (revised edit.), Barnardo's, Tanner's Lane, Barkingside, Ilford, Essex IG6 1QG.

Antecedents

A term used in *behaviour modification* to describe the events which precede the be-haviour causing concern. The two types of antecedents are setting events and dis-criminative stimuli. A setting event is a relatively stable feature of the environment which affects a substantial number of subse-quent events. Discriminative stimuli are more transient events such as instructions or *cues*. Antecedents set the occasion for most behaviours but do not produce them auto-matically with the exception of reflex in-voluntary responses known as *respondents*. Voluntary responses are known as *operants*. Behaviour may be modified by changing the antecedents.

BACHMAN, J.E. & FUQUA, R.W. (1983) Management of inappropriate behaviors of trainable mentally impaired students using antecedent exercise. J. Appl. Behav. Anal., 16:477–484.

Antenatal

A term which literally means 'before birth'. Causes of mental handicap which operate before birth may be referred to as antenatal causes.

Anti-epileptic drugs

= *anticonvulsants*.

Anti-mongolism
A condition which was once thought to be the opposite of *Down's syndrome* (mongolism). This view is no longer held. There is an abnormality of part of the long arm of the chromosomes 21 or 22 and this may occur in a number of forms. Affected individuals may have a broad bridge to the nose, small jaw, low-set ears, genital abnormalities, *club foot*, *cataracts*, tightness of muscles and short stature. Mental handicap usually occurs and may be severe.

WARREN, R.J. & RIMOIN, D.L. (1970) The G-deletion syndromes. J. Pediatr., 77:658.

Anti-mongoloid
This usually refers to a slant of the eyes downward from the nose which is in the opposite direction to that in *Down's syndrome* (mongolism). It occurs quite often in conditions associated with mental handicap including *Treacher-Collins syndrome*, *Rubinstein-Taybi syndrome* and several *chromosome* disorders.

Anti-parkinsonian drugs
Drugs used in the treatment of *Parkinson's disease* and also for drug-induced *parkinsonism*. These include *benzhexol*, *benztropine* and *orphenadrine* which may also be referred to as anti-cholinergic drugs.

Anti-psychotic drugs
A group of drugs, often referred to as major tranquillizers, which are used to treat people with serious psychiatric illnesses (*psychoses*) such as *schizophrenia*. These drugs are frequently used for the management of problem behaviours in people with a mental handicap, although the evidence for their efficacy is limited and they are, almost certainly, over-used. These drugs include *chlorpromazine*, *promazine*, *thioridazine*, *pericyazine*, *fluphenazine*, *trifluoperazine*, *haloperidol*, *pimozide* and *flupenthixol*.

FERGUSON, D.G. & BREUNING, S.E. (1982) Antipsychotic and antianxiety drugs. In: Drugs and Mental Retardation. Breuning, S.E. & Poling, A.D. (Eds.). Illinois: Charles C. Thomas.
JAMES, D.H. (1983) Monitoring drugs in hospitals for the mentally handicapped. Brit. J. Psychiat., 142:163–165.
RUSSELL, O. (1985) Mental Handicap. Edinburgh: Churchill Livingstone. pp. 150–161.

Anticholinergic drugs
See *anti-parkinsonian drugs*.

Anticonvulsant/antiepileptic drugs
Drugs used in the treatment of *epilepsy*. Such drugs cannot cure epilepsy but may control and prevent *seizures* to varying degrees. The aim of the treatment is to maintain a sufficient level of the anticonvulsant in the blood and therefore in the brain. Many drugs are used as anticonvulsants and the particular drug(s) prescribed will depend on the type of seizures, the *electroencephalogram* recording obtained, the cause of the seizures and other factors. Drugs should be monitored carefully by a doctor to make sure that the best dosage is obtained and to detect side-effects. Anticonvulsants are rarely stopped suddenly because of the increased risk of seizures. This group of drugs includes *phenobarbitone, phenytoin, carbamazepine, sodium valproate* and several others.

DAVISON, D.L.W. (1983) Anticonvulsant drugs. Brit. Med. J., 286:2043–2045.
EADIE, M.J. & TYRER, J.H. (1980) Anticonvulsant Therapy (2nd. edit.). Edinburgh: Churchill Livingstone.
GADOW, K.D. (1986) Children on Medication. Epilepsy, Emotional Disturbance and Adolescent Disorders. San Diego: College Hill Press.
GIBBS, E.L. et al (1982) Antiepilepsy drugs. In: Drugs and Mental Retardation. Breuning, S.E. & Poling, A.D. (Eds.). Illinois: Charles C. Thomas.
WOODBURY, D.M., et al (Eds.) (1982) Antiepileptic Drugs. New York: Raven Press.

Antidepressant drugs
Drugs used in the treatment of *depression*.

17

There are two main groups of these drugs (1) the tricyclics including *imipramine, amitriptyline*, and *doxepine* and (2) *monoamine oxidase inhibitors* including phenelzine and isocarboxazid. The indications for using a particular drug relate to the symptoms of the depression and the health of the person. A medical practitioner with psychiatric knowledge should prescribe the appropriate drug and in the case of a severely mentally handicapped person, the skills of the practitioner are important because of the problems of correctly diagnosing depression.

GUALTERI, C.T. & HAWK, B. (1982) Antidepressant and anti-manic drugs, In: Drugs and Mental Retardation. Breuning, S.E. & Poling, A.D. (Eds.) Illinois: Charles C. Thomas.

Anxiety state / anxiety

A psychiatric term for an abnormally intense state of anxiety which can occur regardless of intellectual ability. There is considerable variation in the way anxiety may affect an individual and people who are mentally handicapped may be unable to describe the feelings experienced. Physical problems may be more evident. An acute anxiety state is a sudden reaction to a frightening or worrying situation whereas a chronic anxiety state is a more prolonged response to stress. Avoidance and fear of a particular object or situation is known as a *phobia*.

Anxiolytic drugs

Drugs used in the treatment of anxiety and *anxiety states*. These include the *benzodiazepines*.

Aortic stenosis

Narrowing of the main artery of the body (aorta) as it leaves the heart. This causes the heart to be under strain and may lead to heart failure. This form of *congenital heart disease* may occur in association with conditions which cause mental handicap such as *rubella syndrome* and *infantile hypercalcaemia*.

Apert's syndrome

People with this condition have a very unusual appearance with an abnormally shaped head caused by the skull being taller than usual (*acrocephaly*). The eyes protrude and there may be abnormalities of the eyes, nose, palate, mouth and teeth. Fingers may be joined together or very small and there are similar abnormalities of the feet. The extent of the mental handicap is variable and intelligence may be normal. A number of operations are required to correct the various deformities. Operations on the skull are usually necessary to prevent pressure on the brain. The condition can be inherited from one parent who may be mildly affected (*dominant inheritance*). It is often present without a family history of the condition. Two types of Apert's syndrome are described. In Type I all five fingers on each hand are fused but in Type II the thumb and little finger are free or only partially fused. Type II is sometimes called Apert-Crouzon disease or Vogt cephalosyndactyly. *Crouzon's syndrome, Chotzen's syndrome* and *Pfeiffer's syndrome* are sometimes regarded as subtypes of Apert's syndrome but are usually described separately.

BLANK, C.E. (1960) Apert's syndrome (a type of acrocephalosyndactyly) observations on a British series of 39 cases. Ann. Hum. Genet., 24:157.
COHEN, M. (1975) Overview of craniosynostosis syndromes. Birth Defects Original Article Series. 11(2): 137. New York: National Foundation-March of Dimes.

Apgar score

A system for scoring the condition of a baby at birth. It includes the heart rate, state of breathing, colour of baby, *tone* of muscles and response to the tapping of the sole of the foot. It results in a score out of ten. Apgar scores are recorded at 1 and 5 minutes after birth. A score of 10 indicates that the baby is in good condition and a low score indicates that the baby is at risk. People who are mentally handicapped due to problems at birth may have had low Apgar scores.

Aphakia

Absence of the lens of the eye.

Aphasia

The absence or loss of *language* skills. Receptive aphasia is the absence of the ability to understand language. Expressive aphasia is the absence of the ability to put ideas into words. It is caused by damage to, or abnormality of, certain parts of the brain or may be as a result of severe mental handicap. There are many types of aphasia depending on the classification used.

Aplasia

Complete or partial failure of a part of the body to grow or develop. This may happen to any part of the body including the brain.

Apnoea / apnoeic attacks

The cessation of breathing or episodes when breathing stops. Recovery may be spontaneous or resuscitation may be necessary. Such attacks may occur in babies with *Joubert's syndrome* and *Patau's syndrome*, which are associated with mental handicap.

Approved social workers

The *Mental Health Act (1983)* for England and Wales, under section 114, requires *Local Authority Social Services* to appoint a sufficient number of approved *social workers* with appropriate competence in dealing with persons who are suffering from *mental disorder*, for the purpose of discharging the functions imposed on them by the Act.

Apraxia

Lack of ability to perform a pattern of movements, although the individual understands what is required and has no physical reason for not being able to carry it out. It is caused by damage to, or abnormality of, certain parts of the brain. It may include deficits in the co-ordination of speech so that although sounds can be made, the person may be unable to do so at will in order to form words.

Aqueductal stenosis

See *Dandy-Walker syndrome*.

Arachnodactyly

Excessively elongated, slender fingers and toes. It occurs in *homocystinuria* and a few other conditions associated with mental handicap. When not associated with such conditions it may be a sign of *Marfan's syndrome*.

Argininaemia

= *hyperargininaemia*.

Argininosuccinic aciduria

In this disorder a substance called argininosuccinic acid accumulates in the blood and is excreted in the urine. An *amino acid*, arginine, is not made in the body. It is due to reduced activity of the *enzyme* argininosuccinase which is important in reducing the amount of ammonia in the body. Hair and nails are abnormally brittle and various skin problems may occur. The degree of mental handicap is variable but usually severe. Physical handicaps may include abnormal movements, unsteadiness and sudden jerking of limbs. *Seizures* may occur. In one form of this disorder there is normal development in early infancy with rapid deterioration in the second and third years of life. In the other form there is a more gradual deterioration after birth with poor feeding, enlargement of the liver and *epilepsy*. In this milder type there are less abnormalities of the hair and survival into adult life is usual. On reduced protein intake some improvement has been reported and life expectancy improved. The addition of arginine to the diet may improve the hair. This disorder is inherited by the same abnormal *gene* being carried and passed on by both parents (*recessive inheritance*). Newborn babies can be screened for this condition so that treatment can be started early. It may be detected in the *fetus* following *amniocentesis* so that the pregnancy can be terminated. It can be detected in carriers following *fibroblast culture*.

BATSHAW, M.L. et al (1982) Treatment of inborn errors of urea synthesis. New Engl. J. Med., 306:1387.

BRENTON, D.P. et al (1974) Argininosuccinic acidaemia: clinical, metabolic and dietary study. J. Ment. Defic. Res., 18:1–7.

Arhinencephaly

The absence of the nose as part of a facial deformity. This can occur in a number of *syndromes* especially less common chromosomal abnormalities which are associated with mental handicap. It often occurs with *holoprosencephaly*.

Arnold-Chiari malformation

Malformation of the base of the brain so that it protrudes into the top end of the spinal canal. This causes an obstruction to the flow of the fluid around the brain and the pressure of fluid inside the brain builds up resulting in *hydrocephalus*. This can severely damage the brain, but can be relieved by an operation to by-pass the obstruction. *Meningomyelocoele* usually occurs with this malformation.

Art therapy

There are courses for the training of art therapists who may work with mentally ill or mentally handicapped people. Art Therapy may be of help in the development of self-expression and creativity and provide a useful way of reducing frustration and increasing achievement. It may also help the ability to control movements and to improve posture. Fine movements of the hand and hand-eye co-ordination may particularly benefit.

Arteriogram

= *angiogram*.

Arthrogryposis

Limbs curved at the joints. Abnormal development or structure of joints can occur in many diseases including some conditions associated with mental handicap. In *arthrogryposis multiplex congenita* the severe joint abnormalities are the major disability.

Arthrogryposis multiplex congenita

In this condition multiple malformations of joints and bones are present at birth, affecting the arms and legs. It may involve only one or two limbs. Muscles in affected limbs are much smaller and weaker than normal and the skin is tight and lacks the normal creases at the joints. Abnormalities of other parts of the body have also been described. Intelligence is usually normal but mental handicap occurs more commonly than in the general population. The cause is not known.

FRIEDLANDER, H.L. et al (1968) Arthrogryposis multiplex congenita. J. Bone Jt. Surg., 50A,89.

PENA, C.E. et al (1968) Arthrogryposis multiplex congenita. Neurology, 18:926.

Arthur Adaptation of the Leiter Scale

= *Leiter International Performance Scale*.

Articulation of speech

The process of speaking in distinct and easily understood syllables or words. Some mentally handicapped people have difficulty in speaking clearly and there are many possible causes including impaired hearing, abnormalities of the palate, clumsy tongue and lip movements, *cerebral palsy* and lack of motivation. Hearing and *speech therapy* assessments are recommended, followed by treatment if indicated. There are a number of commercially available standardized articulation tests.

DARLEY, F.L. et al (Eds.) (1977) Evaluation of Assessment Techniques in Special Pathology. Reading, Mass: Addison Wesley.

INGRAM, D. (1976) Phonological Disability in Children. Elsevier: New York.

MURDOCK, J.Y. et al (1977) Generalized articulation training with trainable mentally retarded subjects. J. Appl. Behav. Anal., 10:717–733.

ASD
= *atrial septal defect.*

Ash-leaf marks
Oval pale areas of skin with irregular margins which occur quite frequently in *tuberose sclerosis*. They may be noted at birth and are seen before 2 years of age in more than half the children with this condition. In light-skinned children they may only be demonstrable under ultra violet light (*Wood's lamp*).

GOLD, A.P. & FREEMAN, J.M. (1965) Depigmented nevi: The earliest sign of tuberose sclerosis. Pediatrics, 35:1003.

ASL
= *American Sign Language.*

Asocial
Unaware of, or indifferent to, social values. People who are mentally handicapped may not know or understand social values often because the proper education and training in these values has not been given.

Aspartylglucosaminuria
A rare condition which is inherited as an abnormal *gene* from both parents who do not have the condition themselves (*recessive inheritance*). The features of the face are coarse, *cataracts* develop, there is deterioration in intellectual abilities and *failure to thrive.* The onset is between 6 and 15 years of age. It is thought to be due to lack of a substance (*enzyme*) called N aspartyl-6-glucos-aminidase. The results of treatment are variable. A *carrier* of this condition can be identified by measuring the level of this enzyme from cells obtained by *skin biopsy*. The disorder can be detected by a blood test after birth. There is an excess of glyco-protein in the urine.

AUTIO, S. (1972) Aspartylglucosaminuria – analysis of 34 patients. J. Ment. Defic. Res. Monograph Series I.
ISENBERG, J.N. & SHARP, H.L. (1975) Aspartylglucosaminuria: Psychomotor re-tardation masquerading as a mucopoly-saccharidosis. J. Pediatr., 86:713.

Asperger's syndrome
In this condition the person has difficulty in forming appropriate friendships and is unable to understand how other people might feel. Speech tends to be repetitive and restricted in content often with preoccupation with certain subjects. Language may be stilted and pedantic with a limited capacity for abstract thought and very restricted imagination. Facial expression and use of gesture are also reduced. Movements may be clumsy and co-ordination may be poor. Posture can be odd. It is more common in males than in females and has many similarities to *autism*. It seems likely that there are a variety of causes, *genetic* or environmental, which lead to abnormal brain function. Many people with this syndrome have also been reported as having mild or moderate mental handicap but it can occur in people of normal intelligence.

BOWMAN, E.P. (1988) Asperger's syndrome and autism: the case for a connection. Brit. J. Psychiat., 152:372–382.
SCHOPLER, E. (1985) Convergence of learning disability, higher level autism, and Asperger's syndrome. J. Autism Dev. Dis., 15:359.
VOLKMAR, F.R. et al (1985) The use of 'Asperger's syndrome'. J. Autism Dev. Dis., 15:437–439.
WING, L. (1981) Asperger's syndrome : a clinical account. Psycholog. Med., 11:115–129.
WING, L. (1986) Clarification on Asperger's syndrome. J. Autism Dev. Dis., 16:513–515.

Asphyxia
A state which leads to the tissues of the body being deprived of oxygen. The brain is particularly susceptible to lack of oxygen and, the longer the state of asphyxia continues, the less likely it becomes that the brain will make a full recovery even if breathing and circulation of the blood are

restarted. Asphyxia of the baby may occur during labour and birth if there are complications (asphyxia neonatorum). Asphyxia due to other causes such as drowning and suffocation may occur later in infancy and childhood and result in mental handicap.

PETERSON, B. (1977) Morbidity of childhood near-drowning. Pediatrics, 59:364–370.
THOMPSON, A.J. et al (1977) Quality of survival after severe birth asphyxia. Arch. Dis. Childh., 52:111–119.

Aspiration pneumonia

Severely physically disabled people may have problems with swallowing and food or mucus may be drawn into the windpipe. If the person also has difficulty in coughing and clearing the airways the food and secretions are drawn further into the lungs. The collection of food and/or mucus in the lungs acts as a focus for infections which lead to a pneumonia. This is a particular problem with *bulbar paralysis*.

Assessment

A systematic and thorough evaluation of the strengths, weaknesses and problems of a person. It is carried out by a professional person or a team of staff from different disciplines (*multidisciplinary team* assessment). This should be carried out over a reasonable period of time and may be used to establish the nature or cause of the disabilities; the most appropriate approach, treatment or educational placement; the future potential; and the needs of a person and his or her family. There are a number of questionnaires and interview schedules, developed in recent years, which can be used with parents, teachers or other key informants. These may be used instead of, or as well as, submitting the individual to a test situation using tests to measure *mental age* or *intelligence quotient*. Practical skills are now being regarded as more relevant to the individual than the more abstract criteria such as general intelligence. Interventions should be based on thorough assessments. Re-assessments need to be carried out at regular intervals. Assessments are generally of limited value unless there is a subsequent plan of action to deal with any problems or needs which have been identified.

BEST, A. & BELL, J. (1984) Assessment of children with profound handicaps: an analysis of 12 schedules. Mental Handicap, 12(4):160–163.
COOPER, B. (Ed.) (1981) Assessing the Handicaps and Needs of Mentally Retarded Children. London: Academic Press.
DICKENS, P. & STALLARD, A. (1987) Assessing Mentally Handicapped People. A Guide for Care Staff. Windsor: NFER/Nelson.
HOGG, J. & RAYNES, N. (1986) Guide to Assessment for Professionals Working with Mentally Handicapped People. London: Croom Helm.
LEYIN, A. (1982) Assessing assessments – notes for the non-psychologists. Mental Handicap, 10(4):124–126.
MATSON, J.L. & BREUNING, S.E. (1983) Assessing the Mentally Retarded. London: Grune & Stratton.
PALMER, J.O. (1983) The Psychological Assessment of Children. Chichester: J. Wiley.
WODRICH, D.L. & JOY, J.E. (1986) Multi-disciplinary Assessment of Children with Learning Disabilities and Mental Retardation. Baltimore: Paul H. Brookes.

Assessment unit

A facility designed, staffed and run in order to provide *assessment* of disability. It often refers to paediatric units but may apply to many other types of centres.

Association for the Advancement of Behavior Therapy

An American association of qualified professionals who are skilled in *behaviour therapies*.

Further Information:
Association for the Advancement of

Behavior Therapy 420, Lexington Ave, New York, N.Y. 10017.

Association of Professionals for Mentally Handicapped People

An organization established to support and encourage good practice directed toward the best interests of mentally handicapped people. Local group meetings are held and information is provided on many aspects of mental handicap through a quarterly newsletter.

Further information:
APMH, King's Fund Centre, 126, Albert St., London. NW1 7NF.

Astasia

Inability to stand or walk due to an impairment of co-ordination of muscles.

Astigmatism

An error of *refraction* of light in the eye caused by irregularity in the curvature of the *cornea* or lens of the eye. This gives rise to distortion and blurring of vision.

Asylum

A place which offers refuge and protection. This term was used to describe the large colonies established for mentally handicapped people which later became hospitals. The word asylum came to be associated with the idea of an *institution*.

Asymmetric

The two vertical halves of the body being different in the size or appearance of parts which normally match.

Asymmetric crying facies

= *cardiofacial syndrome.*

Asymmetric tonic neck reflex

= *tonic neck reflex.*

Asynesia

Dull intellect.

Ataxia

The lack of the ability to control movements although the strength to make the movements is present. There are several possible causes related to conditions of the brain or *spinal cord*. Co-ordination of the afflicted part(s) of the body is poor and when the lower limbs are affected walking may be very unsteady. *Cerebellar ataxia* is one example.

HARDING, A.E. (1984) Hereditary Ataxias and Related Disorders. Edinburgh: Churchill Livingstone.

Ataxia telangiectasia

= *Louis-Barr syndrome.*

ATC

= *Adult Training Centre.*

Ateliosis

Incomplete development physically and/or mentally. It includes restricted growth and mental handicap. See *bird-headed dwarfism*.

Athetoid

See *athetosis*.

Athetosis

The term means 'no fixed position' and in this condition there are uncontrolled, slow, continuous movements which are writhing, repeated, often frequent and usually most severe in hands and feet, although the face may also be affected. It is caused by damage to particular parts of the brain and lack of oxygen and/or severe *jaundice* at the time of birth are possible causes. In the first year or two of life the baby is often floppy and the athetosis develops later. The affected person has more control over movements if the nearest joint of the limb is held still e.g. hand control is easier if the wrist is held in place. The movements are made worse by excitement or effort. The abnormal movements are called athetoid movements. Athetosis may occur in people who also have other forms of *cerebral palsy* and/or who are mentally handicapped. If the athetosis is caused by jaundice it is often associated with deafness.

Athyroidism

Absence of thyroid hormone due to *congenital* abnormality of the *thyroid* gland or the hormones it produces. If this condition is not treated with thyroid hormone, *cretinism* will result and this is a cause of mental handicap.

Ativan

= *lorazepam.*

Atlanto-axial instability / subluxation

Approximately 10% of people with *Down's syndrome* have this malalignment of the first two vertebrae in the neck. If the neck is bent too far the *spinal cord* may be injured and this can result in permanent paralysis. An X-ray is required to detect this. The *Special Olympics* Inc. has a policy that people with this condition should avoid gymnastics, diving, butterfly stroke, high jump, pentathlon, soccer and any exercises which place pressure on the head and neck muscles.

COOKE, R.E. (1984) Atlantoaxial instability in individuals with Down's syndrome. Adapted Physical Activity Quarterly, 1: 194–196.

Atonia

Extreme *hypotonia.*

Atresia

Absence of a natural opening in the body or on the outside of the body. Such malformations are usually evident at, or soon after, birth and may occur in association with mental handicap in some *congenital* conditions and *syndromes*. In *Down's syndrome*, atresia of parts of the bowel may occur.

Atrial septal defect

This is a malformation of the heart present at birth which is often referred to as a 'hole in the heart'. There is a defect in the wall between two of the chambers of the heart (atria) which do not normally interconnect. As a result some of the blood which should be pumped to the lungs to collect oxygen may be short-circuited and passed round the circulation of the body again, without going to the lungs first. As a consequence the heart may have to work harder than usual to pump sufficient oxygenated blood round the body. If the hole is small it may cause very few problems and gradually close as the child grows. If it is larger the heart may be under strain and more active medical or surgical treatment will be required. The two other chambers of the heart (ventricles) may also be affected (see *ventricular septal defects*).

It is usually diagnosed when an abnormal sound is heard by a doctor listening to the heart with a stethoscope. The 'murmur' is made by the turbulence of the blood as it passes through the hole. Children with mental handicap caused by factors operating before birth may have an associated abnormality of the heart. It is, for example, more common than usual in people with *Down's syndrome, Smith-Lemli-Opitz syndrome, de Lange syndrome, Goltz's syndrome* and many *chromosome* abnormalities.

Atrophia oculi congenita

= *Norries syndrome.*

Atrophy

The wasting, shrinkage or change of substance of a part of the body due to some interference with normal functioning. Atrophy of the brain may be demonstrated by *CT scan* in some people with mental handicap. It is usually secondary to disease or damage which has affected the brain.

Attachment behaviour

Children normally develop attachment to parental figures from 6 months of age or even earlier, and the trust and security engendered by this process is thought to have a significant effect on the psychological, social and intellectual development of the child. Mentally handicapped children have the same emotional needs as any other child and do form attachments. A disability may sometimes interfere with attachment formation if it causes a lack of response to the parents' nurturing behaviour which then reduces their involvement and emotional commitment. The *institutionalization* of handicapped children is contraindicated because it prevents normal attachment behaviours and exposes the child to psychological stress and deprivation.

BLACHER, J. & MEYERS, C.E. (1983) A review of attachment formation and disorder of handicapped children. Am. J. Ment. Defic., 87:359–371.
RUSSELL, O. (1985) Mental Handicap. London: Churchill Livingstone. pp. 43–49.
STONE, N.W. & CHESNEY,B.H. (1978) Attachment behaviours in handicapped infants. Mental Retardation, 16:8–12.

Attendance allowance

A financial benefit available in the U.K. from the Department of Health and Social Security. It is paid to a person who needs a lot of help from another person because of mental or physical disability. The disability has to have been present for at least six months' duration. Eligibility starts after 2 years of age and most mentally handicapped people, who are not already in the care of the state, are entitled to this benefit. It is tax-free and not means-tested but an individual assessment of the person's disabilities is carried out. Application is made through the local DHSS office. There are separate rates for day and night attendance allowance. When the recipient is receiving care away from the usual home this can affect the allowance depending on the frequency and the amount of time spent elsewhere.

Disability Rights Handbook (updated every year) from The Disability Alliance ERA, 25 Denmark St., London WC2H 8NJ.

Leaflet N.I. 205 obtainable from local DHSS office.

Further information:
Attendance Allowance Unit, DHSS, Norcross, Blackpool FY5 3TA.

Attention seeking

A term sometimes used to describe behaviours which are irritating or antisocial, and which seem to be related to a need for attention from others. The need for attention from other people is very normal but some mentally handicapped people lack the skills to meet this need in a socially acceptable way. Very often such people have been seriously deprived of attention or affection in the past and have learnt to resort to extreme behaviours in order to compete with others. Such deprivation may also lead to an increased need for affection and attention which is often difficult to fulfil. Alternatively some people who are mentally handicapped have required a lot of attention in their childhood and expect always to be the centre of attention. *Behaviour modification* techniques may be necessary to reduce attention seeking behaviours.

Atypical childhood psychosis

A disorder of development which becomes evident between 3 and 12 years of age with some or all of the features of infantile *autism*. Some mentally handicapped people could be described with this term although the term 'autistic features' may be used instead. It is usually considered that autism becomes evident before 3 years of age and children with a later onset have been difficult to categorize.

Aubry's syndrome

= *Hallermann-Streiff syndrome.*

Audiologist

A person trained in the assessment and measurement of hearing and the fitting of suitable aids.

Audiology

The *assessment* and measurement of hearing or loss of hearing. There is a higher incidence of deafness amongst mentally handicapped people and thorough assessment is therefore important.

ELLIS, D. (Ed.) (1986) Sensory Impairments in Mentally Handicapped People. London: Croom Helm.

Audiometry

A term for the measurement of hearing. There are a number of standard procedures which may be used for testing hearing. The audiometer produces sounds of different frequencies and loudness (measured in *decibels*) to measure the amount of hearing loss under different conditions. Impedance audiometry is another technique that can be used (*acoustic impedance testing*). It is important that all mentally handicapped people are screened to exclude hearing loss.

Auditory

A medical descriptive term for things to do with the ear or with hearing.

Aura

The term used to describe the feeling or experience which a person may have just before the onset of an epileptic *seizure*. Sometimes the feeling leads to a characteristic behaviour which may also serve to warn others that the person is about to have a seizure. The aura may take many different forms and may be pleasant or unpleasant.

Aural

Pertaining to the ear or sense of hearing.

Autism / autistic

A term first used by Kanner in 1943 to describe children who had severe problems in relating to people and had abnormal behaviours. Kanner thought it was a major psychiatric disorder, similar to *schizophrenia*, caused by abnormal parenting but this has been disputed. Recent research has described the condition more precisely. It is characterized by great difficulty in understanding and using language and by impaired imagination and social relationship skills. These disabilities lead to many problems in relating to people and the surrounding world. Autistic children find it hard to cope with complex and unstructured situations and tend to resist change. They are often manneristic, with characteristic repetitive movements and habits. The cause is now generally thought to be due to an abnormality of structure or function of certain parts of the brain but the nature of this is not yet known. It is three times more common in boys than in girls and occurs in four to five children in every 10,000. Research has shown that only 20% of autistic people are of normal intelligence and the more severe the mental handicap the worse the outcome. There is no cure for autism but most autistic children make progress with a systematic and carefully planned approach to teaching and *behaviour modification*. The prediction that special education would overcome the autistic handicap has been shown to be over-optimistic and about 60% of autistic people need help and supervision throughout their lives. Autistic features occur two or three times more commonly than the classic autistic syndrome. About one half of children with autistic behaviour also have an additional handicap such as *epilepsy*, *cerebral palsy* or *deafness*. A possible link with *fragile-X syndrome* has recently been described.

DEYMER, M.K. et al (1981) Infantile autism reviewed: a decade of research. Schizo. Bull., 7:388–451.

KIERNAN, C. (1983) The use of non-social communication techniques with autistic individuals. J. Child. Psychol. Psychiat., 24:339–376.

RUTTER, M. (1985) The treatment of autistic children. J. Child Psychol. Psychiat., 26(2):193–214.

RUTTER, M. & SCHOPLER, E. (Eds.) (1978) Autism: A Reappraisal of Concepts and

Treatment. New York: Plenum.

SCHOPLER, E. & MESIBOV, G.B. (1984)
The Effects of Autism on the Family. New
York: Plenum Press.
SCHOPLER, E. & MESIBOV, G.B. (1983)
Autism in Adolescents and Adults. New
York: Plenum Press.
WING, L. (1984) Children Apart. Autistic
Children and Their Families: National
Autistic Society, 276 Willesden Lane,
London NW2 5RB.
WING, L. & GOULD, J. (1979) Severe
impairments of social interaction and asso-
ciated abnormalities in children: epidemiol-
ogy and classification. J. Autism & Develop-
mental Disorders. 9:11–29.
The National Autistic Society also publish a
list of books and articles on the subject of
autistic children and adults.

Further information:
National Autistic Society, 276, Willesden
Lane, London NW2 5RB.
National Society for Children and Adults
with Autism, 1234, Massachusetts Ave.,
N.W., Suite 1017, Washington D.C. 20005–
1599.

Automatism

The performance of an act without conscious intention. This can occur after or
during an attack of *epilepsy* but it is very
unusual.

Autosomal dominant inheritance

= *dominant inheritance.*

Autosomal recessive inheritance

= *recessive inheritance.*

Autosome

= *chromosome.*

Aversive stimulation / aversion therapy

A *punishment* procedure usually restricted to
the management of severe self-destructive
and antisocial behaviours in mentally
handicapped people. Aversive shock (*electric
shock*), delivered immediately after the behaviour occurs, was one of the earliest
approaches used for intractable *self-injurious
behaviour* but, even if successful, *generalization*
is usually poor and withdrawal is difficult.
Mild physical and verbal punishment,
squirts of lemon juice in the mouth, inhalation of aromatic ammonia (smelling salts),
water mist sprayed in the face and facial
screening (covering the face with a cloth)
have also been used. Such procedures
potentially undermine human rights and
very vigorous controls on their use must be
applied.

CORBETT, J. (1975) Aversion for the treatment of self-injurious behaviour. J. Ment.
Defic. Res., 19:79–96.
LUTZKER, J.R. (1978) Reducing self-
injurious behaviors in three classrooms by
facial screening. Am. J. Ment. Defic., 82:
510–513.
MARHOLIN, D. et al (1980) Response-
contingent taste-aversion in treating chronic
ruminative vomiting of institutionalized
retarded children. J. Ment. Defic. Res.,
24:47–56.
SINGH, N.N. (1979) Aversive control of
breath-holding. J. Behav. Ther. Exp.
Psychiat., 10:147.

Axenfeld syndrome

= *Rieger's syndrome.*

B

Babinski reflex

An abnormal response seen when the outside edge of the sole of the foot is scraped. The big toe would normally point downward and the other toes curl. The abnormal response occurs when the big toe is raised up and the other toes spread. It indicates that there is damage to the brain or *spinal cord*. It is very easy to get apparently abnormal responses in normal people especially infants and young children and it should therefore be carried out by professionals skilled in neurological examinations.

Backward chaining

A method of teaching mentally handicapped people a complex behaviour or action. It can be used to teach any skill or activity which occurs in a set sequence. The action is broken down into small steps and the last step is taught first. This has the advantage of immediately leading to success and is rewarding to the person. Once the last step has been learnt the penultimate step is added and so on, until the entire chain of small steps has been learnt and the skill acquired. A backward chaining programme needs to be carefully planned and followed very consistently with appropriate *prompts* and *reinforcements*. It is one of a range of *behaviour modification* techniques practised by the *psychologists*, *teachers*, *care staff* and others who help mentally handicapped people.

MINGE, M.R. & BALL, T.S. (1967) Teaching of self-help skills to profoundly retarded patients. Am. J. Ment. Defic., 71:864–868.
MOORE, P. & CARR, J. (1976) Behaviour modification programme to teach dressing to a severely retarded adolescent. Communication, 11,2:20–27.

Baclofen

A drug used in the treatment of *spasticity*. It helps to relax the limbs. It may be used for people with *cerebral palsy* or with spasticity due to *meningitis* or *head injury*. It is likely to be of most benefit when spasticity is a major handicap to activities or to *physiotherapy*. It may help to counteract painful spasms. Its use should be carefully monitored and the dose increased gradually to reduce side-effects. These include nausea, vomiting, sedation, confusion, muscle weakness and fatigue. It should be used with great caution in people who have *epilepsy* as it can make it worse.

Balanced carrier

See *chromosome translocation*.

Balanced translocation

See *chromosome translocation*.

Baldness

= *alopecia*.

Balthasar Scales of Adaptive Behavior

A detailed scale suitable for people with severe or profound mental handicap. It may be used for assessment, target setting, research and evaluation. It is a very structured system and needs to be used over several days by someone who is both trained in its use and frequently in contact with the client. The first part covers eating, dressing and toileting skills. The second part includes self-directive behaviour, interpersonal behaviour, vocal communication, play activities and response to instructions. The manuals give detailed information on data collection and *goal planning*. Each behaviour is scored and results are drawn onto a profile graph for each area covered.

BALTHASAR, E.E. (1971) Balthasar Scales of Adaptive Behavior for the Profoundly and

Severely Mentally Retarded: A system for program evaluation and development. Illinois: Research Press Champaign.

BALTHASAR, E.E. (1971) The Assessment of Adaptive Behaviour. In: Proceedings for the Second Congress of the International Association for the Scientific Study of Mental Deficiency. Primrose, D.A.A. (Ed.) Warsaw: Polish Medical Publishers. pp. 566–570.

BALTHASAR, E.E. (1976) Balthasar Scales of Adaptive Behavior 1 & 2. Palo Alto, Calif: Consulting Psychologists Press.

Banding techniques

Each *chromosome* has a characteristic marking known as banding. The techniques for staining human tissues so that the chromosome bands can be studied in detail have become increasingly sophisticated. Recent developments have led to most laboratories recognizing between 400 and 800 bands on a chromosome and in some cases up to 2000 bands. Most laboratories now use one or more banding techniques as a routine test. These methods allow identification of an extra or missing chromosome and the accurate localization of breakpoints in chromosome rearrangements.

Barbiturates

A group of drugs with a number of uses. Long-acting barbiturates, mainly *phenobarbitone*, have been used for many years to treat *epilepsy*. Short-acting barbiturates are used in general *anaesthesia*. The intermediate-acting barbiturates were used for the treatment of insomnia and *anxiety states* but are used infrequently nowadays because of the risk of dependence.

Bardet-Biedl syndrome

= *Biedl-Moon-Laurence syndrome*.

Barr body

A mass of chromosomal material seen at the edge of the dark centre (nucleus) of each cell of a normal human female. It can only be seen when the cells obtained, for example, by scraping the inside of the mouth, are stained with a special chemical and looked at under a microscope. The number of Barr bodies is always one less than the number of X-*chromosomes* possessed. Examination of the Barr bodies may be used in the *diagnosis* of abnormalities of the *sex chromosomes* in conditions which are associated with mental handicap e.g. *XXXX syndrome*. More sophisticated techniques for examining *chromosomes* are usually used nowadays.

Basal cell naevus syndrome

People with this rare syndrome are prone to tumours of the skin which usually appear before ten years of age especially on the upper half of the body. They start as small lumps but may increase in size and invade the skin, becoming malignant. The forehead is often protuberant and the base of the nose broad. Cysts may occur in the jawbones. Abnormalities of the eyes, bones (especially ribs and spine) and brain may also occur and mental handicap and *schizophrenia* have been reported. It is inherited from a parent who also has the condition (*dominant inheritance*) sometimes in the milder form.

DAVIDSON, F. (1962) Multiple naevoid basal cell carcinomata and associated congenital abnormalities. Brit. J. Derm., 74: 439.

GORLIN, R.J. et al (1965) The multiple basal cell nevi syndrome. Cancer, 18:89.

Basal ganglia / basal nuclei

These are centres deep in the brain which are involved in the control of movements. Damage to, or abnormalities of, this part of the brain may lead to muscular rigidity, involuntary movements (such as tremor) and weakness of muscles. *Parkinson's disease* or *athetosis* may result.

Baseline

This term describes a measure used in *behaviour modification*. Before intervention is planned it is conventional to record the level of occurrence of the behaviour which is causing concern. This baseline observation should be continued until it is thought that the behaviour is reliably represented and the treatment or intervention is then started. The baseline often provides useful information in itself and also makes it possible to evaluate the effect of the intervention.

Basic Life Skills Screening Inventory

This is a method of assessing the life skills of mentally handicapped *deaf-blind* people 10 years of age and older. It assesses physical functioning, personal management, home management, community living, language, work habits and behaviours, responsibility and social maturity, *maladaptive behaviour* and an actual work sample. Each assessment item is divided into three levels: 1. beginning formal vocational and life skills training; 2. skills required for *sheltered workshop* and supervised living; 3. skills for competitive employment and independent living.

BECKER, H. et al (1983) The Basic Life Skills Screening Inventory: An instrument to assess vocational readiness in the deaf-blind developmentally disabled. Dallas, Texas: South Central Regional Deaf-Blind Center.

Basilar impression of vertebrae
= *platybasia*.

Bassen-Kornzweig syndrome

A rare condition in which a probable *enzyme* deficiency leads to impaired absorption of fat from food and consequently low levels of fat and fat-related substances in the body. Vitamins A, E and K are stored in fat and deficiencies of these vitamins can also be a problem. In the first year of life infants develop abdominal distension, diarrhoea, foul-smelling faeces, decreased fat absorption and occasionally softening of bones. Most are small in weight and height. Between 2 and 17 years of age unsteadiness when walking is usually the first sign of abnormality of the nervous system. Reflexes

and sensation are usually reduced. Mental handicap occurs in about one third of affected people. Deterioration of the *retina* of the eye leads to poor vision and night blindness. Abnormalities of heart rhythm are common. Supplementation of the diet with the deficient vitamins is recommended. The cause of the condition is unknown.

IERBERT, P.N. et al (1983) Familial lipo-rotein deficiency: abetalipo-proteinaemia, hypoabetalipoproteinaemia and Tangier disease. In: The Metabolic Basis of Inherited Disease (5th edit.) Stanbury, J.B. (Ed.) et al. New York: McGraw-Hill. p. 589. ILLINGWORTH, D.R. et al (1980) Abetalipoproteinaemia: Report of two cases and review of therapy. Arch. Neurol., 37:659. MULLER, D.P.R. & LLOYD, J.K. (1982) Effect of large oral doses of vitamin E on the neurologic sequelae of patients with abetalipoproteinaemia. Ann. N.Y. Acad. Sciences, 393:133.

Batten's disease
= *Batten-Vogt disease*.

Batten-Mayou disease
= *Batten-Vogt disease*.

Batten-Spielmeyer-Vogt disease
= *Batten-Vogt disease*.

Batten-Vogt disease

This is a group of disorders (*ceroid lipofuscinoses*) in which abnormal substances accumulate in the cells of the body. These collect in the brain, nerves and eyes and interfere with function. The condition becomes evident in childhood or adolescence and mental handicap, visual loss, *spasticity* and *epilepsy* all increase in severity over a number of years. It is inherited from both parents who are carriers of the condition (*recessive inheritance*). The chemistry of the disorder is not known but the abnormal substances which accumulate are glycolipids and cholesterolesters. The diagnosis is made by microscopically examining a small sample of tissue obtained by rectal or liver *biopsy* and seeing the abnormal materials in the cells using an electron microscope.

The juvenile form (Spielmeyer-Vogt) has an onset between 6 and 10 years of age with death occurring between 15 and 25 years.

The late infantile form (*Bielschowsky-Jansky disease*) has an earlier onset and a rapid course. An early infantile form has recently been described (*Santavuori's disease*).

BRETT, E.M. & LAKE, B.D. (1983) Progressive neurometabolic brain disease. In: Paediatric Neurology (Ed.) Brett,E.M. London: Churchill Livingstone. pp. 133–140.

KRISTENSEN, K. et al (1983) Central nervous system dysfunction as an early sign of neuronal ceroid lipofuscinosis (Batten's disease). Dev. Med. Child Neurology, 25(5):588–590.

MACLEOD, P.M. et al (1985) Prenatal diagnosis of neuronal ceroid-lipofuscinosis. Am. J. Med. Genet., 22(4):781–789.

Battered child syndrome
= *Child abuse.*

Bayley Scales of Infant Development

A test suitable for babies, young children and severely mentally handicapped children. It is in three parts: the mental scale, the motor scale and infant behaviour record. It compares the child's development with the average for children of his or her own age. The scales were standardized on infants aged 1 month to 2 years 6 months and are more suitable for children with even profiles of development, rather than for those with marked discrepancies between different types of skills. It is useful in the evaluation of physically handicapped infants because it separates motor and *cognitive* skills. It is also helpful in planning activities to stimulate the development of the child.

BAYLEY, N. (1969). Bayley Scales of Infant Development. New York: Psychological Corporation.

Bead test

This test is used to assess vision in people who are severely mentally handicapped. The person is invited to eat small sugarbeads with a diameter ranging from 1cm to 1mm. The distance between the sugarbeads and the person is measured.

RICHMAN, J.E. & GARZIA, R.P. (1983) The bead test: a critical appraisal. Am. J. Optometry Physiological Optics, 60:199–203.

BEAM

= brain electrical activity mapping. See *topographic brain mapping.*

Beckwith syndrome / Beckwith-Wiedemann syndrome

People with this syndrome characteristically have a large tongue and are large for their age. Their ears are frequently of an unusual shape and have a groove in the lobes. An *umbilical hernia* may be present. The lower jaw may protrude. Internal organs of the body especially the liver, spleen and pancreas are often enlarged. In infancy there may be problems with low blood sugar levels and there may be a tendency to *diabetes mellitus* in later life. There is often a birth mark on the forehead which fades during the first two years of life. Very many abnormalities involving most body systems have been reported in people with this syndrome. Abnormalities of the kidneys are quite common. Sometimes one side of the body grows faster than the other (*hemihypertrophy*). There is increased risk of childhood malignant disease (estimated at 5%). A mild to moderate degree of mental handicap has been reported but some people with this condition are of normal intelligence. It is thought to be inherited from both parents who are carriers (*recessive inheritance*).

FILLIPI, G. & McKUSICK, V.A. (1970) The Beckwith-Wiedemann syndrome. Medicine, 49:279.

SCHIFF, D. et al (1973) Metabolic aspects of the Beckwith-Wiedemann syndrome. J. Pediatr., 82:258.

Beclamide

A drug used for the treatment of *behaviour disorders* and *epilepsy*. It is said to be indicated for people who are unstable and *aggressive*. It is not widely used and is generally not regarded as the drug of first choice for either behaviour problems or epilepsy. It tends to be used as well as, rather than instead of, other *anticonvulsant* drugs. Side-effects, such as weight loss, dizziness and skin irritation are very unusual and if they do occur are mild and transient.

Bed-wetting

= *enuresis*.

Behaviour analysis

This process is considered an essential part of the *behaviour modification* approach to teaching people or changing behaviours. A behavioural analysis involves careful observation of a previously defined behaviour in a previously defined environment. It includes the events preceding the behaviour (*antecedents* or setting events), the frequency and duration of the behaviour and the events which happen after (consequences). This may be recorded in a number of ways and video filming provides a useful record which can be analysed later. This information is used to understand the relationship between the behaviour and the environment so that either the antecedents or consequences can be changed in order to change the behaviour i.e. a behaviour modification programme can be established. Behaviour analysis can then continue in order to monitor the effects of any interventions.

GELFAND, D.M. & HARTMANN, D.P. (1975) Child Behavior Analysis and Therapy. New York: Pergamon.
KANFER, F.M. & GRIMM, L.G. (1977) Behavioral analysis: selecting target behaviors in the interview. Behav. Mod., 1:7–28.
KIERNAN, C.C. (1973) Functional analysis. In: Assessment for Learning in the Mentally Handicapped. Mittler, P. (Ed.) London: Churchill. pp. 263–283.

Behaviour Assessment Battery

A complex, detailed and comprehensive assessment tool designed to aid the selection of teaching targets for severely and profoundly mentally handicapped people in a variety of areas. Not all sections have to be used and some parts are suitable for use with deaf, blind and physically handicapped people. The areas covered include reinforcement and experience; inspection; tracking; visuo-motor; auditory; play; perceptual problems; search strategies; social; communication and self-help skills. Each area has a score sheet arranged as a 'lattice' which forms a visual profile of progress. Training and practice is necessary to become proficient in its use.

KIERNAN, C.C. & JONES, M.C. (1982) Behaviour Assessment Battery (2nd edit.) Windsor: NFER-Nelson.

Behaviour disorders

Behaviours which seriously interfere with the normal life of a person or the lives of those with whom he or she lives or works. The majority of people with a mental handicap do not show serious behaviour disorders. When problem behaviours do occur there is an unfortunate tendency to attribute them to the fact that the person is mentally handicapped. More usually the cause lies in environmental, emotional or psychiatric factors. Nevertheless, a few mentally handicapped people do have great difficulty in coping with reasonable expectations and with normal life, especially those with *autistic* traits. There is a clear association between social impairments, communication problems, symbolic/imaginative impairments and behaviour disorders. Mentally handicapped people may have behaviour disorders such as *aggression, self-injury*, destructiveness and *overactivity* which are rarely serious enough to endanger themselves or other people. Even if not severe, such behaviours can still be sufficient to interfere with learning or with enjoyment of life and may respond to *behaviour modification* techniques or medication so long as the person is emotionally secure and in an appropriate environment. It is preferable to teach alternative adaptive behaviours rather than to try only to eliminate undesirable behaviours. Behaviour disorders in mildly mentally handicapped people may attract psychiatric diagnoses or be described as conduct or *personality disorders*.

SIGSTON, A. (1987) Meeting the needs of people with severe learning and behaviour difficulties and their families. Newsletter, Association for Child Psychol. and Psychiat., 9(2):23–25.

Behaviour modification

This term is used to describe a particular approach to teaching desirable behaviours and eliminating undesirable behaviours. It was controversial but it is now widely accepted as an important method for improving the skills of mentally handicapped people. It is based on the practical application of a branch of psychology which originated in the 1930's mainly through B.F. Skinner's work with animals. This involved the experimental analysis of behaviour and the development of theories about the way people learn. A behaviour modification programme necessitates defining the problem objectively; setting up hypotheses to account for observations; testing these hypotheses and evaluating the outcome. A number of techniques of *behaviour analysis*, task analysis and behaviour change are used. They include *shaping, chaining, prompting, fading, modelling, imitation, reinforcement* and *generalization*. Behaviour modification is a highly structured form of intervention and, to be effective, must be carefully planned by appropriately skilled practitioners. It does not exclude other approaches and is most likely to be effective when a person is emotionally secure and has an appropriate environment which affords opportunities to have a full and normal life-style. It is now recognized that behaviour modification to eliminate undesirable behaviours is more likely to be successful when *adaptive behaviours* are taught at the same time.

BELLACK, A.S. et al (Eds.)(1982) International Handbook of Behaviour Modification and Therapy. New York: Plenum Press.
CARR, J. (1980) Helping Your Handicapped Child. London: Penguin Books.
CRAIGHEAD, W.E. et al (Eds.) (1976) Behaviour Modification: Principles, Issues and Applications. Boston: Houghton Mifflin.
FOXX, R. (1983) Increasing Behaviours of Severely Retarded and Autistic Persons. Illinois: Research Press.
FOXX, R. (1983) Decreasing Behaviours of Severely Retarded and Autistic Persons. Illinois: Research Press.
KAZIN, A.E. (1980) Behaviour Modification in Applied Settings. Illinois: Homewood.
KIERNAN, C.C. & WOODFORD, F.P. (Eds.) (1975) Behaviour Modification with the Severely Retarded. Elsevier North Holland: Associated Scientific Publishers.
MATSON, J.L. & McCARTHY, J.R. (Eds.) (1981) Handbook of Behavior Modification with the Mentally Retarded. New York: Plenum.
THOMPSON, T. & GRABOWSKI, J. (Eds.) (1977) Behaviour Modification of the Mentally Retarded. (2nd edit.) New York: Oxford University Press.
WHITMAN, T.L. et al (1983) Behavior Modification with the Severely and Profoundly Retarded: Research and Applications. New York: Academic Press.
YULE, W. & CARR, J. (Eds.) (1987) Behaviour Modification for People with Mental Handicaps (2nd edit.). Beckenham: Croom Helm.

Behaviour problem checklists

A variety of checklists and rating scales have been devised to assess the severity and incidence of behaviour problems in children and in people who are mentally handicapped. They vary as to the number of problem areas covered; the age range to which they are applicable; the specificity of the items; the settings in which they can be appropriately used; and whether or not they include a scale which rates the severity or frequency of the problem. The most commonly used are the *Adaptive Behavior Scales* and the *Handicap, Behaviour and Skills Schedule*.

Behaviour problems

= *behaviour disorders*.

Behaviour reinforcement

= *reinforcement*.

Behaviour therapy

A treatment approach consisting of practical procedures based on therapy and research in the behavioural sciences especially in relation to learning theory. The person's problems are formulated in terms of behaviours that need to be changed and these are tackled directly, generally without reference to possible causes in the past. Many techniques are used including desensitization, flooding, assertion training, biofeedback and aversion therapy. Behaviour therapy may be used to help any person regardless of intellectual ability but some of the techniques require active co-operation and motivation. Those approaches described under *behaviour modification* are generally considered to be most applicable to mentally handicapped people.

Behavioural approach

= *behaviour modification*.

Behavioural objectives

The goals and targets of *behaviour modification*. It is important that these are specific and observable behaviours. It is easy to set unrealistic or overambitious objectives. One way of helping people select appropriate objectives is to use a *developmental checklist* or chart which indicates the level of achievements and shows the items which can become the next behavioural objectives.

Bell and pad

An instrument used for training a person who wets the bed at night. A foil mat is put underneath the bottom sheet and is connected to an alarm. When the person first starts to wet the bed the urine, which conducts electricity, completes the circuit between the two strips of foil and sets off the alarm bell or buzzer. It is powered by a small battery. It has been used to train children with nocturnal *enuresis* for many years with a good success rate. It is possible to have the alarm ring in the parents' room so that they can wake and help the child to the toilet. A pillow vibrator can be used instead of a buzzer so that other members of the family are not woken.

Bender Visual Motor Gestalt Test

= *Bender-Gestalt Test*.

Bender-Gestalt Test

This test was originally developed to provide an index of maturity in skills involving perception and motor co-ordination. It consists of nine geometric drawings that are presented one at a time to be copied. Later workers have developed scoring systems for assessing *brain damage* and emotional problems.

KOPPITZ, E.M. (1964) The Bender Gestalt Test for Young Children. New York: Grune & Stratton.
KOPPITZ, E.M. (1975) The Bender Gestalt Test for Young Children: Research and Application, 1963–1973, Vol 2. New York: Grune & Stratton.

Benefits (financial)

= *allowances*.

Benperidol

A tranquillizer which may also help a person to control deviant and antisocial sexual behaviour. It is reported to reduce sexual drive in adults. It should be introduced gradually in order to avoid drowsiness or insomnia. It can cause low blood pressure and allergic reactions but these are rare. The most common side-effects are muscle rigidity, spasms and tremor (*extra-pyramidal signs*). It may be necessary to give drugs to counteract these. Other effects, such as involuntary movements (*tardive dyskinesia*) may also occur.

Benzhexol

This is very similar to *benztropine* in its use and side-effects.

Benzodiazepines

A group of drugs used for the treatment of *anxiety* and as sleeping tablets. Some of these drugs also have *anticonvulsant* properties. The benzodiazepines which are used for the treatment of chronic anxiety include *diazepam*, chlordiazepoxide, *clobazam* and others. Shorter acting drugs such as *oxazepam* and *lorazepam* may be used for acute anxiety and panic attacks. There is little convincing evidence that benzodiazepines remain effective in the treatment of anxiety after 4 months' continuous treatment. Side-effects include impairment of judgement and slowness to react. The ability to drive or operate machinery is affected. The benzodiazepines used to induce sleep include *nitrazepam*, *flurazepam* and others. These have a prolonged action which may give rise to residual effects the following day.

Psychological and physical dependence on benzodiazepines may occur and the withdrawal symptoms include sleeplessness, anxiety, loss of appetite, shakiness and perspiration. The benzodiazepines used as anticonvulsants include diazepam, clobazam, nitrazepam and *clonazepam*.

Benzodiazepines may be used to treat mentally handicapped people who are suffering from anxiety or insomnia but, in children particularly, may have a disinhibitory effect and this may make them unsuitable for the treatment of *behaviour disorders*.

FREEMAN, H. & RUE, Y. (Eds.) (1987) *The benzodiazepines in current clinical practice.* London: Roy. Soc. Med. Serv.

TRIMBLE, M.R. (1983) Benzodiazepines in epilepsy. In: Benzodiazepines Divided. Trimble, M.R. (Ed.). Chichester: Wiley. pp. 65–91.

Benztropine

This drug is used for the treatment of *Parkinson's disease* and also for the treatment of the similar side-effects (*extra-pyramidal signs*) of tranquillizers such as *haloperidol*, *chlorpromazine* and *pericyazine*. Benztropine also has side-effects which include dryness of the mouth, nausea, vomiting, blurring of vision and confusion.

Berardinelli's lipodystrophy

See *lipodystrophy*.

Bereavement reaction

This is an emotional reaction to severe loss. It is usually associated with the death of a loved one and mentally handicapped people are just as susceptible as anyone else to this reaction. Unfortunately they are sometimes deprived of the opportunity to grieve by well-meaning people who try to protect them from the pain of loss.

The bereavement reaction also occurs in parents following the *diagnosis* of mental handicap in their child. This is particularly evident when the diagnosis is made at birth or is due to trauma or illness after birth. They have lost the normal child they were expecting and have to come to terms with a new and unplanned situation. This may be reactivated at various crisis points throughout life. There are three stages of this reaction. The first is numbness and disbelief when it is difficult to take in information. The second is overt grief and distress. The third is the development of strategies for dealing with the situation.

MCLOUGHLIN, I.J. (1986) Bereavement in the mentally handicapped. Brit. J. Hosp. Med., 36(4):256–260.

OSWIN, M. (1981) Bereavement and Mentally Handicapped People. London: King's Fund Centre.

STRACHAN, J. (1981) Reaction to bereavement: a study of a group of mentally handicapped hospital residents. Apex, 9(1): 20–21.

WORTHINGTON, A. (1982) Coming to Terms with Mental Handicap. Whitby: Helena Press.

Bereweeke

A method of *assessing* and teaching skills. There are two checklists, one for adults and one for children. It should be used with *individual programme plans*. Areas covered include language, self-care, motor skills, social skills and cognitive skills. The manual is detailed and precise. A visual summary chart and *goal planning* checklists are available. The main purpose is to develop individual teaching programmes.

JENKINS, J. et al (1986) The Bereweeke Skill Teaching System. Windsor: NFER-Nelson.
MANSELL, J. et al (1979) The Bereweeke Skill-teaching System: Programme Writer's Handbook. Winchester: Health Care Evaluation Research Team.

Berry-Francescetti syndrome
= *Treacher-Collins syndrome.*

Beta-glucuronidase deficiency
= *Sly's syndrome.*

Better Services for the Mentally Handicapped (1971)
= *White Paper 1971.*

Biedl-Moon-Laurence syndrome
= *Laurence-Moon-Biedl syndrome*

Bielschowsky-Jansky disease / Bielschowsky disease
One of a group of disorders (*ceroid lipofuscinoses*) in which abnormal substances accumulate in the cells of the body. The onset is between 1 and 4 years. There is deterioration in vision and increasing brain damage resulting in *seizures*, unsteadiness, weakness, spasticity and mental handicap. The *electroencephalogram* shows a characteristic pattern on *photic stimulation*. Death usually occurs within a few years. It is inherited from both

parents who are carriers but show no symptoms (*recessive inheritance*). The chemistry of the disorder is not known but the abnormal substances which accumulate are called lipofuscins. It is similar to *Batten-Vogt disease* but with an earlier age of onset and a more rapid course.

PAMPIGLIONA, G. & MARDEN, A. (1973) A neuro-physiological identification of a late infantile form of 'neuronal lipidosis'. J. Neurol. Neurosurg. Psychiat., 36:68–74.

Biemond's syndrome
= *Laurence-Moon-Biedl syndrome.*

Bimanual synkinesis
This unusual symptom is described in people with abnormalities of the upper region of the spine (as occurs in *Klippel-Feil syndrome*). Movements of one hand or arm are imitated automatically by the other as if in a mirror. Children under 8 years of age normally tend to mirror complex movements of one hand with the other hand.

BIMH
= *British Institute of Mental Handicap.*

BIMH Developmental Checklist
A simple checklist based on normal child development and designed for assessment and goal planning. It is used for severely and profoundly handicapped children and adults. It covers the areas of social skills, self-help, play and language and is easy to use. A profile summary is provided which gives a general impression of strengths and weaknesses.

PERKINS, E.A. et al (1980) BIMH Developmental Checklist in Helping the Retarded – a Systematic Behavioural Approach. Kidderminster: BIMH.
SIMON, G.B. (1981) Next Step on the Ladder: Assessment and Management of the Multihandicapped Child. Kidderminster: BIMH.

Binet-Simon Scale of Intelligence
This was devised by Binet, a French psy-

chologist, and his colleagues in 1905 and consisted of 30 items graded in difficulty. The items ranged from following a moving object with one's eyes to defining abstract words. The average score for each age group was determined and it was then possible to compare a child's performance with the average for his or her age group. A revised version was produced in 1908, in which test items were grouped according to age at which the majority of a large sample of children passed them. The child was given a *mental age* (MA) from the highest group of tests passed, and this was compared with his or her *chronological age* (CA). The Binet-Simon Scale was later revised and modified at Stanford University and renamed the *Stanford-Binet*.

Bing-Siebenmann dysplasia

An abnormality of the tissues of the inner ear which affects hearing and balance. It occurs in *Usher's syndrome* and *Goldenhar's syndrome* both of which are associated with an increased incidence of mental handicap.

Biopsy

The removal and examination of tissues from the living body for diagnostic purposes. Skin biopsy may be used to obtain cells, known as fibroblasts, which can be grown (*fibroblast culture*). If the cells are unable to make certain enzymes this is diagnostic of some deteriorating conditions which cause mental handicap. Rectal or liver biopsies may be used to examine cells microscopically to help in the diagnosis of *Batten-Vogt disease*.

Bipolar illness / bipolar affective disorder

= *manic-depressive psychosis*.

Bird-headed dwarfism

People with this rare condition are small throughout their lives and have a slender body build. They have a relatively small head (*microcephaly*), rather flat cheeks, narrow face, a prominent beak-like nose and receding chin. Ears are often low set with small or absent lobes. The roof of the mouth is high and may be cleft (*cleft palate*). Teeth may be absent or small with poor enamel. Abnormalities of the genitals have been reported. There may be abnormalities of bones and dislocation of joints and there is a wide space between the first and second toes. Any degree of mental handicap may occur. It is said that mood changes are frequent. It is inherited from both parents who are carriers (*recessive inheritance*). This condition has been described with premature senility, early loss of hair and wrinkling of the skin. This is called Montreal-type bird-headed dwarfism and may be a separate condition.

FRIJNS, J.P. & van den BURG, H.E. (1976) Bird-headed dwarfism. Acta Paediatrica Belgica, 29:79–82.
HARPER, R.G. et al (1967) Bird-headed dwarfs (Seckel's syndrome). A familial pattern of developmental, dental, skeletal, genital and central nervous system anomalies. J. Pediatr., 70:709.
McKUSICK, V.A. et al (1967) Seckel's bird-headed dwarfism. New Engl. J. Med., 277:279–286.

Birth control

= *contraception*.

Birth defects

Abnormalities of the baby noticed at birth but caused by factors operating before birth.

Birth injury

Any damage to the baby as a result of the birth process. External injuries can occur to a baby during birth but these are rare and recovery is usually good. Of greater concern are problems which cause damage to the brain either directly or through lack of oxygen (*anoxia*). Factors which make damage more likely are prematurity and difficult labour. Lack of oxygen due to a difficult birth or to delay in breathing after birth can cause damage to the brain cells. Direct injury to the brain may result from a sudden delivery, prolonged delivery, use of forceps or breech delivery. *Cerebral palsy* and mental handicap may be the consequence.

Bite reflex

People with *cerebral palsy* may have a reflex clamping of the jaws when the mouth is stimulated. This can cause feeding problems. A programme of desensitizing the mouth area using gentle and repeated stimulation may be helpful and the feeding technique in use needs to be carefully considered. Expert advice from a *physiotherapist, speech therapist* or *mental handicap nurse* may be useful. Spastics society centres also offer advice on such problems.

Further information:
Spastics Society, 12 Park Crescent, London, W1N 4EQ.

Blepharitis

Inflammation of the eyelids. This is quite a common problem for people with *Down's syndrome*, due to the absence of a chemical in the tears which normally prevents infection. It can be treated.

Blepharophimosis

Narrowing of the width of the eyelids so that the eyes appear small and may seem widely spaced. This may be associated with a number of conditions including *Down's syndrome*.

Blindisms

These are *mannerisms* like eye pressing and rocking, found among some blind people. Such mannerisms are also common among mentally handicapped people but have been given a special name for visually handicapped people. This is not regarded as a scientific term and is one that has been rejected by many people working in the field of visual impairment.

JAN, J.E. et al (1977) Visual Impairment in Children and Adolescents. New York: Grune & Stratton.

Blindness

Blindness or partial sight occurs in 14% of people with a mental handicap. Blindness, as defined by the World Health Organization, is a measured visual acuity of less than 6/18 Snellen in the person's own home. This fractional score indicates that the person can see, at 6 metres, what a person with normal vision can see at 18 metres. Many countries use some form of registration as the basis of providing aid and services to visually handicapped people. Blindness, in itself, will not limit the learning capacity of a person but when a person already has learning problems it is another obstacle to overcome.

In the U.K. registered blindness is defined as 'so blind as to be unable to do any work for which eyesight is essential' (National Assistance Act (1948)) and the registration form has to be completed by an ophthalmologist.

In the U.S.A. legal blindness is defined as 'a distance visual acuity of 20/200 or less in the better eye, when the eye is fully corrected with optical lenses; or visual acuity better than 20/200 but with visual field reduction in the widest diameter to no greater than 20 degrees'. Partially sighted children, on the other hand, are those who have sufficient vision to be used as the primary modality in their education. There are many state and federal resource centres for visually handicapped and blind people across the U.S.A. which include the following.

1. National Study for the Prevention of Blindness. 16E 40th St., New York, N.Y. 10016.
2. U.S. Department of Health, Education and Welfare, Division of Handicapped

Children and Youth, Washington, D.C. 20225.

3. National Aid to the Visually Handicapped, Inc., 3201 Balboa St. San Francisco, Calif. 94121.

4. American Foundation for the Blind, Inc., 15W 16th St. New York, N.Y. 10011.

The Royal National Institute for the Blind, 224–228, Great Portland St., London, W1N 6AA provides help, advice and publications on the care, training, management and needs of blind people.

ELLIS, D. (1986) Sensory Impairments in Mentally Handicapped People. London: College Hill Press; Croom Helm.

JAN, J.E. et al (1977) Visual Impairment in Children and Adolescents. New York: Grune & Stratton.

Blissymbolics / Bliss Symbol Communication System

A system of symbols based on meaning rather than words. Some of the symbols are like pictures but the majority are abstract. The major use is as a means of *communication* for people who have limited ability in the production of speech and in hand function (as may occur in *cerebral palsy*). It can be used by people who can indicate by some means (eyes, fingers, hand, pointer or electronic) the symbols they wish to use. The symbols are set out on a board or sheet. Although Bliss does not require reading skills it is generally agreed that a *mental age* of 3 or more is necessary to learn the system. The basic vocabulary is taught following the normal developmental pattern and grammatical use of words is attempted. Bliss symbols have logical roots and several symbols can be combined to produce new words. Each symbol has the word written under it so that the 'listener' does not need to know the symbols. It is the most widely used symbol system in the U.K. and is also used in the U.S.A. and many other countries (it is not dependent on the use of English).

BLISS, C. (1975) Teaching Guidelines. Australia: Blissymbolics.

BLISS, C. (1976) Provisional Dictionary (revised edit.). Sydney, Australia: Blissymbolics.

McDONALD, E.T. (1980) Teaching and Using Blissymbolics. Toronto: Blissymbolics Communication Institute.

OWRAM, L. (1982) Introducing Blissymbolics – A Guide for Parents and Friends of Symbol Users. Toronto: Blissymbolics Communication Institute.

Further information:
Blissymbolics Communication and Resource Centre, South Glamorgan Institute of Higher Education, Western Ave, Llandaff, Cardiff, CF5 2YB.

Bloch-Sulzberger syndrome / Bloch-Siemens syndrome

People with this condition have skin problems starting with red blistering linear patches in early infancy. These change over months or years into bands of swollen scars and grey or brown pigmentation. Over the years these gradually fade and may leave thin areas of skin. Baldness or bald patches are common and teeth are often missing or malformed. Nails are thin and poorly developed. Abnormalities of the eyes may occur, and also minor abnormalities of bones. In about a third of people with this syndrome there are signs of brain abnormalities including mental handicap, *cerebral palsy, seizures* and a small head. Life expectancy is normal.

It has only been reported with certainty in females and for this reason is thought to be due to an inherited abnormal *gene* carried on an X *chromosome* which is lethal to males (males only have one X chromosome whereas females have two and it is possible that the normal gene in the female modifies some of the more serious effects of the abnormal gene).

CARNEY, R.G.L. & CARNEY, E.G. (1970) Incontinentia pigmenti. Arch. Derm., 102: 157–162.

O'DOHERTY, N.J. & NORMAN, R.M. (1968) Incontinentia pigmenti with cerebral malformation. Dev. Med. Child Neurology, 10:168.

Blood dyscrasia

Abnormalities of the blood cells which may occur as a serious side-effect of some drugs. The most usual presentation is a reduction in the number of cells in the blood. When the number of white cells is reduced (*leucopenia* or *agranulocytosis*) the person can become very susceptible to infections. Reduction in the number of red cells results in an anaemia. Blood dyscrasias have been reported with the use of *carbamazepine*, *chlorpromazine* and other drugs.

BLSSI

= *Basic Life Skills Screening Inventory.*

Boarding out

A system under which a mentally handicapped person is taken into a private domestic home as a 'boarder' or 'lodger'. This has been used as a part of some *community care* programmes.

Bobath neurodevelopmental therapy

This method of *physiotherapy* was developed in the U.K. and particularly benefits children with *cerebral palsy*. A functional assessment of the child's neurological handicap is made with an understanding of abnormal movements and *tone*. The therapy is designed to inhibit the abnormal movements and postures and to facilitate the normal development of movement and balance reactions which occur as the child matures.

BOBATH, K. (1980) A Neurophysiological Basis for the Treatment of Cerebral Palsy. London: Heinemann Medical Books.

Bobble-head doll syndrome

Bobbing movements of the head seen in children with obstructive *hydrocephalus*. It can be a warning sign of increasing pressure in the *cerebro-spinal fluid*.

TOMASOVIC, J.A. et al (1975) The bobble-head doll syndrome: an early sign of hydrocephalus. Two new cases and a review of the literature. Dev. Med. Child Neurology, 17:777–792.

Bogaert's disease

= *cerebrotendinous xanthomatosis.*

Bonding

This refers to the special bond which exists between most parents and their babies. There are many factors that influence the parent-child relationship and 'bonding' may not come easily even with a healthy normal baby. Unfortunately the birth of a brain damaged or handicapped child can also interfere with this process. The baby may be separated and nursed in an incubator so that the parents cannot relate to her or him. The baby may not be as responsive as usual or may be irritable and difficult. Furthermore parents may be distressed by a difficult birth or by having been told that the child may be mentally handicapped (*bereavement reaction*). Some parents deliberately suppress their feelings for a baby because they know or suspect that there is something wrong or because there is a fear that the baby might not survive. Despite all the potential problems the majority of parents are strongly 'bonded' to their mentally handicapped child and are often especially caring and protective because of the child's special needs. Bonding is a two-way process and is known as *attachment behaviour* in the child.

BOWLBY, J. (1979) The Making and Breaking of Affectional Bonds. London: Tavistock Publications.

Bone marrow transplantation

This treatment has been used for leukaemia for some time but has more recently been used for children with *Hurler's syndrome*. Although there is a risk of the host rejecting the donor bone marrow, a number of these transplants have now taken place with subsequent production of the missing chemical (*enzyme*) and apparently normal development of the children. Some of the existing physical abnormalities in the children improved.

HOBBS, J.R. et al (1981) Reversal of clinical features of Hurler's disease and biochemical improvement after treatment by bone marrow transplantation. Lancet, 2:709.

Bonnet's syndrome
= *Wyburn-Mason syndrome*.

Bonnevie-Ullrich syndrome
= *Noonan's syndrome*.

Borderline mental retardation / borderline mental deficiency / borderline mental handicap

There is no sharp dividing line in terms of *intelligence quotient* (I.Q.) between normal intelligence and mental handicap. The upper limits of mental handicap are set at an I.Q. between 70 and 80 depending on the particular test used. In 1959 the American Association on Mental Deficiency proposed that the range of mental retardation should include all persons with an I.Q. within one standard deviation of the mean in statistical terms. Under this classification persons with I.Q.s of 70–84 were described as 'borderline' retarded. In the 1973 revision of the AAMD definition this category was eliminated. Nowadays the term borderline mental handicap may still be used to refer to the intellectual skills of people who are on the borderline between mild mental handicap and dull normal intelligence.

Borders Assessment Schedule

A behaviour and skills rating scale which consists of schedules. Schedule 'B' is for use with profoundly handicapped people; 'A' is for all other mentally handicapped people and 'C' is an educational attainments test. These can be used for the assessment of individuals or groups or for target setting and evaluation. Schedules A and B are completed by interview and cover social competence, skills, behaviour and special needs. Schedule C is a test which has three levels of difficulty. A booklet contains the criteria and scores and each item passed is marked. There is space for a written summary and targets.

DICKENS, P. & STALLARD, A. (1987) Assessing Mentally Handicapped People. Windsor: NFER/Nelson. pp. 41–43.
HALLAS, C.H. et al (1982) The Care and Training of the Mentally Handicapped. (7th edit.) London: Wright PSG. This book contains a full copy of the schedules.
PATON, X.W.R. (1981) Paton's Assessment Schedules. Borders Area Mental Handicap Team, Dingleton Hosp., Melrose, Scotland.

Börjeson-Forssman-Lehmann syndrome

An extremely rare condition in which there is short stature, small head, underdeveloped genitals and mental handicap. Affected individuals have very full cheeks and tend to be overweight especially on the abdomen and breasts. *Epilepsy* occurs. It has been suggested that it is due to an abnormal *gene* on one of the X *chromosomes* and males are more severely affected because they do not have a normal gene on the Y chromosome to ameliorate the effect.

BAAR, H.S. & GALINDO, J. (1965) The Börjeson-Forssman-Lehmann syndrome. J. Ment. Defic. Res., 9:125–30.

Bossing

A protuberance of the bones of the skull which is particularly noticeable in the frontal bones beneath the forehead. The forehead is then prominent and this is referred to as frontal bossing. Similarly *occipital bossing* refers to the prominence of the occipital region at the back of the skull. Bossing may occur in a number of conditions which are associated with mental handicap such as *infantile hypercalcaemia, Sotos' syndrome* and some rare chromosomal disorders.

Bourneville's disease
= *tuberose sclerosis*.

Brachmann-de Lange syndrome
= *de Lange syndrome*.

Brachycephaly
A skull shape characterized by shortening from front to back and increased height of the skull. The back of the head tends to be flat. The width of the skull should be at least four fifths of the length. Brachycephaly is a feature of several conditions associated with mental handicap including *Down's syndrome, Apert's syndrome, Carpenter's syndrome, de Lange syndrome* and *happy puppet syndrome*.

Brachydactyly
Abnormal shortness of some or all of the fingers and toes. This occurs in several conditions associated with mental handicap including *Down's syndrome, Turner's syndrome, mucopolysaccharidoses* and *Rubinstein-Taybi syndrome*.

Brachymelia
Abnormal shortness of limbs as may occur in *Apert's syndrome, de Lange syndrome* and other conditions associated with mental handicap.

Brachymesophalangy
Shortening of the middle section (phalanx) of a finger between the two joints of the finger. This often occurs in *Carpenter's syndrome*.

Bradyarthria / bradyphasia / bradylalia
Slowness of speech.

Bradylexia
Slowness in reading.

Bradyphrenia
Slowness of thought. This has been used in the past as equivalent to mental handicap but it is generally used to describe a slowness of thought due to a psychiatric disorder.

Braille
A system of printing in raised dots which can be read by a blind person by touch. Letters are represented by different combinations of dots in six possible positions. People who are blind and mildly mentally handicapped may be able to learn braille and should have the opportunity to do so.

Braille Hand Speech
This is a method of holding the initial, middle and ring fingers of both hands in such a position on the receiver's body that the tips represent the six dots of the braille cell. Braille hand speech is especially useful for people who have learnt *braille* in childhood and subsequently lose their hearing.

Brain damage
The brain may be damaged before, during or after birth from a multiplicity of causes. The effects of brain damage also vary from complete recovery to profound mental or physical handicap. Severe damage, especially if affecting both sides of the brain, will almost certainly have a long-term effect on intellectual development and may cause psychiatric disorder or *behaviour problems*. Damage to one side of the brain is less likely to cause intellectual impairment. Severe brain injury is likely to cause persistent impairment if the person is unconscious for 3 weeks or more after the injury. See also *head injury* and *child abuse*.

RUTTER, M. (1981) Psychological sequelae of brain damage in children. Am. J. Psychiat., 138:1533–1544.

Further information:
Association for Brain Damaged Children, Clifton House, 3 St. Pauls Rd., Foleshill, Coventry CV6 5DE.

Brain electrical activity mapping
= *topographic brain mapping*.

Brain lobes

The brain is not a spherical structure and there are deep fissures in its surface which divide it into lobes. These lobes are the *frontal lobes*, in the forehead region; the *parietal lobes*, on the sides and upper parts of the brain; the *occipital lobes* at the back of the brain; and the *temporal lobes* lying just above the ears. Some of the functions of the brain are localized to specific areas and damage to a lobe may produce particular, recognizable, problems. Mental handicap is usually produced by severe and widespread damage involving more than one lobe.

Brain scan

= *CT scan.*

Brain stem

An area at the base of the brain containing important centres which control breathing, blood pressure, heart beat and other vital functions. It also contains centres which control movement of the eyes, face, tongue, jaw and palate and others which act as relay stations for sensations from the head and hearing. The brain stem is a major thoroughfare for the messages passing from the brain to the *spinal cord* to control movements, and for the messages travelling in the opposite direction to give the brain information about the body.

Brain surgery

This is rarely indicated for people with a mental handicap unless it is caused by *hydrocephalus, brain tumour* or bleeding into, or around, the brain. Some rare causes of *epilepsy* may be treated by brain surgery.

Brain tumour

The role of brain tumours in mental handicap is difficult to assess. Some brain tumours are present at birth and are associated with a malformation or abnormal development of the brain. These can cause an early death but may remain symptomless for years although the child may be mentally handicapped. After infancy brain tumours are one of the more common tumours of childhood. Benign, non-invasive, slow growing tumours, are a rare cause of mental handicap and malignant tumours may result in extensive damage to the brain and impaired intellectual functioning. Often malignant tumours are terminal though, if successfully treated, a child may be left mentally handicapped. Benign tumours of the brain are present in *tuberose sclerosis* and these tumours very occasionally become malignant.

FESSARD, C. (1968) Cerebral tumors in infancy: 66 clinicoanatomical case studies. Am. J. Dis. Child., 115:302–308.
KUHN, L.E. et al (1983) Quality of life in children treated for brain tumours: intellectual, emotional and academic functions. J. Neurosurg. 58: 1–6.

Brain-stem evoked response audiometry

A way of measuring high frequency hearing which can be carried out when a person is sedated or asleep. It may therefore be useful if a mentally handicapped person is unable to co-operate with other forms of hearing testing. It involves small electrodes being placed on the forehead, scalp and behind each ear. A headphone is held against the ear and a clicking noise delivered through it. This generates tiny electrical potentials in the nerve of the ear and the pathway to the brain. These potentials are picked up by the electrodes and processed on a computer to give a visual display. The information on hearing is limited to high frequencies and is not always reliable. The response also changes with age. The test should be carried out and interpreted by specially trained staff and other tests and information are necessary before any firm conclusions can be drawn about a person's hearing.

Breast enlargement

= *gynaecomastia.*

Breath-holding attacks

These attacks occurs in early childhood and are brought on by a child being angry, frustrated or in pain. Usually the child looks as if he or she is going to cry, goes red and then blue in the face. The child may then collapse, the eyes may briefly roll and slight twitching may occur. Most children have grown out of these attacks by 6 years of age. It is important to differentiate these from *seizures* which do not have the characteristic precipitating factors.

Brevicollis

Abnormal shortness of the neck as in *Klippel-Feil syndrome, Down's syndrome* and a few other conditions associated with mental handicap. It is caused by fusion or reduction in the vertebrae (bones of the spine) in the neck. The hairline is low and movements of the neck are limited.

British Ability Scales

Relatively new scales of abilities which are flexible and cover a wide range of skills. They incorporate most of the new ideas on intellectual testing and cover an age range of 2 years 6 months to 17 years. These are principally for testing intelligence and generating hypotheses about a child's problems. Different subscales include speed of information processing; reasoning; spatial imagery; perceptual matching; short-term memory; retrieval and application of knowledge and conservation. As well as obtaining a general *intelligence quotient* it is possible to obtain visual, verbal and short form I.Q. estimates and to identify unusual score patterns.

ELLIOTT, C.D. et al (1983) The British Ability Scales (Revised edit.). Windsor: NFER/Nelson.

British Institute of Mental Handicap

An organization, registered as a charity, whose aims and objectives are to promote and advance study and research in all matters relating to mental handicap. The publications of the Institute include 'Mental Handicap' & 'Bulletin' (four issues a year) and many books and information packs. Conferences are sponsored and organized throughout the U.K.

Further information:
British Institute of Mental Handicap, Wolverhampton Rd, Kidderminster, Worcs., DY10 3PP.

British Sign Language (BSL)

A *sign language* evolved and used by the deaf population of the U.K. The deaf people of many other countries also have their own sign languages. BSL is very similar to American Sign Language (ASL) but it has more one-handed signs. BSL includes hand movements representing one idea, finger spellings, limited lip movements, vocalizations and a great deal of facial expression. Signing was suppressed until recently, particularly in schools for deaf children, because it was regarded as ungrammatical and likely to interfere with the acquisition of spoken or written language. It has its own intrinsic grammar which does not easily translate into English. It is now regarded as being different rather than inferior to spoken English and is widely used and accepted. It should always be used as part of *total communication* which includes the use of a hearing aid, lip-reading and voice. It has been simplified and changed to form the basis of the *Makaton* Vocabulary which is the most common signing system used with mentally handicapped people in the U.K.

DEUCHAR, M. (1984) British Sign Language. London: Routledge & Kegan Paul.
JONES, H. & WILLIS, L. (1972) Talking Hands: an Introduction to Communicating with People who are Deaf. London: Stanley Paul.
KILMA, E.S & BELLUGI, U. (1979) The Signs of Language. Cambridge, Mass: Harvard University Press.

Further information:
The Royal National Institute for the Deaf,
105, Gower St., London WC1E 6AE.

Brittle hair
The hair may be abnormally brittle in
conditions where the chemical processes in
the body are abnormal. This occurs in
argininosuccinic aciduria and *hydroxylysinuria*,
both of which also cause mental handicap.

Broad thumb syndrome / Broad thumb-hallux syndrome
= *Rubinstein-Taybi syndrome*.

Brooklands experiment
A pioneer demonstration of the effects of
institutional care on children. It was carried
out in 1960 by Dr. Jack Tizard. He was
appalled at the environmental conditions for
children in mental handicap hospitals in the
U.K. and opened a relatively small residential unit for severely retarded children which
paid attention to their developmental needs
and was run on a family basis. He demonstrated that children who were moved to
this environment had a reduction in *behaviour problems*, better physical health and
improved intellectual functioning. Since
then there have been numerous studies of
various forms of residential care and
increasing recognition of the importance of
appropriate living environments to enable
the development of handicapped persons.

HAYWOOD, H.C. & NEWBROUGH, J.R.
(1981) Living Environments for Develop-
mentally Retarded Persons. Baltimore:
University Park Press.
KING, R.D. et al (1971) Patterns of Resi-
dential Care. London: Routledge & Kegan
Paul.
TIZARD, J. (1964) Community Services for
the Mentally Handicapped. London:
Oxford University Press.

Brushfield spots
A fine white speckling of the *iris* which is
present in the eyes of about 70% of people
with *Down's syndrome* (as compared to 12%
of people without Down's syndrome).
Brushfield spots also commonly occur in
happy puppet syndrome and several other
chromosomal disorders.

Bruxism
The grinding of the teeth so that they are
gradually worn down. This occurs in some
mentally handicapped people as a habit but
also as an involuntary movement usually
associated with *athetosis*. As well as damag-
ing the teeth it can damage their bone-
support. Careful *dental care* is essential. If
teeth are becoming damaged a *behaviour
modification* approach may be appropriate
when there is no physical cause.

BLOUNT, R.L. et al (1982) Reducing severe
diurnal bruxism in two profoundly retarded
females. J. Appl. Behav. Anal., 15:565–571.

BSER
= *brain-stem evoked response audiometry*.

BSL
= *British Sign Language*.

Buccal smear
This is obtained by scraping the inside of
the mouth with a blunt instrument to obtain
tissue which can be examined microscopically. This is particularly useful for
examining the centres (nuclei) of cells for
Barr bodies.

Bulbar paralysis
Damage to the part of the brain called the
medulla oblongata can cause paralysis of
lips, tongue, throat and voice box. This
leads to severe feeding problems and pneumonia commonly develops due to inhalation
of food, saliva or vomit (*aspiration pneumonia*).
It also interferes with the articulation of
speech.

Bulimina
A type of eating disorder characterized by
binge eating during which a large quantity

of food is eaten in a short period of time. Each binge is typically followed by a depressed mood, self-criticism and often self-induced vomiting. It occurs most frequently in females and is difficult to treat. It is very rare in people with mental handicap although excessive eating occurs in the *Prader-Willi syndrome* and is sometimes referred to as bulimina.

Buphthalmos

Abnormal distension and enlargement of the eyeball in early childhood. It may occur in *Sturge-Weber syndrome, homocystinuria* and *Patau's syndrome* all of which are associated with mental handicap. The raised pressure within the eye is due to increased secretion of fluid or failure of the drainage system. This is called *glaucoma*.

Burnout

A loss of enthusiasm and commitment to working which is often seen in people who were previously successful but have become disillusioned or exhausted. It is generally used to describe professional workers or *care staff*, and is particularly likely to occur in people who have been in the same job for a number of years, who are frustrated by lack of achievement, unsupported, and emotionally and physically exhausted. It is characterized by feelings of defeat and despair and loss of concern. It is sometimes seen in the parents and families of mentally handicapped people. They become too tired and frustrated to effectively devote energy to changing the problem which is the source of the exhaustion.

CHERNISS, C. (1980) Staff Burnout: Job Stress in the Human Services. London: Sage.
MASLACH, C. (1976) Burned-out. Human Behaviour, 5:16–22.

Butterfly rash
= *adenoma sebaceum*.

Butyrophenones
A group of drugs which includes *haloperidol, benperidol* and *droperidol*. Butyrophenones all have similar side-effects which are described under haloperidol.

Bzoch-League
= *Receptive Expressive Emergent Language Scale*.

C

CA
= *chronological age.*

Cachexia
A weak state produced by a serious and prolonged disease.

CACL
= *Canadian Association for Community Living.*

Café-au-lait patches
Patches of increased pigmentation of the skin which are usually pale yellow or light brown (coffee coloured). These spots are generally irregular in outline and oval in shape although many different shapes and sizes may occur. They may be present at birth or appear during childhood. Multiple café-au-lait spots are unusual in normal children and are signs of several conditions associated with mental handicap including *Louis-Barr syndrome, tuberose sclerosis, Silver's syndrome* and *Von Recklinghausen's disease.*

Calcaneovalgus foot deformity
See *club-foot.*

Calcification
See *cerebral calcification.*

Callier-Azusa Scales
A set of structured *behaviour checklists* designed for *assessment* of *deaf-blind* children. They cover the developmental range from birth to 9 years. They consist of five sections: socialization, daily living skills, motor development, perceptual abilities and language development. The scales have not been standardized on a deaf-blind population and provide no developmental patterns for these children. The scores are given in terms of developmental age. Scale H has been more recently developed and is an assessment scale of communicative abilities. It is designed to provide the information required for individualized, communication-based intervention programmes.

STILLMAN, R.D. (1978) Assessment of Deaf-blind Children: The Callier-Azusa Scale. Dallas: The Callier Center for Communication Disorders, University of Texas.
STILLMAN, R.D. & BATTLE, C.W. (1983) Callier-Azusa Scale-H: Cognition and Communication. Dallas: University of Texas.
STILLMAN, R.D. & BATTLE, C.W. (1986) Developmental assessment of communicative abilities in the deaf-blind. In: Sensory Impairment in Mentally Handicapped People. Ellis, D. (Ed.). London: Croom Helm, pp. 320–325.

Calvarium
The skull cap or arched roof of the head.

Campaign for People with Mental Handicaps
An organization which promotes the rights, including *self-advocacy* and *integration,* of people with a mental handicap. It is committed to campaigning with and on behalf of people with mental handicaps in order to create and support changes which will enable them to become equal and valued citizens. There is also a CMH Education and Research Association (CMH ERA) which runs workshops for staff and managers of services and disseminates information on *normalization.*

Further information:
Campaign for People with Mental Handicaps, 12a Maddox St, London W1R 9PL.

Camphill village communities

A charitable organization in the U.K. which provides long-term residential care for mentally handicapped people in village communities. These are based on the philosophy of Rudolf Steiner. The Camphill movement has a strong Christian orientation. The villages have up to 150 villagers and approximately the same number of staff or co-workers who live and work together as equals. The villages usually contain a number of households with up to ten villagers in each. Everyone is expected to work for the good of the community in activities such as farming, market gardening and craft work. No wages are paid and the living expenses of the residents are met by DHSS benefits, local authorities or private means. Most of the villages now offer rehabilitation as well as long-term care.

Further information:
Delrow College, Hillfield Lane, Aldenham, Watford WD2 8DJ.

Camptodactyly

The permanent bending inward of a finger or fingers. It particularly affects the little fingers and may run in families as a harmless trait. It also occurs in a number of conditions associated with mental handicap including *cerebro-hepato-renal syndrome, Noonan's syndrome, Goltz's syndrome* and *Down's syndrome*.

Camptomelia

Permanent bending of a limb or limbs as occurs in *camptomelic dwarfism*.

Camptomelic dwarfism

A very rare condition in which a number of abnormalities are present at birth. These may include an unusual appearance with a flat face, widely spaced eyes, a small mouth, *cleft palate* and low-set ears. The shoulder blades, collar bones and ribs are underdeveloped and the bones of the leg are bowed and short. There is *club foot*. The height is short. If a baby is severely affected there are problems with breathing and death is likely to occur in early infancy. Less severely affected children may survive and are likely to be mentally handicapped. It has been suggested that this condition may be caused by certain chemicals affecting the *fetus* including aminopterin and methotrexate (these are used in the treatment of *psoriasis*). Rather similar but milder abnormalities have also been reported in the babies of women taking certain *anticonvulsants* in pregnancy (*phenytoin* and *phenobarbitone*) and this is known as fetal hydantoin syndrome. It may rarely occur as a hereditary condition (*recessive inheritance*).

BIANCHINE, J.W. et al (1972) Camptomelic dwarfism. Lancet, 1:1068.
HANSON, J.W. et al (1976) Risks to the offspring of women treated with hydantoin anticonvulsants, with emphasis on the fetal hydantoin syndrome. J. Pediatr., 89:662–668.
HASSELL, T. et al (1980) Phenytoin-Induced Teratology and Gingival Pathology. New York: Raven Press.
THURMON, T.F. et al (1973) Familial camptomelic dwarfism. J. Pediatr., 83:841.

Canadian Association for Community Living / Canadian Association of Mental Retardation

This charitable organization has managed a partnership between professionals and citizens in the development of a comprehensive community service system for mentally handicapped people (ComServ). It acts as a national planning and co-ordinating body working through its affiliated associations in the provinces and through the participation of both the federal and provincial government representatives on its advisory committees. The *Canadian National Institute on Mental Retardation* shares the same building and provides expertise and research.

NATIONAL INSTITUTE ON MENTAL RETARDATION (1982) Experimenting with Social Change: An Interpretive History of the Southern Alberta ComServ Project. Downsview, Ontario: NIMR.

NEUFELDT, A. (1983) Canada: Canada's ComServ plan – a nationwide strategy of service development. In: A Way of Life for the Handicapped. Jones, G. & Tutt, N. (Eds.) London: Residential Care Assoc.

PELLETIER, J. & RICHLER, D. (1982) Major Issues in Community Living for Mentally Handicapped Persons. Reflections on the Canadian Experience. Downsview, Ontario: NIMR.

Further information:
Kinsman NIMR Building, York University Campus, 4700 Keele St., Downsview, Ontario, Canada M3J 1P3.

Canadian National Institute on Mental Retardation

This organization of professional people sponsors research, programme development, training, public education and publications on mental handicap and supports the *Canadian Association for Community Living* (CACL). It is financially sponsored by CACL with voluntary and government support.

Canavan's disease

A very rare condition in which the development of the baby seems normal until 2 or 3 months of age. Poor head control is often noticed first and the baby then gradually becomes less active and less responsive. Head enlargement is obvious by 6 months of age. Vision gradually deteriorates, the limbs become stiff, *epilepsy* is common and death usually occurs between 7 months and 4 years of age, although children rarely survive into early teens with a profound physical and mental handicap. The cause is not known but *recessive inheritance* is suspected in some cases.

BUCHANAN, D.S. & DAVIS, R.L. (1965) Spongy degeneration of the nervous system. A report of four cases with a review of the literature. Neurology (Minneap.), 15:207.

MAHLOUDJI, M. et al (1970) Familial spongy degeneration of the brain. Arch. Neurol., 22:294.

Cancer

A general term for forms of tumours to which the term 'malignant' is applied. They are different to benign tumours because they can invade and destroy tissue; can reproduce very actively and in a disorderly way; and can produce secondary growths some distance from the original tumour. These properties make such tumours very life-threatening unless treated early. There are a number of conditions which cause mental handicap which are associated with a higher incidence of malignant tumours. These include *Beckwith syndrome, tuberose sclerosis, Louis-Barr syndrome, xeroderma pigmentosum* and *Fanconi's hypoplastic anaemia*.

Cannon communicator

A small machine which straps onto the wrist and has a number of keys. Touching the keys in different combinations makes it possible to print letters onto paper tape which comes out of the machine as a printed message. This may be useful in certain types of physical handicap where speech is impaired. It requires an ability to read and type and good physical co-ordination in one hand. It is therefore of very limited use for people who are mentally handicapped.

Canthus

The angle at either end of the opening between the eyelids.

Capillary haemangioma

A birthmark, often extensive, which is red or purple in colour and is caused by overgrowth of fine blood vessels (capillaries) in the skin. This type of birthmark has been reported in the *Rubinstein-Taybi syndrome* and several *chromosome* disorders. It occurs extensively in the *Sturge-Weber syndrome*.

Carbamazepine

An *anticonvulsant* drug used in the treatment

of most forms of *epilepsy*. It is particularly useful in children because it is less likely to have an adverse effect on behaviour or learning compared with other anticonvulsants. Side-effects include dizziness, unsteadiness, drowsiness, stomach upsets and an allergic rash. Blood disorders have occurred rarely and for this reason regular blood counts should be arranged especially in the early stages of treatment. In order to reduce the likelihood of some side-effects it is usually introduced gradually. It has a relatively short duration of action and has to be given two or three times a day. Carbamazepine has also been used to treat behavioural disturbances in overactive mentally handicapped people and has more recently been advocated for the treatment of *affective disorders*.

BRODIE, M.J. & HALLWORTH, M.J. (1987) Therapeutic monitoring of carbamazepine. Hospital Update, 13(1):57–63.
REID, A.H. et al (1981) A double blind placebo controlled cross-over trial of carbamazepine in overactive severely mentally handicapped patients. Psycholog. Med. 11: 109–113.

Carcinoma
The medical term for certain types of *cancer* such as those which originate in the skin or in the lining of the stomach or bowels.

Cardiac anomalies
= *congenital heart disease*.

Cardiofacial syndrome
A condition in which paralysis of one side of the lower half of the face is associated with *congenital heart disease* and often with defects of other major body systems. The facial weakness is evident from birth when the baby cries but does not interfere with smiling or sucking. Mental handicap and *epilepsy* have been described in some people with this condition. The cause is not known.

PAPE, K. & PICKERING, D. (1972) Asymmetric crying facies: an index of other congenital anomalies. J. Pediatr., 8:21.
SALMON, M.A.(1978) Developmental Defects and Syndromes. Aylesbury, England: HM&M. pp. 183–184.

Care staff
A very general term used to describe qualified or unqualified staff involved in the direct care or support of people who are mentally handicapped.

CARE villages (cottage and rural enterprises)
A non-statutory organization of charitable status, which provides permanent residential care for mentally handicapped people within a village type of community. There are several such villages in the U.K. All are in rural settings and take up to 70 villagers. They live in cottages of up to 12 residents with housestaff offering supervision. Work includes farm work, market gardening, estate maintenance and craft work. No wages are paid and residents must be supported by DHSS benefits, local authorities or private means. Recreation is provided and integration with the local community is encouraged.

Further information:
Care Village, Ide Hill, Nr. Sevenoaks, Kent TN14 6BB.

Caries
Gradual decay. It usually refers to dental caries when it means tooth decay. This occurs commonly in people with poor *dental care* and a sugar-rich diet but some people are particularly prone to this problem. When the protective enamel of the teeth is poorly formed, the teeth are very vulnerable (*enamel hypoplasia*). Good dental hygiene with regular brushing with fluoride toothpaste, attention to diet, and regular dental check-ups are of obvious importance to prevent caries.

MOSS, S.J. (1977) Your Child's Teeth. Harmondsworth, Middx.:Penguin Books.

Carp-mouth

An abnormally shaped mouth with down-turned corners. This has been described in *German's syndrome*. *Deletion of long arm of chromosome 18* causes a syndrome which includes carp-mouth and is sometimes called carp-mouth syndrome.

Carpenter's syndrome

People with this rare condition have an unusual appearance with an abnormally shaped head caused by the skull being taller than usual (*acrocephaly*). The bridge of the nose tends to be flat and the upper jaw underdeveloped. The eyes are widely spaced, protuberant and slope slightly downward. The fingers may be joined together or very small, with similar abnormalities of the feet and extra toes. There may be abnormalities of the leg, joints, the heart, the eyes and other organs. There is a tendency to obesity, small genitals and short stature. Most people with this condition have some degree of mental handicap. Operations may be required to correct the various deformities and operations on the skull may be necessary to prevent pressure on the brain. This condition is inherited from both parents who are carriers (*recessive inheritance*).

SUNDERHAUS, E. & WOLTER, E.R. (1968) Acrocephalosyndactyly. J. Pediatr. Ophthal., 5:118.
TEMTAMY, S.A. (1966) Carpenter's syndrome, acrocephalosyndactyly; an autosomal recessive syndrome. J. Pediatr., 69: 111–120.

Carrier (genetic)

Many normal, healthy people carry abnormal *genes* without ever being aware that this is the case. They will only become aware of this if a relative (most often their child) develops a genetic condition. The detection of the carrier state is particularly valuable in those conditions due to a *dominant gene* but with some individuals only mildly affected. It is also important in

dominant disorders of late onset.
Detection of carriers of *recessive genes* is of value mainly when there is a risk of a couple both carrying the same recessive gene as may occur with marriages between close relatives (e.g. cousins) or within communities where a particular condition is known to be common.
Recent advances in the detection of abnormal genes have made it possible to identify the carrier state in about sixty different disorders. Once a couple are aware of the risks of having an affected child it is frequently possible to detect an affected fetus thus making termination of pregnancy a possibility.

Carrow test of auditory comprehension of language

This is a test of the understanding of spoken English. There is a choice of three pictures for each test item and the person has to point to the relevant picture. It provides an 'age level' upon which to base training programmes. There is no ceiling so the whole test must be administered although the language is sophisticated and abstract at the top of the scale. This can be boring for less able people but the test only takes about twenty minutes.

CARROW, E. (1973) Test for Auditory Comprehension of Language (English). Mass,: Teaching Resources.
CARROW, E. (Actual test kit): The Carrow Test of Auditory Comprehension of Language, Windsor, Berks: NFER/Nelson.

Case conference

A meeting called to discuss a client. It always includes the professional workers involved with the 'case' and nowadays the client, his or her *advocate* and/or close relatives are usually also invited. There has been a trend toward making such meetings more structured and goal-orientated so that needs can be identified and clear objectives set for the future (see *Individual Programme Plan*).

CAT scan
= *CT scan*.

Cat-cry syndrome
= *Cri-du-chat syndrome*.

Cat-eye syndrome
A person with this condition has part of the iris of the eye missing (*coloboma*) and this unusual appearance of the eye gives rise to the name of the syndrome. Some people with chromosome 13 deletion and ring (*Orbeli syndrome*) have coloboma and this used to be called the cat-eye syndrome. The term has also been applied to abnormalities attributed to *partial trisomy* of the long arm of chromosome 22 which include coloboma, small head, small jaw, low-set ears and malformations of the heart, kidneys and anus. The literature on cat-eye syndrome is therefore confusing.

BUHLER, E.M. et al (1982) Cat-eye syndrome, a partial trisomy 22. Humangenetik, 15:150–162.
CHIERI, P.R. de, et al (1974) Cat-eye syndrome: evaluation of the extra chromosome with banding techniques. Case report. J. Genet. Hum., 22,101.
HSU, L.W.F. & HIRSCHHORN, K. (1977) The trisomy 22 syndrome and the cat-eye syndrome. In: New Chromosomal Syndromes. Yunis, J.J. (Ed.) New York: Academic Press. pp. 339–368.

Cataract
The lens of the eye is normally clear but if it becomes cloudy and opaque this is known as a cataract. The size and position of the cataract determines the extent to which it interferes with vision. Cataracts are found in 20% of all visually impaired mentally handicapped children. Cataracts may be present at birth and often other abnormalities of the eye are also present. Four percent of babies with *Down's syndrome* and 15% of babies with *Patau's syndrome* are born with cataracts. Cataracts also occur in *Hallermann-Streiff syndrome, congenital toxoplasmosis,* *Marinesco-Sjögren disease, galactosaemia, homocystinuria, Rothmund-Thomson syndrome, rubella syndrome* and many other conditions which cause mental handicap. Most practitioners now favour early surgery (before 6 months of age) where there is evidence of decreased vision. More than half of all people with Down's syndrome have cataracts but they most commonly occur in older children and adults. There was a tendency to avoid operating on people with Down's syndrome but this is well-tolerated and safe if the person can be kept quiet for a few days after the operation. Spectacles are needed afterwards to get the full benefit but, even without, vision is improved. In recent years artificial lenses have been implanted after the cataract has been removed. Vision deteriorates if the cataract is left unoperated and the older person particularly may become anxious, sometimes hallucinated and often uncooperative. Like any other elderly people, elderly mentally handicapped persons may develop a senile cataract and it is important to be alert to this possibility. Injuries to the eyes may also cause cataract development and in mentally handicapped people injuries are sometimes self-inflicted. Frequent banging of the head with fists may be a cause. The outcome of operation in such individuals is not good.

BLECKER-WAGEMAKERS, E.M. (1981) On the Causes of Blindness in the Mentally Retarded. Doorn, Netherlands: Bartimeus.
ELLIS, D. (Ed.) (1986) Sensory Impairments in Mentally Handicapped People. London: Croom Helm.

Catatonia
This is a stuporose state in which strange postures are adopted and maintained. The state can occur in a number of psychiatric or organic conditions.

Cattel Infant Intelligence Scale (CIIS)
Designed as a lower extension of the *Stanford-Binet* covering the age range of 2 to 30

months. The items are similar to those of the *Gesell development schedules* but the sensori-motor tasks are minimized. It measures language development, perceptual functions and manipulatory skills. It is often used for assessing mentally handicapped people with a *mental age* of less than 2 years. It is less well standardized than the *Bayley scales*.

CATTEL, P. (1947) The Measurement of Intelligence of Infants and Young Children. New York: Psychological Corporation.

Caudate nucleus
One of the *basal ganglia*.

Causation
= *aetiology*.

CDH
= *congenital dislocation of the hip*.

Cebocephaly
A malformation of the nose. There is a proboscis-like structure between the eyes but no bone or cartilage within this. It has a single opening at the lowest end and ends blindly at the upper end. The eyes are abnormally closely spaced. This may occur in a few rare *chromosome* abnormalities and in *holoprosencephaly*.

Cellular therapy
= *sicca cell therapy*.

Central deafness
This type of *deafness* results from damage to, or underdevelopment of, the areas of the brain involved in making sense of sounds. It may be inherited or caused by infections such as *meningitis*.

Central nervous system
This consists of the brain and *spinal cord* which are the centre of the nerves of the body.

Cephalic index
The ratio between the head width and head

length which is measured as width divided by length. The normal value is 0.07 to 0.08. The cephalic index may be increased in some conditions including *de Lange syndrome*.

Cephalocoele / cephalocele
A collective term for abnormalities which occur during the development of the brain in the *fetus*. In this group of abnormalities brain tissue prolapses and protrudes through a defect in the skull to form a sac covered by skin. This includes *encephalocoeles* and *meningocoeles*.

Cerebellar ataxia
Unsteadiness and poor co-ordination due to disease or abnormality of the *cerebellum*. This may occur in *Hartnup's disease*, *Friedreich's ataxia*, *Marinesco-Sjögren syndrome* and several other rare conditions associated with mental handicap.

Cerebellar degeneration
This occurs when a progressive disease or disorder affects the *cerebellum* as in *Friedreich's ataxia* which is occasionally associated with mental handicap.

Cerebello-lental degeneration with mental handicap
= *Marinesco-Sjögren syndrome*.

Cerebellum
Part of the brain found behind and below the bulk of the brain. It is attached to the *brain stem*. It receives and processes information from the muscles and joints of the body and the part of the inner ear which registers balance. The cerebellum is responsible for balance reactions, and for making sure that movements of the body are smooth and co-ordinated. Damage to the cerebellum can cause weakness and floppiness of muscles; disturbances of posture and gait; and disorders of movements which include tremor, jerking eye movements (*nystagmus*), poor co-ordination, slurred speech and involuntary movements (*athetosis*). Several conditions which cause mental handicap

Cerebral

also cause abnormalities of the cerebellum. These include *Hartnup's disease, Cockayne's syndrome* and *Marinesco-Sjögren syndrome*.

WARKANY, J. et al (1981) Mental Retardation and Congenital Malformations of the Central Nervous System. Chicago: Year Book Medical Publishers Inc. pp. 244–255.

Cerebral

Concerning or relating to the brain or *cerebrum*.

Cerebral angiogram

= *angiogram*.

Cerebral atrophy

Atrophy of the brain.

Cerebral calcification

The process of the deposition of lime salts in areas of the brain. These substances normally make up bones. Calcification may occur abnormally in the body especially in scars, tumours or tissues which are diseased or damaged. It usually shows up on X-rays. Calcification may occur in the brain in association with several conditions which cause mental handicap. In *Sturge-Weber syndrome* there is a characteristic pattern seen on X-rays with a double contour following the outlines of the damaged brain (tramline calcification). Calcified areas of the brain also occur in congenital *cytomegalic inclusion disease*, congenital *toxoplasmosis, Cockayne's syndrome* and *herpes simplex encephalitis*.

Cerebral cortex

See *cortex of the brain*.

Cerebral degeneration

Degeneration of the brain as occurs in the *degenerative disorders*.

Cerebral gigantism

An ambiguous term which can mean a brain of abnormal size and weight (*megalencephaly*) or can refer to people with *Sotos' syndrome* which includes a large head.

Cerebral haemorrhage

Escape of blood into the substance of the brain causing damage to the brain tissue. This may be caused by trauma, abnormalities of the blood vessels, high blood pressure or increased bleeding tendency. The most common manifestation in the general population is a 'stroke'.

Brain haemorrhage is also a cause of mental handicap and in this case usually occurs at birth. Premature babies have delicate blood vessels which easily rupture in their brains. A very difficult birth, where the baby's head is large in relation to the mother's pelvis can cause bleeding into the brain, as can very sudden deliveries when the head is compressed in the pelvis and then suddenly released. A very difficult forceps delivery is another possible cause. Mental handicap as a result of brain haemorrhage may also be caused by *head injury* as in a road traffic accident or *child abuse*. When bleeding into the brain occurs some children die, some survive with brain damage and some appear to recover fully. Residual brain damage will vary in extent and severity and may cause mental handicap, *cerebral palsy, epilepsy* and other disabilities.

Cerebral hemispheres

These form the major and most obvious part of the brain. There is one on each side of the brain (right and left). Each cerebral hemisphere can be divided into *frontal, temporal, parietal* and *occipital lobes*. These can be mapped out on the surface of the brain and many of the functions of the brain are localized to particular lobes.

Cerebral palsy

A permanent disorder of movement and posture due to a defect of, or damage to, the brain occurring in early life. The brain damage or defect involves those parts of the brain concerned with movement. The incidence of cerebral palsy is 1 per 500 live births. The most common associated abnormality is impairment of speech. Mental handicap, *epilepsy*, visual problems and/or *deafness* may also occur. There are many possible causes and cerebral palsy may be associated with prematurity, difficult birth, multiple birth and *jaundice*. It is often caused by lack of oxygen to the brain during the birth process. It is rarely transmitted as a hereditary disorder but may occur as part of a condition associated with mental handicap such as *microcephaly*. It is a very general term covering a wide range of physical disability. It may be mild or severe. There are a number of different classifications and there is considerable overlap between categories. Most classifications recognize ataxic, athetotic, dystonic and *spastic* types of cerebral palsy. Ataxic cerebral palsy is uncommon and is often mild although the development of movement skills may be considerably delayed (*ataxia*). Dystonic cerebral palsy is more common than previously recognized and consists of fluctuating muscle tone so that limbs and body may sometimes be tight and tense and at other times much more relaxed. There is considerable overlap with the other categories especially with *athetosis* (sometimes called dyskinetic cerebral palsy). Spastic cerebral palsy is the most common type (about 80%) and refers to weakness and stiffness of muscles. The cause of the stiffness is tightness in the muscles. Muscle *spasm* is often present, and reflex patterns may distort movements. Spastic cerebral palsy is subdivided according to the limbs involved. The six subdivisions are:

1. Hemiplegic – affecting the arm and leg on one side of the body. In about 30% of affected people the limbs on the other side of the body are mildly affected.
2. Monoplegic – predominantly one limb.
3. Diplegic – predominant involvement of both lower limbs although there may be slight involvement of both upper limbs (*Little's disease*).
4. Paraplegic – both legs without involving the arms.
5. Triplegic – predominant involvement of three limbs.
6. Quadriplegic – all four limbs affected.

The terms tetraplegic and double hemiplegic may alternatively be used.

The treatment of the cerebral palsies varies according to severity and type but most people affected will benefit from *physiotherapy* especially in early childhood. Spasticity may sometimes be helped by muscle relaxant drugs such as *baclofen, dantrolene,* and *diazepam*. Orthopaedic surgery may be necessary to release or replant tight muscles.

ABERCROMBIE, M.L.J. (1964) Perceptual and Visuomotor Disorders in Cerebral Palsy. London: Heinemann Medical Books.
FINNIE, N.R. (1974) Handling the Young Cerebral Palsied Child at Home. London: Heinemann Medical Books.
LEVITT, S. (1982) Treatment of Cerebral Palsy and Motor Delay. (2nd. edit.) Oxford: Blackwell.
SAMILSON, R.L. (Ed.) (1975) Orthopaedic Aspects of Cerebral Palsy. London: Heinemann Medical Books.
SCRUTTON, D. (Ed.) (1984) Management of the motor disorders of children with cerebral palsy. Clinics in Dev. Med. No.90. London: Spastics Int. Medical Publ.

Further information:
United Cerebral Palsy Associations, 66 East 34th St., New York NY10016,
The Spastics Society, 12 Park Crescent, London W1N 4EQ.

Cerebral ventricles
Four interconnecting cavities of the brain which are filled with *cerebro-spinal fluid*. The lateral ventricles are the largest and each (left and right) is in the middle of the corresponding *cerebral hemisphere*. In some conditions associated with mental handicap, such as *hydrocephaly*, the ventricles are enlarged due to pressure from the fluid. In other conditions they may be enlarged due to lack of substance of the brain.

Cerebro-hepato-renal syndrome
In this very rare condition abnormalities of the brain, liver and kidneys are present at birth and the baby is very floppy with

feeding problems and failure to thrive. Children have characteristic features with a high prominent forehead, widely spaced eyes and skin folds (*epicanthic folds*) at the inner angle of the eyes. The chin is small and cheeks full. Abnormalities of the eyes, ears, heart and genitals have also been described. A single *palmar crease* is common. Progress is very slow with severe mental handicap. Most children do not survive infancy. *Epilepsy* is common. Pipecolic acid is found in the blood and other biochemical abnormalities are present. This condition is thought to be inherited from both parents who are carriers (*recessive inheritance*).

BURTON, B.K. et al (1981) Hyperpipecolic acidaemia: Clinical and biochemical observations in two male siblings. J. Pediatr., 99:729.

MOSER, A.E. et al (1984) The cerebro-hepatorenal (Zellweger) syndrome. Increased levels and impaired degradation of very-long-chain fatty acids and their use in prenatal diagnosis. New Engl. J. Med., 310:1141.

Cerebro-oculorenal syndrome
= *Lowe's syndrome*.

Cerebro-metacarpo-metatarsal dystrophy
= *Albright's syndrome*.

Cerebro-spinal fluid (CSF)
The fluid which bathes the brain and *spinal cord*. It is produced within the cavities (*cerebral ventricles*) of the brain. It eventually drains into the veins in the membranes surrounding the brain. The pressure and contents of the CSF are normally within a certain range and increased pressure can cause damage to the brain (*hydrocephalus*). A specimen of the fluid can be obtained by lumbar puncture and analysis may demonstrate a number of conditions including infections such as *meningitis*. Such conditions may be a cause of mental handicap.

Cerebromacular degeneration
= *amaurotic familial idiocy*.

Cerebroretinal degeneration
= *amaurotic familial idiocy*.

Cerebroside lipidosis
= *Gaucher's disease*.

Cerebrosideroses
A group of disorders in which biochemical abnormalities result from the inheritance of the same abnormal gene from both parents who are carriers (*recessive inheritance*). The abnormal gene causes a lack of chemicals (*enzymes*) which deal with fatty substances, known as cerebrosides. As a result abnormal substances accumulate throughout the body including the brain. Mental and physical deterioration occur. *Gaucher's disease* and *metachromatic leucodystrophy* are both examples.

Cerebrotendinous xanthomatosis
A very rare condition with a gradual onset. Mental handicap occurs in childhood and there is a very gradual deterioration in mental abilities. In adolescence or even later, shakiness, unsteadiness and stiffness become evident. *Cataracts* may develop. Weakness of muscles and difficulty in swallowing become more evident later in life and death usually occurs between the fourth and sixth decades. Abnormal substances (cholestanols) are found in the *cerebellum* of the brain and in the tendons of muscles where they may be seen as lumps. Treatment with chenodeoxycholic acid has been reported to reduce the blood cholestanol and to give a rise in intelligence and a reversal of neurological symptoms. The disease is probably inherited from both parents who are carriers (*recessive inheritance*).

BERGINER, V.M. et al (1984) Long term treatment of cerebrotendinous xanthomatosis with chenodeoxycholic acid. New Engl. J. Med., 311:1649.

MENKES, J.H. et al (1968) Cerebrotendinous xanthomatosis: the storage of cholestanol within the nervous system. Arch. Neurol., 19:47.

SCHIMSCHOCK, J.R. et al (1968) Cerebro-tendinous xanthomatosis: clinical and pathological studies. Arch. Neurol., 18:688.

Cerebrum

The major and most obvious part of the brain which includes the *cerebral hemispheres* but excludes the *cerebellum* and *brain stem*.

Ceroid-lipofuscinoses

A group of disorders in which biochemical abnormalities result from the inheritance of the same abnormal *gene* from both parents who are carriers (*recessive inheritance*). Large amounts of yellow-brown granules, made of a pigment known as ceroid-lipofuscin, are deposited in the brain and *retina* of the eye which degenerate as a result. *Bielschowsky-Jansky disease, Kuf's disease* and *Batten-Vogt disease* are examples of this group of disorders.

Cervical ribs

Extra ribs arising from the bones (vertebrae) of the neck. This abnormality may occur in a few conditions associated with mental handicap including *Rubinstein-Taybi syndrome, Bloch-Sulzberger syndrome, Klippel-Feil syndrome* and *Noonan's syndrome*.

Cervico-oculo-acoustic dysplasia / cervico-oculo-facial dystrophy

= *Wildervanck's syndrome*.

Chaining

Behaviour often occurs in set sequences, or chains, composed of small stages linked together. Many activities are like this, including feeding, washing, dressing, cooking, puzzles and many work activities. When a complex behaviour is being taught the long chain is broken into its small links and each link is learnt before progressing to the next. The person being taught learns the sequence and is gradually required to do more of the links usually with help being phased out gradually. The most common method of doing this is *backward chaining*, although *forward chaining* is sometimes used.

Chaining of expectancies

A technique used with severely mentally handicapped children which is particularly useful in a child with multiple sensory impairments (e.g. *deaf-blind* child). By structuring daily living routines, such as self-care skills, into a very rigid sequence of events, the child learns to anticipate, and may well carry out, one of the actions in the sequence if it is missed out. It is claimed that this also increases the bond between the child and carers.

Chart of Initiative and Independence

A chart of activities with the contents decided upon by the user. There are ten suggested categories including personal hygiene, domestic, shopping, finances, leisure and social interaction. It is necessary to observe the person's skills over a long period of time (up to two weeks) and to use flow charts and complex forms. The purpose is the selection of tasks requiring increased independence and initiative using the information obtained on the present level of initiative, opportunity and potential for each activity chosen. The coding system needs a lot of practice.

DICKENS, P. & STALLARD, A. (1987) Assessing Mentally Handicapped People. Windsor: NFER-Nelson. pp. 25–27.

MACDONALD, I. & COUCHMAN, T. (1980) Chart of Initiative and Independence. Windsor: NFER-Nelson.

Chatter-box syndrome

A characteristic of a few mentally handicapped people especially those with untreated *hydrocephaly*. The person appears to have language skills which are more advanced than skills in other areas of development. On closer examination much of the language is repetitive and consists of phrases which are repeated with little or no understanding of their meaning. Often the person chatters excessively in this way.

CHD
= *congenital heart disease.*

Cherry-red spot
= *macular degeneration.*

Cheshire Homes
= *Leonard Cheshire Foundation.*

Chest deformities
Several of these deformities are associated with mental handicap. In a barrel-shaped chest the ribs are too horizontal and the chest short. This may occur in *Cockayne's syndrome.* A shield-like chest is one in which the chest is broad and shield-like with wide spaced nipples. This may occur in *Turner's syndrome* and *deletion of short arm of chromosome 18.* Bulging of the chest is generally due to curvature of the spine (scoliosis). Protuberance of the breast bone is known as pigeon chest or *pectus carinatum.* When the breast bone is sunken this is known as *pectus excavatum.*

Chewing
Problems with chewing include inability to chew, *rumination* and excessive chewing of objects.
Inability to chew is a feeding problem mainly encountered with *cerebral palsy.* Often the child still has a strong sucking reflex. Liquidized or mashed foods are necessary until the child learns to chew. The advice of a *physiotherapist* or *speech therapist* may be required. Gradually thickening and coarsening the consistency of foods may help and also gently moving the jaws in a chewing action. Mealtimes should not be hurried and a relaxed atmosphere is important.
Excessive chewing of objects usually occurs as a normal stage of development but may become a persistent habit. It is important to encourage and teach other ways of exploring and using objects and to firmly discourage the abnormal chewing. Chewing of self is a type of *self-injurious behaviour.*

Chickenpox
= *Varicella.*

Child abuse
There has been increasing concern about the problem of physical abuse and neglect of children which appears to be occurring with greater frequency in Europe and the U.S.A. in recent years. Affected children are usually infants, toddlers or pre-schoolers and are often chronically neglected. They may present with minor or major injuries with explanations which often do not fit the injury. The nature of injuries is usually very characteristic and identifiable to well-trained professional workers. Retardation in intellectual and social development is common in deprived, neglected and abused children. Brain damage is usually the result of bleeding under the skull or in the brain following injury, and skull fractures may be evident. Some children subjected to abuse may suffer severe brain damage and be permanently mentally handicapped often with other associated disabilities such as *spasticity, epilepsy* or *blindness.* Handicapped children have been found to be over-represented in the population of abused children and this may be caused by abnormal behaviour from the handicapped child interfering with attachment, or the reaction of the parents to the knowledge that the child is handicapped.

BUCHANAN, A. & OLIVER, J.E. (1977) Abuse and neglect as a cause of mental retardation. Brit. J. Psychiat., 131:458–467.
FRODI, A.M. (1981) Contribution of infant characteristics to child abuse. Am. J. Ment. Defic., 85:341–349.
HANSEN, C. (1980) Child abuse: A cause and effect of mental retardation. In: Prevention of Mental Retardation and other Developmental Disabilities. McCormack, M. (Ed.). New York: Dekker Inc.
KEMPE, R.S. & KEMPE, C.H. (1978) Child

Abuse. Cambridge, Mass.: Harvard University Press.

LYNCH, M.A. & ROBERTS, J. (1982) Consequences of Child Abuse. London: Academic Press.

Child bearing
See *parenthood*.

Childhood psychosis
This includes two very separate and different disorders – *autism* and childhood *schizophrenia*. Whereas autism starts in the first three years of life, childhood schizophrenia has a later onset and is very rare before *puberty*. A large proportion of autistic children are also mentally handicapped, but this is not the case in childhood schizophrenia which is fairly evenly distributed across the range of intelligence.

Childrearing by mentally handicapped parents
See *parenthood*.

Chiropody
The proportion of mentally handicapped people requiring chiropody treatment is high. The conditions necessitating this treatment include the simple problems such as callouses, corns, fungal infections and verrucae and complex problems developing as a result of deformities or unusually shaped feet.

Chloral hydrate
A drug used for sedation which may sometimes be prescribed to help with a sleep problem in a person who is mentally handicapped. It is usually given in a liquid form which makes it easier to take. Side-effects are rare but can include drowsiness, dizziness, unsteadiness, dry mouth, irritation of the stomach and excitement. Allergic rashes can occur. It is said to be suitable for use with children and the elderly because it is unlikely to have side-effects such as confusion. Habituation may develop and sudden withdrawal after long-term use may cause confusion and distress. Withdrawal should be gradual.

Chlordiazepoxide
One of the *benzodiazepine* group of drugs used in the treatment of *anxiety states*.

Chlormethiazole
This drug may be used temporarily as a sedative especially for sleep disturbances. It is not commonly used for mentally handicapped people. The most common side-effect is nasal congestion.

Chlorpromazine
One of the *phenothiazine* group of drugs used in the treatment of *schizophrenia* and some other types of mental illness. It is also used for mentally handicapped people with *behaviour disorders*, but other methods of treatment are usually preferred nowadays (*behaviour modification*) unless there is also a mental illness. It may still be used as an adjunct to treatment by other methods. The most common side-effects are muscle rigidity, spasms and tremor (*extrapyramidal* or *parkinsonian* effects). It may be necessary to give *anti-parkinsonian* drugs to counteract this. Other effects include drowsiness, involuntary movements (*tardive dyskinesia*), low blood pressure, weight gain, sleeplessness, depression, low body temperature and menstrual disturbances. Allergic reactions and sensitivity reactions may occur including abnormalities of the blood, sensitivity of the skin to sunlight and *jaundice*.

Choanal atresia
Absence of the opening between the back of the nose and the upper part of the throat. This may occur in a few conditions associated with mental handicap including *Treacher-Collins syndrome*, *de Lange syndrome* and *cat-eye syndrome*.

Chondro-ectodermal dysplasia
= *Ellis-van Creveld syndrome*.

Chondrodysplasia epiphysialis punctata

= *Conradi's syndrome.*

Chondrodystrophia calcificans congenita

= *Conradi's syndrome.*

Chondrodystrophia fetalis

= *achondroplasia.*

Chondrodystrophia fetalis calcificans

= *Conradi's syndrome.*

Chondrodystrophic epiphysialis punctata

= *Conradi's syndrome.*

Chondrodystrophy

Short-limbed dwarfism which includes *achondroplasia* and *Conradi's syndrome.*

Chorea

A condition or disease in which *choreiform movements* occur.

Choreic movements

= *choreiform movements.*

Choreiform movements

Irrepressible, involuntary, non-repetitive, jerky and abrupt movements of roughly normal patterns resembling incomplete gestures. If mildly affected the person may just seem clumsy and fidgety. If severe there is almost continuous writhing movement. Such movements may occur in limbs or facial muscles. There are several diseases such as *Huntington's chorea* in which these movements are very characteristic but most of these are not associated with mental handicap. Chorea may, however, occur where any form of *brain damage* affects the *basal ganglia* of the brain and has been reported in viral *encephalitis, cerebral palsy, Wilson's disease, argininosuccinic aciduria* and following problems at birth. In these cases it is frequently associated with mental handicap.

Choreo-athetosis

A combination of the features of *chorea* and *athetosis* as may occur in the *Louis-Barr syndrome, Lesch-Nyhan syndrome* and *cerebral palsy*, all of which are associated with mental handicap.

Chorion biopsy

A technique used to obtain a minute piece of the placenta in order to identify abnormalities in the *fetus*. It can be performed between the 6th and 10th week of pregnancy so that abnormalities can be diagnosed much earlier than by *amniocentesis*. A small sample of the chorion, the outermost fetal membrane, which is part of the placenta, is obtained through the cervix using *ultrasound* to locate the placenta and guide the instrument. Sampling is successful in more than 80% of attempts but about 1 in 50 are followed by miscarriage. This early examination of fetal tissue makes it possible to offer an early and safe termination of pregnancy if an abnormality of *chromosomes* or *enzymes* is detected. The conditions which may be detected are the same as in amniocentesis. Early diagnosis may also make possible the early treatment of the fetus in order to prevent or reduce abnormalities.

KAZY, Z. et al (1982) Chorion biopsy in early pregnancy: a method of early prenatal diagnosis for inherited disorders. Prenat. Diagn., 2:39–45.

RODECK, C.H. et al (1983) A single operator technique for first trimester chorion biopsy. Lancet, 2:1340.

SIMONI, G. et al (1983) Efficient direct chromosome analyses and enzyme determinations from chorionic villi samples in the first trimester of pregnancy. Hum. Genet., 63:349–357.

Chorionic villus sampling (CVS) / biopsy

= *chorion biopsy.*

Choroid

The middle of the three coats of the eye. It

lies behind the *retina* and consists mainly of blood vessels.

Choroid plexus
The tissue in the brain responsible for producing *cerebro-spinal fluid*.

Choroido-retinitis / chorio-retinitis
An inflammation of the middle (*choroid*) and inner (*retina*) coats of the eye. It may occur in a number of infections of the fetus or infant which cause mental handicap including *cytomegalic inclusion disease, toxoplasmosis, rubella syndrome, syphilis* and *herpes simplex encephalitis*.

Choroido-retinopathy
An abnormality of the middle (*choroid*) and inner (*retina*) coats of the eye. It may occur in a few conditions associated with mental handicap including *Aicardi's syndrome* and *Klippel-Feil syndrome*.

Chotzen's syndrome
A form of *acrocephalosyndactyly* which is similar to *Apert's syndrome* but less extreme in its manifestations. There may be webbing between fingers and toes but this is not severe. The abnormalities of the skull are the same as in Apert's syndrome but the abnormal facial appearance is absent or mild. There is no protuberance of the eyes. It is also associated with mental handicap and the pattern of inheritance is the same.

Chromosome
Chromosomes are the carriers of the *genes* of heredity. Forty-six chromosomes are present in the centre (nucleus) of every living cell in the body. They are rod-shaped and are arranged in 23 pairs. Each member of a pair consists of two thread-like structures touching at a point known as the centromere. They do not touch at the midpoint and each chromosome therefore has a long arm (designated by the letter 'q') and a short arm ('p'). Twenty-two of the pairs are known as autosomes and the other two are the sex chromosomes. In the female the sex chromosomes are a matching pair known as the X chromosomes. In the male they consist of an X chromosome and a shorter Y chromosome. The 22 pairs of autosomes are all slightly different in shape and length and are grouped accordingly. These groups are designated by letters and the individual pairs identified by numbers 1 to 22. The chromosomes can only be seen at certain stages of the multiplication of cells and after special techniques are used to make them visible under intense magnification using a microscope. *Banding techniques* can show bands running across them which helps to identify them. In the process of forming eggs and sperm the chromosomes in each pair separate so that there are only 23 chromosomes in these cells. The fertilized egg receives 23 chromosomes from the egg of the mother and 23 chromosomes from the sperm of the father. These then sort themselves into pairs. There are a number of ways in which this process can go wrong and about 4% of all fetuses carry a chromosome abnormality but 90% of these spontaneously abort. One in 200 live-born infants have a chromosome abnormality and some of these may cause physical and/or intellectual disability. Chromosome abnormalities include *deletion of chromosomes, chromosome translocation, chromosome constriction, chromosome mosaic, chromosome rings, trisomy, partial trisomy, sex chromosome abnormalities, fragile-X syndrome*.

Chromosome constriction
This is an abnormally narrow place on a *chromosome*, the significance of which is uncertain. It may be more common in people with a mental handicap.

Chromosome deletion
= *deletion of chromosome*.

Chromosome mosaic
As a result of abnormal separation of the *chromosome* during the later stages of cell division, after the fertilization of the egg, chromosome mosaics may occur in which a number of the cells of the body contain an

abnormality of chromosomes while the remainder are normal. The proportion of normal to abnormal cells can vary considerably between mosaic individuals and will affect the extent and severity of the features of the disorder.

Chromosome rings
Rarely it happens that both *chromosomes* in a pair break and that two raw ends are left. The two end fragments are deleted and the ends of the chromosome unite to form a ring known as a ring chromosome. This occurs in *cat-eye syndrome* and *Orbeli syndrome*.

Chromosome translocation
Rarely it happens that a part of, or nearly all of, one *chromosome* becomes joined to or becomes part of another. The *genetic* material is still all present in the cell with such a translocation but is arranged abnormally. The person is healthy and normal. This is a balanced translocation and the person is a translocation carrier. When the cells divide to make the eggs or sperm, however, there cannot be equal division of the translocated pair of chromosomes and one cell may get all or most of the genetic material of the pair while the other gets none or little. Such a person has a high risk of having a child with abnormal chromosomes. The child has an unbalanced translocation or a *deletion of chromosome*. Sometimes an unbalanced translocation can arise as a fresh mutation, a kind of genetic accident, in which both parents have completely normal chromosomes. Translocation is the cause of the extra chromosomal material in 3% of people with *Down's syndrome*.

Chronically Sick and Disabled Persons Act (1970)
This Act in the U.K., and the later amending legislation, places on local authorities the responsibility for providing services to handicapped people. Chronically sick or disabled persons are defined as those who are 'substantially and permanently handicapped' by illness, injury, congenital deformity or old age, and the mentally disordered of any description. The Act does not compel local authorities to provide particular kinds of help unless the person's needs have been assessed and the authority is satisfied that the individual requires such help. Individual circumstances will be taken into account and a contribution may be asked for toward the cost of any service offered.

Chronically Sick and Disabled Persons Act (1970) London: HMSO.

Chronological Age
A term for the actual age of a person which is used in comparison with the *mental age* when estimating the *intelligence quotient*.

CIIS
= *Cattel Infant Intelligence Scale*.

Citizen advocacy
See *advocacy*.

Claw-foot
= *pes cavus*.

Claw-hand deformity
A hand which is deformed with the fingers bending inward like a claw. It may be due to abnormalities of joints or tendons. This may occur in a few conditions associated with mental handicap including *Hunter's syndrome, Hurler's syndrome, Scheie's syndrome* and *Patau's syndrome*.

Cleft lip / cleft palate
Cleft palate is the term applied to a fissure of the roof of the mouth usually present at birth and often combined with a divided or cleft lip (hare lip). The incidence of cleft palate and/or cleft lip is about 0.2% of total births. About one sixth of the children with this problem also have other problems which may include mental handicap. Deafness is also common. Cleft lip and palate commonly occurs in *Patau's syndrome, Wolf's*

syndrome, Treacher-Collins syndrome, Smith-Lemli-Opitz syndrome, camptomelic dwarfism, Edward's syndrome, Apert's syndrome, de Lange syndrome, Goldenhar's syndrome, Pierre Robin syndrome and many other conditions. The cleft can usually be successfully repaired by an operation. The results are generally good but sometimes the movements of the palate and lip are restricted and the voice quality may be poor. *Speech therapy* is frequently required.

Clinical

This means literally 'belonging to a bed' but the word is used to denote anything associated with the practical study or care of sick persons.

Clinical medical officers

Doctors employed by Health Authorities in the U.K. for the developmental assessment and medical screening of children. This includes the medical assessment of children as part of the assessment of special needs under the *Education Act (1981)*.

Clinical psychologist

A professional person who, in addition to a psychology degree, has had further training in the application of psychology to treating or helping people. Whether working individually or as part of a team the clinical psychologist applies psychological principles to the management of mental, emotional and *behaviour disorders* of individuals and groups. In addition the clinical psychologist is skilled in research methodology.

In the U.K. this training now has to take place on a recognized course open only to psychology graduates. In the U.S.A. the American Psychological Association accredits doctoral programs which require four to five years of graduate study and at least two years of supervised experience in a clinical setting. Some psychology departments offer master's degrees in clinical psychology but the APA does not accredit these. Some states will license or certify both master's and doctoral psychologists.

Clinical psychologists have made a major contribution to helping people who are mentally handicapped. The application of techniques for teaching adaptive behaviours (*behaviour modification*) has created far more positive and constructive attitudes. Systematic approaches to *assessment* and intervention and a growing body of research have all added to the understanding of the problems and needs of mentally handicapped people.

WILCOCK, P. (1985) The role of the psychologist. In: Mental Handicap. A Multidisciplinary Approach. Craft, M. et al. London: Baillière Tindall. pp. 304–316.

Clinodactyly

Curving of a finger toward one side or the other. It usually affects the little finger only, the tip of which curves toward the fourth digit. This occurs in several conditions associated with mental handicap including *Down's syndrome* and other chromosomal disorders.

Clobazam

This drug is used for the treatment of *anxiety* and *epilepsy*. When used for anxiety it is very similar to *diazepam* in its effects and side-effects. It is used in epilepsy usually in addition to other *anticonvulsants* when *seizures* are difficult to control. It is introduced gradually to prevent sedation and withdrawn gradually to prevent withdrawal seizures. Tolerance to its effects tends to develop and this necessitates dose increases or breaks in treatment.

Clonazepam

A drug used in the treatment of *epilepsy*. It is used for most types of *seizures* and may be effective where other drugs have given poor control. Side-effects include over-sedation and weakness and are usually minimized if it is introduced gradually. It occasionally causes irritability and agitation. It may cause excessive salivation. Excessive mucus production in the chest can be a problem. Sometimes tolerance develops and necessitates an increase in dose or a break in treatment. Withdrawal of the drug should be gradual to prevent withdrawal seizures. It may be given by injection into a vein in the treatment of *status epilepticus*.

Clonic movement / clonus

A rhythmical jerking contraction of muscle or limb. Clonic movements sometimes occur in limbs affected by *cerebral palsy*, often when placed in a particular position or when stretched.

The clonic stage of an epileptic *seizure* is the stage characterized by regular jerking movements.

Clonus is the state in which clonic movements occur when the muscle is stretched e.g. ankle clonus occurring when the achilles tendon is stretched may be a sign of brain damage.

Clopenthixol / clopixol

= *zuclopenthixol*.

Clouston's syndrome

A very rare condition in which the skin of the palms and soles is thin and pale but other areas of the body are excessively pigmented (*ectodermal dysplasia*). There is baldness and an impaired ability to sweat. Teeth are poorly developed. *Cataracts* may be present. Mental handicap is usual. It is inherited from both parents who are carriers (*recessive inheritance*).

CLOUSTON, H.R. (1939) The major forms of hereditary ectodermal dysplasia. Canad. Med. Ass. J., 40:1.

Clover-leaf skull

= *Kleeblättschädel syndrome*.

Club foot

A deformity also known as talipes in which the foot is permanently twisted at the ankle-joint, so that the sole does not rest on the ground when standing or walking. There are a number of varieties of talipes all of which may occur in conditions associated with mental handicap:

1. talipes equinus – the heel is pulled up so that the person walks on his or her toes.
2. talipes calcaneus – the toes are bent up so that walking is on the heel only.
3. talipes varus – the sole looks inward so that walking is on the outer edge of the foot.
4. talipes valgus – the sole looks outward and walking is on the inside of the foot.
5. talipes equino-varus – the heel is drawn up and the sole turned inward (combination of 1 & 3 above).
6. talipes calcaneovalgus – the heel rests on the ground and the sole looks outward (combination of 2 & 4 above).

The deformity may be present at birth and treatment will depend on severity. Strapping may be necessary or more rarely, operative intervention. Sometimes the deformity will develop as a result of disease or injury after birth and may occur in children with *cerebral palsy* due to the uneven pull of muscles.

CMH / CMH ERA

See *Campaign for People with Mental Handicaps*.

CMMS

= *Columbia Mental Maturity Scale*.

CMV

= *cytomegalic inclusion disease*.

CNS

= *central nervous system*.

Co-ordination

The control, by the brain and the nervous system, which enables muscles to contract in harmony and so produce definite purposeful actions. Poor co-ordination results in clumsy or unwanted movements.

Coarctation of the aorta

Narrowing of the main artery from the heart. This is a *congenital* abnormality which can be corrected surgically. It may occur in a number of conditions associated with mental handicap including *Goldenhar's syndrome, oro-facial digital syndrome, rubella syndrome, cardiofacial syndrome, arthrogryposis multiplex congenita* and *Down's syndrome.*

Cochlea
The part of the inner ear which is sensitive to sound waves and transmits them to the nerve of the ear (auditory nerve).

Cochleography
= *electrocochleography.*

Cockayne's syndrome / Cockayne-Neill dwarfism
A rare condition in which mental handicap is associated with a prematurely senile appearance, deafness, deteriorating vision, small stature, sensitivity of the skin to light, deformities of joints and a characteristic facial appearance with rather sunken eyes. Development during the first year of life is usually normal but there is a steady deterioration from the second year. Walking and speech may never occur or be delayed and once developed may deteriorate. This condition is inherited from both parents who are carriers (*recessive inheritance*).

CROME, L. & KANJILAL, G.C. (1971) Cockayne's syndrome. J. Neurol. Neurosurg. Psychiat., 34:171.

FUJIMOTO, W.Y. et al (1969) Cockayne's syndrome. J. Pediatr., 75:881.

Cocktail party syndrome
= *chatterbox syndrome.*

Coffin-Lowry syndrome
A rare condition in which mental handicap is associated with a small stature, abnormalities of bones, large soft hands with tapering fingers, flat feet, muscle weakness and coarse facial features with downward slanting, widely spaced eyes, prominent brow and broad nose. Males are more severely affected than females who may be only mildly mentally handicapped or of normal

intelligence. It is therefore thought to be due to an abnormal *gene* on an X-*chromosome.* This is an unusual type of *sex-linked inheritance.*

HUNTER, A.G.W. et al (1982) The Coffin-Lowry syndrome: experience from four centres. Clin. Genet., 21:321–335.

TEMTAM, S.A. et al (1975) The Coffin-Lowry syndrome: an inherited faciodigital mental retardation syndrome. J. Pediatr., 86:724–731.

Coffin-Siris syndrome
A very rare condition in which mental handicap is associated with coarse facial features, full lips, sparse hair on the scalp but profuse body hair, floppy muscle *tone,* underdeveloped or absent little finger with absence of some nails and the *Dandy-Walker syndrome.* The cause is not known.

TUNNESON, W.W. et al (1978) The Coffin-Siris syndrome. Am. J. Dis. Child., 132:393.

Cogentin
= *benztropine.*

Cognition / cognitive
Cognition is a general term covering all the ways of knowing including perceiving, remembering, imagining, conceiving, understanding, judging and reasoning. Cognitive skills are therefore those skills necessary to carry out these activities and cognitive tests measure these abilities. Cognitive skills are acquired during human development in a fairly predictable sequence. Mentally handicapped people may be described as having a cognitive deficit or disability because their cognitive skills are poorly developed.

Coloboma
A cleft or defect especially of the eye which may result in a gap in the eyelid, *iris,* lens or lining of the eye (*choroid* and/or *retina*). It may occur in a number of conditions associated with mental handicap including *Apert's syndrome, Crouzon's syndrome, Beckwith*

syndrome, rubella syndrome, Rubinstein-Taybi syndrome and *cat-eye syndrome.*

Coloured progressive matrices

See *Raven's standard progressive matrices.*

Columbia Mental Maturity Scale

A scale which has an age range from 3 to 10 years and was developed to assess people with *cerebral palsy.* Sets of cards with drawings or written words are used. One card in each set is incorrect. The early sets are very simple but the later ones use more abstract ideas and require logical reasoning. A *mental age* and *intelligence quotient* can be calculated from the scores. It does not rely on language skills and the ability to make a simple physical response (e.g. eye pointing) is all that is required. It is also useful for deaf people.

BURGEMEISTER, B. et al (1972) Columbia Mental Maturity Scale. New York: Harcourt Brace Jovanovich Inc.

Committee on Child Health Services

= *Court Report.* See *district handicap teams.*

Committee of Enquiry into the Education of Handicapped Children and Young People

= *Warnock Committee Report (1978).*

Committee of Enquiry into Mental Handicap Nursing and Care

= *Jay Committee.*

Communication / communication disorders

Communication is the art of imparting or conveying information. There are many ways of communicating by *language*, gesture, pictures, facial expression, etc. Language is the most sophisticated method and impaired brain function may prevent or delay the ability to acquire language skills. Other problems, such as deafness, may also interfere with language acquisition. Some people, including those with *autism*, have a

specific problem with communication skills whereas they may be far more able in other areas. The term 'communication disorder' is therefore very general and covers many disabilities. How far communication will develop in a person with a mental handicap will depend largely on the severity of the mental handicap, the opportunities available for stimulation and learning and the nature and extent of other disabilities. People with language disorders may be able to communicate by the use of *gesture systems*, *sign language* or *symbols*.

CULHANE, T. et al (Eds.) (1984) Communication Problems of the Mentally Handicapped. Colchester: University of Essex.
JEFFREE, D. & McCONKEY, R. (1976) Let Me Speak. London: Souvenir Press.
KIERNAN, C. (1985) Communication. In: Mental Deficiency. The changing outlook (4th edit.) Clarke, A.M. et al (Eds.) London: Methuen. pp. 584–638.
LEEMING, K. et al (1979) Teaching Language and Communication to the Mentally Handicapped. London: Evans/Methuen.

Community care

This term has become so general that its significance has been lost. It is used to describe services provided in the community and also to describe a philosophy against which to judge and develop services. The *Social Services Committee Report (1985)* describes the general principles which form the basis for most definitions.
1. A preference for home life over care in an *institution*.
2. The pursuit of the ideals of *normalization* and *integration* and avoidance so far as possible of separate provision, *segregation* and restriction (i.e. the *least restrictive alternative*).
3. A preference for small over large.
4. A preference for local social services over district ones.
The basic principle is that 'Appropriate care should be provided for individuals in such a way as to enable them to lead as

normal an existence as possible given their particular disabilities and to minimize disruption of their life within the community'. The consequences of such a policy means providing for basic needs in ordinary domestic housing, in ordinary occupational settings and through the use of ordinary recreational amenities. The resettlement of the residents of large institutions (*deinstitutionalization*) is a temporary phenomenon and once this is accomplished, community care in the future will be the care of the people within the local community. Comprehensive locally based services are required to make this possible. It should not be assumed that living in the community will always be a satisfactory experience for mentally handicapped people. If supported by family and friends, life may be very rewarding but without the necessary support, opportunities and services, it can be very miserable.

ATKINSON, D. (1982) Distress Signals in the Community. Community Care, 421: 21–23.
BRUININKS, R. et al (1981) Deinstitutionalization and Community Adjustment of Mentally Retarded People. Washington DC.: American Association on Mental Deficiency.
DONEGAN, C. & POTTS, M. (1988) People with mental handicap living alone in the community: A pilot study of their quality of life. Brit. J. Ment. Subn., 66:10–22.
EDGERTON, R.B. & BERCOVICI, S.M. (1976) The cloak of competence: Years later. Am. J. Ment. Defic., 86:485–497.
KING'S FUND CENTRE (1982) An Ordinary Life: comprehensive locally based services for mentally handicapped people. London: King's Fund Centre.
LANDESMAN-DWYER, S. (1981) Living in the community. Am. J. Ment. Defic., 86: 223–234.
SOCIAL SERVICES COMMITTEE REPORT (1985) Community Care with Special Reference to Adult Mentally Ill and Mentally Handicapped People. London: HMSO.
WARD, L. (1982) People First: Developing Services in the Community for People with Mental Handicap. London: King's Fund Centre.

Community homes
In the U.S.A. this refers to homes in the community for ten or less mentally handicapped people.

Community mental handicap nurse
In the U.K. there is nurse training and qualification specifically for people working with mentally handicapped people. The reduction in size and closure of hospitals has resulted in the transfer of many nurses to the community where they advise, train and assist mentally handicapped people and their carers. They are usually members of a *community mental handicap team*.

HALL, V. & RUSSELL, O. (1980) A National Survey of Community Nursing Services for the Mentally Handicapped. Mental Handicap Studies Research Reports No.10, Bristol University.
SINES, D. (1985) The role of the community nurse. In: Mental Handicap. A multidisciplinary approach. Craft, M. et al. London: Baillière Tindall. pp. 288–294.
SINES, D. & BICKNELL, J. (1985) Caring for Mentally Handicapped People in the Community. London: Harper & Row.

Community mental handicap team
These have developed in the U.K. in the last decade since the majority of mentally handicapped people are now living in the community. Teams have developed in various ways in different parts of the country depending on local geographical and historical factors. Teams generally include a *social worker, community mental handicap nurse* and *clinical psychologist*. Several other professional workers may be included or involved. Their role is to support mentally handicapped people living in the community and their carers. This may be directly or through the generic services.

GRANT, G. et al (1986) Community Mental

Community nurse

Handicap Teams: Theory and Practice. Kidderminster: BIMH Conference Series.
HOLLINS, S. (1985) The dynamics of teamwork. In: Mental Handicap. A multidisciplinary approach. Craft, M. et al. London: Baillière Tindall. pp. 281–287.
SINES, D. & BICKNELL, J. (1985) Caring for Mentally Handicapped People in the Community. London: Harper & Row.

Community nurse

In the U.K. this may refer to a *health visitor*, district nurse or specialist nurse such as a *community mental handicap nurse*.

SINES, D. & BICKNELL, J. (1985) Caring for Mentally Handicapped People in the Community. London: Harper & Row.

Community units

Units developed in the early days of *community care* for mentally handicapped people. They offer a residential resource, mainly for part-time forms of care, provide a centre of expertise and may house the *community mental handicap team*. They may have as many as 20–30 beds. While these units were a considerable improvement on the previous institutions they are now being replaced by programmes which use domestic housing as the main residential resource.

KING'S FUND CENTRE (1982) An Ordinary Life : comprehensive locally based services for mentally handicapped people. London: King's Fund Centre.

Complex partial seizure

This type of *seizure* can be difficult to diagnose. It is a type of *epilepsy* in which inappropriate but apparently purposeful and complex behaviour may occur. The same sequence of movements may occur each time and lip-smacking and jerking of the mouth and face is quite a common accompaniment. This is also known as psychomotor epilepsy and often arises from an abnormal area (focus) in the *temporal lobe* of the brain. People with complex partial seizures are also more at risk of overactivity and behaviour problems.

GESCHWIND, N. (1979) Behavioural changes in temporal lobe epilepsy. Psychol. Med., 9:217–219.

Comprehension of language

The ability to understand *language*. When this is impaired a person will hear language or see it written down but it will have little or no meaning. Phrases may be repeated parrot fashion, without knowing their meaning, and this may give the mistaken impression of comprehension. Responses to gestures and situations may also be misleading. It is most important accurately to assess a mentally handicapped person's ability to comprehend language, although this may be difficult if the person has other severe disabilities. There are a number of standard assessments which can be given by a *speech therapist* or *psychologist*.

Compulsory admission to hospital

The *Mental Health Act (1983)* in England and Wales allows compulsory admission for *assessment* for up to 28 days (Section 2) on the grounds of *mental disorder* which includes arrested or incomplete development of the mind. Hospitalization must be for the person's health or safety or for the protection of other persons. The person has a right to appeal within the first 14 days. The nearest relative or *approved social worker* can apply for admission and there must be two medical recommendations. Admission for assessment in an emergency involves only one doctor and lasts up to 72 hours (Section 4). Compulsory admission for more than 28 days (Section 3) is only possible for treatment of *mental impairment* or *severe mental impairment* which includes abnormally aggressive or seriously irresponsible behaviour. The person must be mentally impaired such that hospital care and treatment are appropriate and it must be impossible to provide this elsewhere. In the case of mental impairment it has to be shown that such treatment is likely to alleviate or prevent a deterioration of the patient's condition. If the hospital accepts the patient the detention can last for up to 6 months when it is renewable. A patient may apply to the *Mental Health Review Tribunal* within 6 months following admission under Section 3 and also any time during each period of renewal. If the patient does not ask for a Tribunal hearing the hospital managers are obliged to refer the case.

It is a constitutional requirement in the U.S.A. that hospitalization is the *least restrictive alternative*. The trend is toward admission only for an overt dangerous act on the part of the mentally handicapped person.

ENNIS, B.J. & EMERY, R.D. (1978) The Rights of Mental Patients. New York: Avon Books.
GUNN, M.J. (1984) The Mental Health Act 1983 – guardianship and hospitalization. Mental Handicap, 12:8–9.

Computerized axial tomography / computerized tomographic scanning
= *CT scan.*

Computers / computer-aided learning
Computers may be used as part of the *microelectronic equipment* designed for profoundly mentally handicapped people for environmental control and the teaching of adaptive skills. Computer-aided learning is relevant to the full range of mental handicap and is particularly used in *special education*. In recent years the development of suitable computer hardware (to allow mentally handicapped people to control the equipment) and software (programs designed to respond to the needs of mentally handicapped people) has been a priority. More research needs to be done on evaluating this approach to learning but preliminary experience suggests that it has many applications and can achieve good results so long as it is applied appropriately. Recently teachers have also begun to use computers as an aid to planning and as a tool in assessment and the design of teaching programmes.

BENNETT, R.E. (1982) Applications for microcomputer technology to special education. Except. Child., 49:106–113.
BRINKER, R.P. & LEWIS, M. (1982) Making the world work with microcomputers: a learning prosthesis for handicapped infants. Except. Child., 49:163–170.
GOLDENBERG, E.P. et al (1984) Computers, Education and Special Needs. California: Addison-Wesley.
LOVETT, S. (1985) Microelectronic computer-based technology. In: Mental Deficiency. The changing outlook (4th edit.). Clarke, A.M. et al (Eds.). London: Methuen. pp. 549–583.
STALLARD, C.K. (1982) Computers and education for exceptional children: emerging applications. Except. Child., 49:102–104.

Conductive deafness / conduction deafness
A hearing loss caused by disease or damage which interferes with the conduction of sound from outside in the environment to the inner ear. Normally the eardrums and minute bones in the middle ear conduct the sound to the inner ear (the *cochlea* and auditory nerve) but if the drum or bones are damaged or impeded then they cannot do their job properly and deafness is the result. Such problems may be caused by repeated infections, *glue ear* or traumatic damage. Treatment, usually by an operation on the ear, may help considerably and a hearing aid is also generally effective in this type of deafness. Ear infections and deafness are easily missed in mentally handicapped people and should be promptly and effectively treated.

Conductive education
A method initially introduced to teach sequences of movements to children with *cerebral palsy*. It has been found to be

Congenital

particularly effective for children with *athetosis* who become less able to carry out movements the more they are concentrated upon. A group drill technique of play and motor patterns is used. The regular repetition of a simple sequence of acts is used to make them so automatic that conscious thought is no longer necessary. There is also emphasis on performing movements in the mid-line of the body to maintain symmetry. Recently this approach has been used with physically fit mentally handicapped children though the rationale for this is less obvious.

In Hungary, conductive education is used with the child from 6am to 9pm. Continuity is maintained throughout the day with the conductors working a six-hour shift with an hour overlap. The task series, which the children learn in order to overcome their motor handicap, are incorporated into every activity of daily living.

BUDD, B. & EVANS, J. (1977) What is their future? An experimental project in conductive education with the multiply handicapped. Apex, 4:18–22.
HOOPER, H. (1986) Hungarian therapy goes on trial in the U.K. G.P.News, 12.
ROOKE-COTTAM, P. (1985) Evaluation of a teaching approach for children with profound multiple handicaps based on aspects of Conductive Education. Mental Handicap, 134:159–160.

Congenital

Deformities or diseases which are present at birth although sometimes may not become evident until later.

Congenital aplastic anaemia

= *Fanconi's hypoplastic anaemia.*

Congenital cytomegalovirus infection

= *Cytomegalic inclusion disease.*

Congenital dislocation of hip

Dislocation of one or both hips may be present at birth. Generally the socket for the thigh bone is shallow so that it easily slips out. This may occur in some conditions associated with mental handicap including *bird-headed dwarfism* and several *chromosome* abnormalities. *Cerebral palsy* may be a later cause due to muscles pulling on the hip joint. It is treated in babies by strapping the thigh in a frog-leg position for several months. It is more difficult to treat in older children and an operation may be required.

Congenital facial diplegia

= *Möbius' syndrome.*

Congenital gangliosidosis

= *Norman-Wood disease.*

Congenital goitrous cretinism

A type of *congenital hypothyroidism* in which the thyroid gland is enlarged causing a swelling in the front of the neck. It may be inherited (*recessive inheritance*) and due to an *enzyme* defect. If associated with deafness it is known as *Pendred's syndrome.*

ANDERSEN, H.S. (1961) Studies in hypothyroidism in children. Acta Pediatr. Suppl., 125.

Congenital heart disease / defect

Abnormalities, present at birth, of the heart and/or the large blood vessels joining it. These may include holes between the chambers of the heart, malformations of the heart valves, narrowing of the blood vessels and persistence of a blood vessel which usually closes after birth (*patent ductus arteriosis*). These occur commonly in many conditions associated with mental handicap. All these abnormalities, depending on nature and severity, may be evident at birth or become evident later in childhood. The turbulence of blood as it flows past an abnormality may be heard with a stethoscope as a murmur. Severe defects may cause heart failure and the infant may be very ill. Most defects can be operated on and repaired but the risks can be high.

Examples of congenital heart disease include *atrial septal defect, Fallot's tetralogy* and *ventricular septal defect*.

Congenital hypothyroidism

A deficiency of the thyroid gland secretion, thyroxine at birth. This type of *hypothyroidism* is caused by the body failing to make one or more of the substances necessary for the production of thyroxine or by the thyroid gland failing to develop. There are at least five types of biochemical abnormality and three of these can be inherited (*recessive inheritance*). In most cases, however, it is not inherited. Thyroxine from the mother during pregnancy may prevent the signs of the condition becoming evident at birth but, if *diagnosis* and treatment are delayed, after 3 months the chances of preventing irreparable brain damage become progressively less and *cretinism* will develop. It can be treated by giving the infant thyroxine as a medicine. It can be detected early by testing all newborn infants and this is an important way of preventing this cause of mental handicap. In the U.K. and U.S.A. the majority of children are screened for this at birth. Even after treatment some children perform below the average especially on tests of hearing and speech.

DASSAULT, J.H. & WALKER, P. (1983) Congenital Hypothyroidism. London: Butterworths.
FISHER, D.A. (1983) Second International Conference on neonatal thyroid screening: progress report. J. Pediatr., 98:653–654.
GLORIEUX, J. et al (1983) Preliminary results on the mental development of hypothyroid infants detected by the Quebec Screening Program. J. Pediatr., 102:19–22.
HULSE, J.A. et al (1980) Population screening for congenital hypothyroidism. Brit. Med. J. 280:675–678.
HULSE, J.A. (1984) Outcome for congenital hypothyroidism. Arch. Dis. Childh., 59: 23–30.
VANDERSCHUEREN-LODEWEYCKZ, M. et al (1983) Sensorineural hearing loss in sporadic congenital hypothyroidism. Arch. Dis. Childh., 58:419–422.

Congenital lactic acidosis
= *familial lactic acidosis.*

Congenital malformation
An abnormality of body structure present at birth.

Congenital rubella syndrome
= *rubella syndrome.*

Congenital stippled epiphyses
= *Conradi's syndrome.*

Congenital syphilis

Syphilis is a very rare cause of mental handicap nowadays. If the fetus is infected both mental and physical development may be impaired from birth. Physical abnormalities are most common but mental handicap and *epilepsy* can occur. The physical characteristics are peg-shaped front upper teeth, defective development of the bridge of the nose and abnormalities of the eyes. A child may appear normal until 8 to 10 years of age but then deteriorate (*juvenile paresis*). Treatment with penicillin arrests the course of the disease.

BUDELL, J.W. (1984) Syphilis. In: Practice of Pediatrics. Kelly, V.C. (Ed.) (revised edit.). Philadelphia: Harper & Row. Vol. 3. ch. 103, pp. 1–18.
FINBERG, L. (1977) Syphilis. In: Pediatrics. Rudolf, A.M. (Ed.). New York: Appleton-Century-Crofts.
WIGGELINKHUIZEN, J. & MASON, R. (1980) Congenital neurosyphilis and juvenile paresis: a forgotten entity? Clin. Pediatr., 19:142–145.

Conradi's syndrome / Conradi-Hunermann syndrome

A very rare condition characterized by shortening of the limbs, flat bridge to nose, *cataracts* of the eyes, deformities of the joints and dry scaly skin. X-rays of limb bones

Consanguinity

show stippling of the soft ends of bones. *Congenital heart disease* may be present. Many affected infants die in the first year of life. There are two types only one of which is associated with mental handicap. This type is inherited from both parents (*recessive inheritance*).

ALLANSMITH, M. & SENZ, E. (1960) Chondrodystrophia congenita punctata (Conradi's disease). Am. J. Dis. Child., 100:109.
BRIGGS, J.N. et al (1953) Congenital stippled epiphyses. Arch. Dis. Childh., 28: 209.

Consanguinity

The situation where two people are blood relatives. If the parents of a child are related (e.g. cousins) there is an increased risk of the child having a disorder due to *recessive inheritance*.

Consent to treatment

The *Mental Health Act (1983)* in England and Wales allows any form of treatment to be given to a detained patient under Sections 2 and 3 except psychosurgery, surgical implantation of hormones, electroconvulsive therapy and *psychotropic drugs* after the first 3 months, without the patient's consent provided it is for mental disorder. If a detained patient cannot or will not consent to treatment with drugs three months after they were first given, an independent doctor can say that the treatment should be given, provided he or she has consulted with two non-medical professionals involved with the patient (their advice does not have to be followed). If the patient is in hospital informally he or she may refuse any treatment and has a common-law right to sue for assault if treated without informed consent. Treatment can only be given without consent in cases of urgent necessity when failure to act might be construed as negligence.
The position in the U.S.A. varies, 88% of states recognize a qualified right to refuse medication for psychiatric disorder whereas

12% recognize no right to refuse. If the person cannot consent then technically the treatment cannot be given unless it is a necessary emergency operation. On the other hand a practitioner has a duty to take responsible care of his patient and to enable him to receive the treatment he needs. In the U.S.A. third-party consent by a parent or guardian is possible.

FRIEDMAN, P.R. (1976) The Rights of Mentally Retarded People. New York: Avon Books.
HAYES, S.C. & HAYES, R. (1982) Mental Retardation: Law, Policy and Administration. Sydney: Law Book Co.
MENTAL HEALTH ACT COMMISSION (1985) Consent to Treatment. Hepburn House, Marsham St., London SW1P 4HW.
TURNBULL, H. (Ed.) (1977) Consent Handbook. American Association on Mental Deficiency. Washington DC.

Constriction of chromosome

= *chromosome constriction*.

Consultant

A specialist, generally a doctor, who is consulted in difficult cases. In the U.K. mental handicap is regarded as a sub-specialty of psychiatry and consultants must be members of the Royal College of Psychiatrists as well as having had relevant experience of mental handicap at a senior registrar grade before appointment.

Continence

See *incontinence*.

Contingency

The relationship between a behaviour and the events (consequences) which follow that behaviour. An understanding of contingencies is an important prerequisite to *behaviour modification* programmes.

Contraception

Many mentally handicapped people are living much more independent lives than previously expected. The more aware and informed people become the more they will expect the right to love, marry, have a sexual relationship and to have children. It is therefore very important to include in *sex education* very thorough considerations about birth control, *sterilization* and the responsibility of having children. If the carers supporting mentally handicapped people are concerned about the capacity of individuals or a couple to rear children then they have the responsibility of helping to arrange protection by effective *counselling*, education and birth control should there be any risk of an unwanted pregnancy. Often parents or caregivers have tried to prevent pregnancy by instilling a fear of sex but are often vague about what sex really is, so that they are easily misunderstood, sometimes with disastrous results. Family planning clinics can be helpful in providing suitable information about contraception to mentally handicapped people.

CRAFT, A. & CRAFT, M. (1985) Sexuality and personal relationships. In: Mental Handicap. A multidisciplinary approach. Craft, M. et al (Eds.). London: Baillière Tindall. pp. 192–194.
MCCARTHY, W. & FEGAN, L. (1984) Sex Education and the Intellectually Handicapped. Boston: ADIS Press.

Further information:
Family Planning Association, 27–35, Mortimer St., London W1N 7RJ.
Planned Parenthood Federation of America, Inc. (PPFA), 810 Seventh Avenue, New York, NY 10019.

Contracture
The permanent shortening of a muscle or of fibrous tissue. *Cerebral palsy* often causes contracture of muscles which may fix joints in abnormal positions leading to deformities.

Convulsion
See *epilepsy, grand-mal convulsion* and *febrile convulsions*.

Copewell Scale / System / Curriculum
A comprehensive scale for assessing mildly to severely mentally handicapped adults. It covers self-help, social, academic, interpersonal and vocational skills and also involves the identification of opportunities. The Copewell Curriculum has 174 objectives distributed over the four sections. The teaching packages within the system are intended to act as resource material for staff.

WHELAN, E. & SPEAKE, B. (1979) Learning to Cope. London: Souvenir Press.
WHELAN, E. & SPEAKE, B. (1979) Scale for Assessing Coping Skills. London: Copewell Publications.

Coprophagy
Eating faecal matter. This is a rare behaviour problem seen in severely mentally handicapped people and is a type of *pica*.

FOXX, R.M. & MARTIN, E.D. (1975) Treatment of scavenging behavior (coprophagy and pica) by overcorrection. Behav. Res. Ther., 13:153–162.

Core and cluster
A system which provides accommodation and support services for people who are mentally handicapped. The core consists of a central resource which includes skilled professional workers and often a training facility for the clients usually on a residential basis. Sometimes the core unit also provides accommodation for support care to give clients in the locality a break away from home. The cluster usually consists of a range of living accommodation scattered throughout the local community. It may include staffed and unstaffed *group homes*, lodgings, flatlets etc. The size of the area and the number of clients served by the core unit varies from scheme to scheme. Recently, the model has been questioned, especially the use of the core unit as a residential and training facility. Training people in their own home probably produces better results

and support care can also be provided on a domestic scale in ordinary housing.

Cori disease
= *limit dextrinosis*.

Cornea
The clear layer at the front of the eye through which the light passes to the interior.

Corneal opacity
Clouding of the *cornea* of the eye usually due to damage and scarring (*corneal ulceration*). It may also occur in some conditions associated with mental handicap including some of the *mucopolysaccharidoses* and rarely in *Down's syndrome*. It will interfere with vision depending on extent and density and, if severe, a corneal graft is necessary.

Corneal ulceration
A breach of the surface of the cornea usually caused by injury or infection. *Eye-poking*, as a method of self-stimulation or self-injury, can occur in mentally handicapped people and it is more likely if there is already a loss of vision. This can cause corneal ulceration with the risk of scarring and impairment of vision (*corneal opacity*). It should be treated promptly with the use of an antibiotic or anti-viral drugs to prevent or control infection and to allow healing.

Cornelia de Lange syndrome
= *de Lange syndrome*.

Corpus callosum
A central broad tract of fibres which connects the two halves of the upper brain (*cerebral hemispheres*). It may be abnormal or absent (agenesis of the corpus callosum) in a few rare conditions associated with mental handicap including *Edward's syndrome, Aicardi's syndrome* and *Rubinstein-Taybi syndrome*. There is no consistent pattern of disorder in this condition. A wide variety of signs and symptoms have been attributed to it but many are probably due to other abnormalities of the brain.

ETTLINGER, G. et al (1974) Agenesis of the corpus callosum: A further behavioural investigation. Brain, 97:225.
FIELD, M. et al (1978) Agenesis of the corpus callosum: Report of two preschool children and review of the literature. Dev. Med. Child Neurology, 20:47.
WARKANY, J. et al (1981) Mental Retardation and Congenital Malformations of the Central Nervous System. London: Year Book Medical Publishers. pp. 224–243.

Cortex of the brain
The surface layer of the *cerebral hemispheres* of the brain. This is crinkled into large folds and is composed of nerve cells. It is grey in colour as compared with the white fibrous areas beneath the cortex.

Cortical atrophy
Shrinkage of the *cortex of the brain* due to damage or disease.

Cortical-evoked response audiometry
The measurement of the response of the *cortex of the brain* to pure sound. It requires the subject to be very alert and co-operative and is generally not used for *assessment* of mentally handicapped people. It has now been largely replaced by more specific techniques.

Council for Exceptional Children (CEC)
A non-profit making organization established in the U.S.A. to help those who serve the educational needs of exceptional children. It aims to expand the body of special education knowledge and to ensure that each child has access to skilled educators and the resources required to provide quality education. CEC operates a federally-funded Educational Resources Information Center, produces journals and makes available teaching aids, reports, books and professional materials. CEC has professional divisions which are special organizations concentrating on particular abilities or dis-

abilities of exceptional children or unique aspects of special education. Divisions publish journals and newsletters and also hold conferences and workshops for members.

Further information:
Council for Exceptional Children, 1920 Association Drive, Reston, VA 22091.
CEC, Jefferson Plaza, 1411 S. Jefferson Davis Highway, Arlington, VA 22202.

Counselling
The process of advising and supporting people in a constructive and helpful way. It is a skilled approach from a helper or therapist to a person with a problem. It is based on the assumption that talking will help the client to clarify and explore possible solutions to problems in a non-judgemental atmosphere of equality. It should enable him or her to adapt, cope and, if possible, to solve the problem. Many parents benefit from counselling to help them come to terms with having a handicapped child. See also *genetic counselling*.

ATTWOOD, T. (1981) Counselling parents of handicapped children. Apex 9(2):48.
CUNNINGHAM, C.C. & DAVIS, H. (1985) Early parent counselling. In: Mental Handicap. A multidisciplinary approach. Craft, M. (Ed.) London: Baillière Tindall. pp. 162–176.
TAYLOR, D.C. (1982) Counselling the parents of handicapped children. Brit. Med. J., 284:1027–1028.

Further information:
The British Association for Counselling, 26 Bedford Sq., London WC1 3HQ.

Court committee / Court report
See *district handicap teams*.

Court of Protection (Part VIII of the *Mental Health Act 1959* as amended by Part VII of the *Mental Health Act 1983*)
In the U.K. a person with mental handicap may be accepted into the jurisdiction of the court if there is medical evidence that the person is incapable by reason of mental disorder of managing and administering his or her own property and affairs. The officers of the court are the Master, Deputy Master and judges nominated by the Lord Chancellor. It is their task to 'do or serve the doing of all such things as appear necessary or expedient' for the maintenance or other benefit of the person or his or her family, or for providing for the people or purposes for which the person might have expected to provide were he or she not disordered or for otherwise administering his or her affairs. The Act contains a list of actions which may be taken by the court on behalf of the person. A judge may act in an emergency if necessary. The usual method by which the court deals with the management of the person's affairs is by the appointment of a receiver. Application to the court for the exercise of its jurisdiction can be made to the Chief Clerk, Court of Protection, Staffordshire House, 25 Shore St., London WC1E 7BP.

Coxa valga
Turning inward of the legs at the hip joint usually due to the upper end of the thigh bone developing at an abnormal angle. This may occur in several conditions associated with mental handicap including *Down's syndrome* and *Carpenter's syndrome*.

Coxa vara
Turning outward of the legs at the hip joint usually due to the upper end of the thigh bone developing at an abnormal angle. This may occur in association with mental handicap in the *de Lange syndrome*.

CP
= *cerebral palsy*.

Craniofacial dysostosis
= *Crouzon's syndrome*.

Craniofacial syndrome
A rare condition in which, from birth, the

baby has a weakness of the muscles of one side of the face when crying. This is a pointer to the likelihood of other abnormalities, including *congenital heart disease*, mental handicap, *epilepsy* and *spina bifida*. It occurs in males more than females and there is not thought to be a hereditary cause.

PAPE, K. & PICKERING, D. (1972) Asymmetric crying facies: an index of other congenital anomalies. J. Pediatr., 81:21.

Craniostenosis / craniosynostosis
Premature closure of the flat bones of the skull while the brain is still growing in size. This results in pressure on the brain and if untreated will cause mental handicap. It may be associated with an unusual facial appearance depending on the bones affected but if the majority of the bones fuse together the result is called *acrocephaly* or oxycephaly. An operation is required to separate the bones and to reduce the pressure on the brain.

COHEN, M.M. (1975) An etiologic and nosologic overview of craniosynostosis syndromes. Birth Defects, 2(11):137.
WARKANY, J. et al (1981) Mental Retardation and Congenital Malformations of the Central Nervous System. London: Year Book Medical Publishers. pp. 123–157.

Cranium
The part of the skull enclosing the brain.

Cretinism
A condition caused by absent or low levels of thyroxine (the hormone produced by the thyroid gland) during the development of the child. It is generally caused by *congenital hypothyroidism*. It was common in areas of the world deficient in iodine which is essential to the thyroid gland. It has been prevented in these areas by the introduction of iodized salt. An early sign of cretinism is lethargy especially when feeding. Enlargement of the tongue occurs with noisy breathing. If untreated the baby becomes increasingly slow in development with a lack of interest

in people and surroundings. The skin becomes loose, wrinkled and usually has a yellowish tinge. Puffiness and thickening of the skin occurs with thick eyelids, lips etc. The neck is short and fat and fatty pads develop around the shoulders. Hair is scanty. The tummy protrudes and constipation is usual. Body temperature is low and the baby has a characteristically hoarse cry. The child becomes increasingly mentally handicapped and growth and sexual development is stunted.

If treatment with thyroxine is not started until after the age of 3 months the mental handicap present at the time is unlikely to improve to normal. Subsequent development will be better and physically there will be a considerable improvement.

HOLMES, L.B. et al (1972) Mental Retardation. New York: Macmillan. pp. 10–11.
SMITH, D.W. et al (1975) Congenital hypothyroidism: Signs and symptoms in the newborn period. J. Pediatr., 87:958.

Cri-du-chat syndrome
In this rare condition, which affects females more frequently than males, there is a missing part to the short arm of one of the fifth pair of *chromosomes* (*chromosome deletion*). Children with this condition have a low birth weight and remain small for age. The baby has a mewing cry for the first few months and may have other unusual features or deformities. These may include a small head, squint (*strabismus*), wide spaced eyes with flat bridge to nose, small mouth with high palate, low set ears, downward eye slant and small chin. There may be minor abnormalities of limbs such as flat feet, mild *spasticity* and slight unsteadiness when walking. *Curvature of the spine* may develop. Mental handicap is usually severe. In the majority of cases the abnormality of the chromosome arises as a genetic accident during conception and there is no known cause. In about 10% of individuals one of the parents has an abnormality known as a balanced *chromosome translocation*.

BREG, W.R. et al (1970) The Cri-du-chat syndrome in adolescents and adults: clinical findings in 13 older patients with partial deletion of the short arm of chromosome no. 5. J. Pediatr., 77:782.

NIEBUHR, E. (1978) The cri du chat syndrome. Epidemiology, cytogenetics and clinical features. Hum. Genet., 44:227–275.

Crouzon's syndrome

People with this rare condition have an unusual appearance and usually an abnormally shaped head (*acrocephaly*). The eyes protrude and are widely spaced sometimes with a squint (*strabismus*). Vision may sometimes be reduced. The upper jaw and lip are underdeveloped and the nose is beak-shaped. Operations on the skull may be necessary to prevent pressure on the brain and eyes. Mental handicap is present to a varying degree in about 20% of people with the condition. *Seizures* may occur. It can be inherited from one parent who may be mildly affected (*dominant inheritance*) or, as in one third of cases, it arises anew without a family history.

DODGE, H.W. et al (1959) Cranio facial-dysostosis: Crouzon's disease. Pediatrics, 23:98.

Cryptophthalmos syndrome

People with this rare condition are born with skin covering one or both eyes. The front of the eyeball is also abnormal. There may be other abnormalities of the ears, mouth, chest, limbs or genitals. *Blindness* may be accompanied by some hearing loss. Mental handicap occurs quite frequently. It is probably inherited from both parents who are carriers (*recessive inheritance*).

GUPTA, S.P. & SAXENA, R.C. (1962) Cryptophthalmos. Br. J. Ophthalmol., 46: 629–632.

IDE, C.H. & WOLLSCHLAEGER, P.B. (1969) Multiple congenital abnormalities associated with cryptophthalmia. Arch. Ophthalmol., 81:638–644.

Cryptorchidism

Undescended testes which are inside the abdomen or in the canal between the abdomen and the scrotum. In young children the testes retract easily into the canal above, especially when examined, leading to misdiagnosis. In such children they will stay in place more as the child develops. True cryptorchidism occurs in several conditions associated with mental handicap including some chromosomal abnormalities, *de Lange syndrome*, *Prader-Willi syndrome* and *Smith-Lemli-Opitz syndrome*. An operation is usually necessary to bring down the testes.

CSF

= *cerebro-spinal fluid.*

CT scan

A great breakthrough in the diagnostic investigations available for the study of the brain. A computer is used to analyse the difference in density between the X-ray appearance of water and brain tissue, a distinction not possible with the unaided eye. A series of X-ray images are analysed to provide views of sections of the brain. These provide detailed and informative pictures which may show malformations of the brain, cysts, *brain tumours, haemorrhage* and *hydrocephalus* as well as other diseases and abnormalities. It requires the subject to be still for periods of minutes and sedation may therefore be required. It can also be used to study the rest of the body.

Cubitus valgus

An abnormality of the elbow joint causing the forearm to turn outward when the arm is held by the side. This may occur in conditions associated with mental handicap including *Silver's syndrome, cerebro-hepato-renal syndrome* and *Noonan's syndrome.*

Cues

In *behaviour modification* this refers to the methods used to give clues to a person in order to help remembering, understanding and learning about the tasks required. Cues may be unmistakable, such as reminding with words, but sometimes they are more subtle e.g. using a gesture or facial expression.

Sometimes environmental cues (such as places, events or other people's behaviour) prompt inappropriate behaviour from the individual.

Mentally handicapped people sometimes have difficulty in understanding the cues which indicate that a behaviour is socially unacceptable.

Curvature of the spine
= *scoliosis* and *kyphosis*.

Cutis verticis gyrata
The corrugated appearance of the scalp which sometimes occurs in people with *microcephaly*.

Cyanosis
Blueness, particularly of the face and extremities, due to lack of oxygen in the blood. There are many possible causes including *seizures* and *congenital heart disease*, which may occur in mentally handicapped people.

Cylert
= *pemoline*.

Cyproterone acetate
A drug used for the treatment of severe oversexuality or misdirected sexuality in the male. It blocks the male hormones known as androgens. It has generally reversible side-effects such as breast enlargement and rarely, disturbances of the liver. It can cause sedation and depression. It should not be used in physically inactive men and there are ethical considerations in its use for people who are mentally handicapped and unable to give *consent to treatment*.

Cystathioninuria / cystathionin-aemia
One of the group of disorders known as the *amino acidurias*. A substance (*enzyme*) called cystathionase is absent and as a result an important chemical process cannot take place and a substance, cystathionine, accumulates in the blood and urine. The effect is to slow growth. Abnormalities of the blood also occur including anaemia and a tendency to bleed. The degree of mental handicap is variable. A number of other abnormalities such as *epilepsy*, kidney disease and small ears have been reported but none occur consistently.

It is probably inherited from both parents who are carriers (*recessive inheritance*). Long-term treatment with *pyridoxine* is said to increase the growth rate and reduce the degree of mental handicap. Mothers who are carriers of this condition should be given this vitamin during pregnancy.

BERLOW, S. (1966) Studies in cystathionin-aemia. Am. J. Dis. Child., 112: 135.
HARRIS, H. et al (1959) Cystathioninuria. Ann. Hum. Genet., 23:442.

Cystinuria
In this disorder some of the *amino acids* cannot be absorbed from the intestine and they change to other substances which are absorbed and passed into the urine. The kidneys also function abnormally and cystine is concentrated in the urine and can damage the kidneys and urinary system. Kidney stones are a common complication. People with this condition are more likely to be mentally handicapped or mentally disturbed. It is an inherited condition and if inherited from one parent the person may only be mildly affected or just a *carrier*. If inherited from both parents there is a greater likelihood of being severely affected. Treatment is complicated and includes control of diet, high fluid intake, controlling the acidity of urine and the administration of *pyridoxine*. Other medication may also be required.

SCHRIVER, C.R. et al (1970) Cystinuria: Increased prevalence in patients with mental disease. New Engl. J. Med., 283:783.
SINCLAIR, L. (1979) Metabolic Disease in

Childhood. Oxford: Blackwell Scientific Publications. pp. 240–244.

Cytogenetics

The science of heredity at the microscopic level. It includes the study of the arrangement of *chromosomes*, of *genes* on the chromosomes, the chemical structure of genes and the effects of abnormalities of genes and chromosomes. There have been tremendous advances in the last 20 years in the technical skills, their application and the knowledge acquired.

SCIORRA, L.J. (1980) Chromosomal basis for developmental disabilities and mental retardation. In: Prevention of Mental Retardation and other Developmental Disabilities. McCormack, M.D. (Ed.) New York: Marcel Dekker Inc. pp. 83–112.

Cytomegalic inclusion disease / cytomegalovirus

Infection with cytomegalovirus causes a very mild illness or no illness at all in adults. If a woman is infected with it during pregnancy it may infect the *fetus*. It is estimated that in the U.K., U.S.A. and Australia about one in every hundred live births is infected with the virus and that at least 10% of these will become mentally handicapped. Affected children are usually born prematurely with breathing difficulties, *jaundice*, enlarged liver and spleen and a tendency to bleed especially into the skin where there are small purple spots. Many affected babies die soon after birth but those who survive may have small heads (*microcephaly*), deafness, inflammation of the back of the eye (*choroido-retinitis*), and may develop *epilepsy*, loss of vision, *cerebral palsy* and mental handicap. Microscopic examination of affected tissues in the body with certain stains shows the characteristic inclusion bodies in the centre of cells. Small shadows on X-rays of the skull represent areas of *cerebral calcification*. The virus can be obtained from the urine of affected babies. There is no known treatment.

PANJVANI, Z.F.K. & HANSHAW, J.B. (1981) Cytomegalovirus in the perinatal period. Am. J. Dis. Child., 135:56–60.

PASS, R.F. et al (1980) Outcome of symptomatic congenital cytomegalovirus infection: results of long-term longitudinal follow-up. Pediatrics, 66(5):758–762.

PECKHAM, C. et al (1983) Cytomegalovirus infection in pregnancy: preliminary findings from a prospective study. Lancet, 1:1352–1355.

D

Dalmane

= *flurazepam*.

Dandy Walker syndrome

In this condition there is enlargement of the fluid-filled cavity of the brain known as the fourth *cerebral ventricle*. It expands due to the pressure of the fluid inside it and forms a large sac-like structure which presses on other parts of the brain. This is a type of *hydrocephalus*. It is caused by a malformation of the brain known as Dandy Walker malformation. The holes through which the *cerebro-spinal fluid* usually drains do not open during the development of the fetus (this is known as aqueductal stenosis). The fluid continues to be made by the special lining of the ventricles and so the pressure builds up. Head enlargement may be evident especially at the back of the skull and a prominent brow may also develop. This malformation is often associated with other abnormalities of the brain and sometimes of other organs of the body. In a few of the reported cases there have been *hereditary* factors but in the rest there has either been no cause identified or it has been associated with another abnormality or *syndrome*.

Operations on the brain are usually successful and a valve may need to be inserted to relieve the pressure. Without a successful operation mental handicap is very likely to occur and there may be a residual problem after operation especially if there are other abnormalities of the brain.

AIMOND, J. et al (1969) Atresia of the foramina of Luschka and Magendie: The Dandy Walker cyst. J. Neurosurg., 31:202.
HART, M.N. et al (1972) The Dandy Walker syndrome, Neurology (Minneap.), 22:771.

Dantrium / dantrolene

A drug used for the relaxation of contracted muscles as in *cerebral palsy*. It is only indicated where *spasticity* of muscles interferes significantly with the activities of daily living. Side-effects include drowsiness, dizziness, weakness, fatigue and diarrhoea. It can also damage the liver. It should not be prescribed for children. Dosage should be increased slowly until maximum benefit is obtained.

Day care / day services

Services which involve a mentally handicapped person during the day and which are usually provided outside the place where he or she lives. These include preschool services (opportunity groups, nursery schools, play groups, *assessment units*), schools, colleges, *adult training centres*, sheltered employment and work experience schemes. It is unusual nowadays for hospitals in the U.K. to offer day care. Recently services have become more flexible and more than one type of day service may be available to a person according to need. This may include someone visiting the home for care or training purposes.

INDEPENDENT DEVELOPMENT COUNCIL FOR PEOPLE WITH MENTAL HANDICAP (1985) Living Like Other People – Next Steps in Day Services for People with Mental Handicap. 126 Albert Street, London NW1 7NF.
NATIONAL DEVELOPMENT GROUP FOR THE MENTALLY HANDICAPPED (1977) Day Services for Mentally Handicapped Adults. NDG Pamphlet 5. London: DHSS.
WORKING PARTY OF NATIONAL COUNCIL FOR THE ROYAL SOCIETY FOR MENTALLY HANDICAPPED CHILDREN AND ADULTS

(1986) Day Services Today and Tomorrow. London: Mencap.

De Grouchy syndrome
= *deletion of short arm of chromosome 18.*

De Lange syndrome
People with this condition have a characteristic appearance with thick eyebrows which meet in the middle and eyelashes which are long and curled. The face and the body are excessively hairy. The bridge of the nose is rather flat and the eyes are often widely spaced. The nostrils tend to point forwards and lips are thin with a downward slant to the corners of the mouth. Other abnormalities of eyes and palate have been described. The ears are usually low-set. The stature is short and the genitals underdeveloped. There may be *congenital heart disease.* The arms are usually shortened and hands and feet are small. The thumb is nearer to the wrist than normal and fingers sometimes are clawed. Other abnormalities of hands and feet may occur. Mental handicap is usually severe but walking is acquired and sometimes simple speech. *Self-injurious behaviour* can be a serious problem. *Epilepsy* occurs in 10% of people with this syndrome. Most infants have a low birth weight. Feeding and swallowing problems and a low-pitched cry in infancy occasionally occur. The cause is not known but in some cases hereditary factors are significant (*recessive inheritance*).

BERG, J.M. et al (1970) The de Lange syndrome. Oxford: Pergamon Press.
BISHUN, N.P. & MORTON, W.R.M. (1965) Brachmann-de Lange syndrome. Lancet, 1:439.
JERVIS, G.A. & STIMSON, C.W. (1963) De Lange syndrome: the 'Amsterdam Type' of mental defect with congenital malformation. J. Pediatr., 63:634.
McARTHUR, R.G. & EDWARDS, J.H. (1967) De Lange syndrome: report of 20 cases. Canad. Med. Ass. J., 96:1185.
WILSON, G.N. et al (1978) The association of chromosome 3 duplication and the Cornelia de Lange syndrome. J. Pediatr., 93:783–788.

De Sanctis-Cacchione syndrome
= *Xeroderma pigmentosum.*

Deaf-blind
Various degrees of *deafness* may be associated with various degrees of *blindness.* Mental handicap may be another disability adding to the multiple handicap. The international definition of deaf-blind accepted by most agencies is 'a deaf-blind child is one who has a visual and auditory deficiency to such an extent that he is unable to function satisfactorily in either a school for the deaf or for the blind'. Very close co-operation between a *multidisciplinary team* is required with early *diagnosis* and intervention. The multiply sensory impaired are not just blind who cannot hear or deaf who cannot see. With both distance senses impaired, the magnitude of the disability is far greater with such severe problems of isolation from the surrounding world. Specialist help is essential. In the past *rubella syndrome* was the commonest cause of such multiple handicaps. *Cytomegalic inclusion disease, Down's syndrome, Hurler's syndrome, cerebro-hepato-renal syndrome* and others are now commoner due to the preventative rubella vaccination programmes.

ELLIS, D. (Ed.) (1986) Sensory Impairments in Mentally Handicapped People. London: Croom Helm; San Diego: College-Hill Press Inc.
FREEMAN, P. (1975) Understanding the Deaf/Blind Child. London: Heinemann Medical Books.
WALSH, S.R. & HOLZBERG, R. (Eds.) (1981) Understanding and Educating the Deaf-Blind/Severely and Profoundly Handicapped. An International Perspective. Illinois: Charles C. Thomas.
WYMAN, R. (1986) Multiply Handicapped Children. London: Human Horizon Series. Souvenir Press.

Further information:
National Association for Deaf-Blind and Rubella Handicapped (SENSE) 311, Grays Inn Rd. London WC1X 8PT.
National Association for the Deaf-blind 2703, Forest Oak Circle, Norman, OK 73071.

Deaf mutism

Absence of speech due to, or accompanied by, deafness. People who are deaf mute have sometimes been misdiagnosed as being mentally handicapped. Deaf mutism can, of course, occur with mental handicap.

Deafness

A well used definition of deafness is a deviation in hearing sufficient to impair normal *communication* by the spoken word. The degree of deafness is the result of the degree of hearing loss interacting with a number of other factors such as age of onset, age of detection and intervention, duration, cause, use of hearing aid, intelligence, training given, family factors and adaptive abilities.
There are four types of hearing impairment:
1. *Conductive deafness*
2. *Sensori-neural*
3. *Central deafness*
4. Mixed – more than one of the above.
It is important to distinguish diagnostically between these because treatment may improve conductive deafness but it is unlikely to change sensori-neural and central types. There are many causes of hearing impairment and many of these coincide with the causes of conditions associated with mental handicap. These include chromosomal and *genetic* conditions, injury and infections. The age of onset and the degree of impairment can have serious consequences for language development. In the past some deaf people have been misdiagnosed as having mental handicap. There is no doubt that a hearing impairment in a mentally handicapped person has a multiplicative rather than a simple additive effect. Accurate diagnosis and assessment of hearing loss followed, if possible, by treatment is very important for people who are mentally handicapped. Education and training is important in all areas of development but particular understanding and emphasis needs to be given to the communication skills of the individual. For people with a severe hearing loss the system of *total communication* is generally recommended.

BESS, F. & McCONNELL, F.E. (1981) Audiology, Education and the Hearing Impaired Child. St. Louis: The C.V. Mosby Co.
ELLIS, D. (Ed.) (1986) Sensory Impairment in Mentally Handicapped People. London: Croom Helm.
FREEMAN, R.D. et al (1981) Can't Your Child Hear? A guide for those who care about deaf children. London: Croom Helm.
MILLER, A.L. (1980) Hearing Loss, Hearing Aids and Your Child. Illinois: Chas. C. Thomas.
NOLAN, M. & TUCKER, I.G. (1981) The Hearing Impaired Child and the Family. London: Souvenir Press.

Further information:
International Association for the Deaf, 814 Thayer Ave., Silver Spring, MD 20910.
National Deaf Children's Society, 45, Hereford Rd., London W2.
Royal National Institute for the Deaf, 105 Gower St., London WC1E 6AH.

Death

A person who is mentally handicapped will be just as fearful and anxious when terminally ill as would any other person. Comfort and personal attention from people who are known and trusted is important. If possible the person should be cared for by familiar people in familiar surroundings with advice from hospice staff or MacMillan nurses if necessary. Freedom from pain is essential and if the person has no language it is particularly important to be watchful for any signs of discomfort. Mentally handicapped friends of the person will also

require comfort, support and honest explanations.
See also *bereavement*.

Debrancher deficiency
= *limit dextrinosis*.

Decerebrate rigidity
A state of continuous tightness of muscles due to almost total lack of control by the brain. This occurs as the terminal state in several *degenerative disorders* including the *sphingolipidoses*.

Decibel
This a unit of hearing. One decibel is the least intensity of sound at which a given note can normally be heard. The normal abbreviation for decibel is dB.

Defective
Mental defective is a term used in the past to describe a person who is mentally handicapped. In the 1952 *DSM III* it was described as an intellectual defect existing since birth without demonstrated organic brain disease or known *prenatal* cause.

Degenerative disorders
In relation to mental handicap this applies to a group of disorders in which there is a progressive deterioration in mental and physical ability. These include the *mucopolysaccharidoses, lipidoses, cerebrosideroses*, and *glycogen storage disorders*.

MENKES, J.H. (1985) Textbook of Child Neurology (3rd edit.) Philadelphia: Lea & Febiger. pp. 123–168.

Dehydration
The loss of water from the body. This causes biochemical processes to be upset, generally leading to problems such as *hypernatraemia* and, if severe, can result in brain damage, especially in the infant and young child. Causes include fluid loss by diarrhoea and vomiting as in gastroenteritis.

Deinstitutionalization
Discharge from an *institution*, usually a hospital, to *community care*. *Rehabilitation* of institutionalized people is also important as well as adequate support services after discharge.

BRUININKS, R. et al (Eds.) (1981) Deinstitutionalization and Community Adjustment of Mentally Retarded People. Washington DC: American Association on Mental Deficiency. Monograph 4.
CROSSLEY, R. & CROSSLEY, A. (1982) Annie's Coming Out. Harmondsworth: Penguin Books.
KLEINBERG, J. & GALLIGAN, B. (1983) Effects of deinstitutionalization on adaptive behavior of mentally retarded adults. Amer. J. Ment. Defic., 86:178–183.

Deletion of chromosome
It can happen that a fragment of a *chromosome* breaks off and becomes lost. The loss of a tiny fragment, just a few *genes*, may not have any noticeable effect. Generally a deletion has a major effect and this will vary according to the chromosome affected and the site and extent of the deletion. A deletion of the long arm is written as the letter q, and of the short arm as the letter p. See below for specific examples.

Deletion of long arm of chromosome 13 / deletion 13q
= *Orbeli syndrome*.

Deletion of long arm of chromosome 18 / deletion 18q
In this very rare condition part of the long arm of *chromosome* 18 is missing. A small head is usual. The mid-portion of the face is underdeveloped with deep set eyes and a small bridge to the nose so that the forehead and chin appear to be prominent. The mouth has downward slanting corners and a *cleft palate* may be present. Minor abnormalities of the eyes sometimes occur. The fingers are long and tapering and leg and foot abnormalities are common. Deafness,

congenital heart disease and genital abnormalities often occur. Young infants have very floppy muscles. Children may learn to walk on their knees first but later walk with a poorly co-ordinated gait. Mental handicap ranges from mild to severe and progress in late childhood may be better than initially expected. *Seizures* may occur. It usually occurs sporadically without a hereditary cause but occasionally a parent has a *chromosome translocation*.

WERTELECKI, W. & GERALD, P.S. (1971) Clinical and chromosomal studies of the 18p-syndrome. J. Pediatr., 78:44–52.
WILSON, M.G. et al (1979) Syndromes associated with deletion of the long arm of chromosome 18. Am. J. Med. Genet., 3:155.

Deletion of short arm of chromosome 4 / deletion 4p
= *Wolf's syndrome*.

Deletion of short arm of chromosome 5 / deletion 5p
= *cri-du-chat syndrome*.

Deletion of short arm of chromosome 9 / deletion 9p
In this very rare condition part of the short arm of *chromosome* 9 is missing. The person has a high pointed skull, which is flat at the back. The eyes are prominent and slant upward. The nose is short with a flat bridge. The jaw is small and the ears are poorly formed. The neck, the end bones of the fingers and the nails are all short. Defects of the feet and heart and spinal curvature are common. Mental handicap is moderate to severe.

RETHORE, M. (1977) Syndromes involving chromosomes 4, 9 and 12. In: New Chromosomal Syndromes. Yunis, J.J. (Ed.). New York: Academic Press.

Deletion of short arm of chromosome 18 / deletion 18p
In this very rare condition part of the short arm of *chromosome* 18 is missing. The person often has a small head and *neck webbing*. Abnormalities of the nose are common and often associated with *cleft palate*. Squint (*strabismus*) and drooping of the eyelids are common. Various limb abnormalities and short, broad fingers have been described. Height is below normal and infants may have floppy muscles and be very slow to gain weight. Mental handicap varies from mild to severe and language may be particularly delayed. *Autism* may be another handicap. This condition may arise spontaneously with greater frequency in older mothers. It may also be due to a *chromosome translocation* in one parent.

DE GROUCHY, J. (1969) The 18p-, 18q- and 18r syndromes. Birth Defects, 5(5):74.
LURIE, I.W. & LAZJUK, G.I. (1972) Partial Monosomies 18. Review of cytogenetical and phenotypical variants. Humangenetik, 15:203.

Delinquency
Behaviour by a juvenile which is in violation of the criminal law. It is generally agreed that juvenile offenders psychologically resemble their non-delinquent peers more than they differ from them. The number who suffer from a psychiatric disorder or from mental handicap is small, despite many popular misconceptions to the contrary.

CRAFT, M. (1985) Low intelligence and delinquency. In: Mental Handicap. A multidisciplinary approach. Craft, M. et al (Eds.). London: Baillière Tindall. pp. 51–57.

Delusion
A false belief that is firmly maintained by the person but not shared by others. Mentally handicapped people may sometimes hold delusional ideas because of an inability to understand an alternative and more rational explanation of events. More usually delusional ideas, as with other people, are a manifestation of a psychiatric illness such as *depression* or *schizophrenia*.

Dementia

Reduction or loss of previous intellectual abilities as a result of damage to, or deterioration of, brain tissue. Social or occupational functioning is impaired and memory loss is a major problem. Understanding and judgement may also be impaired and a personality change may occur. The two main types are senile dementia, occurring in old age, and pre-senile dementia, which occurs usually in middle-aged people. One of the commonest causes of pre-senile dementia is *Alzheimer's disease* which is more common than usual in people with *Down's syndrome*. The intellectual deterioration seen in children with *degenerative disorders* is sometimes referred to as a dementia.

REID, A.H. et al (1978) Dementia in ageing mental defectives: a clinical and neuropathological study. J. Ment. Defic. Res., 22:233–241.
RUSSELL, O. (1985) Mental Handicap. Edinburgh: Churchill Livingstone. pp. 128–132.

Demyelination

The process whereby the myelin sheaths of nerve fibres are destroyed. Electrical messages cannot travel along the fibres without the fatty *myelin* acting as an insulating sheath. This occurs in *Alexander's syndrome, Cockayne's syndrome, metachromatic leucodystrophy* and a few other rare *syndromes* associated with mental handicap.

Dental abnormalities

Many conditions associated with mental handicap include abnormalities of the teeth. In *Down's syndrome* and several other chromosomal disorders, the teeth develop late and may be abnormal in size, shape and alignment. In *bird-headed dwarfism* the teeth may be absent or small with poorly developed enamel. Teeth may be delayed and irregular in people with *Apert's syndrome, Hurler's syndrome* and many other conditions.

Dental care / dental hygiene

Prevention of tooth decay (*caries*) by the use of fluoride and good dental hygiene is most important especially for severely mentally handicapped people who have problems in understanding and co-operating with dental treatment and may require an *anaesthetic*. In some conditions there is a susceptibility to tooth decay. Dental hygiene is also an important part of social training and teeth cleaning should be started at a very early age. Ordinary dental services can generally be used but referral to more specialist services may be necessary.

MOSS, S.J. (1977) Your Child's Teeth. Harmondsworth: Penguin Books.
SCULLY, C. (1976) Something to Bite on: Dental Care for Mentally Handicapped Children. London: Mencap.
TESINI, D.A. (1981) An annotated review of the literature of dental caries and periodontal disease in mentally retarded individuals. Special Care Dentist, 1:75–87.

Denver developmental screening test

This is a short test of a child's development and is divided into four sections which are: Personal Social Scale, Fine Motor Adaptive Scale, Language Scale and Gross Motor Scale. It provides a quick estimate of a child's developmental progress using questions and observations. If there is evidence of delay a more detailed assessment is required. The age range is infancy to 6 years and it is more useful after 4 years. No special training is required to administer, score or interpret the scale which is generally regarded as reliable and valid.

FRANKENBURG, W.K. & DODDS, J.B. (1967) The Denver developmental screening test. J. Pediatr., 71:181–191.
FRANKENBURG, W.K. et al (1971) The revised Denver developmental screening test: Its accuracy as a screening instrument. J. Pediatr., 79:988–995.
FRANKENBURG, W.K. et al (1973) Denver Developmental Screening Test Manual/

Depakene

Workbook for Nursing and Paramedical Personnel. Denver CO: LADOCA project and publishing foundation.

Depakene
= *sodium valproate*.

Dependency
In some parts of the U.K. people with mental handicap are classified according to their degree of independence. High dependency refers to individuals who are severely mentally handicapped to the extent that they cannot guard themselves against common dangers and depend on others for care and protection. Medium dependency refers to people with a medium degree of mental handicap such that they require some care and constant supervision. Low dependency refers to individuals with slight mental handicap who require some support but can be fairly independent.

Depigmentation
Pale areas of depigmented skin are a feature of some conditions associated with mental handicap including *tuberose sclerosis* and *Louis-Barr syndrome*. Such areas can be of any size and can occur in any part of the body but are often oval in shape (*ash-leaf marks*).

Depot injections
Long-acting injections introduced in the 1960's for the administration of *phenothiazines* to people with *schizophrenia*. These may also be used for the treatment of mentally handicapped people with severe *behaviour disorders* or with *psychoses*. The most commonly used is *fluphenazine*.

CRAFT, M.J. (1977) Toxic effects of depot tranquillizers in mental handicap. Brit. Med. J., i:835.
CRAFT, M.J. & SCHIFF, A.A. (1980) Psychiatric disturbance in mentally handicapped patients. Brit. J. Psychiat., 137: 250–255.
KINNELL, H.G. (1977) Depot tranquillizers for disturbed behaviour. Brit. Med. J., ii:578.

Depression
Two main types of depression are recognized:
1. Reactive, exogenous or neurotic depression is an extreme reaction to circumstances or events which are likely to cause unhappiness and which cannot easily be resolved.
2. Psychotic, or endogenous depression is a severe depression of mood, often without a cause, when the person becomes very unhappy, slowed up, or agitated with severe disturbances of appetite and sleep. Morbid *delusions* of unfounded guilt and suicidal ideas may be present.
People who are mentally handicapped are just as likely, and probably more likely, to become depressed when compared to people of greater intellectual ability. Difficulty in expressing feelings in words may lead to other symptoms and signs being more relevant. Previously acquired skills may be lost and *hypochondria* may be evident. Friends will notice a change in the person and are likely to be concerned.
Treatment is generally with *antidepressant drugs* but attention must also be given to environmental factors and to *counselling* and support if necesary. Electroconvulsive therapy is avoided as much as possible but may be rarely used as the only treatment approach left for someone with a clearly diagnosed and severe psychotic depression. Psychotic depression may be part of a *manic-depressive psychosis* when the person also has mood swings into elation and overactivity.

MATSON, J.L. (1982) The treatment of behavioural characteristics of depression in the mentally retarded. Behav. Ther., 13: 209–218.
SIRELING, L. (1986) Depression in mentally handicapped patients: diagnostic and neuroendocrine evaluation. Brit. J. Psychiat., 149:274–278.

Deprivation
A person can be deprived of many important things in life. In addition to material deprivations, the most common for mentally

handicapped people are emotional and sensory deprivations. They are predisposed to deprivation by the nature of their disabilities and also by the way in which society responds to these disabilities. Many mentally handicapped people live in circumstances where there are a restricted range of opportunities and experiences available as occurs in institutions and segregated facilities. Even when living in a normalized environment deprivation will occur if there is insufficient support and help to enable the person to take advantage of the opportunities. There are more subtle ways in which a person can be restricted and deprived. The tendency to protect mentally handicapped people may lead to exclusion from opportunities to learn by mistakes or to learn how to make decisions and choices. *Institutionalization* puts a child at risk of emotional deprivation with inadequate or inappropriate relationships being available, instead of a positive and continuous relationship with a parental figure. Whole generations of mentally handicapped people, institutionalized in childhood, have become additionally handicapped by emotional deprivation. This state of affairs has only recently started to change with the encouragement of families to care for their handicapped child, and with the availability of *fostering* and *adoption* as alternatives to institutional care.

Loss of hearing or vision obviously causes a state of sensory deprivation but other disabilities such as physical handicaps, by restricting the mobility of the person, may also limit perception and exploration of the environment. Social and educational deprivation are a contributory causative factor to mild mental handicap in some cases as has been shown by early intervention studies on disadvantaged children.

ANASTASIOW, N.J. (1986) Development and Disability. Baltimore: Paul H. Brookes.

Derbyshire Language Scheme
A scheme used for the assessment and treatment of communication disorders. It is divided into three sections – early vocabulary stage, simple sentence stage and grammar and complex sentence stage. A system of cross-references allows identified weaknesses to relate to appropriate teaching activities. Its main use is with children whose language development is delayed as opposed to deviant.

MASIDSLOVER, M. & KNOWLES, W. (1982) The Derbyshire Language Scheme. Derbyshire County Council.

Dermatoglyphics
The study of fingerprint and palm-print patterns and their correlation with *genetic* and *chromosome* disorders. Three basic fingertip patterns are recognized: whorls, arches and loops. The density of the ridges which make up these patterns can be expressed as the total ridge count for all ten fingers. The point where three ridge systems meet in the palm is known as a triradius and three of these form an angle known as the 'atd' angle. When using the prints for diagnostic purposes particular attention is paid to the atd angle, the total ridge count and to the relative incidence of the different types of fingertip patterns. A single transverse crease of the palm (simian crease) and a single fifth finger crease occurs quite commonly in *Down's syndrome* and in other chromosomal abnormalities. Abnormal configurations are never diagnostic on their own but provide additional information to assist in making a diagnosis.

SCHAUMANN, B. & ALTER, M. (1976) Dermatoglyphics in Medical Disorders. New York: Springer-Verlag.

Desensitization
The gradual exposure of a person to a situation which provokes *anxiety*. At each stage the person needs to have overcome that anxiety before proceeding to the next, more difficult, stage. This *behaviour therapy* technique is frequently used in the treatment of *phobias*.

Development Team for the Mentally Handicapped

= *National Development Team for Mentally Handicapped People.*

Developmental checklists / developmental scales / developmental screening

There are several checklists which assess the developmental progress of a child. These include *Bayley Scales of Infant Development, Denver Developmental Screening Test, Gesell Development Schedules, Stycar Tests, Griffiths Scale* and many others. These cover a broad range of skills and do not just relate to intellectual skills. They are useful for screening populations of children to identify those with developmental problems and may also be used with an individual child in whom *developmental delay* is suspected. There are some checklists devised for use with people who are already diagnosed as being developmentally delayed. These may be used to identify strengths and needs and to measure progress. These include the *BIMH Developmental Checklist, PIP Developmental Chart, Gunzberg Progress Assessment Charts, Portage system* and *Behaviour Assessment Battery.*

DRILLIEN, C.M. & DRUMMOND, M.B. (1983) Developmental screening and the child with special needs. A population study of 5000 children. Clinics in Dev. Med. No. 86. London: Heinemann Medical.

Developmental delay

When a practitioner finds that a child is well behind in any area of development it is most important that this is fully investigated. Delays in language development may be due to *deafness*, mental handicap, *autism* and *dysphasia* as well as other causes. Delays in development of movement skills may be due to *cerebral palsy* or other physical causes. Backwardness in several areas may be due to mental handicap and a cause for this should always be sought. Referral to a *paediatrician* is therefore indicated so that full investigations and assessment can be carried out.

Developmental disability

In the U.S.A. this term has legal implications and a recent U.S.A. government definition was 'a severe, chronic disability of a person which:

a. is attributable to a mental and/or physical impairment.

b. is manifested before the age of 22.

c. is likely to continue indefinitely.

d. results in substantial functional limitations in three or more of the following areas of major life activity.

1. self-care
2. receptive and expressive language
3. learning
4. mobility
5. self-direction
6. capacity for independent living
7. economic self-sufficiency

e. reflects the person's need for a combination and sequence of special, interdisciplinary, or generic care, treatment, or other services which are of lifelong or extended duration and are individually planned and co-ordinated'.

ANASTASIOW, N.J. (1986) Development and Disability. Baltimore: Paul H. Brookes.

Developmental disorder

This includes *developmental disabilities* and also disorders of emotional development. The term 'pervasive developmental disorder' is used in the U.S.A. to describe children previously described as having childhood *schizophrenia*, infantile *autism*, symbiotic childhood psychosis and mental retardation. It is therefore used to describe those children in whom multiple abnormalities of development have occurred. This is compared to the term 'specific developmental disorder' which refers to children who have a delay in one skill area but are otherwise normal as in specific developmental reading disorder (*dyslexia*).

Developmental quotient

Developmental checklists which estimate the developmental level of a child and compare this with *chronological age* may present the result as a developmental quotient. This is similar to an *intelligence quotient* in that it is derived from the same formula of *mental age* divided by chronological age and multiplied by 100. It is, however, a broader based assessment than an *intelligence test*.

Developmentally Disabled Assistance and Bill of Rights Act (1974)

In this Act the U.S.A. Congress presented a concise bill of rights, expressed as findings and government obligations, to ensure the right to appropriate treatment, services and habilitation in the setting that is least restrictive of the person's personal liberty. It stated that *habilitation* programmes should be 'designed to maximize the developmental potential' of the disabled individual. The federal government and the states have obligations to assure that public funds are not provided to any institutional or other residential programme that does not provide treatment, services and habilitation which is appropriate to the needs of developmentally disabled persons. The Secretary of Health and Human Services can deny funds to recipient states that fail to comply with human rights assurances. In order to receive federal funds states must also guarantee that clients receiving residential and other habilitation services have in effect a written, specifically stated, individual habilitation plan (IHP). The client and/or his parents, guardian or other representative, has the right to review the initial plan and to participate in periodic revisions. Congress and federal courts have repeatedly recognized that appropriate habilitation is determined through individual plans describing goals and services suited to the person's particular needs. The law also provides federal funding of systems to protect and advocate the rights of developmentally disabled persons. Independent *advocacy* agencies were authorized to pursue legal, administrative and other appropriate remedies using the rights outlined in the Act as their starting point.

HERR, S.S. (1983) Rights and Advocacy for Retarded People. Massachusetts: Lexington Books.

Dextroamphetamine / dexedrine

A stimulant drug which is sometimes given to hyperactive children because it frequently has the paradoxical effect of calming the child. This approach is common in the U.S.A. but not in the U.K. where the diagnosis of *hyperactivity* is less often made. Side-effects include sleeplessness, restlessness, irritability, dizziness, dry mouth, loss of appetite, sweating and stimulation of the heart. Drug dependence is a hazard.

Dextrocardia

An abnormal position of the heart toward the right side of the body. This usually occurs in association with other *congenital* abnormalities including heart abnormalities and mental handicap.

Di George syndrome

People with this condition have abnormalities from birth which include widely spaced eyes which slant downward, a short upper lip, abnormalities of the heart and *atresia* of the nostrils, anus and the tube from the mouth to the stomach (oesophagus). Most die within the first few months due to poor immunity, *seizures* or heart failure. Those who have survived longer have had mild mental handicap. The cause is unknown but some people have abnormalities of *chromosome* 22.

DE LA CHAPELLE, A. et al (1981) A deletion in chromosome 22 can cause Di George syndrome. Hum. Genet., 57:255–256.
SMITH, D.W. (1982) Recognizable Patterns of Human Malformation (3rd. edit.) Philadelphia: Saunders.

Diabetes mellitus

A disorder in which the pancreas gland reduces or stops the secretion of insulin. Insulin is needed to enable the muscles and other tissues of the body to use sugar.

Weakness and other symptoms appear and the sugar accumulates in the blood and urine. This causes the body to pass more urine and an excessive thirst develops. There is greater susceptibility to infections. The onset is usually gradual but is more rapid in children. Older people with mild diabetes may manage by controlling the amount of sugar in the *diet*. Sometimes drugs are needed which stimulate the production of insulin. In more severely affected individuals the use of insulin by injection is needed. Diabetes occurs more commonly in some conditions associated with mental handicap including *lipodystrophy, Prader-Willi syndrome, Turner's syndrome, Down's syndrome* and *Klinefelter's syndrome*. Diabetes in the mother is also a potential cause of mental handicap either due to abnormal blood glucose levels at birth and/or other complications of pregnancy and delivery.

Further information:
British Diabetic Association, 10, Queen Anne St., London W1M 0BD.

Diagnosis
The art of distinguishing one disease from another or the opinion arrived at as to the nature of a disease. This is based on the medical history of the person, the symptoms, the signs found during examination and investigations carried out. It is essential before scientific treatment can be started. When there is mental handicap, the diagnosis of the cause is important because it will be a guide to the future outlook and likely progress, it will alert professionals to the possible presence of other disabilities and it will enable parents to receive informed advice about the child's condition and the risk of recurrence in other members of the family. It is generally easier for parents to accept that their child is mentally handicapped if the cause is known.

Diagnostic and Statistical Manual
= *DSM III*.

Diagnostic Assessment Procedure
A procedure which is useful for assessment of vision in multi-handicapped children although the level of functioning has to be age 3 or over. It includes an observational checklist to assess the functional use of vision when moving. It also suggests training activities which match the assessment items. These are carefully sequenced and outlined in a format that can easily be adapted for the individual child. For each activity there is a description of the objective, visual task, materials, procedure, response, procedural notes and additional auditory, kinaesthetic and tactile activities.

BARRAGA, N.C. & MORRIS, J.E. (1980) Programs to Develop Efficiency in Visual Functioning. Kentucky: American Printing House for the Blind.

Diazepam
One of the *benzodiazepine* group of drugs. It is used as a *tranquillizer*, muscle relaxant and/ or *anticonvulsant*. Its use as a tranquillizer should be restricted to people who are suffering from short-lived anxiety. Severely mentally handicapped people respond unpredictably and may become disinhibited. It is used as a muscle relaxant in severe *cerebral palsy*. As an anticonvulsant the major use is intravenously or rectally for *status epilepticus*. Side-effects are the same as for other benzodiazepines.

Diet
There are several diets which may be necessary for people with a mental handicap. A reducing diet is important for the overweight person especially if there is a physical disability. The *Feingold diet* is worth trying with a *hyperactive* child. Conditions such *phenylketonuria* and some other *amino acidurias* may require a very specific diet to prevent mental handicap. *Ketogenic diets* may be used for severe *epilepsy*. There is no evidence that food *allergies* (treated by exclusion diets) are a cause of mental handicap. A healthy well-balanced diet is important for everyone.

DAY, S. & HOLLINS, S. (1985) The role of the dietitian. In: Mental Handicap. A multidisciplinary approach. Craft, M. et al (Eds.). London: Baillière Tindall.
WEBB, Y. (1980) Feeding and nutrition problems of physically and mentally handicapped children in Britain: a report. J. Nutrition, 54:201–285.

Differential Reinforcement of Other behaviours (DRO)

There is considerable evidence in *behaviour modification* that any programme aiming to reduce the rate of undesirable behaviours is more effective when the person is also given positive *reinforcement* for other behaviours. This can simply be given for not showing the inappropriate behaviour. This is referred to as differential reinforcement of alternative behaviour (DRA). Rewarding an alternative behaviour which is incompatible with the inappropriate behaviour may be particularly effective. This is known as differential reinforcement of incompatible behaviour (DRI). The last type of differential reinforcement is reinforcement of a lower rate of the unwanted behaviour (DRL). The interval is gradually extended so that lower and lower rates are reinforced. DRO is usually more effective when combined with other behaviour modification techniques such as *time-out* or *extinction*.

CAVALIER, A.R. & FERRETTI, R.P. (1980) Stereotyped behavior, alternative behavior and collateral effects. A comparison of four intervention procedures. J. Ment. Defic. Res., 24:219–230.
REPP, A.C. et al (1983) A comparison of two procedures for programming the differential reinforcement of other behaviors. J. Appl. Behav. Anal., 16:435–445.
SINGH, N.N. et al (1981) Effects of spaced responding DRL on the stereotyped behavior of profoundly retarded persons. J. Appl. Behav. Anal., 14:521–526.
TARPLEY, H.D. & SCHROEDER, S.R. (1979) Comparison of DRO and DRI and rate of suppression of self-injurious behavior. Am. J. Ment. Defic., 84:188–194.

Diffuse angiokeratoma
= *Fabry's syndrome*

Diffuse cerebral sclerosis
= *sudanophilic leucodystrophy*.

Diffuse progressive degeneration of the grey matter of the cerebrum
= *Alper's syndrome*.

Digits

The fingers and toes. Abnormalities of digits occur in many conditions associated with mental handicap. *Ectrodactyly, clinodactyly, arachnodactyly* and *brachydactyly* are all different types of abnormalities.

Dihydrobiopterin
= *tetrahydrobiopterin*.

Dilantin
= *phenytoin*.

Diminished responsibility

In England, in murder cases only, a mentally handicapped person may be able to plead that at the time of the act or omission, he or she was suffering from 'such abnormality of mind as would substantially impair his mental responsibility'. A jury can accept or reject this on the evidence. If accepted the person would be guilty of manslaughter which the judge can deal with by any appropriate means including a hospital order or probation order. For other offences mitigating features including mental handicap may be taken into account. In Scotland, a charge of murder may be reduced to culpable homicide if it is shown that the accused suffered at the time of the act or omission from a state of mind bordering on insanity of sufficient degree to diminish responsibility.

Diphenylhydantoin
= *phenytoin*.

Diplegia

A type of *cerebral palsy* with predominant involvement of both lower limbs.

Disability

The World Health Organization defines disability as 'any restriction or lack (resulting from an *impairment*) of ability to perform an activity in the manner or within the range considered normal for a human being. *Handicap* is the resulting personal and social disadvantage'. There is a move away from the term mental handicap towards terms such as learning disability or intellectual disability. Disability is used when an impairment causes a hindrance to mobility, occupation, *communication* or ability to care for self. It can be continuous or intermittent and may be present from birth or acquired later. See also *developmental disability*.

GOLDFARB, L.A., et al (1986) Meeting the Challenge of Disability or Chronic Illness – A Family Guide. Baltimore: Paul Brookes.
LEES, D. & SHAW, S. (1974) (Eds.) Impairment, Disability and Handicap. London: Heinemann.
STUBBINS, J. (1977) (Ed.) Social and Psychological Aspects of Disability. Baltimore: University Park Press.
WORLD HEALTH ORGANIZATION (1980) International Classification of Impairments, Disabilities and Handicaps. Geneva: WHO.

Disability Alliance

This organization publishes the Disability Rights Handbook which gives simple but full information on the rights and allowances for disabled people in the U.K.

Further information:
Disability Alliance, 25, Denmark St., London WC2.

Disability Assessment Schedule

This is a derivative of the *Handicaps, Behaviour and Skills Schedule* but it is shorter and useful in large-scale surveys. It is suitable for all ages and requires only a short training. It produces precisely categorized functional data suitable for microcomputation on a wide range of specific abilities and disabilities. It can be used for local service planning and research and also for monitoring and individual *habilitation* programming.

SHAH, A. et al (1982) Prevalence of Autism and related conditions in Adults in a Mental Handicap Hospital. Applied Research in Mental Retardation, 3:303–317.

Disabled Living Foundation

This organization provides advice and information for disabled people in the U.K. particularly in relation to aids and equipment in the living environment. Clothing, housing, furniture design and physical recreation are other concerns. A number of booklets and pamphlets have been been published following extensive studies of the range of help available.

Further information:
DLF, 380 Harrow Rd, London W9 2HU.

Disabled person

This term is used in the U.K. in the National Assistance Act (1948) and applies to people who are 'blind, deaf or dumb, and other persons who are substantially and permanently handicapped by illness, injury or *congenital* deformity or who are suffering from a mental disorder within the meaning of the *Mental Health Act*'. The rights of disabled persons have recently been reviewed in the *Disabled Persons Act (1986)*.

Disabled Persons (Services, Consultation and Representation) Act (1986)

The Act in the U.K. is concerned with the rights of disabled persons. The first two sections deal with the appointment of authorized representatives and the rights of such representatives. Sections 3, 4 and 8 describe the procedures which should be followed by local authorities in assessing the needs of a disabled person in relation to the welfare services which the local authority is required to provide. The abilities of the carers must also be taken into account. A written statement must be provided if requested. Sections 5 and 6 refer to disabled children and young people leaving full-time education and their right to a full assessment after the social services have received notification. Section 7 refers to persons discharged from hospital, after an admission of 6 months or more, and the arrangements for assessment which should be made once a discharge date is known.

DISABLED PERSONS (SERVICES, CONSULTATION & REPRESENTATION) ACT (1986). London: HMSO.
RADAR & MIND (1986) Disabled Persons Act 1986: Handbook for Voluntary Organisations. London: Mind.

Disabled persons register
In the U.K. disabled people over the age of 18 years who are capable of *employment* may be registered at the local employment office or job centre. The advantages are: (a) opportunities for participating in suitable training schemes, (b) opportunities for sheltered employment, (c) certain employers have a statutory obligation to employ a certain proportion of registered disabled persons. The *disablement resettlement officer* assists disabled people.

Disablement resettlement officers
In the U.K. these officers are based at job centres to advise, help and support disabled people. They know of local employment possibilities and encourage employers to take on disabled people. They know of the training facilities including assessment and *rehabilitation* courses.

Discrimination
The ability to detect differences and to make the appropriate choice. In *behaviour modification* it means the understanding of the conditions in which a particular behaviour is appropriate. There are subtle cues generally used by people to signal socially accept-

able and unacceptable behaviours but these may not be recognized by people with a mental handicap. Discrimination may be established by differential *reinforcement* of responses. Correct responses are reinforced but incorrect ones are ignored or punished. The person may also need to be taught to recognize *cues* which are a way of knowing how to behave in different situations. Other cues which trigger undesirable behaviours may have to be removed. Most learning tasks involve discriminative skills e.g. learning colours, recognizing words.

Discriminative stimulus
See *antecedents*.

Disintegrative psychosis of childhood
= *Heller's disease*.

Disipal
= *orphenadrine*.

Dislocation (joints)
Any joint of the body can be dislocated by the separation of the surfaces of bones which normally articulate together. Some joints dislocate more readily than other, more stable, joints. *Congenital dislocation of the hip* is one of the more common types of dislocation. Paralytic dislocation of the hip may occur in people with *cerebral palsy* due to the tightness and imbalance of muscles at the hip joint.

Disorientation
Impairment in the understanding of time, space, or personal relationships.

Disphonia
= *dysphonia*.

DISTAR
This is an educational programme used in the U.S.A. as part of the 'follow-through' project, to provide extra education to disadvantaged children in the early elementary

grades and assistance to their parents. It was a sequel to the *head start* programme. It is suitable for mentally handicapped people. The level of achievement of a person is established in a test situation and then systematic teaching applied and monitored by retesting at intervals. Detailed 'Direct Instruction' programmes have been developed for language, reading, arithmetic and spelling.

ENGELMANN, S. & BRUNER, E.C. (1969) DISTAR Reading; An instructional system. Chicago: Science Research Associates.
ENGELMANN, S. & CARNINE, D. (1975) DISTAR Arithmetic,I, (2nd edit.). Chicago: Science Research Associates.
ENGELMANN, S. & OSBORN, J. (1969) DISTAR Language. Chicago: Science Research Associates.

Distraction test of hearing

This is routinely done when an infant reaches the age of 7–9 months. It is usually carried out with the child sitting but satisfactory head control is necessary so if this is lacking the child should be lying on his or her back. A number of quiet sounds of different frequencies are made using a standard procedure. The child's attention is attracted by one person and then the sound presented to each ear by someone who is out of sight. If the child is distracted by the sound it is assumed that he has heard it. A mentally handicapped child may fail to respond because of lack of interest or understanding rather than lack of hearing and more objective tests may need to be carried out.

NOLAN, M. et al (1979) Testing the Hearing of Young Children, London: National Deaf Children's Society.

District Handicap Teams / Child Development Teams

The establishment of these teams in the U.K. was recommended by the Court Report (1976) whose task was to review the existing health services for children, judge how effective they were for the child and his parents and to propose what the new integrated child health service should try to achieve and how it should therefore be organised and staffed. The role of the district handicap team is to ensure that children with special needs receive co-ordinated services. The team should include a paediatrician, clinical medical officer (child health), social worker, psychologist and a representative of the community nursing service. Other professionals may also be involved regularly or as necessary. The team assesses, provides and co-ordinates services to all children assessed as having special needs. Teams review each child regularly and usually nominate a keyworker to be the parents' main point of contact with the team. Frequently the regular members of the district handicap team are based together in a child assessment centre which children may attend for assessments, playgroups and therapy.

Report of the Committee on Child Health Services (Court Report) (1976) Cmnd 6684. London: HMSO.

Divorce

The sole ground for divorce in the U.K. is that the marriage has irretrievably broken down in one of five specific ways. Mental handicap, in itself, is unlikely to be a cause. The incidence of marriages of people known to be mentally handicapped is low and statistics are not available on the divorce rate. It is the impression of most people that so many obstacles are put in the way of marriage, that only the most determined couples succeed, and having achieved this the divorce rate is very low.

Matrimonial Causes Act (1973) London: DHSS.

Doliochocephaly / dolichocephaly

A term meaning long headed. The width of the head is less than four fifths of the length from front to back. This occurs rarely in conditions associated with mental handicap including some of the less common *chromo-some* disorders, *oto-palato-digital syndrome* and *German's syndrome*. *Scaphocephaly* is a type of doliochocephaly.

Doman-Delacato system
A controversial training method for mentally handicapped children. It involves 'patterning' techniques which are repetitive manipulations of the limbs and head in patterns that allegedly simulate pre- and postnatal movements of normal children. It is believed that this will lead to previously unused brain cells taking over the functions of the damaged ones and that lower level functions have to be developed fully before higher ones. This involves an enormous amount of time (up to 8 hours a day) from a large number of people. High expectations are created, with the implication that the usual services will achieve less with the child. Sparrow and Zigler conducted a trial which showed that the group treated by the Doman-Delacato system made no more progress than the control group. Despite the paucity of scientific evidence of its effectiveness and devastating critiques by responsible organizations, some parents continue to be persuaded to try this approach often following uninformed articles in the lay press.

AMERICAN ACADEMY FOR CEREBRAL PALSY ET AL (1968) The Doman-Delacato treatment for neurologically handicapped children. Dev. Med. Child Neurology, 10: 243–246.
SPARROW, S. & ZIGLER, E. (1978) Evaluation of patterning treatment for retarded children. Pediatrics, 62:137–149.
ZIGLER, E. (1981) A plea to end the case of the patterning treatment for retarded children. Am. J. Ortho. Psychiat., 51:388–390.

Domestic housing
This usually refers to the use of ordinary housing stock with ordinary furnishings to provide homes for small groups of mentally handicapped people with the necessary support from staff. This is part of the *community care* policy of most authorities in the U.K.

An Ordinary Life – Comprehensive locally based services for mentally handicapped people (1982). London: King's Fund Centre.

Domiciliary
Services provided in the home.

Dominant gene
The majority of characteristics of human beings are determined by the genetic make-up of the individual. *Genes* are on the *chromosomes* which are paired and carry one set of genes from each parent. When the gene from one parent has the power to suppress or override the activity of the gene from the other (*recessive gene*) this is known as a dominant gene. A dominant gene may be responsible for abnormal development and can be a cause of mental handicap as in *tuberose sclerosis, Apert's syndrome, Crouzon's syndrome, Treacher-Collins syndrome* and *Hallermann-Streiff syndrome*. Some dominant genes are said to have variable penetrance which means that some people are more seriously affected than others when this gene is present.

Dominant inheritance
If a parent passes on a *dominant gene* to a child this is known as dominant inheritance. As each person carries two genes for most characteristics (with the exception of the sex *chromosomes* in the man) there is a 50% chance of passing on the dominant rather than the recessive member of the pair.

Donohue's syndrome
Babies with this very rare condition appear emaciated with relatively large hands, feet and head. They have large wide-set eyes, a broad nose and long low-set ears. Thick lips and a receding chin are features as well as excessive hairiness. Many other abnormalities have been described. They are weak and floppy, have feeding problems and are

susceptible to infections. Most do not survive the first few months of life but if they do the subsequent physical and mental development is slow and mental handicap occurs. The syndrome is inherited from both parents who are carriers (*recessive inheritance*).

DEKABAN, A. (1965) Metabolic and chromosomal studies in Leprechaunism. Arch. Dis. Childh., 40:632.

KALLO, A. et al (1965) Leprechaunism (Donohue's syndrome). J. Pediatr., 66:372.

ROGERS, D.R. (1966) Leprechaunism. Amer. J. Clin. Path., 45:614.

Dothiepin

An *antidepressant* drug used particularly when anxiety is also present. It is similar to *amitriptyline* and has the same side-effects but is said to act more quickly and to have side-effects less often.

Double Y syndrome

= *XYY syndrome*.

Down's syndrome

A common cause of mental handicap with an incidence of approximately one in 600 live births. People with Down's syndrome have many characteristics in common but also have individual features and personalities. Height is small for age, limbs a little short and hands are broad. The little fingers are usually curved and short and a single crease in the palm commonly occurs. Feet tend to be flat and broad with a wide space between first and second toes. Eyes are obliquely set slanting up and outward and the upper lid has an extra fold at the inner angle of the eye (*epicanthic fold*). Frequently there is a white speckling of the iris of the eye known as *Brushfield spots*. The nose has a broad bridge which is rather flat, as is the face. The roof of the mouth is high, arched and short and the tongue furrowed and relatively large. Teeth usually develop late and may be abnormal in size, shape and alignment. The ears tend to be small and are usually low set. The head is wide in relation to length (*brachycephaly*) and hair is straight. Many other abnormalities may occur including *cataracts* and squints (*strabismus*) of eyes, hearing impairment, webbing of fingers or toes and malformations of the heart and bowel. Reduced thyroid gland function (*hypothyroidism*) is also quite common. People with Down's syndrome are prone to chest infections which, before the introduction of antibiotics, usually caused an early death. The average life expectancy is now 50 years of age and *Alzheimer's disease* sometimes occurs in middle age or later.

People with Down's syndrome vary widely in intelligence and achievements. Improved attitudes and techniques of professionals and parents, especially in education, have dramatically improved the outcome. With a caring home and appropriate stimulation and discipline most children with Down's syndrome respond extremely well. Most people with this condition now acquire basic skills in literacy and numeracy by adult life. Speech problems are common, especially difficulty in speaking clearly. Practical and social skills are usually better than reasoning skills and in adult life a wide range of independence can be achieved depending on the ability, skills and personality of the individual. Sheltered or open employment are also within the capabilities of most people.

The cause of Down's syndrome is the presence of an extra chromosome 21. In most instances this is thought to be present in the egg cells before conception, which occurs more often in older mothers (*nondisjunction*). The risk of recurrence in later pregnancies is quite low but *genetic counselling* and *amniocentesis* or *chorion biopsy* are recommended. In 4% the extra chromosome has become attached to a member of another pair of chromosomes (*translocation*). In this case either parent can be a carrier and the risk of recurrence is then high. Occasionally some of the cells of the body have the normal number of chromosomes and some have the extra chromosome. This is known as *chromosome mosaic*. There is no record of a man with Down's syndrome fathering a child and few published cases of women giving birth. In about half of these the child had Down's syndrome.

BURGIO, G.R. et al (1981) Trisomy 21. Berlin: Springer Verlag.
CUNNINGHAM, C. (1982) Down's Syndrome: An Introduction for Parents. London: Souvenir Press.
DE LA CRUZ, F. & GERALD, P.S. (Eds.) (1981) Trisomy 21 (Down's syndrome): Research Perspectives. Baltimore: University Park Press.
GATH, A. (1978) Down's Syndrome and the Family. New York: Academic Press.
HARTLEY, X.Y. (1986) A summary of recent research into the development of children with Down's syndrome. J. Ment. Defic. Res., 30:1–14.
LANE, D. & STRATFORD, B. (Eds.) (1985) Current Approaches to Down's Syndrome. London: Holt, Rinehart & Winston.
PUESCHEL, S.M. et al (1986) New Perspectives on Down's Syndrome. Baltimore: Paul H. Brookes.

Further information:
Down's Syndrome Association, 12–13 Clapham Common South Side, London SW4 7AA.

Doxepin

An *antidepressant* drug similar to *amitriptyline*. It is said to have fewer but similar side-effects to that drug. It may also help to calm *anxiety* if it is also present.

Drama

This is something which most mentally handicapped people enjoy as much as anyone else. Participation is a useful way of self-expression and self-esteem, as well as a valuable leisure activity.

McCLINTOCK, A.B. (1984) Drama for Mentally Handicapped Children. London: Souvenir Press.

Driving licence

In the U.K. an applicant for a driving licence must indicate if he has any disorder for which he is compulsorily or informally being treated in hospital, or if he suffers severe mental impairment for which he is under guardianship. The authorities must also be informed if he is in any form of local authority care or has any disorder which has made it necessary for his property to be in the hands of a receiver. A licence may be refused but there is a right of appeal. A person who has epileptic *seizures* will be refused a licence unless he has been free of daytime seizures for at least 3 years.

DRO

= *differential reinforcement of other behaviours.*

DRO

= *Disablement resettlement officer.*

Drop attack

= *akinetic seizure.*

Droperidol / droleptan

This drug is very similar to *haloperidol* and has the same uses and side-effects.

Drug damage

Some drugs taken by the mother during pregnancy can affect the development of the child and give rise to mental handicap. Aminopterin and methotrexate, used in the treatment of psoriasis, are thought to cause *camptomelic dwarfism* and similar abnormalties may be caused by *phenobarbitone* and *phenytoin*. Excessive intake of vitamin D can cause *infantile hypercalcaemia*. Drugs for *hyperthyroidism* of the mother can cause *cretinism* in the child and drugs which lower the mother's blood sugar can cause damage to the brain of the fetus. Drugs of addiction used by the mother can cause withdrawal symptoms in the baby who can be damaged by this.

Drug serum level

The levels of a number of drugs can be

Drug treatment

measured in the blood. This is particularly useful for those drugs where high levels can cause toxic side-effects. Most *anticonvulsants* are monitored by making regular checks on the blood levels. This is also important for treatment with *lithium*.

Drug treatment
The use of drugs (medication) for the purpose of treatment. Mentally handicapped people do not need drug treatment for their learning disability, but may need it for associated disabilities such as *epilepsy, cerebral palsy, behaviour disorders* or *psychiatric illness*. Sometimes it is necessary to remedy the underlying cause of the mental handicap as in *pyridoxine dependency* and *congenital hypothyroidism*.

Dry-bed training
An intensive night-time *toilet training* programme which requires considerable effort from the trainer over a short period of time, but may solve the problem of *enuresis* very rapidly.

AZRIN, N.H. et al (1973) Dry-bed: A rapid method of eliminating bedwetting (enuresis) of the retarded. Behaviour. Res. Ther., 11: 427–434.

DSM-III. Diagnostic and Statistical Manual of Mental Disorders (Third Edition Revised 1987)
Prepared by the Task Force on Nomenclature and Statistics of the American Psychiatric Association. It is a classification system aiming to provide clear descriptions of diagnostic categories without forming any particular theories regarding the cause. It gives criteria for the use of each category which are based on the judgement of the clinician. Mental retardation is included. It is modelled on the *International Classification of Diseases*, 9th Edition 1978, which has a clinical modification for use in the U.S.A. DSM-III uses a *multiaxial classification*.

AMERICAN PSYCHIATRIC ASSOCIATION (1987) Diagnostic and Statistical Manual of Mental Disorders (3rd edit. revised). Washington DC: American Psychiatric Association.

Duchenne's muscular dystrophy
This progressive condition starts in early childhood with weakness of the muscles of the trunk and upper parts of the limbs and enlargement of calf muscles. A waddling gait and frequent falling are early signs. The muscle weakness gets steadily worse resulting in increasing physical disability and death in childhood or early adult life. Mental handicap occurs in about 30% of people with this condition but is not progressive. This condition is inherited from the mother who is a carrier (*sex-linked inheritance*). Most carriers can be identified by the estimation of the activity of a substance (creatine kinase) in the blood.

DUBOWITZ, V. (1965) Intellectual impairment in muscular dystrophy. Arch. Dis. Childh., 40:296–301.
PROSSER, E.J. et al (1969) Intelligence and the gene for Duchenne muscular dystrophy. Arch Dis. Childh., 44:221–230.

Further information:
Muscular Dystrophy Ass., 810 Seventh Ave, New York. NY 10019.
Muscular Dystrophy Group of Great Britain, Nattrass House, 35 Macaulay Rd, London SW4 0QP.

Ductus arteriosus
= *patent ductus arteriosus.*

Duodenal atresia / stenosis
The duodenum is the part of the bowel below the stomach where food mixes with the digestive juices from the pancreas gland and with the bile from the gall bladder. If it fails to develop (*atresia*) or is severely narrowed (*stenosis*) it causes an obstruction to food with vomiting and death from malnutrition. It is usually operable with good results. This may occur as a *congenital* abnormality in *Down's syndrome, lissencephaly*

and a few other rare conditions associated with mental handicap.

Duplication
= *partial trisomy*.

Dura mater
See *meninges*.

Dwarfism
= *restricted growth*.

Dysarthria
Difficulty in the mechanics of speaking clearly. People with *cerebral palsy* may have unintelligible speech because movements of tongue, lips and mouth muscles are slow and poorly co-ordinated. Rhythm of speech may be impaired and breathing difficulties add to the problems. People with *Down's syndrome* often have dysarthria due to the shape and size of the mouth and tongue as well as muscular and co-ordination problems. There are several other possible causes including *cleft palate* and abnormalities of the *cerebellum*. It is always important to exclude other problems such as hearing loss. Assessment and advice by a *speech therapist* is necessary.

COOPER, J. et al (1978) Helping Language Development: A Developmental Programme for Children with Language Handicaps. London: E. Arnold.
MUELLER, H. (1974) 'Speech'. In: Handling the Young Cerebral Palsied Child at Home. Finnie, N.R. (Ed.). London: Heinemann Medical Books.

Dysautonomia
Abnormal functioning of the autonomic or vegetative nervous system. This system deals with the functioning of the organs of the body and is largely outside voluntary control. It controls sweating, salivation, blood pressure, etc. There is a familial cause of this condition known as the *Riley-Day syndrome*.

Dyscrasia
A diseased constitution. Usually used to describe abnormalities of the blood which may be caused by certain drugs such as *carbamazepine* and *chlorpromazine*.

Dysdiadokokinesis
Impaired ability to perform small rapid alternating movements. It is a sign of damage to, or abnormality of, the *cerebellum* of the brain.

Dysencephalia splanchnocystica
= *Meckel syndrome*.

Dyskeratosis congenita
= *Zinsser-Engman-Cole syndrome*.

Dyskinesia
A disorder of movement with involuntary muscular activity. This includes *tremor, athetosis, parkinsonism* and *tardive dyskinesia*. It may occur in *cerebral palsy*.

HAGBERG, B. et al (1979) Dyskinesia and dystonia in neurometabolic disorders. Neuropaediat., 10:305–320.

Dyslexia
A difficulty in learning to read and spell which is well below the person's general ability. This is also called specific reading difficulty. The disorder may occur at one or more points in the processes necessary to decipher and use written language. It sometimes runs in families. Similar learning difficulties do occur in children with definite *brain damage*. It tends to be associated with clumsiness and poor concentration. Detailed assessment by a *psychologist* is required and special remedial education may be necessary for people who are more severely affected.

BENTON, A.L. & PEARL, D. (Eds.) (1978) Dyslexia: An Appraisal of Current Knowledge. New York: OUP.
BRADLEY, L. (1980) Assessing Reading Difficulties. A Diagnostic and Remedial Approach. London: Macmillan.

CRITCHLEY, M. & CRITCHLEY, E.A. (1978) Dyslexia Defined. London: Heinemann Medical Books.
NEWTON, M. & THOMSON, M. (1975) Dyslexia: A Guide for Teachers and Parents. London: University of London Press.
YOUNG, P. & TYRE, C. (1983) Dyslexia or Illiteracy? Realising the Right to Read. Milton Keynes: Open University Press.

Further information:
British Dyslexia Association, Church Lane, Peppard, Oxon. RG9 5JN.

Dysmorphic

Abnormal shape or form of the body or any part of the body as may occur in many *syndromes* associated with mental handicap.

Dysostosis

Abnormal development and formation of bones as in *Apert's syndrome, Chotzen's syndrome* and *Crouzon's syndrome* all of which are associated with mental handicap.

Dysphagia

Difficulty in swallowing.

Dysphasia

Difficulty with speech which may be due to a problem in understanding *language* (receptive dysphasia) or in the ability to formulate ideas in the spoken form (expressive dysphasia) which is out of proportion to ability levels in other areas of development. In receptive dysphasia the person, despite normal hearing, can make limited or no sense of the language heard. Sometimes there is imitation of language without understanding. In expressive dysphasia the person understands but cannot easily put ideas into spoken words. Sometimes people have a mixed dysphasic disability. Assessment and advice from a *speech therapist* is necessary. The cause is usually damage to, or abnormality of, certain parts of the brain.

COOPER, J. et al (1978) Helping Language Development: A Developmental Programme for Children with Language Handicaps. London: E. Arnold.
MUELLER, H. (1974) 'Speech'. In: Handling the Young Cerebral Palsied Child at Home. Finnie, N.R. (Ed.). London: Heinemann Medical Books.

Dysphonia

The inability to speak louder than a whisper usually due to weakness of the vocal cords. It may also be used to refer to a low pitched and hoarse voice.

Dyspnoea

Difficulty with breathing, breathlessness or laboured breathing.

Dyspraxia

A problem in co-ordinating and sequencing movements despite intact musculature capable of normal movements. The person may be generally clumsy and have difficulties in hopping, running, jumping etc. Whilst able to use single short words, the person may not be able to sequence long words or sentences which become a meaningless jumble.

GORDON, N. & MCKINLAY, I. (Eds.) (1980) Helping Clumsy Children. London: Churchill Livingstone.

Dystonia

Abnormal postures and movements with disordered and fluctuating distribution of muscle tone involving the trunk and often with extreme degrees of bending of the extremities. This may occur as a side-effect of tranquillizing drugs such as *chlorpromazine, haloperidol* and other *phenothiazines*. There is a dystonic type of *cerebral palsy*.

HAGBERG, B. et al (1979) Dyskinesia and dystonia in neurometabolic disorders. Neuropaediat., 10:305–320.

Dystrophia myotonica

= *Steinert's myotonic dystrophy.*

E

Ear abnormalities

Abnormalities of the ear are very commonly associated with conditions which cause mental handicap. The shape, size and position of the external ear can be abnormal as can the ear canal. Abnormalities of the middle and inner ear can also occur. These are frequently associated with *deafness*.

Early infantile autism

= *autism*.

Early Intervention Developmental Profile

A comprehensive assessment scheme for planning developmental programmes for children with all types of handicap who function below the 3 year level. There are six scales, perceptual, fine motor, social, emotional, self-care and gross motor development. Stimulating activities are designed for every item assessed and include suggestions for use with deaf, blind or physically handicapped children. It is also used as an *early intervention programme*.

ROGERS, S.J. & D'EUGENIO, D.B. (1977) Developmental Programming for Infants and Young Children: Assessment and Application. Michigan: University of Michigan Press, Ann Arbor.

Early Intervention Programmes

These programmes assume that the early years of life are particularly important for later development. A programme of stimulation and training based on a developmental assessment is used to encourage progress and to give parents constructive and rewarding experiences with their child. *Head start* programmes in America were used for disadvantaged children and showed that the greatest *cognitive* gains were made by children introduced into structured child-parent programmes at the age of 1 to 2 years. Most gains largely disappeared within 3 years of the cessation of the programme. Later workers who followed up children from high-quality, well-designed programmes showed that significant positive effects on scholastic attainments, attitudes to school and vocational aspirations had occurred. Studies on children who are already at risk of having learning disabilities due to biological factors have been varied in age of starting, length, intensity, place and type of intervention and outcome measures. There is some evidence of limited effectiveness but further research is necessary. The *Portage system* is widely used in the U.K. Recently, as well as recognizing the importance of parents as trainers of the child, there has been emphasis on the early parent-infant interaction patterns and cognitive models of development.

BAROFF, G.S. (1986) Mental Retardation. Nature, Causes and Management. Washington: Hemisphere. pp. 209–218.

CLEMENTS, J. et al (1980) A home advisory service for pre-school children with developmental delays. Child: Care, Health and Development, 6:25–33.

CUNNINGHAM, C.C. (1983) Early support and intervention: the HARC infant project. In: Parents, Professionals and Mentally Handicapped People, approaches to partnerships. Mittler, P. & McConachie, H. London: Croom Helm.

CUNNINGHAM, C.C. & SLOPER, P. (1979) Helping your Handicapped Baby. London: Souvenir Press.

GIBSON, D. & HARRIS, A. (1988) Aggregated early intervention effects for Down's syndrome persons: Patterning and congenuity of benefits. J. Ment. Defic. Res., 32:1–7.

SIMEONSSON, R.J. et al (1982) A review and analysis of the effectiveness of early intervention programmes. Pediatrics, 69: 635–641.

ZIGLER, E. & BERMAN, W. (1983) Discerning the future of early childhood intervention. Am. Psychol., 38:894–906.

Eastern Nebraska Community Office of Retardation (ENCOR)

Eastern Nebraska's community services for people with a mental handicap have become internationally recognized as some of the most comprehensive, well-organized and progressive services in the world. A complete community alternative to institutional care has been pioneered. It stresses the importance of the principle of *normalization* as an effective base for all services and the use of general services and everyday patterns of life for people with a mental handicap, provided the right amount of support and training is made available. The effectiveness is based on the commitment of staff to the organizational goals and to shared aims and objectives. Service planners and managers are close to both clients and to direct care staff. The individual needs of clients are always determined through the *Individual Program Plan*. Services have changed and evolved in response to the needs of individual consumers. *Core and cluster* units were the starting point in 1970 and are now no longer deemed suitable or necessary. Ordinary houses (alternative living units (ALU)) are used with adaptations where necessary. Staff are engaged to work in a flexible manner adapting hours of work to the needs of the client. The importance of public education and public relations is stressed. The services are provided under the umbrella of one agency but include vocational services, residential services, home based programs and respite care. The ENCOR model has been well received in some areas of the U.K. and has provided the basis for many developments.

THOMAS, D. et al (1978) ENCOR – A Way Ahead. Enquiry paper No.6: London: Campaign for Mentally Handicapped People.

ECG
= *electrocardiogram*.

Echoencephalography
= *ultrasound scanning*.

Echolalia

The copying of words without understanding their meaning. Immediate repetition is known as immediate echolalia whereas delayed echolalia is a word sequence which repeats something heard earlier. It tends to give a false impression of the person's ability to use language. It often occurs in *autistic* children. Delayed echolalia is the basis of the *chatter-box syndrome* seen in some people with *hydrocephalus*. It is usually treated with *behaviour modification* techniques.

FREEMAN, B.J. et al (1975) An operant procedure to teach an echolalic, autistic child to answer questions appropriately. J. Autism Childh. Schiz. 5:169–176.

PALYO, W.J. et al (1979) Modifying echolalic speech in pre-school children: training and generalization. Am. J. Ment. Defic., 83:480–489.

Eclampsia
See *toxaemia*.

Ectodermal dysplasia

Abnormal growth or development of the skin, nails, hair and/or teeth. The skin may be abnormally thin or excessively thick and the sweat glands may be absent, underdeveloped or overdeveloped. The pigmentation of the skin may be abnormal. Nails may be absent or underdeveloped and hair may be thin or abnormal in texture. Teeth are underdeveloped, absent or abnormal usually with defects in the enamel.
Ectodermal dysplasia occurs in *Hallermann-Streiff syndrome*, *Clouston's syndrome* and *Goltz's*

syndrome; it also occurs with other abnormalities of development which are associated with mental handicap.

Ectopia lentis

A dislocated lens of the eye. This causes the iris of the eye to be tremulous during eye movements and the pupil is irregular in shape. It occurs in *homocystinuria* and in *Goltz's syndrome* which are often associated with mental handicap.

Ectrodactyly

Congenital absence of all or part of the fingers and toes. This may occur in *Crouzon's syndrome, Goltz's syndrome, de Lange syndrome* and a few other rare conditions often associated with mental handicap.

Ectromelia

Absence or underdevelopment of one or more of the long bones in the limbs. This may very rarely occur in conditions associated with mental handicap.

Ectropion

A condition of the eyelid, usually the lower, in which the inside of the lid turns outward. This is generally due to abnormality of the skin of the eyelid and may occur in *xeroderma pigmentosum*, congenital *hemihypertrophy* and *Zinsser-Engman-Cole syndrome* which are often associated with mental handicap.

Eczema

A disease of the skin which becomes blistered, scaly and cracked with a sticky, watery discharge. It is associated with itching or even pain. It can occur in sensitive people as an *allergic* reaction to some drugs, foods or substances in the environment. It occurs in one third of people with *phenylketonuria* and may be a feature of the *Louis-Barr syndrome*.

Edema

= *oedema*.

Education (Handicapped Children) Act (1970)

In England and Wales this Act made it the duty of the Local Authority Education Department to provide education for all children however severely handicapped. As a result of this legislation, the Department of Education and Science assumed responsibility for the education of all the children who had previously been deemed ineducable. The new schools were referred to as *ESN(S)* schools to distinguish them from schools for moderately mentally handicapped *ESN(M)* children which were already in existence. Other consequences were staff training in special education, standardized curricula and suitably designed and equipped schools.

Education Act (1981)

This Act came into force in England and Wales in 1983 and set up a new framework for the education of children who have *special educational needs*, whether they attend ordinary or special schools. It followed the *Warnock Committee Report* and places emphasis on the individual needs of each child. The Act introduces the principle that children with special needs can be educated in ordinary schools but taking into account the ability of the school to meet the needs of the child, the needs of other children at the school and the efficient use of resources. Local education authorities are responsible for identifying children who have special educational needs and have a duty to make special provision to meet these needs. The views of parents have to be taken into account and parents are involved at all stages. The assessment process should include an analysis of the child's learning difficulties; the specification of his special needs in relation to the approach, facilities and resources required; and the special educational provision required to meet those needs. When a child has been assessed the LEA makes a statement of the child's special educational needs and must indicate the provision which will be made to meet those needs. Parents are given a copy of the statement, have a right of appeal and are given the name of a person to whom they may apply for information and advice about their child. Authorities must review statements at least once a year, drawing upon reports from school and including the views of parents wherever possible.

ACE Special Education Handbook, Ace Publications, 18 Victoria Park Sq., London E2 9PB.
DHSS (1981) Education Act 1981. London: HMSO.
DHSS (1983) Education (Special Educational Needs) Regulations. London: HMSO.
GULLIFORD, R. (1985) Education. In: Mental Deficiency. The Changing Outlook (4th edit.). Clarke, A.M. et al (Eds.). London: Methuen. pp. 637–685.
STAMINA paper number 1, Mencap Bookshop, 123 Golden Lane, London EC1Y 0RT.
WEDELL, K. et al (1982) Challenges in the 1981 Act, Special Education: Forward Trends, 9:6–8.

Education for all Handicapped Children Act (1976) (Public Laws 94–142)

In the U.S.A. this Act requires that all states receiving federal moneys for their schools must assure all handicapped children aged 3 to 21 years the right to a free appropriate public education. Each child must be educated in the 'least restrictive' and most normal environment compatible with his or her handicap and as close as possible to home. This means that whenever possible the child should be placed in mainstream classes (*mainstreaming*). Each child must have a written *individual educational plan* (IEP) that states the goals, short-term instructional objectives and specific educational services to be provided. The procedures used to evaluate children with learning difficulties must not be racially or culturally biased. On an annual basis the special education supervisor, teacher, parent and, whenever appropriate, the child meet to reconsider and update the IEP. The law encourages and requires parental participation. If the legislative requirements are not fulfilled the child is entitled to claim damages. If parents do not agree with the plan they can invoke powerful procedures such as impartial due process hearings. Contested cases can trigger a number of legal protections including an administrative hearing, an appeal to the state education agency and an action in court. There is also a pledge of surrogate parents for children without family support but few states have established such programmes.

CUTLER, B. (1981) Unravelling the Special Education Maze: An Action Guide for Parents. Champaign, Illin.: Research Press.
TURNBULL, H. & TURNBULL, A.P. (1982) Free Appropriate Public Education: Law and Implementation. Denver: Love Publishing Co.

Education of the Developmentally Young (EDY)

A teaching course in the U.K. designed to teach *behaviour modification* techniques, through written materials and guided practice. A pyramid training structure is used through which the course organizers train potential instructors. These then train other staff using materials provided.

FOXEN, T. & McBRIEN, J. (1981) Training Staff in Behavioural Methods: Trainee Workbook, Manchester: Manchester University Press.
McBRIEN, J. (1981) Introducing the EDY project. Special Education Forward Trends, 8:29–30.
McBRIEN, J. & FOXEN, T. (1981) Training Staff in Behavioural Methods: Instructors Handbook. Manchester: Manchester University Press.

Educational psychologist

A graduate *psychologist* who has had teaching experience and has further specialized in assessing children, identifying educational needs and advising on the management of educational problems leading to a postgraduate qualification. Educational psychologists are involved in the decisions regarding school placement under the *Education Act (1981)*. They are usually employed by education authorities but may also be found in child and family psychiatry settings.

CORNWALL, K. & SPICER, J. (1982) The role of the educational psychologist in the discovery and assessment of children requiring special education. Brit. Psychol. Soc., DECP Occasional Papers, 6(2):3–11.

Educational subnormality (ESN)

Used in the U.K. to describe mentally handicapped children before the *Education Act (1981)* came into force. There were two categories: ESN(M) referring to mildly or moderately educationally subnormal children and ESN(S) referring to severely educationally subnormal children. Schools were also designated by these categories. These have now been replaced by the general terms 'children with special needs' and 'schools for children with learning difficulties'.

Edward's syndrome

A condition occurring in approximately 1 per 7000 live births and increasing in frequency with the age of the mother. It is twice as common in girls than boys. The baby's head is elongated from front to back. The back of the head is often prominent. The neck is short and wide with skin folds. Eyes are wide-set with folds of skin at the inner angle. The eyelids are often narrow and the upper lids may droop. The chin tends to be small. Abnormalities of the eyes such as *cataracts*, clouding of the surface of the eyes, small eyes and thin eyebrows and eyelashes have been described. Ears are often small, low-set and malformed. *Cleft palate/lip* may occur. Hernias are common and the testes are usually undescended.

Hands are an unusual shape with the second and fifth fingers often curving inwards. Fingers may be fused together. Nails are often underdeveloped. Thumbs are often abnormal. *Club foot* is common and feet are often described as 'rocker bottom' shaped. *Congenital heart disease* and abnormalities of other organs are common. Growth is slow and size small. Feeding difficulties are common in infancy. Very severe mental handicap, *cerebral palsy* and *epilepsy* are usual. Survival beyond infancy is unusual. The cause is an extra *chromosome* 18 and this occurs in the same way as the extra chromosome 21 in *Down's syndrome*. Following the birth of a child with this condition there is an increased risk of chromosome abnormalities in future pregnancies.

HODES, M.E. et al (1978) Trisomy 18 (29 cases) and Trisomy 13 (19 cases): a summary. Birth Defects, 14(6C):377.
WEBER, F.M & SPARKES, R.S. (1970) Trisomy E(18) syndrome. J. Med. Genet. 7:363.

Further information:
Trisomy 18 Edward's syndrome support group, 20 Gostwich, Orton Brimbles, Peterborough, Cambridgeshire.

EDY
= *education of the developmentally young.*

EEG
= *electroencephalogram.*

EIDP
= *Early Intervention Developmental Profile.*

Elective mutism

Used to describe people who can talk but are silent with everybody except for a small circle of close friends and relatives. This rare, selective, refusal to speak often starts when the child begins to attend school. It can occur in children of any ability level but mentally handicapped children, especially if they have unclear speech, may be particularly reluctant to talk when parents are not there to interpret.

Electric shock

This has been used very infrequently as *aversive stimulation* to eliminate undesirable behaviours as part of a *behaviour modification* programme. It is widely agreed that it should only be used to reduce life-threatening behaviours, when all else has failed, and only as part of an extremely well-planned programme (including staff training and *generalization* procedures) and in combination with a programme for *reinforcement* for alternative behaviours. It is usual to establish an ethical committee to consider each case individually before such procedures are used.

CORBETT, J. (1975) Aversion for the treatment of self-injurious behaviour. J. Ment. Defic. Res., 19:79–96.

Electrocardiogram (ECG)

A method of recording the electrical activity of the heart. It is obtained by means of electrodes placed on the chest. Damage to the heart muscle, the nerves of the heart or abnormalities of functioning or development may be detected by means of the ECG. Abnormal ECGs often occur in *Friedreich's ataxia*, *Pompe's disease* and *Steinert's myotonic dystrophy* all of which are associated with mental handicap.

Electrocochleography

A small needle electrode is placed through the eardrum onto the base of the *cochlea* which is part of the inner ear. It is usually carried out under an anaesthetic. The responses to short, sharp sounds are computerized and analysed to give information about the function of the cochlea and auditory nerve. It is only possible to assess hearing for high frequency sounds. It is useful if a sensory deafness is suspected. It does not require co-operation.

Electroencephalogram (EEG)

A method of recording the electrical activity discharged by the nerve cells in the brain. It is obtained by means of electrodes placed on the scalp. The waves of the electrical potential of the brain are amplified and recorded. Characteristic changes in the type, frequency and potential of the brain waves occur in various conditions of the brain. Different rhythms are characteristic of various stages of alertness or sleep and these change to some extent with age. Abnormal spiky waves may occur in people with *epilepsy* and the origin and type of these may contribute to the diagnosis. Certain techniques are used to accentuate abnormal waves or to bring out latent abnormalities including stroboscopic light, overbreathing and sleep induction. Deviations from the normal brain wave patterns also occur with many other diseases of the brain. EEG abnormalities occur commonly in conditions associated with mental handicap especially those where epilepsy is also a feature. Major abnormalities often occur in the *degenerative disorders*. The EEG may be very characteristic in *infantile spasms* and the *Lennox-Gastaut syndrome*.

LAGET, P. & SALBREUX, R. (1982) Atlas of Electroencephalography in the Child. Paris: Masson.
NIEDERMEYER, E. & LOPES DA SILVA, F. (Eds.) (1982) Electroencephalography. Baltimore: Urban & Schwarzenberg.

Electroretinogram

A method by which electrical signals produced by the *retina* are picked up by a contact lens, recorded and analysed. The type of disorder of the retina can be further differentiated using light of different wavelengths to stimulate the eye. Some conditions which cause mental handicap are also associated with degeneration of the retina including *Batten's disease, Laurence-Moon-Biedl syndrome*, and *Leber's congenital amaurosis*.

Elfin face

A description of the facial features in *Donohue's syndrome* and in *infantile hypercalcaemia*.

Ellis-van Creveld syndrome

A very rare condition in which the person has short stature, short limbs, extra fingers and toes, and abnormal or absent teeth, nails and hair. Only a few people with this syndrome are mentally handicapped. About one third of affected infants have severe heart abnormalities. It is inherited from both parents who are carriers (*recessive inheritance*).

ELLIS, R.W.B. & Van CREVELD, S. (1940) A syndrome characterized by ectodermal dysplasia, polydactyly, chondrodysplasia and congenital morbus cordis. Arch. Dis. Childh., 15:65.

ELSI

= *everyday living skills inventory.*

Emotional development

In normal children the basic emotions appear in the first 2 years of life. Much early childhood training involves teaching the socially accepted way to express and control emotions. The accomplishment of autonomy and competence also involves emotional control and achieving dignity and self-respect. People who are mentally handicapped may have problems in emotional development caused by their disability or by other people's reaction to it. It may, for example, be more difficult to deal with emotions by expressing them in words. People who are mentally handicapped experience normal human emotions and generally follow the normal pattern of emotional development.

ANASTASIOW, N.J. (1986) Development and Disability. Baltimore: Brookes.
BAILEY, R. et al (1986) Feeling – The way ahead. Mental Handicap 14(2):65–67.
CICCHETTI, D. & SCHNEIDER-ROSEN, K. (1984) Theoretical and empirical consider-

ations in the investigation of the relationship between affect and cognition in an atypical population of infants. In: Emotions, Cognitions and Behaviour. Izard, C.E. et al (Eds.). Cambridge: Cambridge University Press.

Emotional disorder

A very general term used to cover a wide range of disorders of behaviour, emotions and mental state.

Empathy

The ability to understand another person's thinking, feeling and behaviour.

Employment

It is difficult, but not impossible, for many mentally handicapped people to obtain open employment. Although competitive employment was regarded as only suitable for mildly mentally handicapped people, the recent development of *work stations* and *supportive work* in places of employment has opened up this possibility for those with moderate or even severe mental handicap. It is generally considered to be important to learn social skills and work habits in readiness for work. The work skills needed are best taught doing the job. A useful assessment is the *prevocational assessment and curriculum guide*. In the U.K. there are *disabled persons registers* and *disablement resettlement officers* to assist. *Sheltered employment* is available in most areas and this can be arranged through the local authority Social Services department. In the U.S.A. the opportunities vary from state to state but sheltered employment and open employment schemes have become established in some areas.

An Ordinary Working Life (1984). King's Fund Project Paper No. 50. London: King's Fund Centre.
KIERNAN, W.E. & STARK, J.A. (1986) Pathways to Employment for Adults with Developmental Disabilities. Baltimore: Paul H. Brookes.

PORTERFIELD, J. & GATHERCOLE, C. (1985) Progress towards an Ordinary Working Life. King's Fund Project Paper No.55. London: King's Fund Centre.
RUSCH, F.R. (1986) Competitive Employment Issues and Strategies. Baltimore: Paul H. Brookes.
SHELTON, C. & LIPTON, R. (1983) An alternative employment model. Canad. J. Ment. Retard., 33(2):12–16, 42.
WEHMAN, P. (1981) Competitive Employment: New Horizons for Severely Disabled Individuals. Baltimore: Paul H. Brookes.
WHELAN, E. & SPEAKE, B.R. (1981) Getting to Work. London: Souvenir Press.

Enamel hypoplasia

Underdevelopment of the hard protective enamel of the teeth making them susceptible to decay. This often occurs in *bird-headed dwarfism, Albright's hereditary osteodystrophy, Prader-Willi syndrome, Chotzen's syndrome, Goltz's syndrome, Sjögren-Larsson syndrome* and *Ellis-van Creveld syndrome* all of which are associated with mental handicap.

Encephalitis

Inflammation of the brain. The most common cause is a viral infection as may occur in *measles encephalitis, cytomegalic inclusion disease, rubella syndrome, congenital syphilis, herpes simplex encephalitis* and *toxoplasmosis* all of which may be a cause of mental handicap. The extent of recovery from encephalitis is variable. It frequently occurs in conjunction with *meningitis* and is then known as meningoencephalitis. It may also occur following certain vaccinations and is then known as *vaccine encephalitis.*

BOSS, S.J. & ESIRI, M.M. (1986) Viral Encephalitis: Pathology, Diagnosis and Management. Oxford: Blackwell Scientific.

Encephalocoele

A protuberance of the brain through the skull to form a bulge covered by skin. Most encephalocoeles occur at the back of the head and the size varies. If large, the infant is stillborn or dies soon after birth. The brain may be abnormal and *hydrocephalus* may develop. Mental handicap is common with encephalocoeles whether or not they are part of a *syndrome*. Encephalocoele often occurs with other abnormalities as in *Klippel-Feil syndrome, Meckel syndrome*, and *Edward's syndrome*. Operations to remove the encephalocoele soon after birth may be successful but it is difficult to predict the extent of future mental handicap, *cerebral palsy, blindness, deafness* and *epilepsy* all of which can be a consequence.

WARKANY, J. et al (1981) Mental Retardation and Congenital Malformations of the Central Nervous System. Chicago: Year Book Medical Publishers Inc. pp. 158–175.

Encephalogram

= *air encephalogram.*

Encephalomeningomyelocoele

A combination of *encephalocoele* with *meningomyelocoele.*

Encephalomyelitis

Inflammation of the brain and *spinal cord* as may occur in *cytomegalic inclusion disease, rubella syndrome, toxoplasmosis, congenital syphilis* and *herpes simplex encephalitis* all of which may cause mental handicap.

Encephalopathy

Any disease of the brain which is general and widespread rather than localized to one part of the brain. There are several types, e.g. *lead encephalopathy* and *Leigh's syndrome* and, depending on the cause, mental handicap may be a consequence.

Encopresis

Incontinence of faeces without a physical cause. The majority of children have control over their bowels before 5 years of age but severely mentally handicapped children may take longer to learn this. Constipation with overflow soiling is another common cause which is often missed. In a few children encopresis is caused by emotional problems but in the majority, with the right approach to training, the problem can be solved. The use of a *behaviour modification* approach with the help of a nurse specialist in mental handicap, or of a *psychologist*, may be necessary. Encopresis occurring during the night is sometimes referred to as nocturnal encopresis.

ASHKENAZI, Z. (1975) The treatment of encopresis using a discriminative stimulus and positive reinforcement. J. Behav. Ther. Exp. Psychiat., 6:155–157.

LAL, H. & LINDSLEY, O.R. (1968) Therapy of chronic constipation in a young child by rearranging social contingencies. Behav. Res. Ther., 6:484–485.

NEALE, D.H. (1963) Behaviour Therapy and encopresis in children. Behav. Res. Ther., 1:139–149.

WRIGHT, D.F. & BUNCH, G. (1977) Parental intervention in the treatment of chronic constipation. J. Behav. Ther. Exp. Psychiat., 2:93–95.

ENCOR

= *Eastern Nebraska Community Office of Retardation.*

Endemic goitrous cretinism

See *goitre.*

Endocrine glands

Organs of the body which secrete hormones or other chemicals which are important for the development and functioning of the body. The chief glands are the *thyroid*, adrenals, *pituitary*, *parathyroids*, pancreas, ovaries and testes. Abnormalities of these glands may cause, or be associated with, mental handicap in a few conditions and *syndromes*.

Engagement

Recently the concept of engagement has been given emphasis and importance as an aspect of improving the quality of life of mentally handicapped people. It refers to the involvement of a person in the surrounding world in a positive and purposeful manner. Staff are trained to promote engagement for the people in their care by encouraging active participation in the social world or physical environment. This is in contrast to many institutions where residents spend long periods of time disengaged. The level of engagement may be used as one measure of quality of life. There are a number of techniques for promoting engagement including *opportunity plans, room management schemes* and *behaviour modification*.

Engelmann's disease

A very rare progressive disorder of the bones. Head enlargement, prominence of the forehead and a small face may occur. The spine is often bent. Leg pains and a waddling walk may be evident in the first years of life. Hearing loss and poor vision may gradually develop. Thin limbs and short stature occur in more severely affected individuals. About 10% of people with Engelmann's disease are mentally handicapped. It is inherited from one parent who may also be affected (*dominant inheritance*). Treatment of children with corticosteroid drugs has been reported to produce improvements in physical symptoms.

ALLEN, D.T. et al (1970) Corticosteroids in the treatment of Engelmann's disease: progressive diaphyseal dysplasia. Pediatrics, 46:523–531.

English Peabody Picture Vocabulary Test

The British version of the *Peabody Picture Vocabulary Test.*

Enopthalmos

Sunken and deep-set eyes. This may occur in a number of conditions associated with mental handicap including *Lowe's syndrome*.

ENT

An abbreviation for ear, nose and throat.

Entropion

A condition of the eyelid, usually the lower, in which the outside of the lid turns inward so that the eyelashes irritate and damage the eye. This may occur in *xeroderma pigmentosum* which is sometimes associated with mental handicap.

Enuresis

Incontinence of urine without a physical cause. The majority of children have reasonable control over their bladder before 3 years of age, but severely mentally handicapped children may take longer to learn this. Continence at night is usually acquired later than in day time and bedwetting (nocturnal enuresis), especially in boys, is a common problem in children of all levels of ability. In a few mentally handicapped children enuresis is caused by emotional problems but in the majority, with the right approach to *toilet training*, the problem can be solved. Nocturnal enuresis may be more difficult to treat effectively but the use of *imipramine, bell and pad* and other *behaviour modification* methods may be successful.

AZRIN, N.H. et al (1973) Dry-bed: a rapid method of eliminating bed-wetting (enuresis) of the retarded. Behav. Res. Ther., 11:427–434.
BUTLER, R.J. (1987) Nocturnal Enuresis: Psychological Perspectives. Bristol: Wright.
DOLEYS, D.M. (1977) Behavioural treatments for nocturnal enuresis in children: A review of recent literature. Psychol. Bull., 84(1):30–54.
SMITH, L.J. (1981) Training severely and profoundly mentally handicapped nocturnal enuretics. Behav. Res. Ther., 19:67–74.

Environmental deprivation

See *deprivation*.

Enzymes

Proteins which catalyse the chemical reactions of the body allowing or speeding up chemical changes. Many conditions which cause mental handicap are due to the absence of an enzyme as in the *amino acidurias*. The absence of an enzyme may prevent important biochemical reactions taking place, and may also lead to abnormal substances building up in the body to act as 'poisons' which can, for example, damage the brain. When the body does not manufacture an enzyme this is usually a *hereditary* problem, most commonly due to *recessive inheritance*.

Epanutin

= *phenytoin*.

Ependyma

The lining of the cavities of the brain (*cerebral ventricles*). This is responsible for secreting the *cerebro-spinal fluid*.

Epicanthic fold / epicanthus

A fold of skin running downward at the inner angle of the eye from the upper eyelid. This may be present in a number of conditions associated with mental handicap including *Down's syndrome* and other chromosomal disorders, *fetal alcohol syndrome, Smith-Lemli-Opitz syndrome, cerebro-hepato-renal syndrome, Rubinstein-Taybi syndrome, Carpenter's syndrome, Prader-Willi syndrome, German's syndrome, de Lange syndrome, infantile hypercalcaemia* and *Noonan's syndrome*. It is also found frequently in people of normal ability and appearance.

Epidemiology

The study of the distribution of particular medical, social or other characteristics in a given population. This may include *incidence, prevalence* and factors and patterns which may contribute to the understanding of an illness or a disability.

BELMONT, L. (1981) (Ed.) Severe mental retardation across the world: epidemiological studies. Internat. J. Ment. Health, 10(1):3–119.
FRYERS, T.(1984) The Epidemiology of Severe Intellectual Impairment. London: Academic Press.

RICHARDSON, S.A. & KOLLER, H. (1985) Epidemiology. In: Mental Deficiency. The Changing Outlook. Clarke, A.M. et al (Eds.) (4th. edit.) London: Methuen. pp. 356–400.

Epidermis

The outer layer of the skin.

Epilepsy

A disorder in which *seizures* occur. There is a sudden and transitory disturbance of brain function with impairment of consciousness and a tendency to recurrence. There are several types of epilepsy described according to the nature of the seizures. These vary depending on the site of origin, the extent of the area of brain involved and the nature of the cause. The frequency of epilepsy in the general population is 1 in 200 with a higher expectancy if a parent is epileptic. Between 5 and 10% of mildly mentally handicapped children have a history of epilepsy compared to 20–30% of severely mentally handicapped children. *Grand-mal convulsions* occurring in people of normal intelligence with no identified cause are often categorized as idiopathic epilepsy. In the majority of mentally handicapped people with epilepsy the seizures are symptomatic of an underlying cause, generally that which also caused the mental handicap (symptomatic epilepsy).

There are two main types of seizures: generalized and partial. Generalized seizures include grand-mal convulsions; *absence seizures; myoclonic seizures; akinetic seizures* and *infantile spasms*. There are several types of *partial seizures* in which consciousness may not be fully impaired. In the motor types there may be jerking or other characteristic movements of part of the body. *Jacksonian epilepsy* is one example. In the sensory types the person may experience particular sensations of the body, taste, vision, hearing or dizziness. Flushing or pallor may occur. *Complex partial seizures* which may include automatic stereotyped behaviour are also called psychomotor seizures or temporal lobe epilepsy. All types of partial seizures may sometimes be followed by a generalized seizure usually of the grand-mal type. Mentally handicapped people with complex partial seizures are also more at risk of *hyperactivity* and behaviour problems.

Status epilepticus occurs when a grand-mal convulsion is very prolonged or a person goes into a succession of convulsions without a full recovery between them. It is a life-threatening condition requiring immediate treatment.

Epilepsy is treated with *anticonvulsant* drugs but some types of epilepsy may be difficult to control especially when there are several points of origin in the brain as occurs in *tuberose sclerosis*.

Electroencephalograms are used to help to make the diagnosis of epilepsy and to identify the source and type of seizures.

It is important that people with epilepsy are encouraged to lead as normal a life as possible and restrictions should only be made where there are unacceptable risks to the person or to others.

LAIDLAW, J. & RICHENS, A. (Eds.) (1982) A Textbook of Epilepsy. (2nd edit.) Edinburgh: Churchill Livingstone.

O'DONOHUE, N.V. (1979) Epilepsies of Childhood. London: Butterworths.

RICHARDSON, S.A. et al (1980) Seizures and epilepsy in a mentally retarded population over the first 22 years of life. Appl. Res. Ment. Retard., 1:123–134.

ROSS, E. & REYNOLDS, E. (Eds.) (1985) Paediatric Perspectives on Epilepsy. Chichester, U.K.: Wiley.

WARD, A.A. et al (Eds.) (1983) Epilepsy. New York: Raven Press.

Further information:
British Epilepsy Association, Crowthorne House, New Workingham Rd., Crowthorne, Berks.
Epilepsy Foundation of America, 4351 Garden City Drive, Landover, MD 29781.

Epileptic equivalents

Behaviours, occurring in people with *epil-*

epsy, which are inappropriate, unpredictable and which have no apparent environmental cause. The evidence for such behaviours being epileptic is slim. *Complex partial seizures* could account for these behaviours in a few people and there is an association between such seizures and *behaviour disorders*. It is generally agreed that in a small number of people with epilepsy there is a tendency to be more irritable before, or sometimes after, seizures. Temper *tantrums* should never be regarded as a form of epilepsy unless there is clear evidence that this is the case in a particular individual.

Epilim
= *sodium valproate*.

Epiloia
= *tuberose sclerosis*.

Epispadia
An abnormal opening of the tube from the bladder (urethra) on the upper side of the penis. This may occur in a few conditions associated with mental handicap including the *Ellis-van Creveld* and *Orbeli syndromes*.

Equinovarus foot deformity / equinus
See *club-foot*.

ESN
= *educational subnormality*.

Esotropia
Cross-eye, a type of *strabismus*.

Ethosuximide
An *anticonvulsant* medication used in the treatment of *absence seizures*. The initial dose is low and is gradually adjusted according to the number of seizures and the presence of any side-effects. Mild side-effects, which are usually transient, may occur initially. These include apathy, drowsiness, headache, unsteadiness, loss of appetite, nausea and vomiting. Skin rashes rarely develop. Changes in blood cells have also been

reported very rarely and include anaemia and lowered resistance to infection. Blood tests are recommended to exclude this reaction to the drug.

Ethotoin
An *anticonvulsant* medication used in the treatment of *grand-mal convulsions* and *partial seizures*. It is not in common use. It is less toxic but also less effective than *phenytoin*. It has the same side-effects.

Etiology
= *aetiology*.

Eugenics
The study and cultivation of conditions that may improve the physical, mental and moral qualities of future generations. At the end of the 19th century the eugenics movement was beginning to provide rationales for institutional *segregation* of mentally handicapped people and later, in Nazi Germany, for the extermination of such people. *Sterilization* programmes were never introduced in the U.K. and constituted a dismal failure in the U.S.A. Segregationist aims were never completely realized and gradually society became uncomfortable with the notion of lifelong confinement on an inadequate scientific and legal basis. This was not before several generations spent childhoods without education and adult lives without hope of release. The philosophy of *normalization* is in complete opposition to the eugenics movement.

HERR, S. (1983) Rights and Advocacy for Retarded People. Massachusetts: Lexington Books.

Euthanasia
Procuring an easy and painless death. There are obvious moral, religious and medical objections to such procedures. There has been much recent debate concerning the care after birth of babies with severe *congenital* abnormalities and the rights of parents, physicians and other authorities in

determining the fate of such infants on whom 'passive euthanasia' is sometimes practised (non-intervention in treatable conditions or failure to provide adequate nourishment in terminal conditions).

CAMPBELL, A. & DUFF, R. (1979) Deciding the care of severely malformed or dying infants. J. Med. Ethics, 5:65–67.

CRANE, D. (1975) The Sanctity of Social Life: Physicians' Treatment of Critically Ill Patients. New York: Russell Sage.

ROBERTSON, J.A. & FOST, N. (1976) Passive euthanasia of defective newborn infants: Legal considerations. J. Pediatr., 88(5):883–889.

WALDMAN, A.M. (1976) Medical ethics and the hopelessly ill child. J. Pediatr., 88(5): 890–892.

Evaluation

The measurement of worth or value and/or the degree of success in achieving a predetermined objective. It is necessary for services for mentally handicapped people to set clear objectives so that the measures and indices for assessing success can be specified. The criteria for success and degrees of success should be defined in terms of output expected within stated periods of time. The information obtained should be fed back into the system so that the programme can be altered if necessary. The aim of evaluation is to determine the efficiency, effectiveness and scope of the system under investigation, to define its strengths and weaknesses and thereby to provide a sound basis for decision making. All services for mentally handicapped people should be properly evaluated although it is not always necessary to have sophisticated measuring techniques to understand the plight of handicapped people in some situations where action is obviously and urgently required.

KEBBON, L. (1981) Evaluation of services for the mentally retarded in Sweden: a conceptual framework. In: Assessing the Handicaps and Needs of Mentally Retarded Children. Cooper, B. (Ed.) New York: Academic Press. pp. 197–233.

MITTLER, P. (1984) Evaluation of services and staff training. In: Scientific Studies in Mental Retardation. Dobbing, J. et al (Eds.) London: Royal Society of Medicine.

RAYNES, N.V. (1981) The evaluation of residential services for mentally retarded children. In: Assessing the Handicaps and Needs of Mentally Retarded Children. Cooper, B. (Ed.) New York: Academic Press. pp. 205–212.

Everyday Living Skills Inventory

A checklist designed to assess a person's independence across a wide range of skills essential for survival and general well-being. It helps to identify areas of everyday living which present the person with major problems. Ten major areas are detailed in the assessment. Some skills are essential to survival and others contribute to quality of life. As well as providing numerical information in the form of ratings for each behaviour it also provides a useful profile with the use of symbols to represent all 86 areas of behaviour. These are shaded according to the degree of independence in this area. There is a scoring manual, two visual profile sheets and an evaluation record and target-setting sheet. The assessment makes it possible to plan ways of reducing the extent of the person's problem by selecting short-, medium- and long-term targets. If ratings are repeated at intervals throughout training they provide an indication of the extent of progress achieved. The symbol profile is designed to be understood by the handicapped person so that he can see his own progress and can also use it as a prompt in learning new skills.

BARKER, P. et al (1978) ELSI. Chalbo Press: Dept. Clinical Psychology, Royal Dundee Liff Hospital, Dundee.

Ewing test

The *distraction test of hearing.*

Exomphalos

A hernia formed by the projection of the abdominal organs through the navel into the base of the umbilical cord with a thin transparent covering (of peritoneum and amniotic membrane). This may be associated with other *congenital* abnormalities and if very severe may not be compatible with life. Milder degrees can be successfully treated by surgery. It occurs uncommonly in babies with *Down's syndrome*, *Beckwith syndrome*, *Goltz's syndrome* and *Patau's syndrome* all of which are associated with mental handicap.

Exophthalmos

Abnormal protrusion of the eyeball. The commonest cause is *hyperthyroidism*. It may also occur in *Crouzon's syndrome*, *Noonan's syndrome* and *Wolf's syndrome*.

Exotropia

Wall-eye, a type of *strabismus*.

Expressive aphasia

See *aphasia*.

Expressive dysphasia

See *dysphasia*.

Extension

This term is applied to the process of straightening or stretching a limb or body part. In *cerebral palsy* the imbalance of muscle *tone* may lead to lack of extension or abnormal extension of joints, impairment of movement and sometimes deformity.

Extension contracture

In *cerebral palsy* and other disorders of nerves and muscles, the imbalance of muscle *tone* and the tightness of some muscles compared to others at a joint, may lead to a permanent state of *extension*. Over time, this becomes a permanent deformity known as extension contracture. An operation may sometimes be indicated to relieve this.

Extensor spasm

Sudden tightness (*spasm*) in the muscles responsible for *extension* may lead to discomfort and abnormal posture. This may occur in children with *cerebral palsy*.

Extensors

Muscles that straighten a limb or body part.

External auditory meatus

The ear canal which has its opening in the external ear and a blind end at the eardrum.

Extinction

A *behaviour modification* technique by which the frequency of an undesirable behaviour is reduced by stopping any *reinforcements* which have been maintaining that behaviour. Once extinction is started there is a temporary rise in the frequency of the behaviour followed by a reduction. The rate at which the behaviour reduces in frequency is partly related to the way in which it was being reinforced previously. Depending on the circumstances, it may take some time to be effective. Extinction has been widely used with 'nuisance' behaviours such as excessive *attention-seeking*, *tantrums*, spitting and destruction of property.

Extradural haematoma

Accumulation of blood between the skull and the fibrous lining of the skull (dura). This causes pressure on the brain. It is usually caused by trauma to the skull but in children this may be only a minor injury. *Child abuse* may be a cause. It is treated by operative removal of the clot. Recovery may be complete but often there is some residual brain damage.

Extrapyramidal signs / extrapyramidal side-effects

These include a *tremor* of hands, tongue and facial muscles; paucity of movements; shuffling gait; muscle spasms and cramps which are sometimes associated with pain. *Oculogyric crises* may occur in which there is involuntary rolling upward of the eyes for minutes or hours. *Dystonia, akathisia,* and *tardive dyskinesia* may develop. These signs occur in *Parkinson's disease* and also in a few conditions associated with mental handicap such as *Louis-Barr syndrome* and *Batten's disease.* They are a common side-effect of *phenothiazine* drugs including *chlorpromazine, fluphenazine, perphenazine, thioridazine, pericyazine* and *haloperidol.* Treatment with *antiparkinsonian drugs* such as *benzhexol, benztropine* and *orphenadrine* varies in effectiveness depending on the cause and severity of the signs. It is less effective for tremor and dystonia. Tardive dyskinesia can be worsened by such drugs.

Eye abnormalities
Abnormalities of the eye are very commonly associated with conditions which cause mental handicap. Abnormalities of the lids include *ectropion* and *entropion*; of the *cornea* include *keratoconus*; of the lens include *cataracts* and of the *choroid* and *retina* include *choroido-retinitis* and *retinal degeneration.* Many eye abnormalities are associated with poor vision or *blindness.*

Eye contact
Making eye contact is a powerful way of communicating with other people and a means of making attachments and evoking care-giving from others. Avoidance of eye contact is a feature of *autism* and occurs in some mentally handicapped children, especially those with autistic behaviours. Making eye contact is therefore frequently identified as a target in basic training programmes.

Eye-poking / eye-gouging
Eye-poking with closed eyelids tends to be a self-stimulating activity in people with visual impairment.

Eye-gouging is a *self-injurious behaviour* which is reported in a few blind people of normal intelligence but is particularly common in visually impaired mentally handicapped people.

JAN, J.E. et al (1983) Eye pressing by visually impaired children. Dev. Med. Child Neurology, 25:755–762.

F

Fabry's syndrome

A rare disorder which usually develops during childhood and *adolescence*. It often begins with unexplained periodic bouts of fever and severe sharp pains in the limbs which are aggravated by changes in environmental temperature. Small red spots develop on the skin and similar abnormalities of small blood vessels in the eyes may affect vision. Blood vessel abnormalities in the brain may cause brain damage and *epilepsy*. The kidneys are generally affected. It is progressive and survival beyond 50 years of age is unusual. The cause is an *enzyme* deficiency leading to accumulation of abnormal substances (glycosphingo lipids) in the body particularly around blood vessels. It is a *lipidosis*. It is inherited through the sex *chromosomes* and the full syndrome only appears in the male. If the mother is the carrier she may have a mild form of the condition (*sex-linked inheritance*). The condition can be detected in carriers.

DE GROOT, W.P. (1970) Fabry's disease in children. Brit. J. Derm., 82:329.
DESNICK, R.J. et al (1973) Enzymatic diagnosis of hemizygotes and heterozygotes: Fabry's disease. J. Lab. Clin. Med., 81:157.
LOCKMAN, L.A. et al (1973) Relief of the pain of Fabry's disease by diphenylhydantoin. Neurology, 23:871.

Facial asymmetry

A difference in size and/or shape of the right and left halves of the face. This may occur in *Apert's syndrome, Riley-Day syndrome, Goldenhar's syndrome, bird-headed dwarfism, Treacher-Collins syndrome* and some rare *chromosome* abnormalities associated with mental handicap.

Facies

The appearance of the face.

Fading

1. Fading of *prompts*. Teaching techniques using verbal or physical prompts may be used in *behaviour modification*. After some repetitions the teacher senses that the person is beginning to participate in the task and then begins to fade out the prompts. Prompts may be first faded from those aspects of the sequence of behaviour closest to the final link in the chain of responses (*backward chaining*). A physical prompt in self-feeding, for example, may be faded out by initially holding the hand over the spoon and over a period of time gradually moving the teacher's hand down the arm of the person until a nudge on the elbow is sufficient.
2. Stimulus fading. In behaviour modification this involves gradual planned changes in the situation in which the behaviour occurs. For example, if a person is disruptive in a large group, but not alone, he may gradually be introduced to the group by having them join him one at a time. This is similar to *desensitization*.
3. *Reinforcement* fading. Once the behaviour is well established the trainer gradually fades out or reduces the reinforcement over a period of time.

DORRY, G.W. & ZEAMAND, D. (1975) Teaching a simple reading vocabulary to retarded children: effectiveness of fading and non-fading procedures. Am. J. Ment. Defic., 79(6):711–716.

Faecal incontinence

= *encopresis*.

Failure to thrive

In some of the more severe conditions associated with mental handicap the child may fail to grow and to gain weight and may eventually die in an emaciated state. Whilst this may not be amenable to treatment in some *degenerative disorders*, it should always be fully investigated to exclude a treatable cause. A possible cause is inadequate food intake due to severe *feeding problems*.

Fairview Self-Help Scale
A short assessment scale suitable for use with severely and profoundly handicapped people. It is not very detailed and can therefore be used for screening a large number of clients or for a brief general assessment of an individual. It covers the areas of motor skills, self-help, communication, social interaction and self-direction. It provides a behavioural age score in months.

ROSS & ROSS (1970) Fairview Self-Help Scale. Fairview State Hospital, Costa Mesa, Calif. 92626, U.S.A.

Fallot's tetralogy
A serious form of *congenital heart disease* in which there is a defect in the wall between the two major chambers of the heart and also the major blood vessels from the heart are wrongly positioned. Blood which should be pumped to the lungs for oxygen is, instead, recirculated around the body. This puts the heart under strain and leads to a number of secondary problems. The success rate following early operation is steadily improving although it is a major operation with high risk. Fallot's tetralogy may occur in a number of conditions associated with mental handicap including *rubella syndrome, Goldenhar's syndrome, Smith-Lemli-Opitz syndrome, Noonan's syndrome, Down's syndrome* and other *chromosome* abnormalities.

Familial
The tendency for a condition or characteristic to be present in several members, or more than one generation, of a family. The term is usually used when the mode of *inheritance* is uncertain or unproven.

Familial amaurotic idiocy
= *Tay-Sachs syndrome*.

Familial dysautonomia
= *Riley-Day syndrome*.

Familial lactic acidosis
A group of disorders some of which are associated with progressive mental deterioration and death in early childhood. Overbreathing when not exercising, muscle twitching, progressive unsteadiness and often *seizures* occur. The types of inheritance and the exact types of biochemical disturbance are not yet fully understood but there is an excess of lactic acid in the blood in these conditions. Further investigations may be indicated in some children in order to identify the cause.

ROBINSON, B.H. et al (1980) The genetic heterogeneity of lactic acidosis. Pediatr. Res., 14:956.
STERN, J. & TOOTHILL, C. (1972) Organic Acidurias. Proceedings of the 9th Symposium of the Society for the Study of Inborn Errors of Metabolism. Edinburgh: Churchill Livingstone.

Familial lipidosis
= *lipidosis*.

Family
The effect on a family of having a handicapped child is very variable. The family has a major effect on the child's development and the child has a major effect on the well-being of the family. There have been conflicting findings on the impact of a handicapped child on the marital relationships but most point towards the importance of a good marriage before the birth if the couple are to cope well with the extra stress. The effect on *siblings* is also very variable but any stress is usually found to be less than usually supposed. Older sisters may resent the extra responsibility and other siblings may find disruptive behaviour a nuisance at times. There are also reports

of many positive aspects to having a mentally handicapped member of the family.

BALLARD, R. (1982) Taking the family into account. Mental Handicap, 10:75–76.
BICKNELL, D.J. (1982) Living with a mentally handicapped member of the family. Postgrad. Med. J., 58:597–605.
GATH, A. (1978) Down's Syndrome and the Family: The Early Years. London: Academic Press.
HUNTER, A.B.J. (1980) The Family and their Mentally Handicapped Child. Ilford: Barnardo Publications Ltd.
MITTLER, P. & MCCONACHIE, H. (1983) Parents, Professionals and Mentally Handicapped People. London: Croom Helm.
MURPHY, M.A. (1982) The family with a handicapped child: a review of the literature. J. Dev. Behav. Pediatr., 3:73–82.
WIKLER, L. (1981) Chronic stresses of families of mentally retarded children. Family Relations, 30:281–288.

Family fund
= *Rowntree trust.*

Family group home
A home provided for a small group of mentally handicapped residents usually in an ordinary domestic house or bungalow. It is run as much as possible like a family. Sometimes 'house parents' may be fully resident but more often staff operate a rota and are present when needed. For mentally handicapped people this is an attempt to provide the next best alternative to family life. See *staffed domestic homes* and *group homes.*

Family placement
Placement in a family is now the preferred alternative to full-time institutional care for mentally handicapped children. This may be by means of *adoption* or *fostering* and is generally arranged through an agency specializing in 'hard to place' children. If arranged on a part-time basis in order to support the natural family, it is often known as a *family support scheme.*

BRITISH INSTITUTE OF MENTAL HANDICAP (1980) Family Placements for Mentally Handicapped Children. Kidderminster: BIMH.
WEDGE, P. & THORBURN, J. (1986) Finding Families for Hard to Place Children. B.A.A.F., 11, Southwark St., London SE1 1RQ.

Family Planning Association
An organization which is able to advise mentally handicapped people and their families on aspects of sexuality and prevention of unwanted pregnancies. It has branches throughout the U.K. and can also provide books, slides, film and other teaching aids.

Further information:
Family Planning Association, 27–35 Mortimer St., London W1N 7RJ.

Family support scheme
This may describe any scheme which offers practical or emotional support to families with a handicapped child. In the U.K. it is more often used to describe schemes which offer *phased care* usually through a link with another family who are trained and paid for this role. In the U.K. this was pioneered by the Social Services Departments in Somerset and Leeds. In the U.S.A. this may be provided in a *family-care home.*

CRINE, A. (1981) Partnership with parents – a real alternative to hospital. Mind Out, 51: July.
CROSBY, I. et al (1978) Time off for parents. Social Work Today, June.
OSWIN, M. (1984) They Keep Going Away. London: King Edward's Hospital Fund for London.

Family therapy / family psychiatry
Emotional problems in children and parents are frequently treated by psychotherapeutic techniques involving the whole family as a unit rather than individual treatment of one or more members of the family. This approach has developed particularly in

child psychiatric centres and usually requires skilled practitioners working as part of a team who provide observation and feedback. It has proved very valuable and is now applied to many families in need of help including those who are finding it hard to adjust to having a handicapped child. The aim is to improve the coping skills and resourcefulness of the family often by helping them to 'pull together' more effectively. It may also facilitate the process of coming to terms with the disabilities of the child.

BLACK, D. (1982) Handicap and family therapy. In: Family Therapy Vol. 2. Bentovim, A. et al (Eds.). New York: Academic Press. pp. 417–439.
TURNER, A. (1980) Therapy with families of a mentally retarded child. J. Marital Family Therapy, pp. 167–171.

Family-care home
An arrangement in which a mentally handicapped person lives with a family in their own home. As well as *fostering* and *adoption* for children this can also be used to provide a home for an adult.

BAKER, B.L. et al (1974) As Close as Possible: Community Residences for Retarded Adults. Boston: Little, Brown.
SCHEERENBERGER, R.C. & FELSENTHAL, D. (1977) Community settings for MR persons: Satisfaction and activities. Ment. Retardation, 15:3–7.

Fanconi's hypoplastic anaemia
In this condition a general reduction in the number of blood cells (aplastic anaemia) is associated with brown pigmentation of the skin, short stature, small head, underdeveloped genitals and often abnormalities of limbs, eyes, fingers, spine, heart and kidneys. Mental handicap occurs in 20% of people with this condition. The patchy pigmentation occurs within the first few years of life. There is a predisposition to malignant tumours and leukaemia. It is inherited from both parents who are carriers (*recessive inheritance*). *Chromosome* abnormalities commonly occur. The outlook for children with this condition is poor.

AUERBACH, A.D. (1981) Prenatal and postnatal diagnosis and carrier detection of Fanconi's anaemia by a cytogenetic method. Pediatrics, 67:120 131.
BLOOM, G.E. et al (1966) Chromosome abnormalities in constitutional aplastic anaemia. New Engl. J. Med., 274:8.
SALMON, M.A. (1978) Developmental Defects and Syndromes. Aylesbury, Bucks: HM+M Publishers. pp. 211–212.

Farber's lipogranulomatosis
A very rare disease due to a deficiency of an *enzyme* (lysosomal acid ceramidase) which is necessary for dealing with lipids (a type of fat) in the body. Within the first few weeks of life the infant becomes irritable, has a hoarse cry and develops red nodular lumps on the wrists. Over the next few months similar lumps develop elsewhere especially on the joints and buttocks. There is usually severe mental and physical handicap and death usually occurs by 2 years of age. Mildly affected people in whom intellectual function is unimpaired have also been described. There is no known treatment. It can be detected in the fetus following *amniocentesis*.

FARBER, S. et al (1957) Lipogranulomatosis. A new lipoglycoprotein storage disease. J. Mount Sinai Hosp. New York. 24:816.

FAS
= *fetal alcohol syndrome*.

Febrile convulsion
A *seizure* that occurs in a child aged between 3 months and 5 years with a high temperature but without any other evident cause. It is usually a *grand-mal convulsion*. Often there is a family history of febrile convulsions or *epilepsy*. Recovery is generally complete but if a convulsion is very prolonged (*status epilepticus*) brain damage may be a consequence. The *temporal lobes* of the brain are particularly susceptible to such damage

and *complex partial seizures* may occur later in childhood as a consequence. Children who are mentally handicapped and epileptic may be more prone to seizures when running a temperature.

ANNEGERS, J.F. et al (1979) The risk of epilepsy following febrile convulsions. Neurology, 29:297–303.
NELSON, K.B. & ELLENBURGH, J.H. (1978) Prognosis in children with febrile seizures. Pediatrics, 61:720–727.

Feeble-minded

This term was used to describe mildly mentally handicapped people under the 1914 *Mental Deficiency Act* in England and the 1913 Act in Scotland.

Feeding problems

Many children have feeding problems often as a part of a battle with parents who worry excessively about food intake. Mentally handicapped children may have feeding problems for other reasons such as poor muscle strength or co-ordination, as may occur in babies with *Down's syndrome, cerebral palsy* and many other conditions associated with mental handicap. Delay in learning to self-feed may be one aspect of *developmental delay* and is generally an easy self-help skill to teach because it is simple and inherently rewarding. Teaching appropriate social behaviour at meal times may be more difficult especially if antisocial behaviours are present. *Behaviour modification* techniques can usually be successfully applied to these problems.

ALBIN, J.B. (1977) Some variables influencing the maintenance of acquired self-feeding behaviour in profoundly retarded children. Ment. Retardation, 15:49–52.
AZRIN, N. & ARMSTRONG, P.M. (1973) The 'mini-meal' – a method of teaching eating skills to the profoundly retarded. Ment. Retardation, 11:9–13.
MATSON, J.L. et al (1980) A comprehensive dining program for mentally retarded adults. Behav. Res. Ther., 18:107–112.
RICHMAN, J.S. et al (1980) Prerequisite in vivo acquisition of self-feeding skills. Behav. Res. Ther., 18:327–332.
STIMBERT, V.E. et al (1977) Intensive feeding training with retarded children. Behav. Mod., 1:517–529.
WEBB, Y. (1980) Feeding and nutrition problems of physically and mentally handicapped children in Britain. J. Human Nutrition, 34:281–286.
WEIR, K. (1979) Psychological factors in feeding disorders occurring in mentally or multiply handicapped children. Child Care, Health & Development, 5:285–294.

Feely box

A box which contains a selection of objects which provide experiences in manipulation for the visually handicapped person.

Feingold diet

A diet based on the work of the American doctor, Ben Feingold. It is recommended for *hyperactive* children in the belief that this is caused by food *allergy*. All synthetic colours or flavours, glutamates, nitrates, nitrites, BHA, BHT and benzoic acid are excluded from food and drink. Foods containing natural salicylates (including most fruits) may be avoided and then reintroduced one at a time to see if they cause problems. The evidence for the success of the diet is still inconclusive especially regarding the type of child who is most likely to benefit.

LESSOF, M.H. (1983) Food intolerance and allergy – a review. Quart. J. Med., 52:111–119.
PEARSON, D.J. et al (1983) Food allergy: how much in the mind? Lancet, 1:1259–1261.
THORLEY, G. (1984) Pilot study to assess behavioural and cognitive effects of artificial food colours in a group of retarded children. Dev. Med. Child Neurology, 26:56–61.
FEINGOLD, B.F. (1975) Hyperkinesis and learning disabilities linked to artificial food flavors and colors. Am. J. Nursing, 75:797–803.

Lancet Editorial (1982) Food additives and hyperactivity. Lancet, 8273:662–663.

Further information:
Hyperactive Children's Support Group. 59, Meadowside, Angmering, West Sussex. BN16 4BW.

Fentazin
= *perphenazine*.

Fertility
Some people who are mentally handicapped may be less fertile than usual. This is particularly the case in *Down's syndrome* and other *chromosome* disorders. There has been no recorded case of a man with Down's syndrome fathering a child, but a few women with Down's syndrome have become pregnant (with a 40% rate of having a child with Down's syndrome). The great majority of mentally handicapped people have normal sexual development and normal fertility. This raises issues of *contraception*, *abortion* and *parenthood*.

Fetal alcohol syndrome
This condition has only been recognized since the late 1960's as a significant cause of mental handicap. The frequency is estimated to be between 1 and 2 per 1000 live births with partial expression of the syndrome in 3 to 5 per 1000 live births. It is seen in the children of mothers who consume more than 80g of alcohol per day during pregnancy. More subtle signs can be found in the children of 'social drinkers' and there is some evidence that even the occasional 'binge' can be harmful. It is manifest by deficient growth before and after birth, characteristic facial appearance, small head and abnormal brain development. Children have a short upturned nose and narrow eyes. The upper jaw and lip are underdeveloped and the mouth is often small. Floppiness in infancy and *hyperactivity* in childhood are often described. Many other abnormalities have been reported including a protuberant chest, *congenital heart disease*, *epicanthic folds*, and genital, joint and skeletal abnormalities. Mental handicap occurs in 85% of children recognized to have the syndrome. In those children with an *intelligence quotient* in the normal range there still may be deficits in *cognitive* skills and language development.

CHERNOFF, G. (1980) The fetal alcohol syndrome: clinical studies and strategies of prevention. In: Prevention of Mental Retardation and Other Developmental Disabilities. McCormack, M.K. (Ed.). New York: Marcel Dekker.

COOPER, S. (1987) The fetal alcohol syndrome. J. Child. Psychol. Psychiat., 2(28): 223–227.

EDWARDS, G. (1983) Alcohol and advice to the pregnant woman: Brit. Med. J., 286: 247–248.

JONES, K.L. et al (1973) Patterns of malformation in offspring of chronic alcoholic mothers. Lancet, 1:1267–1271.

NITOWSKY, H.M. (1982) Fetal alcohol syndrome and alcohol-related birth defects. N.Y. State. J. Med., 82:1214.

SMITHELLS, R.W. (1979) Fetal alcohol syndrome. Dev. Med. Child Neurology, 21: 244–247.

Fetal anoxia
Lack of oxygen to the *fetus*. It can occur at any time during pregnancy but the time of greatest risk is during a prolonged or difficult labour or as a result of other complications of pregnancy. The human brain is capable of surviving deprivation of oxygen for only short periods of time before permanent damage ensues. This may lead to *cerebral palsy* and/or mental handicap. Babies with a low weight for the length of pregnancy (*fetal growth retardation*) are particularly prone to the effects of lack of oxygen.

Fetal distress
There are several signs recognized by the obstetrician and midwife which indicate that the *fetus* is getting insufficient oxygen

(*fetal anoxia*) in the womb. These include an increase in the fetal heart rate. It is nowadays customary to monitor the state of the fetus at risk by using specialized equipment. Caesarean delivery is often indicated when there are signs of distress especially in the early stages of labour.

Fetal growth retardation

A low fetal weight for the length of the pregnancy. The weight of the developing brain is in direct relationship with the general body weight of the *fetus* and nutritional deficiencies during pregnancy may produce deficiencies of brain growth and intelligence which cannot subsequently be made up. An insufficient or a damaged placenta due to complications of pregnancy is the most common cause of fetal growth retardation. Smoking, alcohol and *malnutrition* are other causes.

Fetal hydantoin syndrome

See *camptomelic dwarfism*.

Feto protein

= *alpha-feto protein*.

Fetoscopy

This technique involves direct viewing of the *fetus* by a fibreoptic system passed into the *amniotic fluid* through a needle. As well as viewing the external appearance of the fetus it is possible to take blood samples and even to *biopsy* skin or organs such as the liver in order to diagnose conditions in the fetus. It is still a procedure which involves risk to the fetus and is therefore only used where the risks of abnormality are high, where other procedures (*amniocentesis, ultrasound scanning* and *chorion biopsy*) are inapplicable and where *abortion* is an agreed option.

RODECK, C.H. & NICOLAIDES, K.H. (1983) Fetoscopy and fetal tissue sampling. Brit. Med. Bull., 39:332–337.

Fetus / foetus

The name given to the unborn child within the womb from the eighth week of pregnancy. Prior to this it is known as an embryo.

Feuerstein-Mims syndrome

= *linear naevus sebaceous syndrome*.

Fibroblast culture

Cells known as fibroblasts can be grown outside the body in a laboratory. These cells may be found in many parts of the body but are usually obtained from the deep layer of the skin by means of skin biopsy or from the *amniotic fluid* (which surrounds the fetus in the womb) by means of *amniocentesis*. The culture of fibroblast cells produces chemicals (*enzymes*) and some conditions caused by enzyme deficiencies can be detected. This may be used to make the diagnosis of a number of *genetic disorders* including most of the *lipidoses* and *mucopolysaccharidoses*. As well as detecting a serious condition in the fetus (making *abortion* an option) it can be used to detect the *carrier* state in parents and relatives. This is important for *genetic counselling*.

Fibroma

Benign tumour of fibrous tissues. There are many fibromata throughout the body in *tuberose sclerosis* and in *Von Recklinghausen's disease*.

Financial benefits

= *allowances*.

Fine motor skills

The ability to perform fine movements which require strength and co-ordination of fingers and hands.

Fingerprint patterns

= *dermatoglyphics*.

Finger-thumb opposition

The ability to pick up small objects using a finger and thumb is a significant step in the development of the *fine motor skills* of a child. It occurs on average at, or about, the age of

1 year. It is used in some test scales as a test of motor development. Its acquisition may be delayed if the child is mentally or physically handicapped.

First arch syndromes
A group of disorders which are associated with abnormal development of the structures arising from a part of the embryo known as the first brachial arch (which is in evidence only in the very early stages of pregnancy). There is considerable overlap of the features of various *syndromes* in this group which include *Wildervanck's syndrome, Treacher-Collins syndrome, Hallermann-Streiff syndrome, Rubinstein-Taybi syndrome* and *Smith-Lemli-Opitz syndrome*.

Fitness to plead
In English law a person accused of a criminal offence is unfit to plead if he or she cannot understand the nature of the charge; cannot distinguish between the meaning of 'guilty' and 'not guilty'; or cannot challenge a juror, instruct counsel or follow the proceedings in court. He or she is not put on trial and is sent to a hospital nominated by the Home Secretary and is detained until 'Her Majesty's pleasure be known'.

Fits
= *seizures*.

Flat foot
= *pes planus*.

Flexibilitas cerea
An abnormal state in which the limbs remain in any position into which they are moved.

Flexion
The process of bending a limb or body part.

Flexion contracture
In *cerebral palsy* and other disorders of nerves and muscles the imbalance of muscle *tone* and the tightness of some muscles compared to others at a joint may lead to a permanent

state of *flexion*. Over time, this becomes a permanent deformity which is called a flexion contracture. An operation may sometimes be indicated to relieve this.

Flexion spasm
Sudden tightness (*spasm*) in the muscles responsible for *flexion* may lead to temporary discomfort and abnormal posture. This may occur in children with *cerebral palsy*.

Flexors
Muscles that bend a limb or body part.

Fluanoxol
= *flupenthixol*.

Fluorescent banding
The identification of *chromosomes* is possible by staining with chemicals which reveal fluorescent bands.

Flupenthixol
This is available in tablet form (fluanxol) for the short-term treatment of mild or moderate *depression* and as higher dose tablets or long-acting injection (Depixol) for the treatment of *schizophrenia*. It has been shown to possess activating, alerting and anti-anxiety effects and, in low doses, *antidepressant* activity. The injection is given at 2 to 4 week intervals. The commonest side-effects with the higher doses are *extrapyramidal signs*. *Tardive dyskinesia* is reported very rarely.

Fluphenazine
This drug is available as tablets (Moditen) or as a long-acting injection (Modecate). It is one of the *phenothiazines*. The tablets are used in the management of anxiety; agitated excitement; violent or dangerously impulsive behaviour; *schizophrenia* and in *mania* and *hypomania*. The injection is used for the treatment and maintenance of people with schizophrenia and is particularly valuable when the person is unreliable at taking tablets. Fluphenazine should be used with caution in people with liver disease, heart disease, thyroid disorders and *epilepsy*. It

may impair the effects of *anticonvulsants*. Side-effects include *extrapyramidal signs, tardive dyskinesia*, drowsiness, lethargy, blurred vision, dryness of mouth, constipation, difficulty in passing urine, *incontinence, seizures, jaundice*, skin rashes, hormonal effects, minor abnormalities of the blood and impaired body temperature regulation.

Flurazepam

A drug of the *benzodiazepine* group which is used in the short-term treatment of people who have difficulty in getting to sleep and/or wake frequently. Side-effects include drowsiness, sedation, unsteadiness and confusion. Headache, dizziness, skin rashes and stomach upsets have also been reported.

Focal dermal hypoplasia

= *Goltz's syndrome.*

Focal epilepsy

Epilepsy arising in a focus or particular site in the brain. It is usually used to describe *complex partial seizures* and also for *Jacksonian epilepsy.*

Foetus

= *fetus.*

Folate deficiency / folic acid

Folic acid is one of the B group of vitamins, a deficiency of which can cause anaemia. It has been discovered that the recurrence rate of *meningomyelocoele* in subsequent pregnancies can be reduced considerably by administering folic acid before and following conception.
Anticonvulsant drugs which reduce folic acid levels in the body, such as *phenobarbitone* and *phenytoin*, can cause anaemia as a side-effect and if taken during pregnancy children may have several abnormalities including mental handicap (*camptomelic dwarfism*). The blood folate levels of people taking these anticonvulsant drugs should be checked at regular intervals so that, if necessary, folic acid tablets can be given. It has recently been suggested that treatment with folic

acid may improve the behaviour of some people with *fragile-X syndrome.*

LAURENCE, K.M. et al (1981) Double-blind randomized controlled trial of folate treatment before conception to prevent recurrence of neural tube defects. Brit. Med. J., 282:1509–1511.
SMITHELLS, R.W. et al (1983) Further experience of vitamin supplementation for prevention of neural tube defect recurrence. Lancet, 1:1027.

Fontanelle

An area of the skull in which bone has not yet formed. In the baby the flat bones of the skull do not join together to form a rigid structure and there are still gaps. The largest of these is the anterior fontanelle just above the forehead. By the age of 18 months it is usually completely covered by bone. The fontanelles become more tense and bulge when the pressure of the *cerebro-spinal fluid* is increased as in *hydrocephalus*. They become sunken in dehydration. In some conditions, such as *Down's syndrome, rubella syndrome, Rubinstein-Taybi syndrome, congenital hypothyroidism, Silver's syndrome* and *Hallermann-Streiff syndrome*, the anterior fontanelle is late in closing.

Forced-choice preferential looking

A way of measuring visual acuity in infants. An infant prefers to look at a striped pattern rather than at a blank screen of the same brightness. A procedure is used to adjust the stripe width and determine the acuity of vision. An observer from behind the screen records the direction in which the child is looking. It works best for infants under 9 months or with a *mental age* of less than 9 months.

ATKINSON, J. et al (1982) 'Preferential looking' for monocular and binocular acuity testing of infants. Brit. J. Ophthalmol., 66:264–268.
TELLER, D.Y. (1979) The forced-choice preferential looking procedure: a psycho-

physical technique for use with human infants. Infant Behav. Dev., 2:135–153.

Forensic medicine
Study of medicine as it concerns the criminal law.

Formboard
A board with depressions of various shapes into which appropriate insets can be fitted. It may be used as an educational toy and also as a mental test of the *performance* type. The ability to complete simple formboards starts on average at the age of 2 years.

Forward chaining
A method of teaching a behaviour or skill which occurs in a set sequence. The action is broken down into small steps and the first step is taught first. Once it is learnt the next step is taught and added and so on. It is less frequently used than *backward chaining*. It is one of a range of *behaviour modification* techniques practised by *psychologists*, teachers, *care staff* and others who help mentally handicapped people. See also *chaining*.

Fostering
Foster parents care for children who are not their own and who are the responsibility of another agency. They are carefully selected, vetted and should be well supported. Until a few years ago it was considered impossible to place mentally handicapped children for fostering or *adoption*. It has now been shown to be possible for the majority of children due to pioneering work carried out by specialist fostering agencies in the U.S.A and U.K. Dr. Barnardo's have run a very successful fostering scheme in north-west England since 1979 and even profoundly handicapped and behaviourally disturbed children have been moved from institutions into families. The success rate has been much better than for fostering non-handicapped children and, by 1986, 55 children had been placed. Professional attitudes have gradually changed and it is now very unusual to take a mentally handicapped child into any form of residential care on a permanent basis. Parents are given encouragement and support to rear their mentally handicapped child at home but if they are unable or unwilling to do so it is now the usual practice for the preferred placement to be fostering or adoption.

EYMAN, R.K. & BEGAB, M.J. (1981) Relationship between foster home environment and resident changes in adaptive behaviour. In: Frontier of Knowledge in Mental Retardation, Vol. I. Mittler, P. (Ed.). Baltimore: University Park Press. pp. 327–336.
HARDY, J. (1986) Professional fostering: handicapped children. Adoption and Fostering, 10(2):19–21.
WOLFORTH, P. et al (1986) Professional Foster Care for Mentally Handicapped Children. Barnardo Practice Paper, Dr Barnardo's, Tanner's Lane, Barkingside, Essex IG6 1QG.

Fragile-X syndrome
In 1977 it was discovered that some mentally handicapped people had certain characteristics in common (previously described by Martin and Bell) and when blood or skin cells were grown in the absence of *folic acid* there was an indentation (fragile site) on the long arm of the X *chromosome* and this is known as the marker-X chromosome. The syndrome is commoner and more marked in males than females. The person generally has a somewhat prominent chin, broad forehead, wide jaw, wide nose, long face and large floppy ears. Large testes may be present at birth or become evident at puberty. There are no severe physical defects. The degree of mental handicap varies and there may be specific speech difficulties. Affected girls are usually only mildly mentally handicapped. It is thought to be a fairly common cause of mental handicap occurring in 9% of males with an *intelligence quotient* between 35 and 60 and with no other abnormalities of the nervous system. Approximately 5% of mildly mentally handicapped schoolgirls have a fragile-

X chromosome. In one study treatment of *autistic* patients with fragile-X syndrome using folic acid produced a marked improvement in the symptoms of most of them. Diagnosis of this condition may be made before birth by means of *amniocentesis*. It is inherited from the mother who is a carrier of the condition or mildly affected (*sex-linked inheritance*).

BROWN, W.T. et al (1986) Fragile-X and autism. Am. J. Med. Genet., 23(1–2):341–352.

BROWN, W.T. et al (1986) High dose folic acid treatment of fragile-X males. Am. J. Med. Genet., 23(1–2):643–664.

DE ARCHE, M.A. & KEARNS, A. (1984) The fragile-X Syndrome: the patients and their chromosomes. J. Med. Genet., 21:84–91.

PUESCHEL, S.M. et al (1983) Familial X-linked mental retardation syndrome associated with minor congenital anomalies, macro-orchidism and fragile-X chromosome. Am. J. Ment. Defic., 87:372–376.

RICHARDS, B.W. et al (1981) Fragile X-linked mental retardation: the Martin-Bell syndrome. J. Ment. Defic. Res., 25:253–256.

SHAPIRO, L.R. (1982) Prenatal diagnosis of fragile-X chromosome. Lancet, 1:99.

TOMMERUP, N. et al (1986) Fragile-X: carrier detection in pregnancy. Am. J. Med. Genet., 23(1–2):527–530.

TOWNES, P.E. (1982) Fragile-X syndrome: a jigsaw puzzle with picture emerging. Am. J. Dis. Child., 136:389–391.

Franceschetti-Zwahlen-Klein syndrome
= *Treacher-Collins syndrome.*

Fraser syndrome
= *cryptophthalmos syndrome.*

Frequency recording
The recording of the number of times a specified behaviour occurs within a specific time period. This is used in *behaviour modification* programmes.

Friedreich's ataxia
This condition particularly affects the *spinal cord* and *cerebellum* but nerve cells throughout the body are gradually destroyed. Unsteadiness is usually the first sign and the average age of onset is 10 years. Weakness and poor co-ordination become steadily worse and speech is affected. Deformities of feet and spine develop or may be present from birth. The condition may also affect the brain leading to mental handicap in about 8% or less of cases. Deafness is common. Most people with this condition die in their twenties or thirties. The condition is usually inherited from both parents who are carriers (*recessive inheritance*).

GREENFIELD, J.G. (1954) The Spino-Cerebellar Degenerations. Oxford: Blackwell.

HARDING, A.E. (1981) Friedreich's ataxia: A clinical and genetic study of 90 families with an analysis of early diagnostic criteria and intrafamilial clustering of clinical features. Brain, 104:589.

Further information:
Friedreich's Ataxia Group, The Common, Cranleigh, Surrey GU6 8SB.

Frisium
= *clobazam.*

Frontal bossing
= *bossing.*

Frontal lobes
The lobes at the front of the brain. Severe damage to this part of the brain may lead to disinhibited behaviour. The *pre-central cortex* lies at the back of the frontal lobe.

Frontal-nasal dysplasia
= *median cleft face syndrome.*

Fructose intolerance
This is rare in the U.S.A. but far more common in Europe. The child has bowel disturbances, poor weight gain and faintness after consuming sugar. Mild mental

handicap is frequent and there may be a floppy weakness of limbs. The liver and brain become increasingly damaged. This condition is inherited from both parents who are carriers (*recessive inheritance*). Treatment is with a lifelong fructose-free diet.

CHAMBERS, R.A. & PRATT, R.T.C. (1956) Idiosyncrasy to Fructose. Lancet, 2:340.
RENNERT, O.M. & GREER, M. (1970) Hereditary Fructosemia. Neurology, 20:421.

Fucosidosis

A very rare condition caused by the absence of an *enzyme* (alpha-L-fucidase). Severe mental handicap and *cerebral palsy* occur. In Type (1) the onset is at about 1 year of age. The facial features of the child are coarse, the tongue large and abnormalities of bones are present. Excessive sweating occurs. *Seizures* and poor growth are common. The deterioration is rapid with the child dying by age 3 to 5 years. Type (2) is similar except that there is also a skin rash with small red spots. It is thought to be inherited in a *recessive* manner. It can be diagnosed in the fetus following *amniocentesis*.

KOUSEFF, B.G. et al.(1976) Fucosidosis Type 2. Pediatrics, 57:205.
TROOST, J. et al (1977) Fucosidosis 1. Clinical and enzymological studies. Neuro-paediatrie, 8:155.

Full Scale Intelligence Quotient

In the *Weschler Intelligence Scale for Children* and the *Weschler Adult Intelligence Scale* the Verbal and Performance IQ scores are calculated as well as a Full Scale IQ score based on the sum of Verbal and Performance subtest scores.

Functional analysis

= *behaviour analysis.*

Functional behaviours / handicaps

It is important to know what a person can or cannot do in everyday living and these are called functional behaviours. Checklists of functional behaviours are more often useful in the assessment of a mentally handicapped person than measures of *intelligence quotient* or *mental age*. Types of checklists are *Adaptive Behavior Scale, Bereweeke, Borders assessment schedule, Gunzberg Progress Assessment Charts* and *Pathways to Independence.*

Functional Vision Inventory for the Severely Impaired

An inventory used for the assessment of vision in a multi-handicapped child in the areas of structural defects, reflexive reaction, eye movements, near and distance vision, visual field preference and visual perception. It also recommends goals, objectives and specific intervention strategies. These include ideas for activities to encourage early visual skills such as fixation, tracking and changing focus and then move on to more complex skills such as discrimination, figure-ground recognition and perspective. There is also a helpful discussion on the development and use of residual vision.

LANGLEY, M.B. (1980) Functional Vision Inventory for the Multiple and Severely Handicapped. Chicago: Stoelting Co.

Fundus

The back of the eye as seen by viewing through the pupil using an instrument known as an *ophthalmoscope*. It is possible to see the head of the *optic nerve* and blood vessels on the surface of the *retina*. The state of the retina can also be seen. Fundoscopy is a useful aid to diagnosis in many conditions.

Further education

Mentally handicapped people generally benefit from further education after leaving school. Like many other people, readiness to learn and willingness to concentrate are often improved in adult life. It is therefore important that suitable opportunities are available in colleges, evening classes, adult literacy schemes and, if appropriate, in the course of day-time occupation. In the U.K. many colleges of further education now provide courses for young people with special needs. Most of these are specially designed courses but some students are supported in ordinary courses. Link courses between school and college are usually available in the final school years and full-time courses are offered after leaving school. Adult education centres may provide a service to *adult training centres* and day centres.

BRADLEY, J. & HEGARTY, S. (1982) Stretching the System. London: Further Education Curriculum Review and Development Unit.

BROWNE, G. (1979) Continuing Education: A Programme for the Less Able in Colleges of Further Education. Manchester: National Elfrida Rathbone Society.

DEAN, L. & HEGARTY, S. (1984) Learning for Independence. Windsor: NFER/Nelson.

GRIFFITHS, M. et al (1985) Further education, adult education and self-advocacy. In: Mental Handicap. A Multidisciplinary Approach. Craft, M. et al (Eds.). London: Baillière Tindall. pp. 271–277.

HUTCHINSON, D. (1982) Work Preparation for the Handicapped. London: Croom Helm.

G

G-deletion 1
= *anti-mongolism.*

G6PD
= *glucose-6-phosphate dehydrogenase deficiency.*

GABA
= *gamma-aminobutyric acid.*

Galactosaemia
A condition which usually becomes evident in early infancy when the baby starts to vomit and is reluctant to feed. Lethargy, weight loss and *jaundice* follow. It is caused by deficiency of an *enzyme* necessary to convert galactose (found in milk) and galactose-1-phosphate to glucose in the body. As a result there is an accumulation of chemicals in the blood which damage the liver, kidneys, lens of the eye and brain. Galactose and a number of *amino acids* appear in the urine. If the condition is untreated liver damage, mental handicap and *cataracts* develop and death occurs early. If treated with a lactose-free diet soon after birth, physical health recovers and mental handicap may be prevented or reduced in severity. This condition is inherited from both parents who are carriers (*recessive inheritance*). The diagnosis may be made before birth using cells obtained by *amnio-centesis*. The carrier state can also be detected from *fibroblast culture*. There are some rarer forms of this condition in which the person is less severely affected.

FISHLER, K. et al (1980) Developmental aspects of galactosaemia from infancy to childhood. Clin. Pediat., 19:38.
KOMROWER, G.M. (1982) Galactosaemia thirty years on: The experience of a generation. J. Inherited Metab. Dis. 5 (suppl.2): 96.

MENKES, J.H. (1985) Metabolic diseases of the nervous system. In: Textbook of Child Neurology (3rd edit.). Philadelphia: Lea & Febiger. pp. 31–36.
SEGAL, S. (1983) Disorders of galactose metabolism. In: The Metabolic Basis of Inherited Disease (5th edit.). Stanbury, J.B. et al (Eds.). New York: McGraw-Hill. p.167.

Galactosylceramide lipidosis
= *Krabbe's disease.*

Gamma-aminobutyric acid
A substance involved in the transmission of information in the brain. It stabilizes and reduces the excitability of nerve cells. It is therefore thought to have an important role in preventing *seizures.*

GALE, K. & IADAROLA, M.J. (1980) Seizure protection and increased nerve terminal GABA: Delayed effects of GABA trans-aminase inhibition. Science, 208:288.
OLSEN, R.W. (1982) Drug interactions at the GABA receptor-ionophore complex. Ann. Rev. Pharmacol. Toxicol., 22:245.

Gangliosidoses
A group of rare disorders in which there are abnormalities of the chemical processes involving gangliosides. These are a type of fat found in the brain and nerve cells as well as in the other parts of the body. Mental handicap occurs in these *degenerative* conditions. *Tay-Sachs disease, Sandhoff's disease* and *generalized gangliosidosis* are the most common of these. In a few classifications *Niemann-Pick disease* is included. Generally the gangliosidoses and Niemann-Pick disease are regarded as subgroups of the *sphingolipidoses.*

MENKES, J.H. (1985) Metabolic diseases of the nervous system. In: Textbook of Child

Neurology (3rd edit.). Philadelphia: Lea & Febiger. pp. 60–68.

O'BRIEN, J.S. (1983) The gangliosidoses. In: The Metabolic Basis of Inherited Disease (5th edit.). Stanbury, J.B. et al (Eds.). New York: McGraw-Hill. p. 945.

SANDHOFF, K. & CONZELMANN, E. (1984) The biochemical basis of gangliosidoses. Neuropediat. 15: suppl. 85.

Gardenal

= *phenobarbitone.*

Gargoylism

= *Hurler's syndrome* and *Hunter's syndrome.*

GATE

= *Gestural Assessment of Thought and Expression.*

Gateway Clubs

The Federation of Gateway Clubs was established in 1966. These clubs provide mentally handicapped people in the U.K. with the opportunity to pursue leisure activities on an organized basis with voluntary assistance. Greater emphasis is now being placed on expanding the range of activities and opportunities and on fuller integration into ordinary community leisure activities. Gateway is recognized by the Department of Education and Science as a national voluntary youth and community organization.

Further information:
Royal Society for Mentally Handicapped Children and Adults, 123 Golden Lane, London EC1Y 0RT.

Gaucher's disease

A condition caused by a deficiency of an *enzyme* which deals with fatty substances (cerebrosides) in the body. The lack of this enzyme leads to the accumulation of various cerebrosides in the brain, liver, spleen, bone marrow and other tissues of the body. The infantile form of the disease becomes evident within the first 6 months of life with apathy, anaemia and loss of achievements. *Spasticity*

develops and there is rapid mental and physical deterioration leading to death at about 1 year of age. The juvenile form becomes apparent during the first ten years of life with intellectual deterioration, enlargement of liver and spleen, unsteadiness, spasticity and *epilepsy.* The chronic adult form of this disease is more common and rarely involves the brain.

There is no known treatment. The enzyme deficiency may be detected from *fibroblast culture.* The condition is inherited from both parents who are carriers (*recessive inheritance*). It can be detected in the fetus following *amniocentesis.* The carrier state can also be detected.

MENKES, J.H. (1985) Metabolic Diseases of the Nervous System in: Textbook of Child Neurology (3rd edit.). Philadelphia: Lea & Febiger. pp. 68–70.

SENGERS, R.C.A. et al (1975) Infantile Gaucher's disease: glucocerebroside deficiency in peripheral blood leucocytes and cultivated fibroblasts. Neuropediatrie, 6: 377–382.

Gene

The smallest part of a *chromosome* which can pass on a *hereditary* characteristic from parent to offspring. It carries the code for a sequence of *amino acids* and it is these that eventually determine the structural and chemical make-up of the body. They carry biochemical information to the cells and determine the kinds of proteins the cells will produce. These proteins serve as *enzymes* or catalysts of the many chemical reactions of the body. The genes therefore determine the potential limits of the physical and mental characteristics of each individual. Most genes occur in pairs and one member of each pair is contributed by one parent and the other by the other parent. The genes for some characteristics (*dominant genes*) can override the effects of the corresponding genes derived from the other parent (*recessive genes*). A recessive gene can express itself only when another recessive gene for the

Generic Skills Assessment Inventory

same characteristic is inherited from the other parent. The genes which cause some types of mental handicap are carried on the sex chromosomes and this is known as *sex-linked inheritance*. Many *syndromes* associated with mental handicap are due to abnormal genes.

General Intelligence Quotient (G.Q.)
This is derived from the *Griffiths Scale* and is based on the average of the quotients obtained in each of the five fields of development measured by this test. It provides an indication of the child's developmental level compared to other children of the same age.

Generalization
When a behaviour learnt in certain situations occurs spontaneously in other situations, generalization is said to have taken place. For example a child who has learnt to drink from one cup may generalize this skill and also drink from a cup of a different shape or colour. A child who has learnt to undress at home will usually undress at school without having to relearn the skill. Whereas generalization occurs readily in most children this may not be the case with a mentally handicapped child. *Autistic* children find generalization particularly difficult. This needs to be taken into account when planning training programmes and to reduce such problems it is wise to teach skills in as natural a setting as possible. Once a behaviour has been learnt in more than one situation it is usual for generalization to occur increasingly rapidly in other situations. Generalization of behaviour is an important issue in *behaviour modification*.

STOKES, T.F. & BAER, D.M. (1977) An implicit technology of generalization. J. Appl. Behav. Anal., 10:349–367.

Generalized gangliosidosis
This occurs in three forms. Type 1 is commonest and resembles *Hurler's syndrome* (pseudo-Hurler's syndrome); Type 2

resembles the late infantile form of *Tay-Sachs disease* and Type 3 is characterized by unsteadiness of the *cerebellar* type. In all forms there is storage of abnormally high levels of substances (gangliosides) in the brain and other organs. This is due to a deficiency of the *enzyme* beta-galactosidase. There is no available treatment but it is possible to diagnose following *fibroblast culture*. It can be detected in the *fetus* following *amniocentesis*.

FELDGES, A. et al (1973) GM1-gangliosidosis. Clinical aspects and biochemistry. Helv. Paediatr. Acta, 28:511.
LOWDEN, J.A. et al (1973) Prenatal diagnosis of Gm1-gangliosidosis. New Engl. J. Med., 288:225.
O'BRIEN, J.S. (1969) Generalized gangliosidosis. J. Pediatr., 75:167.

Generalized reinforcer
A term used in *behaviour modification* for a reward which does not have an intrinsic value but which can be used to obtain something which is of value to the individual. *Tokens*, points, stars and money are all examples.

Generalized seizures
These are *seizures* which involve loss of consciousness. *Grand-mal convulsions, absence seizures, myoclonic seizures, akinetic seizures* and *infantile spasms* are examples.

Generic Skills Assessment Inventory
This inventory is divided into 'People skills' and 'Object skills' across four levels of performance on five scales: Object relationships, Representation, Dyadic interaction, Expressive communication and Comprehension and imitation. It covers the developmental range from birth to 2 years and is standardized on a normal population. It was developed for severely handicapped students with language impairments and is prescriptive. It allows great flexibility in administration and scoring. Age scores are not obtained but levels of competence in the five areas can be ascertained.

McLEAN, J. et al (1981) Process-oriented Educational Programs for the Severely / Profoundly Handicapped Adolescent, Bureau of Child Research, University of Kansas, Parsons Research Center, Parsons, Kansas.

Genetic
Determined by the *genes*.

Genetic counselling
The identification of the risk of a person being affected by an inherited disorder and the imparting of this information. In the past it largely relied on observation of the recurrence risks of a particular disorder in a family and a knowledge of the laws of inheritance. Recent advances have improved the accuracy and predictability of counselling especially for single-gene disorders. Genetic counselling may be sought for many reasons but generally because a suspected genetic disorder has occurred and the risks for other members of the family need to be identified. There may be concern about more general risk factors such as age of mother or marriage between cousins.

Full investigation and diagnosis of affected individuals is essential and investigation of other members of the family may be necessary. On the basis of the family history, appropriate tests and a knowledge of the literature, an estimate of recurrence risk is made. Carrier detection is possible in many rare conditions and although screening of the whole population for carriers is uneconomical, for at-risk individuals or groups such screening and counselling may be appropriate. If both parents are carriers of a *recessive gene* then diagnosis by *amniocentesis* and *fibroblast culture* may be possible and *abortion* can be carried out if necessary. Similarly the identification of a mother as a carrier of an X-linked disorder can lead to abortion of affected fetuses or of all male children. Accurate diagnosis before birth is now possible for about 60 single-gene disorders some of which cause mental handicap.

The counsellor may assist in the process of reaching a decision concerning appropriate action. Decisions may include whether to marry, have another baby, use *contraceptive* measures, seek *sterilization*, adopt, have artificial insemination from a donor, have amniocentesis or have a therapeutic abortion. Having understood the information, its implications and possible alternatives, the decision-making process may still not be easy for the client because of emotional reactions to the information. The counselling process may extend to other members of the family at risk of developing the disorder or of having affected children. Genetic screening programmes to identify individuals with treatable genetic diseases and parents at risk of having children with severe genetic diseases, are an important element of genetic counselling programmes. The development of genetic counselling as a health care service raises complex legal, moral and ethical issues. Skilled counselling is very important. In many countries medical genetics is now a recognized speciality. In the U.K. Consultant Clinical Geneticists are qualified doctors with a high level of relevant experience. The American Society of Human Genetics has set up The American Board of Medical Genetics to accredit Geneticists and Genetic Associates.

BIRD, J. (Ed.) (1975) Genetic Counselling in Relation to Mental Retardation. Oxford: Pergamon Press.

CAPRON, A.M. et al (Eds.) (1979) Genetic Counselling: Facts, Values and Norms. Birth Defects Original Article Series 15(2).

EMERY, A.E.H. & PULLEN, I.M. (Eds.) (1984) Psychological Aspects of Genetic Counselling. London: Academic Press.

FALEK, A. (1980) Psychodynamics in genetic counselling of families with mental retardation. In: Prevention of Mental Retardation and other Developmental Disabilities. McCormack, M.K. (Ed.). New York: Marcel Dekker.

HSIA, Y.E. et al (Eds.) (1979) Counselling in Genetics. New York: Alan R. Liss.

WINTER, R.M. (1988) Common problems in genetic counselling. Hosp. Update, 14(2): 1222–1225.

Genetic disorders

Disorders caused by the presence of one or more abnormal *genes*. Many such disorders are a cause of mental handicap. See also *genetic counselling, recessive inheritance, dominant inheritance, sex-linked inheritance*.

FRASER, F.C. & NORA, J.J. (1986) Genetics of Man. Philadelphia: Lea & Febiger.

Genetic engineering

A rapidly developing biological science used in human *genetics* for mapping *genes* on *chromosomes* and for making *diagnoses* before birth (after *amniocentesis*). It has developed following the discovery of *enzymes* which will cut the DNA molecule (the basis of the gene) at specific sites (recombinant DNA techniques). Specific genes can then be cloned to identify their structure in unprecedented detail and to examine the details of their regulation and evolution.

WILLIAMSON, R. (Ed.) (1981) Genetic Engineering. London: Academic Press.

Genetics

The science which deals with the origin of the characteristics of an individual or the study of heredity.

FRASER, F.C. & NORA, J.J. (1986) Genetics of Man. Philadelphia: Lea & Febiger.

Genital hypoplasia

= *hypogenitalism*.

Genitourinary anomalies

Abnormal formation or underdevelopment of the reproductive system or the organs of urination.

Genu recurvatum

An abnormality of the knee joint allowing it to bend backward to a limited extent.

Genu valgum

An abnormality of the knee joint causing the leg to bend inward at the knee (knock knee). This may occur in *Carpenter's syndrome, de Lange syndrome, Engelmann's disease, mucopolysaccharidoses* and several other rare conditions associated with mental handicap.

Genu varum

An abnormality of the knee joint causing the leg to bend outward at the knee (bow leg).

German measles

See *Rubella syndrome*.

German's syndrome

Infants with this condition have *failure to thrive*, small stature, floppiness, delayed development and frequent nose, throat and chest infections. The cry of the baby is weak, high pitched and monotonous. The sides of the mouth are down-turned and the high arched roof of the mouth and small tongue may make swallowing difficult in early infancy. The eyes are widely spaced with *epicanthic folds* and the ears are low set. Various abnormalities of bones and muscles have been reported including the skull shape known as *doliochocephaly*. The cause of this condition is unknown.

GERMAN, J. et al (1975) Generalized dysmorphia of a similar type in two unrelated babies. Birth Defects Original Article Series 11(2):34.

Gesell development schedules

These schedules provide standards of normal development of motor activity, adaptive behaviour, language and social behaviour at various ages. There is one schedule for infants from birth to 3 years and one for children from 15 months to 6 years. These provide an indication of developmental progress. The child's level of functioning is compared with developmental norms and is reported in terms of developmental age and developmental quotient (D.Q.). The relatively heavy emphasis on motor and physical skills is a limitation. They have been modified for the *Griffiths Scale*.

GESELL, A. & AMATRUDA, C.S. (1947) Developmental Diagnosis, Normal and Abnormal Child Development: Clinical Methods and Practical Applications. (2nd edit). New York: Paul B. Hoeber.

Gestural Assessment of Thought and Expression

A method of assessing readiness for *communication*, using gesture or signing, designed for use with multi-handicapped children. Seven components of non-verbal communication are assessed: turn-taking, signalling, *object permanence*, social causality, imitation, behaviours relating to objects and sign behaviour. It covers the developmental range from birth to 3 years and records the most rudimentary to the most sophisticated gestural communication. It was standardized on normal hearing children, *deaf-blind*, multi-sensorily disabled and severely mentally handicapped children. It is administered by observing the child in familiar environments over a period up to 5 days and by directly eliciting target behaviours. The performance profile is used for selecting teaching objectives and activities.

LANGLEY, M.B. (1984) The Gestural Approach to Thought and Expression: An Index to Nonverbal Communicative Behaviours. St. Petersburg, Florida: Nina Harris Exceptional Education Center.

Gesture systems

Communication by gesture has been used successfully with mentally handicapped people who have problems in speaking. Gesture systems use movements which usually represent the action or object that they symbolize. Gestures generally involve more body movements than *sign language* and, unlike signs, do not conform to language rules. Examples of gesture systems used with severely mentally handicapped

non-speakers include mime, generally understood gestures and *Amer-Ind*.

BALICK, S. et al (1976) Mime in language therapy and clinical training. Arch. Phys. Med. Rehab., 57:35–38.

DANILOFF, J. & SCHAFER, A. (1981) A gestural communication program for severely and profoundly handicapped children. Language, Speech and Hearing Services in Schools, 12:258–267.

LEVETT, L.M. (1971) A method of communication for non-speaking severely subnormal children: trial results. Brit. J. Dis. Commun. 6:125–128.

Gigantism

A large stature and head (*cerebral gigantism*) occurs in association with mental handicap in *Sotos' syndrome*.

Gillian-Turner syndrome

= *fragile-X syndrome*.

Gingival hyperplasia / hypertrophy

= *gum hypertrophy*.

Glaucoma

A condition in which raised pressure of the fluid inside the eye destroys the *optic nerve* fibres. It is caused by blockage of the part of the eye where the fluids filter out into neighbouring blood vessels. This is the sharp angle at the junction of the *iris* and the clear front of the eye (*cornea*). If the angle becomes closed, as may occur if the iris is pushed forward at its outer margin against the cornea, or in congenital abnormalities of the eye, the filtration stops and pressure builds up. If untreated there is deteriorating vision leading to blindness in that eye. Operation is usually successful but if it is not possible, drugs may help the condition to a limited extent. Glaucoma may occur in a number of conditions associated with mental handicap including *rubella syndrome, toxoplasmosis, homocystinuria, Norries syndrome, Rieger's syndrome, Laurence-Moon-Biedl syndrome, Pierre Robin syndrome, Lowe's syndrome,*

Sturge-Weber syndrome, cerebro-hepato-renal syndrome, Aniridia-Wilm's tumour syndrome and *Noonan's syndrome*.

Globoid cell leucodystrophy
= *Krabbe's disease*.

Glossoptosis
A condition in which the tongue easily falls backward and downward in the mouth obstructing the airway. This occurs in infants with *Pierre Robin syndrome* due to the small jaw bone and weak muscles.

Glucose-6-phosphate dehydrogenase deficiency
The deficiency of this *enzyme* predisposes affected males to respond to certain substances and infections by developing an anaemia and *jaundice* (caused by destruction of red blood cells). Aspirin, sulphonamides, some antimalarial drugs and other less used drugs may cause this. Jaundice may be present at birth if the mother has taken these drugs during pregnancy. It may cause damage to the brain resulting in mental handicap. Further brain damage may be prevented by avoiding these drugs. Several different forms of this condition have been described. It is inherited in a *sex-linked* manner. Type A occurs most frequently in negro races. Type B is more severe and occurs in the Mediterranean peoples and in orientals.

Glucosphingolipid lipidosis
= *Fabry's disease*.

Glucosyl ceramide lipidosis
= *Gaucher's disease*.

Glue ear
A condition in which the middle ear is filled with a viscous fluid. This is an after-effect of ear infections and impairs hearing. The fluid is removed by an operation known as *myringotomy*. The viscosity of the middle ear fluid removed at myringotomy is very variable but in children with *Down's syndrome* it is nearly always very thick or almost solid. The reasons for this are not known. The fluid often recurs and to prevent this, tiny tubes (T-tubes or grommets) are usually inserted into the eardrum in order to keep the middle ear aerated and free from infection.

FRIEDMANN, I. (1987) Catarrhal otitis media (Glue ear). Hosp. Update, 13(10): 797–804.

Glycinaemia
= *hyperglycinaemia*.

Glycogen storage disorders / glycogenoses
This is a group of eight disorders in which there is a problem with the storage of glucose as glycogen. There is either an inability to form normal glycogen or to convert stored glycogen back into glucose. Glycogen accumulates in the tissues and blood levels of glucose are inadequate. For some disorders in this group there is no known treatment and death occurs in infancy or early childhood. In others there is no intellectual impairment and survival into adult life. In two disorders mental handicap is evident. These are *Pompe's disease* Type II and *limit dextrinosis* Type III.

HOWELL, R.R. & WILLIAMS, J.C. (1983) The glycogen storage diseases. In: The Metabolic Basis of Inherited Disease (5th edit.). Stanbury, J.B. et al (Eds.). New York: McGraw-Hill.

Gm1-gangliosidosis
= *generalized gangliosidosis*.

Gm2-gangliosidosis
= *Tay-Sachs disease* and *Sandhoff's disease*.

Gm3-gangliosidosis
One of the *gangliosidoses* in which there is poor physical development, coarse facial appearance, large tongue, overgrowth of gums, clawing of fingers and enlarged liver

and spleen. Deterioration is rapid and death occurs in infancy.

MAX, S.R. et al (1974) GM3 (hematoside) sphingolipodystrophy. New Engl. J. Med., 291:929.

Goal analysis

The function of goal analysis, as used in mental handicap services, is to establish, analyse and make explicit the goals of the service based on the special needs of its clients. This assists in the process of *evaluation*.

Goal planning / setting

This is a method of providing specific behavioural targets for a person. There are many types of goal-planning systems in use, generally based on an initial assessment of a person's skills which is then used to set targets or goals to help tackle needs or problems. Goals are set for specific items of behaviour but if necessary are split into small steps that are easily attainable. The goal plan should be written down and should also state clearly who will do what and when. Goals are reviewed at regular predetermined intervals and new ones set as a result of the review.

One of the best known examples is the *Portage system* but there are many other similar systems. *Individual programme plans* are a feature of many modern service provisions and are essentially goal planning in nature.

HOUTS, P. & SCOTT, R. (1975) Goal Planning with Developmentally Disabled Persons. Hershey, Pa.: The Mitton Hershey Medical Center.

Goitre

An enlargement of the thyroid gland in the neck which sometimes indicates an abnormality of function of the gland. It is associated with *hypothyroidism* in *congenital goitrous cretinism* due to *enzyme* deficiency in the thyroid gland. The degree of hypothyroidism varies widely as does the impairment of intelligence. The association of deafness (caused by a defect in nerve conduction) with goitrous hypothyroidism has been termed *Pendred's syndrome*. Mental handicap, *deaf-mutism* and *spasticity* are also seen in children with endemic goitrous cretinism which is caused by iodine deficiency in the diet and was a common cause of *cretinism* in some areas of the world. It has been prevented in these areas by the introduction of iodised salt.

Goldenhar's syndrome

A condition in which defects of the eyes and ears are associated with abnormalities of the spine, heart and lungs. The commonest eye abnormalities are cysts and defects (*coloboma*) of the upper eyelids and iris. The ear is usually abnormal in shape often with skin tags or pits in the skin in front of it. Deafness often occurs. There may be a prominent forehead, flat cheek bones, small receding chin and a difference in shape between the two sides of the face. The corners of the mouth may be extended with *cleft palate* and tongue abnormalities. About 10% of people with this condition are mentally handicapped, usually mildly. In some cases it is inherited from one parent (*dominant inheritance*).

GORLIN, R.J. et al (1963) Oculoauriculo-vertebral dysplasia. J. Pediatr., 63:991–999.
MELLOR, D.H. et al (1973) Goldenhar's syndrome: oculo-auriculo-vertebral dysplasia. Arch. Dis. Childh., 48:537.
SUMMIT, R.L. (1969) Familial Goldenhar syndrome. Birth Defects Original Article Series, 2:106–109.

Goltz's syndrome / Goltz-Gorlin syndrome

A condition in which there are abnormalities of the skin, nails, teeth and bones. The skin is thin in places so that the underlying fat bulges through. Pigmentation is patchy and may be reduced or increased. Abnormalities of the blood vessels may show as red areas through the skin. The hair is usually thin, sparse and short. Small, absent and abnormally arranged teeth are common with deficient enamel. Thin poorly formed nails are common. Abnormalities of the bones, especially of the spine, collar bones and fingers, and of the eyes frequently occur. Most affected people are short and thin. Mental handicap, deafness and *epilepsy* are quite common in this condition. It is thought to be inherited and occurs much more commonly in females. The exact mode of inheritance is not known.

GOLTZ, R.W. et al (1970) Focal dermal hypoplasia syndrome. A review of the literature and report of two cases. Arch. Derm., 101:1–11.
WARBURG, M. (1970) Focal dermal hypoplasia. Ocular and general manifestations with a survey of the literature. Acta Ophthalmol., 48:525–536.

Goodenough Draw-a-person Test
A child's drawing of a person is scored according to criteria of intellectual maturity. This is a simple way of assessing the *mental age* of a child in terms of *visuo-motor* skills, *perception* and conceptual skills.

HARRIS, D.B. (1963) Children's Drawings as Measures of Intellectual Maturity. New York: Harcourt, Brace & World.

Gorlin syndrome
= *basal cell naevus syndrome.*

Gorlin-Psaume syndrome
= *oro-facial digital syndrome I.*

Gower's phenomenon
In 1881 Gower wrote that 'The effect of a convulsion on the nerve centres is such as to render the occurrence of another more easy, to intensify the predisposition that already exists. Thus every fit may be said to be, in part, the result of those which have preceded it, the cause of those which follow it.' This argument for the early and active treatment of *epilepsy* is still upheld by some experts.

SHORUON, S.D. & REYNOLDS, E.H. (1982) Early prognosis of epilepsy. Brit. Med. J., 285:1699–1701.

G.Q.
= *General Intelligence Quotient.*

Graded change
A gradual alteration of one aspect of the environment in order to obtain a required response. It is a technique used in *behaviour modification*. A common example is the use of feeder mugs as an intermediate stage between the bottle and an open cup. Another example is the treatment of attachment to a blanket or similar object in a child by cutting small pieces off in gradual stages until it is so small that the child abandons it.

MARCHANT, R. et al (1974) Graded change in the treatment of the behaviour of autistic children. J. Child Psychol. Psychiat., 15: 221–227.
WICKINGS, S. et al (1974) Modification of behaviour using a shaping procedure. Apex, 2:6.

Graduated guidance
See *overcorrection.*

Grand-mal convulsion
A type of *seizure* in which there is a tonic stage in which all the muscles tighten and breathing stops (rarely lasting more than 30 seconds) followed by a clonic stage in which there is short, sharp jerking of muscles causing irregular movements of the limbs. Throughout these two stages the person is unconscious and may be incontinent. This is usually followed by heavy sleep or confused behaviour from which normal consciousness is regained. In some types of *epilepsy* a grand-mal convulsion is preceded by an *aura*.
Prolonged or repeated grand-mal convulsions are referred to as *status epilepticus*. During a grand-mal convulsion the person should be laid on his or her side in a comfortable position as soon as possible.

Obtain medical help if status epilepticus develops.

Grasp reflex

The fingers or toes of a baby close into a grasp when the palm or sole is stroked. This reflex is usually lost by about the 4th month of life as the nervous system develops. It may persist longer in children with *developmental delay*.

Greenfield's disease

= late infantile *metachromatic leucodystrophy*.

Gregg's syndrome

= *rubella syndrome*.

Greig's syndrome

A condition in which there is an excessive distance between the eyes with a broad and flattened bridge of the nose (*hypertelorism*). This is due to overgrowth of the bone in the base of the skull (sphenoid bone). The roof of the mouth is usually high and narrow. In some cases the fingers and toes are broad and stubby. It is often associated with *congenital heart disease* and mental handicap. This condition is usually inherited from both parents who are carriers (*recessive inheritance*). Life expectancy is normal. Hypertelorism occurs more commonly as a feature of other conditions associated with mental handicap.

GAARD, R.A. (1961) Ocular hypertelorism of Greig: A congenital craniofacial deformity. Am. J. Orthodont., 47:205.
SALMON, M.A. (1978) Developmental Defects and Syndromes. Aylesbury: HM+M. pp. 28–29.

Grief reaction

= *bereavement reaction*.

Griffiths scale

A set of developmental scales designed for handicapped as well as normal children and modified from the *Gesell development schedules*. There are five subscales: Locomotor, Per-sonal-Social, Hearing and Speech, Hand / Eye and Performance (which includes the ability to reason and to manipulate material intelligently). It covers the developmental range from birth to 8 years. It is standardized on a normal population of children but handicapped and multi-handicapped children were included in the sample. It is flexible and the practical items are easy to administer. There are profiles in the manual for the performance of sensorily impaired children. It is advised that training in its administration should be given to ensure reliability. It provides a *general intelligence quotient* based on the average of the quotients obtained in each of the five subscales.

GRIFFITHS, R. (1970) The Abilities of Young Children. London: Child Development Research Centre.

Grinding of teeth

= *bruxism*.

Grommet

See *glue ear*.

Gross motor skills

Skills involving large movements of body and limbs as compared to *fine motor skills*. Gross motor skills include sitting, running, walking, jumping, climbing, etc. Their acquisition may be delayed in children who are mentally handicapped and delayed or permanently impaired in children who are physically handicapped by conditions such as *cerebral palsy*.

Group homes

In North America the term 'group home' has been applied to boarding houses, hostels, halfway houses and modified motels and hotels. Such board or care facilities may cater for 15 or more residents. The average size of group homes has tended to be less in recent years. In the U.K. it generally refers to a much smaller group of people (usually 2 to 6) living in ordinary domestic housing. In the past these were generally unstaffed houses for more able people who were supported by community services or by the hospital from which they came. Nowadays the concept is also applied to staffed houses (*staffed domestic homes* and *family group homes*).

GATHERCOLE, C. (1981) Group Homes – Staffed and Unstaffed. Kidderminster: British Institute of Mental Handicap.
JANICKI, M.P. et al (1983) Availability of group homes for persons with mental retardation in the United States. Ment. Retardation, 21:45–51.
MALIN, N. (1982) Group homes for mentally handicapped adults: resident's views on contacts and support. Brit. J. Ment. Subn., 28(1):29–34.

Group therapy

A group set up for therapeutic purposes. Such a group may be established to help parents come to terms with having a handicapped child. It provides the opportunity for sharing experiences and learning from each other in a supportive setting. A group may also be set up to help mentally handicapped people with adjustment and/or interpersonal problems. The relationships set up within the group provide a learning and adjustment experience as well as offering support.

Groups

1. Parent groups are an important source of support to many parents with disabled children. These may be part of a larger organization or small local informal groups. Professional workers often help to organize and lead such groups which may have an educational purpose as in parent *workshops*. Parent groups may become pressure groups to attempt to improve local services or to influence policies.

HOLLAND, J.M. & HATTERSLEY, J. (1980) Parent support groups for the families of mentally handicapped children. Child: Care, Health and Development, 6:279–289.
TAVORIMA, J.B. (1975) Relative effectiveness of behavioural and reflective group counselling with parents of mentally retarded children. J. Cons. Clin. Psychol., 43(1): 22–31.
TAVORIMA, J.B. et al (1976) Participant evaluations of the effectiveness of their parent counselling groups. Ment. Retardation, 14(6):8–9.

2. Groups may be established for mentally handicapped people because social relationships are an essential aspect of development. Participation in groups is therefore an important learning experience. There are many groups such as youth groups and interest groups available in the local community as well as special groups set up for mentally handicapped people. See also *Gateway clubs* and *group therapy*.

Gruber's syndrome
= *Meckel syndrome.*

Guardianship

In law a guardian is a person who has the custody of a minor. In the case of mentally handicapped adults, however, the term has other connotations. In England and Wales the *Mental Health Act (1983)* under Section 7 authorizes the reception into guardianship of any person who has attained the age of 16 years who is suffering from mental illness, *mental impairment, severe mental impairment* or *psychopathic disorder* which warrants his reception into guardianship. The person may be received into the guardianship of either a social services authority or of any other person (including the applicant) approved by the social services authority. This is provided that it is in the interests of the welfare of the person or for the protection of other persons. Section 8 of the Act describes the method of application and the need for medical recommendation. If accepted by the local social services, the application confers on the guardian the power to require the person to reside in a specified place, to attend at specified places and times for medical treatment, occupation, education and training and power to require access to be given at any place where the person is residing to any registered medical practitioner, approved social worker or other specified person. There are safeguards built into the Act in Sections 9 and 10.

In the *Mental Health Act (1959)* guardianship was intended to ensure that people could be treated in the community with some sort of overview but results were poor and guardianship was hardly ever used. The new regulations reduce the powers of guardians and thereby reduce the burden on local authorities. This could result in its being used more frequently in the future. On the other hand there is a general move away from the paternalism of guardianship towards the partisanship of *advocacy*.

GUNN, M.J. (1984) The Mental Health Act 1983 – guardianship and hospitalization. Mental Handicap, 12:8–9.

Guardianship order

See *hospital order* and *guardianship*.

Guilt

Many parents experience guilt about having a handicapped child. In the past this was reinforced by the attitudes of society but nowadays parents are always repeatedly reassured by professional workers that it is not their fault (with the obvious exception of *child abuse*) and that anyone can have a handicapped child. Even in the case of *genetic* conditions it is explained that everyone carries abnormal *genes* and it is unfortunate if the genetic make-up of the child includes a combination of genes which leads to a disability. Nevertheless, despite these reassurances, some parents continue to experience irrational guilt as a reaction to having a disabled child. This is part of the process of coming to terms with the problem but if guilt is severe or protracted it may interfere with healthy adjustment.

Gum hypertrophy / hyperplasia

Overgrowth of the gums. This is most commonly seen as a side-effect of *phenytoin* especially when the blood levels of the drug are high. It may require surgical excision by a dental surgeon.

Gunzberg Progress Assessment Charts

A series of checklists which record development in four areas: self-help, communication, socialization and occupation. A number of skills are included under each area and marked on charts which provide a clear visual comparison of skills in different areas and makes skill deficits evident. It is also easy to compare charts so that progress can be seen. Separate charts are used for different age groups and levels of functioning. The Primary Progress Assessment Chart (PPAC) is for very young children and for profoundly handicapped people. The Progress Assessment Chart 1 (PAC1) is for the age group 6–16 years with a modified form (M/PAC1) for children with *Down's syndrome*. The Progress Assessment Chart 2 (PAC2) is for teenagers and for older mentally handicapped people. A Progress Evaluation Index has been developed for use with each Progress Assessment Chart to enable the achievements of an individual on that chart to be compared with the average attainments of other mentally handicapped people of comparable intelligence. The emphasis is on assessment, goal setting and evaluation on a continuous basis.

GUNZBERG, H.C. (1963) Progress Assessment Charts. London: N.A.M.H.
GUNZBERG, H.C. (1966) The Primary Assessment of Social Development. Birmingham: SEFA Publications.
GUNZBERG, H.C. (1972) Progress Assessment Charts (P.A.C.) Manual. Birmingham: SEFA Publications.

Guthrie Test

This is a laboratory test used in the diagnosis of *phenylketonuria*. A sample of blood is taken between 6 and 14 days of age and absorbed by thick filter paper onto a disc which is dried. This is then autoclaved and placed for incubation on a special substance. This is a gel (agar) in which a microorganism (Bacillus subtilis) is suspended with a substance to inhibit its growth. If phenylalanine is added in sufficient concentration it overcomes the effect of the inhibitor and the organism grows. The extent to which it grows is a measure of the concentration of phenylalanine. Modifications of this method are used for the recognition of *histidinaemia, maple-syrup urine disease* and *galactosaemia*. Its use other than for phenylketonuria is cumbersome and expensive in laboratory time and *Scriver chemical methods* are increasingly used.

GUTHRIE, R. & SUSI, A. (1963) A simple phenylalanine method of detecting phenylketonuria in large populations of new born infants. Pediatrics, 32:338.

Gynaecomastia / gynecomastia

Abnormal enlargement of the male breast which may be associated with female bodily proportions in a few conditions in which there are abnormal sex *chromosomes*. Examples are *Klinefelter's syndrome, XXYY syndrome* and *XXXY syndrome* in all of which mental handicap may occur. Gynaecomastia may also occur as a side-effect of certain drugs. These include *cyproterone acetate* and *phenothiazine* tranquilizers such as *chlorpromazine*.

Gyrus

A fold of the surface of the brain. Certain gyri of the brain are associated with particular functions. For example the precentral gyrus is part of the *frontal lobe* of the brain and is a major area for the initiation of movements of the body. Gyri are absent or abnormal in *lissencephaly*.

H

Habilitation

This is the process by which individuals acquire and maintain the life skills necessary to cope with the demands of self, others and the environment and raise their levels of physical, mental and social functioning. As a concept it recognizes that mentally handicapped people, like everyone else, undergo behavioural changes that are influenced by learning and living environments. It stems from a developmental model which believes that all mentally handicapped people can benefit from education and training.

BELAMY, G.T. (Ed.) (1976) Habilitation of Severely and Profoundly Retarded: Reports from the Specialized Training Program. Eugene, Center on Human Development, University of Oregon.
BERNSTEIN, G.S. et al (1981) Behavioral Habilitation through Proactive Programming. Baltimore: Paul H. Brookes.
ROSEN, M. et al (1977) Habilitation of the Handicapped. Baltimore: University Park Press.
WHELAN, E. (1985) The habilitation of adults. In: Mental Deficiency. The changing outlook (4th edit.). Clarke, M.E. et al (Eds.). London: Methuen. pp. 686–714.

Habit training

1. The acquisition of socially specified behaviour patterns mainly related to eating, continence, sleep and dress.
2. In *behaviour modification* it is often used as a description of one of the most commonly used methods of training a child to be continent of urine. The child is taken to the toilet at regular intervals (between a half and one hour) and sat there for several minutes. If he or she urinates a reward is immediately given. This may teach the child to use the toilet but it does not necessarily teach him or her to stay dry in between and rewards for dry pants may be necessary for this. The habit training method does not work with all mentally handicapped people and other more intensive *toilet training* methods may be required.

YULE, W. & CARR, J. (1980) Behaviour Modification for the Mentally Handicapped. London: Croom Helm. pp. 135–136.

Haemangioma / hemangioma

= *angioma*.

Haematuria

Blood in the urine. This occurs in conditions in which the kidneys are affected including *Lesch-Nyhan syndrome* and *hydroxyprolinaemia* which are associated with mental handicap.

Haemolytic disease of the newborn

Incompatibility of the blood of the fetus with that of the mother (usually due to the mother being Rhesus negative and the baby Rhesus positive) resulting in the destruction of the blood of the fetus (haemolysis) by antibodies formed by the mother. This leads to anaemia and *jaundice* in the baby which can cause widespread brain damage if the baby survives, but it is particularly likely to cause *sensori-neural deafness* and *athetosis*. In recent years the injection of mothers with antibodies obtained from previously immunized mothers destroys any fetal blood cells before the mother can make antibodies against them. Improved *antenatal* care to detect 'at risk' mothers has resulted in haemolytic disease of the newborn becoming uncommon and when it does occur it can usually be successfully treated by exchange blood transfusion of the baby at birth. Consequently this is now a very rare cause of mental handicap.

FRASER, F.C. & NORA, J.J. (1986) Genetics of Man. Philadelphia: Lea & Febiger. pp. 255–257.
PHIBBS, R.H. (1977) Haemolytic disease of the newborn. In: Pediatrics (16th edit.) Rudolph, A.M. (Ed.) New York: Appleton-Century-Crofts.

Haemorrhage
See *cerebral haemorrage*.

Haeussermann Scale of Developmental Potential of Preschool Children
A structured interview and observation used to assess sensory processes, fine motor, receptive and expressive communication abilities, motor planning, concept of self, self-help functions, perceptual abilities, the ability to abstract above the level of identity, the ability to arrive at a solution by the process of elimination, spatial reconstruction of configuration done mentally, counting, the ability to shift from previous mind set and rate of learning. It is a clinical assessment and does not provide standardization data but is based on 25 years of experience with handicapped, including multiply handicapped, children. It covers developmental levels from 2 to 6 years and provides directions for assessing lower functioning children. The manual specifies the concepts tapped by each item and suggests numerous innovative ways of eliciting the concepts from the child. The tactile, auditory and visual motor screening items are also very useful.

HAEUSSERMANN, E. (1958) Developmental Potential for Preschool Children. New York: Grune & Stratton.

Hallermann-Streiff syndrome
People with this condition have an unusual appearance with a prominent brow. The back of the head is flat. The nose is long with a thin tip and the chin, mouth and tongue are small. The eyes are small, *cataracts* and other abnormalities are commonly present at birth. The ears are low-set and the cheeks are flat. Teeth erupt irregularly and are often malformed or absent. Abnormalities of the jaw joint may occur. The roof of the mouth is high and narrow. The skin is thin and the hair is thin and sparse. Genitals tend to be underdeveloped. The stature is short. Mental handicap, from mild to severe, occurs in about 16% of people with this condition. A few *familial* cases have occurred and it may be inherited from one parent (*dominant inheritance*). It more often arises as a fresh mutation.

STEELE, R.W. & BASS, J.W. (1970) Hallermann-Streiff syndrome. Clinical and prognostic considerations. Am. J. Dis. Child, 120:462.
SUZUKI, Y. et al (1970) Hallermann-Streiff syndrome. Dev. Med. Child Neurol., 12: 469–506.

Hallervorden-Spatz disease
There is considerable variability in time of onset (usually before 10 years) and in the major manifestation of this condition. There is usually progressive impairment of walking caused by a *club-foot* deformity of the feet, rigidity of the legs and slowing and reduction of movement. Slurring of speech and mental deterioration also occur. About half the people affected have abnormal movements (*choreo-athetosis*). It is slowly progressive with death 10–20 years after it first becomes evident. It is thought to be inherited from both parents who are carriers (*recessive inheritance*).

DOOLING, E.C. et al (1974) Hallervorden-Spatz syndrome. Arch. Neurol., 30: 70.
VAKILI, S. et al (1977) Hallervorden-Spatz syndrome. Arch. Neurol., 34:729.

Hallucination
An apparent perception of an external object when no such object is present. Such perceptions may be heard, seen or felt. Hallucinations occur mainly in confusional

states and in *psychoses* especially *schizophrenia*. People who are mentally handicapped can have difficulty in describing hallucinatory experiences.

Hallux-broad thumb syndrome
= *Rubinstein-Taybi syndrome*.

Hallux valgus
A deformity in which the big toe points toward the other toes making the joint protuberant. It may occur in *arthrogryposis*, *club-foot*, and *cerebral palsy* all of which may be associated with mental handicap. If severe it will interfere with walking and cause discomfort.

HALO
= *Hampshire Assessment for Living with Others*.

Haloperidol
One of the *butyrophenone* group of drugs used in the treatment of *mania* and *schizophrenia*. It is a tranquillizer and can be used for the treatment of behavioural disturbances and *anxiety states*. It is also used in low doses for the treatment of tics and stuttering. Sudden introduction can cause drowsiness and low blood pressure. The most common side-effects are muscle rigidity, spasms and tremor (*extrapyramidal signs*). It may be necessary to give drugs to counteract these. Other effects such as involuntary move-ments (*akathisia, tardive dyskinesia*) may also occur. Allergic reactions are rare. It can also be given in a liquid form and as a long-acting injection.

VAISANEN, K. et al (1981) Haloperidol, thioridazine and placebo in mentally sub-normal patients – serum levels and clinical effects. Acta Psychiat. Scand., 63:262–271.

Hamartoma
A benign tumour present at birth and consisting of an abnormal mixture of tissues arising as a developmental defect. Many hamartomas may be present in *Von Reckling-hausen's disease* and *tuberose sclerosis* both of which are associated with mental handicap.

Hamartoses
= *neurocutaneous syndromes*.

Hampshire Assessment for Living with Others
A system of detailed assessment useful for identifying the residential and training needs of mentally handicapped adults. Each skill can be rated at four levels of independ-ence. Other items are on a multiple-choice basis. As well as a manual there is a book of 'Behavioural Anchors' that gives detailed descriptions of each level of independence on each item. It covers self-care, domestic skills, community living skills, communi-cation, personality and social adjustment, personal relations, use of leisure, health / disability, group membership and employ-ment. The mentally handicapped person's own evaluation can be included as part of the assessment. Visual profiles can be drawn as bar charts showing service requirements. Training needs are recorded on a separate sheet.
Similar assessments are available for use in other settings. These are HANC-2 (Hamp-shire New Curriculum), for use by training centre staff and the handicapped person; HANC-F, for use with families; and HANC-S, for use with school leavers.

SHACKLETON BAILEY, M.J. (1980) Hamp-shire Assessment for Living with Others (HALO). Hampshire Social Services, Winchester. SO23 8UQ.

Hand-eye co-ordination
The ability to co-ordinate the movement of the hands by watching that movement with the eyes.

Handicap
A disadvantage for an individual resulting from an *impairment* or *disability*, that limits or prevents the fulfilment of a role that is normal (depending on age, sex, social and cultural factors) for that individual. A handicap has been described as something imposed on a disability to make it more

limiting than it must necessarily be. It is very difficult to classify handicap, but for individuals the components of handicap, and factors affecting handicap, may be analysed. Handicap, as experienced by a person, is far more than the direct result of impairments and disabilities. It is also affected by the response and adjustment of the family, the financial and social situation, the response of the wider community and the extent, philosophy, style and quality of services.

SHEARER, A. (1981) Disability: Whose Handicap? Oxford: Blackwell Scientific Publications.
THOMAS, D. (1982) The Experience of Handicap. New York: Methuen.
WORLD HEALTH ORGANIZATION (1980) International Classification of Impairments, Disabilities and Handicaps. Geneva: WHO.

Handicaps, Behaviour and Skills Schedule

This uses a semi-structured, informal interview, which follows a standard procedure, to obtain a detailed profile of a child's abilities, handicaps and behaviour as shown in his ordinary life-situation. Instructions for the interviewer are incorporated in the schedule but it is suitable for use only by people trained to administer it. There are 31 sections, 17 covering developmental skills and 14 covering abnormalities of behaviour. Each section has one or more sub-sections and each sub-section is made up of a series of items. Items for developmental skills are in the sequence of normal development. Items to do with abnormalities of behaviour are arranged according to severity. It is possible to extract from the HBS Schedule the information required to complete the *Vineland Social Maturity Scale*. Children can be grouped according to the patterns of their profiles and it may be useful for assessment, diagnosis, individual planning, *epidemiology* and research. The second edition is slightly shortened and modified to make it suitable for adolescents and for mentally handicapped children. The second edition has two appendices, one for problems in sexual behaviour and the other for psychiatric conditions.

BERNSEN, A.H. (1980) An interview technique in assessing retarded children: a comparative study of the reliability of the children's handicaps, Behaviour and Skills (HBS) Schedule. J. Ment. Defic. Res., 24:167–179.
WING, L. (1981) A schedule for deriving profiles of handicaps in mentally retarded children. In: Assessing the Handicaps and Needs of Mentally Retarded Children. Cooper, B. (Ed.) London: Academic Press. pp. 133–141.
WING, L. & GOULD, J. (1978) Systematic recording of behaviours and skills of retarded and psychotic children. J. Autism Childh. Schiz., 8:79–97.
WING, L. & GOULD, J. (1978) Children's Handicaps, Behaviour and Skills. (2nd edit.) London: Medical Research Council.

Happy puppet syndrome

A very rare condition in which there are easily provoked and prolonged paroxysms of laughter, *epilepsy*, jerky unsteadiness and mental handicap. The lower jaw of the person protrudes and the head tends to be small and flattened from front to back. The tongue can be protruded to an unusual degree. All the children described have had widely spaced eyes and abnormalities of vision often occur. Floppiness of muscles but a stiff jerky walk is characteristic. A variety of *seizures* occur and usually first appear at the age of 1 year. The *electroencephalogram* shows a characteristic spike and wave record. The cause of this syndrome is unknown and no familial cases have been reported.

BERG, J.M. & PAKULZA, Z. (1972) Angelman's ('happy puppet') syndrome. Am. J. Dis. Child., 123:72.
BOWER, B.D. & JEAVONS, P.M. (1967) The 'Happy Puppet' syndrome. Arch. Dis. Childh., 42:298.

MAYO, O. et al (1973) Three more 'happy puppets'. Dev. Med. Child Neurology, 15:63.

Further information:
Angelman's syndrome support group. 15, Place Cres. Waterlooville, Portsmouth, U.K.

Hare lip
= *cleft lip*.

Hartnup disease
The transport of a number of important chemicals in the intestine and kidneys is impaired in this rare condition. Important *amino acids* such as tryptophan are not absorbed in the intestine and this results in a deficiency of nicotinic acid of which it is a precursor. There is an abnormal excretion of a number of amino acids in the urine. The commonest symptom of this condition is the development of a rash on exposure to sunlight. In untreated cases there is weight loss and signs of nicotinic acid deficiency (*pellagra*) with mental disturbances and unsteadiness. Mental handicap occurs to varying degrees in 17% of people with this condition even if treated with large doses of nicotinamide (vitamin B) and a high protein diet. It is inherited from both parents who are carriers (*recessive inheritance*) and the carrier state can be detected. The condition can be identified during pregnancy following *amniocentesis*.

JEPSON, J.B. (1978) Hartnup disease. In: The Metabolic Basis of Inherited Disease. Stanbury, J.B. et al (Eds.) (4th edit.). New York: McGraw-Hill. p. 1563.
WILCKEN, B. et al (1977) Natural history of Hartnup disease. Arch. Dis. Childh., 52:38.

HBS Schedule
= *Handicaps, Behaviour and Skills Schedule*.

Head banging
This is one type of *self-injurious behaviour*.

Head circumference
The circumference of the head in the widest place i.e. upper forehead to occipital protuberance at the lower back of the head. Charts are available to compare the head circumference of a person with the normal distribution for age and sex. There are persons with small heads who are intellectually normal and although serious reductions of head measurements should draw attention to the strong probability of *developmental delay*, a diagnosis of mental handicap should never be made by head measurement alone. See *microcephaly*, *macrocephaly* and *hydrocephalus*.

Head control
The ability to control the position of the head.

Head injury
The frequency of head injury has increased in the last 20 years within the western world and serious head injuries are the most common *neurological* condition resulting in the hospitalization of children under 19 years of age. These include skull fractures, concussion and direct damage to the brain itself by trauma, bleeding, bruising and swelling. The outlook for full intellectual function in children suffering minor head injuries (those without any neurological signs) is excellent. The outlook for major head injuries is better in children than adults with the exception of children under 2 years of age. In a series of children treated for major head injuries in hospital 29% were normal on follow up and 53% had returned to school with only mild behavioural or *cognitive* problems. The outcome was worse in children who had been in prolonged coma. The children with residual problems are often left both physically and mentally handicapped.

AKUFFO, E.O. & SYLVESTER, P.E. (1983) Head injury and mental handicap. J. Roy. Soc. Med., 76:545–549.
BROWN, G. et al (1981) A prospective study

of children with head injuries. III Psychiatric sequelae. Psychol. Med., 11:63–78.
MAHONEY, W.J. et al (1983) Long-term outcome of children with severe head trauma and prolonged coma. Pediatrics, 71:756.
MENKES, J.H. & BATZDORF, U. (1985) Postnatal trauma and injuries by physical agents. In: Textbook of Child Neurology. Menkes, J.H. (Ed.) (3rd edit.). Philadelphia: Lea & Febiger. pp. 471–505.

Further information:
National Head Injury Foundation, 280 Singletary Lane, Framlington, Manchester, U.K.

Head Start
In the early 1960's the theory that intelligence is innate was questioned and there was recognition of the effects of environmental experiences on development. This led to formation of programmes in the U.S.A. for children living in deprived circumstances through poverty or inadequate parenting skills (often attributed to low intelligence of the mother). These programmes aimed to enrich the child's experiences usually through teaching parents but sometimes also by nursery school tuition. Head Start was federally funded and designed for 4- to 5-year-olds. There were many similar programmes (*early intervention programmes*). The early programmes did not specifically identify the techniques or strategies used and there were several different curriculum approaches. This led to equivocal results although there were some clear positive gains for participants compared to the matched comparison group who did not have intervention. They were later develop into more sophisticated programmes such as the *High/Scope programme*. Although Head Start and similar educational programmes have improved the academic and social aspirations of many young children, it has been claimed that they have not been as effective in raising overall intellectual functioning as have programmes that began before 2 years of age. Head Start established grants to various agencies to set up child development centres in which underprivileged preschool children were offered educational, nutritional, psychological, social, medical and dental services. Many centres offered day care and some offered home intervention programs. After 1970 all Head Start centres were also required to enrol 10% handicapped children.

ZIGLER, E. & VALENTINE, J. (Eds.) (1979) Project Head Start: A Legacy of the War on Poverty. New York: Free Press.

Health visitor
In the U.K. this refers to a registered general nurse (RGN) who has further qualified in prevention and early detection of disease and disability. Involvement is usually greatest with young children and the elderly. Involvement with mentally handicapped people was small when institutionalization was common but nowadays health visitors are often closely involved in helping families and sometimes with *early intervention programmes*.

CUNNINGHAM, C.C. et al (1982) Health visitor services for families with a Down's syndrome infant. Child: Care, Health and Development, 8:311–326.

Hearing aid
A method of helping a hearing impaired person by amplifying sound. Unfortunately amplified sound is distorted to some extent and this is greater as amplification is increased. Before selecting a suitable aid it is essential to diagnose the quantity of loss at the various frequencies as accurately as possible. The likelihood of a person tolerating body-worn aids or those worn behind the ear (post-aural) must also be decided and there are advantages and disadvantages to each. In order to reduce background noise, and increase the amount of non-distorted amplification, children may be supplied with radio aids. The microphone is

hung around the neck of the parent or teacher and radio signals transmit the sound to the aid of the child. This is particularly useful in teaching situations. It is particularly important that the ear mould fits well or noisy feedback will occur. People who are mentally handicapped already have difficulties in understanding the environment so the prescription of aids is even more, not less, important. It is always essential to dispense aids as a part of the total training programme especially for severely mentally handicapped people who may need a programme of very small stages toward accepting the use of the mould and aid. With perseverance and patience the results can be very good.

YEATES, S. (1986) Medical and otological aspects of hearing impairment in mentally handicapped people. In: Sensory Impairments in Mentally Handicapped People. Ellis, D. (Ed.). London: Croom Helm. pp. 141–144.

Hearing loss
= *deafness*.

Heart defects
= *congenital heart disease*.

Hebephrenic schizophrenia
This form of *schizophrenia* begins insidiously in adolescence or early adulthood and can occur in people who are mentally handicapped. There may be periods of excitability but mainly lethargy. Emotions tend to be shallow. There is a marked disturbance of thought. Obscure or idealistic ideas may be a preoccupation. Senseless, impulsive, erratic behaviour is common. *Hallucinations* are common especially in the later stages.

Heller's disease
A condition in which the first symptom, at age 3 or 4, is loss of speech followed by *autistic* or schizophrenic symptoms. This was one of the alternatives to be considered when diagnosing autism. In fact there are a number of disorders which present in this way including several childhood *degenerative disorders* (especially *ceroid-lipofuscinoses*), childhood *schizophrenia*, autism and mental handicap. The term is therefore no longer commonly used.

Hemianopia
Loss of half the usual area of vision. The position of the blind area is important in localizing the damage or disease responsible for the condition.

Hemifacial
Affecting only one side of the face as with hemifacial microstomia in which one side of the mouth is smaller. This may occur in *Goldenhar's syndrome*.

Hemihypertrophy
Increased growth in one side of the body as may occur in *Silver's syndrome* and *Beckwith syndrome* which are associated with mental handicap. Hemihypertrophy may also occur as a *congenital* syndrome present at birth. There is an association with malignant disease of the liver, kidneys and adrenal glands as well as with defects of the heart, kidneys, bones and eyes. About 20% of affected people are mentally handicapped.

GERLOCZY, F. & SCHULER, D. (1968) Hemihypertrophy: Incidence and chromosomal examinations. Acta Paed. Acad. Sci. (Hung.), 9:323.
HENRY, M. et al (1973) Congenital hemihypertrophy with aortic, skeletal and ocular abnormalities. Brit. Med. J., 1:87.

Hemiparesis / hemiplegia
Paralysis of one side of the body. It occurs when brain damage or disease predominantly affects the opposite side of the brain including the motor areas (*pre-central cortex*). It occurs in a few conditions associated with mental handicap including *cerebral palsy* and the *Sturge-Weber syndrome*.

Hemivertebrae
Absence of one side of one or more of the

bones of the spine (vertebrae). This may occur in *Goldenhar's syndrome, Treacher-Collins syndrome, Silver's syndrome, Aicardi's syndrome, Noonan's syndrome, Bloch-Sulzberger syndrome, arthrogryposis*, and *meningomyelocoele*.

Hepatitis
Inflammation of the liver as may occur in *cytomegalic inclusion disease* and *rubella syndrome* both of which are associated with mental handicap.

Hepatitis B (HSV) virus infection
This virus is the cause of serum hepatitis which is a severe inflammation of the liver which can lead to liver failure and death. It can be carried by people who have had an infection with the virus even if they have had no signs, or only mild signs of the disease. It is particularly common amongst people living or working in mental handicap institutions and people with *Down's syndrome* are thought to be particularly susceptible to the carrier state. It is transmitted only by direct contact with the body fluids, especially blood, and the recipient is only likely to be affected if there is a break in his or her skin. There is now a vaccination available if staff and other residents are likely to be bitten or scratched by a client who is a carrier.

McGREGOR, M.A. et al (1988) Hepatitis B in a hospital for the mentally subnormal in South Wales. J. Ment. Defic. Res., 32: 75–77.

Hepatolenticular degeneration
= *Wilson's disease*.

Hepatomegaly
Enlargement of the liver which may occur in some conditions associated with mental handicap including *cytomegalic inclusion disease, toxoplasmosis* and *rubella syndrome*. It also occurs in many of the *degenerative disorders* and *Beckwith syndrome*.

Hepatosplenomegaly
Enlargement of the liver and spleen which

may occur in those conditions listed under *hepatomegaly*.

Hereditary / heredity
Descending from parents to offspring by inheritance. Many conditions which cause mental handicap are hereditary, although often carried in such a way that their presence is not evident in the parents (*recessive inheritance*). See also *dominant inheritance* and *sex-linked inheritance*.

Hereditary ataxia
= *Friedreich's ataxia*.

Hereditary cerebellolental degeneration
= *Marinesco-Sjogren disease*.

Hereditary choreo-athetosis, self-mutilation, and hyperuricaemia
= *Lesch-Nyhan syndrome*.

Hereditary fructosaemia
= *fructose intolerance*.

Heredodegenerative diseases
= *degenerative disorders*.

Herpes simplex encephalitis
The herpes simplex virus is a widespread organism that commonly affects humans. Type I virus is associated with herpes (cold sore) infections on the face and mouth. Type II is the cause of genital herpes. Infection of the *fetus* or of babies under 1 month of age is commonly due to Type II and is known as congenital herpes. The infection in the baby is usually recognized within the first 3 weeks and either presents as chest problems, fever and *jaundice* or as *encephalitis* (nearly always due to Type II). Localized or widespread damage to brain and nerves may result from the encephalitis and this may cause *microcephaly, hydrocephalus*, areas of *cerebral calcification*, cysts in the brain, mental handicap, *cerebral palsy*, abnormal movements, small eyes, abnormal *retina, cataracts* or death. Often an infected baby has the character-

istic skin rash with small 'blisters'. In another group of Type II infections infants develop symptoms at 4 months or later with antibodies in their blood suggesting reinfection or reactivation of an existing infection. Infection of a person after 6 months of age is usually with Type I virus acquired from a fresh infection or by reactivation of an existing infection. The person may rarely develop symptoms of *meningitis* and encephalitis. The mortality rate is high but complete recovery may occur. There is often residual brain damage. This may cause mental handicap, personality change, poor co-ordination, memory problems, speech problems, paralysis and/or *epilepsy*. The diagnosis can be made from the antibodies in the blood but this is unreliable and brain biopsy is a more reliable but controversial method. Treatment with acyclovir or vidarabine should be started as soon as possible after the onset of infection if permanent brain damage is to be minimized.

NAHMIAS, A.J. et al (1970) Infection of the newborn with Herpesvirus hominis. In: Advances in Pediatrics, Vol.17. Chicago: Year Book Medical Publishers. pp. 185–226.
SOUTH, M.A. et al (1969) Congenital malformation of the central nervous system associated with genital (Type 2) herpesvirus. J. Pediatr., 75:13–18.
TORPHY, D.E. et al (1970) Herpes simplex virus infection in infants: a spectrum of disease. J. Pediatr., 76:405–408.
WHITLEY, R.J. et al (1981) Herpes simplex encephalitis. Vidarabine therapy and diagnostic problems. New Engl. J. Med., 304: 313.
WHITLEY, R.J. et al (1982) Herpes simplex encephalitis. Clinical assessment. J. Am. Med. Assoc., 247:317.

Heterophoria

A latent squint (*strabismus*) so that the eye has a tendency to become misaligned. This is generally controlled but when a person is tired or unwell the squint becomes evident.

Heterotropia

A squint.

Heterozygote / homozygote

A *gene* can exist in one of several different states. Alternative forms of the same gene are called alleles. Each individual carries two sets of genes, one from the mother and one from the father. If the two members of a pair of genes are alike the individual is said to be a homozygote for this allele; if they are different, the individual is a heterozygote. In the case of *recessive inheritance* the parents, who are carriers of the disorder, each have the abnormal and normal gene and are heterozygous for the condition whereas their affected offspring are homozygous.

High frequency deafness

A type of hearing loss in which the person is deaf only to high frequency sounds. This is demonstrable with thorough audiological assessment but may otherwise be difficult to recognize, especially in a mentally handicapped child. The person appears to respond to quiet sounds but has greater difficulty in understanding speech because only the low frequency parts of it are heard. Hearing loss in children with *Down's syndrome* is often of the high frequency type.

DAVIES, B. & PENNICEARD, R.M. (1980) Auditory function and receptive vocabulary in Down's syndrome children. In: Disorders of Auditory Function III. Taylor, I.G. & Markides, A. (Eds.) London: Academic Press.
KEISER, H. et al (1981) Hearing loss of Down's syndrome adults. Am. J. Ment. Defic., 85(5):467–472.

High/Scope Program

This was developed from the *Head Start Program*. Children were randomly assigned to different treatment groups and care was taken to describe the nature of the curriculum intervention. At age 16 to 17 the young adults, compared to a control group, were doing better on a large number of criteria of success.

BERRUETTA-CLEMENT, J.R. et al (1984) Changed Lives (Monograph of the High/Scope Education Research Foundation No.8). Ypsilanti, M.I.: High Scope Press.
SCHWEINHART, L. & WEIKART, D. (1980) Effects of Early Childhood Intervention on Teenage Youths (Monograph of the High/Scope Education Research Foundation No.8). Ypsilanti, M.I.: High Scope Press.

High-arched palate

A high-arched roof of the mouth which occurs in many conditions associated with mental handicap including *Down's syndrome*.

Hip dislocation

See *congenital dislocation of the hip*.

Hirschsprung's disease

An abnormality of the nerve supply to the large bowel. This results in a section of bowel being unable to contract and empty. Instead it becomes increasingly dilated, as it fills with faeces, and an obstruction of the bowel develops. This uncommonly occurs in infants with *Down's syndrome* and surgery is generally necessary for survival.

Hirsutism

Excessive hair growth on the body. It occurs in a number of conditions associated with mental handicap including *de Lange syndrome, Rubinstein-Taybi syndrome, Hurler's syndrome, Hunter's syndrome* and *Donohue's syndrome*.

Histidinaemia

This rare condition is caused by a deficiency of an *enzyme* which converts histidine to other substances in the body. As a result histidine accumulates in the blood and in the urine along with other abnormal substances. Birth and early development is normal but in about one third of people with histidinaemia a delay in mental and physical development has been reported with a high incidence of speech defects, *epilepsy* and *ataxia*. It is inherited from both parents who are carriers (*recessive inheritance*). Treatment consists of restricting the amount of histidine in the diet so as to minimize the presumed brain damage. More recent research has suggested that this is probably a completely harmless condition and that low intelligence and other handicaps occur no more in histidinaemia than in the general population. The original surveys took place in mental handicap hospitals and the finding of histidinaemia was probably a coincidence. Treatment by diet is therefore no longer recommended.

SCRIVER, C.R. & LEVY, H.L. (1983) Histidinaemia 1. Reconciling retrospective and prospective findings. J. Inherited Metab. Dis., 6:51–53.

Holoprosencephaly / holotelencephaly

A failure of the brain to divide normally into two halves (hemispheres). The front part of the brain is not properly formed. Severe facial abnormalities may be associated with this condition including *arhinencephaly, cebocephaly, cleft lip* and *hypotelorism*. This condition is most commonly associated with *Patau's syndrome, deletion of short arm of chromosome 18* and *Meckel syndrome*. It can also arise as a *genetic* disorder with either *recessive* or *dominant inheritance*. The severity of the mental handicap and life expectancy are in proportion to the severity of the defect.

KHAN, M. et al (1970) Familial holoprosencephaly. Dev. Med. Child Neurology, 12:71.
WARKANY, J. et al (1981) Mental Retardation and Congenital Malformation of the Central Nervous System. Chicago: Year Book Medical Publishers Inc. pp. 176–190.

Home Farm Trust

A charitable organization in the U.K. which runs twelve homes and plans to open at least one every year. This provides for over 300 mentally handicapped people. The Trust's homes each contain smaller homes, some within the grounds and others in the neighbouring community. This provision, in a wide range of settings, aims to cater for the residential, training, work and social needs of people with a wide range of disabilities. There is emphasis on an adult and personalised life-style and residents are encouraged to assist in the running of the home and also to participate in the life of the local community. Placements are paid from DHSS benefits, sponsoring authorities or private means.

Further information:
The Home Farm Trust, Merchants House North, Wapping Rd., Bristol BS1 4RW.

Home leader

The person in charge of a *staffed domestic home* for mentally handicapped people. It does not indicate a specific professional qualification although one may be required. It is one of several terms used in the U.K. to indicate this role in a system of *community care* based on the principles of *normalization*.

Home-based care

This type of service to mentally handicapped people and their families is provided in the person's home on a planned (*phased care*) or an emergency basis. In the U.S.A. these are often called homemaker services and utilize trained and licensed staff who take over some aspects of care often while the parents leave the home. In the U.K. general or specialist home-help services may be used in a similar way although help with the general household tasks is more usual. Sitter or companion services more often provide a one-to-one link between the sitter and the family. These may utilize paid staff, volunteers or individuals, such as relatives or friends, already known to the family. The role of the homecarer service may also be extended to that of increasing the skills of the mentally handicapped person or the carers by the use of various training strategies or by introducing the person to community leisure activities. Many innovative schemes have developed along these lines in recent years.

ARNOLD, I.L. & GOODMAN, L. (1975) Homemaker services to families with young retarded children. In: Community Services for Retarded Children. Dempsey, J. (Ed.). Baltimore: University Park Press.
WIKLER, L.M. et al (1986) Home-based respite care and family stress. In: Respite Care. Salisbury, C. & Intagliata, J. (Eds.). Baltimore: Paul H. Brookes.

Homes Foundation Scheme

A scheme established in the U.K. by the *Royal Society for Mentally Handicapped Children and Adults (Mencap)*. Parents, or anyone else who owns property, can give or bequeath their houses to Mencap Homes Foundation for mentally handicapped people. Houses may also be made available by housing associations, by local councils or given by charities. The intention is to provide a wide variety of homes so that there will eventually be suitable accommodation for people with varying degrees of handicap. Staffing is according to the needs of the residents. Homes are run by an Area Management Committee.

Further information:
Mencap National Centre, 123 Golden Lane, London, EC1Y 0RT.

Homocystinuria

A condition caused by the deficiency of an *enzyme* (cystathionine synthatase) which is normally involved in converting the *amino acid* methionine into cystine. As a result the levels of methionine and homocystine are raised in the blood and homocystine is excreted in the urine which is said to have a characteristic sulphurous smell. It can be detected in the urine by chemical tests. People with this condition have fair hair and skin, a flush of the cheeks and may dislocate the lens of the eyes and develop *glaucoma*. They have excessively long limbs, knock knees, shuffling walk and weakening of the bones with a tendency to spontaneous fractures. They may later develop a bending of the spine. The circulation at the extremities is poor and there is a tendency to thrombosis (blood clots in blood vessels). Thrombosis in the brain can cause problems such as *epilepsy* and paralysis. The signs of homocystinuria are not obvious at birth but gradually develop. Approximately 50% of people with this condition are of normal intelligence and severe mental handicap is rare. The development of mental handicap may be prevented by treatment with a diet low in methionine and supplemented with cystine and folic acid. Large doses of pyridoxine (vitamin B6) may bring about an improvement in some people. Homocystinuria is inherited from both parents who are carriers (*recessive inheritance*) and the carrier state can be detected. The condition can be diagnosed before birth following *amniocentesis*.

KANG, E.S. et al (1970) Homocystinuria: response to pyridoxine. Neurology (Minneap.), 20:503–507.
McKUSICK, V.A. et al (1971) The clinical and genetic characteristics of homocystinuria. In: Inherited Disorders of Sulphur Metabolism. Proceedings 8th Symposium of the Society for the Study of Inborn Errors of Metabolism. Carson, N.A.J. & Raine, D.N. (Eds.) Edinburgh: Churchill Livingstone. p. 179.
SINCLAIR, L. (1979) Metabolic disease in childhood. Oxford: Blackwell Scientific Publications. pp. 434–444.
WILCKEN, B. & TURNER, G. (1978) Homocystinuria in New South Wales. Arch. Dis. Childh., 53:242.

Homosexuality

In the U.K. if a male is over the age of 21, he may enter into a private homosexual partnership with another male so long as that person is not regarded as being severely mentally handicapped. Legally staff have no right to prevent such relationships but clearly have a moral duty to provide *sex education* and *counselling*.

Homozygote

See *heterozygote*.

Horse-riding

= *riding for the disabled*.

Horse-shoe kidney

An abnormality, present at birth, in which the kidneys are fused together in a horseshoe shape. This has been reported to occur in some people with *Rubinstein-Taybi syndrome, Goltz's syndrome, arthrogryposis multiplex congenita, aniridia-Wilm's tumour syndrome, Edward's syndrome, Turner's syndrome* and *Noonan's syndrome*. It is only likely to cause problems for the individual if associated with other abnormalities (such as cystic kidneys) or repeated infections.

Hospital order

Section 37 of the *Mental Health Act (1983)* in the U.K. refers to Hospital orders. This section authorizes a Crown Court (in the case of a person convicted before it of an offence punishable with imprisonment), or a Magistrate's Court (in the case of a person convicted of an offence punishable on summary conviction), to order that person's admission to, and detention in, a specified hospital (hospital order) or to place him under the *guardianship* of a local social services authority (guardianship order). Before making this order the court must be satisfied on the written or oral evidence of two medical practitioners, at least one of whom must be approved by the Secretary of State, that the offender is suffering from mental illness, psychopathic disorder, *mental impairment* or *severe mental impairment* which makes it appropriate for him to be detained in hospital for medical treatment, and, in the case of psychopathic disorder or mental impairment, that such treatment is likely to alleviate or prevent a deterioration of his condition. There are other conditions in which the court must also be satisfied. Under Section 41 of the Act a restriction order can be made to restrict discharge from hospital although the *Mental Health Review Tribunal* retains the power of discharge.

Mental Health Act (1983) London: HMSO.

Hospitals for mentally handicapped people

Hospitals became the major providers of care for mentally handicapped people in the U.K. in the last 40 years. Many started as educational institutions or workhouses which developed a custodial and asylum role as the *eugenics* movement gained hold. These later became designated as hospitals and new hospitals were built as a result of medical labelling and the historical pre-dominance of the medical position in the field. Hospitals assumed the mixed purpose of residence, education and treatment. Overcrowding, underfunding, isolation and poor staff morale contributed to the poor standards of care in many of these institutions and there were a number of enquiries in the 1960's and 70's which highlighted these problems. These concerns combined with the changing attitudes towards community care and *normalization* have led to a steady reduction in the number of people in hospital care, especially in the case of children. Most health authorities aim to close or dramatically reduce the size of the hospitals by the 1990's and most aspects of care are gradually being taken over by the local authority Social Services. The residential role of hospitals is likely to be that of treatment especially for mentally handicapped people who also have psychiatric disorders.

NATIONAL DEVELOPMENT GROUP (1978) Helping Mentally Handicapped People in Hospital. London: HMSO.
OSWIN, N.M. (1978) Children Living in Long-stay Hospitals. London: Spastics International Medical Publications. Heinemann Medical Books.
RYAN, J. & THOMAS, F. (1980) Politics of Mental Handicap. Harmondsworth. Middx: Penguin Books.

Hostels

In the U.K., Local Authority Social Service departments have been the major providers of hostel care. From the 1950's hostels, usually purpose built and offering approximately 24 places, increased in number and were the earliest type of 'community care'. It gradually became evident that hostels were also institutional and isolated within a community. The popularity of hostels as a model of care is now in decline and they are mainly used for part-time forms of support care with any long-stay residents moving into more domestic accommodation. They generally have a policy of training more able residents with a view to independent or minimal support living.

SHEARER, A. (1975) No Place like Home? Hostels and Homes for Mentally Handicapped Adults. London: Campaign for Mentally Handicapped People.
TYNE, A. (1978) Looking at Life... in a Hospital, Hostel, Home or Unit. London: Campaign for Mentally Handicapped People.
WARD. L. (1982) People First. Project Paper No.37. London: King's Fund Centre.

Human rights

The changes internationally in the rights of mentally handicapped people began in the 1960's. In 1968 the International League of Societies for the Mentally Handicapped sought major changes through the Declaration of General and Special Rights of the Mentally Retarded. The first article was 'The mentally retarded person has the same basic rights as other citizens of the same country and the same age.' In 1971 the United Nations Declaration on the rights of mentally retarded persons was adopted and member states pledged to promote the integration of mentally handicapped people 'as far as possible in normal life'. This has influenced the course of legal reform in many countries.

HERR, S.S. (1984) Rights and Advocacy for Retarded People. Lexington, Mass.: Lexington Books, pp. 37–41.

Hunchback
= *kyphosis*.

Hunter's syndrome
This is one of a group of disorders known as *mucopolysaccharidoses*. There is a deficiency of an *enzyme* (iduronosulphate sulphatase) and large quantities of abnormal substances (dermatan sulphate and heparan sulphate) are excreted in the urine and are deposited throughout the body including the brain. Several forms of Hunter's syndrome have been distinguished which differ in severity. In the mild form (Type B) the unusual facial appearance is first noted in early childhood. This consists of coarse features with a flat broad bridge to the nose, thick lips and large tongue. Restricted growth, large liver and spleen, *umbilical hernia*, excess hair on body and frequent chest infections occur. Heart disease is also common and a major cause of death. There is usually widespread involvement of joints especially in the hands, which may become claw shaped. Mental deterioration is slight and progressive head growth, sensory deafness and a deterioration of the retina and nerve of the eye is present. In the severe form (Type A) of the disease the signs are the same but there is also gradual onset of mental handicap starting between 2 and 3 years. *Epilepsy* occurs in 62% and persistent diarrhoea occurs with the same frequency. Death occurs at an average age of 12 years. The condition is inherited from the mother

who is a carrier (*sex-linked inheritance*) and occurs only in males. It can be detected in the *fetus* following *amniocentesis*. Research is progressing into treatment by *bone marrow transplants* or fibroblast transplants.

GIBBS, D.A. et al (1983) A clinical trial of fibroblast transplantation for the treatment of mucopolysaccharidoses. J. Inherited Metab. Dis., 6:62.
YOUNG, I.D. & HARPER, P.S. (1982) Mild forms of Hunter's syndrome: clinical delineation based on 31 cases. Arch. Dis. Child, 57:828.
YOUNG, I.D. & HARPER, P.S. (1983) The natural history of the severe form of Hunter's syndrome: A study based on 52 cases. Dev. Med. Child Neurology, 25:481.

Hunter-Hurler syndrome
This is now recognized as two separate but similar conditions – *Hunter's syndrome* and *Hurler's syndrome*.

Huntington's chorea
This disease usually begins between the ages of 25 and 35 but it may develop as early as 3 years of age. The clinical picture in children differs from adults. There is paucity of movements, rigidity of limbs, *epilepsy* and mental deterioration. The disease progresses rapidly with an average duration of less than 8 years. It is inherited from a parent by *dominant inheritance*.

BARBEAU, A. et al (Eds.) (1973) Huntington's Chorea 1872–1972. New York: Raven Press.
GOEBEL, H.M. et al (1978) Juvenile Huntington's chorea: clinical, ultrastructural and biochemical studies. Neurology, 28:23.

Further information:
Association to Combat Huntington's Chorea, 108 Battersea High St., London SW11 3HP.

Hurler's syndrome
This is one of a group of disorders known as the *mucopolysaccharidoses*. There is a

deficiency of an *enzyme* (alpha-I-iduronidase) and large quantities of abnormal substances (dermatan sulphate and heparan sulphate) are excreted in the urine and are deposited throughout the body including the brain. The baby appears normal at birth but in the first year of life begins to develop the characteristic facial appearance and is slow to develop. Bony abnormalities of the upper limbs develop early. The child is small with a large head and coarse features. The eyes are widely spaced with a flat broad bridge to the nose. The forehead is prominent, lips thick and the tongue large. The teeth are small and irregular. A hump back appears early. Hands are wide and the fingers, which are short and stubby, may become bent. There is severe enlargement of the liver and spleen causing a protuberant abdomen often with an *umbilical hernia*. Body hair is profuse and coarse. The *cornea* of the eyes become opaque and progressive mental deterioration and *spasticity* occur. Deafness may develop later. Chest infections and heart disease are very common and death usually occurs by the second decade.

The condition is inherited from both parents who are carriers (*recessive inheritance*). It can be detected in the *fetus* following *amniocentesis*. The most promising approaches to treatment are the *bone marrow transplants* and fibroblast transplants.

GIBBS, D.A. et al (1983) A clinical trial of fibroblast transplantation for the treatment of mucopolysaccharidoses. J. Inherited Metab. Dis., 6:62.

HOBBS, J.R. et al (1981) Reversal of clinical features of Hurler's disease and biochemical improvement after treatment by bone marrow transplantation. Lancet, 2:709.

IKENO, T. et al (1982) Prenatal diagnosis of Hurler's syndrome – biochemical studies in the affected fetus. Hum. Genet., 59:353.

MCKUSHICK, V.A. (1972) Heritable Disorders of Connective Tissue (4th edit.). St. Louis: C.V. Mosby.

Hutchinson's teeth

An abnormality of the growth of the teeth which occurs in 63% of children with *congenital syphilis*. The central teeth (incisors) are widely spaced and have a peg-shaped appearance with a crescentic notch of the biting edge.

Hutchinson-Gilford syndrome

= *progeria*.

Hydantoins

The group of drugs which includes *phenytoin*. The use of these drugs in pregnancy is thought to cause *camptomelic dwarfism* (fetal hydantoin syndrome).

Hydramnios

An excessive amount of *amniotic fluid* formed in the womb during pregnancy (more than about 1,500 ml or 3 pints). This causes the mother's abdomen to be more distended than usual. There are several possible causes due to fetal or maternal disorders. Abnormalities of the *fetus* are found in 50% of pregnancies with hydramnios and include *anencephaly, cleft lip, club foot, congenital heart disease* and obstruction of the passage between the mouth and stomach (oesophageal atresia). A high incidence of hydramnios in pregnancy has also been reported with the *Beckwith syndrome, Steinert's myotonic dystrophy* and *Edward's syndrome*.

Hydranencephaly / hydrencephaly

A severe brain malformation characterized by the absence of the *cerebral hemispheres* (the upper, largest part of the brain) in the presence of an intact skull. It results from destruction of a brain that had at first developed normally. The brain deterioration usually occurs quite late in fetal life or more rarely soon after birth. The space within the skull is filled with *cerebro-spinal fluid*. There are various possible causes including infections (*toxoplasmosis, congenital syphilis, cytomegalic inclusion disease* and other causes of *encephalitis*), drugs, trauma before, during or after birth and abnormalities of the blood vessels of the brain. Very rarely familial cases have been reported. Quite often the baby appears normal at birth and reflex movements are present although often reduced. After the first few weeks, if the child survives, it becomes increasingly evident that there is severe *developmental delay*. The head usually enlarges in size due to pressure of fluid and *cerebral palsy* may develop. *Epilepsy* is common. Feeding difficulties, poor weight gain, restlessness and irritability with a high pitched whining cry are common. Eyes are usually normal but there is little reaction to visual stimuli due to absence of the *occipital lobes*. Many infants with this condition are stillborn or die soon after birth. The chances of survival are largely dependent on the amount of brain present, but only a few survive more than 1 year. Normal development has been known but is extremely rare. The majority of survivors are profoundly mentally and physically disabled.

CROME, L. (1972) Hydrancephaly. Dev. Med. Child Neurology, 14:224.
PHILIP, A.G.S. (1975) Hydranencephaly. Pediatrics, 56:616.
WARKANY, J. et al (1981) Mental Retardation and Congenital Malformation of the Central Nervous System. Chicago: Year Book Medical Publishers, Inc. pp. 83–100.

Hydrocephalus / hydrocephaly

An abnormal accumulation of *cerebro-spinal fluid* inside (non-communicating hydrocephalus) or around (communicating hydrocephalus) the brain. There is an imbalance between fluid formation inside the brain and absorption into the blood sinuses inside the skull. As a result the fluid is under increased pressure. The extent of this generally depends on the underlying cause. Non-communicating hydrocephalus is due to an obstruction to the flow of fluid within the cavities (ventricles) of the brain or at the outlet point from the brain. As a consequence the ventricles distend pressing the substance of the brain outwards. In communicating hydrocephalus the obstruction occurs between the brain and its covering (*meninges*). Arrested hydrocephalus occurs when fluid formation and absorption come into balance and there is no further accumulation of cerebro-spinal fluid.

Hydrocephalus may be caused by malformations of the brain of which the *Arnold-Chiari malformation* of the lower part of the brain accounts for 80%, and tumours and the *Dandy-Walker syndrome* for most of the rest. It may be caused by trauma during or after birth or by infections (including *toxoplasmosis* and *cytomegalic inclusion disease*). In about 80% of live-born infants with hydrocephalus there is also *meningomyelocoele*. About 3% have other disorders of the nervous system. A few hydrocephalies are familial (*X-linked hydrocephalus*) and even more rarely are associated with chromosomal abnormalities. Hydrocephalus may be a consequence of another syndrome associated with mental handicap such as *achondroplasia*, *Apert's syndrome*, *Hunter's syndrome* or *Hurler's syndrome*.

The course of hydrocephalus is variable according to the time of onset (the earlier the onset the potentially worse the outcome), the duration of increased pressure, the rate at which the pressure rises and the nature and extent of any structural abnormalities of the brain. Before 2 years of age progressive enlargement of the head is the usual presenting feature. Disturbances of eye function, *spasticity* and *developmental delay* usually occur. When hydrocephalus starts after infancy, headache, vomiting and mental deterioration are common signs. Head bobbing is often an early sign. If untreated there may also be disorders of growth, early or delayed puberty, menstrual irregularities and other hormonal problems. Language skills are generally in advance of *cognitive* skills (seen in the *chatter-box syndrome*) and learning problems are common. Emotional lability and overactivity are common.

The advent of *CT scans* has revolutionized the diagnosis and management. Treatment is based on either surgical correction of the obstruction or, much more commonly, on by-passing the obstruction using a shunt (by-pass tube) inserted into a *ventricle* and running into a freely draining compartment of the body (usually the abdomen or heart). Several types of valves are used and the main complications are blockage or infection of the shunt. It has to be revised as the child grows. Surgery is a major advance in reducing mortality and improving outcome. Untreated hydrocephalus has a 50% mortality rate and less than 10% of survivors are intellectually normal. Over two thirds have major physical handicaps. In surgically treated hydrocephalus the survival rate is greater than 90% and intelligence is normal or nearly normal in two-thirds of cases.

BURTON, B.K. (1979) Recurrence risks for congenital hydrocephalus. Clin. Genet., 16:47.

DENNIS, M. et al (1981) The intelligence of hydrocephalic children. Arch. Neurol., 38:607–615.

EPSTEIN, F. et al (1977) Role of computerized axial tomography in diagnosis, treatment and follow-up of hydrocephalus. Childs Brain, 3:91.

GABRIEL, R.S. & McCOMB, J.G. (1985) Malformations of the central nervous system. In: Textbook of Child Neurology. Menkes, J.H. (Ed.). pp. 234–253.

SCHNEIDER, D. (1983) Workshops in Hydrocephalus. New York: Raven Press.

TEW, B. & LAWRENCE, K.M. (1975) The effect of hydrocephalus on intelligence, visual perception and school attainment. Dev. Med. Child Neurology (suppl.), 35: 129.

WARKANY, J. et al (1981) Mental Retardation and Congenital Malformation of the Central Nervous System. pp. 48–82.

Hydrocoele / hydrocele

A collection of fluid around the testicle or spermatic cord usually due to some inflammation of the sac in which these are enclosed. This very occasionally occurs in association with *genitourinary anomalies*. It has been reported in the *craniofacial syndrome* which is associated with mental handicap.

Hydronephrosis

A condition in which the kidney gradually becomes distended with fluid. It is due to incomplete or intermittent blockage of the ureter (the tube connecting the kidney to the bladder). When associated with mental handicap it is most commonly caused by a malformation of the kidney, ureter or bladder. It has been described in people with *Apert's syndrome*, *Carpenter's syndrome*, *Beckwith syndrome*, *Lesch-Nyhan syndrome*, *Laurence-Moon-Biedl syndrome*, *cerebro-hepatorenal syndrome*, *Noonan's syndrome*, *camptomelic dwarfism*, *Down's syndrome* and several other rare *chromosome* abnormalities.

Hydrotherapy

Physiotherapy in a pool of very warm water. It can be helpful for a person with *cerebral palsy* to relax and improve joint mobility. In other conditions such as *athetosis* and *ataxia* the buoyancy eliminates the effects of gravity and this improves co-ordination and increases confidence. Some people with a *diplegia* gain and enjoy independence in the pool and it may improve muscle strength especially in the arms.

MASON, C. (1975) Pool activities with the multiply handicapped child. Nursing Mirror, 71:50–52.

Hydroxylysinuria / hyperlysinaemia

A very rare condition in which an *enzyme* deficiency causes increased levels of lysine in the blood and urine. Severe mental handicap, *epilepsy*, lax ligaments, unusual facial appearance and *hyperactivity* have been reported to occur. The mode of inheritance is uncertain but probably *recessive* in some cases. There is no known treatment. It has been reported in normal infants and its association with mental handicap has been questioned.

DANCIS, J. et al (1976) Multiple enzyme

Hyperactivity / hyperactive children

defects in familial hyperlysinemia. Pediatr. Res., 10:686.

VAN GELDEREN, H.H. & TEIMJEMA, H.L. (1973) Hyperlysinaemia. Harmless error of metabolism. Arch. Dis. Childh., 48:892.

Hydroxyprolinaemia

Several biochemical abnormalities in the body are characterized by increased excretion of proline and hydroxyproline in the urine. These are the two principal imino-acids in the body. Types I and II hyperprolinaemia were associated with mental handicap and *epilepsy* and treated with a low proline diet. Type III hydroxyprolinaemia was associated with mental handicap, kidney problems and *overactivity*. All are inherited from both parents who are carriers (*recessive inheritance*). Like so many other similar disorders these conditions were discovered by examining populations of mentally handicapped children and cause and effect were assumed. It is now fairly certain that these disorders are harmless and the initial association with mental handicap was coincidental.

POTTER, J.L. & WAICKMAN, F.J. (1973) Hyperprolinaemia I. A study of a large family. J. Pediatr., 83:635.

Hyperactivity / hyperactive children

A term describing an excessive amount of activity in a child. It is sometimes referred to as hyperkinetic syndrome, especially when associated with distractability, short attention span, disturbed sleep, excitability, tantrums and low frustration tolerance. The frequency with which this disorder occurs depends on the way it is defined and the enthusiasm with which it is sought. Some children are described as overactive if they are physically 'on the move' for a great deal of the time whilst the third edition of the Diagnostic and Statistical Manual of the American Psychiatric Association renamed the condition 'attention deficit disorder' and subdivided it according to the presence or absence of hyperactive movement patterns.

Hyperactivity, as defined in the U.S.A., is common. Its incidence has been reported to be particularly high in mentally handicapped and epileptic children. It is far more common in boys. Feeding difficulties and sleep disturbances in infancy are common precursors. It is later associated with learning problems and truancy. In the U.S.A. it is regarded as a major problem and commonly treated with stimulant drugs (*amphetamine, methylphenidate* or *pemoline*).

In the U.K. this condition is recognized less frequently and more attention has been paid to the effects of additives in the diet with individual success stories frequently quoted as a result of the *Feingold diet*. In the U.S.A. trials with additive-free diets have met with little success. *Behaviour modification* and *family therapy* are other approaches to the problem and are both reported to have been successful with some individuals. Children who are severely mentally handicapped appear to respond less well to stimulant therapy or to special diets. Behaviour modification and/or the use of tranquillizers (such as *thioridazine* or *haloperidol*) tend to be the main approach with these children in the U.K.. If *epilepsy* or an abnormal *electroencephalogram* is also present the use of *carbamazepine* may have a calming effect.

BIDDER, R.T. et al (1978) Behavioural treatment of hyperkinetic children. Arch. Dis. Childh., 53:574–579.

RUTTER, M. (Ed.) (1984) Developmental Neuropsychiatry, Section III Hyperkinetic/Attentional Deficit Syndrome. Edinburgh: Churchill Livingstone. pp. 259–452.

SCHRAG, P. & DIVOKY, D. (1981) The Myth of the Hyperactive Child. Harmondsworth: Penguin Books.

TAYLOR, E.A. (1986) The Overactive Child (Clinics in Developmental Medicine No. 97) Oxford: Blackwell Scientific Publications.

TAYLOR, J.F. (1983) The Hyperactive Child and the Family: the complete what-to-do handbook. New York: Dodd.

YEPES, L. et al (1977) Amitriptyline and methylphenidate treatment of behaviourally disordered children. J. Child Psychol. Psychiat., 18:39–52.

Hyperacusis

An abnormally acute sense of hearing which may result in some sounds (especially loud noises) being experienced as painful or unpleasant. Some *autistic* people appear to suffer from this.

Hyperammonaemia / hyperammonemia

An abnormally high level of ammonia in the blood. This occurs in *argininosuccinic aciduria, hyperargininaemia* and *ornithine transcarbamylase deficiency* and a few other rare conditions.

Hyperargininaemia

A very rare condition characterized by mental handicap, *epilepsy, spasticity* of the legs, unsteadiness and recurrent bouts of vomiting. It is due to an *enzyme* deficiency and is treated by a diet which excludes arginine. It can be detected in pregnancy following *amniocentesis*. It is inherited from both parents who are carriers (*recessive inheritance*). Carriers can be identified following *fibroblast culture*.

CEDARBAUM, S.D. et al (1977) Hyperargininaemia. J. Pediatr., 90:569.
SNYDERMAN, S.E. et al (1979) Argininemia treated from birth. J. Pediatr., 95:61.

Hyperbilirubinaemia

An abnormally high level of bilirubin in the body which causes a person to be jaundiced. When severe *jaundice* occurs at, or soon after, birth the bilirubin damages the brain and is particularly likely to cause rigidity (*cerebral palsy*) and *athetosis*. Deafness is also common. Phototherapy (light therapy) may reduce mild degrees of jaundice but exchange blood transfusion may be necessary if the baby is severely affected. The commonest cause of severe jaundice at birth is *haemolytic disease of the newborn*.

Hypercalcaemia

An excessive amount of calcium in the body.

This occurs in *infantile hypercalcaemia*, a condition which often causes mental handicap. It can also occur in other diseases which are not associated with mental handicap.

Hyperglycinaemia

A disorder in which the level of glycine in the blood is greater than normal. There are two types of hyperglycinaemia known as ketotic hyperglycinaemia and non-ketotic hyperglycinaemia. Ketotic hyperglycinaemia can be caused by a few very rare *enzyme* deficiencies of which propionic acidaemia is one example. This is characterized by episodes of vomiting, lethargy and the presence of ketones (breakdown products of fats) in the blood and urine. These symptoms may start soon after birth or later in infancy or childhood. They may be precipitated by infections or by certain proteins in the diet. About 50% of affected children have *epilepsy* and mental handicap is usually severe. Muscle weakness and poor coordination often occurs. Growth is retarded. The condition may be inherited probably in a *recessive* manner. It is treated with a low-protein diet which particularly restricts substances containing certain *amino acids*. This does not always prevent the mental handicap. Diagnosis may be made before birth following *amniocentesis*.

Non-ketotic hyperglycinaemia is a little more common and characterized by lethargy, floppy muscles and epilepsy. It may begin on the first day of life but severity varies considerably. The *electroencephalogram* is characteristic. If infants do not succumb, the development of mental handicap and *extra-pyramidal signs* is usual. It is probable that there are several variants of this condition and the mode of inheritance is uncertain but probably *recessive*. Recently treatment with *diazepam* has been recommended.

ANDO, T. et al (1971) Propionic acidaemia in patients with ketotic hyperglycinaemia. J. Pediatr., 78:827.

CARSON, N.A.J. (Ed.) (1982) Selected reviews from the 'Workshop on non-ketotic hyperglycinaemia', Leeds, U.K. 1979. J. Inherited Metab. Dis., 5: (suppl. 2) 2:105–128.

MATALON, R. et al (1983) Nonketotic hyperglycinaemia: Treatment with diazepam – a competitor for glycine receptors. Pediatrics, 71:581.

OKKEN, A. et al (1970) Nonketotic hyperglycinaemia. J. Pediatr., 77:164.

WOLF, B. et al (1981) Propionic acidaemia: A clinical update. J. Pediatr., 99:835.

Hyperhidrosis / hyperhydrosis

Excessive sweating. This sometimes occurs in *Goltz's syndrome, Zinsser-Engman-Cole syndrome, Riley-Day syndrome, fucosidosis* and *Krabbe's disease* which are associated with mental handicap.

Hyperkeratosis

Excessively thick outer layer to the skin which is usually hard and dry. This is widespread in *Sjögren-Larsson syndrome* and may occur in more localized areas such as palms, soles or ankles in other rare conditions associated with mental handicap.

Hyperkinetic syndrome

= *hyperactivity*.

Hyperlexia

Mechanical reading skills developed in excess of comprehension and verbal expression skills. This may occur very occasionally in children with *autism, Down's syndrome* and *hydrocephalus* and sometimes in other forms of mental handicap.

Hyperlipoproteinaemia

= *Cockayne's syndrome*.

Hyperlysinaemia / hyperlysinemia

= *hydroxylysinuria*.

Hypermethioninaemia

An increased blood level of methionine (an *amino acid*) which occurs in several disorders including *tyrosinosis*. It has also been reported as a condition associated with weakness and deterioration of muscles and with mental handicap.

GAULL, G.E. et al (1981) Methioninemia and myopathy. A new disorder. Ann. Neurol., 9:423.

Hypermetropia

Long-sightedness with consequent poor vision for near objects. The eye is too short from front to back and rays of light therefore tend to be focused behind the retina. This is a fairly common problem in the general population but people with some causes of mental handicap, such as *Down's syndrome*, are particularly prone to this abnormality. It can be corrected with spectacles.

MANLEY, J.N. & SCHULDT, W.J. (1970) The refractive state of the eye and Mental Retardation. J. Optometry Arch. Amer. Acad. Optometry, 47(3):236–241.

Hypernatraemia

Increased concentration of sodium in body fluids. This is most commonly caused by excessive fluid loss from the body (as with diarrhoea and vomiting) or insufficient fluid intake. It can cause shrinkage of the brain which leads to haemorrhages. Infants under 6 months of age are particularly susceptible to dehydration, hypernatraemia and its effects on the brain. These include *seizures, spasticity*, impaired consciousness and high temperature. The mortality in children with evidence of brain damage is between 10% and 20% and about one third of survivors have permanent problems especially *epilepsy*, spasticity and mental handicap.

MORRIS-JONES, P.H. et al (1967) Prognosis of the neurologic complications of acute hypernatraemia. Lancet, 2:1385.

SWANSON, P.D. (1977) Neurological manifestations of hypernatraemia. In: Handbook of Clinical Neurology. Vol. 28. Vinken, P.J. & Bruyn, G.W. (Eds.). Amsterdam: North Holland Publish. Co. p. 443.

Hyperopia
= *hypermetropia*.

Hyperphagia
Excessive eating usually compulsively. This occurs in *Prader-Willi syndrome* which is associated with mental handicap. Certain drugs such as *thioridazine* and *sodium valproate* may lead to weight gain probably through stimulating the appetite.

Hyperphenyl-alaninaemia
An excessively high level of phenylalanine in the blood as occurs in *phenylketonuria* and a few other conditions most of which are harmless. Those which are associated with progressive *brain damage* are called the *phenyl-alaninaemias*.

WRONA, R.M. (1979) A clinical epidemiologic study of hyperphenyl-alaninaemia. Am. J. Publ. Health., 69:673–679.

Hyperpigmentation
An excessive amount of pigment (colour) in a part, or all, of the body. It usually refers to areas of the skin and the excess pigment is melanin, the brown pigment of the skin. Hyperpigmentation of the skin occurs in *Fanconi's hypoplastic anaemia, Zinsser-Engman-Cole syndrome, Bloch-Sulzberger syndrome, Rothmund-Thomson syndrome, tuberose sclerosis* and *Hartnup disease* all of which may be associated with mental handicap.

Hyperpipecolic acidaemia
See *cerebro-hepato-renal syndrome*.

Hyperprolinaemia
= *hydroxyprolinaemia*.

Hyperpyrexia
Excessively high body temperature. Very rarely *brain damage* and mental handicap may follow high temperatures due to infections or heat stroke. Usually brain damage is caused by complications of these disorders rather than by the hyperpyrexia. Very rarely severe trauma or infection can damage the deep centres of the brain, which control bodily functions, and cause a hyperpyrexia which may be difficult to control and may prove fatal (malignant hyperpyrexia).

Hypersensitivity
= *allergy*.

Hypertelorism
Excessive distance between the eyes usually with a broad and flattened bridge of the nose. It is due to overgrowth of the bone in the base of the skull (sphenoid bone). Hypertelorism occurs as the main feature of *Greig's syndrome* but also occurs in *Apert's syndrome, cerebro-hepato-renal syndrome, Chotzen's syndrome, de Lange syndrome, Conradi's syndrome, happy puppet syndrome, Laurence-Moon-Biedl syndrome, infantile hypercalcaemia, Noonan's syndrome, Lowe's syndrome, Rubinstein-Taybi syndrome, bird-headed dwarfism*, several of the *chromosome* disorders and a few other rare conditions associated with mental handicap.

Hypertension
Abnormally high blood pressure. When this occurs in pregnancy it can give rise to *toxaemia*, a condition which can put the baby at risk.

Hyperthyroidism
Overactivity of the thyroid gland producing an excess of thyroid hormones in the body. This causes anxiety, restlessness, increased pulse, sweating and often protuberance of the eyes. It is not particularly associated with mental handicap although people with *Down's syndrome* are thought to have a slightly higher incidence than normal.

Hypertonic / hypertonia
An increase in the tension (tone) of muscles. This makes movement more difficult, and the affected part of the body stiff and rigid. This occurs in *spasticity* which is the commonest type of *cerebral palsy*.

Hypertrichosis
= *hirsutism*.

Hypertryptophanaemia
= *tryptophanaemia*.

Hypertyrosinaemia
= *tyrosinosis*.

Hyperuricaemia
= *Lesch-Nyhan syndrome*.

Hypervalinaemia
Increased levels of valine (an *amino acid*) in the blood. This rare condition causes vomiting soon after birth, *failure to thrive*, *nystagmus* and mental handicap. Treatment with a low valine diet is indicated but may not entirely improve the mental state.

TADA, K. et al (1967) Hypervalinaemia. Am. J. Dis. Child., 113:64.

Hyperventilation
Abnormally fast and deep breathing sometimes referred to as overbreathing. This may occur in *Lowe's syndrome* due to the abnormally high acidity of the blood. A very small number of mentally handicapped people with *epilepsy* may hyperventilate in order to induce a *seizure*, presumably because it provokes an enjoyable sensation or *aura*.

Hypocalcaemia
A reduced amount of calcium in the blood. The effects of this vary with age and it occurs most commonly in the newborn baby. It is seen in the first two days of life in premature infants, and infants who were short of oxygen during the birth. It is also seen in the offspring of diabetic mothers, mothers with high blood pressure and also mothers with malnutrition. Another form of hypocalcaemia occurs between the 5th and 10th day of life and may be caused by feeding with cow's milk combined with low parathyroid hormones in the baby. Hypocalcaemia is one of the major causes of *seizures* in small babies. These are occasionally *grand-mal convulsions* but are more usually jittery, twitching movements. The *electroencephalogram* is usually abnormal.

It is treated by giving calcium salts and between 80% and 85% of children develop normally. The remainder develop *epilepsy* and/or mental handicap.

BAUM, D. et al (1968) Hypocalcaemic fits in neonates. Lancet, 1.598.
COCKBURN, F. et al (1973) Neonatal convulsions associated with primary disturbance of calcium, phosphorus and magnesium metabolism. Arch. Dis. Childh., 48:99.
KEEN, J.H. (1969) Significance of hypocalcaemia in neonatal convulsions. Arch. Dis. Childh., 44:356.
KEEN, J.H. & LEE, D. (1973) Sequelae of neonatal convulsions. Arch. Dis. Childh., 48:542.

Hypochondria / hypochondriasis
A state of mind in which a person has a melancholy attitude especially about his or her own health. The belief in a non-existent illness or disability may be very strong despite firm medical evidence that there is nothing wrong. It is usually a symptom of *depression* and people who are mentally handicapped and depressed are considered to be particularly likely to describe their feelings and problems in terms of bodily malfunction.

REID, A.H. (1979) Clinical features of psychotic illness in adult mental defectives. In: Psychiatric Illness and Mental Handicap. James, F.E. & Snaith, R.P. (Eds.). London: Gaskell Press, p. 83.

Hypochromid
= *hypopigmentation*.

Hypodontia
A deficiency in the formation or number of teeth. This may occur in *Down's syndrome* and a few other rare conditions associated with mental handicap.

Hypogenitalism
Underdevelopment of the genitals. This may occur in *Carpenter's syndrome*, *Apert's*

syndrome, Hallermann-Streiff syndrome, Laurence-Moon-Biedl syndrome, Prader-Willi syndrome and *de Lange syndrome* all of which are associated with mental handicap.

Hypoglycaemia

An abnormally low level of glucose in the blood. Initially this causes sleepiness and slowed brain activity but, if prolonged, coma supervenes and *seizures* may occur. In children who have experienced prolonged unconsciousness or repeated hypoglycaemic attacks, the chance of complete recovery is poor and about one half remain mentally handicapped.

Newborn babies may develop signs of hypoglycaemia especially if small for dates, following a stressful birth or if the mother has diabetes or high blood pressure.

Hypoglycaemia may also occur in the *glycogen storage disorders* due to inability to break down the stores of glycogen to provide glucose when it is needed. Episodes of hypoglycaemia also occur quite commonly in people with *Beckwith syndrome* and with *hypoglycemosis*.

GUTBERLET, R.L. & CORNBLATH, M. (1976) Neonatal hypoglycaemia revisited. Pediatrics, 58:10.

HAWORTH, J.C.(1974) Neonatal hypoglycaemia: How much does it damage the brain? Pediatrics, 54:3.

Hypoglycemosis

Babies with this rare condition have an abnormal sensitivity to proteins containing leucine which produce a rapid and prolonged fall in blood glucose (*hypoglycaemia*). It usually becomes evident in the first year of life often with the development of *seizures* after a milk feed. If it starts later in childhood symptoms tend to occur after high protein meals. Drowsiness or loss of consciousness may feature. Irreversible brain damage and mental handicap are a consequence if prolonged hypoglycaemia is not treated early. It is treated with a low leucine and high carbohydrate diet. For-

tunately children often improve with age and by 5 years may be able to resume a normal diet. It is probably inherited from both parents who are carriers (*recessive inheritance*).

HARMER, C. & SINCLAIR, L. (1964) Leucine-sensitive hypoglycaemia. Proc. Roy. Soc. Med., 57:119.

ROTH, H. & SEGAL, S. (1964) Dietary management of. leucine-sensitive hypoglycaemia. Pediatrics, 34:831.

SINCLAIR, L. (1979) Metabolic Diseases in Childhood. Oxford: Blackwell Scientific Publications. pp. 106–107.

Hypogonadism

Deficient production of the hormones secreted by the testes or ovaries (gonads). This may occur in the *Laurence-Moon-Biedl syndrome, Louis-Barr syndrome, Rothmund-Thomson syndrome, Prader-Willi syndrome, Smith-Lemli-Opitz syndrome, sex chromosome abnormalities* and a few other rare conditions associated with mental handicap.

Hypohidrosis

Reduced ability to sweat. This may be a feature of *Goltz's syndrome* and *Sjögren-Larsson syndrome* both of which are associated with mental handicap.

Hypomagnesaemia

Reduced levels of magnesium in the blood. In the last few years the importance of magnesium has been recognized. Some infants with a combined *hypocalcaemia* and a hypomagnesaemia have been found to respond only to the administration of magnesium. It is thought that the low magnesium impairs the secretion of parathyroid hormone and thus causes the low calcium levels. It is sometimes due to an inherited deficiency of an *enzyme*. Hypomagnesaemia also occurs in the babies of diabetic mothers, mothers with hypoparathyroidism, in small for dates babies and in babies with liver disease. The baby with hypomagnesaemia is irritable and jumpy and likely to develop hypocalcaemia. In older children it may occur in *malnutrition* or where the child has a problem in absorbing foods. The magnesium nutritional deficiency syndrome (infantile tremor syndrome) is seen in Indian infants between 6 months and 3 years when there is severe malnutrition. There is often a prior history of slow development and the child develops a tremor, *chorea* and/or *epilepsy*. Children are pale, apathetic and have sparse light-coloured hair. Even if treated with magnesium some degree of mental handicap may remain.

CHAPARWAL, B.C. et al (1980) Meningo-encephalitic syndrome (infantile tremor syndrome): Magnesium cum nutritional deficiency syndrome. Dev. Med. Child Neurology, 22:252.
TEEBI, A.S. (1983) Primary hypomagnesaemia, an X-borne allele? Lancet, 1:701.

Hypomania
A mild form of *mania*.

Hypomelanosis of Ito syndrome
Individuals with this very rare condition have white or pale patches, streaks or whorls on the skin, *epilepsy*, large skull, eye abnormalities including squints and a variable degree of mental handicap. A difference in leg length may occur leading to spinal curvature. It is possibly due to *dominant inheritance* in some cases.

ROSS, D.L. et al (1982) Hypomelanosis of Ito (incontinentia pigmenti achromians) – a clinicopathologic study: Macrocephaly and gray matter heterotopias. Neurology, 32: 1013.

Hypopigmentation / hypochromic
A decreased amount of colour in a part of the body. It usually refers to the eyes, hair or skin. Underpigmented areas of skin occur in *Louis-Barr syndrome, Goltz's syndrome, Bloch-Sulzberger syndrome, Rothmund-Thomson syndrome, tuberose sclerosis* and *xeroderma pigmentosum*. Generalized hypopigmentation occurs in untreated *phenylketonuria*.

Hypoplasia
Underdevelopment of a part of the body.

Hyporeflexia
Reduction in the reflexes tested during neurologic examination of the body (the knee jerk, ankle jerk, etc.). This is often associated with a generalized floppiness as occurs in babies with *Down's syndrome*. Hyporeflexia is also a feature of *Cockayne's syndrome*.

Hypospadias
An abnormality in which the opening of the urethra (outlet point for urine) in the male is situated on the underside of the penis. This may occur in *cerebro-hepato-renal syndrome, de Lange syndrome, Meckel syndrome, Smith-Lemli-Opitz syndrome, Silver's syndrome, bird-headed dwarfism, rubella syndrome, cardio-facial syndrome, Fanconi's hypoplastic anaemia, arthrogryposis multiplex congenita, Aniridia-Wilm's tumour syndrome* and several *chromosome* disorders, all of which are associated with mental handicap.

Hypotelorism
A condition in which the eyes are abnormally closely set. Closely set eyes are a striking feature in *holoprosencephaly*. Hypotelorism occurs in *Down's syndrome* although the combination of a low nasal bridge with *epicanthic folds* may not give this impression. It also occurs in *Patau's syndrome, infantile hypercalcaemia* and *Meckel syndrome* all of which are associated with mental handicap.

Hypothalamus
A deep part of the base of the brain. It is involved in the control of basic bodily functions such as sleep, body temperature and appetite. It can occasionally be affected in *Sturge-Weber syndrome* and *Laurence-Moon-Biedl syndrome* in which obesity may occur.

Hypothenar
The area of the hand below the thumb. The palm print patterns of the hypothenar area (hypothenar eminence) may be of significance in *dermatoglyphics*.

Hypothyroidism

Reduced activity of the thyroid gland so that insufficient thyroid hormone (thyroxine) is produced. The way in which this affects the individual depends on the degree of thyroid insufficiency and time of its onset.

If the onset is at birth (*congenital hypothyroidism*) the child has *cretinism* unless treated early. When hypothyroidism develops after 3 years of age, intelligence is not irreversibly damaged. Impaired memory, poor performance and generalized slowing of movement and speech occur. Muscles are weakened and the person is very sensitive to the cold. There is weight gain, a poor appetite, constipation, loss of hair, dry skin, hoarseness, deafness and disturbances of menstrual function. The skin of the face is often puffy and pale, the lips thick and the tongue enlarged. Anaemia is common. Hypothyroidism is sometimes referred to as myxoedema due to the puffiness and swelling under the skin. It is treated by giving thyroxine. Hypothyroidism is particularly common in people with *Down's syndrome* and is easily missed. Regular screening should be carried out by testing for the blood levels of thyroxine.

BAXTER, R.G. et al (1975) Down's syndrome and thyroid function in adults. Lancet, ii:794–796.

LOBO, E. de H. et al (1980) Community study of hypothyroidism in Down's syndrome. Brit. Med. J., 280:1253.

McAVOY, B.R. & McDOWELL, I. (1983) Down's syndrome and hypothyroidism – psychological effects of treatment. Mental Handicap, 11:159.

MURDOCH, J.C. et al (1977) Thyroid function in adults with Down's syndrome. J. Clin. Endocrinology & Metabolism, 44:453–458.

THASE, M.E. (1982) Reversible dementia in Down's syndrome. J. Ment. Defic. Res., 26:111–113.

Hypotonia / hypotonicity

Floppiness of muscles due to lack of muscle *tone*. This is present in babies with *Down's syndrome* but becomes less evident as they get older. It is also a feature of several other conditions associated with mental handicap including *happy puppet syndrome, Aicardi's syndrome, Prader-Willi syndrome, German's syndrome, Lowe's syndrome, cerebro-hepato-renal syndrome, Rud's syndrome, infantile hypercalcaemia* and several *chromosome* disorders.

Hypotrichosis

= *alopecia*.

Hypoxia

Reduced supply of oxygen to the tissues of the body. See *anoxia*.

Hypsarrhythmia

A high voltage epileptic slow wave *electroencephalogram* pattern which usually occurs in conjunction with *infantile spasms*.

Hysterical symptoms

Hysterical symptoms may occur in a stressful situation. Two types of hysterical reactions are (1) Dissociative symptoms whereby the person dissociates from the event by loss of memory or regression in behaviour. (2) Conversion symptoms whereby the conflict is resolved by producing a symptom such as paralysis, blindness or physical illness without a physical cause. These are different to malingering because the person believes in them and does not recognize his or her motivation. There is generally some gain from the symptom which is evident to others. People of low intelligence are said to be more likely to develop hysterical symptoms.

I

I cell disease
= *mucolipidosis II.*

Iatrogenic
A sickness of mind or body caused by the words or actions of a doctor. Overtreatment, complications of treatment and the unwise use of drugs are all responsible for iatrogenic illness.

ICAN (Physical Activity Programme)
This is a combination of an assessment of physical motor skills and a curriculum for developing these skills. The steps necessary to accomplish a task are listed and each step has clear criteria to measure successful completion.

WESSEL, J.A. (1983) Quality programming in physical education and recreation for all handicapped persons. In: Adapted Physical Activity: From Theory to Application. Eason, R.L. et al (Eds.). Champaign, Illinois: Human Kinetic.

ICD-9
= *International Classification of Disease.*

Ichthyosis
A skin disorder in which the skin is dry, scaly, rough and cracked. It occurs in several conditions associated with mental handicap including *Refsum's syndrome, Rud's syndrome* and the *Sjögren-Larsson syndrome.*

Ictal
Relating to epileptic *seizures.*

Icterus
= *jaundice.*

Ictus
An epileptic *seizure* or a stroke.

Idiopathic
A disorder of unknown cause.

Idiopathic hypoglycaemia
= *hypoglycemosis.*

Idiot / idiocy
This was a legal definition in the U.K. under the *Mental Deficiency Act 1913*, for 'persons in whose case there exists mental defectiveness of such a degree that they are unable to guard themselves against common physical dangers'. The term became obsolete when the Act was abolished. Such individuals are now referred to as severely or profoundly mentally handicapped people.

Idiot-savant
An outdated term for a mentally handicapped person who has an isolated ability of normal or outstanding quality. Most people described in this way would now be called *autistic.*

IEP
= individual education plan. See *Education for All Handicapped Children Act (1976).*

IHP
= individual habilitation plan. See *Developmentally Disabled Assistance and Bill of Rights Act (1974).*

Illinois Test of Psycholinguistic Abilities
A diagnostic test that determines a language age, with a range of 2–10 years, for nine specific areas of language. Precise areas of disability can be identified and an appropriate remedial programme planned.

KIRK, S.A. et al (1968) Illinois Test of Psycholinguistic Abilities. Urbana: University of Illinois Press.

ILSMH

= *International League of Societies for Persons with Mental Handicap*.

Imbecile

This was a legal definition in the U.K. under the *Mental Deficiency Act 1913*, for 'persons in whose case mental defectiveness, though not amounting to *idiocy*, is yet so pronounced that they are incapable of managing themselves and their affairs, or, in the case of children, of being taught to do so'. It became an obsolete term when the Act was abolished and such individuals would now be referred to as moderately or severely mentally handicapped.

Iminoacidurias

A group of disorders in which there is increased excretion in the urine of substances known as iminoacids. The two principal iminoacids are proline and hydroxyproline. See *hydroxyprolinaemia*.

Imipramine

A drug used in the treatment of *depression* and also for nocturnal *enuresis* in children. It has also been advocated for the treatment of overactive behaviour. It should not be used for children under 6 years of age or when there is heart or liver disease. Elderly people are particularly likely to experience adverse reactions especially agitation, confusion and low blood pressure. It may lead to behavioural changes in children and can affect the control of *epilepsy*. When used for depression it takes 2–4 weeks to work and close observation is required during that time if there is any suicide risk. Side-effects include dry mouth, blurring of vision, low blood pressure, constipation, tremor and skin rashes. Very rarely epileptic *seizures*, liver function impairment and bone marrow depression have been reported. It should be withdrawn gradually to avoid relapse and withdrawal symptoms.

Imitation

Imitation is an important way of learning new behaviours and skills. It may be necessary to teach a mentally handicapped person how to imitate by *reinforcement* of any attempt to copy. *Modelling* and imitation are recognized *behaviour modification* approaches. Community care and *integration* into services used by ordinary people are important ways of providing mentally handicapped people with the opportunity to learn from observing and copying the behaviours of ordinary members of society.

GARCIA, E. et al (1971) The development of generalized imitation with topographically determined boundaries. J. Appl. Behav. Anal., 4:101–12.
STREIFEL, J.S. & PHELAN, J.G. (1972) Use of reinforcement of behavioural similarity to establish imitative behaviour in young mentally retarded children. Am. J. Ment. Defic., 77:239–241.

Immunization

Protection against disease by inoculation with a substance which will stimulate the powers of resistance of the body against that disease. The bacteria, viruses or the poisons are rendered harmless by various methods and when injected into the body, the immune response is triggered so that the person can resist any infections in the future. This has led to the control (or in the case of smallpox the eradication) of many diseases some of which can damage the brain. These include diphtheria, tetanus, polio, *whooping cough*, measles and tuberculosis. The immunization of schoolgirls against german measles has dramatically reduced the incidence of *rubella syndrome*. Unfortunately in an extremely small number of children a severe adverse reaction to a vaccine can occur as in *vaccine encephalitis*.

Immunoglobulin deficiency

A deficiency of the proteins in the blood

which carry resistance against infections. About half the people with *deletions* or *rings of chromosome 18* have been described as having immunoglobulin IgA deficiency and this also occurs in the *Louis-Barr syndrome* making affected people susceptible to infections of the lungs, ears, nose and throat. It has been reported in a few other conditions associated with mental handicap. Older people with *Down's syndrome* often have a decreased immunoglobulin IgM thought to be due to abnormalities in their immune system.

HANN, H.L. et al (1979) Lymphocyte surface markers and serum immunoglobulins in persons with Down's syndrome. Am. J. Ment. Defic., 84:245–251.

Impairment

The concept of impairment is that of a basic biological fault in a tissue or organ. The World Health Organization definition incorporates a functional as well as a structural component: 'In the context of health experience, an impairment is any loss or abnormality of psychological, physiological or anatomical structure or function.' Impairments may be temporary or permanent and can be present at birth or acquired later. The description of an impairment is an objective account of the site, nature and severity of loss of structure or function. See also *disability, handicap, mental impairment, intellectual disability*.

LEES, D.S. & SHAW, S. (Eds.) (1974) Impairment, Disability and Handicap. London: Heinemann.
WORLD HEALTH ORGANIZATION (1980) International Classification of Handicaps, Disabilities and Impairments. Geneva: WHO.

Imperforate anus

A *congenital* abnormality in which there is no opening to the anus. This causes a bowel obstruction evident soon after birth and requires an operation for survival. It may occur in association with other congenital abnormalities and has been reported in babies with *Rieger's syndrome, Down's syndrome, cardiofacial syndrome* and a few other rare conditions associated with mental handicap.

In Touch

An organization in the U.K. which is a national contact and information service for parents and professionals involved in the care of mentally handicapped children and adults.

Further information:
In Touch, Mrs Ann Worthington, 10, Norman Rd, Sale, Cheshire M33 3DF.

In-home respite

= *home-based care.*

Inborn error of metabolism

A disorder in which there is deficiency or absence of an *enzyme* leading to abnormal functioning of the body. This may lead to an accumulation of substances which would normally be broken down in the body and/or to a deficiency of substances essential to health. Many of these disorders cause mental handicap which is generally progressive. The *amino acidurias, mucopolysaccharidoses* and *lipidoses* are all examples.

Incidence

The number of new cases of a particular condition occurring within a defined population during a particular time period (usually 12 months). This may be used in the *epidemiology* of a particular condition but is not usually used for mental handicap as a whole which is more usefully described in terms of *prevalence*. Incidence of a handicapping disorder is usually expressed as cases per thousand live births in a particular year.

Inclusion bodies

Inclusion bodies are abnormal substances in the cells which have been stained and examined under a microscope. They are characteristic in *mucolipidosis II*, congenital *cytomegalic inclusion disease* and *Batten-Vogt disease*.

Incompatible behaviour

In *behaviour modification* it refers to the replacement of an undesirable behaviour with a desirable but incompatible behaviour. For example, a person could be taught to use his hands in purposeful activities in order to prevent self-injurious eye-poking behaviour. See *differential reinforcement of other behaviours*.

Incontinence

Lack of control over bladder and/or bowel function. Incontinence of urine may be referred to as *enuresis* and of faeces as *encopresis* if occurring without a physical cause. It is important to the individual and carers that appropriate *incontinence aids* are available, and emphasis on promotion of continence by the use of training programmes is an important part of any service for mentally handicapped people. *Behaviour modification* approaches to *toilet training* are nearly always successful (although perseverance may be needed) so long as there is not a major physical cause.

Incontinence aids

In the U.K. most Health Authorities supply such aids, free of charge, to mentally handicapped people over a certain age. There is usually a specialist service to advise on the use of such aids. The aids available include disposable nappies, pads, trainer pants, plastic pants, mattress covers, catheters, bags and incontinence sheets. The *Rowntree Trust* may help a family to purchase an automatic washing machine and/or tumble drier if a child is severely mentally handicapped and incontinent.

Incontinentia pigmenti

= *Bloch-Sulzberger syndrome*.

Incontinentia pigmentosa achromians

= *hypomelanosis of Ito syndrome*.

Index of Social Competence

A simple assessment for use with mentally handicapped adults. It covers additional handicaps, communication skills, self-care skills and community skills. It is useful for screening a large group or for a brief general assessment of an individual. A profile on the test form is shaded with the totals in each section so that an appropriate ability level can be seen.

McKONKEY, R. & WALSH, J. (1982) Index of Social Competence. J. Ment. Defic. Res., 26:27–61.

Individual Education Plan

See *Education of All Handicapped Children Act (1976)*.

Individual Habilitation Plan

See *Developmentally Disabled Assistance and Bill of Rights Act (1974)*.

Individual Programme Plan

A system for making plans for an individual provisions can be based on the needs of the strengths and needs of that person as identified with the assistance of people who know him/her well. A meeting is held to draw up an individual programme plan at which realistic objectives are set to be achieved within a specified time span. The person responsible for meeting each of these objectives is identified. Any service deficits which prevent the needs from being met are also identified and the managers of the service informed. In this way the service provisions can be based on the needs of the clients. This system originated in the U.S.A. in the *Eastern Nebraska Community Office of Retardation* and is now widely used in the U.K.

BLUNDEN, R. (1980) Individual Plans for Mentally Handicapped People: A draft procedural guide. Cardiff: Mental Handicap in Wales, Applied Research Unit.

CARLE, N. (1981) Individual programme plans. Campaign for People with Mental Handicap Newsletter, 26:3–4.
HOUTS, P.S. & SCOTT, R.A. (1975) Goal planning with developmentally delayed persons: procedures for developing an individualized client plan. Hershey, Pennsylvania: Hershey Medical Center.

Industrial therapy / industrial units

In the 1950's and 60's these were an addition to the conventional occupational therapy in *hospitals for mentally handicapped people*. The *adult training centres* were also developed on this model. It was an attempt to provide clients with realistic work experiences in preparation for outside employment. The work was usually subcontracted from industrial firms and tended to be very limited and repetitive. It was gradually realized that this provided a very restricted learning experience which did little to help the majority of clients who never had the opportunity to enter outside employment. The emphasis then began to shift towards social education in training centres and work experience is nowadays usually provided by *sheltered work* situations which may later lead to some form of *employment*.

An Ordinary Working Life (1984) King's Fund Project Paper No.50. London: King's Fund Centre.
PORTERFIELD, J. & GATHERCOLE, C. (1985) Progress Towards an Ordinary Working Life. King's Fund Project Paper No.55. London: King's Fund Centre.

Ineducable

This was used to describe moderately and severely mentally handicapped children in order to exclude them from school. The term became obsolete after the introduction of the *Education (Handicapped Children) Act of 1970* in which all children were considered educable.

Infantile autism

= *autism*.

Infantile hypercalcaemia

This rare condition is evident soon after birth with *failure to thrive*, an elfin-like facial appearance and high blood levels of calcium in the first year of life. There is also narrowing of the main blood vessel to the body from the heart. This narrowing occurs just above the valve from the heart and is called supravalvular aortic stenosis. Other blood vessels may also be affected. The facial characteristics include a prominent forehead, a short upturned nose, widely spaced eyes, *epicanthic folds*, full cheeks, a wide mouth and a small chin. The ears tend to be low-set and to stand out from the head. Poor or abnormal development of the teeth is common. Short stature is usual. There is a mild form of this condition which is reversible with restriction of calcium and vitamin D in the diet. In this form physical and mental development is normal.

In the severe form, mental handicap is moderate or severe and progressive damage to the kidneys occurs. There may be an early death from heart or kidney failure. The condition probably originates during pregnancy in some infants but there may be a *familial* element as well.

BEJAR, R. et al (1970) Mental retardation, unusual facial appearance and abnormalities of the great vessels. J. Ment. Defic. Res., 14:16.
JONES, K.L. & SMITH, D.W. (1975) The Williams elfin facies syndrome. J. Pediatr., 86:718.
JOSEPH, M.C. & PARROT, D. (1958) Severe infantile hypercalcaemia with special reference to the facies. Arch. Dis. Childh., 33:385.
MARTIN, N.D.T. et al (1984) Idiopathic infantile hypercalcaemia – a continuing enigma. Arch. Dis. Childh., 59:605–613.
UDWIN, O. et al (1987) Cognitive abilities and behavioural characteristics of children with idiopathic infantile hypercalcaemia. J. Child Psychol. Psychiat., 2(28):297–309.

Further information:
The Infantile Hypercalcaemia Group, 37 Mulberry Green, Old Harlow, Essex.

Infantile hyperuricaemia
= *Lesch-Nyhan syndrome.*

Infantile neuroaxonal dystrophy
= *neuroaxonal dystrophies.*

Infantile neuronal ceroid lipofuscinosis
= *Santavouri disease.*

Infantile osteopetrosis
= *osteopetrosis.*

Infantile psychosis
= *autism.*

Infantile spasms
A type of *epilepsy* which most commonly starts in infants between 3 and 8 months of age and rarely after 2 years. Attacks are characterized by a series of sudden muscular contractions in which the head, and often the body, jerks forward, the arms outstretch, and the legs are drawn up (salaam seizure). A cry or smile may precede or follow the spasm. The infant may turn pale, flush or go blue. Other forms of seizure occur less commonly and include falling backwards with arms and legs outstretched and lightning attacks in which there is a single, momentary, shock-like contraction of the entire body. Rarely a *grand-mal convulsion* follows an attack. Clusters of attacks recur frequently, particularly on waking, and some children have from 5 to 100 spasms each day. In up to half the children mental development is normal before the onset of the spasms. In two thirds of infants the *electroencephalogram* (EEG) has the characteristics of *hypsarrhythmia.*
Infantile spasms are almost always associated with major underlying abnormalities of the brain. A minority (about 15%) occur in a group of infants with normal birth and development in whom no obvious cause can be demonstrated. In the group with predisposing factors, abnormalities of pregnancy, such as infections and *prematurity*, are particularly common. Difficulties at birth are reported less often. Seizures after birth are a common precursor especially those due to *hypoglycaemia.* Other underlying abnormalities include *tuberose sclerosis, lissencephaly, cytomegalic inclusion disease, Von Recklinghausen's disease, phenylketonuria* and *maple-syrup urine disease.* In most children the outlook for normal intellectual development is poor but the degree of mental handicap is variable. Infantile spasms have usually stopped by 3 years of age but are often replaced by other forms of epilepsy. *Cerebral palsy* and *autism* may also become evident later in some children. Infantile spasms are usually treated with a course of *adrenocorticotrophic hormone* injections which improves the seizures and EEG in some infants but probably does not affect the outcome.

BELLMAN, M.H. et al (1983) Infantile spasms and pertussis immunization. Lancet, 1:1031.
CAROLLO, C. et al (1982) CT and ACTH treatment in infantile spasms. Child's Brain, 9:347.
FAVATA, I. et al (1987) Mental outcome in West's syndrome: Prognostic value of some clinical factors. J. Ment. Defic. Res., 31: 9–15.
JEAVONS, P.M. et al (1970) Long-term prognosis in infantile spasms: A follow up report on 112 cases. Dev. Med. Child Neurology, 12:413.
LACY, J.R. & PENRY, J.K. (1976) Infantile Spasms. New York: Raven Press.
RIIKONEN, R. (1982) A long-term follow-up study of 214 children with the syndrome of infantile spasms. Neuropaediat., 13:14.

Infantile subacute encephalopathy
= *Leigh's syndrome.*

Infantile tremor syndrome
See *hypomagnesaemia.*

Infantilism
Incomplete or imperfect sexual development in *puberty*, resulting in lack of adult sexual characteristics.

Infection

The invasion of the body by micro-organisms such as bacteria, viruses, parasites or fungi. Usually this is manifest as a disease. The term is also used to describe the process by which a disease is passed on from one person to another.

Informal admission to hospital

Admission of a person to a hospital in the U.K. without the power of detention under the *Mental Health Act (1983)*.

Informing interview

The interview, usually with the physician, at which parents are told the diagnosis of a disabling condition and its implications for their child. Parental reactions are nowadays better understood and there are recognized ways of helping at this difficult time.

GABEL, S. (1980) The informing interview. In: Child Development and Developmental Disabilities. Gabel, S. & Erickson, M.T. (Eds.) Boston: Little, Brown & Co. pp. 223–237.

Inguinal hernia

A protrusion of abdominal contents, usually bowel, under the skin in the region of the groin. This occurs in men through the inguinal canal in which lies the spermatic cord. The hernia may descend into the scrotum. This is a common condition in the general population but is particularly likely to occur in some conditions associated with mental handicap including *cytomegalic inclusion disease, rubella syndrome, lissencephaly, mucopolysaccharidoses, Patau's syndrome, Beckwith syndrome, Smith-Lemli-Opitz syndrome* and *Goltz's syndrome*.

Inheritance

The passing on of a characteristic from parents to their children. Parents may not be aware that they carry this trait. Many conditions which cause mental handicap are inherited. This may be by *dominant inheritance*, *recessive inheritance* or *sex-linked inheritance*. A few *chromosome* disorders may be inherited from a parent who has a balanced *chromosome translocation*.

Institutes of Human Potential

These institutes in the U.S.A. and U.K. follow the *Doman-Delacato system* and make claims of debatable validity regarding the effectiveness of this approach in curing children who are mentally handicapped.

Institution

In its sociological use, this refers to an organized pattern of group behaviour established and generally accepted as part of a culture. The nature of communities for mentally ill or handicapped people led to the use of the term 'institution' particularly to describe hospitals which offered long-term care. As the bad effects of *institutionalization* have become recognized so the term has come to represent the worst aspects of care on a large scale.

KLABER, M.M. (1971) Retardates in Residence: A Study of Institutions. Connecticut: University of Hartford.
LANDESMAN-DWYER, S. & VIETZE, P. (Eds.) (1983) The Social Ecology of Residential Environments: Person x Setting Transactions in Mental Retardation. Baltimore: University Park Press.
WOLFENSBERGER, W. (1975) The Origin and Nature of Our Institutional Models. Syracuse: Human Policy Press.

Institutionalization

Group living in *institutions*. This has a number of common features which tend to develop as the group is organized by the staff and managers. These were described in the 1960's and include lack of personal possessions, fixed routines, lack of personal freedom, lack of individual identity and generally a bureaucratic and hierarchical system which ensures that the smooth running of the institution takes priority over the individual needs of its inmates.

As a result institutionalized people tend to be emotionally deprived, conforming, lacking in initiative, achieving little and to have a poor sense of personal worth. Any attempt to assert individuality tends to be regarded as a behaviour problem which warrants punitive or 'therapeutic' intervention.

A number of studies have shown that children with a mental handicap make better progress if brought up in a normal family environment rather than in an institution.

CONROY, J. et al (1982) A matched comparison of the developmental growth of institutionalized and deinstitutionalized mentally retarded clients. Am. J. Med. Defic., 86(6):581–587.

GOFFMAN, E.(1961) Asylums. Harmondsworth, Middx.: Penguin Books.

MEINDL, J.L. et al (1983) Mental growth of non-institutionalized and institutionalized children with Down's syndrome. Brit. J. Ment. Subn., 29(1):50–56.

MORRIS, P. (1969) Put Away. London: Routledge & Kegan Paul.

OSWIN, M. (1978) Children in Long-Stay Hospitals. London: Spastics International Medical Publications.

TIZARD, J. (1971) Patterns of Residential Care. London: Routledge & Kegan Paul.

Integration

A part of the philosophy of *normalization* in which a person with a mental handicap is integrated into community life by living in ordinary housing, participating in ordinary community activities and leading a normal life-style. This is opposed to the process of *segregation* of mentally handicapped people into *institutions*.

The *Warnock Committee Report* distinguished between three different types of integration for the purpose of education. These are locational (the placement of special provision in ordinary schools); social (participation in the social events of the school such as assemblies, mealtimes and playtimes); and functional integration (participation in the academic curriculum). In the U.S.A. educational integration is known as *mainstreaming*.

BOOTH, A. & POTTS, P. (Eds.) (1983) Integrating Special Education. Oxford: Blackwell.

GULLIFORD, R. (1985) Education. In: Mental Deficiency. The Changing Outlook (4th edit.). Clarke, A.M. et al (Eds.) London: Methuen. pp. 644–653.

HEGARTY, S. & POCKLINGTON, K. (1981) Educating Pupils with Special Needs in the Ordinary School. Windsor: NFER/Nelson.

Intellectual impairment / disability / handicap

These terms are generally regarded as synonymous with mental handicap but are in fact more specific. An *impairment* of intellectual functioning refers to a loss or lack of intelligence. Intellectual *disability* is any restriction or lack (resulting from intellectual impairment) of ability to perform an activity in the manner or within the range considered normal. Intellectual *handicap* is the resulting personal and social disadvantage that limits or prevents the fulfilment of a role that is normal (for age, sex, social and cultural factors) for that individual.

Intelligence / intellectual ability

The ability to reason, to understand, to acquire knowledge and to learn and benefit from experience. It may also include the speed of response, the ability to adapt to different situations and the will to succeed. *Intelligence tests* are used to measure and compare the intelligence of individuals.

BAROFF, G.S. (1986) Mental Retardation: Nature, Cause and Management. (2nd edit.) Washington: Hemisphere Publishing Corp. pp. 2–11.

STERNBERG, R.J. (1981) The nature of intelligence. New York University Education Quarterly, 12:10–17.

Intelligence Quotient (I.Q.)

This is the percentage obtained by dividing

the *mental age* of a person by the *chronological age* and multiplying the result by 100. Intellectual ability is thought to reach a maximum by 15 years of age and therefore the chronological age is taken as 15 even if the actual age exceeds this. This method was used for scoring a number of *intelligence tests* for many years but nowadays I.Q.s are computed by the more accurate statistical method of estimating the deviation from the norm which does not involve consideration of mental age and which makes an individual's I.Q. at different ages more strictly comparable. Intelligence, as measured by tests, should not be the only basis on which an individual is assessed because experience, personality, education, social skills and adjustment are equally important. The average I.Q. of the general population is 100. In the *International Classification of Diseases* mild mental retardation is an I.Q. of 50–70; moderate mental retardation is I.Q. 35–49; severe mental retardation is I.Q. 20–34; and profound mental retardation is less than I.Q. 20.

Intelligence tests

Some intelligence tests assess general *intelligence* including knowledge, whereas others mainly assess particular abilities. Results can be influenced by culture, previous experience and education. Most tests measure verbal and/or performance skills. The tests in most general use include *Weschler Adult Intelligence Scale, Weschler Intelligence Scale for Children, British Ability Scales, Stanford-Binet, Raven's standard progressive matrices, Porteus maze, Kent Oral Test* and the *Merrill-Palmer Test.*

Interdisciplinary approaches / programmes

The recognition of the multiple needs of most mentally handicapped people has led to the need to combine the skills of professionals from different backgrounds. Interdisciplinary teams specifically organized for this purpose first appeared in the 1950's. In the U.S.A. and U.K. this approach rapidly gained popularity. By the mid 1960's interdisciplinary developmental evaluation clinics were operating in the majority of states in the U.S.A.. Unlike the *multidisciplinary teams* in which professionals work side by side with little interaction except to share recommendations, the truly interdisciplinary team involves extensive sharing and interdependence among its members. With the right climate and guidance a cohesiveness can develop in which all team members have a firm sense of each other's roles and functions in which several disciplines may contribute to a part of the evaluation and in which members of one discipline can in part perform some of the functions of others.

Members of such teams may include *social workers,* doctors, *physiotherapists, occupational therapists, speech therapists, nurses, psychologists* and teachers.

Interim Hospital Orders

Section 38 of the *Mental Health Act (1983)* in the U.K. refers to the Interim Hospital Orders. Where a Crown Court is satisfied on the written or oral evidence of two medical practitioners, of whom at least one must be approved by the Secretary of State, that an offender convicted before it of an offence punishable with imprisonment (other than an offence the sentence for which is fixed by law) is suffering from *mental illness, psychopathic disorder, mental impairment* or *severe mental impairment,* and the court has reason to suppose that it may be appropriate for a hospital order to be made, it may make an interim hospital order authorizing his admission to a specified hospital and his detention there for up to twelve weeks. Other conditions also have to be satisfied and the section also specifies the circumstances under which renewal, making of a *hospital order* and termination of the interim hospital order can take place.

Mental Health Act (1983). London: HMSO.

Intermediate Care Facilities

In the U.S.A. some programmes of *rehabili-*

tation from institutions include highly structured support and training within intermediate care facilities before discharge to independent living in the community.

International Classification of Disease
An official list of disease categories, injuries and causes of death which is based on the recommendations of the Ninth Revision Conference, 1975, and adopted by the Twenty-Ninth World Health Assembly. It uses broad categories and each subdivision is given a numerical code. It was issued by the World Health Organization in 1977. The *DSM III* is based on this and is extensively used in the U.S.A..

International Classification of Diseases (1977). 1975 Revision. Geneva: WHO.

International League of Societies for Persons with Mental Handicap
A world-wide federation of parent and professional organizations from over sixty countries. This league, through its symposia and congresses, has sought major reforms in the rights of mentally handicapped people. The Declaration of General and Special Rights of the Mentally Retarded was made at the Jerusalem Congress in 1968. This led to the *United Nations Declaration on the Rights of Mentally Retarded Persons* adopted in 1971. The International League has monitored the implementation of this Declaration of Rights and continues to act as an international pressure group. The league has also established a number of working parties and publishes position papers and guidance documents.

MITTLER, P. (1984) What is the International League of Societies for Persons with Mental Handicap? Brussels: ILSMH.

Intrauterine infection
An infection of a *fetus* within the womb as occurs in *congenital syphilis, cytomegalic inclusion disease, rubella syndrome, toxoplasmosis* and *herpes simplex encephalitis.*

Intracranial
Within the skull.

Intracranial pressure
The pressure of the *cerebrospinal fluid* within the brain. Increased intracranial pressure produces *hydrocephalus* in an infant and other symptoms, such as vomiting, headaches and impaired vision, once the skull bones are joined together after infancy. In addition to the causes of hydrocephalus described elsewhere, a brain tumour is a common cause of raised intracranial pressure later in childhood.

Invalid care allowance
An allowance payable in the U.K. to a person who is under retirement age and who is prevented from working by caring for a disabled person in receipt of *attendance allowance*. The disabled person must be over 2 years of age and in the care of the claimant for 35 hours or more each week. This allowance is taxable and is treated as income when determining other benefits.

Disability Rights Handbook (updated each year), The Disability Alliance ERA, 25, Denmark St., London WC2H 8NT.
Leaflet N.I. 212. Invalid Care Allowance. Obtainable from local social security offices.

Involuntary movements
Movements which are made without conscious control.

IPP
= *Individual Programme Plan.*

Iris
The muscular coloured part of the front of the eye which lies behind the *cornea*. It controls the amount of light entering the eye by changing the size of the pupil (the round hole in its centre).

Isovaleric acidaemia
A very rare condition caused by an *enzyme* deficiency, in which a striking smell,

resembling stale perspiration, is characteristic. An affected infant becomes ill and
comatose usually during the first week of
life. The mortality rate is high and those
who survive experience recurrent attacks of
vomiting, lethargy and *ataxia* usually triggered by infections or excessive protein
intake. Treatment involves a low-protein
diet and glycine. This promotes reasonably
good mental and physical development.
This condition may be diagnosed before
birth following *amniocentesis*.

BUDD, M.A. et al (1967) Isovaleric
acidemia. New Engl. J. Med., 277:321
COHN, R.M. et al (1978) Isovaleric acidemia: use of glycine therapy in neonates.
New Engl. J. Med., 299:996.

J

Jacksonian epilepsy

A type of *epilepsy* in which the *seizures* consist of jerking convulsive movements beginning in a single muscle or group of muscles. The seizure may remain localized or spreads gradually. Consciousness is usually retained unless it spreads to the other side of the body at which point a generalized *grand-mal convulsion* usually occurs. The spread of the seizure is on anatomical and/or physiological lines. This type of epilepsy nearly always indicates disease or damage to the *pre-central cortex* of the brain.

Jansky-Bielschowsky disease

= *Bielschowsky-Jansky disease.*

Jaundice

Yellowness of the tissues of the body which is visible in the whites of the eyes and the skin. It is due to an excess of bile pigment (*hyperbilirubinaemia*). It may occur in a number of conditions associated with mental handicap including *galactosaemia*, *Wilson's disease*, *glucose-6-phosphate dehydrogenase deficiency*, *cytomegalic inclusion disease* and *cretinism*. Severe jaundice, from any cause, can damage the brain of a newborn baby causing *athetosis* and *deafness* and this used to be a common complication of *haemolytic disease of the newborn*.

Jay Committee

The Committee of Enquiry into Mental Handicap Nursing and Care was chaired by Peggy Jay. It reported in 1979. It tried to avoid categorizing mentally handicapped people and suggested that, instead of trying to match particular groups of residents to certain types of buildings, each individual should be regarded as having a unique constellation of general and special needs. These needs were viewed as dynamic and not static. They recommended that handicapped people should be encouraged to make choices and to interact with professionals and others in the community when making these choices. This report recommended that mental handicap nurses should eventually be replaced by a 'new caring profession' and that mental handicap hospitals should be replaced by small homes in the community. Dissent was expressed by those members of the committee who felt that the needs of severely handicapped people might not be adequately safeguarded. Although the proposals of the committee have never been formally implemented, the report stimulated many professionals and planners to reconsider existing policies and approaches.

Report of the Committee of Enquiry into Mental Handicap Nursing and Care (1979). Cmnd. 7468. London: HMSO.

Joint contracture

= *contracture.*

Joseph Rowntree Memorial Trust

= *Rowntree Trust.*

Joubert's syndrome

A very rare condition in which an infant has episodes of overbreathing, episodes of cessation of breathing (*apnoea*), abnormal eye movements, poor co-ordination and mental handicap. Malformation of the central part of the *cerebellum* is the cause. Only half the affected children survive beyond 5 years and respiratory and cardiac arrest is a common cause of death during an apnoeic attack. Survivors are usually mentally handicapped. It is inherited from both parents who are carriers of the disease (*recessive inheritance*).

BOLTSHAUSER, E. & ISLER, W. (1977) Joubert's syndrome: episodic hyperpnoea, abnormal eye movements, retardation and ataxia associated with dysplasia of the cerebellar vermis. Neuropaediat., 8:57–66.
CAMPBELL, S. et al (1984) The prenatal diagnosis of Joubert's syndrome of familial agenesis of cerebellar vermis. Prenat. Diagn., 4:391–395.
CURATOLO, P. et al (1980) Joubert syndrome. Dev. Med. Child Neurology, 15:208–210.
FRIEDE, R.L. & BOLTSHAUSER, E. (1978) Uncommon syndromes of cerebellar vermis aplasia. I. Joubert syndrome, Dev. Med. Child Neurology, 20:758.

Junior Training Centre

These centres were run by the local health departments in the U.K. before the *Education Act (1970)*. They provided day care and occupation for some of the children who were deemed *ineducable* because of a mental handicap.

Juvenile amaurotic idiocy

= *Batten-Vogt disease.*

Juvenile paresis / juvenile taboparesis

A form of *congenital syphilis*. Mental handicap and behaviour disorders are more common in people with congenital syphilis than in the general population. Juvenile paresis is the most common form of congenital syphilis and usually starts between 6 and 21 years of age. It begins with the loss of previously learned skills. The regression is accompanied by confusion, restless purposeless behaviour and flat emotional responses. *Spasticity* of limbs, *cerebellar* deficits, *epilepsy*, visual defects and abnormalities of nerves and spinal cord also commonly occur. Unless treated with large doses of penicillin or other antibiotics the disease steadily progresses to death in 2 to 5 years.

HALLGREN, B. & HALLSTROM, E. (1954) Congenital syphilis: A follow-up study with reference to mental abnormalities. Acta Psychiatr. Neurol. Scand. Suppl., 93.

K

Kanner's syndrome
= *autism*.

Karyotype
The *chromosome* make-up of an individual. It also refers to a photograph of a set of chromosomes arranged in a standard format. This is used to detect an abnormality in the number or structure of the chromosomes.

Kayser-Fleisher ring
A ring of greenish-yellow or greenish-brown pigment on the undersurface of the *cornea* in the front of the eye near the junction with the *iris*. The presence of this ring is a sign of *Wilson's disease* which is a cause of mental deterioration.

Kemadrin
= *procyclidine*.

Kent Language Acquisition Program for the Retarded
This is a teaching programme consisting of activities which are required for language development such as 'attending' and motor and vocal imitation. It moves on to initial receptive and expressive language.

KENT, L.R. et al (1972) A language acquisition program for the retarded. In: Language Intervention with the Retarded. McLean, J.E. et al (Eds.) Baltimore: University Park Press.

Kent Oral Test
A quick test used to demonstrate the level of intellectual ability. It consists of a series of questions ranging from very simple to complex. It assumes that hearing is satisfactory and that there is no specific language problem.

Keratitis
Inflammation of the *cornea* in the front of the eye. This may occur in *congenital syphilis* and *Bloch-Sulzberger syndrome* which are associated with mental handicap. It may also be a result of self-injurious *eye-poking*.

Keratoconus
A conical protrusion at the central area of the *cornea* of the eye. There is usually generalized and progressive thinning of the cornea. This abnormality can cause *blindness* due to severe *astigmatism* and corneal scarring. It rarely occurs in *Down's syndrome* and a few other conditions which are associated with mental handicap. It is often associated with other abnormalities of the eye such as *cataract* and *glaucoma*.

Kernicterus
Damage to the *basal ganglia, brain stem* and *cerebellum* of the brain due to severe *jaundice* in the newborn as can be caused by *haemolytic disease of the newborn* and *prematurity*. The result is lethargy and stiff muscles soon after birth and later *cerebral palsy* of the *athetoid* type. Impaired vertical gaze, deafness and difficulty in understanding language may also occur. Mental handicap is relatively uncommon. Kernicterus is uncommon nowadays due to the improvements in the medical care of newborn infants.

KIM, M.H. et al (1980) Lack of predictive indices in kernicterus: A comparison of clinical and pathologic factors in infants with and without kernicterus. Pediatrics, 66:852.
RITTER, D.A. et al (1982) A prospective study of free bilirubin and other risk factors in the development of kernicterus in premature infants. Pediatrics, 69:260.

RUBIN, R.A. et al (1979) Neonatal serum bilirubin levels related to cognitive development at ages 4 to 7 years. J. Pediatr., 94:601.

Ketogenic diet
A diet used in the treatment of intractable *epilepsy* which does not respond to *anticonvulsants*. It involves restricting protein and carbohydrate intake and supplying 80% of calorie intake through fats. The urine must be checked twice a day to ensure that ketones, produced by the breakdown of fats, are present. A multi-vitamin preparation should be given. The diet is most effective in children between 2 and 5 years of age and in children with minor *myoclonic epilepsy* and with the *Lennox-Gastaut syndrome*. *Grand-mal convulsions* and *complex partial seizures* may also respond. If there is identified brain damage causing the epilepsy there is less likelihood of response. Modified ketogenic diets have also been described.

HUTTENLOCHER, P.R. et al (1971) Medium-chain triglycerides as a therapy for intractable childhood epilepsy. Neurology (Minneap.), 21:1097.
KEITH, H.M. (1963) Convulsive Disorders in Children with Reference to Treatment with Ketogenic Diet. Boston: Little, Brown & Co.

Ketotic hyperglycinaemia
= *hyperglycinaemia*.

Kinky hair disease
= *Menkes' syndrome*.

Kinnier-Wilson disease
= *Wilson's disease*.

Kleeblättschädel syndrome
A severe and rare malformation of the head characterized by a large protrusion of the skull and marked broadening of the face. The eyes protrude and the ears are low-set. Restricted growth and abnormalities of the bones are often associated. *Hydrocephalus* usually occurs. Most babies with this condition are stillborn or die soon after birth. If a child survives, the degree of mental handicap is severe. The cause is unknown.

ANGLE, C.R. et al (1967) Cloverleaf skull: Kleeblättschädel deformity syndrome. Am. J. Dis. Child, 114:198
FEINGOLD, M. et al (1969) Kleeblättschädel syndrome. Am. J. Dis. Child, 118:589.
HALL, B.D. & SMITH, D.W. (1972) Kleeblättschädel syndrome: severe form of Crouzon's disease?. J. Pediatr., 80:526.

Klinefelter's syndrome
A condition in which each cell has two X *chromosomes* and one Y (compared to the normal male who has one X and one Y). About 25% of men with this condition are mildly mentally handicapped and low normal intelligence is common in the remainder. Affected boys develop normally until puberty when male secondary sexual characteristics fail to appear and female bodily proportions and breast enlargement may develop. Genitals are underdeveloped. Skeletal abnormalities may be present and affected men are tall and infertile. Intelligence testing usually shows non-language skills to be significantly higher than the verbal skills and *dyslexia* is common. An increase in the incidence of behavioural abnormalities and psychiatric problems has been reported.

BENDER, B. et al (1983) Speech and language development in 41 children with sex-chromosome anomalies. Pediatrics, 71:262.
RATCLIFFE, S.G. et al (1982) Klinefelter's syndrome in adolescence. Arch. Dis. Childh., 57:6.
WALZER, S. et al (1982) Preliminary observations on language and learning in XXY boys. Birth Defects Original Article Series, 18(4):185–192.

Klippel-Feil syndrome
A condition characterized by a fusion or reduction in the bones of the neck (*brevicollis*). Affected people have a short, wide neck and a low hairline. Movements of the

neck are limited. A progressive paralysis may occur due to compression of the spinal cord and this requires operative treatment to prevent permanent damage. Some affected people are mentally handicapped or have learning difficulties. Associated malformations are common including *meningomyelocoele, congenital heart disease*, spinal curvature, deafness and eye abnormalities. The cause is unknown.

MORRISON, S.G. et al (1968) Congenital brevicollis (Klippel-Feil syndrome). Am. J. Dis. Child., 115:614.

Klippel-Trenaunay-Weber syndrome

A condition of unknown cause which is similar to *Sturge-Weber syndrome*. Birthmarks, consisting of blood vessels, can occur anywhere but usually on the lower half of one side of the body. Other skin disorders may be present. Overgrowth of one or both limbs and sometimes one side of the face may be present at birth or develop in infancy. Swelling of the leg and joint discomfort may occur. Mental handicap and *epilepsy* are usual when the birthmark is on the face.

BAREK, L. et al (1982) The Klippel-Trenaunay syndrome. A case report and review of the literature. Mt. Sinai. J. Med. (N.Y.), 49:66.
KRAMER, W. (1968) Klippel-Trenaunay syndrome. In: Handbook of Clinical Neurology. Vol.14. (Ed.) Vinken, P.S. & Bruyn, G.W. (Eds.). Amsterdam: North Holland Publishing. p. 390.
SALMON, M.A. (1978) Developmental Defects and Syndromes. Aylesbury, U.K.: HM+M. pp. 104–105.

Knock-knee
= *genu valgum*.

Kocher-Debré-Sémélaigne syndrome

In this rare condition generalized muscle enlargement occurs with *congenital hypothy-*

roidism. The cause of the association is not known.

CROSS, H.E. et al (1968) Familial agoitrous cretinism accompanied by muscular hypertrophy. Pediatrics, 41:413.
WILSON, J. & WALTON, J.N. (1959) Some muscular manifestations of hypothyroidism. J. Neurol. Neurosurg. Psychiat., 40:313.

Koenen's tumour

A fibrous benign nodule under or around the nail which, characteristically appearing after *puberty*, is virtually diagnostic of *tuberose sclerosis*, a cause of mental handicap.

Krabbe's disease

A rare condition caused by deficiency of an *enzyme* (galactosidase) which is very important in the use of lipids (a type of fat) in the brain. It is a type of *leukodystrophy*. Early development is normal but at 4 to 6 months there is a sudden onset of restlessness, irritability and progressive stiffness. Muscle spasms may be triggered by sudden stimulation. Unexplained fever, sweating and excessive dribbling occur. Mental deterioration, loss of movement, loss of vision, loss of hearing and *epilepsy* develop and survival beyond 3 years is unusual. The diagnosis can be made by enzyme study of blood or skin cells or of amniotic fluid obtained by *amniocentesis*. It is inherited from both parents who are carriers (*recessive inheritance*). There is no known treatment. A few people have been reported to have a later onset and slower course of the disease.

FARRELL, D.F. & SWEDBERG, K. (1981) Clinical and biochemical heterogeneity of globoid cell leukodystrophy. Ann. Neurol., 10:364.
KOLODNY, E.H. et al (1980) Late onset globoid cell leukodystrophy. Ann. Neurol., 8:219.
MENKES, J.H. (1985) Heredodegenerative diseases. In: Textbook of Child Neurology. (3rd edit.) Philadelphia: Lea & Febiger. pp. 156–158.
SUZUKI, K. (1984) Biochemical patho-

genesis of genetic leukodystrophies: Comparison of metachromatic leukodystrophy and globoid cell leukodystrophy (Krabbe's disease). Neuropediatrics, 15 (suppl): 32.

Kuf's disease

A disorder similar to *Batten-Vogt disease* but with an onset in teens or adult life following normal development in childhood and generally regarded to be one of the *ceroid-lipofuscinoses*. There is mental deterioration often with psychotic symptoms; unsteadiness; muscle rigidity and deterioration in vision. It is inherited but the cause of the condition and the mode of inheritance is uncertain. There is an abnormality of the use of lipids (a type of fat) presumably due to an *enzyme* defect.

Kyphoscoliosis

A curvature of the spine in both an outward (*kyphosis*) and sideways (*scoliosis*) direction. It occurs in many conditions associated with mental handicap especially when a physical disability is also present.

Kyphosis

An outward curvature of the spine (humpback) which occurs in many conditions associated with mental handicap especially when a physical disability is also present.

L

L'Arche communities

Communities established in many countries but founded in France in 1964. By 1983 there were 60 communities all of which were members of the federation of L'Arche which has no legal or statutory powers. It is a separate charity in each country. The communities provide a place to live and work for mentally handicapped and non-mentally handicapped people and vary in size from 12 to 400 members usually with about half of the members having a handicap. In 1983 there were 5 communities in the U.K. One of the aims is to build a community which does not depend on material success or intellectual achievement. It is based on a belief that each individual has something unique to offer and can grow toward freedom in an atmosphere of love and respect.

SHEARER, A. (1976) L'Arche. Richmond Hill, Canada: Daybreak Publications.
VANIER, J. (Ed.) (1982) The Challenge of L'Arche. London: Darton, Longman & Todd.

Further information:
L'Arche Registered Office & Secretariat, 14 London Rd. Beccles, Suffolk NR34 9NH.
L'Arche U.S.A., The Hearth, 502W 8th St., Eire Penn. 16507.

Lacrimal duct

The passage which drains tears from each eye into the nose. This is a fine tube which is sometimes blocked in infants (lacrimal duct obstruction) but often clears itself. The lacrimal ducts are particularly small and liable to obstruction in *Rubinstein-Taybi syndrome* and are absent or malformed in the *cryptophthalmos syndrome*. The opening of the duct into the eye (lacrimal puncta) may be absent in *Treacher-Collins syndrome*.

Lactic acidosis

An accumulation of lactic acid in the blood. There are six known *enzyme* deficiencies which can affect the chemical process known as pyruvate dehydrogenation and each of these can cause lactic acidosis. *Leigh's syndrome* is an example. There are also various impairments of the enzymes which are involved in changing glucose to glycogen (the form in which it is stored) and vice versa. These include *glucose-6-phosphate dehydrogenase deficiency*. There are several other identified deficiencies which can also induce lactic acidosis. In 65% of children with persistent lactic acidosis the enzyme defect has not been identified and in some of these there is a *familial* incidence. Some children with this condition have episodes of vomiting, overbreathing and low blood sugar. Others have intermittent unsteadiness, poor co-ordination and *choreoathetosis* usually following a fever. In another form children have severe mental handicap and *infantile spasms* which improve with thiamine supplements.

MENKES, J.H. (1985) Textbook of Child Neurology. Philadelphia: Lea & Febiger. pp. 57–59.
ROBINSON, B.H. et al (1980) The genetic heterogeneity of lactic acidosis: Occurrence of recognizable inborn errors of metabolism in a pediatric population with lactic acidosis. Pediatr. Res., 14:956.

Lactosyl ceramidosis

A subtype of *Niemann-Pick disease* Type C.

Lafora's disease

= *Unverricht's myoclonus epilepsy.*

Lakeland Village Adaptive Behavior Grid

This is a checklist designed for assessing

skills, training needs and progress of institutionalized clients. There are ten categories: eating, toileting, dressing, health and growing, communicating, mobility, dexterity, vocation and recreation, socialization, orientation and behaviour control. It covers the developmental range from birth to 16 years and was standardized on an institutional population with an average developmental level of 4 years. It is based on observed performance or on information from care givers. Individual developmental levels can be assigned to each category.

The Lakeland Village Adaptive Behaviour Grid (1976), Lakeland Village, Medical Lake, Washington.

Langer-Giedion syndrome
A condition of unknown cause which has sometimes occurred with a *deletion of chromosome* 8. People with this condition have a rather small head and short stature, large protruding ears, bulbous nose, heavy brows, thin upper lip, sparse hair, floppy muscles, excess skin folds especially on the neck in infancy, bone abnormalities, hearing loss and mild to moderate mental handicap.

HALL, B.D. et al (1974) Langer-Giedion syndrome. Birth Defects Original Article Series, 10(12):147–164.
ZABEL, B.U. & BAUMANN, W.A. (1982) Langer-Giedion syndrome with interstitial 8q-deletion. Am. J. Med. Genet., 11:353.

Language / language disorders
This usually refers to the spoken word but *sign languages* also exist. Problems in acquiring language may be due to severe mental handicap, *aphasia* or *autism*. Problems in *articulation* may also occur. There are a number of assessment and training procedures available including *Reynell developmental language scale, Derbyshire language scheme, Illinois test of psycholinguistics abilities, Kent oral test, Peabody language scale* and the *Receptive Expressive Emergent Language scale.* Assessment and treatment of language disorders may be obtained from a *speech therapist*

in the U.K. or a specialist in communication disorders in the U.S.A. (see also *communication*).

BERRY, P. (Ed.) (1976) Language and Communication in the Mentally Handicapped, London: Edward Arnold.
CRYSTAL, D. (1982) Profiling Linguistic Disability. London: Edward Arnold.
HARRIS, J. (1984) Early language intervention programmes: an update. Assoc. Child Psychol. Psychiat. Newsletter 6(1).
JEFFREE, D. & McCONKEY, R. (1976) Let Me Speak. London: Souvenir Press.
McCONKEY, R. & PRICE, P. (1986) Let's Talk. Learning Language in Everyday Settings. London: Souvenir Press.
MILLER, J.F. & CHAPMAN, R.S. (1984) Disorders of communication: investigating the development of language of mentally retarded children. Am. J. Ment. Defic., 88:536–45.
MULLER, D.J. et al (1981) Language Assessment for Remediation. London: Croom Helm.
YULE, W. & RUTTER, M. (Eds.) (1987) Language Development and Disorders. London: MacKeith Press.

Largactil
= *chlorpromazine.*

Late infantile systemic lipidosis
= *generalized gangliosidosis.*

Late onset lipidosis
= *Kuf's disease.*

Late onset progeria
= *Werner's syndrome.*

Laterality
The side of the body preferred by an individual when performing *motor skills*, especially those requiring good coordination e.g. right or left handedness, right or left footedness and eye preference. Mixed laterality such as right handedness with left footedness, or ambiguous hand

preference are said to be more often associated with learning difficulties, stuttering, language disorders, dyslexia and brain damage.

McANULTY, G.B. et al (1984) Personal and familial sinistrality in relation to degree of mental retardation. Brain and Cognition, 3:349.

ZANGWILL, O.L. (1960) Cerebral Dominance and its Relation to Psychological Function. London: Oliver & Boyd.

Laurence-Moon-Biedl syndrome / Laurence-Moon-Biedl-Bardet syndrome

People with this syndrome tend to be obese and to have underdeveloped genitals, short stature, extra fingers and toes, a progressive deterioration of vision and night blindness (*retinitis pigmentosa*). Mild or moderate mental handicap occurs in 80% of cases. Eyes are often widely spaced (*hypertelorism*) and slant upward. Squint and *glaucoma* may occur. Deafness is sometimes present and kidney and heart defects have been reported. Life expectancy is usually normal. It is inherited from both parents who are carriers (*recessive inheritance*).

McLOUGHLIN, T.G.C. et al (1960) Heart disease in the Laurence-Moon-Biedl syndrome. J. Pediatr., 65:388.

MOINI, A.R. et al (1975) The Laurence-Moon-Biedl syndrome. Clin. Pediat., 14(9): 812–815.

NADJMI, B. et al (1969) Laurence-Moon-Biedl syndrome associated with multiple genitourinary tract anomalies. Am. J. Dis. Child, 117:352.

Lay advocacy

See *advocacy*.

Lazy eye

= *amblyopia*.

Lead poisoning / lead encephalopathy

Lead poisoning is more likely to affect the brain (*encephalopathy*) in younger children, and the nerves (polyneuropathy) in older children and adults. There are many possible sources of lead and the extent of the poisoning is in proportion to the amount absorbed. Small and malnourished children are particularly susceptible. The infant or child with encephalopathy may first be pale, irritable, listless and have poor appetite. Stomach pains, vomiting and constipation are common. This is usually followed by the sudden onset of a series of *grand-mal convulsions*, drowsiness or loss of consciousness. The *seizures* respond poorly to *anticonvulsants* and may be followed by weakness of one side of the body or other signs of brain damage. There are signs of increased *intracranial pressure* due to swelling of the brain or *hydrocephalus*. Anaemia and kidney problems may also occur. It is thought that children with less dramatic symptoms but with chronic low level lead poisoning may have a lower *intelligence quotient* than normal. Some studies have failed to show this and it may be that low-ability, emotionally disturbed children are more at risk of lead poisoning. A number of screening procedures have been proposed to detect unsuspected cases of lead poisoning using blood tests or measurement of substances in the urine. Characteristic lines (lead lines) may be seen in X-rays of the bones.

Treatment of lead encephalopathy involves reducing the intracranial pressure by the use of intravenous urea or mannitol; removing lead from the tissues and blood by intravenous edathamil calcium disodium (versene; calcium versanate) using a process known as chelation; treatment of seizures with anticonvulsants such as *diazepam, paraldehyde* or *barbiturates*; and prevention of further lead absorption. The chances of complete recovery in children is not good because, by the time the symptoms become apparent, lasting damage has been done. A few children die but of the survivors *epilepsy* continues in 40% and another 20% have other brain damage such as *hemiplegia, blindness, spasticity*, mental handicap, deafness and *autistic* features.

Least restrictive alternative / least drastic alternative

BICKNELL, J. et al (1968) Lead in mentally retarded children. J. Ment. Defic. Res., 12:282–293.

FREEMAN, R. (1970) Chronic lead poisoning in children. A review of 90 children diagnosed in Sydney 1948–1967 2. Clinical features and investigations. Med. J. Aus., 1:648.

PIOMELLI, S. et al (1984) Management of childhood lead poisoning. J. Pediatr., 105: 523–532.

RUTTER, M. (1980) Raised lead levels and impaired cognitive / behavioural functioning: A review of the evidence. Dev. Med. Child Neurology, 22 (suppl.) 42.

SACHS, H.K. et al (1978) I.Q. following treatment of lead poisoning. A patient-sibling comparison. J. Pediatr., 93:428.

WALDRON, H.A. (1984) Exposure to lead as an environmental factor in mental retardation. In: Scientific Studies in Mental Retardation. Dobbing, J. et al (Eds.) London: The Royal Society of Medicine and Macmillan Press. pp. 183–201.

Learning difficulties

A term suggested in the *Warnock Committee Report*. Children with mild learning difficulties can usually be helped to follow a school curriculum and may not be mentally handicapped. Children with moderate learning difficulties are generally in the mildly retarded range as defined by *intelligence quotient* and children with severe learning difficulties are usually below this range.

Learning disability

Any difficulty in performing an activity within the normal range because of an *impairment* of learning. In the U.K. this term is sometimes used synonymously with 'mental handicap' but is more specific and informative. On the other hand the term can lead to confusion because in the U.S.A. it has been used to describe specific learning disabilities in people of normal intelligence, e.g. *dyslexia* and specific language difficulties.

Learning Potential Assessment Device (LPAD)

See *learning tests*.

Learning tests

In recent years learning tests have been introduced as an alternative or supplement to the more conventional *intelligence tests*. Learning tests are a procedure in which the child's levels of achievement in test situations are first established, then systematic teaching methods applied and the levels of achievement retested to measure the progress that has occurred. Tests such as *Raven's progressive matrices* can be used but special programmes are now available including *DISTAR* and the Learning Potential Assessment Device (LPAD). These techniques make it possible to compare a child's performance over time rather than trying to establish a position on a normative scale. It is claimed that learning tests have a predictive function in special education e.g. in the differentiation between those children who will need further special help after leaving school and those who will cope without it.

BUDOFF, M. & CORMAN, L. (1976) Effectiveness of a learning potential procedure in improving problem-solving skills of retarded and non-retarded children. Am. J. Ment. Defic., 81:260–264.

CLARKE, A.D. & CLARKE, A.M. (1973) Assessment and prediction. In: Assessment for Learning in the Mentally Handicapped. Mittler, P.J. (Ed.) London: Churchill Livingstone. pp. 23–47.

HAYWARD, H.D. (1977) Alternatives to normative assessment. In: Research to Practice in Mental Retardation. Mittler, P.J. (Ed.) Vol.2 Education and Training. Baltimore: University Park Press.

Least restrictive alternative / least drastic alternative

The doctrine of the least restrictive alternative (LRA) developed in the U.S.A. as a response to the intolerable conditions and

187

government interference in the lives of handicapped people. It was developed by the courts in constitutional adjudication and is now widely accepted by professionals. The LRA principle recognizes that when the state restricts fundamental rights, it has the duty to do so in the least drastic manner compatible with the purpose of the restriction. When rights such as personal liberty are at stake, the court may require an enquiry into the alternatives to the challenged regulation or practice.

The LRA principle has also developed other meanings. It is a concept for testing service provisions against *normalization* philosophies, individual needs and individual freedoms.

In recent years the LRA doctrine has been widely accepted as a limitation on civil commitment powers. Congress and state legislatives have used the principle as a check on inappropriate *institutionalization* (See *Developmentally Disabled Assistance and Bill of Rights Act*). Federal courts have applied it to placement and retention decisions affecting residents of many institutions. State courts have also invoked this doctrine to impose limits on state powers to admit and detain mentally retarded persons. State statutes can give rise to an enforceable right to least restrictive care. Statutory commands that dictate exploration and development of least restrictive care plans are frequently made.

HERR, S.S. (1983) Rights and Advocacy for Mentally Retarded People. Lexington, Mass.: Lexington Books.

Leber's congenital amaurosis

A *degenerative disorder* in which there is a progressive loss of central vision due to damage to the optic nerves. The onset is usually between 18 and 25 years of age. Some people with this condition also suffer from *epilepsy*, *spasticity*, mental handicap, deafness, kidney problems and poor co-ordination. It is inherited from the mother who is a carrier (*sex-linked inheritance*) and

may be mildly affected. It is thought to be due to an *enzyme* deficiency which affects the ability of the body to deal with even small quantities of cyanide. There is no known treatment.

BRUYN, G.W. & WENT, L.N. (1964) A sex-linked heredodegenerative neurological disorder associated with Leber's optic atrophy. J. Neurol. Sci., 1:59.

CAGIANUT, B. et al (1981) Thiosulfate-sulfur transferase (rhodanese) deficiency in Leber's hereditary optic atrophy. Lancet, 2:981.

NIKOSKELAINEN, E. (1984) New aspects of the genetic, etiologic and clinical puzzle of Leber's disease. Neurology, 34:1482.

Legal advocacy
See *advocacy*.

Leigh's syndrome / Leigh's encephalopathy

A condition in which degeneration of the brain and nerves progresses from infancy. Between the sixth and tenth month the infant starts to vomit and is reluctant to feed. Following this there is floppiness of the muscles with minimal movements of limbs apart from facial grimacing and rolling eye movements. Periods of gradual slight recovery are followed by further episodes of vomiting and physical and mental deterioration. There may be *lactic acidosis* and pyruric acid levels in the blood may also be high. The cause is thought to be a deficiency of the *enzyme* pyruvate carboxylase. It is probably inherited from both parents who are carriers (*recessive inheritance*). There is no cure but some improvement may occur on a high-carbohydrate, low-protein diet with thiamine supplements.

HOMMES, F.A. et al (1968) Leigh's encephalomegalopathy: An inborn error of gluconeogenesis. Arch. Dis. Childh., 43:423.

SINCLAIR, L. (1979) Metabolic Disease in Childhood. Oxford: Blackwell Scientific Publications. pp. 336–340.

TOSHIMA, K. et al (1982) Enzymologic

studies and therapy of Leigh's disease associated with pyruvate decarboxylase deficiency. Pediatr. Res., 16:430.

Leisure

The importance of enjoyable and purposeful leisure time for people with a mental handicap has been more clearly recognized in recent years. The philosophy of *normalization* has emphasized the importance of integrated leisure opportunities with non-handicapped people. The *Gateway clubs* in the U.K. have developed in response to the needs of mentally handicapped people in the community.

JEFFREE, D.M. & CHESELDINE, S. (1985) Let's Join In. London: Souvenir Press.
MATSON, J.L. & ANDRASIK, F. (1982) Training leisure-time social-interaction skills to mentally retarded adults. Am. J. Ment. Defic., 86:542–553.
WUERCH, B.B. & VOELTZ, L.M. (1982) Longitudinal Leisure Skills for Severely Handicapped Learners. Baltimore: Paul H. Brookes.

Leiter International Performance Scale

This is a type of intelligence test which does not rely on language for the tasks or instruction. The materials consist of a series of picture cards and sets of small wooden cubes each with a picture on one face. The picture cards are displayed in turn in a frame. The subject has to match the pictures on the blocks with those on the cards and then place the blocks in the holes provided in the frame, adjacent to the appropriate picture on the card. The instructions are given entirely by demonstration. The earlier items include matching by colour, shape and design and number. Some depend on matching by analogy. Later items in the scale involve the ability to visualize in three dimensions. It covers a developmental age range from 2 to 18 years and gives a mental age score and an *intelligence quotient*. It is particularly useful for mentally handi-

capped people who do not have language skills and for deaf people.

ARTHUR, G. (1952) The Arthur Adaptation of the Leiter International Performance Scale. Los Angeles: Western Psychological Services.
LEITER, R.G. (1969) The Leiter International Performance Scale. Chicago: Stoelting Co.

Lejeune Syndrome

= *cri-du-chat syndrome*.

Lennox-Gastaut syndrome / Lennox syndrome

People with this condition have minor *seizures (myoclonic seizures)*, are often mentally handicapped and have an *electroencephalogram* pattern characterized by rhythmical spike and wave activity usually at a slower cycle (1.5 to 2.5 Hz) than the typical absence *seizure* rhythm. Typically a child between 1 and 6 years of age develops minor motor seizures, consisting of staring, muscle jerks and falls, due to sudden loss of body tone. This type of *epilepsy* is very resistant to *anticonvulsant* drugs and mental handicap occurs in up to 90% of cases. A child with *infantile spasms* may later develop this syndrome. It can persist into adult life especially if associated with severe or profound mental handicap.

There are many possible causes of the syndrome including head injury, *measles encephalitis*, prolonged *febrile convulsions, lead poisoning, degenerative disorders, rubella syndrome, toxoplasmosis* and *cytomegalic inclusion disease*. There is a group for whom no cause can be found and some of these retain a normal *intelligence quotient*. Children with the Lennox-Gastaut syndrome sometimes have 20 or more seizures a day and injury from sudden falls is common. Major complications are a progressive mental deterioration and episodes of minor status in which the abnormal brain activity is persistent. In these episodes the person is withdrawn, *autistic* or aggressive. Speech may deteriorate and the child is unsteady. Minor twitching of the face and hands may occur. It may last for hours, days, weeks or months.

Treatment is with a major anticonvulsant such as *carbamazepine* or *phenytoin* to lessen the risk of *grand-mal convulsions* or *status epilepticus*, and a *benzodiazepine* such as *clonazepam, nitrazepam, clobazam* or *diazepam*. Steroids or a *ketogenic diet* may be tried. *Sodium valproate* may be effective in a small number of cases. If a drug does not reduce the seizures then it should be gradually withdrawn. As the child gets older the seizure type and pattern may change to a mixture of *complex partial seizures*; grand-mal convulsions and *absence seizures*. At this stage drugs such as carbamazepine and sodium valproate may be more effective. Intellectual performance may vary from day to day causing schooling difficulties and behavioural problems such as *hyperactivity*, distractability and aggression.

BOWER, B.D. (1972) Minor epileptic status. Dev. Med. Child Neurology, 14:80–81.
CHEVRIE, J.J. & AICARDI, J. (1972) Childhood epileptic encephalopathy with slow spike-wave. A statistical study of 80 cases. Epilepsia, 13:259.
PAPINI, M. et al (1984) Alertness and incidence of seizures in patients with Lennox-Gastaut syndrome. Epilepsia, 25: 161–167.
YAMATOGI, Y. et al (1979) Treatment of Lennox syndrome with ACTH. A clinical and electro-encephalographic study. Brain. Dev., 4:267–276.

Lenticular opacity
= *cataract*.

Lentigines
Small dark brown patches of skin which develop progressively during the first few years of life in the *multiple lentiginosis syndrome* in which they become numerous.

Lenz syndrome
In this condition small eyes and eye abnormalities occur in association with abnormalities of collar bones, hands, kidneys, teeth and genitals. Mental handicap and a small head have been described in this disorder.

HERRMANN, J. & OPITZ, J.M. (1969) The Lenz microphthalmia syndrome. Birth Defects, 5(2):138.

Leonard Cheshire Foundation
A foundation that runs 74 residential homes in the U.K., mainly for severely physically handicapped adults but also caters for a small number of mentally handicapped children and adults. In addition, there are 147 Cheshire Homes in 45 countries throughout the world caring for physically and mentally handicapped people.

Further information:
Leonard Cheshire Foundation, 28–29 Maunsel St., London SW1.

Leprechaunism
= *Donohue's syndrome*.

Leroy's disease
= *mucolipidosis II*.

Lesch-Nyhan syndrome
A disorder caused by a deficiency of an *enzyme* (hypoxanthineguanine-phosphoribosyl transferase). This causes extra uric acid to be produced in the body. Other biochemical abnormalities cause damage to the brain and nervous system. Affected children appear normal at birth. During the first year of life delays in motor skills are noticed. In the second year involuntary movements (*extrapyramidal signs*) are noticed until stopped by progressive *spasticity* and *athetosis*. *Epilepsy* occurs in about half of those affected and self-injurious biting of fingers, arms and lips necessitates restraints or even removal of teeth. Hitting other people, vomiting and spitting have been frequently observed. Kidney damage leads to blood in the urine and kidney stones. Gout is a late complication. Mental handicap is rarely severe and

intelligence may be normal. Height and weight are below average. Life expectancy is considerably reduced. The condition occurs only in males and is inherited from the mother who is a carrier (*sex-linked inheritance*). The level of the enzyme can be measured in the blood or following *skin biopsy* or *amnio centesis*. Treatment is with allopurinol to reduce the uric acid and to alleviate some of the kidney damage and gout.

BOYLE, J.A. & RAIVIO, K.O. (1970) Lesch-Nyhan syndrome: Preventive control by prenatal diagnosis. Science, 169:688.
BULL, M. & LAVECCHIO, F. (1978) Behaviour therapy for a child with Lesch-Nyhan syndrome. Dev. Med. Child Neurology, 20:368–375.
CHRISTIE, R. et al (1982) Lesch-Nyhan disease: clinical experience with nineteen patients. Dev. Med. Child Neurology, 24: 293–306.
DASHEIFF, R.M. (1980) Benzodiazepine treatment for Lesch-Nyhan syndrome. Dev. Med. Child Neurology, 22:101–102.
NYHAN, W.L. (1978) The Lesch-Nyhan syndrome. Dev. Med. Child Neurology, 20:376–379.
WATTS, R.W.E. et al (1982) Clinical, postmortem, biochemical and therapeutic observations on the Lesch-Nyhan syndrome with particular reference to the neurological manifestations. Quart. J. Med., 51:43–78.

Leucine-sensitive hypoglycaemia
= *hypoglycemosis*.

Leucodystrophy / leukodystrophy
This term applies to a group of disorders in which there is degeneration primarily affecting the white matter of the brain. All these disorders are progressive, usually with physical and mental deterioration. The group includes *sudanophilic leucodystrophy*, *Pelizaeus-Merzbacher disease*, *Canavan's disease*, *Alexander's disease*, *metachromatic leucodystrophy* and *Krabbe's disease*.

Leucopaenia / leucopenia
A reduction in the number of white blood cells. This occurs very rarely as a sensitivity reaction to some drugs and has been reported with *carbamazepine, thioridazine, pericyazine* and *chlorpromazine*. If severe it increases the person's susceptibility to infection and can be life threatening.

Leukaemia
A disease in which the number of white cells in the blood is excessive. It is a *malignancy* (cancer) of the white blood cells. There is usually enlargement of the lymph glands and spleen. Infiltration of the bone marrow occurs interfering with the formation of normal blood cells. There are a number of different types of leukaemia and some progress more rapidly than others. Recent advances in treatment are producing a higher cure rate but are unpleasant for the recipient. Leukaemia occurs more commonly than usual in *Louis-Barr syndrome, Fanconi's hypoplastic anaemia* and *Down's syndrome* all of which are associated with mental handicap.

Further information:
Leukaemia Society of America, 800 Second Ave., New York, NY 10017.
Leukaemia Research Fund, 43 Great Ormond St., Camden, London WC1N 3JJ.

Librium
= *chlordiazepoxide*.

Licensed physical therapist
= *physiotherapist*.

Lightning attacks
A type of *seizure* which may occur in an infant suffering from *infantile spasms*. It consists of a single, momentary, shock-like contraction of the entire body.

Lightwood's syndrome
= *infantile hypercalcaemia*.

Limit dextrinosis
One of the *glycogen storage disorders* caused by

a deficiency of the *enzyme* debrancher amylo-1,6-glucosidase. Normally glucose is stored in the body, mainly in the liver, as glycogen. This is broken down to make glucose when the body needs energy. In this rare disorder the glycogen cannot be broken down and *seizures* occur due to low blood glucose (*hypoglycaemia*). Muscle wasting and weakness usually occur and chest infections are frequent. Excess glycogen is stored in the liver which becomes very large. This may improve in puberty. It is inherited from both parents who are carriers (*recessive inheritance*). Treatment is with a special diet and drugs may be used to raise the blood sugar levels. An operation may be necessary on the blood vessels from the bowel to divert blood past the liver (portacaval shunt). The disorder is progressive but survival into adult life can occur. Mental handicap is rare and usually due to brain damage from recurrent seizures and low blood sugar.

BROWN, B.I. & BROWN, D.H. (1968) Glycogen-storage disease Types I, III, IV, V, VII and unclassified glycogenoses. In: Carbohydrate Metabolism and its Disorders, Vol. 2, New York: Academic Press. p. 123.
SINCLAIR, L. (1979) Metabolic Disease in Childhood. Oxford: Blackwell Scientific Publications. pp. 264–265.

Linear naevus sebaceous syndrome

In this very rare syndrome there is a long thin birth-mark, often on the face, scalp and/or neck, consisting of yellow or brown nodules and lumps. After puberty it increases in size and tumours develop within it which may be *malignant*. It is often associated with *epilepsy*, mental handicap and behavioural disturbances. Abnormalities of the eyes, brain and kidneys have been reported. *Dominant inheritance* is usual with a parent being only mildly affected.

LOVEJOY, F.H. Jr. & BOYLE, W.E. (1973) Linear nevus sebaceous syndrome: Report of two cases and a review of the literature. Pediatrics, 52:383.

WARKANY, J. et al (1981) Mental Retardation and Congenital Malformations of the Central Nervous System. Chicago: Year Book Medical Publishers. Inc. pp. 347–349.

Lioresal
= *baclofen*.

Lipidosis / lipid storage disease

This group of disorders includes a number of hereditary diseases characterized by abnormal *metabolism* of fatty substances (lipids), especially sphingolipids, leading to the deposition of lipid materials in the cells of the brain and nervous system. There is a progressive course to the diseases with intellectual and visual deterioration. *Gangliosidoses* such as *Tay-Sachs disease* are within this group as are *Gaucher's disease*, *Fabry's disease* and *Niemann-Pick disease*.

Lipodystrophy / lipoatrophic diabetes mellitus

The absence of fat tissue (adipose tissue) is referred to as lipodystrophy. This may be partial or complete. The *congenital* form is also known as Berardinelli's lipodystrophy, Seip syndrome and lipodystrophic muscular hypertrophy. Infants with the congenital form are usually of average or increased birth weight. It is more common in girls. The absence of fat makes the skin look thin and the veins prominent. The cheeks appear hollow. Hairiness and increased pigment in the skin are common. The tongue, liver and spleen are enlarged and the muscles are bulky. The hands, feet and genitals are relatively large. During the first few years of life growth is rapid but is usually normal by teenage years. Bone age, as determined by X-ray, is greatly advanced for the actual age. About 20% of people with this condition are mildly or moderately mentally handicapped. The exact cause is not known. It is thought to be inherited from both parents who are carriers (*recessive inheritance*). There is no known treatment.

SEIP, M. & TRYGSTAD, O. (1963) Generalized lipodystrophy. Arch. Dis. Childh., 38: 447–453.

SENIOR, B. & GELLIS, S.S. (1964) The syndromes of total lipodystrophy and of partial lipodystrophy. Pediatrics, 33: 593–612.

Lipofuscinosis / lipofuscin storage disease
= *ceroid-lipofuscinoses.*

Lipogranulomatosis
= *Farber's lipogranulomatosis.*

Lissencephaly
Literally translated this means a brain without surface folding and without convolutions (agyria). It is often also used to describe brains with shallow convolutions. Partial lissencephaly occurs when only certain areas of the brain are smooth. If some of the convolutions (gyri) are abnormally thick and broad the term pachygyria may be used. Some writers use the term lissencephaly for both agyria and pachygyria. Complete lissencephaly (agyria) is very rare.

There are probably many different causes of lissencephaly. Some *familial* cases have been reported suggesting *recessive inheritance.* These are known as lissencephaly syndrome or Miller-Dieker syndrome. In these families the lissencephaly was associated with other *congenital* abnormalities of the heart, intestine, liver, kidneys, eyes, bones and/or genitals. In some affected children the lissencephaly is part of another syndrome such as *cerebro-hepato-renal syndrome.* In most children with lissencephaly the head circumference is small. The forehead may slant and the face may have a rather flat appearance with a small lower jaw. There is often a history of breathing difficulties at birth, feeble movements and a weak cry. Sucking and swallowing problems may lead to inhalation of feeds and bronchopneumonia. The initial floppiness is usually gradually replaced by increasing rigidity, *spasticity* and arching of the back and neck.

Many children have *seizures* which may be *grand-mal convulsions* or *infantile spasms.* The *epilepsy* is difficult to control. Profound mental and physical handicap is the rule. Many affected children die within a few months of birth and in only three recorded cases have the children lived beyond the first decade. There is no known treatment for this condition.

DIGNAN, P.ST.J. & WARKANY, J. (1978) Congenital malformation: lissencephaly, agyria and pachygyria. In: Mental Retardation and Developmental Disabilities. Wortis, J. (Ed.) New York: Brunner/Mazel.
DOBYNS, W.B. et al (1983) Miller-Dieker syndrome: lissencephaly and monosomy 17p. J. Pediatr., 102:552–558.
GARCIA, C.A. et al (1978) The lissencephaly (agyria) syndrome in siblings. Computerized tomographic and neuropathologic findings. Arch. Neurol., 35:608.
WARKANY, J. et al (1981) Mental Retardation and Congenital Malformation of the Central Nervous System. Chicago: Year Book Medical Publishers. Inc. pp. 200–210.

Lithium
A drug used for the treatment of *manic-depressive psychosis*, recurrent *mania* or recurrent *depression.* It is also given to prevent recurrence of such disorders. It has been used in the treatment of mentally handicapped people with aggressive and *self-injurious behaviours.* It has to be introduced and monitored carefully because the therapeutic dose is near to the toxic dose. Kidney, heart and thyroid function should be checked before and during treatment and the blood levels of lithium must be taken regularly. Toxic effects include nausea, diarrhoea, vomiting, muscle weakness, tremor, drowsiness, passing excess urine and excessive thirst. It should be stopped immediately if the person is ill.

CRAFT, M. et al (1987) Lithium in the treatment of aggression in mentally handicapped patients. Brit. J. Psychiat., 150: 685–689.

DALE, P.G. (1980) Lithium therapy in aggressive mentally subnormal patients. Brit. J. Psychiat., 137:469–474.

JOHNSON, F.N. (1980) Handbook of Lithium Therapy. Lancaster, U.K.: MTP Press.

NAYLOR, G.J. et al (1974) A double blind trial of long term lithium therapy in mental defectives. Brit. J. Psychiat., 124:52–57.

RIVINUS, T.M. & HARMATZ, J.S. (1979) Diagnosis and lithium treatment of affective disorders in the retarded: five case studies. Am. J. Psychiat., 136:551–554.

Little leopard syndrome
= *multiple lentiginosis syndrome.*

Little's disease
A type of *cerebral palsy* with a spastic diplegia. The legs are stiff and tend to cross (*scissoring*). There is a strong association between this type of cerebral palsy and the infant being premature and small for dates.

Livido reticularis
A red mottling of the skin present over the limbs and chest in *homocystinuria.*

Lobes of brain
A lobe is a major division of an organ. There are four lobes visible on each half of the brain; the *frontal, temporal, parietal* and *occipital lobes.* Certain functions of the brain can be located in particular lobes.

Lobster claw hand
A deformity of the hand sometimes seen in the *de Lange syndrome.* The thumb is situated nearer the wrist than usual and the fingers are short and partially bent.

Local authority social services
In the U.K. each county council has a Social Services department. This department runs *social work* services and also *adult training centres, hostels, family support care schemes* and many other services for mentally handicapped people. Information about a local department and the services offered can be obtained from a local social services office or from the county council headquarters. County councillors are the elected representatives of people within the county and are involved in major decisions about the service provided.

Local education authority
In the U.K. since, the *Education (Handicapped Children) Act 1970* the local education authorities run by the county council have had a statutory responsibility for providing education for mentally handicapped children. The duties of the education authorities were increased in the *Education Act (1981).*

Locomotor skills
The skills involved in moving the body around. These include crawling, walking and running abilities.

Long-term care
This usually refers to full-time residential care on a long-term basis as compared to *phased care* where the major part of the care is elsewhere.

Lorazepan
A drug used for the treatment of anxiety. It is one of the *benzodiazepine* group. It has also been recommended for intravenous use in the treatment of *status epilepticus* because it is effective for longer than *diazepam.*

Lordosis
An abnormal forward curve of the spine. This generally occurs in the lower part of the back (lumbar lordosis) where there is normally a slight forward curve. Severe lumbar lordosis occurs in *Duchenne's muscular dystrophy* and a few other rare conditions associated with mental handicap.

Louis-Barr syndrome
A condition in which multiple biochemical abnormalities occur in the body. The mechanism by which these occur is not understood. Unsteadiness (*cerebellar ataxia*) develops in early childhood and involuntary

movements (*choreoathetosis*) also occur. Small patches of fine tortuous blood vessels (*telangiectasia*) appear in the skin and whites of the eyes usually between 3 and 10 years of age. They are characteristically located over the exposed areas of the body, the bridge of the nose, ears, neck and front of the elbow. They become more marked with exposure to sunlight. There is loss of skin elasticity and lack of fat under the skin. Brown patches (*café-au-lait patches*) appear on arms and legs and dermatitis is common. The hair thins and goes prematurely grey. Later unsteadiness and unco-ordination of eye movements, floppiness of muscles and generalized weakness occur. Although intelligence is initially normal there is a progressive impairment. *Epilepsy* often occurs.

Susceptibility to infection is a problem and this is due to abnormalities in the immune system of the body. About half the affected people develop an unusual form of *diabetes* in adolescence. Life expectancy is considerably reduced through recurrent chest infections or *malignancy*. It is inherited from both parents who are carriers (*recessive inheritance*). Carriers may be more susceptible than usual to malignant diseases.

McFARLIN, D.E. et al (1972) Ataxia-telangiectasia. Medicine, 51:281.

SHAHAM, M. et al (1982) Prenatal diagnosis of ataxia-telangiectasia. J. Pediatr., 100:134.

SWIFT, M. & CHASE, C. (1983) Cancer and cardiac death in obligatory ataxia-telangiectasia. Lancet, 1:1049.

TOLEDANO, S.R. & LANGE, B.J. (1980) Ataxia-telangiectasia and acute lymphoblastic leukaemia. Lancet, 45:1675.

Lowe's syndrome

A rare condition present at birth in which severe mental handicap is associated with abnormalities of the eyes, poor growth, functional abnormalities of the kidneys and floppiness and weakness of muscles. A characteristic facial appearance occurs with a prominent brow and sunken eyes. *Cataracts* and *glaucoma* of the eyes frequently occur.

Amino acids and proteins are lost through the kidneys and can be detected in the urine. This leads to *dehydration* and biochemical disturbances in the body and is a cause of softening of the bones (rickets). Life expectancy is considerably reduced and death often occurs from infections when the person is already very weak from kidney failure. Treatment with vitamin D has been recommended to reduce the rate of deterioration. It occurs in males and is inherited from the mother who is a carrier (*sex-linked inheritance*).

ABBASSI, V. et al (1968) Oculo-cerebro-renal syndrome: a review. Am. J. Dis. Child., 115:145–168.

MARTIN, M.A. & SYLVESTER, P.E. (1980) Clinicopathological studies of oculo-cerebro-renal syndrome of Lowe, Terry and MacLachlan. J. Ment. Defic. Res., 24:1.

WISNIEWSKI, K.E. et al (1984) Ultrastructural, neurological and glycosaminoglycan abnormalities in Lowe's syndrome. Ann. Neurol., 16:40.

Lumbar kyphosis

A *kyphosis* of the lower part of the back (also known as the loin or lumbar region).

Lumbar lordosis

See *lordosis*.

Lumbar scoliosis

A *scoliosis* of the lower part of the back (also known as the loin or lumbar region).

Luminal

= *phenobarbitone*.

Lymphoedema

Swelling as a result of fluid accumulation caused by obstruction of the lymph drainage system. Lymphoedema of the skin occurs at birth in *Turner's syndrome* and lymphoedema of the hands and feet may occur in *Noonan's syndrome*.

Lysosomal diseases

Many of the storage diseases (those in which

Lysosomal diseases

abnormal substances accumulate in the cells of the body causing damage) fit into the category of lysosomal diseases. The lysosomes are organelles inside cells which consist of a fat (lipid) membrane enclosing a particular group of *enzymes* (acid hydrolytic enzymes). If a lysosomal enzyme is missing the chemical it normally deals with may accumulate in the lysosomes and the cell becomes laden. The first example in which this was discovered was *Pompe's disease* and other examples are *Tay-Sachs disease, Hurler's syndrome* and *Hunter's syndrome*. The discovery of this process has considerably enhanced the understanding of these disorders.

FRASER, F.C. & NORA, J.J. (1968) Genetics of Man. (2nd edit.) Philadelphia: Lea & Febiger. pp. 108–110.

NEUFIELD, E.F. & McKUSICK, V.A. (1983) Disorders of lysosomal enzyme synthesis. In: The Metabolic Basis of Inherited Disease. (5th edit.) (Ed.) Stanbury, J.B. et al. New York: McGraw-Hill.

M

Macomb-Oakland Regional Center (MORC)

This service in Michigan, U.S.A., has established not only a small residential centre in bungalow-type accommodation, but also a community placement programme in which intellectually disabled children are placed in community training homes (CTH). These are private homes in which care and training are provided by 'foster parents' who are specially trained. The majority of residential placements for children are in the CTH's which are closely monitored and supported. For adults there are group homes mainly in rented accommodation with involvement of the owner and a staff team to support the residents. This service is generally regarded as a very successful example of community care.

HERON, A. & MYERS, S. (1983) Intellectual Impairment. London: Academic Press. pp. 104–106, 132–133.

Macrencephaly

= *megalencephaly*.

Macro-orchidism

Abnormally large testicles. This is a characteristic of the *fragile-X syndrome*.

Macro-orchidism marker X syndrome

= *fragile-X syndrome*.

Macrocephaly

An abnormally large head with a circumference that is, in statistical terms, more than two standard deviations above the norm for age, sex and race. It may be caused by *hydrocephalus* or *megalencephaly*. A thickened skull can also cause macrocephaly as in *osteopetrosis*. Macrocephaly may be associated with mental handicap and other abnormalities in a variety of conditions. These include *Beckwith syndrome, Klippel-Trenaunay-Weber syndrome, tuberose sclerosis, Sturge-Weber syndrome* and *Sotos' syndrome*. Although there is increased prevalence of macrocephaly in children with mental handicap, there are also many examples of macrocephaly associated with normal intelligence.

GABRIEL, R.S. & McCOMB, J.G. (1985) Malformations of the central nervous system. In: Textbook of Child Neurology. Menkes, J.H. (3rd edit.). Philadelphia: Lea & Febiger. pp. 232–234.
LORBER, J. & PRIESTLY, B.L. (1981) Children with large heads. Dev. Med. Child Neurology, 23:494.
SMITH, R.D. (1981) Abnormal head circumference in learning disabled children. Dev. Med. Child Neurology, 23:626.

Macroglossia

An abnormally large tongue. This may occur in many conditions associated with mental handicap including *Greig's syndrome, Beckwith syndrome, cretinism, Down's syndrome, Rud's syndrome* and the *mucopolysaccharidoses*.

Macrogyria

See *pachygyria* and *lissencephaly*.

Macrostomia

An abnormally large mouth. This may occur in *Goldenhar's syndrome* and a few other rare conditions associated with mental handicap.

Macula / macula lutea

A small circular area of the *retina* of the eye. No blood vessels run through it and it is used for fine central vision.

Macular degeneration

Degeneration of the *macula* of the eye may occur in a number of conditions associated with mental handicap. A bright red coloration of the macula (cherry-red spot) is characteristic of *Tay-Sachs disease, Niemann-Pick disease, Farber's lipogranulomatosis* and *generalized gangliosidosis*. Grey discoloration with a red spot in the centre occurs in *metachromatic leucodystrophy*. In these conditions there is a progressive loss of visual acuity.

Magnesium nutritional deficiency syndrome

= *hypomagnesaemia*.

Magnetic resonance imaging

= *nuclear magnetic resonance imaging*.

Mainstreaming

In the U.S.A. this refers to the *integration* of children with special educational needs with other children in ordinary classes. This concept is central to the *Education for All Handicapped Children Act (1976)* which requires the least restrictive educational environment appropriate to the individual child's needs. Special classes, separate schooling, or other forms of removal from the ordinary educational environment should be limited to children who cannot be educated in regular classes even with supplemental and supportive services. Court decisions have upheld this principle even when this has led to costly educational facilities.

CORMAN, L. & GOTTLIEB, J. (1978) Mainstreaming mentally retarded children: a review of research. In: International Review of Research in Mental Retardation. Ellis, N.R. (Ed.) Vol. 9. New York: Academic Press. pp. 251–275.

GOTTLIEB, J. (Ed.) (1980) Educating Mentally Retarded Persons in the Mainstream. Baltimore: University Park Press.

GOTTLIEB, J. (1981) Mainstreaming: fulfilling the promise? Am. J. Ment. Defic., 86(2): 115–126.

STRAIN, P.S. & KERR, M.M. (1981) Mainstreaming of Children in Schools. New York: Academic Press.

Makaton

In the U.K. this sign language was developed following a project which explored the use of sign language with hearing impaired mentally handicapped adults. The Makaton vocabulary consists of about 350 whole word translations of *British Sign Language* signs. Some of the BSL signs had to be simplified. The signs are arranged in eleven stages each consisting of thirty-five to forty signs. Signs are depicted by line drawings and 'language programmes' are also available. Signs are used in the sequence of spoken English. It has been claimed that the language development of mentally handicapped people with normal hearing is also facilitated by the use of Makaton signing as the words are spoken.

WALKER, M. (1976) The Makaton Vocabulary (revised edit.) London: RADD.

WALKER, M. (1978) The Makaton vocabulary. In: Ways and Means. Tebbs, T. (Ed.). Basingstoke: Globe Education.

Malabsorption

Faulty absorption of food substances from the small bowel. This may cause vitamin deficiencies, *hypoglycaemia* and *hypomagnesaemia* which are rare causes of mental handicap.

Maladaptive behaviour

A behaviour which is a poor strategy for dealing with the natural and social demands of the environment. It is the cause of problems for the individual.

Malar flush

A redness of the cheeks of the face as often occurs in *homocystinuria*.

Malar hypoplasia

Underdevelopment of the cheek bones. This may occur in a few conditions associated with mental handicap including *bird-headed dwarfism*, *Treacher-Collins syndrome* and *Hallermann-Streiff syndrome*.

Malformation
See *congenital malformation*.

Malignant
A disease which progresses and/or spreads rapidly and which is often fatal. It is particularly used to refer to cancerous conditions and is the opposite of benign (harmless).

Malnutrition
Severe early malnutrition has been shown to affect the developing brain leading, in some cases, to varying degrees of mental handicap. Minor malnutrition and hunger undermine learning by causing listlessness and worry which can lead to underachievement even when the learning potential is normal. As malnourished children are usually raised in profound poverty or in institutions, it is not easy to identify single causative factors.

BIRCH, H.G. et al (1971) Relation of kwashiorkor in early childhood and intelligence at school age. Pediatr. Res., 5:579.
CRAVIOTO, J. & ARRIETA, R. (1984) Malnutrition in childhood. In: Developmental Neuropsychiatry. Rutter, M. (Ed.). Edinburgh: Churchill Livingstone. pp. 32–51.
CROSBY, W.M. et al (1977) Fetal malnutrition: an appraisal of correlated factors. Am. J. Obstet. Gynec., 128:22–31.
EVANS, D. et al (1980) Intellectual development and nutrition. J. Pediatr., 97:358.
RICHARDSON, S.A. (1984) The consequences of malnutrition for intellectual development. In: Scientific Studies in Mental Retardation. Dobbing, J. et al (Eds.). London: Royal Society of Medicine and Macmillan Press.

Malocclusion
Faulty alignment between the teeth of the upper and lower jaw when the mouth is closed. This is a fairly common dental problem which is particularly likely to occur in some conditions associated with mental handicap including *Apert's syndrome*, *Crouzon's syndrome*, *homocystinuria*, *Noonan's syndrome* and *Treacher-Collins syndrome*.

Mandible
The bone of the lower jaw. Overgrowth of this bone is known as *prognathism*. Underdevelopment of the mandible, often with the appearance of a receding chin, occurs in a number of conditions associated with mental handicap including *Carpenter's syndrome*, *Goldenhar's syndrome*, *Treacher-Collins syndrome*, *oro-facial-digital syndrome I*, *Cockayne's syndrome*, *Hallermann-Streiff syndrome*, *Rubinstein-Taybi syndrome*, *Noonan's syndrome* and *infantile hypercalcaemia*.

Mandibulo-facial dysostosis
= *Treacher-Collins syndrome*.

Mandibulo-oculo-facial dyscephaly
= *Hallermann-Streiff syndrome*.

Mania
A mental illness characterized by elated, euphoric but unstable mood; increase in speed of thinking and speaking with rapid shifting from one topic to another (flight of ideas); restlessness, agitation, overactivity; and often grandiose ideas of self-importance. If severely affected the person may get very little sleep and eventually become physically exhausted. Irrational and grandiose behaviour may cause problems. It is more difficult to diagnose when a person is severely mentally handicapped and cannot communicate. An increase in activity, irritability and changes in mood, sleep and appetite may be evident. It is more likely to be diagnosed if, as is often the case with mania, it recurs on a cyclical basis. It may alternate with episodes of *depression* in *manic-depressive psychosis*. Milder degrees of mania are referred to as *hypomania*. Treatment is by the use of tranquillizers such as *haloperidol*. *Lithium carbonate* may be used in order to

reduce the likelihood of recurrence. Mentally handicapped people are twice as susceptible to mental illness compared to the general population.

COOK, E.H. & LEVANTHAL, B.L. (1987) Down's syndrome with mania. Brit. J. Psychiat., 150:249–250.
REID, A.H. (1979) Clinical features of psychotic illness in adult defectives. In: Psychiatric Illness and Mental Handicap. James, F.E. & Snaith, R.P. (Eds.). London: Gaskell. pp. 83–84.

Manic-depressive psychosis

A severe psychiatric illness characterized by episodes of *mania* and episodes of *depression*. These mood swings may be on a sporadic basis or, less commonly, on a regular cycle. It is treated according to the presentation at the time and preventative treatment with *lithium carbonate* is often indicated.

HASAN, M.K. & MOODY, R.P. (1979) Three cases of manic depressive illness in mentally retarded adults. Am. J. Psychiat., 136:1069–1071.
REID, A.H. (1979) Clinical features of psychotic illness in adult defectives. In: Psychiatric Illness and Mental Handicap. James, F.E. & Snaith, R.P. (Eds.). London: Gaskell. pp. 83–84.
REID, A.H. & NAYLOR, G.J. (1976) Short cycle manic depressive psychosis in mental defectives: a clinical and psychological study. J. Ment. Defic. Res., 20:67–76.
RIVINUS, T.M. & HARMATZ, J.S. (1979) Diagnosis and lithium treatment of affective disorders in the retarded: five case studies. Am. J. Psychiat., 136:551–556.

Mannerism

A repetitive movement or gesture usually occurring when a person is anxious or bored. Some mentally handicapped people, especially those with *autistic* features, have very noticeable manneristic behaviours. Rocking and *self-injurious behaviours* may be included but are more often regarded separately.

Mannosidosis

A disease caused by a deficiency of *enzymes* (mannosidoses A and B). This leads to the accumulation of mannose-containing substances in the tissues of the body and these appear in the urine in large amounts. The condition is characterized by a prominent forehead, enlarged tongue, coarse facial features, small *cataracts*, enlarged liver and spleen, abnormal outward curve of the lower region of the back (*kyphosis*), restlessness and progressive physical and mental deterioration. There is a severe infantile form and a milder form occurring in late childhood or adulthood. In the severe infantile form death occurs in early childhood. It is inherited from both parents who are carriers (*recessive inheritance*).

BEAUDET, A.L. (1983) Disorders of glycoprotein degradation: Mannosidosis, fucosidosis, sialidosis and aspartylglycosaminuria. In: The Metabolic Basis of Inherited Disease (5th edit.) Stanbury, J.B. et al (Eds.). New York: McGraw-Hill. p. 788.
KISTLER, J.P. et al (1977) Mannosidosis. New clinical presentation, enzyme studies and carbohydrate analysis. Arch. Neurol., 34:45.

Manual communication

This refers to any form of non-speech communication which involves gestures or signs. It may be used with mentally handicapped people who are deaf or who have a problem with spoken language. There are several *gesture systems* and many *sign languages* including *American Sign Language, British Sign Language, Makaton* and *Paget-Gorman sign system*.

Maple syrup urine disease

A rare condition caused by deficiency of an *enzyme* (alpha-ketoacid decarboxylase). This leads to abnormalities in the processes dealing with some of the *amino acids* in the body. Abnormal substances are present in the blood and are excreted in the urine causing the characteristic smell. Babies with this condition appear normal at birth but within the first week have tightness of muscles, irritability, feeding problems, convulsions and irregularities in breathing. If untreated most die within the first few months. Low blood sugar is a frequent problem (*hypoglycaemia*). Treatment consists of a special diet with restricted intake of certain amino acids which should be started within the first few days of life. Blood levels of amino acids have to be carefully watched and there is a susceptibility to infections which require prompt treatment. Even in those children treated early, one quarter die. Of the survivors, one third have severe *cerebral palsy* and the others have various handicaps including mental handicap and *epilepsy*. A small proportion are completely normal. There is a variant of the disease in which the typical urine is excreted only in infections or under stress when there is also unsteadiness, drowsiness, behaviour disturbances and often *seizures*. Mental handicap is mild or absent. The condition is inherited from both parents who are carriers (*recessive inheritance*). The enzyme deficiency is detectable following *amniocentesis*.

BELL, L. et al (1975) Dietary management of maple syrup urine disease: Extension of equivalency systems. J. Am. Diet. Assoc., 74:357.

CLOW, C.L. et al (1981) Outcome of early and long-term management of classical maple syrup urine disease. Pediatrics, 68: 856.

MENKES, J.H. (1985) Textbook of Child Neurology (3rd edit.). Philadelphia: Lea & Febiger. pp. 14–17.

NAUGHTON, E.R. et al (1982) Outcome of maple syrup urine disease. Arch. Dis. Childh., 57:918.

Marble-bone disease

= *osteopetrosis*.

Marden-Walker syndrome

A rare condition in which mental handicap is associated with an unusual facial appear-

ance and tightness of the joints (*contractures*). There is narrowing of the eyelids, a small jaw, low-set ears and restricted growth. Abnormalities of bones are common. The degree of intellectual disability is variable and often mild. The cause of the condition is not known but it is probably inherited from both parents who are carriers (*recessive inheritance*).

HOWARD, F.M. & ROWLANDSON, P. (1981) Two brothers with Marden-Walker syndrome: case report and review. J. Med. Genet., 18:50–53.

JAATOUL, N.Y. et al (1982) Brief clinical report and review: the Marden-Walker syndrome. Am. J. Med. Genet., 11:259–271.

Marfan's syndrome

People with this condition have long narrow fingers and toes, dislocated lens of the eyes, abnormalities of the heart and blood vessels, a high arched palate and chest deformities. Mental handicap is rarely present. It is inherited from a parent as a *dominant* condition. It has some similarities to *homocystinuria*.

BRENTON, D.P. et al (1972) Homocystinuria and Marfan's syndrome: A comparison. J. Bone Jt. Surg., 54B:277.

Marinesco-Sjögren syndrome

People with this condition have a small head, abnormalities of the ribs, curvature of the spine, short broad fingers, *club foot*, flat foot and small stature. Squints and *cataracts* occur and visual impairment is usual. Hair is scanty or absent with little colour. Unsteadiness (*cerebellar ataxia*), lax muscle tone, slurred speech and progressive weakness develop early in life. *Epilepsy* generally occurs. Walking is usually achieved but is generally late and never good. Mild to severe mental handicap is usual but not progressive. The cerebellar ataxia tends to progress and some adults lose the ability to walk. Life expectancy is slightly reduced. It is inherited from both parents who are carriers (*recessive inheritance*).

ALTER, M. & KENNEDY, W. (1968) The
Marinesco-Sjögren syndrome. Hereditary
cerebello-lental degeneration with mental
retardation. Minn. Med., 51:901–906.
NORWOOD, W.F. (1964) The Marinesco-
Sjögren syndrome. J. Pediatr., 65:431–437.

Marker-X syndrome
= *fragile-X syndrome.*

Marmoration
A marbled appearance which may occur
when there is poor circulation of the blood
to the skin. This is quite common in
children with *Down's syndrome* and does not
have any serious consequences.

Maroteaux-Lamy pycnodysostosis syndrome
= *pycnodysostosis*

Maroteaux-Lamy syndrome
One of the *mucopolysaccharidoses.* It is caused
by an *enzyme* deficiency. People with this
condition have facial features similar to
Hurler's disease but little or no intellectual
impairment. There are two forms. In the
severe form there is a rapid deterioration
with abnormalities of bones and joints and
clouding of the *cornea* of the eye. The liver
and spleen are enlarged. Death occurs
before adulthood. In the mild form corneal
clouding, deafness and claw hands may
occur but death is delayed until the third or
fourth decades. Short stature, heart abnormalities and hip problems are sometimes
present in this syndrome. Intellectual impairment can be caused by the development
of *hydrocephalus.* It is inherited from both
parents who are carriers (*recessive inheritance*).

MAROTEAUX, P. & LAMY, M. (1965)
Hurler's disease, Morquios' disease and
related mucopolysaccharidoses. J. Pediatr.,
67:312.

Marriage
There is no law in the U.K. which specifically prevents mentally handicapped people
from marrying. The Matrimonial Causes
Act 1950 makes a marriage invalid if, at the
time of the marriage, either of the parties
was suffering from a *mental disorder*, within
the meaning of the *Mental Health Act 1983*, of
such a kind or to such an extent as to be
unfitted for marriage (incapable of living in
a married state and carrying out the
ordinary duties and other functions of marriage) and the procreation of children or
subject to recurrent attacks of insanity or
epilepsy. This is provided that the petitioner
was, at the time of the marriage, ignorant of
the alleged facts, that the proceedings were
instituted within a year from the date of the
marriage and that marital intercourse, with
the consent of the petitioner, has not taken
place since the discovery by the petitioner of
the existence of the grounds for a decree.
Under the Matrimonial Causes Act 1973 a
marriage is void (as if it had not taken
place) if either party did not give proper
consent to it because of 'unsoundness of
mind'. This would apply if, at the time of
the ceremony, one of the partners could not
understand the nature of the contract being
entered into and 'appropriate its basic
responsibilities.'
Marriage of mentally handicapped people is
restricted in a number of states of the U.S.A.
This is generally on the basis of the supposed inability of mentally handicapped
people to understand the responsibilities of
marriage and also because of the assumed
risks in allowing procreation.
Marriage can pose many problems for
mentally handicapped people and their
advocates. Some couples talk about marriage
and about being engaged without ever
taking any action to suggest that they wish
to get married. Usually couples who want to
be married will agitate and find an advocate
to help them achieve their goal. Since it is
usual for people to marry it is likely that
mentally handicapped people will wish to
do the same. Most such couples face opposition and are given much more counselling
and advice than other couples. Like any
other marriage the chances of success are

greater if they are mature, have sufficient income, are emotionally stable and have a good model in their parents' marriages. Access to a strong support system is very important. *Parenthood* is a concern and requires very careful consideration.

CRAFT, A. & CRAFT, M. (1985) Sexual and personal relationships. In: Mental Handicap: A Multidisciplinary Approach. Craft, M. et al (Eds.). London: Baillière Tindall. pp. 185–190.
FLOOR, L. et al (1975) A survey of marriages among previously institutionalized retards. Ment. Retard., 13(2):33.
GUNN, M. (1986) The law and mental handicap: 7. Marriage. Mental Handicap 14(1):37–38.
MATTINSON, J. (1973) Marriage and mental handicap. In: Human Sexuality and the Mentally Retarded. De la Cruz, F.F. & La Veck, G.D. (Eds.). New York: Brunner/Mazel.

Martin-Bell syndrome / Martin-Bell-Renpenning syndrome

= *fragile-X syndrome*.

Masturbation

Self-stimulation of the genitals which creates a pleasurable feeling of sexual gratification. Masturbation is not harmful and is generally regarded as a natural and normal part of sexual development. Mentally handicapped people, like everyone else, are likely to turn to whatever sources of distraction, amusement, enjoyment or escape that are available and not harmful. It is important for them to learn that masturbation is an activity which is not socially acceptable in any public place. At the same time as teaching this, it is necessary to avoid making the person feel guilty about carrying out the act in private. Masturbation only becomes a serious issue if the person cannot learn and accept the social rules or if relatives, teachers and care givers differ in their ideas about what constitutes permissible behaviour. There are a number of agencies which specialize in helping disabled people with sexual problems. See *sex education*.

Maxfield-Buchholtz Scale of Social Maturity for Preschool Blind Children

This scale is an adaptation of the *Vineland Social Maturity Scale* and covers the developmental range from birth to 5 years. It is standardized on the performance profiles of blind and partially sighted children and is not an intelligence test but an interview scale given to the main care giver. The categories are the same as for the Vineland Scale. A broader picture of the child's development is obtained by using the scale in conjunction with the *Reynell-Zinkin Scales*.

MAXFIELD, K.E. & BUCHHOLTZ, S.B. (1957) A Social Maturity Scale for Blind Preschool Children. New York: American Foundation for the Blind.

Maxilla

The bone of the upper jaw. It is prominent in a few conditions associated with mental handicap including *Cockayne's syndrome* but is more commonly underdeveloped (hypoplastic) as in *Apert's syndrome, Conradi's syndrome, Crouzon's syndrome, Hallermann-Streiff syndrome, Pfeiffer's syndrome* and *Treacher-Collins syndrome*.

Measles encephalitis

This complication occurs late in the course of a measles infection in about 1 in 1000 cases. Symptoms of *encephalitis* appear 1 to 8 days after the start of the rash. In the more severe cases there is an impairment of consciousness with *seizures* and abnormal signs on neurological examination. There is a mortality of 10%, and at least one third of survivors are left with *epilepsy*, mental handicap, *hyperactivity* and perceptual abnormalities. Often a progressive deterioration in intelligence is seen. *Subacute sclerosing panencephalitis* is another form of measles encephalitis. There is no effective treatment apart from drugs to control the seizures.

BOUGHTON, C.R. (1964) Morbilli in Sydney II. Neurological sequelae of measles. Med. J. Aus., 2:908.

MEYER, E. & BYERS, R.K. (1952) Measles encephalitis: A follow-up study of 16 patients. Am. Med. Assoc. J. Dis. Child, 84:543.

TYLER, H.R. (1957) Neurological complications of rubeola (measles). Medicine (Balt.) 36:147.

Measles vaccine encephalitis

This is a rare complication of vaccination with live measles virus, with an incidence of 1.68 per million vaccine doses. The course of the illness is the same as for *measles encephalitis* and may also be a cause of *subacute sclerosing panencephalitis*.

Measles live attenuated vaccine should not be given to children whose immune responses might be impaired or to children with an infectious illness. Children with a history of convulsions, with *epilepsy* in the immediate family, with chronic lung or heart disease or who are seriously underdeveloped, should only be given the vaccine with simultaneous administration of diluted normal immunoglobin for use with measles vaccine (this contains antibodies against measles). It may reduce the effectiveness of the vaccine and immunity should be checked later.

LANDRIGAN, P.J. & WHITE, J.J. (1973) Neurologic disorders following live measles virus vaccination. J. Am. Med. Assoc. 223:1459.

NADER, P.R. & WARREN, R.J. (1968) Reported neurologic disorders following live measles vaccine. Pediatrics, 41:997.

Mebaral

= *methylphenobarbital*.

Meckel syndrome / Meckel-Gruber syndrome

Infants with this condition have a number of abnormalities present at birth which may include a small head with an *encephalocoele* at the back, malformed eyes and ears, small chin, *cleft lip, cleft palate*, extra fingers and toes, *club feet*, genital abnormalities, underdeveloped lungs and cystic kidneys. Abnormalities of the heart are sometimes present. Nearly all affected infants are stillborn or die soon after birth. It is inherited from both parents who are carriers (*recessive inheritance*).

FRIED, K. et al (1971) Polycystic kidneys associated with malformations of the brain, polydactyly, and other birth defects in newborn sibs. A lethal syndrome showing autosomal recessive pattern of inheritance. J. Med. Genet., 8:285–290.

HSIA, Y.E. et al (1971) Genetics of the Meckel syndrome (dysencephalic splanchnocystica) Pediatrics, 48:237–247.

OPITZ, J.M. & HOWE, J.J. (1969) The Meckel syndrome (dysencephalic splanchnocystica, the Gruber syndrome). Birth Defects, 5:167–179.

Meconium

Meconium is the substance present in the bowel of the newborn infant. It is dark green in colour and is a mixture of mucus, bile and bowel secretions. It is generally passed four or five times in the first 24 hours but, if the *fetus* has been physically stressed due to lack of oxygen and/or complications of labour, much of the meconium may have passed in the uterus leading to meconium staining of the fluid draining during labour. This is regarded as a sign of problems which could lead to mental handicap.

If no meconium is passed after 24 hours the infant should be examined to exclude the possibility that it is suffering from an *imperforate anus* or abnormality of the bowel.

Medial canthus

The inner angle of the eye. The distance between the medial canthi is increased in *hypertelorism*.

Median cleft face syndrome

Individuals with *hypertelorism* and a cleft

nose have been found to have many abnormalities of the middle of the face and sometimes of the brain as well. Most affected people are of normal intelligence but, especially in association with a short neck and shoulder deformity, mental handicap may occur. Squints, deafness and abnormalities of fingers, toes and eyes have also been described.

SEDANO, H.O. et al (1970) Frontonasal dysplasia. J. Pediatr., 76:906–913.

Medical model

A method of understanding a problem based on the medical approach and incorporating ideas of illness, diagnosis, cause and treatment. It provides a useful framework for the understanding of diseases which are either acute or curable but is less useful when there are prolonged effects of illness causing disabilities which interfere with personal development and social function. The medical model has not only been used as a method of understanding the causes of mental handicap but also as an approach to the care of mentally handicapped people. The latter was established in the U.K. in 1946 when colonies and institutions became hospitals. This approach is nowadays regarded as inappropriate, hospitals are closing and resources are being transferred to social and educational services. It is now thought that mentally handicapped people should have access to the same medical assistance as anyone else when they are ill but should not be regarded as ill because they have a disability.

Medical Research Council Handicaps, Behaviour and Skills Schedule
= *Handicaps, Behaviour and Skills Schedule.*

Medulla oblongata
= *brain stem.*

Medulloblastoma

A type of tumour of the *cerebellum* of the brain which varies in the degree of *malig-*

nancy. It is often diagnosed following signs of raised *intracranial pressure* such as headache and vomiting. Unsteadiness when standing and walking are often early signs and are followed by other signs of cerebellar damage such as speech and movement disorders. Diagnosis is usually confirmed by *CT scan.* Treatment usually consists of removal of the bulk of the tumour, by-pass drainage of the *cerebro-spinal fluid* and radiotherapy. If treatment is successful there may sometimes be residual brain damage from surgery or radiotherapy.

MEALEY, J. & HALL, P.V. (1977) Medulloblastoma in children. Survival and treatment. J. Neurosurg., 46:56.
PARK, T.S. et al (1983) Medulloblastoma: Clinical presentation and management. Experience at the hospital for sick children, Toronto. J. Neurosurg., 58:543.

Megacephaly
= *macrocephaly.*

Megalencephaly

A brain of unusually large size and weight. In life this can only be diagnosed by special techniques, such as *ultrasound scans* and *CT scans.* It occurs in many forms and with or without an underlying diagnosed abnormality or disease of the brain. There are various classifications used. When it is the only abnormality present and the cause is unknown, it may be referred to as primary or idiopathic megalencephaly. Sometimes this is associated with severe malformations of the brain or with microscopic abnormalities and then the majority of affected people are mentally handicapped. In a few people the brain structure and intelligence are normal. Megalencephaly may rarely affect only one side of the brain and the face and/or the body may be correspondingly enlarged. *Achondroplasia, tuberose sclerosis, Canavan's disease, Alexander's disease, Schilder's disease, Sotos' syndrome, gangliosidoses* and *mucopolysaccharidoses* are conditions in which megalencephaly is frequently present.

Megalencephaly may be associated with varying degrees of mental handicap, visual defects, squint, *cerebral palsy*, high body temperature, *epilepsy*, abnormalities of the genitals and bones and *congenital heart disease*.

DEMYER, W.W. (1972) Megalencephaly in children. Clinical syndromes, genetic patterns and differential diagnosis from other causes of megalocephaly. Neurology (Minneap.), 22:634.
PORTNOY, H.D. & CROISSANTI, P.D. (1978) Megalencephaly in infants and children. Arch. Neurol., 35:306.
WARKANY, J. et al (1981) Mental Retardation and Congenital Malformations of the Central Nervous System. Chicago: Year Book Medical Publishers Inc. pp. 101–122.

Melleril

= *thioridazine*.

Menarche

The time during *puberty* at which a girl first menstruates. This may be early in *Sotos' syndrome, congenital hypothyroidism, Silver's syndrome* and *hydrocephalus*. It may be late in *Noonan's syndrome, Engelmann's disease, xeroderma pigmentosum* and untreated *hypothyroidism*.

Mencap

= *Royal Society for Mentally Handicapped Children and Adults*.

Mendelian inheritance

Mendel described laws which seemed to govern the way in which characteristics were passed from one generation to the next. He described two main types of single gene inheritance, *recessive* and *dominant inheritance*.

Meninges

The membranes surrounding the brain and *spinal cord*. There are three layers: a tough, fibrous outer membrane, the dura mater, which is closely applied to the inside of the skull; the arachnoid mater, surrounding the brain but separated from it by spaces containing *cerebro-spinal fluid*; and the pia mater, a delicate network of fibres and blood vessels which closely covers the brain.

Meningioma

A benign tumour of the *meninges* which leads to problems only if it causes an obstruction to the flow of cerebro-spinal fluid (*hydrocephalus*) or pressure on brain or nerve tissue. It is unusual for such tumours to become *malignant*. It may be present in *Von Recklinghausen's disease*.

Meningitis

Infection of the *meninges*. Many bacteria and a few viruses and parasites may cause an infection but certain organisms are particularly likely to do so. Examination of *cerebro-spinal fluid* obtained by lumbar puncture confirms the diagnosis and identifies the responsible organism. Symptoms include fever, headache, nausea, vomiting, neck stiffness and reluctance to bend the neck and spine. Impairment of consciousness, *seizures* and paralysis are later signs. Treatment is primarily with antibiotics. Complications include *hydrocephalus, encephalitis* and collection of fluid under the skull (subdural effusion). The outcome depends on the nature and severity of the infection; the age when infected; the time lapse before treatment; and the type and amount of antibiotic used. Residual problems include deafness, *epilepsy*, mental handicap and *spasticity*. The outcome is likely to be particularly poor when meningitis occurs in a very young baby.

Editorial (1976) Diagnosis and prognosis in pyogenic meningitis. Lancet, 1:1361.
JEFFERY, H. et al (1977) Deafness after bacterial meningitis. Arch. Dis. Childh., 52:555.
OVERALL, J.C. (1970) Neonatal bacterial meningitis. J. Pediatr., 76:499–511.
SELL, S.H. (1983) Long-term sequelae of bacterial meningitis in children: Pediatr. Inf. Dis., 2:90–93.

Meningo-encephalitis

Infection of the *meninges* and brain producing the symptoms of *meningitis* and *encephalitis*.

Meningocoele

A protrusion of the *meninges* through a bony cleft in the backbone or skull. This sac does not contain spinal cord (*meningomyelocoele*) or brain tissue. Meningocoele is only rarely associated with *hydrocephalus* or abnormalities of the spinal cord (unlike meningomyelocoele) and the outcome is usually good.

Meningoencephalocoele

= *encephalocoele*.

Meningomyelocoele

A failure in the fusion of the backbone leaving a bony cleft through which the spinal cord and *meninges* protrude. It is probably caused by a failure of the closure of the nerve tube in the fetus. It is often associated with the *Arnold-Chiari malformation* of the brain leading to *hydrocephalus* and up to half the children are intellectually impaired. Eighty percent of meningomyelocoeles occur in the lower part of the back. The extent and situation determine the degree of paralysis of the legs, the type of bladder and bowel incontinence and the extent of the loss of sensation in the legs. Surgical repair of the defect is usually undertaken within the first few days of life. In addition to early neurosurgical treatment affected children are likely to require the ongoing help of orthopaedic surgeons, *physiotherapists*, *paediatricians*, neurologists and the nursing and social services. Recurrence rates in later pregnancies are high (2% with one previously affected child and 6% with two affected children). The recurrence risk is also higher in close relatives. Measurement of the *alpha-feto protein* levels in later pregnancies is therefore recommended if *abortion* of affected children is acceptable to the parents. Folic acid supplements in pregnancy are believed to have a strongly preventative effect. In many areas the routine assessment of serum alpha-feto protein in all pregnant women, supplemented by *ultrasound scanning* and *amniocentesis*, enables meningomyelocoele to be identified in any affected fetuses.

ACTION COMMITTEE ON MYELODYSPLASIA, SECTION ON UROLOGY (1979) Current approaches to evaluation and management of children with myelomeningocoele. Pediatrics, 63:663.

BROCKLEHURST, G. (1976) Spina Bifida for the Clinician. London: William Heinemann Med. Books.

GABRIEL, R.S. & McCOMB, J.G. (1985) Malformations of the central nervous system. In: Textbook of Child Neurology (3rd edit.). Menkes, J.H. Philadelphia: Lea & Febiger. pp. 200–211.

GROSS, R.H. et al (1982) Early management and decision making for the treatment of myelomeningocele. Pediatrics, 70:941.

HUNT, G.M. & HOLMES, A.E. (1976) Factors relating to intelligence in treated cases of spina bifida cystica. Am. J. Dis. Child., 130:823.

SOARE, P.L. & RAIMONDI, A.J. (1977) Intellectual and perceptual motor characteristics of treated myelomeningocele children. Am. J. Dis. Child., 131:199.

WILLIAMSON, G.G. (1987) Children with Spina Bifida. Early Intervention and Pre-school Programming. Baltimore: Paul H. Brookes.

Further information:
Association for Spina Bifida and Hydrocephalus, 22, Upper Woburn Place, London WC1U 0EP.
Spina Bifida Association of America, 343 South Dearbon Ave., Suite 319, Chicago, Illin., 60604.

Menkes syndrome

A condition in which copper cannot be absorbed from the diet and, even if given by injection, cannot be fully used in the body due to a biochemical defect. Symptoms appear soon after birth and include low body temperature, feeding problems and poor weight gain. *Seizures* occur, muscles are floppy and head control poor. The face of the baby is often described as cherubic with a flat bridge to the nose, full cheeks and little expression. Movements are reduced. The hair is colourless, short and breaks easily and its structure, as observed under a microscope, is very abnormal. The skin is dry and thick. Abnormalities of the bones, arteries, eyes, bladder and kidneys are also present. Mental handicap is the rule and life expectancy rarely exceeds 3 years.

It occurs only in males and is inherited from the mother who is a carrier (*sex-linked inheritance*). Several less severe variants have been recognized which may present with unsteadiness, involuntary movements and mild mental handicap.

Treatment with copper injections may help to improve health to a very limited extent but does not avert the progressive deterioration in the brain in the severe form of the disease. It is possible to diagnose before birth by measuring the increased copper content of a *fibroblast culture* following *amniocentesis*. Carriers of the condition may be diagnosed by milder abnormalities of their hair.

BUCKNALL, W.E. et al (1973) Kinky hair syndrome: Response to copper therapy. Pediatrics, 52:653.

COLLIE, W.R. et al (1978) Pili torti as marker for carriers of Menkes disease. Lancet, 1:607.

GROVER, W.D. et al (1979) Clinical and biochemical aspects of trichopoliodystrophy. Ann. Neurol., 5:65.

WHEELER, E.M. & ROBERTS, P.F. (1976) Menkes' steely hair syndrome. Arch. Dis. Childh., 51:269.

Menstruation / menses

Although the *menarche* may be early or late for a few girls with mental handicap, the majority will menstruate in the normal way. It is important that, like any girl, they are prepared for this event and taught to manage it. See *sex education*.

Mental age

The average age at which the intellectual skills of an individual would be acquired by non-handicapped children. The *intelligence quotient* can be derived by dividing the mental age of a child by the *chronological age* up to 16 years and multiplying the result by 100. Mental age may be a useful guide when assessing and understanding the needs and problems of children but can easily be misunderstood when applied to adults. It refers only to the intellectual and reasoning skills of a person and has little relevance to maturity in other areas of development. Physical and social needs may be better understood in relation to the person's actual age and the importance of *age-appropriateness* should be emphasized. Mental age may be measured by a number of tests including *Griffiths Scale, Merrill-Palmer Test of Mental Abilities* and *Stanford-Binet*.

Mental deficiency

A term introduced in the U.K. in the early part of the 20th century but much less used nowadays. It acquired legal usage in the *Mental Deficiency Acts* where it was defined as 'a condition of arrested or incomplete development of mind whether arising from inherent causes or induced by disease or injury'. It was subdivided into four main groups: *feeble minded, idiots, imbeciles* and *moral imbeciles*. It was replaced by the terms *mental subnormality* and *severe subnormality* in the *Mental Health Act 1959* with the exception of the category of moral imbecile which was abandoned.

Mental Deficiency Acts 1913, 1914 and 1927

In 1904 the Royal Commission on the Care and Control of the Feeble Minded was set up in the U.K. This interviewed about 250 witnesses and sent representations far and wide. In 1908 the commission published a report in eight Blue Books on the basis of which the government passed the Mental Deficiency Lunacy (Scotland) Act 1913 and the Mental Deficiency and Lunacy Act for

England and Wales in 1914. Mentally ill people were defined as lunatics and mentally handicapped people were included in the term *mental deficiency*. The Act was amended, for England only, in 1927 when it was specified that the 'defect' must have been present before the age of 18 years. Under these Acts people could be certified as mentally defective and compulsorily admitted to local authority institutions although informal admission was possible. It was also possible to place a person under guardianship and supervision in the community. These Acts were replaced by the *Mental Health Act (1959)*.

Mental disorder
In the U.K. under the *Mental Health Act (1983)* mental disorder means mental illness, arrested or incomplete development of mind, *psychopathic disorder* and any other disorder or disability of mind. It does not include promiscuity, immoral conduct, sexual deviancy or dependence on alcohol or drugs.

Mental handicap
A term used in the U.K. to describe people who have a significant *impairment* of intellectual skills which results in them being *handicapped*. This is not a legal term but was introduced by relatives and professionals as an alternative to the terms *subnormality* and severe subnormality which were defined in the *Mental Health Act (1959)* but which were thought to be less acceptable. It is generally agreed that, in terms of *intelligence quotient*, mental handicap is present when the I.Q. is 70 or below on a standard I.Q. test. Mild mental handicap refers to an I.Q. between 51 and 70 and severe or profound mental handicap refers to an I.Q. of 50 or less. Most professionals prefer to use the *Diagnostic and Statistical Manual (DSM)-III* definition of mental retardation which includes an I.Q. of 70 or less; deficits or impairments in adaptive behaviour taking age into account and onset before 18 years of age. In the U.S.A. the term mental retardation is synonymous with the term mental handicap as used in the U.K.

Mental handicap nurses
See *nurse*.

Mental Health Act (1959)
The Mental Health Act 1959 applied to England and Wales. Mental disorder was subdivided into four categories: mental illness, *subnormality*, severe subnormality and *psychopathic disorder*. Compulsory admission to hospital was possible, without using a Court of Law, for people in these categories so long as certain criteria were met. Long-term admission was only applicable to subnormal people under 21 years of age but to severely subnormal people of all ages. People in both categories could be held on a long-term basis on an order made by a court. *Mental Health Review Tribunals* were established to review the need to continue to detain patients on compulsory orders. Guardianship orders would also be made using similar criteria and used to control the lives of people living in the community. This part of the Act was very infrequently used. This Act has been replaced by the *Mental Health Act (1983)*.

Mental Health Act (1983)
The Mental Health Act 1983 consolidates the law relating to mentally disordered persons in the *Mental Health Act (1959)* and the Mental Health (Amendment Act) 1982. It applies to England and Wales. Part I of the Act states that mental disorder means mental illness, arrested or incomplete development of mind, *psychopathic disorder* and any other disorder or disability of mind. *Severe mental impairment* and *mental impairment* are the categories in which mental handicap is relevant. The Act includes the procedures for *compulsory admission to hospital* or *guardianship* (Part II); patients concerned in criminal proceedings or under sentence (Part III); *Mental Health Review Tribunals* and the rights of patients who do not give *consent to treatment* (Part IV); Management of

Property and Affairs of Patients (Part VII); miscellaneous functions of local authorities and the Secretary of State (Part VIII); and Ill-Treatment of Patients (Part IX).

Mental Health Act (1983). London: HMSO.

BLUGLASS, R. (1983) A Guide to the Mental Health Act 1983. Edinburgh: Churchill Livingstone.

GOSTIN, L.O. (1985) The law relating to mental handicap in England and Wales. In: Mental Handicap. A Multidisciplinary Approach. Craft, M.A. et al (Eds.) London: Baillière Tindall. pp. 58–64.

HAMILTON, J.R. (1983) The Mental Health Act, 1983. Brit. Med. J., 286:1720–1725.

Mental Health Act Commission

Section 121 of the *Mental Health Act (1983)* requires the Secretary of State to establish a Mental Health Act Commission to appoint medical practitioners and others for the purposes of carrying out certain parts of the Act. The commission is required to prepare a report on its activities every 2 years.

Mental Health Review Tribunals

These were established in England and Wales in each Regional Health Authority Area under the *Mental Health Act (1959)* and retained under the *Mental Health Act (1983)*. They review the detention of patients on compulsory *hospital orders* or under *guardianship*. The 1983 Act gave patients and their nearest relatives increased opportunities to apply to a Tribunal and also the opportunity to apply for legal aid in order to obtain advice to assist them in presenting a case, to obtain an independent medical opinion and to cover the cost of representation at a Tribunal hearing. The Tribunal has the power to direct the discharge of patients or to recommend leave of absence, transfer to another hospital or guardianship.

Mental Health Act (1983) Mental Health Tribunals. London: HMSO. Chapter 20 Part V.

Mental illness

= *psychiatric illness*.

Mental impairment

Under the *Mental Health Act (1983)* this is defined as a state of arrested or incomplete development of mind (not amounting to *severe mental impairment*) which includes significant impairment of intelligence and social functioning and is associated with abnormally aggressive or seriously irresponsible conduct on the part of the person concerned.

Mental retardation

A term synonymous with mental handicap. Mental retardation is used more commonly in the U.S.A. and Canada. The definition of mental retardation in the DSM III Classification of the American Psychiatric Association includes a significantly subaverage general intellectual functioning (an *intelligence quotient* of 70 or below on an individually administered standard *intelligence test*); concurrent deficiency or impairments in adaptive behaviour (taking the person's age into account); and onset before the age of 18 years. In the *International Classification of Diseases* mental retardation is defined as a condition of arrested or incomplete development of mind which is especially characterized by subnormality of intelligence. Mild mental retardation (mild mental subnormality, feeble minded, high grade defect) on a standard I.Q. test covers the range 50–70; moderate mental retardation (moderate mental subnormality, imbecile) covers the I.Q. range 35–49; severe mental retardation (severe mental subnormality) covers the I.Q. range 20–34; and profound mental retardation (profound mental subnormality, idiocy) refers to an I.Q. under 20.

Mental subnormality

A term used in the *Mental Health Act (1959)* which is synonymous with *mental handicap* and *mental retardation* but not with *mental impairment* under the Mental Health Act 1983.

Mephenytoin

An *anticonvulsant* chemically related to *phenytoin* and used for the prevention of *grand-mal convulsions* and *complex partial seizures*. It is reported to have fewer side-effects than phenytoin but a higher risk of *agranulocytosis* which is usually reversible on stopping the drug. If used it must be monitored by regular blood tests in the first six months. Less common side-effects are skin rashes, fever and enlarged lymph glands. It is not available in the U.K.

BEST, W.R. & PAUL, J.T. (1950) Severe hypoplastic anaemia following anticonvulsant medication: Review of the literature and report of a case. Am. J. Med., 8:124.
TROUPIN, A.S. et al (1979) Clinical pharmacology of mephenytoin and ethotoin. Ann. Neurol., 6:410.

Mercury poisoning

This is very uncommon but can lead to disturbances in sensation, progressive visual impairment, unsteadiness, impaired hearing and mental deterioration. The degree of recovery is variable. It has been reported that children born to mothers who ate mercury-contaminated shellfish during pregnancy have developed mental handicap and *cerebral palsy*.

AMIN-ZAKI, L. et al (1978) Methylmercury poisoning in Iraqi children: clinical observation over two years. Brit. Med. J., 1:613.
MARSH, D.O. et al (1980) Fetal methylmercury poisoning: clinical and toxicological data on 29 cases. Ann. Neurol., 7:348.
SNYDER, R.D. (1971) Congenital mercury poisoning. New Engl. J. Med., 284: 1014.

Merrill-Palmer Test of Mental Abilities

This is a scale which assesses mental abilities under the headings of: sensori-motor problem-solving skills; long- and short-term memory; goal directedness; visual-motor integration; gross and fine motor skills; receptive and expressive language abilities; visual sequential skills; seriation and spatial relationships; body image; and inductive and deductive reasoning. The emphasis is on non-verbal abilities such as motor skill and extra credit can be gained by performing tasks within specified time limits. Non-verbal items include fitting pegs into boards, assembling picture puzzles and matching shapes. Verbal items involve abilities such as comprehension where the subject is required to carry out simple instructions or give word meanings. The scale consists of 93 items. It covers a developmental range from 18 months to 6 years. It was standardized on a large population of 'normal' children. There are a variety of interesting materials used and the administration and scoring systems are flexible enough to allow for language difficulties, deafness, visual problems or omissions. The norms are rather outdated and the time factor on the items can be a drawback. It may be liable to give false results owing to social training influences. It provides useful information about *mental age*, learning style and potential. It does not give an *intelligence quotient*.

STUTSMAN, R. (1931) Merrill-Palmer Scale of Mental Tests. Chicago: Stoelting Co.

Mesantoin

= *mephenytoin*.

Metabolism / metabolic disease / metabolic disorder

Metabolism refers to the process by which the body uses food and drink to provide energy, to grow and to repair and renew itself. These complex multiple biochemical processes depend on the presence of many *enzymes*. A metabolic disease or disorder is caused by absent or deficient biochemical processes. This leads to abnormal functioning of the body and may have serious or fatal consequences. Many of the metabolic disorders can cause mental handicap.

AMPOLA, M.G. (1982) Metabolic Diseases in Pediatric Practice. Boston: Little, Brown & Co.

CRAWFORD, M. D'A. et al (1982) Advances in the Treatment of Inborn Errors of Metabolism. Chichester: John Wiley.
SINCLAIR, L. (1979) Metabolic Diseases in Childhood. Oxford: Blackwell Scientific Publications.

Metacarpals

The five bones in each hand which lie between the bones of the wrist and the fingers. Metacarpal bones may be absent in *Rothmund-Thomson syndrome* and abnormal in a few other rare conditions associated with mental handicap.

Metachromatic leucodystrophy / leukodystrophy

There are three main forms of this disease recognized by their time of onset (late infantile, juvenile and adult). In each of these there is a deficiency of the *enzyme* arylsulphatase A. This is involved in the *metabolism* of fats (lipids). In the two other rare forms there are other enzyme deficiencies which lead to the same outcome. There is widespread damage to the *central nervous system* with accumulation of sulphatide granules which stain characteristically with certain dyes to be seen under the microscope (metachromatic staining). There is also demyelination of nerves (loss of the fatty insulating *myelin* sheath). In the late infantile form the first signs appear at about 2 years with a squint, poor balance and gradual stiffening of muscles. Impairment of speech, *spasticity* (with reduced tendon reflexes) and intellectual deterioration appear gradually. Unexplained bursts of fever or severe abdominal pain may develop as the disease advances. Vision deteriorates and *seizures* may appear in the later stages. Death occurs between 6 months and 4 years after onset. The juvenile form is less common with onset between 5 and 7 years of age and slower progress. In the adult form there is progressive mental and physical deterioration. Previously the diagnosis was confirmed by finding metachromatic granules in the urine but this has been superseded by measuring enzymes from *fibroblast culture*. This can also be used to identify carriers and *amniocentesis* can be used to make a diagnosis before birth. The condition is inherited from both parents who are carriers (*recessive inheritance*). There is no known treatment.

AUSTIN, J.H. (1973) Studies in metachromatic leukodystrophy. Arch. Neurol., 28: 258.
MACFAUL, R. et al (1982) Metachromatic leukodystrophy: Review of 38 cases. Arch. Dis. Childh., 57:118.
PERCY, A.K. et al (1977) Metachromatic leukodystrophy: Comparison of early and late onset forms. Neurology, 27:933.

Metaphyses

The junction between the end of a long bone and its shaft. This is the point at which growth takes place in a child. Metaphyseal abnormalities occur in a few conditions associated with mental handicap including *rubella syndrome* and *Conradi's syndrome*.

Metatarsals

The five bones in each foot which lie between the bones of the ankle and the toes. Abnormalities of these bones occur in a few rare conditions associated with mental handicap.

Metatarsus adductus

Turning inward of the foot as has been reported in the *Smith-Lemli-Opitz syndrome*.

Metatarsus varus

A deformity of the foot in which the *metatarsal* bones are curved so that the foot bends toward the other foot. This has been reported in a few rare *chromosome* disorders.

Methioninaemia

= *hypermethioninaemia*.

Methionine malabsorption syndrome

= *oast house urine syndrome*.

Methylmalonic acidaemia / aciduria

An abnormal amount of methylmalonic acid in the blood. This suppresses the formation of blood cells and the acidity causes vomiting and lethargy. It is caused by an *enzyme* deficiency and there are six different types. Routine screening of newborn infants has shown that 50% of babies with persistent methylmalonic acidaemia have no symptoms and have normal physical and mental development. When it is a symptomatic type it may progress rapidly with death in the first month. More commonly the symptoms appear in the first week following protein feeds. Floppiness, lethargy, vomiting and constipation occur, often episodically. Most infants die within 2 months of the onset but the survivors suffer from recurrent episodes of illness and from poor physical and intellectual growth. Long-term treatment is with a low-protein diet. Injections of cyanocobalamin or hydroxycobalamin are effective in some types. It is inherited from both parents who are carriers (*recessive inheritance*). It can be diagnosed following *amniocentesis* and the fetus has benefited from treatment of the mother with vitamin B12 in the last nine weeks of pregnancy.

AMPOLA, M.G. et al (1975) Prenatal therapy of a patient with vitamin B12 – responsive methylmalonic acidemia. New Engl. J. Med., 293:313–317.

MARTSUI, S.M. et al (1983) The natural history of the inherited methylmalonic acidemias. N. Engl. J. Med., 308:857.

Methylphenidate

A stimulant drug sometimes used in the treatment of *hyperactivity* in children. It is widely used in the U.S.A. where the diagnosis is more commonly made. It is no longer marketed in the U.K. It is thought to act by sensitizing the child to incoming stimuli. Side-effects include loss of appetite and weight, sleeplessness and possible growth retardation with prolonged use.

AMAN, M.G. (1982) Stimulant drug effects in developmental disorders and hyper-activity: towards a resolution of disparate findings. J. Autism Dev. Dis., 12:385–398.

AMAN, M.G. & SINGH, N.N. (1982) Methylphenidate in severely retarded residents and the clinical significance of stereotypic behaviour. Appl. Res. Ment. Retard., 3:345–358.

KALACHNIK, J.E. et al (1982) Effect of methylphenidate hydrochloride on stature of hyperactive children. Dev. Med. Child Neurology, 24:556.

SHEA, V.T. (1982) State-dependent learning in children receiving methylphenidate. Psychopharmacology, 78:266.

Methylphenobarbital / methylphenobarbitone

An *anticonvulsant* drug used in the treatment of *epilepsy*. It is a barbiturate. It is sometimes used as an alternative to *phenobarbitone* because it is believed to have fewer side-effects but, as it is broken down into phenobarbitone in the liver, it probably has no real advantages.

Micrencephaly / microencephaly

A small brain. This usually occurs in association with *microcephaly*.

Microbrachycephaly

A combination of *microcephaly* and *brachycephaly* as may occur in *de Lange syndrome*.

Microcephaly

A small head. This is usually applied to a head circumference which is less than three standard deviations below the mean for age, sex and race (in statistical terms). Body size also needs to be taken into account. Serious reduction of head size is generally, but not always, associated with mental handicap. Most classifications differentiate between primary and secondary microcephaly. If brain development stops early in fetal life it is the primary form (microcephaly vera) but, if a well-formed brain is damaged or destroyed before or after birth, secondary microcephaly results. Some authors restrict the primary type to those who have *genetic* microcephaly with no other identified cause or condition. This is nearly always due to *recessive inheritance* from both parents who are carriers. Microcephaly can also be a symptom of very many diseases. Many of these are conditions in which microcephaly is associated with other *congenital* abnormalities as in *Alper's syndrome, Carpenter's syndrome, Crouzon's syndrome, de Lange syndrome, Meckel syndrome, lissencephaly, phenylketonuria, Pierre Robin syndrome, Rubinstein-Taybi syndrome, bird-headed dwarfism, Smith-Lemli-Opitz syndrome* and many of the *chromosome* disorders including *Down's syndrome*. Microcephaly occurs infrequently in the *degenerative disorders* but frequently follows congenital infections in *rubella syndrome, cytomegalic inclusion disease, toxoplasmosis* and *herpes simplex encephalitis* It may also follow *meningitis* or *meningo-encephalitis*. A well established cause of microcephaly is radiation during pregnancy. Other toxic causes are *hydantoin* drugs and alcohol during pregnancy (*fetal alcohol syndrome*). Maternal phenylketonuria is another recognized cause. Brain injury or lack of oxygen at birth may also cause brain growth to stop and microcephaly to develop. Severe primary microcephaly may be recognized at birth due to the receding forehead, flat back of the head, reduced head measurements and small *fontanelles*. Often it becomes more evident as the head fails to grow normally after birth. There is great variation in physical and mental development. Sometimes *spasticity* and *seizures* occur. Walking and speech may be delayed and speech may not be acquired. There is no particular personality type or behaviour pattern. Intellectual skills vary from normal to profound mental handicap. In the hereditary form the skin over the skull may be loose and in folds, the hair thick and rough and the ears large and imperfectly formed. *Epilepsy* is quite common. The stature is usually small.

BOOK, J.A. et al (1953) A clinical and genetical study of microcephaly. Am. J. Ment. Defic., 57:637–660.

BRANDON, M.W.G. et al (1959) Microcephaly. J. Ment. Sci., 105:721.

MARTIN, H.P. (1970) Microcephaly and mental retardation. Am. J. Dis. Child., 119:128–131.

NELSON, K.B. & DEUTSCHBERGER, J. (1970) Head size at one year as a predictor of four year I.Q. Dev. Med. Child Neurology, 12:487.

WARKANY, J. et al (1981) Mental Retardation and Congenital Malformations of the Central Nervous System. Chicago: Year Book Medical Publishers, Inc. pp. 13–40.

Microcornea
An abnormally small *cornea* of the eye. This may occur in *Carpenter's syndrome, Rieger's syndrome, rubella syndrome, Laurence-Moon-Biedl syndrome* and a few other conditions associated with mental handicap. It is often associated with other abnormalities of the eye and with impaired vision.

Microdontia
Abnormally small teeth as may occur in *Greig's syndrome, Rothmund-Thomson syndrome* and a few other rare conditions associated with mental handicap.

Microelectronic equipment
Microelectronic technology is being increasingly used to stimulate and assist mentally handicapped people. It can increase the person's control over the environment and for profoundly handicapped people this may be the first step in the process of learning adaptive skills.
Pethna toys and *Possum* devices are examples of this type of equipment. *Computers* are often used in such equipment.

LOVETT, S. (1985) Microelectronics and computer-based technology. In: Mental Deficiency. The changing outlook (4th edit.) Clarke, A.M. et al (Eds.). London: Methuen. pp. 551–566.

ROSTRON, A. & SEWELL, D. (1984) Microtechnology in Special Education. London: Croom Helm.

Microencephaly
= *micrencephaly*.

Micrognathia
An abnormally small jaw. This usually refers to the lower jaw. It occurs in *Pierre Robin syndrome, bird-headed dwarfism, cytomegalic inclusion disease, Prader-Willi syndrome, Smith-Lemli-Opitz syndrome, German's syndrome, de Lange syndrome* and many of the *chromosome* disorders associated with mental handicap.

Microgyria
Abnormally small folds of the brain (*gyri*) usually as a consequence of brain damage around the time of birth. It has been described in *megalencephaly* and *cytomegalic inclusion disease*.

Micromelia
Abnormally small limbs as may occur in a few rare conditions associated with mental handicap and in some types of *restricted growth*.

Microphthalmia
Abnormally small eye or eyes. This may occur in *de Lange syndrome, Goldenhar's syndrome, Hallermann-Streiff syndrome, Meckel syndrome, Lowe's syndrome, Lenz syndrome, Treacher-Collins syndrome* and *tuberose sclerosis*. It has also been described in several *chromosome* abnormalities and in *rubella syndrome, cytomegalic inclusion disease* and *toxoplasmosis*. It is often associated with other abnormalities of the eye and with impaired vision.

WARBURG, M. (1971) The heterogeneity of microphthalmia in the mentally retarded. Birth Defects Original Article Series, 7(3): 136–154.

Micropolygyria
An excess of small folds and grooves on the surface of the brain. Microscopically the brain is abnormal. It is thought to result from damage to the developing nervous system before the fifth month of pregnancy. Mental handicap and *spasticity* or floppiness

of muscles are the consequence. It has been described in the *cerebro-hepato-renal syndrome* and *Bloch-Sulzberger syndrome*.

Microstomia
A small opening to the mouth caused by a decrease in width. This has been reported in a few *chromosome* disorders associated with mental handicap.

Microtia
Abnormally small ear(s). This may occur in association with mental handicap in *Treacher-Collins syndrome* and a few other rare conditions.

Middle ear deafness
Deafness caused by problems with the small bones (ossicles) in the middle ear which conduct sound from the eardrum to the inner ear. This is known as *conductive deafness*. By far the most common cause is infection of the middle ear which results in *glue ear*. Chronic infection with discharge through the eardrum may permanently damage or destroy the ossicles. In a few *congenital* conditions associated with mental handicap such as *Treacher-Collins syndrome* there may be abnormality or absence of the middle ear.

Mild mental handicap
See *mental handicap*.

Milestones
Major achievements in a child's development, such as sitting, crawling, walking, talking etc., are sometimes referred to as developmental milestones. If a child does not achieve these milestones within the normal time this *developmental delay* may be due to *disability*.

Miller Assessment of Preschoolers
A test developed to identify children in need of further *assessment*. It covers the developmental range from 2 years 9 months to 5 years 8 months using 27 items which assess sensory and motor abilities, memory, sequencing, comprehension, verbal

expression, visualizations, mental manipulations and visual-spatial interpretation. There are five performance indices which are called foundations, co-ordination, verbal, non-verbal and complex behaviours. An estimated developmental age range can be obtained for each item and individual profiles are also provided.

MILLER, L. (1982) The Miller Assessment of Preschoolers. Colorado: KID Foundation.

Miller-Dieker syndrome
See *lissencephaly*.

Milwaukee experiment
This project was carried out in the early 1960's in an area of Milwaukee which had poor socio-economic status. Mothers were selected who had an *intelligence quotient* (I.Q.) of below 75 on the *Weschler Adult Intelligence Scale*. Twenty children and their families were used as matched controls where no intervention took place. The twenty experimental families were subjected to a six-year intensive intervention programme which included attendance from the age of 3 months at a special day centre where there was a very structured programme of stimulation and education. The mothers were involved in a vocational and social education programme which included job training. The children were followed up and the experimental group children's average I.Q. was more than 30 I.Q. points greater than that of the control group at 6 and 9 years of age. A number of criticisms have been levelled at the design of the project.

GARBER, H. & HEBER, F.R. (1977) The Milwaukee Project. In: Research and Practice in Mental Retardation, Vol. 1. Care and Intervention. Mittler, P. & de Jong, J.M. (Eds.) Baltimore: University Park Press.
PAGE, E.B. (1972) Miracle in Milwaukee: raising the I.Q. Educ. Res., 1:8–16.
THRONE, J.M. (1975) The replicability fetish and the Milwaukee project. Ment. Retardation, 13:14–17.

MIND (National Association for Mental Health)
An organization in the U.K. concerned with the welfare of mentally ill and mentally handicapped people. As well as organizing courses and conferences it plays an important part in informing the general public about the needs of mentally handicapped people and in supporting them and their relatives. It is a politically active pressure group. It runs local and regional offices throughout the U.K.

Further information:
MIND, 22 Harley St., London W1N 2ED.

Minimal brain dysfunction (MBD) / minimal brain damage / minimal cerebral dysfunction
A term used increasingly in the last 20 years to describe a broad group of behavioural and learning disabilities in childhood. The main features are based on *hyperactivity* but *perceptual, cognitive* and *specific learning disabilities* may be included. The diagnosis has, especially in the U.S.A., been extended to include more and more childhood psychological disorders. Children with neurological signs are usually excluded. At one time it was argued that the behavioural characteristics of MBD were characteristic and easily recognized but this is now challenged on the basis of insufficient evidence.

There are three major theories concerning the underlying deficit in MBD. The first is as a minor degree of brain damage (e.g. by birth injury, infection or some other cause) and the second is as a biochemical abnormality which affects the level of arousal. The third, more recent, proposal is that there is more than one *syndrome* but each is related to damage to a specific area of the brain.
The most commonly used treatments for this ill-defined condition are described under hyperactivity.

CAPUTE, A.J. & ACCARDO, P.J. (1980) The minimal cerebral dysfunction – learning disability syndrome complex. In: Child Development and Developmental Disabil-

ities. Gabel, S. & Erickson, M. (Eds.)
Boston: Little, Brown & Co.

GROSS, M. & WILSON, W.C. (1974)
Minimal Brain Dysfunction: A Clinical
Study of Incidence, Diagnosis and Treat-
ment in Over 1000 Children. New York:
Brunner/Mazel.

RIE, II.E. & RIE, E.D. (Eds.) (1980)
Handbook of Minimal Brain Dysfunctions:
A Critical View. New York: Wiley.

RUTTER, M. (1982) Syndromes attributed
to minimal brain dysfunction in childhood.
Am. J. Psychiat., 139:21–33.

RUTTER, M. (1984) Concepts of minimal
brain dysfunction. In: Developmental
Neuropsychiatry. Rutter, M. (Ed.) Edinburgh: Churchill Livingstone. pp. 575–598.

Minimal support unit
A place of residence for disabled people
where support is provided by regular visits
from professional workers rather than by
residential staff. It usually refers to a small
group home or *hostel* for more able residents.

Minimata disease
A form of *mercury poisoning*.

Minor motor seizures
See *Lennox-Gastaut syndrome*.

Minor status epilepticus
= *absence status*.

Mirror movements
= *bimanual synkinesis*.

Mobility allowance
An allowance payable in the U.K. to people
between 5 years and 66 years of age whose
ability to walk is very limited or whose
health may be damaged by exertion. The
person must be able to benefit from it in
some way. It is not means-tested or taxable.
A payment made before pension age will
continue until the age of 75 years. An
independent medical assessment is carried
out. Appeals can be made on medical or
non-medical grounds. Application can be
made through any DHSS office.

COOKE, K.R. (1980) An evaluation of the
mobility allowance for families with handicapped children. Child: Care, Health and
Development, 6:279–289.

Disability Rights Handbook (updated every
year) from the Disability Alliance ERA, 25
Denmark St., London WC2H 8NJ.

Leaflet N1 211, obtainable from local DHSS
office.

Further information:
Mobility Allowance Unit, DHSS, Norcross,
Blackpool, Lancs. FY5 3TA.

Möbius' syndrome
A non-progressive condition present at birth
in which there is paralysis of the nerves of
the muscles of the face. As a result all or part
of the face is immobile and incomplete
closure of the eyes may lead to damage to
the *cornea*. Eyelids may droop. Often the jaw
and tongue are underdeveloped. There may
be considerable feeding problems in infancy.
Communication problems may occur.
When it occurs alone it may be due *dominant
inheritance*. It is sometimes associated with
mental handicap, protruding ears, *club foot*,
webbed fingers and toes and skeletal abnormalities. It may occur with other conditions
as in *arthrogryposis multiplex congenita* and
Klippel-Feil syndrome.

BARAITSER, M. (1977) Genetics of Möbius
syndrome. J. Med. Genet., 14:415.

MEYERSON, M.D. & FOUSHEE, D.R. (1978)
Speech, language and hearing in Möbius
syndrome. Dev. Med. Child Neurology,
20:357.

SPROFKIN, B.E. & HILLMAN, J.W. (1956)
Möbius' syndrome – congenital oculofacial
paralysis. Neurology (Minneap.), 6:50.

WARKANY, J. et al (1981) Mental Retard-
ation and Congenital Malformations of the
Central Nervous System. Chicago: Year
Book Medical Publishers Inc. pp. 211–223.

Modecate
= *fluphenazine*.

Modelling

Learning by means of observation and *imitation*. The person acting as a model demonstrates the required behaviour. This is a common way in which children normally learn, but for mentally handicapped people it may have to be more carefully planned and structured. It requires observation, memory and physical skills as well as motivation. The person may first have to be taught how to imitate. Modelling, in combination with other approaches, is used in teaching and *behaviour modification*. It is important to provide good models for mentally handicapped people. Approaches to care which involve *integration* into the community and mixing with ordinary people (*normalization*) are far more likely to achieve this.

CARR, J. (1980) Imitation, generalization and discrimination. In: Behaviour Modification for the Mentally Handicapped. Yule, W. & Carr, J. (Eds.). London: Croom Helm. pp. 77–89.

Moditen

= *fluphenazine*.

Moebius syndrome / Moebius sequence

= *Möbius' syndrome*.

Mogadon

= *nitrazepam*.

Mohrs' syndrome

A very rare condition in which there are malformations of the mouth, face, fingers and toes. There is a small head with abnormalities of the brain including fluid-filled spaces (cysts) or *hydrocephalus*. The tongue is lobed and nodular, the upper lip is cleft and there are extra toes. The central teeth are usually absent and the lower jaw underdeveloped. The base of the nose is broad and the tip may be divided. There is usually *conductive deafness* in both ears. Episodes of overbreathing and floppiness of muscles have also been described. Some people with this syndrome have mental handicap and early death may occur. In about two thirds of cases, however, intelligence and life expectancy are normal. It is inherited from both parents who are carriers (*recessive inheritance*).

GUSTAVSON, K.H. et al (1971) Syndrome characterized by lingual malformations, polydactyly, tachypnoea and psychomotor retardation (Mohr syndrome). Clin. Genet., 2:261.

RIMION, D.L. & EDGERTON, M.T. (1967) Genetic and clinical heterogeneity in the oral-facial-digital syndromes. J. Pediatr., 71:94.

Mongolian Quotient

A proposed method for expressing the *intelligence quotient* in children with *Down's syndrome*. It is found by the formula M.Q.= $100 \times$ *mental age* / mental age estimate. The mental age estimate is equal to 20.87 log *chronological age* minus 5.77. Mental age, mental age estimate and chronological age are all in months. This approach has been standardized on institutionalized children. In general the usefulness of this approach is questionable and the figures derived from it have little advantage over the original data.

CARR, J. (1985) The development of intelligence. In: Current Approaches to Down's syndrome. Lane, D. & Stratford, B. (Eds.) London: Holt, Rinehart & Winston. pp. 170–171.

MEINDL, J.L. et al (1983) Mental growth of non-institutionalized and institutionalized children with Down's syndrome. Brit. J. Ment. Subn., 29(1):50–56.

SILVERSTEIN, A.B. (1966) Mental growth in mongolism. Child Dev., 37(3).

Mongolism / mongoloid / mongol

= *Down's syndrome*.

Monoamine oxidase inhibitors

A group of drugs used in the treatment of some types of *depression* and *phobia*. These are used much less frequently than tricyclic *antidepressants* such as *amitriptyline* because of the dangers of dietary and drug interactions. The most commonly used are phenelzine and isocarboxazid. They are very rarely used for people with a mental handicap.

Monoplegia
Paralysis of one limb as may occur in *cerebral palsy*.

Monosomy
Absence of all, or an arm, of a *chromosome*.

Monosomy 4p
= *Wolf's syndrome*.

Monosomy 5p
= *cri-du-chat syndrome*.

Monosomy 9p
= *deletion of short arm of chromosome 9*.

Montreal-type bird-headed dwarfism
See *bird-headed dwarfism*.

Moro reflex
A reflex response seen in very young babies. The body, neck, arms and legs straighten, often with the head back. The hands open as arms outstretch. The arms are then closed together. It is elicited by suddenly removing support from the back of the head. In babies with *Down's syndrome* in early weeks this reaction may be partial or absent, probably due to the floppiness of the muscles. It is normally lost by the end of the fourth month unless there is damage to the *central nervous system*.

Moron
A term which used to be applied to mildly mentally handicapped people or those of dull normal intellectual ability (described as a *mental age* of 8 to 12 years in adults). It was usually regarded as synonymous with *feeble-minded*.

Morquios' syndrome
One of the *mucopolysaccharidoses* in which an *enzyme* deficiency causes large amounts of keratan sulphate to be excreted in the urine and abnormal substances to be deposited in body cells. Onset is between 1 and 3 years of age and growth is severely limited with abnormalities of the bones of the spine, rib cage and long bones of the limbs. There is clouding of the *cornea* of the eye, *sensori-neural deafness* and damage to the aortic valve of the heart. Facial features may be characteristic. Intelligence is normal in most cases. The syndrome is inherited from both parents who are carriers (*recessive inheritance*). There are severe (A) and mild (B) forms of the disease.

KOTO, A. et al (1978) The Morquios syndrome: Neuropathy and biochemistry. Ann. Neurol., 4:26.
MAROTEAUX, P. & LAMY, M. (1965) Hurler's disease, Morquios' disease and related mucopolysaccharidoses. J. Pediatr., 67:246.

Mortality
The death rate for mentally handicapped people used to be much greater in children and young adults than for the general population. This is still the case but to a much lesser extent. It is due to the increased rate of *congenital* abnormalities such as *congenital heart disease* and increased susceptibility to infection in some physically handicapped people. *Degenerative disorders* also take their toll. In 1958 70% of all children with *Down's syndrome* failed to survive the first 10 years but from 1960 to 1970 mortality was reduced by 50–60%. The situation has continued to improve.

THASE, M.E. (1982) Longevity and mortality in Down's syndrome. J. Ment. Defic. Res., 26:177.

Mosaic
= *chromosome mosaic*.

Motability
A charity set up in the U.K. to help recipients of *mobility allowance* to obtain and run a suitable vehicle. This may be done through leasing or hire purchase agreements.

Further information:
Motability, The Adelphi, John Adam St., London WC2N 6AZ.

Motor development / skills
Achievement of co-ordinated and purposeful movements in recognized developmental stages. *Gross motor* refers to larger movement skills and *fine motor* to more delicate skills which require finer co-ordination. Motor development may be delayed in children who are mentally handicapped and permanently impaired when a child is physically handicapped as in *cerebral palsy*. The elements necessary for normal motor development are *tone*, *co-ordination* and strength.

Motor handicap
= *physical disability*.

Motor seizures (minor)
See *Lennox-Gastaut syndrome*.

Mourning
= *bereavement*.

MRI
= magnetic resonance imaging. See *nuclear magnetic resonance imaging*.

Mucolipidoses
These rare conditions have features of both the *mucopolysaccharidoses* and the *lipidoses*. At least four mucolipidoses have been distinguished. They are characterized by storage of mucopolysaccharide substances in the body but excess amounts are not excreted in the urine.
Mucolipidosis I or *sialidosis* is very rare with only a few reported cases. *Mucolipidosis II* is

the most common of this group. Mucolipidosis III is *pseudo-Hurler polydystrophy*. *Mucolipidosis IV* is very rare and would be better classified with the *gangliosidoses*. All these disorders are caused by *enzyme* deficiencies and are usually due to *recessive inheritance*.

Mucolipidosis I
= *sialidosis*.

Mucolipidosis II
The *enzyme* deficiency in this disorder leads to abnormal substances accumulating in the lysosomes of cells. These are called *inclusion bodies* and can be seen microscopically. Features of the disease are evident at birth when the baby is floppy and has a coarse facial appearance, overgrowth of gums, *congenital dislocation of hips*, restricted movements of joints, and tight thickened skin. Poor growth, small head and progressive mental deterioration gradually become apparent. Most affected people die in childhood. It is inherited from both parents who are carriers (autosomal *recessive inheritance*). It can be detected in pregnancy following *amniocentesis*.

CIPOLLONI, C. et al (1980) Neonatal mucolipidosis II (I-cell disease): Clinical, radiological and biochemical studies in a case. Helv. Paediatr. Acta, 35:85.
TONDEUR, M. et al (1971) Clinical, biochemical and ultrastructural studies of chondrodystrophy presenting the I-cell phenotype in culture. J. Pediatr., 79:366.

Mucolipidosis III
= *pseudo-Hurler polydystrophy*.

Mucolipidosis IV
A very rare disorder due to an *enzyme* deficiency which affects the body processes and causes abnormal substances to be deposited in cells. It is characterized by mental deterioration, floppiness and early clouding of the *cornea* of the eye. There are no abnormalities of bones and the liver is not enlarged. It is difficult to diagnose and

requires electron microscopy of skin or nerves. The urine contains large quantities of abnormal substances including gangliosides and as the enzyme deficiency is thought to be a partial defect of ganglioside sialidase this is probably better classified as a *gangliosidosis*. It is probably inherited from both parents who are carriers (*autosomal recessive inheritance*). It can be detected in pregnancy following *amniocentesis*.

CRANDALL, B.F. et al (1982) Review article: Mucolipidosis IV. Am. J. Med. Genet., 12:301.
TELLEZ-NAGEL, I. et al (1976) Mucolipidosis IV. Arch. Neurol., 33:828.

Mucopolysaccharidoses (MPS)

The diseases of this type cause abnormalities in the chemical processes of the body which deal with body constituents known as mucopolysaccharides (complex sugars). These abnormalities are caused by various *enzyme* deficiencies which are *genetic* in origin. There are seven different types in this group of disorders but only in types I to III is mental handicap usually a feature. In each type an abnormal accumulation of mucopolysaccharides occurs in the body and tissues undergo degeneration giving rise to the particular features of each disorder. Diseases in this group include *Hurler's syndrome (MPS I)*, *Hunter's syndrome (MPS II)*, *Sanfilippo syndrome (MPS III)*, *Morquios' syndrome (MPS IV)*, *Scheie's syndrome (MPS V)*, *Maroteaux-Lamy syndrome (MPS VI)* and *Sly's syndrome (MPS VII)*.

Mucopolysaccharidosis I

= *Hurler's syndrome*.

Mucopolysaccharidosis II

= *Hunter's syndrome*.

Mucopolysaccharidosis III

= *Sanfilippo syndrome*.

Mucopolysaccharidosis IV

= *Morquios' syndrome*.

Mucopolysaccharidosis V

= *Scheie's syndrome*.

Mucopolysaccharidosis VI

= *Maroteaux-Lamy syndrome*.

Mucopolysaccharidosis VII

= *Sly's syndrome*.

Mucosulfatidosis

A rare variant of *metachromatic leucodystrophy*.

Multiaxial classification

A system for classifying diseases or impairments which allows for more than one diagnosis. Diagnoses are made under a number of different headings known as axes. Many people with a mental handicap have other associated problems and doctors, especially child psychiatrists, may use a multiaxial system to allow diagnoses to be made under headings such as medical disorders, psychiatric disorders, intellectual level, *specific learning difficulties* and psychosocial problems.

RUTTER, M. et al (1975) A Multi-axial Classification of Child Psychiatric Disorder. Geneva: World Health Organization.

Multidisciplinary team

People from different professions (disciplines) working together as a team for the purposes of *assessment*, treatment, training, *rehabilitation* or support of patients or clients. The *interdisciplinary approach* occurs when there is an overlap of roles. The *community mental handicap team* is an example of a multidisciplinary team.

PLANK, M. (1982) Teams for Mentally Handicapped People: A Report on an Enquiry into the Development of Multidisciplinary Teams. Enquiry Paper No.10. London: Campaign for Mentally Handicapped People.

Multifactorial inheritance

A type of inheritance involved in many common malformations such as *hydrocephalus*, congenital heart disease and cleft lip/palate. These parts of the body are thought to involve many genes in their formation and environmental factors also play a part. Therefore, in some families, there is a predisposition to a disorder which does not follow a clear pattern of inheritance.

CLARK-FRASER, F. & NORA, J.J. (1986) Genetics of Man. Philadelphia: Lea & Febiger. pp. 173–183.

Multiple lentiginosis syndrome

A rare condition in which restricted growth and a skin condition may be associated with mental handicap, heart abnormalities, eye defects, abnormal genitals and deafness. The skin condition consists of numerous small dark brown patches (lentigines) which are not usually present at birth but develop progressively during the first few years of life. The eyes are often widely set with a slight downward slant from the nose. The lower jaw may protrude. It is due to dominant inheritance or may arise anew. The degree of mental handicap is variable and life expectancy depends on the nature of any heart condition.

GORLIN, R.J. et al (1969) Multiple lentigines syndrome. Am. J. Dis. Child., 117: 652.
MACMILLAN, D.C. (1969) Profuse lentiginosis, minor cardiac abnormality and small stature. Proc. Roy. Soc. Med., 62, 1011.
PICKERING, D. et al (1971) 'Little Leopard' syndrome. Arch. Dis. Childh., 46:85.

Mumps encephalitis

The mumps virus may cause a meningitis from which recovery is nearly always complete or a meningo-encephalitis. With the latter there is a fever, vomiting, neck stiffness, lethargy, headache and less often seizures and delirium. Permanent consequences include paralysis of face muscles, damage to the nerves of the eye, deafness, epilepsy and behaviour disorders. Mental handicap is an extremely rare outcome.

LEVITT, L.P. et al (1970) Central nervous system mumps. A review of 64 cases. Neurology (Minneap.), 20:829.
OLDFELT, V. (1949) Sequelae of mumps meningoencephalitis. Acta Med. Scand., 134:405.

Murmur

This usually refers to an abnormal sound heard with a stethoscope in the area of the heart. It is caused by turbulence in the flow of blood due to abnormalities in the heart or major blood vessels. In congenital heart disease the nature, timing and location of the murmur may assist in making the diagnosis.

Muscle tone

See tone.

Muscular dystrophy

The muscular dystrophies are a group of hereditary diseases with a gradual onset in early life, progressive weakness affecting the central more than the peripheral muscles, and loss of tendon reflexes such as knee jerks. There are six major forms recognized: Duchenne's muscular dystrophy, Becker muscular dystrophy, Emery-Dreifuss muscular dystrophy, the facioscapulohumeral form, congenital muscular dystrophies and various limb-girdle dystrophies. It is only the Duchenne type which is often associated with mental handicap, although people with a subtype of the congenital muscular dystrophies may also have mental handicap and seizures.

FORSYTHE, E. (1979) Living with Muscular Dystrophy. London: Faber & Faber.
MENKES, J.H. (1985) Textbook of Child Neurology (3rd edit.) Lea & Febiger. Philadelphia. pp. 688–694.

Further information:
Muscular Dystrophy Group of Great Britain, Nattrass House, 35 Macaulay Rd. London SW4 0QP.
Muscular Dystrophy Association, 810 Seventh Ave, New York, NY 10019.

Music therapy

People with a mental handicap can enjoy and benefit from music in the same way as anyone else. It can be developed as a leisure activity and may be used for relaxation. Accomplishments in this field may enhance self confidence and self-esteem. Music should therefore be readily available so long as the person shows pleasure and indicates a desire to pursue this activity. Music also has a therapeutic value by improving listening skills and the ability to discriminate sounds and rhythms. Playing an instrument can also improve muscle strength and co-ordination in mouth and/or limbs.

ALVIN, J. (1978) Music for the Handicapped Child. Oxford: Oxford University Press.
BUNT, L. (1984) Research in music therapy in Great Britain: outcome of research with handicapped children. Brit. J. Music Ther., 15(3):2–8.
OLDFIELD, A. & PEIRSON, J. (1985) Using music in mental handicap. Mental Handicap, 13(4):156–158.
STREETER, E. (1980) Making Music with the Young Handicapped Child: A Guide for Parents. London: Music Therapy Publications.
WOOD, M. (1983) Music for Mentally Handicapped People. London: Souvenir Press.

Further information:
British Society for Music Therapy, 48 Lanchester Rd., London. N6 4TA.

Mutation

A permanent change in *genetic* material. This usually refers to a change in a single *gene* (point mutation) but includes the occurrence of *chromosome* aberrations. A disorder caused by mutation is not, therefore, present in, or carried by, the parent but arises anew in the offspring. It can, however, be passed on to future generations in the usual way. *Tuberose sclerosis* is an example of a disorder which may be passed on by *dominant inheritance* but may also arise as a new mutation. The cause of a mutation is usually not known. Certain factors, like radiation, are known to increase the mutation rate.

Mutism

The state of being voiceless, dumb or silent when there is no physical abnormality in the vocal apparatus. *Elective mutism* is a selective refusal to speak. Deafness is one of the commonest causes of mutism and should always be considered. Some severely and profoundly mentally handicapped people may not have the intellectual skills necessary to produce speech and some *autistic* people never speak.

Mycoplasma infection

The mycoplasma pneumoniae organism usually causes infections of the lungs, nose and throat but may, infrequently, infect the *central nervous system* especially in children. *Meningo-encephalitis* may develop and survivors make a slow recovery. Residual brain damage may occur and cause mental handicap.

CASSEL, G. & COLE, B. (1981) Mycoplasmas as agents of human disease. New Engl. J. Med., 304:80.
PONKA, A. (1980) Central nervous system manifestations associated with serological verified mycoplasma pneumoniae infections. Scand. J. Infect. Dis., 12:175.

Myelin

An insulating sheath of fatty substance which surrounds nerve fibres in the *central nervous system*. Loss of myelin (demyelination) may occur in a number of conditions associated with mental handicap and impairs the function of the brain and nerves.

Myelocoele

= *meningomyelocoele.*

Myelomeningocoele

= *meningomyelocoele.*

223

Myeloschisis

= *rachischisis*.

Myoatonic seizures

= *akinetic seizures*.

Myocardium

The muscular part of the heart.

Myoclonic-astatic seizures

= *akinetic seizures*.

Myoclonic encephalopathy

This condition which is seen in infants and young children is characterized by a fairly sudden onset (often following a cold or chest infection) of severe *myoclonus*, unsteadiness and chaotically irregular eye movements (*opsoclonus*). The abnormal eye movements are worse whenever the child moves his or her eyes. Recovery from the condition occurs and steroid drugs may bring about a rapid improvement. More than half of the affected children are left with mental handicap and/or abnormalities of movement, speech and behaviour. In half the children a malignant tumour (*neuroblastoma*) is discovered but the long-term outcome is similar to that for children in whom a tumour is not present. In the majority of these children a viral infection is thought to be the cause.

ALTMAN, A.J. & BACHNER, R.L. (1976) Favourable prognosis for survival in children with coincident opsomyoclonus and neuroblastoma. Cancer, 37:846.
BOLTSHAUSER, E. et al (1976) Myoclonic encephalopathy of infants or 'dancing eyes syndrome'. Helv. Paediatr. Acta, 34:119.
KUBAN, K.C. et al (1983) Syndrome of opsoclonus-myoclonus caused by Coxsackie B3 infection. Ann. Neurol., 13:69.

Myoclonic epilepsy / myoclonic seizures

In myoclonic *epilepsy* the *seizures* are characterized by irregular muscle jerks or spasms which may be single or repetitive. Con-sciousness may, or may not, be impaired. Myoclonic seizures may occur in association with other types of seizures. The onset is often at an early age and the *electroencephalogram* is often very abnormal with a spike and wave form. The outcome is then poor in terms of long-term seizure control and ultimate intellectual development. The picture is that of the *Lennox-Gastaut syndrome*. Myoclonic seizures also occur in a variety of degenerative diseases such as *amaurotic familial idiocy, subacute sclerosing panencephalitis* and *Unverricht's myoclonus epilepsy*. By comparison isolated myoclonic attacks may have a relatively favourable outcome and sometimes show a good response to *anti-convulsant* drugs.

Myoclonus

Rhythmic involuntary muscular contractions which generally persist during sleep. These are caused by abnormalities of, or damage to, the *spinal cord* or *brain stem* and may be seen in viral *encephalitis, cerebral palsy* and in a few progressive *degenerative disorders* such as *Unverricht's myoclonus epilepsy* although in these it should probably be regarded as *myoclonic epilepsy. Myoclonic encephalopathy* is a condition described in infants which may leave the child mentally handicapped.

LOMBROSO, C.T. & FEJERMAN, N. (1977) Benign myoclonus of early infancy. Ann. Neurol., 1:138.

Myopia

Shortsighted. Near objects are clearer than distant objects which are more blurred the further away they are. This can be corrected with spectacles which have concave lenses. The image which had been previously focused in front of the *retina* can then be brought to a focus on the retina. People with *Down's syndrome* are more prone to myopia than the general population.

Myotonia

Delay in the relaxation of muscle after

voluntary contraction. This is most evident in the muscles of the hand, face and tongue. Repetitive movements lessen myotonia and exposure to cold aggravates it. It occurs in a number of *genetic* conditions which are not associated with mental handicap and also in *Steinert's myotonic dystrophy*.

Myotonia atrophia
= *Steinert's myotonic dystrophy*.

Myotonic dystrophy
= *Steinert's myotonic dystrophy*.

Myringotomy
An operation on the ear by which sticky fluid (*glue ear*) is removed through an incision in the eardrum. *Grommets* or T-tubes are often inserted to prevent recurrence of the fluid. Children with *Down's syndrome* are particularly prone to ear infections and glue ear but the narrow ear canal may make the operation impossible until the child is older.

DAVIES, B. (1985) Hearing problems. In: Current approaches to Down's syndrome. Lane, D. & Stratford, B. (Eds.). London: Holt, Rinehart & Winston. pp. 97–99.

Mysoline
= *primidone*.

Myxoedema
= *hypothyroidism*.

N

Naevoid amentia
= *Sturge-Weber syndrome.*

Naevus / nevus
A mark in the skin caused either by blood vessels (*haemangioma*) or excess pigment cells (melanoma or mole). Naevi are characteristic of a few conditions associated with mental handicap such as *Sturge-Weber syndrome.*

Naevus sebaceous linearis
= *linear naevus sebaceous syndrome.*

Naevus sebaceous of Jadassohn
= *linear naevus sebaceous syndrome.*

Naevus unius lateris / lateralis
A skin condition characterized by raised streaks or bands consisting of small lumps which are pink, brown or black in colour. They are nearly always confined to one side of the body. They are present at birth or develop within the first year of life. They do not progress further. *Cancer* may develop within them and can be a cause of early death. A number of other abnormalities may also be present at birth including underdevelopment of the affected side of the body, abnormalities of bones, deficient hearing on the affected side, *Möbius' syndrome* and, in a few people, *epilepsy* and mental handicap. This rare condition is not thought to be inherited.

HOLDEN, K.R. & DEKABAN, A.S. (1972) Neurological involvement in naevus unius lateris and naevus linearis sebaceous. Neurology (Minneap.), 22:879.
PACK, G.T. & SUNDERLAND, D.A. (1941) Naevus unius lateralis. Arch. Surg. (Chicago), 43:341.

Nail-patella syndrome
An inherited disorder in which fingernails and kneecaps (patellae) are absent or underdeveloped. It is very often associated with other abnormalities of bones and joints and also with kidney disease which may cause premature death. Mental handicap has been reported but is unusual. It is inherited from a parent as a *dominant* condition.

DARLINGTON, D. & HAWKINS, C.F. (1967) Nail-patella syndrome with iliac horns and hereditary nephropathy. J. Bone. Jt. Surg., 49B:164.
SALMON, M.A. (1978) Developmental Defects and Syndromes. Aylesbury, England: HM&M Publishers. pp. 298–299.

Nanocephalic dwarfism
= *bird-headed dwarfism.*

Nasolacrimal ducts
= *lacrimal ducts.*

National Association for Deaf-Blind and Rubella Handicapped
See *deaf-blind.*

National Association for Mental Health
= *MIND.*

National Association for the Deaf
See *deafness.*

National Autistic Society
See *autism.*

National Deaf Children's Society
See *deafness.*

National Development Group

An independent advisory body to the government set up in the U.K. in 1975 to make recommendations on the policies, development and implementation of better services for mentally handicapped people. A series of pamphlets translated the philosophies of better services into codes of practice. It has now been disbanded.

National Development Team

An independent body, set up by the Secretary of State for Social Services in 1976, to advise health authorities and local authority social services departments in the U.K. on the development of their services to mentally handicapped people. It visits areas by invitation only and although it has a professional directorate it calls on a panel of between 80 and 100 people, all of whom have personal or professional experience of caring for mentally handicapped people. About 10 panel members are seconded for the duration of a study. The team look at every aspect of the services provided and consult with consumer groups and voluntary organizations. A verbal report is followed by a written report which the authorities are required to make public. The NDT is not an inspectorate and has no power to impose its advice on the health service or local authorities.

Further information:
The Team Secretary, National Development Team, Room C411, Alexander Fleming House, Elephant and Castle, London SE1 6BY.

National Federation of Gateway Clubs

= *Gateway Clubs*.

National Physically Handicapped and Able Bodied

An organization in the U.K. which promotes leisure opportunities based on clubs involving physically handicapped and able-bodied people.

Further information:
PHAB, Tavistock House North, Tavistock Sq., London WC1H 9HJ.

National Society of Phenylketonuria and Allied Disorders

See *phenylketonuria*.

NDG

= *National Development Group*.

NDT

= *National Development Team*.

Neck webbing

Folds of skin on either side of the neck which make it appear wide and thick. This may occur in *Turner's syndrome*, *Noonan's syndrome*, *arthrogryposis multiplex congenita* and some *chromosome* disorders all of which are associated with mental handicap.

Necrotizing encephalitis

A severe form of *encephalitis* in which a large amount of brain tissue is destroyed by the infection. This may occur in *cytomegalic inclusion disease* and *toxoplasmosis*.

Necrotizing encephalopathy

= *Leigh's syndrome*.

Negative reinforcement

See *reinforcement*.

Neill-Dingwall syndrome

See *Cockayne's syndrome*.

Neonatal

New born. Applying to the first few weeks of life. A number of problems may occur at this time which can damage the brain, e.g. neonatal *hypoglycaemia*.

Neonatal screening

It is possible to screen babies for several treatable genetic disorders by means of a blood test soon after birth. *Phenylketonuria*, *homocystinuria*, *congential hypothyroidism*, *galactosaemia*, *maple syrup urine disease* and

Neoplasia / neoplasm

histidinaemia can all be identified by this means and screening tests are carried out routinely in many countries.

GUTHRIE, R. (1980) Newborn infant screening and the prevention of mental retardation. In: Prevention of Mental Retardation and other Developmental Disabilities. McCormack, M. (Ed.) New York: Marcel Dekker Inc. pp. 269–278.

Neoplasia / neoplasm
New tissue forming in the body as occurs with a tumour.

Nephritis
Inflammation of the kidney.

Nephroblastoma
= *Wilm's tumour.*

Nerve deafness
= *Sensori-neural deafness.*

Neulactil
= *pericyazine.*

Neural tube defects
A malformation of the *central nervous system* caused by an abnormality in the early stages of the development of the *fetus* in the womb. *Anencephaly, encephalocoele* and *meningomyelocoele* are examples.

Neuroaxonal dystrophies
A group of rare *degenerative disorders* of the nervous system characterized by swellings in the nerves of the *spinal cord* and brain. The most common form is infantile neuroaxonal dystrophy (Seitelberger's disease). The onset is between 1 and 2 years of age with progressive weakness, floppiness and mental deterioration. Reflexes are overactive and there may be problems in passing urine. Vision deteriorates. *Seizures* are rare. Survival beyond 10 years of age is unusual. There are also similar forms with earlier and later onsets. The juvenile form begins between 9 and 17 years of age. The nature of

the assumed *enzyme* defect is not known. These disorders are probably inherited from both parents who are carriers (*recessive inheritance*).

COWEN, D. & OLMSTEAD, E.V. (1963) Infantile neuroaxonal dystrophy. J. Neuropathol. Exp. Neurol., 22:175.
WILLIAMSON, K. et al (1982) Neuroaxonal dystrophy in young adults: A clinicopathological study of two unrelated cases. Ann. Neurol., 11:335.

Neuroblastoma
A tumour of nerve cells which can occur anywhere in the body and is malignant to a variable extent. It may be associated with *myoclonic encephalopathy.*

Neurocutaneous melanosis
A very rare condition with large, brown, thick, birthmarks present on the skin especially on the trunk, abdomen and thighs, with similar malformations involving the brain, *spinal cord* and *meninges*. These sometimes become malignant. *Epilepsy* is usual and there is slow development with progressive mental handicap and very reduced life expectancy. *Hydrocephalus* is a common complication. The cause is unknown.

HARPER, C.G. & THOMAS, D.G.T. (1974) Neurocutaneous melanosis. J. Neurol. Neurosurg. Psychiat., 37:760.
SALMON, M.A. (1978) Developmental Defects and Syndromes. Aylesbury, England: HM+M. pp. 111–112.

Neurocutaneous syndromes
A group of hereditary diseases characterized by a tendency for malformations and tumours to arise in numerous organs especially the skin, brain and *spinal cord*. In order of frequency these include *Von Recklinghausen's disease, tuberose sclerosis, Sturge-Weber syndrome*, and *Louis-Barr syndrome*. There are several other rare conditions included in this group. Many of them are of uncertain heredity. Many, but not all, disorders in this group are associated with mental handicap.

228

HOLMES, L.B. et al (1972) Mental Retardation. New York: Macmillan. pp. 353–383.
MENKES, J.H. (1985) Textbook of Child Neurology (3rd edit.). Philadelphia: Lea & Febiger. pp. 566–580.

Neurodegenerative disease
= *degenerative disorders.*

Neurodevelopmental therapy
= *Bobath.*

Neurofibromatosis
= *Von Recklinghausen's disease.*

Neuroleptic medication / drugs
Drugs which have a specific effect on the *central nervous system.* This includes *tranquillizers, antidepressants* and sedatives.

Neurological
To do with the nervous system of the body (brain, *spinal cord* and nerves).

Neurology
The branch of medicine and science which deals with the nervous system of the body (brain, *spinal cord* and nerves) and its diseases.

Neuron / neurone
A nerve cell and the fibres emerging from it.

Neuronal ceroid lipofuscinoses
= *Batten-Vogt disease.*

Neuronal lipidoses
= *lipidoses.*

Neuroses / neurotic disorders
Psychiatric disorders in which the person retains contact with reality (as compared to the *psychoses*) and in which language is not disturbed. It includes *anxiety states, phobias, hysterical symptoms, obsessive-compulsive disorders, hypocondriasis* and milder forms of *depression.* All of these can occur in mentally handicapped people when under stress.

FORREST, A.D. (1979) Neuroses in the mentally handicapped. In: Psychiatric Illness and Mental Handicap. James, F.E. & Snaith, R.P. (Eds.) London: Gaskell Press. pp. 45–51.
REID, A.H. (1985) Psychiatry and mental handicap. In: Mental Handicap. A Multi-disciplinary Approach. Craft, M. et al (Eds.). London: Baillière Tindall. pp. 328–330. ·

Neurosyphilis
= *congenital syphilis.*

Neurovisceral lipidoses
= *generalized gangliosidosis.*

Nevus
= *naevus.*

Next Step on the Ladder
A detailed developmental checklist and training schedule for use with multiply and/or profoundly handicapped children or adults. It covers the use of sight and hearing, movement, manual dexterity, social development and personal contact, self-help skills and communication. The manual gives clear instructions for training but assessment is not so simple and two assessors are recommended.

SIMON, G.B. (1981) Next Step on the Ladder (revised edit.). Kidderminster, U.K.: BIMH Publications.

Niemann-Pick disease
This degenerative condition is now known to include at least six major forms of the *lipidoses.* In these disorders an *enzyme* deficiency causes accumulation of abnormal substances (particularly sphingomyelin) in the body especially in the liver, spleen and lymph glands. In Type A the onset is during the first year of life with poor physical and mental development. The liver and spleen are grossly enlarged and *seizures,* particularly *myoclonic seizures* are common. Muscles are floppy but later may become spastic.

A deterioration in sight may accompany cloudiness of the *cornea* and lens of the eye and a characteristic cherry-red spot on the back of the eye in the *macula* region (*macular degeneration*). The progression is variable but death usually occurs before 5 years of age. Type B becomes evident between 2 and 6 years of age with enlargement of liver and spleen but normal intelligence until late in the disease. Type C includes several sub-types and is the most common form. The course is extremely variable. It may present in infancy with prolonged *jaundice*, enlarged liver and spleen and rapid progression but more commonly the onset is between 2 and 4 years with unsteadiness, *spasticity*, seizures (usually myoclonic or *akinetic*) and the cherry-red spot on the macula of the eye. Enlargement of the liver and spleen may be less marked. In some there is a rapid course and in others a very slow progression. Impairment of upward gaze (supranuclear *ophthalmoplegia*) and a variety of seizure disorders have been described. The degree of intellectual impairment is very variable. Life expectancy is reduced usually to teens or early 20's. Type D is slowly progressive and only seen in Nova Scotia.

These disorders are inherited from both parents who are carriers (*recessive inheritance*). A deficiency of the enzyme sphingomye-linase in body cells can be used to confirm the diagnosis in types A and B and this can also be measured following *amniocentesis*. There is no known treatment. Removal of the spleen may sometimes be necessary.

CROCKER, A.C. & FARBER, S. (1958) Niemann-Pick disease: A review of 18 patients. Medicine (Baltimore), 37:1–95.
ELLEDER, M. & JIRASEK, A. (1983) International symposium on Niemann-Pick disease. Eur. J. Pediatr., 140:90.
EPSTEIN, C.J. et al (1971) In utero diagnosis of Niemann-Pick disease. Ann. Hum. Genet., 23:533–535.
MENKES, J.H. (1985) Textbook of Child Neurology (3rd Ed). Philadelphia: Lea & Febiger. pp. 72–74.

NIMROD

The name of a pioneering scheme in South Glamorgan, Wales, U.K. NIMROD stands for New Ideas for the care of Mentally Retarded people in Ordinary Dwellings. It aims to offer all the mentally handicapped people in a defined area, whatever their degree of disability, the services they need to remain in their own home community, either with their families or in alternative ordinary housing. Its catchment area has a 60,000 total population. All clients have *individual programme plans* and services respond with individual training and problem solving. Staffed and unstaffed houses have been established.

EVANS, G. et al (1987) Evaluating the impact of a move to ordinary housing. Brit. J. Ment. Sub., 33(64):10–18.
MATHIESON, S. & BLUNDEN, R. (1980) NIMROD is piloting a course. Health & Soc. Services J., 122–124.

Further information:
NIMROD, The White Houses, 40–42 Cowbridge Road East, Canton, Cardiff CF1 9DU.

Nitrazepam

One of the *benzodiazepine* group of drugs which is used as a sedative. It is used in the treatment of insomnia in adults but side-effects include drowsiness and impaired performance at skilled tasks during the day. It may cause confusion in the elderly and withdrawal effects if stopped suddenly after prolonged use. Rashes and stomach upsets are unusual side-effects. It is occasionally effective in the treatment of *epilepsy*, particularly *infantile spasms* and *myoclonic epilepsy* but the problem of oversedation severely limits its usefulness.

It is not available in the U.S.A. because of the fears of liver damage.

NMR

= *nuclear magnetic resonance imaging*.

Noack's syndrome
= *Pfeiffer's syndrome.*

Nocturnal enuresis
See *enuresis.*

Non-accidental injury
= *child abuse.*

Non-ketotic hyperglycinaemia
See *hyperglycinaemia.*

Non-verbal communication
Communication without the use of the spoken word. This is generally by means of *gestures systems, sign language* or *symbols.*

Nondisjunction
The failure of the two members of a *chromosome* pair to separate during the division of the cell. Both pass to the same daughter cell. This causes the presence of an extra chromosome in that cell. This abnormal process is the most common cause of the extra chromosome in the cells of people with *Down's syndrome.*

Noonan's syndrome
A condition that includes short stature and a webbed, short, broad neck. The eyes are widely spaced, slanting and the eyelids often drooping. Squint and *myopia* are common. Abnormalities of the teeth, spinal curvature and other abnormalities of bones may occur. Genitals are underdeveloped and kidneys and heart abnormalities are often a problem. *Sensori-neural deafness* and variable degrees of mental handicap are common but social competence is relatively good. It is very similar to *Turner's syndrome* but the *chromosomes* are normal and it can occur in both sexes. It is a genetic disorder with *dominant inheritance.*

COLLINS, E. & TURNER, G. (1973) The Noonan syndrome: Review of clinical and genetic features of 27 cases. J. Pediatr., 83:941.
NOONAN, J. (1968) Hypertelorism with Turner phenotype: a new syndrome with associated congenital heart disease. Am. J. Dis. Child., 116:373.
SALMON, M.A. (1978) Developmental Defects and Syndromes. Aylesbury, England: HM+M Publishers. pp. 199–200.

Further information:
Noonan Syndrome Support Group, Mrs. Sheila Brown, 27 Pinfold Lane, Cheslyn Hay, Walsall, W50 7HP, U.K.

Normalization
An approach which was originally developed in Scandinavia and refers to the principle of providing the opportunity for mentally handicapped people to have a life-style which is as close as possible to normal life in the community. It relates to the living conditions, circumstances and activities of a person and carries the expectation that a disabled person should not be further handicapped by an abnormal life-style. It is related to the recognition that disabled people are members of society and have the same rights and human needs as anyone else. Gradually the North American workers have developed the idea that adoption of the principle of normalization demonstrates that disabled people are valued in our society. A more recent definition (O'Brien & Tyne 1981) is 'The use of means which are valued in our society in order to develop and support personal behaviour, experiences and characteristics which are likewise valued.' This includes the provision of personal dignity, choice and valued experiences while at the same time providing any special help and services required to lead to characteristics, behaviour and experiences which are accepted and valued and which will minimize any disability. The principle of normalization therefore applies to the services provided for the individual and is not a description of the individual himself. The *Programme Analysis of Service Systems* (PASS) is a method which can be used to specify the implications of normalization in particular situations.

FLYNN, R.J. & NITSCH, K.E. (Eds.) (1981) Normalization, Social Integration and Community Services. Baltimore: University Park Press.

O'BRIEN, J. & TYNE, A. (1981) The Principle of Normalization: A Foundation for Effective Services. London: Campaign for Mentally Handicapped People.

ROSE-ACKERMAN, S. (1982) Mental retardation and society: the ethics and politics of normalization. Ethics, 93:81–101.

RUSSELL, O. (1985) Mental Handicap. Edinburgh: Churchill Livingstone. pp. 174–177.

WOLFENSBERGER, W. (1972) The Principle of Normalization in Human Services. Toronto: National Institute on Mental Retardation.

Norman-Wood disease

A *gangliosidosis* which presents at birth but is otherwise similar to *Tay-Sachs disease*.

Norries syndrome

A rare condition in which blindness is present from birth or develops very early in infancy. A white mass of abnormal tissue develops in the eyes which become small and sunken. Mental handicap occurs to a variable extent. Intellectual development is usually normal in the preschool years but mental deterioration occurs later, often with behaviour problems and/or *autistic* features. *Self-injurious behaviour* may occur. Older people with this syndrome sometimes show mental deterioration and develop deafness. It is inherited from the mother who is a carrier and affects only males (*sex-linked inheritance*).

HOLMES, L.B. (1971) Norries disease: an X-linked syndrome of retinal malformation, mental retardation and deafness. J. Pediatr., 79:89–92.

WARBURG, M. (1971) Norries disease. Birth Defects, 8(3):117.

Nuclear magnetic resonance imaging

This very technical procedure is versatile and safe. It provides pictorial information on the structure of organs of the body such as the brain. It provides a clearer definition than a *CT scan* in certain areas and also shows chemical differences. It will, for example, contrast the white (fibres) and grey (cells) layers of the brain and show the presence or absence of *myelin*. It is very valuable in the diagnosis of some types of tumours of the brain and *spinal cord*.

GOODING, C.A. et al (1984) Nuclear magnetic resonance imaging of the brain in children. J. Pediatr., 104:509.

KARSTAEDT, N. et al (1983) Nuclear magnetic resonance imaging. Surg. Neurol., 19:206.

Nurse

In the U.K. there is a qualification for nursing mentally handicapped people (Registered Nurse Mental Handicap). This originated from the *medical model* of care established when the mental handicap colonies became hospitals in the 1940's. It is now widely accepted that a nursing qualification is not necessary to provide adequate care for disabled people. If a person is ill the proper medical services should be provided. There is a difference between illness and disability. Some profoundly handicapped people do require a high standard of physical care which may include some nursing techniques but these can nearly always be taught to non-qualified care-givers including relatives. Nevertheless, during the course of their work, many RNMH qualified nurses gain a lot of experience and skill in supporting, teaching and assisting mentally handicapped people and their families. These skills can be very useful in the community setting where *community mental handicap nurses* form part of a multidisciplinary *community mental handicap team*.

The future role of nurses and the continuing need for such a qualification has been strongly questioned and it is probable that a new training and qualification will emerge which is more in line with the Local Authority Social Services qualifications. While this is being resolved the training continues and extra courses are available for nurses who wish to work in the community. In the U.S.A. the qualifications of nurses who work with mentally handicapped people are as varied as the settings that serve these people. There is no specific qualification as in the U.K. Although licensing is required for a nursing post, decisions on the qualifications are the prerogative of the employer.

HALLAS, C.H. et al (1982) The Care and Training of the Mentally Handicapped. Bristol: Wright.

Nutrition / nutritional amentia
See *malnutrition*.

Nydrane
= *beclamide*.

Nystagmus
Fine jerking movements of the eyeball which usually occur from side to side but many follow an up and down or rotatory pattern. Nystagmus is sometimes more evident when looking in a particular direction. It may occur in people of normal intelligence without any impairment of vision but it often occurs in people who are mentally handicapped with or without other visual defects such as diseases of the *retina*. It is particularly associated with abnormalities of the *cerebellar* region of the brain. It has been described in *Cockayne's syndrome, Hallermann-Streiff syndrome, Louis-Barr syndrome, Klippel-Feil syndrome* and a number of *chromosome* abnormalities including *Down's syndrome*.

O

Oast house urine syndrome

An extremely rare condition in which there is an inability to absorb methionine (an important *amino acid*) from the gut. This leads to the collection of abnormal substances in the blood and their excretion in the urine which has a distinctive smell resembling dried celery, burnt sugar or an oast house. Affected children have fine hair, blue eyes and episodes of overbreathing and diarrhoea. Severe mental handicap and *epilepsy* are present. The early introduction of a low methionine diet may improve physical and mental development. The condition is probably inherited from both parents who are carriers (*recessive inheritance*).

HOOFT, C. et al (1964) Methionine malabsorption in a mentally defective child. Lancet, ii:20.

SMITH, A.J. & STRANG, L.B. (1958) An inborn error of metabolism with the urinary excretion of X-hydroxybutyric acid and phenylpyruric acid. Arch. Dis. Childh., 33:109.

Obese / obesity

Significantly overweight compared to others of the same age, height and sex. This usually occurs from a combination of overeating and insufficient exercise. It is also characteristic of a few conditions associated with mental handicap including *Laurence-Moon-Biedl syndrome* and *Prader-Willi syndrome*. Drugs such as *thioridazine* and *sodium valproate* may stimulate the appetite and lead to obesity.

Object permanence

A stage of intellectual development, which normally occurs between 7 and 9 months of age, in which the child will look for an object which he or she has seen being hidden under or behind another object. In mentally handicapped children the acquisition of this skill may be delayed and it may be learnt more slowly.

MORSS, J.R. (1985) Early cognitive development: difference or delay? In: Current Approaches to Down's Syndrome. Lane, D. & Stratford, B. (Eds.). London: Holt Reinhardt & Winston. pp. 242–259.

Observational learning

= *imitation*.

Obsession / obsessional neurosis / obsessive-compulsive disorder

An obsession is an idea, emotion or impulse that repetitively and insistently forces itself into consciousness even though it is unwelcome. When this becomes a preoccupation which causes distress or problems for the person or those he lives with it is regarded as an obsessional neurosis which is a type of psychiatric disorder. An obsessive-compulsive disorder includes repetitive impulses to perform acts (rituals, handwashing, checking, etc.). Ritualistic behaviours seen in *autistic* people are not usually included. Obsessional ideas or fears sometimes occur as symptoms of anxiety or *depression*. Very little has been published on the prevalence or presentation of these disorders in mentally handicapped people. In mildly mentally handicapped people there is probably very little difference to the general population although it has been suggested that they occur less frequently.

REID, A.H. (1985) Psychiatry and mental handicap. In: Mental Handicap. A Multidisciplinary Approach. Craft, M. et al. London: Baillière Tindall. pp. 328–330.

Occipital bone / occiput
The part of the skull in the lower region of the back of the head where it joins the neck.

Occipital bossing
Protuberance of the *occipital bone* at the back of the head. This may occur in a number of conditions associated with mental handicap including *Patau's syndrome* and *Edward's syndrome*.

Occipital lobes
The lobes of the brain which lie at the back of the head and are mainly concerned with vision.

Occupational therapy / occupational therapist (OT)
The skills of an occupational therapist may be used to initiate or improve the skills of a mentally handicapped person in any area of life. An OT also assesses disabilities and recommends suitable aids, adaptations and therapy. Occupational therapists may provide self-help training programmes, work training, training in the skills of daily living and training in leisure skills such as art, music and craft.

In the U.K. there are both diploma and degree courses in occupational therapy. These equip therapists to deal with the rehabilitation and habilitation of ill and disabled people. Specialization in mental handicap is gained by relevant experience or by a post-registration degree course.

In the U.S.A. the profession may be entered at two levels each providing general skills. This is by means of an undergraduate degree in occupational therapy or by completion of work for a master's degree following an undergraduate degree in another subject. Certification and national registration are managed by the American Occupational Therapy Association. Individual states may also insist on licensing. Specialization in mental handicap is gained through continuing education programmes, specialized master's curricula and/or doctoral programmes in occupational therapy.

ANSTICE, B. & BOWDEN, R. (1985) The role of the occupational therapist. In: Mental Handicap. A Multidisciplinary Approach. Craft, M. et al (Eds.) London: Baillière Tindall.

Further information:
College of Occupational Therapists, 20 Rede Place, Bayswater, London W2.

Ocular
To do with the eye.

Ocular hypertelorism
= *hypertelorism*.

Ocular hypotelorism
= *hypotelorism*.

Oculoauriculovertebral dysplasia
= *Goldenhar's syndrome*.

Oculocerebral degeneration
= *Norries syndrome*.

Oculocerebrorenal syndrome
= *Lowe's syndrome*.

Oculogyric crisis
An episode of involuntary spasm of the muscles of the eye causing them to roll upward so that only the whites are visible. This occurs rarely when brain damage causes *Parkinson's disease*. It is also an *extrapyramidal side-effect* of the *phenothiazine* and *butyrophenone* drugs.

Oculomandibulodyscephaly
= *Hallermann-Streiff syndrome*.

Oculovertebral syndrome
= *Goldenhar's syndrome*.

Oedema / edema
Swelling due to fluid accumulating in tissues. Accumulation of lymphatic fluid is called *lymphoedema*.

Oesophageal atresia / oesophageal stenosis

The oesophagus is the canal between the throat and the stomach. It may be closed (*atresia*) or narrowed (*stenosis*) in a few conditions associated with mental handicap including *Down's syndrome* and *Edward's syndrome*.

OFD I

= *oro-facial-digital syndrome I.*

OFD II

= oro-facial-digital syndrome II. See *Mohrs' syndrome.*

Offerton Self-Care Checklist

A checklist for a broad assessment of the self-care skills and independence of a mentally handicapped person. It covers basic self-care skills such as toilet use, dressing, eating and drinking and personal hygiene. Each item also identifies the opportunities required for the skill to be used. There are initial questions which assess the environment, restrictions and opportunities.

BURTON, M. et al (1981) Offerton Self-Care Checklist. Manchester: Hester Adrian Research Centre.

Olfactory

To do with the sense of smell. The nerves which transmit the sense of smell (olfactory nerves) may be absent in a few conditions associated with mental handicap including *cytomegalic inclusion disease, Patau's syndrome* and *Edward's syndrome.*

Oligodactyly

Fewer fingers and toes than normal. This may occur in a few conditions associated with mental handicap including *de Lange syndrome.*

Oligophrenia

A term for mental handicap which is little used in the U.K. and U.S.A. but is sometimes used in mainland Europe.

Omphalocoele / omphalocele

= *exomphalos.*

OPD syndrome

= *otopalatodigital syndrome.*

Operant conditioning

A method widely used in *behaviour modification*, in which behaviours are changed by changing their consequences. The four types of operant conditioning are positive *reinforcement*, negative reinforcement, *punishment* and *extinction.*

Operants

A term used in *behaviour modification* to describe voluntary behaviours which are purposeful or instrumental in attaining goals. *Antecedents* set the occasion for operants but do not automatically elicit them. Consequent events exert a controlling effect on operants (see *operant conditioning*).

Operational plan

A plan outlining the way in which staff and other resources will be developed in a particular locality or situation in order to meet the goals of an overall policy or strategy. This is a process used by a central authority to impose priorities and objectives. This method of planning for priority groups has been challenged and planning based on individual client needs (as identified in *individual programme plans*) has been proposed as a more satisfactory model.

GLENNERSTER, H. (1982) Planning for Priority Groups. Oxford: Martin Robertson.

Ophthalmic specialist / ophthalmologist / ophthalmic surgeon

A doctor who has specialized in diseases of the eyes and visual problems. Full and regular ophthalmological assessments are important for a mentally handicapped person because abnormalities of the eyes and vision are commonly associated with many disorders which cause mental handicap.

Ophthalmoplegia

Paralysis of muscles which move the eyes. This often occurs in one type of *Niemann-Pick disease* and in *Bloch-Sulzberger syndrome*.

Ophthalmoscope

An instrument used to look into the eye. It can be focused on the *cornea*, the lens of the eye, the *retina* or any abnormalities between them. It is used to detect diseases of, or damage to, the eye. It can also be used to diagnose disorders of the body including some conditions associated with mental handicap.

Opisthotonus

A position of the body in which the back is arched and head bent backward. This is due to spasm and tightness of the muscles of the back and neck. It may be a sign of *meningitis* and may also be a form of *extensor spasm* as occurs sometimes in *cerebral palsy*.

Opitz syndrome

A very rare condition reported only in males in whom there are defects in structures occurring in the midline of the body. The eyes are wide set (*hypertelorism*) and the skull broad (*brachycephaly*). *Cleft lip / palate*, squint, low-set ears and a downward slant to the eyes have also been reported. The opening from the bladder is situated on the underside of the penis and the testes are often undescended. *Congenital heart disease* is common. Mild to moderate mental handicap was apparent in about half the people described. It is inherited from one parent (*dominant inheritance*).

OPITZ, J.M. et al (1969) The BBB syndrome – Familial telecanthus with associated congenital abnormalities. Birth Defects Original Article Series II, 5(2):86.

Opportunity plan

A method of planning the activities of a mentally handicapped person so that the necessary opportunities and experiences are provided in the weekly timetable. These are usually identified at an *individual programme planning* meeting.

Opsoclonus

Chaotically irregular eye movements. The eyes are constantly making fine movements that are interrupted by rapid and unequal larger movements which usually take place from side to side. When the person attempts to change the position of the eyes the abnormal eye movements become more evident. Opsoclonus characteristically occurs in *myoclonic encephalopathy*.

Optic atrophy

The shrinkage and wasting of the *optic nerve*. This can be seen at the *optic disc*, by using an *ophthalmoscope*. As a result vision is lost or severely impaired. The term optic atrophy is less often used to describe shrinkage and wasting of the eye itself. Atrophy of the optic nerve may occur in a number of conditions associated with mental handicap including *cytomegalic inclusion disease, toxoplasmosis, congenital syphilis, Conradi's syndrome, Crouzon's syndrome, de Lange syndrome, Goldenhar's syndrome, happy puppet syndrome, hydrocephalus, Laurence-Moon-Biedl syndrome, Niemann-Pick disease, Tay-Sachs disease* and several other rare conditions.

Optic disc

The place on the *retina* of the eye at which the *optic nerve* joins the retina. At the optic disc it is possible to see the nerve itself by using an *ophthalmoscope* and to detect abnormalities such as *optic atrophy* or *papilloedema*.

Optic nerve

The nerve which runs from the *retina* of the eye to the brain. It transmits all the information concerning vision from that eye. It can be seen at the *optic disc*. Abnormalities of the optic nerve may be associated with conditions which cause mental handicap. See *optic atrophy* and *papilloedema*.

Oral

To do with speech or with the mouth.

Oral-facial-digital syndrome

= *oro-facial-digital syndromes I & II*.

Orap

= *pimozide*.

Orbeli syndrome

A condition caused by loss of material from chromosome 13 (*deletion of chromosome*) and often the formation of a ring (*chromosome ring*). Infants with this condition are small at birth and have restricted growth. Development is slow and severe mental handicap is usual. The head is small and the head shape may be abnormal.

The *corpus callosum* of the brain may not be developed. In the case of a deletion, a tumour of the *retina* of the eyes (retinoblastoma) frequently develops at about 2 years of age. Other eye abnormalities may also occur including defects in the iris which led to the term *cat-eye syndrome* being used. The nose has a broad and prominent bridge and the mouth and lower jaw are small with a protuberant upper jaw. Absent or small thumbs are common and the fifth finger may also be short. *Congenital dislocation of the hip* and deformities of the leg or foot can be a problem. Abnormalities of bowel, kidneys, heart and genitals have also been reported. The cause of the abnormal chromosome arrangement is rarely *hereditary*. It is not related to parental age.

McCANDLESS, A. & WALKER, S. (1976) D 13 ring chromosome syndrome. Arch. Dis. Childh., 51:449.
ORBELI, D.J. et al (1971) The syndrome associated with the partial D-monosomy. Case report and review. Humangenetik, 13:296.

Organic acidurias

A group of disorders due to *enzyme* deficiencies which can result in intermittent episodes of vomiting, lethargy, acidity in the blood and abnormal substances (generally ketones) in the urine. These disorders include *hyperglycinaemia, methylmalonic acidaemia, isovaleric acidaemia* and *lactic acidosis*. These are all rare disorders and many infants do not survive to adulthood. Screening for organic acidurias in infants with unexplained *developmental delay* is regarded as unproductive and not cost effective and is usually reserved for severely ill newborn infants and young children when there are suggestive symptoms.

CHALMERS, R.A. et al (1980) Screening for organic acidurias and aminoacidopathies in newborns and children. J. Inherited Metab. Dis., 3:27–43.
MENKES, J.H. (1985) Textbook of Child Neurology. Philadelphia: Lea & Febiger. pp. 54–59.

Organic brain damage / disorder

A general term used to describe any structural damage to the brain caused by trauma, disease or other disorder. It may also include any secondary effects on the brain caused by disease or malfunction of other organs.

Organic brain syndrome

A psychiatric or emotional disorder caused by abnormality of the brain or its function as in delirium or in *dementia*.

Organic disorder / disease

A disorder of an organ or organs of the body which produces structural change. It is used to denote physical disease as opposed to psychological disorder.

Ornithinaemia

The presence of ornithine in the blood. This is caused by several disorders all of them due to different *enzyme* deficiencies. A partial deficiency of ornithine decarboxylase causes, in the newborn baby, prolonged *jaundice, infantile spasms*, mental handicap and intermittent unsteadiness. A partial deficiency of ornithine-ketoacid aminotransferase causes liver disease, kidney dysfunction and a variable degree of mental handicap. A severe deficiency of ornithine-ketoacid aminotransferase causes damage to the *retina* of the eye but does not cause intellectual impairment. Symptoms are helped by a diet low in arginine (an *amino acid*).

Each of this group of conditions is inherited from both parents who are carriers (*recessive inheritance*).

McINNES, R.R. et al (1981) Hyperornithinaemia and gyrate atrophy of the retina. Improvement of vision during treatment with low arginine diet. Lancet, 1:513.

VALLE, D. & SIMELL, O. (1983) The hyperornithinemias. In: The Metabolic Basis of Inherited Disease (5th edit.). Stanbury, J.B. et al.(Eds.) New York: McGraw-Hill, p. 382.

Ornithine transcarbamylase (OTC) deficiency

A very rare condition caused by a deficiency of the *enzyme* OTC. As a result ammonia accumulates in the blood and excess *amino acids* are excreted in the urine. Affected children have poor appetite, stunted growth and attacks of vomiting, headache and screaming. Later there is lethargy and sometimes a coma. Severe mental handicap, *epilepsy* and delayed speech are usual. It is sometimes fatal in early infancy. Attacks often follow protein foods and treatment is with a low-protein diet supplemented with essential amino acids. Citric acid and aspartic acid may be given to reduce the blood ammonia levels and the degree of brain damage.

It is due to *sex-linked inheritance* and in boys the enzyme is almost completely absent so that they have a very severe form of the disease. Girls only have a partial deficiency and are more mildly affected. In some boys several months of normal development are followed by progressive intellectual deterioration with or without liver damage resembling *Reye syndrome*.

BATSHAW, M.L. et al (1980) Cerebral dysfunction in asymptomatic carriers of ornithine transcarbamylase deficiency. New Engl. J. Med., 302:482.

KRIEGER, I. et al (1979) Atypical clinical course of ornithine transcarbamylase deficiency due to a new mutant (comparison with Reye's disease). J. Clin. Endocrinology & Metabolism, 48:388.

SNYDERMAN, S.E. et al (1975) The therapy of hyperammonemia due to ornithine transcarbamylase deficiency in a male neonate. Pediatrics, 56:61.

Oro-cranio-digital (OCD) syndrome

A very rare condition in which there is *cleft-lip / palate*, small head and underdevelopment of the thumbs which are nearer the fingers than usual. It may not be possible to straighten the arm at the elbow. The eyes may be widely spaced. Mild mental handicap is frequently present.

JUBERG, R.C. & HAYWARD, J.R. (1969) A new familial syndrome of oral, cranial and digital anomalies. J. Pediatr., 74:755.

Oro-facial-digital syndrome I

In this rare condition people have a midline cleft of the upper lip, cleft tongue, *cleft palate*, webbing between tongue and cheek, a broad bridge of the nose and the tip of the nose is often short and thin. In profile the brow is relatively prominent and the middle of the face flattened. Central teeth may be absent. There are abnormalities of fingers, and less often toes, include incurving, fusing together, shortness and extra fingers or toes. Scalp hair is often sparse and coarse. It is often associated with agenesis of the *corpus callosum*. One third to one half of affected people are mentally handicapped usually only mildly. It mainly occurs in females and the type of inheritance is uncertain but it is probably a *sex-linked* dominant *gene* lethal in males.

BARAISTER, M. (1986) The orofaciodigital syndromes. J. Med. Genet., 23(2)116–119.

RIMOIN, D.L. & EDGERTON, M.T. (1967) Genetic and clinical heterogeneity in the oral-facial-digital syndromes. J. Pediatr., 71:94–102.

Oro-facial-digital syndrome II
= *Mohrs' syndrome.*

Orphenadrine
A drug used in the treatment of *Parkinson's disease* and also for the *extrapyramidal side-effects* induced by *phenothiazines* and *butyrophenones.*

Orthopaedic
The branch of medicine dealing with abnormalities and deformities of bones, joints and muscles. An orthopaedic specialist has had special experience and qualification in this subject. Many mentally handicapped people have associated physical problems which require orthopaedic treatment.

SAMILSON, R.L. (1975) (Ed.) Orthopaedic Aspects of Cerebral Palsy. London: Heinemann Medical Books. Lippincott.

Oseretsky Test of Motor Proficiency
This was introduced as a measure of *motor development*. It has been modified for use for different purposes but each version includes short tests involving *gross motor skills* (such as balancing on one leg or walking backwards in a straight line) and *fine motor skills* (such as picking up small objects individually). It is scored on accuracy and speed. It has reasonable agreement with *neurological* assessment. It correlates with age and differentiates mentally handicapped children from children of normal intellectual ability.

RUTTER, M. et al (1970) A neuropsychiatric study in childhood (Clinics in Developmental Medicine Nos. 35–36). London: Spastics International Publications / Heinemann Medical Books.
SLOAN, W. (1955) The Lincoln-Oseretsky motor development scale. Genetic Psychology Monographics, 51:183–252.

STOTT, D.H. (1966) A general test of motor impairment for children. Dev. Med. Child Neurology, 8:523–531.

Ospolot
= *sulthiame.*

Osteomalacia
Softening of the bones usually due to lack of vitamin D. If this leads to deformities it is known as rickets. It can rarely occur as a complication of a few disorders associated with mental handicap such as *Lowe's syndrome.*

Osteopetrosis
A disorder in which there is over-production of poorly formed bone leading to thickening but increased fragility of bones. The thickening of the skull can narrow some of the openings and this may cause damage to the nerves of the eyes (*optic atrophy*), hearing (causing deafness) and to other nerves of the head. It may also cause *hydrocephalus*. The head appears enlarged with a prominent brow. Defects in teeth are frequent. Bones may break with very little stress. Anaemia and enlargement of the liver and spleen are also problems. Growth is stunted. A variable degree of mental handicap is often present. Life expectancy is usually limited due to the loss of bone marrow and resulting inability to make blood. Removal of the spleen and blood transfusions are usually necessary. A low calcium diet and treatment with steroid drugs may also help. The progression tends to be more rapid the earlier the onset. As well as the infantile form, which is inherited from both parents who are carriers (*recessive inheritance*) there is a milder later onset form which is usually passed on by *dominant inheritance*. The severe infantile form can be diagnosed in the womb by X-rays.

DENT, C.E. et al (1965) Studies in osteopetrosis. Arch. Dis. Childh., 40:7–15.
JOHNSTONE, C.C. et al (1968) Osteopetrosis. A clinical, genetic, metabolic and

morphological study of the dominantly inherited benign form. Medicine, 47: 149–167.

LEHMAN, R.A.W. et al (1977) Neurological complications of infantile osteopetrosis. Ann. Neurol., 2:378.

MOE, P.J. & SKAEVELAND, A. (1969) Therapeutic studies in osteopetrosis. Acta Paediatr. (Uppsala), 58:593.

Osteoporosis

A condition in which the bones loose calcium and become porous and weak. They break more easily than normal. It may occur due to dietary deficiencies, lack of use (as may happen in physical disabilities) or to particular chemical problems in the body. The latter may be caused by a few conditions associated with mental handicap including *homocystinuria, Cockayne's syndrome, Hallermann-Streiff syndrome* and *Donohue's syndrome*.

Otitis media

Inflammation of the middle ear usually due to infection. If recurrent or untreated it can lead to *glue ear* and *middle-ear deafness*. Children with *Down's syndrome* are particularly prone to ear infections.

Oto-palato-digital (OPD) syndrome

A very rare condition in which there is *conductive deafness, cleft palate,* abnormalities of bones and short stature. The appearance is a little unusual with a prominent forehead and back of head. Eyes are widely spaced and slant downward from the bridge of the nose. The mouth is small and teeth defects are common. A small sunken chest is usual. Second and third toes are very long and curved, with a wide space between first and second fingers and toes. Thumbs are short and broad. Limitation of elbow movement is usual. The intellectual ability is usually in the low normal range but mild mental handicap may be present. The mode of inheritance is uncertain but it is probably *sex-linked inheritance*, only affecting males and carried by females.

DUDDING, B.A. et al (1967) The oto-palatal-digital syndrome. Am. J. Dis. Child., 113:214–21.

GALL, J.C. et al (1972) Oto-palatal-digital syndrome: comparison of clinical and radiographic manifestations in males and females. Am. J. Hum. Genet., 24:24–36.

TURNER, G. (1970) Inheritance of the oto-palatal-digital syndrome. Am. J. Dis. Child., 119:377.

Ovarian dysgenesis

= *Turner's syndrome*.

Overactivity

= *hyperactivity*.

Overcorrection

A technique used in *behaviour modification*. The required behaviour is rehearsed excessively whenever the unwanted behaviour occurs and is therefore used as a *punishment*. Restitutional overcorrection requires that the person repairs or clears up any damage caused. Positive practice overcorrection (PPOC) requires the person to practise behaviours which are usually, but not always, forms of relevant and appropriate behaviours. It is sometimes difficult to insist on the carrying out of the overcorrection procedure and a technique of graduated guidance may be used in which physical guidance is kept to a minimum but any attempts to do anything apart from the required behaviour are immediately blocked. Overcorrection has been applied to a wide range of behaviour problems such as furniture throwing, threatening, biting, eating indigestible objects, physical assaults, screaming and toileting accidents. There are many successful accounts of the use of overcorrection but it can sometimes reinforce rather than reduce a behaviour. Such procedures are open to abuse and must always be carefully supervised and monitored.

AZRIN, N.H. & WESOLOWSKI, M.D. (1974) Theft reversal: An overcorrection procedure for eliminating stealing by retarded persons. J. Appl. Behav. Anal., 7:577–81.

AZRIN, N.H. & WESOLOWSKI, M.D. (1975) The use of positive practice to eliminate persistent floor sprawling by profoundly retarded persons. J. Appl. Behav. Anal., 6:627–632.

CAREY, R.G. & BUCHER, B. (1983) Positive practice overcorrection: the effects of duration of positive practice on acquisition and response reduction. J. Appl. Behav. Anal., 16:101–110.

EPSTEIN, L.H. et al (1974) Generality of side-effects of overcorrection. J. Appl. Behav. Anal., 7:385–390.

FOXX, R.M. (1976) The use of overcorrection to eliminate the public disrobing (stripping) of retarded women. Behav. Res. Ther., 14:53–61.

MURPHY, G.H. (1978) Overcorrection: A critique. J. Ment. Defic. Res., 22:161–173.

ROLLINGS, J.P. et al (1977) The use of overcorrection procedures to eliminate stereotyped behaviours in retarded individuals. Behav. Mod., 1:29–46.

Overdependence

The tendency for a disabled person to rely on others for help more than is necessary. Nowadays there is much more emphasis on education and training in order to be as self-sufficient as possible but for a person with poor motivation or very protective carers, this can still be a problem.

Overlearning

The opportunity to practise previously learnt skills so that they become well established.

Overprotection

The natural protective feelings which parents have for children may be exaggerated when the child is perceived as being vulnerable because of disability. This may lead to unnecessary restrictions or low expectations unless parents are given the encouragement and support needed to allow their child to acquire new experiences and skills toward greater independence. It is not easy for most parents to let their child grow up and eventually leave home. The child may often force the pace but an intellectually disabled child may be less able to express or demonstrate a wish for more choice or freedom.

Oxazepam

A tranquillizer which is one of the *benzodiazepine* group of drugs used in the treatment of anxiety. It has a short duration of action. Side-effects are similar to those of other benzodiazepines.

Oxycephaly

= *acrocephaly*.

Oxygen shortage / deprivation

= *anoxia*.

P

PAC
= *Gunzberg Progress Assessment Charts.*

Pachygyria
Abnormally broad and thick convolutions on the surface of the brain. See *lissencephaly.*

Paediatrician
A doctor who specializes in *paediatrics.*

Paediatrics
The branch of medicine concerned with childhood diseases and disabilities.

Paget-Gorman sign system
A system in which the hands are used to make signs in a grammatically correct sequence. It was originally developed for deaf people and later used for people with a specific language difficulty or a mental handicap. Each category of items has a basic sign upon which modifications indicate members of that group. It is very systematic unlike *British Sign Language.* In the U.K. it is used less than *Makaton.* It should be used in conjunction with speech and staff training is important. It is not generally used in deaf communities.

CRAIG, E. (1978) Introducing the Paget-Gorman sign system. In: Ways and Means. Tebbs, T. (Co-ordinator). Hampshire, U.K.: Globe Education. pp. 162–163.
FENN, G. & ROWE, J. (1975) An experiment in manual communication. Brit. J. Disord. Commun., 10:3–16.

Palate
The roof of the mouth. The front is hard and made of bone whereas the back is soft and muscular. Malformations of the palate occur in many conditions associated with mental handicap. The palate may be abnor-mally high and arched as in *congenital syphilis, Conradi's syndrome, Down's syndrome, Friedreich's ataxia, Menkes' syndrome, Pfeiffer's syndrome, Pierre Robin syndrome* and *Smith-Lemli-Opitz syndrome.* It may be high, arched and narrow in *Apert's syndrome, Crouzon's syndrome, homocystinuria, Rubinstein-Taybi syndrome* and *Treacher-Collins syndrome.* It may also be cleft (see *cleft lip / palate*).

Palm-print patterns
= *dermatoglyphics.*

Palmar crease
A single transverse crease of the palm (simian crease) occurs quite commonly in *Down's syndrome* and other *chromosome* abnormalities. It occurs less commonly in the general population. See *dermatoglyphics.*

Palpebral fissure
The gap between the eyelids. The palpebral fissures may be abnormal in a number of conditions associated with mental handicap. They are absent in the *cryptophthalmos syndrome* and often narrow in *Edward's syndrome, de Lange syndrome* and *congenital hypothyroidism.* They slant upward in *Down's syndrome, Laurence-Moon-Biedl syndrome* and often in *lissencephaly.* They slant downward in *Apert's syndrome, Carpenter's syndrome, cri-du-chat syndrome, Crouzon's syndrome, de Lange syndrome, Rubinstein-Taybi syndrome, Noonan's syndrome, Treacher-Collins syndrome* and many other conditions.

Pancytopaenia
A reduction in the numbers of all types of cells in the blood. It is rare but potentially very serious especially if due to inactivity of the bone marrow (aplastic anaemia). If severe, infection and bleeding are the most troublesome complications. It may be a very

rare sensitivity reaction to certain drugs including *carbamazepine* and *chlorpromazine*. It also occurs in *Fanconi's hypoplastic anaemia*.

Panencephalitis

An *encephalitis* affecting all of the brain and causing widespread damage. It is slowly progressive and characterized by gradual mental deterioration, physical deterioration and *epilepsy*. It is ultimately fatal. It is thought to be a sensitivity reaction following second contact with a virus and has been described with the measles virus (*subacute sclerosing panencephalitis*) and the rubella virus (*rubella panencephalitis*).

Papilloedema

Swelling of the *optic disc* which can be seen on the *retina* of the eye using an *ophthalmoscope*. The most common cause is increased *intracranial pressure*.

Papillon-Léage syndrome

= *oro-facial-digital syndrome I*.

Paraldehyde

A drug which was once used as a tranquilizer but is now largely restricted to the treatment of *status epilepticus* in which it is a relatively safe and effective drug. It is unpleasant to use due to the smell, which lingers on the breath of the patient. It can be given by rectum but not by mouth. Injections are painful. It must not be given in a plastic syringe.

Parallelogram head

= *plagiocephaly*.

Paralysis

Loss of the strength and voluntary movement of a muscle. This is due to interference with the nerve supply or with control from the brain. *Cerebral palsy* is the commonest type of paralysis in people who are mentally handicapped.

Paranoid / paranoia

A condition in which there is a firmly held but false belief (*delusion*) which includes ideas of persecution or jealousy. This may be a sign of a serious psychiatric illness (such as *schizophrenia*) but it should be remembered that mentally handicapped people can be persecuted or exploited and referral to a psychiatrist should take place before a diagnosis of mental illness is made. In an older person paranoia is often associated with disorders of vision or hearing. Paranoid ideas may develop suddenly when a person is confused due to an operation, illness or intoxication or when under intense stress. When associated with schizophrenia there is generally a more gradual onset usually in an older person. Voices may be heard (*hallucinations*) which criticize, accuse or taunt.

Paraplegia

Paralysis of the lower half of the body which often includes the bladder and bowel. This can be caused by *meningomyelocoele* and by injuries to the spinal cord.

Parathyroid glands

Four small glands situated in the neck. They secrete hormones which are involved in dealing with calcium and phosphorus. The levels of these hormones are high in *Albright's syndrome* but this is caused by the low calcium blood levels and there is no abnormality of the glands themselves.

Parent groups

See *groups*.

Parent-professional partnership

Modern services for families of mentally handicapped people generally recognize the importance of a close working relationship on the basis of mutual respect between parents and professionals. Professionals should build on each parent's own style, accept their own perceptions and develop the family's own unique resources. This should be assisted by skilled counselling and the imparting of information and skills held by the professional worker.

McCONACHIE, H. (1986) Parents and Young Mentally Handicapped Children: A Review of Research Issues. London: Croom Helm.

MITTLER, P. & McCONACHIE, H. (1983) Parents, Professionals and Mentally Handicapped People: Approaches to Partnership. London: Croom Helm.

PUGH, G. (Ed.) (1981) Parents as Partners. London: National Children's Bureau.

Parental Involvement Project

= *PIP development charts*.

Parental reactions / adjustment

No parent finds the diagnosis of mental handicap easy to accept and it is particularly difficult when told soon after birth or when the child had previously been of normal ability.

The process of coming to terms with the child's disability is usually painful and difficult and sensitive support and counselling should always be available from professional workers who understand the emotional and practical needs of the family and can provide accurate information about the child's problems. The phases of reaction are usually recognized as shock, reaction, adaptation and orientation and are similar to the phases of any *bereavement reaction*. The support of other parents who have been through the same experiences is often valuable (see *groups*).

CUNNINGHAM, C.C. & DAVIS, H. (1985) Early parent counselling. In: A Multidisciplinary Approach to Mental Handicap. Craft, M. et al (Eds.) London: Baillière Tindall.

EMDE, R.N. & BROWN, C. (1978) Adaptation to the birth of a Down's syndrome infant. J. Am. Acad. Child Psychiat., 17: 299–323.

HANNAM, C. (1980) Parents and Mentally Handicapped Children. Harmondsworth: Penguin Books.

LONSDALE, G. et al (1979) Children, Grief and Social Work. Oxford: Blackwell.

McCONACHIE, H. (1986) Parents and Young Mentally Handicapped Children: A Review of Research Issues. London: Croom Helm.

MILUNSKY, A. (1981) Coping with Crisis and Handicap. New York: Plenum Press.

WORTHINGTON, A. (1982) Coming to Terms with Mental Handicap. Whitby, U.K.: Helena Press.

Parenthood

The question of parenthood for mentally handicapped people presents a major dilemma between the human rights of the potential parents and the rights of the potential child. The procreation of children is highly valued in our society and there is a view that every couple ought to have the right to choose freely and responsibly whether or not to have children. Experience with parenthood for mentally handicapped couples has not been encouraging. Parenthood is a demanding and difficult task and there is some evidence that the larger the family the greater the problems for intellectually disabled parents. A high proportion of such children have been taken into the care of the local authority or are heavily supported and monitored in the family. This may be as much a reflection of the lack of skills and investment by the authorities in these families as it is of the inadequacy of the parents.

Genetic counselling is particularly important and couples must be given the best information possible to help them decide whether or not to have children and, if they do, the chances of the child being born handicapped. It is most important for mentally handicapped couples to understand that *marriage* does not necessarily imply parenthood. They should also be fully informed about sexual relationships and family planning and fully aware of the responsibilities and disadvantages of parenthood. Professional workers, when trying to assess the adequacy of mentally handicapped parents, should remember that intelligence of parents may not be as important for good child care as other factors, such as marital harmony and stability, psychiatric health, finances, number of children, use and availability of support services and support from other relatives. See also *sex education*.

ATTARD, M.T. (1988) Point of view: mentally handicapped parents. Some issues to consider in relation to pregnancy. Brit. J. Ment. Subn., 66:3–9.
MATTINSON, J. (1975) Marriage and Mental Handicap (2nd edit.). London: Institute of Marital Studies. The Tavistock Institute of Human Relationships.
SHAW, C.H. & WRIGHT, C.H. (1960) The married mental defective: a follow-up study. Lancet, 1:273–274.

Parents Encouraging Parents
In 1978 the Special Education Division of Colorado State Department of Education developed workshops for parents of handicapped children. Parents shared their problems with each other and with professionals and administrators and were then trained to form a support network throughout the state. They offered each other emotional support and taught each other how to work through the educational and health systems to obtain assistance for their child. The goal of the programme is to enable parents to become effective advocates as well as trainers of their own children and to be a ready resource for parents of other handicapped children.

AMON, C. & SMITH, D. (1983) Parents Encouraging Parents. Denver: Colorado Department of Education.

Paresis
The reduced ability of a part of the body to function normally. This usually refers to weakening or slight paralysis of limbs and sometimes occurs in *cerebral palsy*.

Parietal lobes
The right and left parietal lobes are situated in the upper central area of the brain. Body sensations, such as touch, are received and analysed in the parietal lobes. These lobes are also involved in *cognitive* skills. Damage to this part of the brain may interfere with these functions.

Parkinson's disease / parkinsonism
A condition in which there is impairment of voluntary movement, rigidity of muscles and a characteristic tremor (*extrapyramidal signs*). It is caused by damage to, or disease of, the *basal ganglia* of the brain or the interconnections between them and the rest of the brain. There are biochemical abnormalities in this condition including a deficiency of dopamine. Parkinsonism can also be caused by some tranquillizing drugs especially the *phenothiazines* and *butyrophenones* and in this case is reversible when the drugs are stopped. Treatment includes the use of drugs such as *benzhexol, benztropine* and *orphenadrine* in drug-induced parkinsonism. In Parkinson's disease levodopa, amantidine and bromocriptine may be used.

Paroxysmal disorders
Conditions manifested by sudden, recurrent and potentially reversible alterations of brain function. *Epilepsy* is one such disorder. Others are migraine, *breath-holding attacks* and fainting.

Partial deletion
= *deletion of chromosome*.

Partial hearing
See *deafness*.

Partial seizures
This group of *seizures* represents a subgroup in the classification of *epilepsy* and is characterized by the fact that consciousness is not fully interrupted by a seizure. There are motor types in which there may be jerking of part of the body, *Jacksonian seizures* or other patterns of movements which are characteristic. There are also sensory types in which particular sensations may be experienced. *Complex-partial seizures* may involve complex

behaviours which always follow a similar pattern and occur inappropriately and out of context with the environment.

Partial trisomy (duplication)

A few very rare *chromosome disorders* have been described in which there is an extra part of a chromosome in each body cell. It may be a duplication of part of a long arm of a chromosome (q) or of a short arm (p). The type and extent of the disorder probably depends on the extent and position of the duplication. Most of these disorders are associated with mental handicap. Sometimes they are associated with *deletion of a chromosome*. For particular partial trisomies see below.

Partial trisomy 1q

This very rare *partial trisomy* of the long arm of chromosome 1 causes restricted growth and an unusual appearance with wide-set eyes, prominent ears, beaked nose, *cleft lip/palate*, long-tapered fingers, hairiness, undescended testes, heart abnormalities and *exomphalos*. Mental handicap and *holoprosencephaly* have been described. Some people with this chromosome abnormality are perfectly normal.

CHEN, H. et al (1979) Omphalocoele and partial trisomy 1q syndrome. Hum. Genet., 53:1.
GARDNER, R.J.M. et al (1974) Are 1q + chromosomes harmless? Clin. Genet., 6:383.

Partial trisomy 2p

This very rare *partial trisomy* of the short arm of chromosome 2 causes restricted growth, short nose with prominent tip, wide-set eyes which slant downward, small jaw, pointed chin, squint, long fingers, widely spaced toes and underdeveloped genitals. Severe mental handicap is present.

FRANCKE, U. (1978) Clinical syndromes associated with partial duplication of chromosomes 2 and 3. Birth Defects, 14 (6c):191.

Partial trisomy 2q

This very rare *partial trisomy* of the long arm of chromosome 2 causes restricted growth, prominent forehead, broad and flat bridge of nose, wide-spaced eyes, low-set abnormal ears, short neck, incurved fingers and malformed feet. A small head, floppiness of muscles and severe mental handicap occur.

ZANKL, M. et al (1979) Distal 2q duplication: Report of two familial cases and an attempt to define a syndrome. Am. J. Med. Genet., 4:5.

Partial trisomy 3p

This very rare *partial trisomy* of the short arm of chromosome 3 causes restricted growth, prominent forehead and cheeks, wide-spaced eyes, prominent upper lip, large mouth, small jaw, short neck, and abnormalities of the heart and genitals. Mental handicap is usually present.

FRANCKE, U. (1978) Clinical syndromes associated with partial duplication of chromosomes 2 and 3. Birth Defects, 14 (6c):191.
SAY, B. et al (1976) Familial translocation (3q 15q) with partial trisomy for the upper arm of chromosome 3 in two sibs. J. Pediatr., 88:447.

Partial trisomy 3q

This very rare *partial trisomy* of the long arm of chromosome 3 causes restricted growth, excessive hairiness, forward pointing nostrils, small jaw, incurving fingers and abnormalities of the heart and kidneys. A small head, mental handicap and *epilepsy* are usual. There are many similarities to the *de Lange syndrome*.

CHIYO, H.A. et al (1976) A case of partial trisomy 3q. J. Med. Genet., 13:525.
YUNIS, E. et al (1979) Partial trisomy 3q. Hum. Genet., 48:315.

Partial trisomy 4q

This very rare *partial trisomy* of the long arm of chromosome 4 causes restricted growth, sloping forehead, low or wide bridge of nose, small jaw, malformed or low-set ears, short neck, abnormalities of the heart and kidneys, undescended testes, hernia and malformed hands and feet. A small head with severe mental handicap is usual.

BONFANTE, A. et al (1979) Partial trisomy 4q: Two cases resulting from a familial translocation. Hum. Genet., 52:85.

CERVENKA, J. et al (1976) Partial trisomy 4q syndrome: Case report and review. Hum. Genet., 34:1.

Partial trisomy 5p

This very rare *partial trisomy* of the short arm of chromosome 5 causes a large unusually shaped head (*doliochocephaly*) due to *craniostenosis*, floppiness of muscles, breathing difficulties, abnormalities of the kidneys and short big toes. Severe mental handicap is usual.

DILIBERTI, J.H. et al (1977) Trisomy 5p: delineation of clinical features. Birth Defects, 13 (3c): 185.

OPITZ, J.M. & PATAU, K. (1975) A partial trisomy 5p syndrome. Birth Defects, 11(5): 191.

Partial trisomy 5q

This very rare *partial trisomy* of the long arm of chromosome 5 causes mild abnormalities of the head and face and severe mental handicap.

JALBERT, P. et al (1975) Partial trisomy for the long arms of chromosome 5 due to insertion and further 'aneusomie de recombination'. J. Med. Genet., 12:418.

KESSEL, E. & PFEIFFER, R.A. (1979) Tandem duplication in a mentally deficient girl. Hum. Genet., 52:217.

Partial trisomy 6p

This very rare *partial trisomy* of the short arm of chromosome 6 causes restricted growth, high prominent forehead, close-set eyes, *nystagmus*, low-set and malformed ears, small mouth and heart and kidney abnormalities. Mental handicap is present.

BREUNING, M.H. et al (1977) Partial trisomy 6p due to familial translocation: A new syndrome? Hum. Genet., 38:7.

Partial trisomy 6q

This very rare *partial trisomy* of the long arm of chromosome 6 causes restricted growth, feeding difficulties, prominent forehead, flat face, low bridge to nose with eyes slanting downward, high arched palate, small jaw, squint, short webbed neck, *club foot, scoliosis* and webbing of fingers. A small head with *acrocephaly* and severe mental handicap is usual.

CHEN, H. et al (1976) Familial partial trisomy 6p syndromes resulting from inherited insertion. (5;6). Clin. Genet.,9:631.

TIPTON, R.E. et al (1979) Duplication 6q syndrome. Am. J. Med. Genet., 3:325.

Partial trisomy 7q

This very rare *partial trisomy* of the long arm of chromosome 7 causes restricted growth, prominent forehead, wide-set eyes which slant downward, short nose with low bridge, small jaw, *cleft palate*, low-set malformed ears, cat-like cry, squint, misshapen spine and *congenital heart disease*. Muscles are floppy and mental handicap is severe. *Hydrocephalus* may be present.

BERGER, R. et al (1977) Partial 7q trisomy. Clin. Genet., 11:39.

SCHINZEL, A. & TOENZ, O. (1979) Partial trisomy 7q and probable partial monosomy of 5p in the son of a mother with reciprocal translocation between 5p and 7q. Hum. Genet., 53:121.

Partial trisomy 8p

This very rare *partial trisomy* of the short arm of chromosome 8 causes restricted growth, squint, high arched palate, joint *contractures*, abnormal genitals and *congenital heart disease*. Mental handicap is present and agenesis of the *corpus callosum* has been described.

FINEMAN, R.M. et al (1979) Complete and partial trisomy of different segments of chromosome 8: Case reports and review. Clin. Genet., 16:390.

Partial trisomy 8q

This very rare *partial trisomy* of the long arm of chromosome 8 causes abnormalities of the face and head shape, joint *contractures* and abnormalities of the heart, kidneys and genitals. Mental handicap occurs.

FINEMAN, R.M. et al (1979) Complete and partial trisomy of different segments of chromosome 8: Case reports and review. Clin. Genet., 16:390.

Partial trisomy 9p

= *Rethoré's syndrome.*

Partial trisomy 9q

This very rare *partial trisomy* of the long arm of chromosome 9 causes low birth weight, poor growth, unusual head shape (*doliochocephaly*), deep-set ears, a straight slightly beaked nose, small mouth and jaw and long thin fingers clenched over the thumbs.

TURLEAU, C. et al (1975) Partial trisomy 9q: a new syndrome. Humangenetik, 29: 233.

Partial trisomy 10q

This very rare *partial trisomy* of the long arm of chromosome 10 causes restricted growth, small head, flat oval face, high broad forehead with arched eyebrows, downslanting small widely spaced eyes, small nose with flat nasal bridge, small jaw, *cleft palate*, low-set ears, abnormalities of fingers and toes, spinal curvature and other skeletal abnormalities, *congenital heart disease*, kidney defects and mental handicap.

LACA, Z. & KALICANIN, P. (1974) A case of partial trisomy 10q. J. Ment. Defic. Res., 18:285.

MONENO-FUENMAYOR, H. et al (1975) Familial partial trisomy of the long arm of chromosome 10. Pediatrics, 56:756.

Partial trisomy 11q

This very rare *partial trisomy* of the long arm

of chromosome 11 may cause restricted growth, small head and facial and skeletal abnormalities. The eyes are usually wide-set and and the jaw small. Mental handicap frequently occurs. Survival is often short.

JACOBSEN, P et al (1973) An (11,21) translocation in four generations with chromosome 11 abnormalities in the offspring. Human Hered., 23:568.

WRIGHT, Y.M. et al (1974) Craniorachischisis in a partially trisomic 11 fetus in a family with reproductive failure and a reciprocal translocation. J. Med. Genet., 11:69.

Partial trisomy 12p

This very rare *partial trisomy* of the short arm of chromosome 12 may cause restricted growth, a flat round face with prominent cheeks, a flat bridge to a short narrow nose, a broad prominent lower lip, low-set ears, spade-shaped fingers, single *palmar creases*, increased spaces between first and second toes, floppiness of muscles and severe mental handicap.

CARLIN, M.E. & NORMAN, C. (1978) Case report: partial trisomy 12p associated with 4p deletion due to paternal translocation. Birth Defects, 14(6C):399.

HOO, J.J. (1976) 12p trisomy: a syndrome? Ann. Genet., 19:261.

Partial trisomy 13q

Partial trisomy of the long arm of chromosome 13 varies in its effect depending on the position of the duplication. Duplication nearer the centre of the chromosome may cause small head, scalp defects, ear abnormalities, abnormal nose, abnormalities of fingers and mental handicap. It often presents as a milder form of *Patau's syndrome.* Duplication nearer the end of the chromosome causes ear abnormalities, small head, *seizures*, abnormal skull shape, short neck, hernias, abnormalities of hands and feet, mental handicap and short life expectancy.

ESCOBAR, J.I. et al (1974) Trisomy for the

distal segment of chromosome 13. Am. J. Dis. Child., 128:217.

ESCOBAR, J.I. & YUNIS, J.J. (1974) Trisomy for the proximal segment of the long arm of chromosome 13. Am. J. Dis. Child., 128:221.

WILROY, R.S. et al (1975) Partial trisomy for different segments of chromosome 13 in several individuals of the same family. Birth Defects Original Article Series, 5(5):217.

Partial trisomy 14q

This very rare *partial trisomy* of the long arm of chromosome 14 may cause restricted growth, small head, wide-spaced small eyes, broad prominent nose, wide mouth, high arched or *cleft palate*, low-set ears, *congenital heart disease*, abnormalities of limbs and mental handicap.

FAWCET, W.A. et al (1975) Trisomy 14q. Birth Defects Original Article Series, 11(5): 223.

RAY, M. et al (1979) Partial trisomy 14. Ann. Genet., 22:47.

Partial trisomy 15q

This very rare *partial trisomy* of the long arm of chromosome 15 may cause restricted growth, small head, *epilepsy*, abnormalities of face and palate, low-set ears, abnormalities of fingers and toes and mental handicap.

CENTERWALL, W.R. & MORRIS, J.P. (1975) Partial D15 trisomy. Human Hered., 25: 442.

MAGENIS, R.E. et al (1972) Partial trisomy 15. Lancet, 2:1356.

Partial trisomy 17q

This very rare *partial trisomy* of the long arm of chromosome 17 may cause restricted growth, small head, facial abnormalities, *cleft palate*, malformed ears, short broad neck, floppy abnormal limbs, *congenital heart disease*, kidney abnormalities and severe mental handicap.

BERBERICH, M.S. et al (1978) Duplication (partial trisomy) of the distal long arm of chromosome 17: A new clinically recognisable chromosome disorder. Birth Defects, 14(6C):287.

TURLEAU, C. et al (1979) Distal trisomy 17q. Clin. Genet., 16:54.

Partial trisomy 18q

This *partial trisomy* of the long arm of chromosome 18 may cause slightly restricted growth, high small forehead, high narrow bridge of small upturned nose, short upper lip, small jaw, short neck, small chest and mild to moderate mental handicap.

FRYNS, J.P. et al (1979) New chromosomal syndromes II. Partial distal 18q trisomy syndrome. Acta Paediatr. (Belgium), 32: 217.

Partial trisomy 20p

This very rare *partial trisomy* of the short arm of chromosome 20 may cause a round face with wide-spaced eyes slanting upward from a short upturned nose. A squint, abnormalities of teeth and spine, coarse hair, speech defects, *congenital heart disease*, poor muscle co-ordination and mental handicap may also occur.

RUDD, N.L. et al (1979) Partial trisomy 20 confirmed by gene dosage studies. Am. J. Med. Genet., 4:357.

Partial trisomy 22q

= *cat-eye syndrome*.

Partial vision / partial sight

See *blindness*.

PASS

= *Program Analysis of Service Systems*.

Patau's syndrome

A very rare cause of mental handicap with an incidence of approximately 1 in 5000 live births. Babies with this condition usually have feeding difficulties, jitteriness, *apnoeic attacks* and obvious developmental delay. *Cleft lip/palate* and a small lower jaw are usual. The head and eyes are small and there may be other eye defects. The eyes are often close together and abnormalities of the nose are common. *Congenital heart disease* is present in 80% and abnormalities of the lungs, gut and kidneys are frequent. There may be extra or fused fingers and deformities of fingers, toes and feet often occur. A single *palmar crease* is usual. The ears are often low-set and deformed and deafness is common. Restricted growth and a severe degree of mental handicap are usual. Minor *seizures* are frequent. Abnormalities of the blood have been described. Many babies with this condition are stillborn or die within the first few months of life. Less than 10% survive their first birthday.

The condition is caused by an extra *chromosome* 13 in all body cells. Like *Down's syndrome* the incidence increases with the age of the mother. Most occur without any hereditary factors (*nondisjunction*) but in a few families a parent has *chromosome mosaicism* or a *chromosome translocation*. It can be diagnosed during pregnancy following *amniocentesis*.

ADDOR, C. & COX, J.N. (1975) Patau's syndrome: a pathological and cytogenetic study of two cases. J. Genet. Hum., 23:83.
BORAZ, R.A. (1987) Trisomy 13 syndrome: A rare case of long term survival. J. Pedodontics, 11:288–294.
MAGENIS, R.E. et al (1968) Trisomy 13 (D) syndrome: studies on parental age, sex ratio and survival. J. Pediatr., 73:222–228.
TAYLOR, A.I. (1968) Autosomal trisomy syndromes: A detailed study of 27 cases of Patau's syndrome. J. Med. Genet., 5: 227–252.

Patella

The knee cap. It may be absent or underdeveloped in a few rare syndromes associated with mental handicap such as *bird-headed dwarfism* and *nail-patella syndrome*.

Patent ductus arteriosus

One of the common *congenital heart defects*.

The ductus arteriosus is a blood vessel which runs between the blood supply to the lungs (pulmonary artery) and the main artery to the body (aorta). In the womb, because the *fetus* does not breathe, blood bypasses the lungs through this passage. At birth it should close so that all the blood passes to the lungs to collect oxygen before being pumped through the body. If it fails to close it is referred to as patent ductus arteriosus and it reduces the efficiency of the heart. This causes poor growth and eventually heart failure. Other congenital abnormalities may be associated with this and it has been reported in *rubella syndrome, Goldenhar's syndrome, Carpenter's syndrome, Rubinstein-Taybi syndrome, cerebro-hepato-renal syndrome* and some *chromosome* abnormalities. It can usually be corrected by a simple operation. It occurs in many conditions in which congenital heart disease is associated with mental handicap such as *Down's syndrome*.

Pathological

To do with disease, especially the structural and functional changes caused by diseases.

Pathway Scheme

A scheme sponsored in the U.K. by the *Royal Society for Mentally Handicapped Children and Adults* (Mencap). It aims to provide *employment* opportunities for adults with a mental handicap. The Pathway officer finds potential employers in the neighbourhood. The employer identifies someone in the work setting who will support the mentally handicapped employee. The employee receives the normal wage for the job but half of this is provided by Mencap for the first six months. The support worker is also paid. At the end of the trial period the employer decides whether to employ the person. The Pathway officer monitors and supports the placements. The results have been good with a high proportion of people being offered employment.

Further information:
Mencap National Centre, 123 Golden Lane, London.

Pathways to Independence

A checklist designed for individual assessment, goal planning and reassessment. It covers self-care, domestic, communication, time, money and community living skills. Each section has a main goal and several subgoals which do not need to be scored if the main goal has been achieved. The checklist brings together the skills required by anyone who wants to lead an independent life in the community. The booklet is self-contained and easy to use with a score sheet. Extra copies of the profile score sheet can be purchased.

JEFFREE, D. & CHESELDINE, S. (1982) Pathways to Independence. Sevenoaks, U.K.: Hodder & Stoughton Educational.

Paton's Borders Assessment Schedule

= *Borders Assessment Schedule.*

Patterning

A treatment approach advocated by the *Doman-Delacato system* of training.

Peabody Developmental Motor Scales and Activity Cards

Scales used to assess the *gross motor skills* and *fine motor skills* of mentally handicapped children. They are suited for children who also have visual impairment. The activity cards prescribe suitable activities according to the scales.

FOLIO, M.R. & FEWELL, R.R. (1983) Peabody developmental motor scales and activity cards. Hengham, Maryland: Teaching Resources Corporation.

Peabody Language Development Kit

A teaching programme linked to the *Illinois Test of Psycholinguistic Abilities*. It provides a comprehensive remedial programme for language development.

DUNN, L. & SMITH, J. (1965) Peabody Language Development Kit. Minneapolis: American Guidance Service.

Peabody Mobility Scale and Kit

A scale used to assess orientation and mobility in mentally handicapped, visually impaired children. The sensory assessment scales include sound localization, tactile discrimination with hands and feet and olfactory discrimination. The scale was later revised and adapted for low-vision multi-handicapped children. The scale is divided into four major areas: motor development, sensory training, concept development and mobility skills.

There are training activities designed for each scale item. These are easy to follow and a step-by-step programme of instruction is provided. Sensory training for low-vision children emphasizes visual tasks whereas that for visually impaired children emphasizes sound localization and tactile and olfactory discrimination. The scale and training materials were tried out on 40 multiply handicapped children in nine centres in a 16-week field test. The experimental group demonstrated significant overall gains in performance compared to the control group.

HARLEY, R.K. et al (1975) The development of a scale in orientation and mobility for multiply impaired blind children. Education of the Visually Handicapped, 7:1–5.
HARLEY, R.K. & MERBLER, J.B. (1980) Development of an orientation and mobility program for multiply impaired low vision children. J. Visual Impairment and Blindness, 74:9–14.

Peabody Picture Vocabulary Test

A test for assessing the vocabulary of a child using pictures. It covers a developmental level from 30 months to 18 years. The test consists of a graded series of plates each of which contains four drawings. The examiner presents a word and the child is asked to point to the picture that best describes the word. The number of pictures correctly identified can be converted to a mental age score. It is a useful test for children who have expressive language problems but good hearing. It measures only vocabulary and is not a measure of general intelligence.

DUNN, L. et al (1982) British Picture Vocabulary Scale. Windsor: NFER Publishing Co.
DUNN, L.M. (1959) Peabody Picture Vocabulary Test. Minneapolis: American Guidance Service.
DUNN, L.M. (1965) Expanded Manual for the Peabody Picture Vocabulary Test. Minnesota: American Guidance Service.
SHAW, H.J. et al (1966) The equivalence of WISC and PPVT I.Q.'s. Am. J. Ment. Defic., 70:601–606.

Peabody Rebus Reading Scheme
= *Rebus Reading Symbols.*

Pectus carinatum
A protruding chest. This may occur in a few conditions associated with mental handicap including *homocystinuria*, *Hunter's syndrome*, *Sanfilippo syndrome* and *Noonan's syndrome*.

Pectus excavatum
A sunken chest due to the lower part of the breast bone being indented. It causes round shoulders. It may occur in a few conditions associated with mental handicap including *homocystinuria*, *Greig's syndrome*, *Noonan's syndrome*, *oto-palato-digital syndrome* and *Turner's syndrome*.

Peganone
= *ethotoin.*

Pelizaeus-Merzbacher disease
A very rare, slowly progressive condition which appears in several forms. The most commonly reported type begins in infancy often within a few weeks of birth. There is a side-to-side head tremor and trembling and roving eye movements (*nystagmus*). Head control is poor. Poor co-ordination (*cerebellar ataxia*) is usual. Often speech is unintelligible or limited to a few words. Deafness frequently develops. Over the years vision and voluntary movements deteriorate and *spasticity* increases while the nystagmus may disappear. By 3 to 6 years of age many children are immobile. Intellectual deterioration and *epilepsy* occur. Difficulty with swallowing develops later. Survival to adult life is unusual and most children die by the age of 6 years. The exact cause is not known but it is thought to be due to a defect in the tissues that produce the *myelin* which insulates nerve fibres. In most families it is inherited from the mother as a *sex-linked* disorder and only affects males. Other families have affected females, suggesting *recessive inheritance*. There are no biochemical tests to confirm the diagnosis or to diagnose affected fetuses before birth. The diagnosis can only be confirmed at post-mortem (autopsy).

RENIER, W.O. et al (1981) Connatal Pelizaeus-Merzbacher disease with congenital stridor in two malformed cousins. Acta Neuropathol., 54:11.
TYLER, H.R. (1958) Pelizaeus-Merzbacher disease. Acta Neurol. Psychiatry, 80:162.
ZEMAN, W. et al (1964) Pelizaeus-Merzbacher disease. A study of nosology. J. Neuropathol. Exp. Neurol., 23:334–354.

Pellagra
A form of malnutrition in which the principal deficiency is of nicotinic acid, an essential vitamin derived mainly from meat. This causes a characteristic skin condition and diarrhoea. Mildly affected children are irritable or apathetic but in the more severe cases children are delirious, *spastic* or have impaired vision. Pellagra-like symptoms occur in *Hartnup disease* due to nicotinic acid deficiency.

SPIES, T.D. et al (1939) Pellagra in infancy and childhood. J. Am. Med. Ass. 13:1481.
STILL, C.N. (1977) Nicotinic acid and nicotinamide: pellagra and related disorders

of the nervous system. In: Handbook of Clinical Neurology. Vol. 28. Vinken, P.J. & Bruyn, G.W. (Eds.) Amsterdam: North Holland Publ. Co. p. 59.

Pemoline

A drug used in the U.S.A. but not the U.K. for the treatment of *hyperactivity* in children. It has a longer duration of action than *methylphenidate* and is less likely to be misused as a stimulant drug.

Pendred's syndrome

A condition in which there is *deafness*, due to defects in the nerves from the ear (sensorineural deafness), and *hypothyroidism*. There is enlargement of the thyroid gland at the front of the neck. It is inherited from both parents who are carriers (*recessive inheritance*) and is due to a biochemical defect in the manufacture of the hormone thyroxine in the thyroid gland.

BATSAKIS, J.G. & NISHIYAMA, R.H. (1962) Deafness with sporadic goitre: Pendred's syndrome. Arch. Otolaryngol. (Chicago), 76:401.

Penta X-syndrome

= *XXXXX syndrome*.

People First Organizations

The *self-advocacy* movement in the U.S.A. led to the establishment of groups of people with a mental handicap who called themselves 'People First'. Similar groups in Canada also adopted this title which is now beginning to be used in the U.K. and elsewhere.

Further information:
People First of Washington, PO Box 381, Washington, D.C. 98401.
Speaking for Ourselves of Colorado, PO Box 338, Glenwood Springs, CO 81602.
People First of Canada, Kinsman Building, 4700 Keele Street, Downsview, Ontario M3J 1P3.
People First of London and Thames, C/O King's Fund Centre, 126 Albert St., London NW1 7NF.

PEP

= *Parents Encouraging Parents*.

Perception / perceptual abnormalities

Perception is the ability to interpret experiences obtained through the senses (sight, hearing, touch, smell, etc.). *Cognitive* processes are involved in understanding this information. Abnormalities in perception may therefore seriously affect understanding, skills and behaviour. This may be due to damage to, or abnormalities of, the brain, especially to those parts which receive information from the body. When brain damage has caused *hemiplegia* it is often forgotten that this is usually associated with a perceptual disorder on the same side of the body. The lack of awareness of this half of the body adds to reluctance to use the limbs. Other more subtle perceptual disorders include problems with understanding spatial relationships, distorted body image and difficulty with right-left orientation.

Performance skills / tests

Skills which do not require the use of language. It is particularly used to describe those parts of *intelligence tests* which do not require a verbal response and the scores on such performance items are used to derive the performance *intelligence quotient*.

Pericyazine

A major tranquillizer used in the treatment of *schizophrenia*, anxiety and violent or dangerously impulsive behaviour. It is sometimes used for the treatment of mentally handicapped children or adults with severe problem behaviours. It is a *phenothiazine* similar to *chlorpromazine* but is more of a sedative. Side-effects are. as for chlorpromazine.

Perinatal

The period between birth and 4 weeks of age.

Perinatal herpes virus infection
See *herpes simplex encephalitis*.

Perphenazine
A major tranquillizer of the *phenothiazine* group of drugs. It is used in the treatment of *schizophrenia*, *mania*, anxiety and violent or dangerously impulsive behaviour. It can be given by mouth or by injection. It is not recommended for children under 14 years of age. It may be used in the treatment of mentally handicapped people with severe behaviour problems. Side-effects are as for *chlorpromazine*. Severe *extrapyramidal side-effects* may occur. It should be used with caution in people who are *epileptic*.

Perseveration
A response (usually verbal) triggered by a question or situation, but which is repeated subsequently when it is no longer appropriate. It occurs in some types of brain damage and is occasionally a problem for a person who is mentally handicapped.

Personality disorder
Personality disorders occur regardless of intelligence and include *psychopathy* (sociopathy, antisocial personality disorder) and paranoid, obsessional, schizoid and hysterical personality disorders. Little research has been done on the combination of mental handicap and personality disorder. It is difficult to diagnose personality disorder in severely mentally handicapped people.

BALLINGER, B.R. & REID, A.H. (1987) A standardized assessment of personality disorder in mental handicap. Brit. J. Psychiat., 150:108.

Personal relationships
Mentally handicapped people often need guidance, education and sometimes training in personal relationships. This may include *sex education* when appropriate.

Pertussis
= *whooping cough*.

Pes cavus
A foot deformity in which there is a very high arch with the heel and toes pointing downward. The foot is short and deep. This has been described in some conditions associated with mental handicap including *homocystinuria, Friedreich's ataxia, Hunter's syndrome* and *Rud's syndrome*.

Pes equinovarus
See *club foot*.

Pes planus
A foot deformity in which the arch is flattened and the inner edge of the foot touches the ground. This has been described in some conditions associated with mental handicap including *Noonan's syndrome, homocystinuria, XXXY syndrome, XXXXY syndrome* and *Engelmann's disease*. People with *Down's syndrome* tend to have flat feet.

PET scan
= *Positron Emission Tomography*.

Pethna toys
An electronic toy system designed for profoundly and multiply handicapped children. It consists of two interchangeable components known as in-boxes and out-boxes. The in-boxes are designed to be operated by the child. They vary in complexity from touch pads and devices which are squeezed when placed in the hand, to switches which demand complex manipulative and discriminative skills. Some can be adjusted to gradually increase the demands made on the child. The out-boxes deliver some form of sensory stimulation which acts as a reward. This may be auditory (usually a cassette player on which favourite music, voices etc. are recorded), visual (flashing lights, moving objects etc.) or vibration. The system is portable and flexible and can be adapted and added to according to individual needs.

WOODS, P. & PARRY, R. (1981) Pethna tailor-made toys for the severely retarded and multiply handicapped. Apex: BIMH. 9:53–54.

Petit-mal

A term used to describe epileptic seizures which are nowadays known as *absence seizures*. It is sometimes misused to describe other varieties of seizures which are not typical *grand-mal convulsions*, such as *partial seizures*.

Petit-mal status

= *absence status*.

Petit-mal variant

= *Lennox-Gastaut syndrome*.

Peto conductive educational system

= *conductive education*.

Pfaundler-Hurler syndrome

= *Hurler's syndrome*.

Pfeiffer's syndrome

This is a condition similar to *Apert's syndrome*. The person has an unusual appearance and an abnormally shaped head (*acrocephaly*). The eyes protrude and are widely spaced. The nose is flat and chin prominent. There is often a squint. There may be abnormalities of the palate and teeth. The thumb and big toe are short, wide and point inward and fingers may be joined by skin but this may not affect all the fingers or toes and may not extend to the end of them. The extent of any mental handicap is variable. Treatment and inheritance are the same as in Apert's syndrome.

HOLMES, L.B. et al (1972) Mental Retardation. An Atlas of Diseases with Associated Physical Abnormalities. New York: Macmillan. pp. 228–229.
MARTSOLF, J.T. et al (1971) Pfeiffer syndrome. An unusual type of acrocephalosyndactyly with broad thumbs and great toes. Am. J. Dis. Child., 121:257–262.

PHAB

= *National Physically Handicapped and Able Bodied*.

Phacomatoses

= *neurocutaneous syndromes*.

Phaeochromocytoma

A tumour of the tissue, mainly found in the adrenal glands, which secretes noradrenaline and adrenaline. This causes high blood pressure, sweating, pallor, palpitations, headache and chest and stomach pain, usually episodically. It sometimes occurs in *neurofibromatosis* which is occasionally associated with mental handicap. Treatment is by excision of the tumour which is sometimes difficult to locate and remove.

Phakoma

Grey or white patches seen on the *retina* of the eye in the *neurocutaneous syndromes* particularly *tuberose sclerosis*.

Phakomatoses

= *neurocutaneous syndrome*.

Phalanges

The bones of the thumbs, fingers and toes. These may be abnormal in many conditions associated with mental handicap.

Phased care

A system for supporting and relieving families with a member who is mentally handicapped. Time away from home is planned at regular intervals for predetermined time periods. The time away from home should be beneficial to the individual concerned by offering new experiences, opportunities for independence and/or further training. At the very least any stress to the individual should be minimized and, in the case of younger children, a family placement is nearly always preferable. Phased care should be monitored and reviewed at regular intervals to ensure that it is meeting the needs of the individual and the family. It may be provided in hostels, hospitals, *family support schemes* or holiday schemes.

Discussion Paper (1981) Short Term Care

for Mentally Handicapped Children. London: King's Fund Centre.
OSWIN, M. (1984) They Keep Going Away. London: King Edward's Hospital Fund for London.
PUGH, G. & RUSSELL, P. (1977) Shared Care: Support Services for Families with Handicapped Children. London: National Children's Bureau.
SALISBURY, C.L. & INTAGLIATA, J. (1986) Respite Care: Support for Persons with Developmental Disabilities and Their Families. Baltimore: Paul H. Brookes.

Phenobarbitone / phenobarbital
A drug used in the treatment of *epilepsy* and *febrile convulsions*. Dosage is adjusted carefully in small amounts until seizures are controlled or side-effects occur. Blood levels of the drug can be measured to help to find the therapeutic dose. Side-effects include drowsiness, sedation, unsteadiness, dizziness, and poor co-ordination especially in the first week of starting medication. In children and the elderly excitement, restlessness and confusion are more likely to occur. Anaemia may occur with prolonged use. Skin rashes may be an allergic reaction. Alcohol should not be taken with phenobarbitone. Withdrawal seizures are a serious problem especially if phenobarbitone is stopped suddenly. An injection into a muscle can be used in the treatment of *status epilepticus*. Phenobarbitone is used less often nowadays and other drugs such as *carbamazepine* and *sodium valproate* have taken its place because side-effects, especially excitement or impairment of learning, are less often a problem with these newer drugs.

Phenothiazines
A group of drugs used as major tranquillizers for the treatment of *schizophrenia* and *mania* and less commonly for *anxiety states*. They may be used to calm people exhibiting very disturbed or difficult behaviours. Side-effects can be troublesome especially the *extrapyramidal signs* and *tardive dyskinesia*. This group of drugs includes *chlorpromazine, pericyazine, fluphenazine, promazine* and *thioridazine*.

Phenylalaninaemias / hyperphenylalaninaemias
Three conditions are now recognized to have an excessive amount of phenylalanine in the blood which is severe enough to cause brain damage (there are other types which are harmless). Classical *phenylketonuria* is the commonest type and this responds to dietary treatment. Phenylalaninaemias due to dihydropteridine reductase deficiency or dihydrobiopterin synthetase deficiency are called malignant because, even with good dietary control, there is a progressive deterioration with *epilepsy* and floppiness or stiffness of muscles.

Editorial (1979) New varieties of P.K.U. Lancet, i:304.
KAUFMAN, S. (1983) Phenylketonuria and its variants. Advances in Human Genetics. London: Plenum Press. 13:217–299.

Phenylketonuria
A condition caused by a deficiency of an *enzyme* (phenylalanine hydroxylase) in the body. Phenylalanine cannot be converted to tyrosine, an *amino acid*. As a result phenylalanine builds up in the body causing damage to the brain. Phenylpyruvic acid is excreted in the urine. The baby is normal at birth but in the first two months vomiting and irritability are frequent. By 9 months of age delayed development becomes apparent. Severe mental handicap, *infantile spasms* and *epilepsy* develop. There is some *spasticity*, especially in the legs. *Hyperactivity* and *autistic* behaviours are usual. The degree of mental handicap is usually severe. Untreated children have fair hair, blue eyes and dry, often eczematous skin. This disorder is routinely tested for in infancy in the U.K. and U.S.A. and early treatment results in normal development. The *Guthrie test* is generally used. A positive result leads to further investigations to confirm the diagnosis. Treatment is with a low

phenylalanine diet monitored by blood phenylalanine measurements. When treated from birth the *intelligence quotient* (I.Q.) of children with phenylketonuria is lower than that of healthy brothers and sisters. Even when the I.Q. is in the normal range there is significant impairment in perceptual functioning and progress in school is slower than expected. The diet is usually continued until at least 8 years of age and often into teenage years. There is a very high incidence of mental handicap in the children of phenylketonuric mothers even when the diet in pregnancy is carefully monitored. Their babies have an unusual facial appearance with upturned nose and thin upper lip, restricted growth, a high incidence of *congenital heart disease* and small heads. Phenylketonuria is inherited from both parents who are carriers (*recessive inheritance*). Carriers can be identified by blood tests. See also *phenylalaninaemias*.

BERRY, H.K. et al (1979) Intellectual development and academic achievement of children treated early for phenylketonuria. Dev. Med. Child Neurology, 21:311–320.

CEDERBAUM, S.D. et al (1984) Symposium on genetic engineering and phenylketonuria. Pediatrics, 74:406–427.

FLANNERY, D.B. et al (1983) Dietary management of phenylketonuria from birth using a phenylalanine-free product. J. Pediatr., 103:247.

KOCH, R. & FRIEDMAN, E.G. (1981) Accuracy of new-born screening programs for phenylketonuria. J. Pediatr., 98:267.

KOCH, R. et al (1982) Preliminary report on the effect of diet discontinuation in PKU. J. Pediatr., 100:870–875.

LIPSON, A. et al (1984) Maternal hyperphenylalaninaemia fetal effects. J. Pediatr., 104:216.

MENKES, J.H. (1985) Textbook of Child Neurology (3rd edit.). Philadelphia: Lea & Febiger. pp. 2–13.

Further information:
National Society of Phenylketonuria and Allied Disorders, Worth Cottage, Lower Scholes, Pickels Hill, Keighley, West Yorkshire BD22 0RR.

Phenytoin

An *anticonvulsant* drug used in the treatment of *grand-mal convulsions* and *partial seizures*. The therapeutic dose is not far below the toxic dose and the blood levels of the drug should therefore be closely monitored until the person is stabilized. Involuntary eye movements (*nystagmus*), slurring of speech and unsteadiness are signs of toxicity. During initial treatment minor side-effects include nausea, discomfort in the stomach, nervousness, weight loss, sleeplessness and a feeling of unsteadiness. These usually become less as treatment continues. Allergic reactions, especially skin reactions, may occur. Long-term side-effects include overgrowth of gums, hairiness, acne, coarsening of features, restlessness, blood disorders and anaemia. Anaemia is caused by a deficiency of the vitamin folic acid. Long-term toxicity is thought to cause damage to the *cerebellum* and possibly other parts of the brain.

DAVIS, V.J. et al (1981) Effects of phenytoin withdrawal on matching to sample and workshop performance of mentally retarded persons. J. Nerv. Ment. Dis., 169:718–725.

HALLWORTH, M.J. & BRODIE, M.J. (1987) Therapeutic monitoring of phenytoin. Hosp. Update, 13(10):830–842.

THOMPSON, P. et al (1981) Phenytoin and cognitive function: effects on normal volunteers and implications for epilepsy. Brit. J. Clin. Psychol., 20:155–162.

Philtrum

The area of the upper lip below the nose. Abnormalities, usually in the size of the philtrum, are sometimes described in conditions associated with mental handicap.

Phobia

An irrational fear of an object or situation. There is no difference in the manifestations of phobias in mentally handicapped people. The approaches to treatment are the same.

Phocomelia

A deficiency or absence of the upper part of a limb so that the hand or foot is situated abnormally close to the body. This infrequently occurs in a few conditions associated with mental handicap including *de Lange syndrome* and *Edward's syndrome*.

Phonology

The study of the *articulation of speech*.

Photic stimulation / photic induced seizures / photosensitive epilepsy

People undergoing *electroencephalograms* are usually subjected to photic stimulation. This is stimulation using a light flickering or flashing at regular intervals. This stimulation may induce an epileptic *seizure* in susceptible individuals. This type of sensitivity to flashing light is often age and sex dependent and also related to genetic factors. Abnormal photic responses occur in people with a variety of seizure disorders. They are not particularly common in people with a mental handicap.

JEAVONS, P.M. & HARDING, G.F.A. (1975) Photosensitive Epilepsy: A Review of the Literature and Study of 460 Patients. London: Heinemann.
NEWMARK, M.E. & PENRY, J.K. (1979) Photosensitivity and Epilepsy: A Review. New York: Raven Press.

Photosensitivity

Sensitivity to light. This usually refers to sensitivity of the skin to sunlight. This occurs as a side-effect of a few drugs including *chlorpromazine*. It is also a symptom of *Hartnup disease*. The skin reaction is generally that of reddening, roughening and sometimes cracking and ulceration.

Physical disability / handicap

A *disability* or *handicap* of the body which is a consequence of physical *impairment*. Many conditions cause physical impairment and a large number of these are associated with mental handicap either as part of a *syndrome*, or as a consequence of brain damage, as in *cerebral palsy*.

Physiotherapy / physical therapy / physical therapist / physiotherapist

Methods of treatment which aim to correct posture and locomotion and the specific functions on which these depend. This involves external physical measures such as exercises, movements, positioning, aids and the therapeutic use of heat, vibration, water, etc. In recent years physiotherapists have tended to specialize in certain areas such as developmental physiotherapy with disabled and handicapped children; respiratory and chest physiotherapy; *orthopaedic* physiotherapy and neurological / rehabilitative physiotherapy. Mentally handicapped people with physical disabilities (such as *cerebral palsy* and *meningomyelocoele* or severe delay in *motor development*) benefit from physiotherapy started as early as possible in childhood. The developmental physiotherapist carries out a careful assessment to establish the level of function and range of physical abilities and then starts a treatment plan usually based on the concepts of normal development and often incorporating special techniques and approaches (such as the *Bobath* approach). Aids and appliances may need to be provided in consultation with medical staff. Advice on positioning, exercises and use of appliances is given to the people caring for the child on a day-to-day basis.

In the U.K. the physiotherapist receives a broad academic and practical training over three years and has to pass qualifying examinations. In the U.S.A. all physical therapy schools or programmes must be approved by the American Physical Therapy Association. Licensure for practice in each state is gained by examination. Successful candidates are designated as a registered or licensed physical therapist (RPT or LPT) depending on the state regulations.

BLYTHE, B. (1985) The role of the

physiotherapist. In: Mental Handicap. A Multidisciplinary Approach. Craft, M. et al (Eds.). London: Baillière Tindall. pp. 342–3
HARRYMAN, S.E. (1976) Physical therapy. In: Developmental Disorders: Assessment, Treatment and Education. Johnstone, R.B. & Magrab, P.R. (Eds.). Baltimore: University Park Press.
MOLNAR, G.E. (1978) Analysis of motor disorder in retarded infants and young children. Am. J. Ment. Defic., 83:213–222.
PARETTE, H.P. & HOURCADE, J.J. (1984) How effective are physio-therapeutic programmes with young mentally handicapped children who have cerebral palsy? J. Ment. Defic. Res., 28:167–175.

Further information:
Chartered Society of Physiotherapy, 14 Bedford Row, London, WC1R 4ED.

Phytanic acid storage disease
= *Refsum's syndrome.*

Pica
The habit of eating substances which are regarded as inedible or unpleasant. This habit may develop in young children and is occasionally attributable to dietary deficiencies. It is usually short-lived but when it does persist into adult life the person is usually very severely mentally handicapped often with *autistic* tendencies. Institutionalization and boredom may encourage persistence of the problem. It frequently occurs in the *Prader-Willi syndrome.*

ALBIN, J.B. (1977) The treatment of pica (scavenging) behavior in the retarded. A critical analysis and implications for research. Ment. Retardation, 15(4):14–17.
FOXX, R.M. & MARTIN, E.D. (1975) Treatment of scavenging behavior (coprophagy and pica) by overcorrection. Behav. Res. Ther., 13:153–162.
MCALPINE, C. & SINGH, N.N. (1986) Pica in institutionalized mentally retarded persons. J. Ment. Defic. Res., 30:171–178.

Pick's disease
A type of *pre-senile dementia.*

Pickwickian syndrome
= *Prader-Willi syndrome.*

Pictographs
The use of pictures or diagrams to represent objects and ideas for the purposes of communication. A picture board is provided for the person to identify, usually by pointing, the meaning he wishes to communicate. Some of the *Blissymbolics* are pictographic as are *Rebus-reading symbols.*

Pierre Robin syndrome
A condition in which the person is born with a small lower jaw, *cleft palate* and a tongue which falls backward and downward (*glossoptosis*). There may be associated abnormalities of the heart, eyes and bones. About one in five people with this condition has a degree of mental handicap. In early infancy the major problems are feeding and breathing but these improve as the child gets older. The cause is unknown but in a few families it is inherited. More than one pattern of inheritance has been reported.

DENNISON, W.M. (1965) The Pierre Robin syndrome. Pediatrics, 36:336–341.
SALMON, M.A. (1978) Developmental Defects and Syndromes. Aylesbury, England: HM+M Publishers. pp. 42–43.
SINGH, R.P. et al (1970) Pierre Robin syndrome in siblings. Am. J. Dis. Child., 120:560.
SMITH, J.L. & STOWE, F.R. (1961) The Pierre Robin syndrome. A review of 39 cases with emphasis on associated ocular lesions. Pediatrics, 27:128.

Pigeon chest
= *pectus carinatum.*

Pigeon-toed
= *metatarsus varus.*

Pili torti

Kinky, twisted stubble-like hair which breaks easily and is therefore short. This occurs in *Menkes syndrome*.

Pimozide

A drug used in the treatment of *schizophrenia*, *mania* and other *psychoses*. It is less often used to treat anxiety, excitement or agitation. Side-effects are similar to those of *chlorpromazine*.

Pincer grasp

= *finger-thumb opposition*.

Pink's disease

= *mercury poisoning*.

PIP developmental charts

A developmental checklist based on normal infant development. It is designed to be easy to complete. It relies on the report of carers or direct observation of the child in daily life. It is arranged in sections from birth to a 5-year-old level and is very comprehensive. It can be used for developmental assessment, target setting and evaluation. It covers motor development, eye-hand skills, development of play and language.

DICKENS, P. & STALLARD, A. (1987) Assessing mentally handicapped people. London: NFER/Nelson. pp. 43–44.
JEFFREE, D. & McCONKEY, R. (1976) PIP Developmental Charts. Sevenoaks, England: Hodder & Stoughton.

Pipecolataemia

= *Cerebro-hepato-renal syndrome*.

Pituitary gland

A small gland at the base of the brain which produces hormones which have a controlling effect on other glands of the body and on growth. Deficiencies of the hormones from this gland have been described in a few rare conditions associated with mental handicap.

PKU

= *phenylketonuria*.

Placebo

An inactive medicine or pill given to a person in order to make him or his carers believe that he is receiving active treatment.

Placenta / placental insufficiency

The placenta (afterbirth) is the organ in which food and oxygen pass from the mother's to the baby's blood while the baby (*fetus*) is in the womb. The placenta lines much of the inside of the womb. Insufficiency of the placenta may be a cause of poor fetal growth (which in turn leads to *hypoglycaemia*) and may be due to developmental abnormalities of the placenta or to various problems in the mother. Haemorrhage behind the placenta is particularly likely to cause serious problems for the baby especially lack of oxygen (*anoxia*) leading to risk of brain damage.

Plagiocephaly

An asymmetrical shape of the head so that, when viewed from above, it is a rhomboid. It is usually associated with asymmetry of the face with one side appearing to be squashed backward and a protuberant eye on that side. It is usually an isolated occurrence not associated with mental handicap or other malformations but may occur in *Aicardi's syndrome* which is associated with mental handicap. It is caused by some of the skull bones on one side fusing earlier than normal. It can be relieved by surgical procedures if it does not resolve in the first 2 or 3 years or if it causes problems.

Plantar reflex

The reflex movement of the toes when the skin on the outer aspect of the sole of the foot is stroked. In adults the normal reaction is curling under of the toes but, when brain damage has caused spasticity, the toes spread outward and the big toe upward.

Plastic surgery

Plastic surgery may be recommended for several conditions associated with mental handicap. It may improve the appearance of the person leading to psychological and social benefits and may possibly improve breathing, eating and speech development. This particularly applies to the malformations of the face which occur in *Apert's* and *Crouzon's syndromes*. Recently facial plastic surgery has also been recommended by some specialists for people with *Down's syndrome*.

Leading Article (1983) Plastic surgery in Down's syndrome. Lancet, i:1314.

LEMPERLE, G. & RADU, D. (1980) Facial plastic surgery in children with Down's syndrome. Plast. Reconstr. Surg., 66: 337–42.

OLBRISCH, R.R. (1982) Plastic surgical management of children with Down's syndrome: indications and results. Brit. J. Plast. Surg., 35:195–200.

Platybasia

A *congenital* malformation of the base of the skull with upward displacement of the upper vertebrae (bones of the spine) in the neck. A short neck may suggest the diagnosis. The opening at the base of the skull is often narrowed so that the spinal cord becomes compressed where it emerges from the brain and it may be necessary to treat it surgically. It is sometimes associated with *hydrocephalus* and often occurs in *Hallermann-Streiff syndrome* and *Klippel-Feil syndrome* which are associated with mental handicap.

Play

Children with a mental handicap enjoy and learn from play as much as any child. Play should be encouraged and, if necessary, taught. Children with *autistic* tendencies do not play normally due to particular difficulties in the use of imagination and in being flexible in thought and action. Their play tends to be stereotyped and repetitive to a far greater degree than normal. When children are able to play this can be a very useful way of learning and acquiring skills and dexterity. Initially play is exploratory and manipulative but as a child develops it becomes more complex and imagination and fantasy become involved.

DARBYSHIRE, P. (1986) Play. In: Mental Handicap – A Handbook of Care. Shanley, E. (Ed.) Edinburgh: Churchill Livingstone. pp. 249–263.

JEFFREE, D. et al (1977) Let Me Play. London: Souvenir Press.

JONES, E. (1980) Play, toy libraries and adventure playgrounds. In: Modern Management of Mental Handicap. Simon, G.B. (Ed.) Lancaster, England: MTP Press Ltd. pp. 241–247.

McCONKEY, R. (1982) Learning to Pretend: Handbook for Staff and Parents. Dublin: St. Michael's House Research.

McCONKEY, R. & JEFFREE, D. (1980) Developing children's play. Special Education: Forward Trends, 7(2).

WEHMEN, P. (1977) Helping the Mentally Retarded Acquire Play Skills. Illinois: Thomas.

Further information:
Play Matters/ Toy Libraries Association, 68 Church Way, London, NW1 1LT.

Pneumoencephalogram

= *air encephalogram*.

Poikiloderma

A condition in which the skin first becomes red and then thin with the appearance of small tortuous blood vessels (*telangiectasia*) and increased pigmentation (brownness) sometimes with pale patches. This occurs in the *Rothmund-Thomson syndrome* which is sometimes associated with mental handicap.

Poikiloderma congenita

= *Rothmund-Thomson syndrome*.

Poliodystrophy cerebri progressiva

= *Alper's syndrome*.

Pollett's syndrome
A very rare condition in which there is non-progressive mental handicap, *epilepsy* and *spasticity*. The hair is brittle (*trichorrhexis nodosa*). It is inherited from both parents who are carriers (*recessive inheritance*).

COULTER, D.L. et al (1982) Neurotrichosis: Hair-shaft abnormalities associated with neurological diseases. Dev. Med. Child Neurology, 24:634.
POLLETT, R.T. et al (1968) Sibs with mental and physical retardation and trichorrhexis nodosa with abnormal amino acid composition of the hair. Arch. Dis. Childh., 43:211.

Polycystic kidneys
The presence of many fluid-filled sacs (cysts) in the kidneys. These are usually present at birth. If severe they interfere with the function of the kidney and may also predispose the person to kidney infections. Kidney failure may develop later in life. Polycystic kidneys may be present in *de Lange syndrome* and *cerebro-hepato-renal syndrome* both of which are associated with mental handicap.

Polydactyly
Extra finger(s) or toe(s). This may occur in a number of conditions associated with mental handicap including *Carpenter's syndrome, Down's syndrome, Treacher-Collins syndrome, Mohrs' syndrome, Beckwith syndrome, Laurence-Moon-Biedl syndrome, de Lange syndrome, Patau's syndrome, Goltz's syndrome, partial trisomy 13q*, and *Edward's syndrome*.

Polydipsia
Excessive drinking of fluid. This may be a symptom of *diabetes mellitus* and can rarely be caused by a hormone deficiency in the *pituitary gland* (diabetes insipidus), but more usually it is a habit acquired for psychological reasons. It is occasionally seen in mentally handicapped people who are institutionalized and lacking stimulation and occupation. It can also develop in individuals with *autistic* tendencies for whom it becomes an obsession or ritual. If very excessive an imbalance of body fluids can occur causing the person to be physically ill and swollen with fluid.

Polydystrophic dwarfism
= *Maroteaux-Lamy syndrome.*

Polydystrophic oligophrenia
= *Sanfilippo syndrome.*

Polygenic inheritance
= *multifactorial inheritance.*

Polymicrogyria
In this condition the surface of the brain is abnormally formed with many small folds (*gyri*). This may be seen in the *cerebro-hepato-renal syndrome* and in congenital *cytomegalic inclusion disease* both of which are associated with mental handicap.

Polysyndactyly
Extra fingers or toes which are joined together. This commonly occurs in *oro-facial-digital syndrome I* and *Carpenter's syndrome*.

Pompe's disease
Glucose is normally stored as glycogen in the body but in this condition the glycogen cannot be broken down to glucose when it is needed. This is due to an *enzyme* (acid maltase) deficiency in muscles, the heart, the liver and the *central nervous system*. As a result glycogen accumulates in these tissues. The first symptoms appear by the second month of life and include difficulty in feeding, breathlessness and exhaustion. Muscle weakness and impaired heart function gradually become apparent. The heart enlarges. The muscles are floppy but firm and rubbery and the infant makes few spontaneous movements. *Epilepsy*, mental handicap and coma develop. Children are susceptible to infections and rarely survive the first two years of life. A milder form of acid maltase deficiency has also been

described in older children and adults and a high-protein diet is said to help in this late-onset form of the disease. It is inherited from both parents who are carriers (*recessive inheritance*). It can also be detected before birth following *amniocentesis* and in carriers following *fibroblast culture*.

BUTTERWORTH, J. & BROADHEAD, D.M. (1977) Diagnosis of Pompe's disease in cultured skin fibroblasts and primary amniotic fluid cells using 4-methylumbel-liferyl-alpha-D-glycopyranoside as substrate. Clin. Chim. Acta, 78:335.

ENGEL, A.G. et al (1973) The spectrum and diagnosis of acid maltase deficiency. Neurology, 23:95.

MARTIN, J.J. et al (1973) Pompe's disease: An inborn lysosomal disorder with storage of glycogen. Acta Neuropathol., 23:229.

SMITH, H.L. et al (1966) Type II glycogenosis: report of a case with four year survival and absence of acid maltase associated with abnormal glycogen. Am. J. Dis. Child., 111:475.

Porencephalic cysts / porencephaly

Extensive fluid-filled cavities (cysts) in the brain usually formed as the result of destruction of brain tissue following severe viral infection (*encephalitis*), lack of oxygen to the brain (*anoxia*) or bleeding into the brain (haemorrhage). Anoxia and haemorrhage may occur following a difficult labour or birth. Porencephaly may also occur in a few conditions associated with abnormal development of the brain such as *de Lange syndrome*. It is frequently found following congenital *cytomegalic inclusion disease*. Occasionally there are other associated malformations including a small or large head, *cataract*, malformed ears, agenesis of the *corpus callosum* and *encephalocoele*. The age of onset of symptoms can vary considerably but is often within the first year of life. Initial symptoms frequently include *cerebral palsy* and *epilepsy*. The *seizures* can be progressive and have many forms. Visual impairment, speech defects and other prob-

lems may be present depending on the site and size of the cyst. Mental handicap is frequently present.

NAEF, R.W. (1958) Clinical features of porencephaly. A review of thirty-two cases. Arch. Neurol. Psychiat. 80:133.

SHURTLEFF, D.B. et al (1973) Congenital brain cysts in infancy: Diagnosis, treatment and follow-up. Teratology, 7:183.

WARKANY, J. et al (1981) Mental Retardation and Congenital Malformations of the Central Nervous System. Chicago; Year Book Medical Publishers Inc. pp. 191–199.

Port-wine naevus

= *capillary haemangioma*.

Portage system

An *early intervention programme* originally devised to encourage mothers to stimulate deprived children in Wisconsin, U.S.A. It has been adapted for use in the U.K. and is now widely used. It consists of a developmental checklist which focuses attention on strengths and needs and a set of guidelines and suggestions about what to teach next. The checklist is colour-coded and 580 items are divided into five developmental areas: cognitive, self-help, motor, language and socialization. There is also an infant stimulation section for young babies or children with severe developmental delay. Items are listed in each section in the normal sequence of development from birth to 6 years of age. The checklist provides an ongoing record of the time each behaviour is learnt and shows the next step to be acquired. The card file includes a colour-coded and numbered card to match each item on the checklist. On each card the skill is described and a list of ideas and materials to teach the skill is provided. The system should be used with the help of a trained home visitor who is able to translate the ideas into a practical activity chart which can be followed by the carers. It is important that the goals set on each visit are realistic and an important part of the process is the breaking down of any goal into segments which are achievable in a short time scale. There is constant reassessment usually at weekly intervals. Very often the skills of more than one professional worker are needed at different times and the home visitor needs support from a multidisciplinary service. The scheme is designed for use in a home visiting scheme but can also be useful in the school or residential setting. There is evidence to suggest that pre-school children, especially children with *Down's syndrome*, do gain in *cognitive skills*, at least in the short term, following the use of such a programme.

BIDDER, R. et al (1983) Evaluation of teaching methods in a home-based training scheme for developmentally delayed preschool children. Child: Care, Health and Development, 9:1–12.
BLUMA, S. et al (1976) Portage Guide to Early Education. Portage, Wisconsin: Cooperative Educational Service Agency, 12.
CAMERON, R.J. (Ed.) (1982) Working Together. Portage in the U.K. Windsor: NFER/Nelson.
CLEMENTS, J.C. et al (1980) A home advisory service for pre-school children with developmental delays. Child: Care, Health and Development, 6:25–33.
DALY, B. et al (Eds.) (1985) Portage: The Importance of Parents. Windsor: NFER/Nelson.
LLOYD, J.M. (1986) Jacobs Ladder. A Parent's View of Portage. Tunbridge Wells: Costello.
REVILL, S. & BLUNDEN, R. (1980) A Manual for Implementing a Portage Home Training Service for Developmentally Handicapped Pre-school Children. Windsor: NFER.
SHEARER, M.S. & SHEARER, D.E. (1972) The portage project: a model of early childhood education. Except. Child., 36: 210–217.

Further information:
National Portage and Home Teaching Association, Silver Hill, Winchester SO23 8AF.

Porteus Maze

A very crude test of *mental age* based on the ability to complete mazes of increasing complexity. There is one maze for each year of age from 3 to 14 years (except year 13). There are two mazes for adults. The person is credited with the mental age associated with the most difficult maze traced.

Positive practice
See *overcorrection*.

Positive reinforcement
See *reinforcement*.

Positron Emission Tomography

The PET scanner can detect and display functional areas in the brain during *cognitive* processing. This technique is based on monitoring the rate at which a radioactive isotope of glucose is taken up by the regions of the brain engaged in the cognitive task.

BUCHSBAUM, M.S. et al (1982) Cerebral glucography with positron tomography. Use in normal subjects and in patients with schizophrenia. Arch. Gen. Psychiat., 39: 251–259.

Possum

A term derived from POSM, an acronym for patient-operated selected mechanisms. This refers to electronic or electromechanical devices which can be controlled be people with severe physical handicaps. The early devices were designed to provide a method of communication for use by severely physically handicapped people who could not speak. An electronic board with letters, words or symbols was used with a light as a pointer. Movements of the light were controlled by any part of the body able to perform voluntary movements. More recently the company have developed and marketed many new electronic devices for communication and learning. Most of these are computer based.

Further information:
Possum Controls Ltd. Middlegreen Rd, Langley, Slough, Berks. SL3 6DF.

Post-central cortex

An area on the surface (*cortex*) of the brain which lies at the front of the *parietal lobe*. Body sensations, such as touch, from the opposite side of the body are received and appreciated here. Damage to this area of the brain can cause loss of sensation.

Postnatal

After birth. This refers to any factors operating after the birth.

Post-vaccine encephalitis / encephalopathy

Encephalitis or *encephalopathy* occurring after vaccination. See *vaccine damage*.

PPAC

= Primary Progress Assessment Charts. See *Gunzberg Progress Assessment Charts*.

PPOC

= Positive practice overcorrection. See *overcorrection*.

Prader-Willi syndrome / Prader-Labhart-Willi syndrome

Babies with this condition are commonly very floppy and have severe feeding difficulties. Increased appetite, compulsive overeating and obesity begin in infancy or early childhood. *Developmental delay* becomes evident and there is a variable degree of mental handicap. People with this condition usually have a long face, narrow forehead and almond-shaped eyes. Restricted growth in adolescence is usual, leading to short stature. Spinal curvature may develop. There is a susceptibility to tooth decay. Hands and feet are proportionally small. Men have a small penis and small testes (which may be undescended). Most do not develop a beard or masculine voice. Some women menstruate but most do so irregularly or not at all. Infertility is usual. A large proportion of people with this condition have a small part of *chromosome* 15 missing or have other abnormalities of this chromosome. The cause of this is not known. Mild

diabetes mellitus may develop and life expectancy is reduced by severe obesity. Treatment of the compulsive overeating is very difficult.

BUTLER, M.G. et al (1986) Clinical and cytogenetic survey of 39 individuals with Prader-Labhart-Willi syndrome. Am. J. Med. Genet., 23(3):793–809.
HALL, B.D. & SMITH, D.W. (1972) Prader-Willi syndrome. J. Pediatr., 81:286.
LEDBETTER, D.H. et al (1982) Chromosome 15 abnormalities and the Prader-Willi syndrome: A follow-up report of 40 cases. Am. J. Hum. Genet., 34:278.
MATTEI, J.F. et al (1983) Prader-Willi syndrome and chromosome 15: A clinical discussion of 20 cases. Hum. Genet., 64:356.

Pre-central cortex

An area on the surface (*cortex*) of the brain which lies at the back of the *frontal lobe*. Voluntary movements of one side of the body are initiated in the pre-central cortex of the opposite side. Damage to the pre-central cortex can cause paralysis and *spasticity* and is a cause of *cerebral palsy*.

Pre-eclamptic toxaemia

A common condition during pregnancy in which the blood pressure is raised, swelling and weight gain occur and albumin is present in the urine. It requires close observation because of the risk of it developing into eclampsia (*toxaemia*) in which the blood pressure is dangerously increased putting the mother and baby at risk.

Pre-school services

In some parts of the U.K. and the U.S.A. there are services available to help mentally handicapped children and their families before the child is old enough to attend school. These services may be based on resource centres which offer playgroups, *physiotherapy, assessment, counselling* etc. or may be run on the basis of home visits. Some services advise parents on a structured approach to training, teaching and stimulating the child using *early intervention programmes* such as *Portage*.

WARD, L. (1982) The pre-school child. In People First. London: King's Fund Centre. pp. 25–42.

Pre-senile dementia
A deterioration of the brain (*dementia*) with an onset before old age. There is generally loss of memory, concentration and other intellectual skills. *Alzheimer's disease* is the commonest type and people with *Down's syndrome* are very susceptible to this condition.

Preauricular skin tags
Small tags of skin in front of the ears. These may occur in *Goldenhar's syndrome, cri-du-chat syndrome* and a few other rare *chromosome* disorders all of which are associated with mental handicap. Pits in front of the ears (preauricular fistulae) may also be present.

Precipitate labour / delivery
A rapid birth. This can sometimes lead to tearing of the delicate structures within the skull of the baby as it suddenly expands following compression through the pelvis. It is a possible cause of bleeding into the brain and consequent brain damage and mental handicap.

Precocious puberty
The onset of *puberty* in early childhood or infancy well before the usual time. This may occur in *hydrocephalus, Sotos' syndrome, tuberose sclerosis, congenital hypothyroidism* and *Silver's syndrome* all of which are associated with mental handicap.

Premack principle
The use of an activity, which the person prefers and enjoys, as a reward for a less preferred but more socially desirable behaviour. This is usually part of a *behaviour modification* or teaching programme.

Prematurity
Occurring before the expected time. The premature infant is usually defined as either born before 38 weeks of gestation or having a birth weight of less than five and a half pounds (2500g). Premature birth can put the infant at risk of life-threatening conditions and also of brain damage and mental handicap. This tends to be in proportion to the degree of prematurity. The outlook for normal development improves with birth weight for any given gestational age and is also enhanced by greater gestational age at any birth weight.

LUBCHENCO, L.O. et al (1972) Long-term follow-up of premature infants. II: Influence of birth weight and gestational age on sequelae. J. Pediatr., 80:509–512.

Prenatal
Describes the time from conception to birth.

Prenatal diagnosis
There are now a large number of diseases of which the diagnosis can be made during pregnancy. This includes many causes of mental handicap such as *Down's syndrome* and the other *chromosome* disorders. Many *enzyme* deficiencies can now be detected. In nearly all of these conditions the diagnosis is made following *amniocentesis. Chorion biopsy* is also becoming available. A few disorders may be suspected from blood tests on the mother for *alpha-feto protein* levels or antibodies to infections such as german measles (see *rubella syndrome*).

Presbyacusis
The hearing loss of old age which often appears in the 50's or 60's and occurs regardless of intellectual ability. *Deafness* in a mentally handicapped person is often missed unless regular assessments are carried out. The use of a hearing aid should be encouraged.

Presbyopia
Loss of the ability to focus the eyes on near

objects. This occurs as a result of ageing. It is easily missed in people who are mentally handicapped and who cannot draw attention to the problem. It can be corrected by the use of spectacles.

Presidential Committee on Mental Retardation

In the U.S.A., as a result of President Kennedy's initiative, there is a standing Presidential Committee on Mental Retardation which tries to co-ordinate interests and to direct policies and initiatives. It is a federal body with no legal powers. It has deplored institutional care and advocated *community care* and has made recommendations regarding the reappraisal of the laws relating to the care of mentally handicapped people.

Pretend play

See *play*.

Prevalence

The measure of the number of people found to have a particular disorder within a given population at a specific point in time. Prevalence of a handicapping disorder is usually expressed as cases per thousand population of a particular age (the age specific rate). Studies in North America and North West Europe show an apparent consistency in the prevalence rate of mental handicap over time and between countries but detailed inspection shows considerable fluctuation especially over time. There are many factors which influence this including the degree of handicap. Most studies find the prevalence rate of *severe mental handicap* to lie between 2 and 5 per thousand.

FRYERS, T. (1981) Measuring trends in prevalence and distribution of severe mental retardation. In: Assessing the Handicaps and Needs of Mentally Retarded Children. Cooper, B. (Ed.). London: Academic Press. pp. 13–31.
FRYERS, T. (1984) The Epidemiology of Severe Intellectual Impairment. The Dynamics of Prevalence. London: Academic Press.

Prevocational Assessment and Curriculum Guide

A scale for assessing the areas of competence relevant to employment. The nine areas identified and incorporated into the scale are – attendance / endurance, independence, production, learning, behaviour, communication skills, social skills, grooming / eating skills and toileting skills.

MITHAUG, D.E. et al (1978) Prevocational Assessment and Curriculum Guide. Seattle: Exceptional Education.
MITHAUG, D.E. et al (1980) Assessing prevocational competencies of profoundly, severely and moderately retarded persons. J. Assoc. Severely Handicapped, 5:271–284.

Primary embryonic hypertelorism

= *Greig's syndrome*.

Primary Progress Assessment Charts

= *Gunzberg Progress Assessment Charts*.

Primidone

An *anticonvulsant* drug used in the treatment of *grand-mal convulsions* and *partial seizures*. It is sometimes used in the treatment of other types of *seizures*. It is usually started as a very low dose and gradually increased to avoid undue sedation. Primidone is converted into *phenobarbitone* in the body. Side-effects are usually those of sedation or behavioural disturbance in children. Disturbances of vision, nausea, headache, vomiting, *nystagmus* and unsteadiness have been described but are rare. Occasionally allergic reactions occur such as skin rashes. Exceptionally there is anaemia due to folic acid and/or vitamin B12 deficiency.

Primitive reflexes

Involuntary posture and movement patterns typical of very immature *central nervous system* development.

Private residential homes

In the U.K. private residential homes for mentally handicapped people now have to be registered with the local authority and have to reach a certain standard. There is a similar system in the U.S.A.

Procyclidine

A drug used in the treatment of *parkinsonism* of the type which is a side-effect of some tranquillizing drugs. It should not be used for *tardive dyskinesia*. Side-effects include dry mouth, blurring of vision and constipation. At higher doses dizziness, confusion and hallucinations may occur.

Profound mental handicap / profound mental retardation

Under the *International Classification of Diseases* (9th edition) profound mental retardation refers to an *intelligence quotient* of less than 20. This represents the most severe degree of mental handicap.

Progeria

Premature ageing usually referring to a rare condition in which normal development during the first year of life is followed by premature senility. This condition is not associated with mental handicap and should not be confused with *Cockayne's syndrome* which includes a progressive intellectual deterioration. For late-onset progeria see *Werner's syndrome*.

Prognathia / prognathism

Projection of the jaw, usually referring to the lower jaw. This makes the chin prominent. This may occur in many conditions associated with mental handicap including *Apert's syndrome, Chotzen's syndrome, Crouzon's syndrome, happy puppet syndrome, homocystinuria, Pfeiffer's syndrome* and several *chromosome* disorders.

Prognosis

The forecast or estimation of the course and outcome of a disease.

Program Analysis of Service Systems (PASS)

A procedure for specifying the practical implications of *normalization* in given situations and of objectively measuring (in terms of normalization) the quality of a wide range of service projects, systems and agencies. This evaluation system has provided a structure within which new patterns of service organization can be assessed and existing services evaluated. The procedure can be used on small or large institutions run by any agency or to evaluate community services and attitudes. It enables continuous or repeated assessments to take place. It can also be used for the purposes of accreditation, teaching, setting of defined objectives for staff or to enable comparative studies of services. There are 50 items which are rated and weighted according to the judgements of the designers of PASS. They include areas such as *integration, age-appropriateness* of activities, appropriateness of programme model, growth orientation and quality of setting. The evaluations are supposed to be carried out by four assessors each acting independently. Average ratings give a total score for each facility or agency which can range from -947 to $+1000$. Comparison between programmes on all 50 items is possible.

ANDREWS, R.J. & BERRY, P.B. (1978) The evaluation of services for the handicapped promoting community living. Internat. J. Rehab. Res., 1(4):451–461.
WOLFENSBERGER, W. & GLENN, L. (1975) Program Analysis of Service Systems PASS 3. Toronto: National Institute for Mental Retardation.

Programmed care

= *phased care.*

Progress Assessment Charts

= *Gunzberg Progress Assessment Charts.*

Progressive degeneration of the CNS in infancy

= *Alper's syndrome.*

Progressive diaphyseal dysplasia
= *Engelmann's disease.*

Progressive disorders
= *degenerative disorders.*

Progressive hepatolenticular degeneration
= *Wilson's disease.*

Progressive infantile cerebral poliodystrophy
= *Alper's syndrome.*

Progressive matrices
These are tests which do not depend on language skills but require skills involving discrimination, *visuo-motor* skills and logic. *Raven's Standard progressive matrices* include a Standard Progressive Matrices test and a Simpler Coloured Progressive Matrices test which is more often used with mentally handicapped people. Norms exist to permit scoring of intelligence down to an *intelligence quotient* of about 40.

Project Head Start
= *Head Start.*

Promazine
A tranquillizing drug used in the treatment of agitation and restlessness. It is one of the *phenothiazine* group of drugs and side-effects are similar to those of *chlorpromazine.*

Prominal
= *methylphenobarbital.*

Prompts / prompting
A teaching technique used in *behaviour modification.* Prompting means giving as much help as necessary in order to accomplish a target behaviour. A physical prompt involves physically guiding the person through the required action and a verbal prompt involves telling him what to do. Prompting by the use of gesture or *modelling* may also be used. Once the desired behaviour is established (and a *reinforcement* identified) the prompt can generally be faded out in a systematic way (*fading*).

WHITMAN, T.L. (1971) Effects of reinforcement and guidance procedures on institution-following behaviour of severely retarded children. J. Appl. Behav. Anal., 4:283–290.
ZELLER, M.D. & JERVEY, S.S. (1968) Development of behaviour: Self-feeding. J. Cons. Clin. Psychol., 32:164–168.

Propionic acidaemia
See *hyperglycinaemia.*

Proptosis
A prominence of part of the body usually referring to the eyes. This may occur in *Engelmann's disease, Apert's syndrome* and *Crouzon's syndrome* all of which are associated with mental handicap.

Prosthesis
An artificial appliance or device used to compensate for, or to replace, an *impairment.*

Prothiadin
= *dothiepin.*

Pseudo-Hurler polydystrophy
This condition is one of a group of disorders known as the *mucolipidoses.* The biochemical abnormalities are similar to those seen in *mucolipidosis II* but symptoms do not appear until 2 years of age or later and mental handicap is mild. Growth is restricted and there are severe abnormalities of the bones of the spine and the pelvis. Joints are stiff. Disease of the valves of the heart is common and small areas of clouding of the *cornea* of the eye may be present. There is a mild coarsening of the facial features. It is similar to *Hurler's syndrome* but less severe. The condition is inherited from both parents who are carriers (*recessive inheritance*). It can be detected during pregnancy following *amniocentesis.*

KELLY, T.E. et al (1975) Mucolipidosis III (Pseudo-Hurler polydystrophy). Clinical and laboratory studies in a series of 12 patients. Johns Hopkins Med. J., 137:156.

Pseudo-Hurler syndrome
See *generalized gangliosidosis.*

Pseudo-hypoparathyroidism / Pseudo-pseudo-hypoparathyroidism
= *Albright's syndrome.*

Pseudo-Turner's syndrome
= *Noonan's syndrome.*

Pseudohydrocephalus
Some children born after poor growth in the womb (intra-uterine growth retardation) have heads and brains which are relatively large in comparison to their facial structure and body size. This is sometimes referred to as pseudohydrocephalus. If the brain weight is excessive for the body weight it should be considered as *megalencephaly.* In *Silver's syndrome* the term pseudohydrocephalus has been used to describe the apparently large head of a person with a small face and body. The head circumference is, in fact, normal.

SZALAY, G.C. (1963) Pseudohydrocephalus in dwarfs: The Russell dwarf. J. Pediatr., 63:622–633.

Pseudotrisomy 18
A very rare condition in which the person is very similar to, or has most of the features of, *Edward's syndrome* but studies of the *chromosomes* fail to show any abnormalities. Mental handicap is present. Survival beyond 6 months of age is unusual. It is probably inherited as a single *gene* disorder from both parents who are carriers (*recessive inheritance*).

HOOK, E.B. & YUNIS, J.J. (1965) Trisomy 18 syndrome in a patient with normal karyotype. J. Am. Med. Ass., 193:840–843.
SIMPSON, J.L. & GERMAN, J. (1965) Developmental anomaly resembling the trisomy 18 syndrome. Ann. Genet. (Paris), 12:107–110.

Psittacorhina
A beak-shaped nose as described in a few conditions associated with mental handicap such as *Crouzon's syndrome.*

Psychiatric illness / psychiatric disorder
A disturbance of the mind of a person commonly called a 'nervous breakdown'. This includes many different disorders usually categorized as *neuroses* or *psychoses*. *Personality disorders* may also be regarded as psychiatric disorders. Mentally handicapped people are more susceptible to psychiatric illness than the general population. See also *mental disorder.*

BALLINGER, B.R. & REID, A.H. (1977) Psychiatric disorder in an adult training centre and a hospital for the mentally handicapped. Psycholog. Med., 7:525–528.
REID, A.H. (1982) The Psychiatry of Mental Handicap. Oxford: Blackwell Scientific.
WRIGHT, E.C. (1982) The presentation of mental illness in mentally retarded adults. Brit. J. Psychiat., 141:496–502.

Psychiatrist
A doctor who has specialized in the field of *psychiatry.* In the U.K. medical specialists in mental handicap are psychiatrists who were, until recently, mainly responsible for mentally handicapped people residing in hospitals. It is now argued that psychiatrists should confine themselves to dealing with the psychiatric needs and problems of mentally handicapped people wherever they live and no longer be responsible for their day-to-day care or general medical needs.

GODBER, G. (1973) The responsibilities and role of the doctor concerned with the care of the mentally handicapped. Brit. J. Psychiat., 123:617–620.
GOST, N.L. & DAVIS, D.R. (1983) Mental handicap policy in Great Britain. Mental Handicap, 11:40.

Psychiatry

The medical speciality concerned with the study, diagnosis, treatment and prevention of emotional disorders and *psychiatric illness*.

Psychological Stimulus – Response Evaluation

This test for severely multiply handicapped children was designed to minimize the physical aspects of tasks while tapping behaviour which shows the acquisition of concepts usually associated with levels of intellectual development. It covers the developmental range from birth to 5 years and there is an Auditory Language Scale, a Visualmotor Scale and a Tactile Differentiation Scale.

MULLEN, E.M. et al (1977) Psychological S-R Evaluation for Severely Multiple Handicapped Children. East Province, R.I.: Meeting Street School.

Psychological tests

Tests, such as *intelligence tests*, which assess the psychological functioning of an individual.

WODRICH, D.L. (1984) Children's Psychological Testing. A Guide for Non-psychologists. Baltimore: Paul H. Brookes.

Psychologist

A person trained as a professional in the science of *psychology* and with a degree in psychology. Psychologists often specialize in one of the branches of psychology and the areas concerned with mentally handicapped people are covered by *educational psychologists* and *clinical psychologists*.

WILCOCK, P. (1985) The role of the psychologist. In: Mental Handicap: A Multidisciplinary Approach. Craft, M. et al. London: Baillière Tindall. pp. 304–316.

Psychology

The science that deals with the mind and mental processes.

Psychometric tests

= *intelligence tests*.

Psychomotor development

The development of skills consciously controlled by the brain and apparent in behaviour. These include movements, speech and other types of learning.

Psychomotor epilepsy / seizures

= *complex partial seizures*.

Psychomotor retardation

Impairment of *psychomotor development*.

Psychomotor status

A very rare state in which prolonged *complex partial seizures* occur. Consciousness is impaired usually with wandering eye movements and intermittent staring and automatic behaviours. Afterwards, the person may be confused and has no memory of the attack.

Psychoneuroses

= *neuroses*.

Psychopathic disorder / psychopathy

A type of *personality disorder* in which antisocial behaviours occur without remorse or shame. There is a failure to learn by experience and an egocentricity and inability to form close relationships involving mutual trust.

Psychoses

A group of mental disorders which includes *schizophrenia, manic-depressive psychoses, paranoid* states and confusional states. There is no single acceptable definition but most include a degree of impairment of appreciation of reality as perceived by other people. These disorders can cause severe problems. Emotions may be qualitatively or quantitatively different from normal. *Autism* is sometimes referred to as infantile psychosis. It is thought that psychoses occur more commonly in mentally handicapped people compared to the general population and this is certainly the case if autism is included.

HEATON-WARD, A. (1977) Psychosis in mental handicap. Brit. J. Psychiat., 130: 525–533.

HUCKER, S.J. et al (1979) Psychosis in mentally handicapped adults. In: Psychiatric Illness and Mental Handicap. James, F.E. & Snaith, R.P. (Eds.) London: Gaskell Press. pp. 27–36.

Psychosomatic
A bodily symptom or disease caused or influenced by psychological factors.

Psychotherapy
A form of treatment for emotional or behavioural disorders in which a trained person (known as a psychotherapist) establishes a professional relationship with the person and uses it to promote positive emotional growth and development and to change disturbed patterns of behaviour. Its use with mentally handicapped people is mainly restricted to those who can communicate adequately.

Psychotropic drugs
Drugs with an effect on mental function, behaviour or experience. It includes the *tranquillizers*, *antidepressant drugs* and stimulants such as *methylphenidate*.

BREUNING, S.E. & POLING, A.D. (Eds.) (1982) Drugs and Mental Retardation. Illinois: Charles C. Thomas.

TU, J. & SMITH, J.J. (1979) Factors associated with psychotropic medication in mental retardation facilities. Comprehensive Psychiatry, 20:289–295.

Pterygium
A thin piece of body tissue present where there should be a space. This generally applies to webbing of skin between fingers and toes, in front of the elbow or at the back of the knee. It may also be used to describe tissue forming in front of the *cornea* of the eye.

Pterygium coli
= *neck webbing*.

Ptosis
Drooping of the upper eyelid. If severe, the head may be tilted back in order to see. This may occur in a few condition associated with mental handicap including *de Lange syndrome, Chotzen's syndrome, Hartnup disease, Noonan's syndrome, Rubinstein-Taybi syndrome, Smith-Lemli-Opitz syndrome* and a few rare *chromosome* disorders.

Puberty
The age at which a person begins to develop sexual maturity and the potential to produce children. It starts with the acquisition of secondary sexual characteristics and continues for 2 or 3 years merging with the start of *adolescence*. Puberty is a time at which emotional adjustment may be precarious in any child including children who are mentally handicapped. This emotional vulnerability may be due to physical factors such as body and hormonal changes as well as psychological factors such as the increase in self-awareness, and increased responsibilities and expectations from self and others. There is considerable individual variation but most mentally handicapped people will need help in understanding the changes that are taking place and in coping with them. See also *sex education*.

Public Laws 94–142
= *Education for All Handicapped Children Act 1976*.

Pudenz-Heyer-Schulte
A pump and valve used in the treatment of *hydrocephalus* to drain off excess fluid from the brain. It consists of a plastic bubble placed under the scalp with its far end connected to a slit valve. It can then be pumped to check that it is working and to clear obstructions.

Pulmonary stenosis
Narrowing of the artery which carries blood from the heart to the lungs in order to obtain

oxygen. This form of *congenital heart disease* occurs, sometimes with other heart defects, in a number of conditions associated with mental handicap including *Greig's syndrome, Carpenter's syndrome, Apert's syndrome*, congenital *cytomegalic inclusion disease, Laurence-Moon-Biedl syndrome, Rubinstein-Taybi syndrome, de Lange syndrome, Noonan's syndrome, arthrogryposis multiplex congenita, infantile hypercalcaemia, Edward's syndrome, Turner's syndrome* and *rubella syndrome*.

Punishment

In *behaviour modification* this refers to the introduction of unpleasant consequences of a behaviour so as to reduce the probability of that behaviour occurring again. *Aversive stimulation* is one example. Unpleasant aversive procedures undermine human rights and are open to abuse. They should therefore be restricted to the management of the most severe self-destructive or antisocial behaviours. A clear procedure combined with very close and systematic monitoring is essential for all punishment techniques. *Time-out, response cost, restraint* and *overcorrection* are sometimes considered to have an element of punishment.

KIERNAN, C. (1985) Behaviour modification. In: Mental Deficiency – The Changing Outlook (4th edit.). Clarke, A.M. et al. London: Methuen. pp. 484–488.
REPP, A.C. & DEITZ, S.M. (1978) On the selective use of punishment. Suggested guidelines for administrators. Ment. Retardation, 16:200–254.

Pure-tone audiometry

A hearing test used for those children whose development is above the 3-year level. The child is asked to demonstrate by a particular action (pressing buttons, putting a ball in a box, etc.) each time he hears a whistle. Once he is doing this reliably the pitch (frequency) and loudness of the whistle are systematically changed to cover the full speech range. Each ear is tested separately using headphones.

Purine

A substance found in the body. Disturbances in the biochemical processes involving purines occur in a few disorders associated with mental handicap including the *Lesch-Nyhan syndrome*.

Purpura

Small purple areas or spots in the skin. It is caused by the leakage of blood from small blood vessels and this may occur at birth in a few conditions associated with mental handicap including *toxoplasmosis, congenital syphilis* and *rubella syndrome*.

Pycnodysostosis

A rare condition in which growth is restricted, bones are dense and fragile and the head is large. The person's face is small compared to the head and the chin is underdeveloped. The eyes may be rather prominent and the mouth may be large. Abnormalities and deformities of teeth and bones are common. Intelligence may be in the normal range but mental handicap is more common than usual. It is inherited from both parents who are carriers (*recessive inheritance*).

ELMORE, S.M. (1967) Pycnodysostosis: a review. J. Bone. Jt. Surg., 49A: 153–62.
SEDANO, H. et al (1968) Pycnodysostosis: clinical and genetic considerations. Am. J. Dis. Child., 116:70–77.

Pyknolepsy

= *absence status*.

Pyloric stenosis

Narrowing and tightness of the muscular lower end of the stomach around the opening where food passes to the next part of the bowel (the duodenum). Usually an infant is born with this condition in which severe vomiting becomes evident soon after birth. Sometimes it is acquired later in life. Occasionally pyloric stenosis occurs as part of a syndrome associated with mental handicap as in *Apert's syndrome, Beckwith syndrome, Smith-Lemli-Opitz syndrome, Edward's syndrome* and *Down's syndrome*.

Pyridoxine / vitamin B6

A vitamin of the B6 group which is necessary for many important biochemical processes to take place in the body. It is used in the treatment of *pyridoxine dependency*, some types of *homocystinuria* and *cystathioninuria*. Pyridoxine may also be effective in the treatment of premenstrual tension. Pyridoxine is water soluble, readily excreted and harmless

Pyridoxine dependency / pyridoxine deficiency syndrome

This is a disorder in which an abnormal *enzyme* requires much higher levels of *pyridoxine* than usual if it is to function effectively. Without these high pyridoxine levels there is a tendency to have *epilepsy* and excess irritability. This becomes evident at birth or soon after. Untreated children are mentally handicapped, epileptic and have *cerebral palsy*. Treatment in the early stages prevents brain damage but later treatment does not.

SCRIVER, C.R. (1960) Vitamin B6 dependency and infantile convulsions. Pediatrics, 26:62.

SCRIVER, C.R. & HUTCHISON, J.H. (1963) Vitamin B6 deficiency syndrome in human infancy: Biochemical and clinical observations. Pediatrics, 31:240.

Q

Quadriplegia / quadriparesis
A type of *cerebral palsy*.

Quality assurance / quality of care
The guarantee of a service which provides quality as defined by criteria such as effectiveness; appropriateness; acceptability to consumers and providers; fairness of access and distribution; and economy. In the *evaluation* of services for mentally handicapped people it is important to include measurements of the quality of care. The *Program Analysis of Service Systems* is one way of doing so. It is generally understood that such evaluation will lead to corrective or remedial action if services do not meet the desired standards.

Quiet room
See *time out*.

R

Rachischisis

A type of *meningomyelocoele* in which the *spinal cord* (neural tube) is wide open, commonly in the middle of the back. Sometimes this term is used to refer to complete splitting of the back of the entire vertebral column (backbone) and skull with exposure of the brain and spinal cord.

Radio-ulnar synostosis

The two bones of the forearm (radius and ulnar) are fused together and movements of the forearm at the elbow are restricted. This may occur in *Treacher-Collins syndrome, arthrogryposis multiplex congenita* and several conditions in which there are abnormalities of the sex *chromosomes*.

Ramsay Hunt syndrome

A condition in which there is *myoclonic epilepsy* and unsteadiness (*cerebellar ataxia*) sometimes associated with deterioration in mental function.

BIRD, T.D. & SHAW, C.M. (1978) Progressive myoclonus and epilepsy with dentatorubral degeneration: a clinicopathological study of the Ramsay Hunt syndrome. J. Neurol. Neurosurg. Psychiat., 41:140.
NAITO, H. & OYANAGI, S. (1982) Familial myoclonus epilepsy and choreoathetosis: hereditary dentatorubral pallidoluysian atrophy. Neurology, 32:798.

Rate recording

The recording of the frequency with which a particular behaviour has occurred. This measure is used in *behaviour modification*.

Raven's Standard Progressive Matrices

An *intelligence test* which does not depend on any language skills. It is particularly useful for assessing people with a hearing impairment. Diagrammatic shapes and patterns are presented in 60 sets of increasing difficulty (5 groups of 12) and the person has to select the correct piece from a number of alternatives in order to complete a design which has one piece missing. The coloured progressive matrices are more suitable for mentally handicapped people because they start from a lower ability level.

RAVEN, J.C. (1965) The Progressive Matrices Scales. London: H.K. Lewis.

Reactive depression

See *depression*.

Reading disability

= *dyslexia*.

Reading-Free Vocational Interest Inventory

This is a test which does not depend on reading ability and which provides systematic information on the vocational interests of mentally handicapped people. It is suitable for adults and teenagers who need help in selecting areas of work which will suit their interests. The inventory has a male and female section. The female interest areas include personal service, laundry service and light industrial while the male areas include building trades, automotive and animal care. It is standardized by separate norms for people in institutions and people in schools. The student is asked to point to the one of three pictures which is the type of work he or she would enjoy. This scale particularly helps to distinguish between preferences for mechanical rather than person-orientated vocations.

BECKER, R.L. (1975) A.A.M.D. – Becker Reading-free Vocational Interest Inventory.

Washington, D.C.: American Association on Mental Deficiency.

Rebus Reading Symbols / Peabody Rebus Reading Scheme

These symbols are diagrammatic represent-ations (*pictographs*) which were designed to interest and help children in learning to read. They have also been used as a communication system for people who are able to point but unable to speak. They were regarded as too complex for most mentally handicapped people to use and *Blissymbolics* were generally preferred. Recently they have been reported to be extremely useful in developing language and reading skills in mentally handicapped children.

CLARK, C.R. & WOODCOCK, R.W. (1976) Graphic systems in communication. In: Communication, Assessment and Interven-tion Strategies. Lloyd, L. (Ed.). Baltimore: University Park Press.

VAN OOSTERAM, J. & DEVEREAUX, K. Learning with Rebuses – Glossary of Rebus and Teaching Packs, EARO, The Resource Centre, Back Hill, Ely, Cambridgeshire, U.K. CB7 4DA.

WOODCOCK, R.W. (1967) Peabody Rebus Reading Program. American Guidance Service. Windsor, U.K.: NFER/Nelson.

Receptive dysphasia

See *dysphasia*.

Receptive Expressive Emergent Language Scale

A scale for assessing the understanding and use of language. It covers the developmental age range from birth to 3 years. The items are grouped as either receptive or expres-sive. It is completed with the primary carer and does not require the active co-operation of the subject. The person administering the test does need a specialist knowledge of language assessments although some technical jargon is used. It is based on normal development and the stages are small and detailed specific equipment is required for some items. Three behaviours are used to assess comprehension and expression at each age level. Language is scored as typical, emergent or absent.

BZOCH, K.R. & LEAGUE, R. (1970) The Bzoch-League Receptive, Expressive, Emergent Language Scale. Florida: Anninya Press.

BZOCH, K.R. & LEAGUE, R. (1971) Assess-ing Language Skills in Infancy (Handbook for the Receptive Expressive Emergent Language Scale). Gainesville, Florida: Tree of Life Press.

Receptive Expressive Language Assessment for the Visually Im-paired (RELA)

A specific language test covering the developmental range from birth to 6 years. It is intended for use with severely visually impaired and blind children. It covers auditory awareness; imitation; vocalization; vocabulary; knowledge of use of objects; body image; concept development; verbal reasoning; memory and use of grammar.

ANDERSON, G.M. (1977) Receptive Expres-sive Emergent Language Assessment for the Visually Impaired 0–6, Ingham Inter-mediate School District. Michigan: Mason.

Recessive gene / recessive inheri-tance

The majority of characteristics of human beings are determined by the genetic make-up of the individual. *Genes* are on the *chromosomes* which are paired and carry one set of genes from each parent. The effects of a recessive gene can be suppressed or over-ridden by the activity of the gene from the other parent (*dominant gene*). The presence of one abnormal recessive gene may not, therefore, be evident because of the normal activity of the dominant gene. The person is a carrier of that abnormal gene but has no symptoms or signs of the condition it may cause. It is likely that the majority of people carry one or more abnormal recessive genes. If, however, a person inherits the same abnormal gene from both parents, there is no normal gene to suppress the effects (by making the necessary *enzyme*) and the person has the symptoms and signs of the condition. This is known as recessive inheritance. There are many examples of recessive inheritance associated with mental handicap including the *amino acidurias, gangliosidoses* and *ceroid lipofuscinoses*. When both parents carry the same abnormal gene, at each conception there is a 1 in 4 (25%) chance that the child will inherit the same defective gene from both parents and will be affected. There is a 1 in 2 (50%) chance that the child will be a carrier and a 1 in 4 (25%) chance that the child will have 2 normal genes. Carriers should avoid marrying relatives as there is a greater likelihood that they will carry the same abnormal gene.

Recklinghausen's disease
= *Von Recklinghausen's disease.*

REEL Scale
= *Receptive, Expressive, Emergent Language Scale.*

Reflex
The involuntary and immediate response of a muscle to stimulation of the nerves which receive sensations from the muscle, tendon or skin. There are many characteristic reflex actions seen in the body as a response to different types of stimulation in different places. The knee jerk is one example. Faults in these reflexes provide important diagnostic information as to the presence and location of disorders of the nervous system. Excessive reflex jerks are a sign of *spasticity* due to damage to the upper parts of the nervous system.

Reflex epilepsy
Seizures that are repeatedly initiated by a particular type of stimulus. *Photic induced seizures* are the most common form.

Refraction / Refractive error
Refraction is the deflection of rays of light as they pass from one substance to another of different density. This occurs in the eye and is one of the ways in which light is focused on the *retina*. Spectacles are used to correct refractive abnormalities (*myopia, presbyopia, astigmatism, hypermetropia*, etc.) of the eyes.

Refsum's syndrome
A disease which does not become evident until 4 to 7 years of age. It is caused by increased quantities of certain fats (lipids) being deposited throughout the body and the blood levels of phytanic acid are abnormally high due to an *enzyme* (phytanic acidoxidase) deficiency. The disease usually starts with abnormal functioning of the nerves in the limbs (peripheral neuropathy) and gradual wasting of the muscles. Unsteadiness, impaired vision (*retinitis pigmentosa*), hearing loss and dry skin gradually develop. It is treated with a phytol-free diet and vitamin A and E supplements. It is not associated with severe mental handicap but affected individuals are reported as having below-average intelligence. Mental development is arrested and followed by varying degrees of mental deterioration.

An infantile phytanic acid storage disease has been described in which there is severe mental handicap, enlargement of liver and spleen and the other symptoms of Refsum's syndrome with the exception of peripheral neuropathy. Refsum's syndrome is inherited from both parents who are carriers (*recessive inheritance*) and can be diagnosed from enzyme estimation following *amniocentesis* and in carriers following *fibroblast culture*.

GIBBERD, F.B. et al (1979) Heredopathia atactia polyneuritiformis (Refsum's syndrome) treated by diet and plasma-exchange. Lancet, I:575–578.

SCOTTO, J.M. et al (1982) Infantile phytanic acid storage disease, a possible variant of Refsum's syndrome. J. Inherited Metab. Dis., 5:83.

STEINBERG, D. et al (1970) Phytanic acid in patients with Refsum's syndrome and response to dietary treatment. Arch. Intern. Med., 125:75.

Registered Nurse for the Mentally Handicapped (RNMH)

This a statutory qualification in the U.K. which is gained after completing a three-year course. In 1982 the General Nursing Council published a revised syllabus which covers a wide range of opportunities and experiences which nurses are likely to encounter in a professional career in hospitals or in the community. It defines their role as 'directly and skilfully to assist the individual and his family, whatever the handicap, in the acquisition, development and maintenance of skills . . . and to do it in such a way as to enable independence to be gained as rapidly and as fully as possible, in an environment that maintains the quality of life that will be acceptable for those citizens of this day and age.'

Regression

To go backwards. This usually refers to a loss of skills previously acquired especially those basic skills related to early childhood. This may be seen in those *degenerative disorders* which have an onset later in infancy or childhood. It may also occur in some *psychiatric illnesses* such as *depression*.

Regurgitation

The bringing up of food or fluid from the stomach to the mouth. This may be caused by over-feeding or wind. It may occur in people who have paralysis of the throat or soft palate. It is sometimes a behaviour problem perpetuated by the attention received or by *rumination*.

BALL, T.S. et al (1974) A special feeding technique for chronic regurgitation. Am. J. Ment. Defic., 78:486–493.

Rehabilitation

A process which aims to restore a handicapped person to a situation in which he can make best use of his abilities within a social context which is as normal as possible. It is the same process as that of *habilitation* but is applied to people who have lost skills or opportunities due to *institutionalization*, illness or *disability*.

Rehabilitation Act (1973) (Public Laws 93–112)

In the U.S.A. this law requires agencies with government contracts to have an active programme for employing disabled people. Discrimination against disabled people is forbidden. Section 504 states that 'No other qualified handicapped individual in the United States . . . shall solely by reason of his handicap, be excluded from the participation in, be denied the benefits of, or be subjected to discrimination under any program or activity receiving federal financial assistance or under any program or activity conducted by any executive agency or by the United States Postal Service.' Detailed regulations emphasize the importance of *integration*, although the idea of access to equally effective services cannot guarantee or require that the handicapped persons be effected 'equal opportunity to obtain the same result, to gain the same benefit . . . in the most integrated setting appropriate to the person's needs.'

HERR, S.S. (1983) Rights and Advocacy for Retarded People. Lexington, Mass.: Lexington Books. pp. 169–170.

Reinforcement / reinforcer

A term used in *behaviour modification* for the consequences of a behaviour which will affect the frequency of that behaviour. A positive reinforcement (reward) is the provision of something the person is known to like, as a direct reward for a particular appropriate or desirable behaviour. It should increase the frequency of that behaviour. A negative reinforcement involves the removal of an unpleasant stimulus as soon as the desired behaviour occurs so that the person changes his behaviour in order to avoid the negative reinforcement. The undesirable behaviour is therefore weakened and the desired behaviour increased. This is different from *punishment* techniques. Sometimes it is sufficient just to eliminate the reinforcement of a behaviour; this is called *extinction*.

Many things can act as reinforcers and these generally fall into two groups: primary (food, drink, warmth, etc.) and secondary (money, praise, attention, tokens, etc.). It is important to identify rewards which will be reinforcing to a particular individual. When none can be found the *Premack principle* may be used. In order to be successful reinforcement must also be provided immediately, consistently, frequently, clearly and only in association with that behaviour. Continuous reinforcement is a schedule of reinforcement in which a behaviour is reinforced every time it occurs. Intermittent reinforcement is a schedule of reinforcement in which a behaviour is not reinforced every time. This is usually very effective in strengthening behaviour. Fixed interval reinforcement is a schedule of intermittent reinforcement under which a specified behaviour is only reinforced following a fixed time interval since the previous reinforcement. Fixed ratio reinforcement is a schedule of intermittent reinforcement under which reinforcement is presented following a specified number of correct responses. Systematic and specific reinforcement should be used as part of a well-planned behaviour-modification programme but it is always a good principle to positively reinforce desirable behaviours and to avoid reinforcing undesirable behaviours. See also *differential reinforcement of other behaviours*.

HEMSLEY, R. & CARR, J. (1980) Ways of increasing behaviour reinforcement. In: Behaviour Modification for the Mentally Handicapped. Yule, W. & Carr, J. London: Croom Helm. pp. 33–47.

Relief care
= *phased care.*

Remedial gymnastics
There is very little difference between the work of a remedial gymnast and that of a *physiotherapist* when working with mentally handicapped people. The aim of remedial gymnasts is to gain as much active movement as possible from the person and to encourage the motivation to continue exercises without help. Very often sports, games and group activities are used.

Renal
To do with the kidneys. Abnormalities of the kidneys are sometimes found in conditions associated with mental handicap.

Renpenning's syndrome
A condition occurring only in males (*sex-linked inheritance*) in which there is short stature, abnormal ears, a prominent jaw, small head and mental handicap. Some authors consider it to be the same as *fragile-X syndrome* but in the original family described by Renpenning fragile sites were not found and therefore other authors restrict the term to sex-linked mental handicap with a small head (*microcephaly*) but without fragile sites on the X-*chromosome*.

FOX, P. et al (1980) X-linked mental retardation: Renpenning revisited. Am. J. Med. Genet., 7:491–495.
RENPENNING, H. et al (1962) Familial sex-linked mental retardation. Canad. Med. J., 87:954–956.

Resonance board
Some therapists use resonance boards for mentally handicapped people who have a visual handicap. A wooden board is supported an inch or so off the floor and the person lies or sits on it. Sounds and movement made by the client are accentuated due to resonance and therefore provide more feedback than usual. This may motivate the client to move.

Respite care
= *phased care.*

Respondents

A term used in *behaviour modification* to describe responses which are elicited by preceding stimulation. These occur in a reflex and involuntary manner. Examples are salivation, knee-jerks and dilation of the pupils of the eyes. Such responses are controlled by *antecedents*.

Response co-variation

A term used in *behaviour modification* to refer to a situation in which two or more responses are related in such a way that changes in one affects the others. Extinguishing aggressive behaviour, for example, could lead to an increase in friendly behaviour or an increase in *self-injurious behaviour*. Behaviours therefore need to be assessed so that negatively and positively correlated responses can be identified.

KAZDIN, A.E. (1982) Symptom substitution, generalization and response co-variation: implications for psychotherapy outcome. Psychol. Bull., 91:349–65.

Response cost

A procedure sometimes used when a person is on a *behaviour modification* training programme using *tokens* (points, stars, plastic discs, etc.). A number of tokens are deducted when a particular undesirable behaviour occurs and this is known as response cost. It should not be used with primary *reinforcers* and, because it is a *punishment* procedure, should always be carefully planned and monitored.

BURCHARD, J.D. & BARRERA, F. (1972) Analysis of time-out and response cost in a programmed environment. J. Appl. Behav. Anal., 5:271–82.
GATHERCOLE, C. & CARR, J. (1980) The use of tokens with individuals and groups. In: Behaviour Modification for the Mentally Handicapped. Yule, W. & Carr, J. (Eds.). London: Croom Helm; Baltimore: University Park Press. pp. 48–68.
KAZDIN, A.E. (1971) The effect of response cost in suppressing behaviour in a pre-

psychotic retardate. J. Behav. Ther. Exp. Psychiat., 2:137–140.
SALEND, S.J. & KOVALICH, B. (1981) A group response-cost system mediated by free tokens: an alternative to token reinforcement. Am. J. Ment. Defic., 86:184–7.

Response shaping

See *shaping*.

Restitution / restitutional overcorrection

See *overcorrection*.

Restraint

On the rare occasions when a mentally handicapped person is violent or aggressive to himself or others, circumstances may arise where physical restraint is necessary. The use of restraint is a means of managing a potentially dangerous situation and restoring calm. It should never be a punishment. In a care situation any management which involves physical restraint should be written down and approved by a team which includes senior members of staff. There are a number of recognized restraint techniques including the use of a large duvet, the Warrendale technique for holding children, holding the person against a wall and other techniques for particular forms of attack. These cannot be easily described and a training workshop with role play is essential if staff are to use physical restraint effectively and therapeutically. Many authorities issue their own guidelines on the use of sanctions and restraint.

Restricted growth

Underdevelopment of the body particularly in relation to height. There are a number of types depending on the underlying cause. Short stature with a low birth weight occurs in several *chromosome* disorders, congenital *cytomegalic inclusion disease, rubella syndrome, Donohue's syndrome, Prader-Willi syndrome, Rubinstein-Taybi syndrome, bird-headed dwarfism, Silver's syndrome, Smith-Lemli-Opitz syndrome* and other rare conditions. Short stature with normal birth weight occurs in *Chotzen's syndrome, congenital hypothyroidism,* and several other rare conditions. Short-limbed dwarfism occurs in *achondroplasia, camptomelic dwarfism, Apert's syndrome, de Lange syndrome, Rothmund-Thomson syndrome, Silver's syndrome* and a few other rare conditions.

Further information:
Association for Research into Restricted Growth, 2 Mount Court, 87 Central Hill, London SE19 1BS.

Restriction order
Section 41 of the *Mental Health Act 1983* allows a crown court to impose a restriction order if, following an offence, it is thought necessary for the protection of the public from serious harm. This restricts the offender's discharge from hospital for a specified period or indefinitely. Leave or discharge from hospital are only possible with the consent of the Home Secretary.

Retardation
= *mental retardation.*

Rethoré's syndrome
A condition caused by *partial trisomy* of the short arm of *chromosome* 9. Most affected infants survive to have a normal life expectancy although feeding may be poor and weight below normal for age. Walking is attained before 4 years of age but speech is poorly developed. Mental handicap is variable from mild to severe. The forehead, nose and upper lips are prominent with deeply set eyes and a small lower jaw. The eyes tend to be widely spaced, small and a squint is common. The corners of the mouth are downturned and the ears are large, often low-set and prominent. A small size and *brachycephalic* shape to the head are usual. The fingers are small and/or abnormal especially the fifth finger which is curved. Single transverse *palmar creases* and a single crease on the fifth finger are usual. Fingernails may be abnormal. The shoulders are narrow and sloping and spinal curvature is

common. The genitals are underdeveloped. *Congenital heart disease* has been described in a few people with this condition. Behaviour problems are not reported. Very often this condition is caused by a parent being a balanced carrier of a *chromosome translocation*. The average parental age is not increased. It can be detected during pregnancy following *amniocentesis.*

BLANK, C.E. et al (1975) Physical and mental defect of chromosomal origin in four individuals of the same family. Trisomy of the short arm of 9. Clin. Genet., 7:261.
ZAREMBA, J. et al (1974) Four cases of 9p trisomy resulting from a balanced familial translocation. Clinical picture and cytogenetic findings. J. Ment. Defic. Res., 18:153.

Retina
The light-sensitive lining on the inside of the back of the eye. Images are received by the retina and transmitted, via the *optic nerve*, to the visual area of the brain (*occipital lobe*).

Retinal degeneration
Deterioration of the special light-sensitive cells in the *retina* resulting in impairment of vision. It occurs in a few conditions associated with mental handicap including *Hunter's syndrome, Cockayne's syndrome, Laurence-Moon-Biedl syndrome* and *Hallermann-Streiff syndrome*. It is usually associated with *retinitis pigmentosa.*

Retinal detachment
Detachment of the *retina* of the eye from the layer surrounding it (*choroid*) into the jelly-like fluid in the centre of the eye. This detachment, if complete, causes total blindness in that eye. This may rarely occur in *tuberose sclerosis, aniridia-Wilm's tumour syndrome* and *homocystinuria.*

Retinitis pigmentosa / retinal pigmentation
A degeneration of the *retina* of the eye due to the deposition of abnormal amounts of

pigment. This can occur as an isolated, usually inherited, disease of gradual onset in childhood. It sometimes occurs as a feature of another disease as in *Hunter's syndrome, Sanfilippo syndrome, Laurence-Moon-Biedl syndrome, Rud's syndrome* and *Refsum's syndrome*.

Retinoblastoma

This is a tumour of the eye present in childhood. Some children with this condition have abnormalities of *chromosome* 13. Although many of the children with retinoblastoma are mentally and physically normal, it may be associated with a small head, high-arched palate, low-set ears and abnormalities of eyes, fingers, genitals and limbs. Mild to severe mental handicap is then common.

HOWARD, R.O. (1982) Chromosome errors in retinoblastoma. Birth Defects Original Article Series. 18(6):703–727.
VOGEL, F. (1979) Genetics of retinoblastoma. Hum. Genet., 52:1–54.

Retinodiencephalic degeneration
= *Laurence-Moon-Biedl syndrome*.

Retinoscopy

A method for measuring the *refractive error* in the eye of a person who cannot understand the usual eye-testing procedures. Eye drops are used to dilate the pupil of the eye and to temporarily paralyse the focusing. It is then possible to measure the point at which light is focused by the lens of the eye using an instrument known as a retinoscope.

Retrolental fibroplasia / retinopathy of prematurity (ROP)

A condition caused by oxygen treatment of premature infants. In severe cases a fibrous plate develops behind the lens of the eye. Less serious damage causes a wrinkling or folding of the *retina* but visual impairment becomes severe if the *macula* of the eye is involved or if the retina becomes detached. Since the cause has been discovered the oxygen levels are kept as low as possible in the incubators for severely premature infants. *Prematurity* is also sometimes followed by mental handicap and, among blind mentally handicapped children with retrolental fibroplasia, *spasticity* is common. Behavioural disturbances such as rocking, handflapping and *eye-poking* are also often seen.

Rett's syndrome

A very rare disorder which only affects girls. There is an apparently normal development up to at least 9 months of age followed by a *regression* in behaviour and skills. There is usually a reduction in the rate of head growth and a particular loss of manipulative ability. This is replaced by characteristic hand-wringing movements usually by the age of 4 years. Over-breathing, breath holding, air swallowing and grinding of teeth often occur. There is usually a marked change in emotional development and behaviour especially with withdrawal and anxiety (*autistic* features). *Spasticity* of limbs increases with age and if walking is achieved this is usually with an unsteady, wide-based, stiff-legged gait. Curvature of the spine may develop. *Epilepsy* is common. Mental handicap is usually severe. Life expectancy is reasonable. No cause has yet been found for this condition.

HAGBERG, B. et al (1983) A progressive syndrome of autism, dementia and loss of purposeful hand use in girls: Rett's syndrome – Report of 35 cases. Ann. Neurol., 14:471.
KERR, A.M. (1987) Report on the Rett syndrome workshop, Glasgow, Scotland, 1986. J. Ment. Defic. Res., 31:93–113.

Further information:
U.K. Rett Syndrome Association, 150, Kingsway, Pettswood, Orpington, Kent. BR5 1PU.

Reward
See *reinforcement*.

Reye syndrome

A condition which has a sudden onset in a child of previously normal development. Vomiting, impaired consciousness, *seizures*, liver damage, *hypoglycaemia* and raised blood ammonia levels are usual. Brain damage, probably due to ammonia intoxication, may leave the child with mental and/or physical handicap. It has sometimes occurred following viral infections and there is a possible association with treatment with aspirin.

BENJAMIN, P.Y. et al (1982) Intellectual and emotional sequelae of Reye's syndrome. Crit. Care Med., 10: 583.
BRUNNER, R.L. et al (1979) Neuropsychologic consequences of Reye syndrome. J. Pediatr., 95:706.

Reynell Developmental Language Scales

A test designed to assess the development of verbal expression and comprehension in children. It covers a developmental age range from 5 months to 7 years and scores the person on a verbal comprehension age and expressive language age in years and months. The test materials consist of a set of manipulative objects including small dolls, furniture, clothing, domestic and farmyard animals and a set of five pictures illustrating the everyday activities of a family. The verbal comprehension scale is in nine sections which follow the normal pattern of development of understanding of language. There is an alternative scale designed for physically handicapped children which requires a minimum of response from the child. The expressive scale is in three sections: language structure, vocabulary and content.

REYNELL, J. (1977) Reynell Developmental Language Scales. Windsor, England: National Foundation for Educational Research (NFER).

Reynell-Zinkin Scales

Scales designed specifically to enable professionals concerned with young visually handicapped children to have some guidelines and developmental advice. It covers the developmental range from 2 months to 5 years and includes scales on social adaptation, sensori-motor understanding, exploration of environment, response to sound and verbal comprehension, and expressive language. A special subscale for communication is available for assessing people who have *cerebral palsy, deafness*, specific language difficulties or who are *deaf-blind*. The scales were standardized on visually impaired children including those with multiple handicaps.

REYNELL, J. (1975) The Reynell-Zinkin Scales: Developmental Scales for Young Visually Handicapped Children – Part I: Mental Development. Windsor: NFER.
REYNELL, J. & ZINKIN, P. (1975) New procedures for the developmental assessment of young children with severe visual handicaps. Child: Care, Health & Development, 1:69–75.

Rhabdomyoma

A tumour occurring in the heart muscle in about half the people with *tuberose sclerosis*. Characteristically these tumours are multiple, benign and well circumscribed. They may cause heart failure especially immediately after birth.

Rhesus incompatibility

See *haemolytic disease of the newborn*.

Rickets

A softening of the bones in childhood usually due to vitamin D and calcium deficiency in the diet. If untreated deformities of the bones, especially of the legs, may develop. Prolonged use of *phenytoin* and *phenobarbitone* may very rarely cause rickets by inducing low calcium levels in the body. Rickets may develop in *Lowe's syndrome* and *cerebro-hepato-renal syndrome*.

Riding for the Disabled

Riding can be introduced from 4 years of

age or earlier. It helps the child with *cerebral palsy* by improving balance, promoting relaxation, establishing a good position with legs apart, encouraging co-ordination and providing mobility. All children benefit by gaining confidence and self-esteem and from the new range of experiences provided.

WALKER, G.M. (1978) Riding for the Disabled. Physiotherapy, 64(10):297.

Further information:
Riding for the Disabled Association, Avenue R, National Agricultural Centre, Kennilworth, Warwickshire, U.K.

Rieger's syndrome
A rare disorder in which abnormalities of the front of the eye may cause visual impairment. There are various abnormalities of the teeth and the lower jaw protrudes. Weakness of muscles (*muscular dystrophy*) and abnormalities of the bones are often present. Mental handicap sometimes occurs. It is inherited from one parent who may be only mildly affected (*dominant inheritance*) or may arise as a spontaneous mutation.

FEINGOLD, M. et al (1969) Rieger's syndrome. Pediatrics, 44:564.
SALMON, M.A. (1978) Developmental Defects and Syndromes. Aylesbury, Bucks: HM+M Publishers. p. 144.

Rights
See *human rights*.

Riley-Day syndrome
A condition in which there is excessive sweating, poor temperature control, skin blotching, defective tear production, indifference to pain, poor co-ordination and loss of *reflexes*. The face is thin and often lacking in expression. The eyes are often widely spaced. Floppy muscles and a weak cry may be evident at birth and regurgitation and vomiting of food can be a problem. During childhood slow physical development is often accompanied by a mild degree of

mental handicap. Spinal curvature frequently occurs. It is inherited from both parents who are carriers (*recessive inheritance*).

AXELROD, F.B. & ABULARRAGE, J.J. (1982) Familial dysautonomia. A prospective study of survival. J. Pediatr., 101:234.
MAHLOUDJI, M. et al (1970) Clinical neurological aspects of familial dysautonomia. J. Neurol. Sci., 11:383.

Ring 13q
= *Orbeli syndrome*.

Ring chromosomes
= *chromosome rings*.

Risk-taking
In the past there has been a tendency for carers to be very protective toward mentally handicapped people. It is now recognized that learning and decision-making require trial and error. Mentally handicapped people have a need and right to learn in this way in order to have access to the learning opportunities required to increase independence and self-confidence. When making decisions on risk-taking, carers should estimate both the seriousness of the risk and the probability of its occurring. When there is a risk with potentially very serious consequences (e.g. injury or death) then the probability of such a risk should be reduced to the minimum possible. Where the consequences are minor, e.g. public embarrassment or burnt toast, then a far higher probability of such a consequence occurring can be tolerated. To ensure that properly informed decisions are made it is necessary for all interested and involved people to be consulted when planning training programmes which involve risk. Procedures should include ways of reducing the risk element and ways of dealing with any harm which could occur. Careful records should be kept.

FERGUSON, H. (1985) Risk-taking and Mentally Handicapped People. Guidelines for Staff. Isle of Wight District Health

Authority and Isle of Wight County Council: Mental Handicap Joint Management Team.

PERSKE, R. (1972) The dignity of risk and the mentally retarded. Ment. Retardation, 10: 24–26.

Ritalin

= *methylphenidate.*

Rivotril

= *clonazepam.*

RNMH

= *Registered Nurse for the Mentally Handicapped.*

Robert's syndrome

A very rare condition in which there is a marked shortening of all limbs and *cleft lip / palate.* The head size is small and the eyes are protuberant, widely spaced and often abnormal in structure. The lower jaw is small. Severely restricted growth and severe mental handicap occur in the few children who survive infancy. It is inherited from both parents who are carriers (*recessive inheritance*).

FREEMAN, M.V.R. et al (1974) The Robert's syndrome. Clin. Genet., 5:1–16.
HOLMES, L.B. et al (1972) Mental Retardation. New York: Macmillan. pp. 344–345.

Robin sequence

= *Pierre Robin syndrome.*

Rocker-bottom foot / heel

The heel of the foot is wide and prominent in this deformity which may be due to an abnormal shape or position of the talus bone. It is often associated with a *club foot* (talipes equino-varus) in which the shape of the foot curves outward giving it a 'rocker bottom' appearance. This may occur in *German's syndrome, Edward's syndrome* and a few other rare *chromosome* abnormalities.

Rocky Mountain Spotted Fever

This condition, caused by infection with a microscopic organism (rickettsia), has been reported from almost all parts of the U.S.A. It is carried by animal ticks and infection occurs when bitten in the presence of the faeces of the tick. The rickettsia damage the lining of the small blood vessels throughout the body causing small thromboses (blood clots) and haemorrhages (bleeding). *Meningo-encephalitis* and various *neurological* abnormalities develop after an incubation period of 4 to 8 days. There is also a fever and a rash. After apparent recovery residual damage to the nervous system may remain including mental handicap, poor co-ordination and floppy muscles. It is treated with suitable antibiotics.

ROSENBLUM, M.J. et al (1952) Residual effects of rickettsial disease on the central nervous system. Arch. Intern. Med., (Chicago) 90:444.
WRIGHT, L. (1972) Intellectual sequelae of Rocky Mountain Spotted Fever. J. Abnorm. Psychol., 80:315.

Room management model / scheme

When mentally handicapped people are cared for in groups with poor staff ratios it is difficult to provide the individual attention and stimulation required by each client. A number of approaches to this problem have been devised which make maximum and most efficient use of staff time and skills. Each day is carefully structured and planned so as to provide time for group work and one-to-one work. One example, using two or more staff to a group, is the arrangement of activity periods of a specified duration during which one member of staff acts as room manager. This person provides each client with a choice of materials and encourages their use. The other member of staff works with one client at a time on an individual basis following detailed instructions on the programme for that client. All clients have at least one individual session during an activity period.

These procedures ensure that a member of staff is responsible for *prompting* and *reinforcing* appropriate behaviour of clients on a systematic basis.

MANSELL, J. et al (1982) Increasing purposeful activity of severely and profoundly mentally handicapped adults. Behav. Res. Ther., 20:593–604.
MCBRIEN, J. & WEIGHTMAN, J. (1980) The effects of room management procedures on the engagement of profoundly retarded children. Brit. J. Ment. Subn., 26:38–46.
PORTERFIELD, J. & BLUNDEN, R. (1981) Establishing activity periods in day settings for profoundly handicapped adults: a replication study. J. Practical Approaches to Developmental Handicap, 5:10–17.

Roseola

A common infection in infancy which causes a rapid rise in body temperature for 3 to 5 days. This subsides with the appearance of a characteristic rash. Sometimes, in very young children, the *intracranial pressure* is raised in the early stages and *seizures* may occur. Although they are usually harmless, persistent complications have been reported very rarely. These include weakness of one side of the body, *epilepsy* and mental handicap.

BURNSTINE, R.C. & PAINE, R.S. (1959) Residual encephalopathy following roseola infantum. Am. J. Dis. Child., 98:144.

Rothmund-Thomson syndrome

A rare condition in which there is a skin rash (*poikiloderma*) usually associated with sparse or short hair, small head, abnormalities of teeth and nails, *cataracts* of the eyes, abnormalities of the bones, restricted growth, underdeveloped genitals and low fertility. Several people with this condition have been described as being mentally handicapped but most are of normal intelligence. The expectation of life is normal so long as skin tumours are not allowed to develop. It is inherited from both parents who are carriers (*recessive inheritance*).

OATES, R.K. et al (1971) The Rothmund-Thomson syndrome: Case report of an unusual syndrome. Aust. Pediatr. J., 7:103.
SILVER, H.K. (1966) Rothmund-Thomson syndrome: An oculocutaneous disorder. Am. J. Dis. Child., 111:182.

Rowntree Trust / Rowntree Memorial Trust

This is a trust which administers, on behalf of the U.K. government, a fund known as the Family Fund. It is designed to help in situations not covered by other benefits such as the provisions of washing machines, tumble driers, holidays, transport problems, unusual aids or adaptations, driving lessons, extra clothing, special play equipment and many other items. It is available for severely disabled children who are 16 years of age or under and all families making first application receive a helpful and sympathetic *assessment* of their needs before a decision is made regarding the eligibility of the child and the suitability of the request.

BRADSHAW, J. (1980) The Family Fund. London: Routledge & Kegan Paul.

Further information:
Family Fund, P.O. Box 50, York, YO1 1UY.

Royal National Institute for the Blind

See *blindness*.

Royal National Institute for the Deaf

See *deafness*.

Royal Society for Mentally Handicapped Children and Adults (Mencap)

A registered charity in the U.K. with membership mainly consisting of parents and friends of mentally handicapped people. It was founded in 1946 as the Association of Parents of Backward Children and membership has steadily increased. The primary objectives are to create a sympathetic climate of public opinion toward mentally handicapped people, to increase public awareness and understanding of their problems and to secure the provisions that they need. It is supported by voluntary contributions. There are over 500 local groups which provide a wide variety of services and support to families. These are supported by regional offices. Mencap offers some residential services including the *Homes Foundation Scheme*. The leisure services are provided by the *Gateway Clubs* and the Mencap Holiday Services. There are welfare, legal, counselling, education, training and employment services. A journal, 'Parents Voice', is published quarterly.

Further information:
Mencap National Centre, 123 Golden Lane, London EC1Y 0RT.

Rubella Panencephalitis

A very rare progressive condition occurring after rubella (german measles) infection before birth, in childhood or in adult life. About 4 to 14 days after reinfection there is a gradual loss of intellectual skills (*dementia*), unsteadiness, increasing physical disability and *seizures*, usually *myoclonic seizures*. The condition progresses over several years and ultimately proves fatal. This disorder is caused by an unusual immune response to the virus and there is no known treatment. It can be diagnosed by the high levels of antibodies to rubella in the blood and *cerebro-spinal fluid* and the ratio between the two.

TOWNSEND, N.N. et al (1975) Progressive rubella panencephalitis: Late onset after congenital rubella. New Engl. J. Med., 292:990.
WEIL, M.L. et al (1975) Chronic progressive panencephalitis due to rubella virus. Arch. Neurol., 32:501.
WOLINSKY, J.S. et al (1976) Progressive rubella panencephalitis. Arch. Neurol., 33: 722.

Rubella syndrome

The rubella (german measles) virus causes a relatively harmless rash and mild illness in children and adults but if a mother has an infection during pregnancy the fetus is at risk of serious damage. Defects occur in almost all infants infected before the eleventh week of pregnancy and these include *congenital heart disease, cataracts,* other eye abnormalities, *sensori-neural deafness*, mental handicap, small head, *epilepsy* and *spasticity*. If the infection occurs between 13 and 16 weeks of pregnancy about one third of affected children develop deafness. Infection between the fourth and sixth month of pregnancy causes, in about two thirds, more subtle abnormalities such as communication problems and *developmental delay*. At birth infants may bleed more readily than normal and develop small haemorrhages in the skin (*purpura*). Low birth weight is usual. Enlargement of the liver and spleen may occur. Signs of *encephalitis* may also be present. These all improve in the first few weeks but babies showing signs of encephalitis are more likely to be mentally handicapped and to have quadriplegic *cerebral palsy*. *Autism* occurs much more frequently in children whose mothers have had rubella in pregnancy than in the general population. Problems which may develop some time after infancy are *rubella panencephalitis* and hormonal abnormalities (*diabetes mellitus, hypothyroidism* and *hyperthyroidism*). Developmental delay in the early years is not a reliable predictor of the degree of mental handicap in later years. Improvement or deterioration in the degree of mental handicap may occur. About 20% of infected babies die in the first year of life. There is no known treatment against rubella virus but the introduction of widespread vaccination of schoolgirls has had a major impact in reducing the frequency of this syndrome. It can be diagnosed by the presence of a specific antibody in the blood of the baby. The virus is present in the urine and throat swabs for at least twelve months.

CHESS, S. et al (1978) Behavioural consequences of congenital rubella. J. Paediat., 93:699–703.

KRUGMAN, S. & KATZ, S.L. (1981) Infectious Diseases of Children (7th edit.). St. Louis: C.V. Mosley. Chap. 25.

MENSER, M.A. et al (1969) Congenital rubella. Am. J. Dis. Child., 118:32.

MILLER, E. et al (1982) Consequences of confirmed maternal rubella at successive stages of pregnancy. Lancet, 2:781–784.

Rubinstein-Taybi syndrome

A condition in which mental handicap is associated with broad thumbs and toes and facial abnormalities. Feeding difficulties, due to poorly co-ordinated swallowing, can be a problem in the early weeks of life with the risk of inhaling fluids and developing pneumonia. This improves with time. The person's nose tends to be thin and widely spaced eyes slant downward from the nose. The jaw is small and the palate narrow and high-arched. The most common eye abnormalities are squint, *cataracts* and *refractive errors*. The ends of the thumbs and toes are particularly broad and sometimes bend toward the body. The other fingers and toes may be slightly longer than normal. All joints may bend more than usual and the person tends to walk with a stiff gait. Many affected people have an excessive amount of dark hair over the body. Restricted growth is usual. Mental handicap of variable extent generally occurs. *Epilepsy* is present in about 25% of people with this condition. Undescended testes are usual in the male. Abnormalities of the eyes, heart and kidneys have also been described. Survival to adult life is usual. Although this condition has occasionally been *familial*, the pattern of inheritance has not been established. No other causative factors have been found.

NAVEH, Y. & FRIEDMAN, A. (1976) A case of Rubinstein-Taybi. Clin. Pediat., 15: 779–783.

PADFIELD, C.J. et al (1968) The Rubinstein-Taybi syndrome. Arch. Dis. Childh., 43: 94–101.

RUBINSTEIN, J.H. (1969) The broad thumb syndrome – progress report 1968. Birth Defects Original Article Series, 5(2):25–41.

RUBINSTEIN, J.H. & TAYBI, H. (1963) Broad thumbs and toes and facial abnormalities. Am. J. Dis. Child., 105:588–608.

Rud's syndrome

A rare condition in which mental handicap is associated with dry, fissured scaly skin (ichthyosis) which is thickened especially over the elbows, knees, palms and soles. The skin condition may not appear until the second year of life and the nails and hair are also brittle and abnormal. Sweating is usually reduced and the body readily overheats. *Epilepsy* can start at any time in childhood. The genitals of the men are underdeveloped, the voice high pitched and infertility is usual. Many other *congenital* abnormalities have been described. Intellectual ability varies from dull normal to severe mental handicap. It is inherited from both parents who are carriers (*recessive inheritance*).

EWING, J.A. (1956) The association of oligophrenia and dsykeratosis. A clinical investigation and an enquiry into its implications. Am. J. Ment. Defic., 60:575.

YORK-MOORE, M.E. & RUNDLE, A.F. (1962) Rud's syndrome. J. Ment. Defic., 6:108.

Rumination

The chewing of *regurgitated* food for a while before spitting it out. If the problem becomes a persistent habit it may result in a loss of nourishment. It is more likely to occur in severely mentally handicapped people who are overactive or bored. It may be reduced if the person is kept quiet, but occupied, following meals. *Behaviour modification* techniques may be necessary to treat severe rumination.

FOXX, R.M. et al (1979) A food satiation and oral hygiene punishment program to suppress chronic rumination by retarded persons. J. Autism Dev. Dis., 9:399–412.

MARHOLIN, D. et al (1980) Response contingent task-aversion in treating chronic ruminative vomiting of institutionalized children. J. Ment. Defic. Res., 24:47–56.

Russell's dwarfism syndrome

= *Silver's syndrome.*

S

Saddle-back deformity

A deformity in which there is defective development of the bridge of the nose giving it a sunken appearance. This occurs in *congenital syphilis*.

Saethre-Chotzen syndrome

= *Chotzen's syndrome*.

Safety mechanics

= *restraint*.

Salaam seizures

= *Infantile spasms*.

Salivary levels

In some centres it is now possible to measure *anticonvulsants* in the saliva which avoids the necessity of blood tests when monitoring these drugs.

Sandhoff's disease

One of the *gangliosidoses* which is very similar to *Tay-Sachs disease*. It is caused by a deficiency of two *enzymes* (hexosaminidases A & B) whereas in Tay-Sachs disease only Type A is deficient. As well as the symptoms of Tay-Sachs disease there is also greater involvement of the internal organs of the body, such as the heart, kidneys, liver and spleen which are enlarged. The function of the heart may be impaired. Methods of inheritance and diagnosis are the same as for Tay-Sachs disease. Death most commonly occurs between 4 and 10 years of age.

JOHNSON, W.G. (1983) Genetic heterogeneity of hexosaminidase-deficiency disease. Res. Publ. Assoc. Res. Nerv. Ment. Dis., 60:215.
SANDHOFF, K. et al (1968) Deficient hexosaminidase activity in an exceptional case of Tay-Sachs disease with additional storage of kidney globoside in visceral organs. Life Sci., 7:283.

Sanfilippo syndrome

This is the most common of the *mucopolysaccharidoses* and is a disorder characterized by intellectual deterioration during the first few years of life. Four types (A, B, C and D) have been recognized which can be distinguished biochemically although the course of the disease is very similar in each. The condition is first noticed between 2 and 5 years of age and the degree of mental handicap gradually becomes more severe. There is some coarsening of the facial features but this is not as severe as in *Hunter's* or *Hurler's syndromes*. There is more hair than usual and the eyebrows may meet in the middle. Growth is only slightly reduced, the eyes are not affected and deafness only occasionally occurs due to recurrent infections. Diarrhoea occurs in more than half of the affected children. Difficulty in straightening the joints of the fingers is usual. Unsteadiness and shakiness develop and difficulty in swallowing is a late complication. The disease is steadily progressive and survival beyond 20 years of age is unusual. Deterioration is most rapid in Type A. The diagnosis is sometimes difficult to establish and may be missed on urine testing unless a 24-hour urine collection shows the presence of heparan sulphate which is produced in excess in this disease due to an *enzyme* deficiency. The measurement of enzyme levels in the blood or *fibroblast culture* confirms the diagnosis and identifies the type. There is no known treatment. It is inherited from both parents who are carriers (*recessive inheritance*) and can be detected during pregnancy following *amniocentesis*. It is also possible to diagnose the carrier state by means of enzyme estimation.

DANKS, D.M. et al (1972) The Sanfilippo syndrome. Clinical, biochemical, radiological, haematological and pathological features of nine cases. Aus. Paediatr. J., 8:174.

VAN DE KAMP, J.J. et al (1981) Genetic heterogeneity and clinical variability in the Sanfilippo syndrome (Types A, B and C). Clin. Genet., 20:152.

Santavuori's disease

One of the *ceroid-lipofuscinoses* in which there is intellectual deterioration becoming apparent between 9 months and 2 years of age. Unsteadiness, *myoclonic seizures* and *blindness* develop. The head ceases to grow and the *electroencephalogram* is abnormal. Two thirds of affected children never learn to walk. There is a steady deterioration leading to death. It is caused by an *enzyme* deficiency which is inherited from both parents who are carriers (*recessive inheritance*).

HABERLAND, C. & BRUNNGRABER, E.G. (1970) Early infantile neurolipidosis with failure of myelination. Arch. Neurol., 23:481.

SANTAVUORI, P. et al (1974) Infantile type of so-called neuronal ceroid-lipofuscinosis. Dev. Med. Child Neurology, 16:644.

Satiation

A term applied in *behaviour modification* to the situation in which a *reinforcer* has lost its effectiveness through over-use. It tends to occur most quickly with foods and least with social reinforcers. It can be minimized by the use of several reinforcers or by depriving the person of the reinforcer at all other times.

Scaphocephaly

A condition in which the skull is very long and narrow due to *craniostenosis*. There is early closure of the sagittal suture (a line along which skull bones join). The bridge of the nose is often depressed. Mental handicap is sometimes present and may be the result of failure to treat raised *intracranial*

pressure. Marked, untreated scaphocephaly has been described in people of normal intelligence. It is the usual skull shape in *Hunter's syndrome, Hurler's syndrome* and *Smith-Lemli-Opitz syndrome*.

Schedules of reinforcement

See *reinforcement*.

Scheie's syndrome

One of the *mucopolysaccharide* group of disorders. Intelligence is not impaired in this condition.

Schilder's disease / Schilder's diffuse sclerosis

This term has been considerably confused and applied to a variety of familial progressive conditions in which *demyelination* occurs. The *leucodystrophies* and *subacute sclerosing panencephalitis* are now regarded as different entities and the term restricted to a condition which is closely related to multiple sclerosis but which has an unremittingly progressive course. The onset is between 5 and 12 years of age in a previously healthy child. The demyelination of the nervous system causes the development of progressive intellectual impairment and abnormal gait. Various kinds of *seizures* are common as are attacks of screaming and crying. Neurological abnormalities which may develop later include visual impairment, deafness, weakness of one side of the body, unsteadiness and disturbances in swallowing. Progression is rapid with severe disability or death within 2 years. Sometimes there is raised *intracranial pressure* so that a brain tumour has to be excluded. The cause is not known.

POSER, C.M. & VAN BOGAERT, L. (1956) Natural history and evolution of the concept of Schilder's diffuse sclerosis. Acta Psychiat. Neurol. Scand., 31:285.

Schizencephaly

Abnormal development of the brain. It is cleft from the surface to the deep structures.

Such clefts usually follow the lines of the fissures which divide the *lobes* of the brain. The part of the brain affected is usually underdeveloped. It is generally caused by damage to the brain during the first 30 days of fetal life. The effect is a wide range of disabilities according to the site and extent of the cleft. These include floppiness, *cerebral palsy, seizures*, small head and mental handicap.

MILLER, G.M. et al (1984) Schizencephaly: A clinical and CT study. Neurology, 34:997.

Schizo affective disorder

A type of *psychiatric illness* in which there are symptoms of *schizophrenia* and *affective disorder*.

Schizophrenia

A *psychiatric illness* with the onset most usually in the second or third decade. It is slightly more common in mentally handicapped people. The diagnosis can only be made with certainty in people who have some language skills. The person may have ideas that he or she is being influenced by other people or objects, have disjointed thoughts or may have *hallucinations* or *delusions*. The person's level of functioning deteriorates and he often becomes more withdrawn and less accessible. Emotions may be flat or inappropriate. In mentally handicapped people hallucinations are generally simple or assumed from the person's behaviour. Delusions are often naïve and wish-fulfilling or paranoid in nature. *Paranoid* schizophrenia generally has a later onset. Treatment with *phenothiazines* or similar drugs brings about an improvement in most people and the disorder may run a chronic and persisting course or there may be prolonged remissions. Relapse may occur when under emotional stress or when phenothiazines are withdrawn. *Rehabilitation* and support within the community is an important aspect of care.

HEATON-WARD, W.A. (1977) Psychoses in

mental handicap. Brit. J. Psychiat., 130: 525–533.
REID, A.H. (1972) Psychoses in adult mental defectives. II Schizophrenia and paranoid psychoses. Brit. J. Psychiat., 120: 213–218.

Further information:
National Schizophrenia Fellowship, 17 Cannon St., Birmingham. B2 5EN.

Schonell Evaluation and Accreditation Procedure (SEAP)

A method for evaluating residential services. It was developed in Australia for the Federal Department of Social Security. There are three stages. In the first stage each facility in the services completes a form about the aims, objectives, size, staffing, clients and activities. The next stage is a visit by a team with different backgrounds and expertise. The final stage is based on a report consisting of recommended objectives and service developments. There is a handbook describing the procedure. It is a more structured, but similar, approach to that of the *National Development Team* in the U.K.

ANDREWS, R.J. et al (1983) Evaluation, Standards and Accreditation of Government-subsidized Services for Handicapped People: Schonell Evaluation and Accreditation Procedure (SEAP). Canberra: Department of Social Security.

Scissoring

Some people with severe *cerebral palsy* have stiff legs which are held tightly together at the hips and cannot easily be held apart. The legs tend to cross over at the knees. It is caused by tightness of the *adductor* muscles and can be improved by an operation on the tendons of these muscles. If untreated it can lead to problems with personal hygiene and dislocation of the hips.

Scoliosis

A curvature of the spine to one side. It occurs in many conditions associated with mental handicap especially when a physical disability is also present. It may occur with a *kyphosis* in which case it is called *kyphoscoliosis*.

Screening

The testing of a particular 'at risk' group within the population for a particular disorder. Newborn babies are usually screened, by means of a blood test, for *phenylketonuria* and *congenital hypothyroidism*, both of which are treatable causes of mental handicap. In most developed countries *developmental checklists* are used for the screening of preschool children.

Scriver chemical methods

A chemical method for *screening* blood of newborn children for many *metabolic* disorders. Techniques such as chromatography or fluorimetry are used. It is generally only used for treatable conditions such as *phenylketonuria*.

SCRIVER, C.R. (1965) Screening newborn infants for hereditary metabolic disease. Pediatr. Clin. North Am., 12:807.

SDH

= *staffed domestic home*.

SEC

= Social Education Centre. See *adult training centre*.

Seckel's bird-headed dwarfism

= *bird-headed dwarfism*.

Seclusion

= *time-out*.

Sedative

A substance, such as a *tranquillizer*, which calms and reduces excitability.

Segregation

The process of separating mentally handicapped people from other members of society as has happened in the past in hospitals, hostels and other forms of residential provision. *Adult training centres, special schools* and other forms of day care are also segregated. This is in opposition to *integration* into the community as emphasized in the philosophy of *normalization*.

MORRIS, P. (1969) Put Away. London: Routledge & Kegan Paul.

Seguin form board

A wooden board with different shaped holes into which wooden pieces can be fitted. Children with *specific language difficulties* and *autism* may be able to complete this even though their abilities in other areas may be at a much lower level. It is part of the *Merrill-Palmer Test of Mental Abilities*.

Seip syndrome

See *lipodystrophy*.

Seitelberger's disease

See *neuroaxonal dystrophies*.

Seizure

An episode caused by a sudden and transitory disturbance of brain function with impairment of consciousness. *Epilepsy* is a disorder characterized by recurrent seizures. The many types of seizures are described under epilepsy.

Self-advocacy

The principle and process of mentally handicapped people speaking or communicating for themselves. This developed in the U.S.A. and Sweden in the 1970's where self-help groups were established to assist members in self-esteem and self-assertion so that they could speak for themselves and influence attitudes and services. This may be achieved on an individual basis and also through groups such as *People First*. There are now self-advocacy groups in many other countries and international conferences have been organized. Mentally handicapped people may need help in acquiring the skills to listen to one another, to share ideas, to express views clearly and to gain confidence. Making decisions and choices and weighing up the facts are also skills to be learnt. Nevertheless people with only a few communication skills can self-advocate if their helpers are prepared to interpret their means of self-expression (see *advocacy*). These developments in self-advocacy make it necessary for professionals and parents to accept that there should be full consultation with mentally handicapped people over decisions affecting their lives. This may involve attitude-changes, training (in listening to and talking with mentally handicapped people) and a willingness to accept a threat to the status quo.

CITY LITERARY INSTITUTE (1983) Have We a Future? (videotape and information pack). London: City Literary Institute.
CRAWLEY, B. (1983) Self-advocacy manual: An overview of the development of self-advocacy by mentally handicapped people and recommendations for the development of trainee committees. Manchester: Hester Adrian Research Centre, University of Manchester.
ELKIN, E. & TEMBY, E. (1984) Participation and Self-advocacy, Position Paper. Brussels: ILSMH.
SANG, B. & O'BRIEN, J. (1984) Advocacy. The U.K. and American Experiences. King's Fund Project Paper Number 51. London: King's Fund Centre.
SCHAAF, V. et al (1977) People First: A self-help organization of the retarded. In: Mental Retardation and Developmental Disabilities. Vol. IX. Wortis, J. (Ed.). New York: Brunner/Mazel.
WILLIAMS, P. & SCHOULTZ, B. (1982) We Can Speak for Ourselves. London: Souvenir Press.

Self-feeding
See *feeding problems*.

Self-injurious behaviour / self-mutilation
A number of self-injurious behaviours may be shown by people who are mentally handicapped. The most common are head-banging, *eye-poking*, ear-poking, gouging or picking at skin and self-biting. Such behaviours occur more commonly amongst people who are *autistic* or have autistic traits, those who are severely or profoundly mentally handicapped and in particular conditions, notably *Lesch-Nyhan syndrome, de Lange syndrome* and blindness. Such behaviours are very difficult to change especially once well established. They appear to be compulsive and self-stimulatory but may be further reinforced by attention or other responses. The reasons for such behaviours are not known but the two main hypotheses are either a biochemical abnormality of the brain or a behavioural cause based on the accidental reinforcement of a developmental stage which is normally short-lived. Physical prevention using splints or protective devices is the treatment method most commonly used and *aversive stimulation* is reserved as a last resort. Careful assessment followed by a planned *behaviour modification* programme is essential and is usually initiated by a *psychologist* and implemented by the carers. Other treatments include drugs such as *tranquillizers, lithium* and *baclofen*.

CORBETT, J.A. (1975) Aversion for the treatment of self-injurious behaviour. J. Ment. Defic. Res., 19:79–95.
HOLLIS, J. & MEYERS, C. (1982) Life Threatening Behaviour: Analysis and Intervention. Washington D.C.: American Association on Mental Deficiency.
LUISELL, J.K. (1986) Modification of self-injurious behaviour: An analysis of the use of contingently applied protective equipment. Behav. Mod., 10(2):191–204.
MAISTO, C.R. et al (1978) An analysis of variables related to self-injurious behaviour amongst institutionalized retarded persons. J. Ment. Defic. Res., 22:27.
MATIN, R.A. & RUNDLE, A.T. (1980) Physiological and psychiatric investigations into a group of mentally handicapped subjects with self-injurious behaviour. J. Ment. Defic. Res., 24:77–85.

MURPHY, G. & WILSON, B. (1985) Self Injurious Behaviour. Kidderminster, U.K.: B.I.M.H.

Self-stimulation
Behaviours which are thought to be used to provide stimulation for the individual. These include *stereopathies*, *eye-poking* and other *self-injurious behaviours*, flicking fingers in front of the eyes (especially in visually handicapped children) and *rumination*. These occur more commonly in people who are severely mentally handicapped especially if they have *autistic* traits or are under-stimulated. The idea that such behaviours are self-stimulating is difficult to prove.

Senile dementia
Deterioration of the intellect, emotions and behaviour in old age as a result of disease or damage to the brain. In most people with this condition the problems are the same as in *pre-senile dementia* but the onset is later and the progress is often less rapid. The lack of information on elderly mentally handicapped people makes it impossible to identify the frequency or nature of the problem in this group of people. It is reasonable to assume that it is the same as for the general population although senile dementia may be more difficult to diagnose in more severely mentally handicapped people. The major causes are *Alzheimer's disease* and narrowing of the arteries of the brain. It is important to exclude treatable physical illness such as *hypothyroidism*.

Sense
See *deaf-blind*.

Sensori-motor skills
The basic skills acquired by normal children in the first 2 years of life. These include grasp, basic hand-eye co-ordination and the exploration of, and experimentation with, the environment. One of the key skills is the development of the concept of *object permanence*.

Sensori-neural deafness
A hearing *impairment* caused by abnormalities of the inner ear (*cochlea*) and/or auditory nerve (the nerve from the ear to the brain). The cochlea receives sound impulses and translates them into messages which can be carried by the auditory nerve. This type of hearing loss cannot be improved so much by the use of hearing aids. Infections such as *meningitis*, *encephalitis*, measles and mumps give rise to sensori-neural loss as do damage from noise and the hearing loss of old age (*presbyacusis*). Some of the *genetic* and *chromosome* abnormalities associated with mental handicap may cause sensori-neural deafness.

Sensory handicaps / impairments
See *blindness*, *deafness* and *deaf-blind*.

Separation anxiety
Anxiety shown about separation from a parental figure. This is normal in young children and must be understood and taken into account when preparing children for *phased care* experiences. As children gain in independence, confidence and self-esteem, their ability to separate from the family improves. Separation anxiety may lead to problems such as school refusal.

Serenace
= *haloperidol*.

Serotonin
A chemical substance found in the body which is derived from tryptophan, an *amino acid*. It is involved in the transmission of messages between nerve cells and is very important in the functioning of the brain.

Serum anticonvulsant levels
The levels of *anticonvulsant* drugs in the blood can be measured when monitoring the use, effectiveness and possible side-effects of these drugs. It is now possible to do this by *salivary levels* in some centres.

Setting events
See *antecedents*.

Setting-sun sign
The eyes deviate downward so that the lower part of the *iris* is hidden by the lower eyelid. This is a characteristic sign of *hydrocephalus* in infants.

Severe Disablement Allowance
An allowance paid in the U.K. to people who are severely disabled or long-term sick and who have not paid National Insurance contributions. Women can claim it between 16 and 60 years of age and men between 16 and 65. It is tax free and is not means tested. It will continue to be paid after retirement age.

Further information:
Disability Rights Handbook (updated each year), The Disability Alliance, 25 Denmark St., London WC2H 8NJ.
Leaflet N1252 Severe Disablement Allowance. DHSS: Available from local Social Security offices.

Severe mental handicap / retardation
See *mental retardation*.

Severe mental impairment
A term defined in the *Mental Health Act 1983* as 'a state of arrested or incomplete development of mind which includes severe impairment of intelligence and social functioning and is associated with abnormally aggressive or seriously irresponsible conduct on the part of the person concerned.'

Severe (mental) subnormality
See *subnormality*.

Sex chromatin
= *Barr body*.

Sex chromosome
See *chromosomes*.

Sex chromosome abnormalities
It is generally agreed that people with an abnormal sex *chromosome* constitution are not necessarily prone to being mentally handicapped but as a group have a higher incidence of speech difficulties and reading problems. The more severe the abnormality of the sex chromosomes the more likely it is that an affected person is mentally handicapped. These abnormalities include *Turner's syndrome, XXX syndrome, XXXX syndrome, Klinefelter's syndrome* and *XYY syndrome*.

BENDER, B. et al (1983) Speech and language development in 41 children with sex chromosome anomalies. Pediatrics, 71:262–267.
NIELSON, J. et al (1982) Chromosome abnormalities in children in two Danish countries during the period 1967–1978. Hereditas, 96:195–210.
RATCLIFFE, S.G. (1982) Speech and learning disorders in children with sex chromosome abnormalities. Dev. Med. Child Neurology, 24:80–84.

Sex education / sexual counselling
In recent years the increasing recognition of the rights of disabled people has led to the promotion of the rights of people to deal knowledgeably with their own sexuality. The trend toward *community care* has exposed disabled people to the same risks and the same demands as experienced by everyone else and has drawn attention to the need for education and counselling in the whole sphere of personal relationships. Mentally handicapped people vary as much as the general population in their sexual interest, sexual activity and reproductive ability and there is no direct connection between the sexuality of a person and their intelligence. There is a wide range of views and expectations about the sexuality of mentally handicapped people and this is a very controversial area. Nevertheless, there is a growing body of opinion that people with a mental handicap should receive appropriate counselling, of a type commensurate with

their level of understanding, about their bodies, their relationships and their sexuality. This is not only to increase their knowledge about themselves but also to promote understanding of the values and rules of the society in which they live so that they know the behaviours expected if they are to adapt to life in that society. The myth that mentally handicapped people have no sexual needs, desires or behaviours is gradually being eliminated and replaced with education, counselling and support. Modern research has shown that many of society's fears concerning the sexuality of mentally handicapped people are ill-founded.

CHAMPAGNE, M.P. & WALKER-HIRSCH, L.W. (1982) Circles: a self-organization system for teaching appropriate social/sexual behaviour to mentally retarded/developmentally disabled persons. Sexuality & Disability, 5(3):172–4.

CRAFT, A. (1987) Mental Handicap and Sexuality. Issues and Perspectives. Tunbridge Wells, U.K.: Costello Press.

CRAFT, A. & CRAFT, M. (Eds.) (1983) Sex Education and Counselling for Mentally Handicapped People. Tunbridge Wells, U.K.: Costello Press.

CRAFT, A. & CRAFT, M. (1985) Sexuality and personal relationships. In: Mental Handicap. Craft, M. et al. London: Baillière Tindall. pp. 177–196.

EDMONSON, B. (1980) Sociosexual education for the handicapped. Except. Ed. Quart., 1:67–76.

HAAVIK, S.F. & MENNINGER, K.A. (1981) Sexuality, Law and the Developmentally Disabled Person: Legal and Clinical Aspects of Marriage, Parenthood and Sterilization. Baltimore: Paul H. Brookes.

HAMRE-NIETUPSKI, S. & FORD, A. (1981) Sex education and related skills: a series of programs implemented with severely handicapped students. Sexuality & Disability, 4(3):179–193.

JOHNSON, P.R. (1981) Sex and the developmentally handicapped adult. A comparison of teaching methods. Brit. J. Ment. Subn., 27:I(52)8–17.

KEMPTON, W. (1975) Love, Sex and Birth Control for the Mentally Retarded. Planned Parenthood Assoc. of S.E. Pennsylvania.

KEMPTON, W. & FORMAN, R (1976) Guidelines for Training in Sexuality and the Mentally Handicapped. Philadelphia: Planned Parent Assoc. of S.E. Pennsylvania.

LIVOCK, P. (1985) Sex Education for People with Mental Handicaps. London: Croom Helm

MCCARTHY, W. & FEGAN, L. (1984) Sex Education and the Intellectually Handicapped. Sydney: Adis Press.

MIND (National Association for Mental Health) (1983) Getting Together: Sexual and Social Expression of Mentally Handicapped People. London: MIND.

Further information:
Family Planning Association, 27–35 Mortimer St., London W1N 7RJ.
American Assoc. of Sex Educators, Sex Counselors and Therapists, 2000 N. St. NW, Washington DC 20036.
Planned Parent Federation of America, Inc., 810, 7th Ave, New York NY 10019.

Sex-linked ichthyosis
= *X-linked ichthyosis.*

Sex-linked inheritance / X-linked inheritance

Inheritance determined by a *gene* which is present on the X of the sex *chromosomes*. Most *genetic* disorders carried on the X chromosomes are manifest only in the males where there is not a normal gene on the Y chromosome to counteract the effects. Such disorders are carried by the females who have a 25% chance of having an affected son, a 50% chance of having an unaffected son or daughter and a 25% chance of having a daughter who is a carrier of the gene. A few conditions associated with mental handicap are carried on the X-chromosome including *Albright's syndrome, Hunter's syndrome, Lesch-Nyhan syndrome, Lowe's syndrome,*

Menkes' syndrome and *Norries disease*. Most sex-linked conditions are *recessive* and are not manifest in females but occasionally female *carriers* may be mildly affected as in the *fragile-X syndrome*. Sometimes sex-linked conditions are present in females only and it is presumed that the condition is lethal to males.

HERBST, D.S. & MILLER, J.R. (1980) Non-specific X-linked mental retardation. Am. J. Med. Genet., 7:443–469.
McKUSICK, V.A. (1978) Mendelian Inheritance in Man (5th edit.). Baltimore: Johns Hopkins Press.

Sexual development
See *sex education*.

Sexual Offences Act (1956)
In the U.K. it is an offence under Section 7 of this Act for a man to have unlawful sexual intercourse with a woman suffering from severe mental handicap unless he does not know, and has no reason to suspect, that she is severely mentally handicapped. Under Sections 14(4) and 15(3) neither a severely handicapped man nor woman can give consent which, for any other person, would prevent any act from becoming an indecent assault. Section 27 of this Act makes it an offence for the owner or manager of any premises to induce or allow a severely mentally handicapped woman to be on the premises for the purpose of having unlawful sexual intercourse with a man.

Sexual Offences Act (1967)
In the U.K. Section 1(3) of this Act states that a man suffering from a severe mental handicap, within the meaning of the Act, cannot in law give 'consent' to homosexual acts. Section 1(2) provides that an act which would otherwise be treated for the purposes of this Act as being done in private shall not be so treated if more than two persons take part or are present.

Shagreen patch
A raised and thickened area of skin often pink in colour with a slight sheen. These are usually found over the loin or lower back. This characteristically occurs in *tuberose sclerosis*.

Shaping
A *behaviour modification* technique in which existing behaviours are built on and expanded. Initially a response similar to the desired one is selected and reinforced so that it occurs frequently. The next stage is to reinforce it selectively when it is a nearer approximation to the required response. The criterion for *reinforcement* is gradually changed over time so that the person goes further toward the target before being reinforced. This method is sometimes called successive approximation.

TSOI, M. & YULE, W. (1980) Building up new behaviours. In: Behaviour Modification for the Mentally Handicapped. Yule, W. & Carr, J. London: Croom Helm. pp. 69–72.
WOLF, M. et al (1964) Applications of operant conditioning procedures to the behaviour problems of an autistic child. Behav. Res. Ther., 1:305–312.

Shared care
= *phased care*.

Sheltered housing
Any form of housing in which more support or help is provided than is usually available in ordinary life. This includes *group homes*, *staffed domestic homes* and warden-controlled flats.

Sheltered Industrial Groups
A system in the U.K. by which an employer pays a disabled employee for the work done and the Manpower Services Commission also contributes in order to provide an adequate wage.

Sheltered work / sheltered work-shops

Any form of work in which there are fewer demands or more support and help than is usually the case in employment. See also *workstations* and *supportive work*.

Short sight

= *myopia*.

Short stature

See *deletion of chromosome*.

Short-arm deletion of chromosomes

See *deletion of chromosome*.

Short-limbed dwarfism

A type of *restricted growth* in which the limbs are short in relation to the trunk which is usually of normal size. This occurs in *achondroplasia*, *Apert's syndrome* and *de Lange syndrome*.

Short-term care

= *phased care*.

Shunt / shunting

A by-pass tube used in the treatment of *hydrocephalus*. The *Pudenz-Heyer-Schulte* pump and valve and the *Spitz-Holter valve* are examples. Shunting operations are carried out in *hydrocephalus* in order to by-pass the obstruction by the use of a tube and valve and to thus reduce the raised *intracranial pressure*.

Sialidosis

One of the rare group of disorders known as *mucolipidoses* and caused by *enzyme* deficiencies. There are two forms of sialidosis. In Type I the onset is after 10 years of age with diminished visual acuity, unsteadiness and *myoclonic seizures*. In Type II there is usually an earlier onset, generally in infancy, and there is also coarsening of the features and abnormal development and formation of bones. Hearing may be impaired and co-ordination poor. It is slowly progressive and usually associated with moderate mental handicap. In both types there is a deficiency of an enzyme known as neuraminidase or sialidase and there may be other deficiencies as well. These disorders are inherited from both parents (*recessive inheritance*). They can be detected during pregnancy following *amniocentesis*.

AYLSWORTH, A.S. et al (1980) A severe infantile sialidosis. J. Pediatr., 96:662.
LOWDEN, J.A. & O'BRIEN, J.S. (1978) Sialidosis: A review of human neuraminidase deficiency. Am. J. Hum. Genet., 31:1.

SIB

= *self-injurious behaviour*.

Sibling / Sib

A brother or sister.

GATH, A. & GUMLEY, D. (1987) Retarded children and their siblings. J. Child Psychol. Psychiat., 28:715–730.
KEW, S. (1975) Handicap and Family Crises: A Study of the Siblings of Handicapped Children. London: Pitman.

Sicca cell therapy

A treatment approach which involves the injection of cell preparations obtained from animals. This is said to activate the corresponding cells of the person to improve their function. Following the injection of sicca cells from the *central nervous system* tissues of animals it has been claimed that benefits have occurred for mentally handicapped people. These claims have been anecdotal and a study by Black et al (1966) found no evidence of improvement in mentally handicapped children.

BLACK, D.B. et al (1966) A study of improvement in mentally retarded children accruing from sicca cell therapy. Am. J. Ment. Defic., 70:499–508.
GOLDSTEIN, H. (1956) Sicca cell therapy in children. Arch. Pediatr., 73:234–249.
KARP, L.E. (1983) New hope for the retarded? Am. J. Med. Genet., 16:1–5.

Sickle cell disease
An inherited abnormality of red blood cells which causes obstruction of blood vessels and bleeding especially when the person is ill. This can affect the brain and cause transient or irreversible neurological problems including mental handicap and *seizures*.

BAIRD, R.L. et al (1964) Studies in sickle cell anaemia XXI. Pediatrics, 34:92.

Sign language / system
A language or system in which information is mainly transmitted by hand and arm postures and movements. There are many different types of sign language in use including *British Sign Language, American Sign Language, Makaton* and *Paget-Gorman Sign System*. These are used by people who cannot speak or who have problems with speech. Makaton is most often used by mentally handicapped people in the U.K.

FAW, G.D. et al (1981) Involving institutional staff in the development and maintenance of sign language skills with profoundly retarded persons. J. Appl. Behav. Anal., 14:411–23.
JONES, P.R. & CREGAN, A. (1986) Sign and Symbol Communication for Mentally Handicapped People. London: Croom Helm.
KIERNAN, C. et al (1982) Signs and Symbols: A Review of Literature and Survey of the Use of Non-Vocal Communication. London: Heinemann Educational Books.
KIRSCHNER, A. et al (1979) Manual communication systems: a comparison and its implications. Education & Training of the Mentally Retarded, 14:5–10.
LLOYD, L.L. & KARLAN, G. (1984) Nonspeech communication symbols and systems. Where have we been and where are we going? J. Ment. Defic. Res., 28:3–20.
SCHEPIS, M.M. et al (1982) A programme for increasing manual signing by autistic and profoundly retarded youth within the daily environment. J. Appl. Behav. Anal., 15:363–79.

Signed English / Signs Supporting English
A derivative of *American Sign Language* which is designed for educational purposes and is often used as part of *total communication*. It is generally used for teaching deaf people of normal intelligence or who are only mildly mentally handicapped. The signs are placed into the order of spoken English and additional signs are introduced to improve grammatical correctness. It is not a true language but a manual coding of English.

BORNSTEIN, H. & HAMILTON, L. (1978) 'Signed English'. In: Ways and Means. Tebbs, T. (Ed.) Basingstoke, U.K.: Globe Education.
BORNSTEIN, H. et al (1983) The Signed English Dictionary for Preschool and Elementary Levels. Washington D.C.: Galludet College Press.
LINVILLE, S.E. (1977) Signed English: A language teaching technique with totally non-verbal, severely mentally retarded adolescents. Language, Speech and Hearing Services in Schools, 8:170–175.

Silver's syndrome / Silver-Russell syndrome
A condition associated with low birth weight and *restricted growth*. The body proportions are small compared with the head which is of normal size. People with this condition tend to have a broad forehead and narrow chin. The lips are thin and the corners of the mouth turn downward. The overall appearance is described as elfin-like. Brown patches on the skin (*café-au-lait patches*) are often present. Excessive sweating has been noted. Hair is often fine and light in colour. Sometimes the two sides of the body grow unevenly and there may be a spinal curvature. The little finger curves inward (*clinodactyly*) and the second and third toes may be joined. *Puberty* may occur early or late. In many people with this condition intelligence is normal although early motor development may be delayed because of muscle weakness. A significant

number of people do, however, have a moderate degree of mental handicap. The cause of this condition is unknown. Familial incidence is rare.

CALLAGHAN, K.A. (1970) Asymmetrical dwarfism or Silver's syndrome in two male siblings. Med. J. Aus., 2:789–92.
FULEIHAN, D.S et al (1971) The Russell-Silver syndrome: a report of three siblings. J. Pediatr., 78:654–57.
SALMON, M.A. (1978) Developmental Defects and Syndromes. Aylesbury, England: HM+M Publishers. pp. 62–64.

Simian crease
See *palmar crease*.

Sinequan
= *doxepin*.

Sjögren-Larsson syndrome
A very rare disorder in which there is moderate or mild mental handicap, short stature, *spasticity* and a characteristic skin condition. The skin is red from birth and becomes thickened, dry and scaly. It is most severe in the armpits and around the neck and the face is often spared. Sweating is diminished. The teeth are poorly developed and scalp hair may be sparse. Spasticity develops, especially in the lower limbs. *Seizures* and poor vision (*retinitis pigmentosa*) develop in about a third of people with this condition. Slurring of speech and other speech disorders have occurred. This condition is inherited from both parents who are carriers (*recessive inheritance*).

HERNELL, O. et al (1982) Suspected faulty essential fatty acid metabolism in Sjögren-Larsson syndrome. Pediatr. Res., 16:45.
JAGELLS, S. et al (1981) Sjögren-Larsson syndrome in Sweden: A clinical, genetic and epidemiological study. Clin. Genet., 19:233–256.
SELMANOWITZ, V. & PORTER, M.J. (1967) The Sjögren-Larsson syndrome. Am. J. Med., 42:412.

Skin biopsy
See *biopsy*.

Skull deformity
See *craniostenosis*.

Slosson Intelligence Test
An *intelligence test* which requires only 15 to 20 minutes to administer. It is not generally considered adequate for diagnostic purposes or for making decisions about intervention but can be used for screening.

SLOSSON, R.L. (1963) Slosson Intelligence Test for Children and Adults. New York: Slosson Educational Publications.

Sly's syndrome
One of the *mucopolysaccharidoses* in which there is a deficiency of the *enzyme* beta-glucuronidase. Some people with this condition are of normal intelligence or only mildly mentally handicapped whereas others are severely mentally handicapped. There is a wide variation in other symptoms. There may be obvious enlargement of the brain and liver with facial and bone abnormalities similar to *Hurler's syndrome* or there may be little evidence of disease. The severe form may become apparent in infancy. It is inherited from both parents who are carriers (*recessive inheritance*).

BEAUDET, A.L. et al (1975) Variation in the phenotypic expression of beta-glucuronidase deficiency. J. Pediatr., 86:388.

Smith-Lemli-Opitz syndrome
A condition in which there is small stature, mental handicap, abnormal genitals in males, and a characteristic facial appearance. People with this condition usually have a small head, a broad, short nose with an upturned tip, wide folds at the inner angle of the eye, drooping eyelids, a small chin, low-set ears and a squint. There may be *cataracts*. The roof of the mouth is narrow, high arched and may be cleft. Muscles are floppy in infancy but may become tighter later. The shoulders are narrow and the

neck is short. The second and third toes may be joined. Other abnormalities of bones and limbs may be present. *Seizures* and *spasticity* may develop. Abnormalities of the heart have been described. Severe or moderate mental handicap is usual. Feeding problems and irritability are common in infancy. It is generally inherited from both parents who are carriers (*recessive inheritance*).

DALLAIRE, L. (1969) Syndrome of retardation with urogenital and skeletal anomalies (Smith-Lemli-Opitz syndrome). J. Med. Genet., 6:113.
FINE, R.N. et al (1968) Smith-Lemli-Opitz syndrome. Am. J. Dis. Child., 115:483.
GARCIA, C.A. et al (1973) Neurological involvement in the Smith-Lemli-Opitz syndrome: clinical and neuropathological findings. Dev. Med. Child Neurology, 15: 48.
HOEFNAGEL, D. et al (1969) The Smith-Lemli-Opitz syndrome in an adult male. J. Ment. Defic. Res., 13:249–57.

SMR

= severe *mental retardation*.

Snellen Illiterate E Letter Test

A test of acuity of vision which uses only one letter, E, in different positions. It is designed for an illiterate person who is asked to indicate the different positions by gestures or words.

Social education centre

See *adult training centre*.

Social Learning Curriculum

An approach to teaching which stresses problem solving rather than rote learning. The aim is to develop the thinking processes which underpin independence. It is called a logical-inductive strategy and the steps identified are: label, detail, infer, predict, verify and generalize. This achieves skills that are not often attained by *behaviour modification*.

GOLDSTEIN, H. & GOLDSTEIN, M.T.

(1980) Reasoning Ability of Mildly Retarded Learners. Resten, VA: Council for Exceptional Children.

Social quotient

A measure of the degree of social self-reliability derived from the *Vineland Social Maturity Scale* and compared to a 'normal' population of the same age.

Social role valorization

= *normalization*.

Social Training Achievement Record

A checklist scoring the degree of social competence in a large number of practical living skills. It is divided into six sections which cover self-help skills, communication, social relationships, domestic skills, discrimination skills, education skills, use of equipment and use of public amenities. It can be presented visually by shading in segments of a star shape. It is then possible to see, at a glance, the profile of an individual and the areas in which further training could be concentrated.

DICKENS, P. & STALLARD, A. (1987) Assessing Mentally Handicapped People. Windsor: NFER/Nelson. pp. 49–50.
WILLIAMS, C. (1986) STAR Profile – Social Training Achievement Record (2nd edit.). Kidderminster, U.K.: BIMH Publications.

Social workers / social work

In the U.K. social workers receive a social work qualification after two years' full-time training, having also obtained a previous qualification and/or relevant experience. The standard is set by the Central Council for Education and Training in Social Work (CCETSW). In the U.S.A. it is usually through a master's degree and two years' supervised post-master's experience, leading to certification by the Academy of Certified Social Workers. In the U.K. social workers are employed by the local authority or by charitable organizations. Social workers provide a personal service which offers skilled assistance to people to facilitate the resolution of material or emotional problems and to enhance the personal and social functioning of an individual, family or group. The main models of social work practice are casework, family therapy, group work and community work.

Social workers also have to work within a legislative framework especially in relation to child care and the *Mental Health Act 1983* (see *approved social worker*).

Social workers have an important part to play in helping mentally handicapped people and their families. Counselling, information, support and practical help are required and the social work services can provide these as part of a co-ordinated service. Social workers are important members of *community mental handicap teams*, and generic social workers also have an important role in the community care of mentally handicapped people.

ANDERSON, D. (1982) Social Work and Mental Handicap. London: Macmillan.
BRITISH ASSOCIATION OF SOCIAL WORKERS (BASW) (1982) Guidelines on Social Work with Severely Handicapped Infants. BASW, 16, Kent St., Birmingham, B5 6RD.
GILBERT, P. (1985) The role of the social worker. In: Mental Handicap. Craft, M. et al. London: Baillière Tindall. pp. 295–303.
HANVEY, C. (1981) Social Work with Mentally Handicapped People. London: Heinemann.

Further information:
BASW, 16, Kent St., Birmingham, B5 6RD.

Sodium valproate

An *anticonvulsant* drug used in the treatment of *epilepsy*. It is particularly effective in the control of *grand-mal convulsions* and also for *absence seizures* and *myoclonic seizures*. Abnormal liver function has occurred in people whose treatment has included this drug and for this reason liver function should be monitored and any illness including vomiting, lethargy, drowsiness, loss of appetite, jaundice or loss of seizure control is an indication for immediate withdrawal of the drug. Inflammation of the pancreas may cause abdominal pain and is another indication for withdrawal. The clotting capacity of the blood may be reduced leading to spontaneous bruising or bleeding and the numbers of blood cells can be reduced. An increase in alertness or sedation may occur and, particularly in children, *aggression* and *overactivity* may be a problem. Increase in appetite and weight gain are quite common and nausea may also occur. Transient hair loss and cessation of menstruation are other, less common, problems.

COVANIS, A. et al (1982) Sodium valproate: monotherapy and polytherapy. Epilepsia, 23:693.
EGGER, J. & BRETT, E.M. (1981) Effects of sodium valproate in 100 children with special reference to weight. Brit. Med. J. 283:577.
JEAVONS, P.M. et al (1977) Treatment of generalised epilepsies of childhood and adolescence with sodium valproate. Dev. Med. Child. Neurology, 19(1):9–25.

Soft play

A total soft play environment is an area in which all play materials, floor and walls are soft and covered in a tough, washable, vinyl. It is very useful for active and clumsy children with a mental handicap. It provides a safe and enjoyable way of learning *gross motor*, spatial and perceptual skills.

KNIGHT, L. (1984) Soft-play-movement, motivation and fun. Association of Chartered Physiotherapists Newsletter, Feb. pp. 7–8.

Soiling
= *encopresis.*

Sonar
= *ultrasound scanning.*

Sonoencephalogram
= *ultrasound scanning.*

Sotos' syndrome
A condition characterized by high birth weight, excessive growth during childhood, mental handicap and characteristic features. The head size is larger than normal for age and is long from front to back. The person has a characteristic posture with the head and neck thrust forward and there may be a spinal curvature. The face is long with a high and prominent forehead. The eyelids may be droopy and the eyes slanting downward from the nose. The chin may be large and the roof of the mouth high and narrow. Early teething is common. Ears are large and often protruding. Hands and feet are disproportionately large. *Puberty* is usually early. Clumsiness and unsteadiness are frequent. About one third of affected people have *seizures.* Intelligence varies from normal to severe mental handicap. Most people with this condition are good natured, lacking in *aggression* and insensitive to pain. Overactive behaviour and short attention span are usual. *Hypothyroidism* occasionally occurs. The cause is not yet known but does not appear to be genetic.

ABRAHAM, J.M. & SNODGRASS, G.J.A. (1969) Sotos' syndrome of cerebral gigantism. Arch. Dis. Childh., 44:203–10.
BEEMER, F.A. et al (1986) Cerebral gigantism (Sotos' syndrome) in two patients with fragile-X chromosome. Am. J. Med. Genet., 23(1–2):221–226.
EVANS, P.R. (1971) Sotos' syndrome (cerebral gigantism) with peripheral dysostosis. Arch. Dis. Childh., 46:199.
SALMON, M.A. (1978) Developmental Defects and Syndromes. Aylesbury, U.K.: HM+M Publishers. pp. 86–88.

Spache Diagnostic Reading Scales
A scale used in the U.S.A. which is designed to evaluate oral and silent reading skills as well as comprehension. It includes word recognition lists, reading passages and phonic tests. The scores obtained reflect grade levels at which the child can read independently with satisfactory comprehension and can comprehend material read aloud by someone else. The phonic tests provide a classification of errors made in reading.

SPACHE, G.D. (1963) Spache Diagnostic Reading Scales. Monterey: California Test Bureau.

Sparine
= *promazine.*

Spasm
An involuntary contraction of a muscle or group of muscles which can be painful. Prolonged spasms sometimes occur as an *extrapyramidal side-effect* of certain drugs. Spasms of shorter duration occur in *cerebral palsy. Seizures* are sometimes inappropriately referred to as spasms. A *clonic spasm* is a rapidly alternating contraction and relaxation of muscle whereas a *tonic spasm* is a sustained firm contraction of muscle causing it to be rigid.

Spasmus nutans
The rhythmic nodding of the head sometimes seen in normal infants in the first year of life. It may also be a sign of a disorder of the brain. It sometimes occurs in *hydrocephalus* when it is known as *bobble-head doll syndrome.*

Spastic / Spastics Society
See *cerebral palsy.*

Spasticity
An overexcitability of muscles due to loss of control from the upper part of the nervous system, usually the brain. The muscles become abnormal in their tension and are most commonly too tight. They sometimes go into *spasm.* The onset of spasticity in infancy is generally caused by brain damage or abnormality at birth and is usually referred to as *cerebral palsy.*

Spate-Hurler disease
= *Scheie syndrome*.

Special care
Usually applied to a day care or residential department which provides a service for profoundly handicapped people who require a great deal of physical assistance in their daily needs and personal hygiene. In the U.K. it particularly refers to the care of people with severe physical and mental handicap in *special education* or in *adult training centres*.

Special education / special schools
In the U.K. this generally refers to schools for children with *special educational needs* such as mental handicap. In some parts of the country there are separate schools for children with moderate learning difficulties and for those with severe learning difficulties. Nowadays more mentally handicapped children, especially those with moderate learning difficulties, are being integrated into ordinary schooling either within a special class or in the mainstream (usually with special help, see *integration* and *mainstreaming*). Teachers in special schools usually have had specialist training and have a qualification in special education. Special education in the U.K. is generally only available following the procedures in the *Education Act (1981)*. The *Warnock Committee Report* defined special education as access to appropriately qualified or experienced teachers, to other trained professional personnel and to an educational and physical environment appropriate for the child's requirements.

ADAMS, F. (1986) Special Education. Harlow: Longman.
BRENNAN, W.K. (1979) The Curricular Needs of Slow Learners. London: Evans / Methuen Educational.
CUTLER, B. (1981) Unravelling the Special Education Maze: An Action Guide for Parents. Champaign, Illin.: Research Press.
FISH, J. (1985) Special Education: The Way Ahead. Milton Keynes: Open University Press.
TOMLINSON, S. (1981) Educational Subnormality: A Study in Decision-Making. London: Routledge & Kegan Paul.
TURNBULL, H. & TURNBULL, A.P.(1982) Free Appropriate Public Education: Law and Implementation. Denver: Love Publishing Co.

Special educational needs
A term used in the *Education Act (1981)* to describe a child with a learning difficulty significantly greater than most children of his age or with a physical or mental disability which prevents or hinders him from making use of the educational facilities generally provided. The *Warnock Committee Report* defines special educational needs as 'requiring the provision of special means of access to the curriculum through special equipment, facilities or resources, modification of the physical environment or specialist techniques; through the provision of a special or modified curriculum; or through particular attention to the social structure and emotional climate in which education takes place'. See *special education*.

Special Olympics
A competitive sports programme which originated in the U.S.A. and has grown to involve more than forty other countries. It is sponsored by the Joseph P. Kennedy, Jr. Foundation. It was started in 1969 and since then thousands of disabled athletes have participated. Its philosophy and aims are to provide people with a mental handicap an opportunity, a challenge and a sense of achievement through sport. There are local, regional, national and international competitions. There are booklets on the rules and training programmes and individual booklets for each sport.

Materials and information are available from Special Olympics Inc., Joseph P. Kennedy, Jr. Foundation, 1701 K Street NW, Suite 205, Washington, DC 20006,

U.S.A. or MIND Olympic Co-ordinating Committee, 23 Mansfield, Writtle, Chelmsford, Essex.

Specialist social worker

A *social worker* who works in a particular field such as mental handicap.

Specific learning difficulties

Learning problems in a particular area such as reading, spelling and writing (*dyslexia*), language (*dysphasia*) or arithmetic.

TANSLEY, P. & PANCKHURST, J. (1981) Children with Specific Learning Difficulties. Windsor: NFER/Nelson.

Speech defects / speech disorders

See *language / language disorders*.

Speech therapist / speech therapy / speech pathologist

Speech therapy training differs from one country to another. In the U.K. it is a specialized training course at degree level. It involves the theoretical study of the development of the various forms of human communication, the factors which influence them, and the problems which interfere with them. Training in assessment and treatment methods is given and practical experience obtained. Related subjects such as anatomy, physiology, neurology, psychology, linguistics and phonetics are also studied. Some speech therapists specialize in a particular area such as mental handicap or child development.

WALKER, M. (1985) The role of the speech therapist. In: Mental Handicap. Craft, M. et al. London: Baillière Tindall. pp. 333–341.

Further information:
College of Speech Therapists, Harold Poster House, 6 Lechmore Rd., London NW2 5BU.

Spelencephaly

In this condition the major part of the brain tissue (*cerebral hemispheres*) is absent and replaced with an enlargement of the *cerebral ventricles* to make a fluid-filled cavity inside the ventricular walls. This is a type of *hydranencephaly*.

Sphingolipidoses / sphingolipodystrophies

A rare group of disorders in which abnormal substances (sphingolipids) are deposited in the cells of the body. This includes those disorders known as *gangliosidoses* and also *Gaucher's disease, Niemann-Pick disease, Fabry's syndrome* and *metachromatic leucodystrophy*.

Sphingomyelin lipidosis

= *Niemann-Pick disease.*

Spielmeyer-Sjögren disease

= *Batten-Vogt disease.*

Spielmeyer-Vogt disease

= *Batten-Vogt disease.*

Spina bifida / spina bifida cystica

= *meningomyelocoele.*

Spina bifida occulta

A defect in the bones of the back (vertebral column) which is closed over by skin and through which there is no protrusion of the spinal cord or its covering. It is the mildest form of spina bifida and does not usually cause any problems.

Spinal cord

The lower part of the *central nervous system* situated inside the backbone (vertebral column). It continues into the brain above and it is the major connection between the nerves of the body and the brain.

Spinal fluid

= *cerebro-spinal fluid.*

Spinocerebellar ataxia

= *Friedreich's ataxia.*

Spitz-Holter valve

A *shunt* and valve used to by-pass the obstruction in *hydrocephalus*.

Splenomegaly

Enlargement of the spleen, an organ deep in the abdomen, involved in the blood and lymphatic systems of the body. The spleen may become enlarged in some conditions associated with mental handicap including *cytomegalic inclusion disease, toxoplasmosis, rubella syndrome* the *lipidoses* and some *mucopolysaccharidoses*.

Splink word board

A means of *communication* which uses a computer to associate a word board, the alphabet and some commonly used phrases (preprogrammed into the board) with one or more television screens. The user touches the letters, words or phrase and the screen displays the required message. It is suitable for people who cannot speak but who can learn to operate the system.

Spongy degeneration of the central nervous system in infancy

= *Canavan's disease.*

Sprengel's anomaly / deformity

A deformity of the shoulder blade so that it protrudes outward (winging). This may occur in a few conditions associated with mental handicap including *Greig's syndrome, multiple lentiginosis syndrome, Klippel-Feil syndrome* and *arthrogryposis multiplex congenita.*

S.Q.

= *social quotient.*

Squint

= *strabismus.*

SSPE

= *subacute sclerosing panencephalitis.*

Staffed domestic house / staffed group home

A home provided for a small group of mentally handicapped people in an ordinary house or bungalow. If it is a home for children the staff assume a parental role although generally operate a rota rather than live-in. The staff are responsible for all aspects of care including household duties. The staff support and assist adults, but encourage as much autonomy as possible. This type of residential provision has been developed in response to the principle of *normalization* and should follow this principle when determining the location, type of housing, staffing and staff training. This type of care was pioneered by the *Eastern Nebraska Community Office of Retardation* in the U.S.A. and by *NIMROD* and other similar projects in the U.K. It is usual for the residents to have an individualized programme of care as provided by *individual programme plans.*

Stanford-Binet

A revised and modified version of the *Binet-Simon Scale of Intelligence*. This test of intellectual functioning is frequently used in the assessment of children. It consists of 120 items and there are several alternative tests for the age range 2 years to adulthood. The tests have a variety of activities of graded difficulty designed to cover both verbal and performance skills. Areas covered include memory, free-association, time orientation, language comprehension, knowledge of common objects, comparison of concepts, perception of contradictions, understanding of abstract ideas, the ability to deal with normal situations and the use of practical judgements. There are also tests of visual-motor co-ordination. The score is in months of *mental age* which can be used to derive an *intelligence quotient.*

TERMAN, L.M. & MERRILL, M.A. (1973) The Stanford-Binet Intelligence Scale – Third revision. Boston: Houghton Mifflin.

STAR

= *social training achievement record.*

Startle reflex
= *Moro reflex.*

Statement of special educational needs
See *Education Act (1981).*

Status epilepticus
A state in which a person has a very prolonged *seizure* or a succession of seizures without gaining consciousness between them. Some people with *epilepsy* are more prone to this condition and it may also be induced by infections, head injury or changes in *anticonvulsant* medication. Treatment is urgently required and consists of maintenance of vital functions; drug therapy to control the convulsions; identification and, if necessary, treatment of the cause; and prevention of further convulsions. Convulsions which last longer than 20 to 30 minutes may cause brain damage probably through the development of a high body temperature and low blood pressure. The most commonly used anticonvulsant for the treatment of status is *diazepam*, either given by a doctor into a vein or given rectally. Non-convulsive status may result from *petitmal* epilepsy and is known as *absence status*. Status resulting from *focal seizures* is usually called continuous partial epilepsy or temporal lobe status.

DELGARDO-ESCUETA, A.V. et al (1982) Management of status epilepticus. New Engl. J. Med., 306:1337.
HUNTER, R.A. (1959) Status epilepticus. History, incidence and problems. Epilepsia (Aust.), 1:162.
STORES, G. (1987) Recent developments in childhood non-convulsive status epilepticus. In: Epilepsy in Young People. Ross, E. et al (Eds.) Chichester: John Wiley. pp. 125–130.
WARD, C.D. (1987) Status epilepticus. Hospital Update, 13(3):190–202.

Steely-hair syndrome
= *Menkes syndrome.*

Steeple skull
= *acrocephaly.*

Steinert's myotonic dystrophy / Steinert's syndrome
An uncommon disorder in which there is wasting of muscles, abnormality of muscle action, *cataracts*, intellectual impairment and abnormal development of the testes and ovaries. The disease usually appears in late *adolescence* or early adult life but may be manifest at birth (congenital form) or in the first decade (juvenile form).
In the infantile form the baby may have a low birth weight and be floppy at birth. Weakness of the muscles of the face and neck, and breathing problems may occur. *Club foot* is common. Motor and speech development is delayed. Cataracts do not develop until after 10 years of age. The hands may be weak and toward the end of the first decade or later *myotonia* (as shown by the inability to relax the grip) may appear. The face, neck, shoulders and hip muscles are first affected and the face is expressionless with a drooping lower lip. *Developmental delay* may be apparent from early in the disease. The conduction of the nerves of the heart is often affected causing abnormal rhythms or irregularities which may cause death from heart failure. Infertility in men is common with shrinkage of the testes. In women periods are irregular and there are often ovarian cysts and infertility. Other hormonal abnormalities may lead to hair loss and diabetes. In the infantile form small head size and abnormalities of bones may occur. Infants who survive the first few years of life appear to improve in early childhood but later deteriorate. The condition is *genetic* in origin and is inherited from one parent, usually the mother, in a *dominant* manner. Diagnosis during pregnancy is possible following *amniocentesis*.

CAUGHEY, J.E. & MYRIANTHOPOULOS, N.C. (1963) Dystrophia Myotonica & Related Disorders. Springfield, Illinois: Thomas.

HARPER, P.S. (1975) Congenital myotonic dystrophy in Britain. I. Clinical aspects II. Genetic Basis. Arch. Dis. Childh., 50:505.
KOH, T.H. (1984) Do you shake hands with mothers of floppy babies? Brit. J. Med., 289:485.
PRUZANSKI, W. (1965) Myotonic dystrophy – a multisystem disease; report of 67 cases and a review of the literature. Psychiat. Neurol., 149:302.

Stelazine
= trifluoperazine.

Stenosis
Abnormal narrowing of a passage or opening of the body.

Stereognosis
The ability to recognize and discriminate the shape and form of objects held in the hand, without using vision. This ability may be impaired in some types of brain damage.

Stereopathy / stereotypy
Behaviours in which there are repetitive actions or words as in *mannerisms* and some *self-injurious behaviours* occurring particularly in severely and profoundly mentally handicapped people. These include rocking, swaying, head banging, *eye-poking*, hand waving and finger movements. Such behaviour is often regarded as *self-stimulation*.

AZRIN, N.H. & WESOLOWSKI, M.D. (1980) A reinforcement plus interruption method of eliminating behavioural stereotypy of profoundly retarded persons. Behav. Res. Ther., 18:113–119.
BAROFF, G.S. (1986) Mental Retardation: Nature, Cause and Management (2nd. edit.). Washington: Hemisphere. pp. 437–445.
McGONIGLE, J.J. et al (1982) Visual screening: an alternative model for reducing stereotyped behaviours. J. Appl. Behav. Anal., 15:461–7.

Sterilization
A surgical procedure that permanently prevents either a male fathering a child or a female conceiving one. For the man it is called vasectomy and is a simple low-risk procedure that can be performed under local anaesthetic. For the woman an abdominal operation is required which requires a general anaesthetic.

It is generally agreed that the only times sterilization should be considered as a method of *contraception* are: when it is certain that other birth control methods cannot be used; when sexual activity or marriage are possibilities but it is certain that the couple could not take care of children; when it is certain that the person's intellectual handicap is inheritable; or if it is the choice of the person who is well informed and capable of making such a decision.

The legal position must also be considered. Parents are not able to make decisions for their children over the age of 18 years and their consent to a sterilization operation may not be legal. The trend of legal opinion in the U.S.A. and the U.K. is toward making it more difficult for parents and legal guardians to have their children sterilized. Because of the permanence of the procedure the question of valid consent becomes very important. In many American states and in Canada it is virtually impossible to obtain sterilization, even when it is the wish of a mentally handicapped person, because no doctor will risk litigation.

EVANS, K.G. (1980) Sterilization of the mentally retarded – a review. Canad. Med. Ass. J., 123:1066–1070.
GILLON, R. (1987) On sterilising severely mentally handicapped people. J. Med. Ethics, 13:59–61.
GONZALES, B. (1982) The international medico-legal status of sterilization for mentally handicapped people. J. Reproduct. Med., 27(5):257–258.
GOSTIN, L. (1980) Sterilization and the law. Parents' Voice, 30(4): 16–17.
HAAVIK, S.F. & MENNINGER, K.A. (1981)

Sexuality, Law and the Developmentally Disabled Person: Legal and Clinical Aspects of Marriage, Parenthood and Sterilization. Baltimore: Paul H. Brookes.

KARP, L.E. (1981) Sterilization of the retarded. Am. J. Med. Genet., 9:1–3.

WOLF, L. & ZARFAS, D.E. (1982) Parents' attitudes towards sterilization of their mentally retarded children. Am. J. Ment. Defic., 87(2):122–129.

Sternum

The breast bone. This can be protuberant as in *pectus carinatum* or sunken as in *pectus excavatum*.

Stigma

A mark or defect which is especially characteristic of a condition or disorder. It may also refer more generally to an attribute that is discrediting.

GOFFMAN, E. (1963) Stigma: Notes on the Management of Spoiled Identity. Englewood Cliffs, New Jersey: Prentice-Hall.

SHEARER, A. (1984) Think Positive: Presenting a Positive Image of Persons with Mental Handicap. Brussels: ILSMH.

Stimulation

The rousing or activation of a person by means of events or surroundings. *Institutionalization* of mentally handicapped people has created artificial environments in which lack of stimulation is a common factor. This increases the developmental and learning problems of the individual. It has been shown that with appropriate stimulation mentally handicapped people can learn more and have a better quality of life. *Early intervention programmes* aim to provide a child with appropriate stimulation at a time when he is most likely to benefit.

Stimulus control

There is a view of behaviour which attributes its occurrence to the events (stimuli) which have preceded it (as well as to the predicted consequences of that behaviour).

If the analysis of an undesirable behaviour shows that it only occurs in one situation then a method for reducing the frequency of that behaviour is the removal of the stimulus which precedes and triggers the inappropriate behaviour. This is known as stimulus control which is a *behaviour modification* technique. Usually avoidance of the stimulus is impractical as a long-term solution especially as the behaviour may generalize to other situations. In practice, stimulus control is usually combined with other methods such as avoidance of *reinforcement* of the undesirable behaviour and/or reinforcement of appropriate behaviours. It may also be necessary to use *fading*.

MURPHY, G. (1980) Decreasing undesirable behaviours. In: Behaviour Modification for the Mentally Handicapped. Yule, W. & Carr, J. London: Croom Helm. pp. 90–116.

SAJWAJ, T. & HEDGES, D. (1973) A note on the effect of saying grace on the behaviour of an oppositional retarded boy. J. Appl. Behav. Anal., 6:711–712.

TERRACE, J.S. (1966) Stimulus control. In: Operant Behaviours: Areas of Research and Application. Honig, W.K. (Ed.). New York: Appleton-Century-Crofts.

Storage disorders

A group of disorders in which there is a defect in the breakdown of particular substances in the body causing their accumulation over a period of time. These include the *glycogen storage disorders, mucopolysaccharidoses, sphingolipidoses, lipidoses* and *Wilson's disease*.

Strabismus

A condition in which the two eyes do not look in the same direction at one time. The movements of the eyeball depend upon the action of six muscles and imbalance between the action of these muscles causes the squint. Often a squint is associated with *hypermetropia, myopia* or defective vision in one eye. A squint may cause *amblyopia*.

Treatment of a squint includes the correction of any *refractive error*, covering up the good eye, exercises to strengthen the weaker muscles and, if necessary, an operation to correct the strength of the eye muscles principally affected.

Sturge-Weber syndrome

A condition in which an extensive birthmark of the skin (*capillary haemangioma*) is associated with a similar malformation of the blood vessels of the covering of the brain (*meninges*). *Epilepsy* and, frequently, mental handicap and paralysis of the opposite side of the body occur. The birthmark is usually confined to one side of the body and affects the face, including at least one eyelid, and often the trunk and limbs as well. Capillary haemangiomas may also occur in other organs of the body. *Seizures* usually start in the first year of life, and are often focal and may be frequent and resistant to *anticonvulsants*. Surgery of the brain may sometimes be indicated. Malformations of the lining of the eye may cause *glaucoma* and there may be other defects of the eye. Skull X-rays show characteristic *cerebral calcification*. The condition is usually sporadic in occurrence without *familial inheritance* but may rarely be transmitted genetically, possibly by *dominant inheritance*. The cause is unknown.

ALEXANDER, G.L. & NORMAN, R.M. (1960) The Sturge-Weber syndrome. Bristol: Wright.
CHAO, D.H-C. (1959) Congenital neurocutaneous syndromes of childhood III Sturge-Weber disease. J. Pediatr., 55:635.
HOFFMAN, H.J. et al (1979) Hemispherectomy for Sturge-Weber syndrome. Child's Brain, 5:233–248.

Stycar tests / Stycar battery

A comprehensive series of tests which are valuable for the assessment of multi-handicapped children. They include the Stycar balls test of vision which involves the detection of a single object (balls of variable size) against a background. More able children can be tested by showing toys or letters which can be matched by toys or letters placed in front of the child. This gives some indication of the distance over which a person will attend visually and can be used to give appropriate measure of visual acuity if more accurate tests are not possible. The Stycar hearing tests consist, at the most simple level, of distraction by rattles, hand-bells etc. There is also a Stycar language test and a developmental scale.

SHERIDAN, M.D. (1973) Children's Developmental Progress from Birth to Five Years: The STYCAR Sequences. Windsor: NFER.
SHERIDAN, M.D. (1975) The Stycar Language Test. Dev. Med. Child Neurology, 17:164.
SHERIDAN, M.D. (1976) Manual for the STYCAR Vision Tests. Windsor: NFER.

Subacute necrotizing encephalo-myopathy

= *Leigh's syndrome.*

Subacute sclerosing panencephalitis

This condition is caused by a measles-like virus infection in a person who is unable to make antibodies to one of the proteins in the virus. The age of onset ranges from 5 to 15 years and boys are more frequently affected. It is less likely to occur if the person has been vaccinated against measles and more likely to occur after infection with the natural measles virus. Initial symptoms are personality changes and a gradual intellectual deterioration. *Myoclonic seizures* usually appear within two months and are characteristically muscle jerks which do not interfere with consciousness, are exaggerated by excitement and disappear during sleep. Spontaneous speech and movements decrease and *spasticity* becomes more evident with involuntary movements. Progressive visual loss may occur. Swallowing difficulties and breathing problems develop terminally. There may be a slow progressive deterioration or variable periods of remission but the average duration is one year. Remissions have been reported up to 3 years and survival of 20 years has been described. The *electroencephalogram* abnormalities are characteristic and, with high levels of measles antibodies, help to confirm the diagnosis.

DURANT, R.H. & DYKEN, P.R. (1983) The effect of inosuplex on the survival of subacute sclerosing panencephalitis. Neurology, 33:1053.
JABBOUR, J.T. et al (1969) Subacute sclerosing panencephalitis: A multidisciplinary study of eight cases. J. Am. Med. Assoc., 207:2248.
TERMEULEN, V. et al (1972) Subacute sclerosing panencephalitis. A review. Curr. Top. Microbiol. Immunol., 57:1.
WEIL, M.L. (1985) Infections of the nervous system. In: Textbook of Child Neurology. Menkes, J.K. (Ed.). Philadelphia: Lea & Febiger. pp. 387–390.

Subarachnoid cysts / arachnoid cysts

Fluid-filled cysts, the walls of which are formed by one of the coverings (*meninges*) of the brain. Such cysts may be caused by infection, bleeding or trauma. Sometimes they are present at birth and no cause is evident (congenital cysts). This type may be associated with other *congenital* abnormalities. Sometimes people with such cysts have no symptoms. When problems do occur the nature and extent will depend on the location and size of the cyst and any associated abnormalities. *Seizures*, headache, mental handicap, unsteadiness and paralysis may all occur and some cysts may cause *hydrocephalus*.

ROBINSON, R.G. (1971) Congenital cysts of the brain: Arachnoid malformations. Prog. Neurol. Surg., 4:133.
STARKMAN, S.P. (1958) Cerebral arachnoid cysts. J. Neuropathol. Exp. Neurol., 17:484.
WARKANY, J. et al (1981) Mental Retardation and Congenital Malformations of the Central Nervous System. Chicago: Year Book Medical Publishers Inc. pp. 256–265.

Subarachnoid haemorrhage

Bleeding beneath the arachnoid membrane which is the middle of the three *meninges* which cover the brain. The *cerebro-spinal fluid* (CSF) usually fills this space. Blood from a ruptured or malformed vessel may destroy brain substance and also passes into the CSF where it acts as an irritant and can cause spasm of blood vessels which may do further damage. Headache, *seizures* and impairment of consciousness usually have an abrupt onset as the haemorrhage occurs. Residual damage is variable.

Subcutaneous

Beneath or under the skin.

Subdural haematoma

A collection of bloody fluid between the two outer membranes (*meninges*) covering the brain. It is a common complication of head injuries especially in infants. It often occurs on both sides of the head and child abuse is one cause which should always be excluded. It also occurs more readily in infants who have an underdeveloped brain. When it has a sudden onset after injury the diagnosis is more obvious but the outcome is poor even after an operation. A more gradual onset may present as personality change, variable impairment of consciousness, headache and later *seizures* and loss of consciousness. In small infants seizures may develop early with vomiting, fever and irritability. The final outcome depends on the extent of the damage to the underlying brain but residual brain damage is common and may cause mental handicap.

MCLAURIN, R.L. & TUTOR, F.T. (1961) Acute subdural haematoma: Review of ninety cases. J. Neurosurg., 18:61.
RAHME, E.S. & GREEN, D. (1961) Chronic subdural haematoma in adolescence and early adulthood. J. Am. Med. Ass., 176:424.
RUSSELL, P. (1965) Subdural haematoma in infancy. Brit. Med. J., 2:446.

Subluxation
Partial dislocation of a joint. This may occur in children with *cerebral palsy* due to tightness of some muscles or it may occur due to abnormalities of bones.

Subnormality / severe subnormality
A term which was used in the U.K. to describe people with a mental handicap. In the *Mental Health Act 1959* severe subnormality was described as 'a state of arrested or incomplete development of mind which includes subnormality of intelligence and is of such a nature or degree that the patient is incapable of living an independent life or of guarding himself against serious exploitation or will be so incapable when of an age to do so'. Subnormality is 'a state of arrested or incomplete development of mind (not amounting to severe subnormality) which includes subnormality of intelligence and is of a nature or degree which requires, or is susceptible to, medical treatment or other special care, training and occupation'. These legalistic definitions are incompatible with current ideas about mental handicap and no longer apply under the *Mental Health Act 1983*. Degrees of subnormality are described under *mental retardation*.

Substitute family care
See *adoption*, *fostering* and *family support scheme*.

Subungual fibroma
A benign fibrous tumour under the nail of a finger or toe. These are often seen in *tuberose sclerosis*.

Successive approximation
See *shaping*.

Sudanophilic leucodystrophy / sudanophilic cerebral sclerosis
A general term for several conditions all of which are characterized by visual and intellectual impairment, *seizures*, *spasticity* and progressive deterioration until death. The most common of these conditions is adrenoleucodystrophy (*Addison-Shilder's disease*) which is accompanied by insufficiency of the adrenal cortex which causes abnormal pigmentation (brownness) of the skin, weakness, low blood pressure, low body temperature, anaemia and loss of salt from the body. The onset of the condition is usually between 5 and 8 years of age with unsteadiness and slight intellectual deterioration. Seizures and attacks of crying and screaming are common. Swallowing is often disturbed and visual problems develop later. Spasticity of the lower limbs occurs. It is inherited as a *sex-linked* condition and female carriers may be very mildly affected. There is no known treatment.

FORSYTH, C.C. et al (1971) Adrenocortical atrophy and diffuse cerebral sclerosis. Arch. Dis. Childh., 46:273.
O'NEILL, B.P. et al (1984) Adrenoleukodystrophy: clinical and biochemical manifestations in carriers. Neurology, 34:798.
SCHAUMBURG, H.H. et al (1975) Adrenoleukodystrophy: a clinical and pathological study of 17 cases. Arch. Neurol., 33:577.

Sulci
The grooves or fissures seen on the surface of the brain.

Sulphatide lipidosis
= *metachromatic leucodystrophy*.

Sulthiame
A drug, previously used for the treatment of *epilepsy* and *behaviour disorders*. Troublesome side-effects and drug interactions led to reconsideration of its use and it is generally no longer available.

Supersensitivity psychosis
A sudden deterioration in behaviour after discontinuation of an anti-psychotic drug. The characteristics of the behaviour are different from the inappropriate behaviour for which the drug was originally prescribed. This may occur following the withdrawal of *phenothiazines*, *butyrophenones* and

thioridazine. A gradual withdrawal followed by 12 to 16 weeks without the drug are required to assess the true effects of drug withdrawal.

BREUNING, S.E. & POLING, A.D. (1982) Drugs and Mental Retardation. Illinois: Charles C. Thomas.

Supplemental Security Income (SSI)

In 1976 an amendment to the Social Security Act in the U.S.A. provides income maintenance payments and automatic eligibility for Medicaid medical benefits to low-income persons with medically documented long-term disabilities. Income and disability must be certified and medical care is available only as part of a comprehensive service plan.

Support care

= *phased care.*

Supportive work

Mentally handicapped people can often be placed in carefully selected jobs, trained in those jobs and, if successful, progress to being independently employed. They may need to be supported by intensive follow-up.

BELLAMY, G.T. et al (1987) Supported Employment. A Community Implementation Guide. Baltimore: Paul H. Brookes.
WEHMAN, P. (1981) Competitive Employment: New Horizons for Severely Disabled Individuals. Baltimore: Paul H. Brookes.
WEHMAN, P. et al (1982) Job placement and follow-up of moderately and severely handicapped individuals after three years. J. Assoc. Severely Handicapped, 7:5–16.

Sutures of the skull

The lines along which the bones of the skull join. These bones are separate at birth but grow together gradually during the first two years of life. In some disorders sutures close too early causing skull deformity as in *craniostenosis.*

Sydney line

A line seen in the palm of the hand. It is formed by the extension of the transverse crease nearest the wrist, to the outside margin of the palm on the side of the little finger. This is of significance in *dermatoglyphics* and may, for example, be present in congenital *rubella syndrome.* It also occurs in some normal people.

Symbolic play

Play which makes reference to previous experiences as shown by words, drawings, imitated actions, gestures, etc. Initially a child tends to depict his own activities in play but then becomes able to pretend the behaviours of others. These skills are thought to be necessary for language development to proceed and can be assessed using the *symbolic play test.*

Symbolic play test

A test standardized on normal children aged 1 to 3 years. It is based on observation of the play behaviour of the child and provides information on the acquisition of 'inner language'. The materials consist of a series of common objects and a series of miniaturized objects.

LOWE & COSTELLO (Actual test kit): Symbolic Play Test: Experimental edition. Windsor, U.K.: NFER-Nelson.

Symbols

Symbol systems may be used as a method of *communication* for people who cannot make themselves understood by speech. Such systems include *Blissymbolics* and *Rebus Reading Symbols.*

JONES, P.R. & CREGAN, A. (1986) Sign and Symbol Communication for Mentally Handicapped People. London: Croom Helm.
LLOYD, L.L. & KARLAN, G. (1984) Non-speech communication symbols and systems. Where have we been and where are we going? J. Ment. Defic. Res., 28:3–20.

Symbrachydactyly

Syndactyly involving the hand and foot.

Symptom

A change or discomfort of the body which is experienced by the person and provides evidence of disease or abnormality.

Syndactyly

Partial or complete fusion of two or more fingers or toes often known as webbing. Usually the fusion is only of skin but sometimes bones as well. It occurs in several conditions associated with mental handicap including *Apert's syndrome, Carpenter's syndrome, Chotzen's syndrome, de Lange syndrome* and, more rarely, in *chromosome* disorders such as *Down's syndrome, Edward's syndrome* and *Patau's syndrome*.

Syndrome

A group of symptoms or signs of disease or abnormality which are noticed to occur together and to which a name has been given. A minor abnormality on its own is not indicative of a syndrome and a particular abnormality may occur in several different syndromes. The number and severity of features may vary between people with the same syndrome and it is not necessary for every feature to be present in order to constitute the syndrome.

Synophris / synophrys

The eyebrows meeting in the midline as occurs in *de Lange syndrome* and often in *Sanfilippo syndrome*.

Synostosis

The fusion together of two bones which are normally separate as may occur in the skull in *craniostenosis*.

Syphilis

A venereal disease which can be passed on to the *fetus* of a pregnant affected female causing *congenital syphilis*. If detected during pregnancy treatment can be given to prevent damage to the baby.

Syringobulbia / syringomelia

The characteristic abnormality in syringomelia consists of cavities filled with fluid and surrounded by nerve tissue, lying near to the centre of the *spinal cord*. The symptoms are usually those of loss of pain and temperature sensation while touch, vibration and position sense are preserved. Sometimes pain may be an early symptom. It may also develop into *spasticity* of limbs. Upward extension of the cavities to involve the lower *brain stem* (syringobulbia) causes the same symptoms on the face, paralysis of the *palate* and *nystagmus*. One of the commonest causes of this condition is *hydrocephalus* caused by obstruction to, or absence of, the holes joining the cavities of the brain to the surface. Syringobulbia and syringomelia may occur in the *Klippel-Feil syndrome, Sturge-Weber syndrome* and *Rieger's syndrome*.

T

Tabes dorsalis
A rare complication of *congenital syphilis*. The first symptoms are often failing vision or incontinence of urine. Squint and abnormalities of the movements of the pupils of the eye are often present. It is caused by damage to nerve tissue in the *spinal cord* and brain. *Juvenile paresis* is the more usual complication of congenital syphilis.

Taboparesis
= *juvenile paresis*.

Talipes
= *club foot*.

Tall stature
Excessive height occurs in a few conditions associated with mental handicap including *Sotos' syndrome*, *Klinefelter's syndrome* and *XXYY syndrome*.

Talpism
= *Rubinstein-Taybi syndrome*.

Tantrum / temper tantrum
A dramatic outburst of crying, kicking, screaming, etc. in response to frustration. This is normal for children of 2 or 3 and may be seen in older children who are mentally handicapped. It is an expression of uncontrolled anger, rage, *aggression* and defiance and an attempt to obtain gratification and to dominate the situation. The child works himself up into a rage in which extremes of behaviour may occur. Tantrums are seen more commonly in the children of overindulgent or inconsistent parents or in mentally handicapped children whose parents are understandably, but unwisely, making too many allowances for immature behaviour. Children with *partial seizures* or *autism* are particularly prone to irritable behaviour and tantrums. Tantrums should be treated calmly and without alarm. It may be possible to intervene early with a face-saving solution but there should never be any question of giving in to the demands. It is best to leave the child alone until he is calm. Attention must be given to alternative outlets and methods of expression for the child and counselling for the family should be available.

Tapeto-retinal degeneration
= *retinal degeneration*.

Tardive dyskinesia
Involuntary movements which particularly occur in the mouth, tongue and jaw muscles. These movements can be controlled to some extent for short periods of time but at rest are almost continuous. They are a troublesome and sometimes persistent side-effect of long-term treatment with some *phenothiazines* and similar drugs. The drugs (*procyclidine*, *benzhexol* and *benztropine*) used to treat other side-effects of the phenothiazines, may exacerbate or precipitate a tardive dyskinesia.

BREUNING, S.E. & POLING, A.D. (1982) Drugs and Mental Retardation. Illinois: Charles C. Thomas.
GLAZER, W.M. et al (1988) Heterogeneity of tardive dyskinesia. Brit. J. Psych., 152: 253–259.
GUALTIERI, C.T. et al (1986) Tardive dyskinesia in young mentally retarded individuals. Arch. Gen. Psychiat., 43(4): 335–340.

Target behaviour
When using *behaviour modification* techniques it is most important to define the aspect of an individual's behaviour which is to be

changed or established by training. This must be described quite specifically to avoid confusion.

Task analysis
The analysis of the task, skill or behaviour required so that it can be taught along a given sequence with clear objectives for each stage. This is one of the techniques used in *special education* and *behaviour modification*.

KLEIN, N.K. et al (1979) Curriculum Analysis and Design for Retarded Learners. Columbus, Ohio: Merrill.

Tay-Sachs disease
The most common of the *gangliosidoses*. It particularly occurs in Jewish families. It is caused by a deficiency of an *enzyme* known as hexosaminidase A. *Sandhoff's disease* is a variant. As a result GM2 gangliosides (lipids) accumulate in the body especially in the brain. Development in infancy is normal but between 3 and 10 months of age listlessness, irritability and sensitivity to noise are usually the first signs. An arrest in intellectual development and loss of acquired abilities then becomes evident. The child is floppy and the characteristic cherry-red spot (*macular degeneration*) is seen on examination of the lining of the eye. There is rapid progression to blindness and loss of all spontaneous movements. *Spasticity* and *epilepsy* develop and there is progressive enlargement of the head. Death by 3 years of age is usual. The condition is inherited from both parents who are carriers (*recessive inheritance*) and the carrier state can be detected. The condition can also be detected in the fetus during pregnancy following *amniocentesis*.

ELLIS, R.B. et al (1973) Prenatal diagnosis of Tay-Sachs disease. Lancet, 2:1144.
KABACK, M. & RIMOIN, D. (1977) Tay-Sachs disease: Screening and Prevention. New York: Alan R. Liss.
MENKES, J.H. (1985) Textbook of Child Neurology. Philadelphia: Lea & Febiger. pp. 60–66.
VOLK, B.W. (Ed.) (1964) Tay-Sachs disease. New York: Grune & Stratton.
VON SPECHT, B.U. et al (1979) Enzyme replacement in Tay-Sachs disease. Neurology, 29:848.

Taybi syndrome
= *oto-palato-digital syndrome*.

Teachers
Teachers in *special education* in the U.K. undertake a 3-year course equivalent to the training for primary school teachers. Before the *Education (Handicapped Children) Act 1970* the staff in Junior Training Centres had a variety of qualifications and skills but were not teachers.

Tegretol
= *carbamazepine*.

Telangiectasia
Abnormally dilated fine blood vessels in the skin causing a web-like or radiating pattern. These are particularly likely to occur in the delicate skin of the face. They are characteristic of the *Louis-Barr syndrome* and also occur in a few other conditions associated with mental handicap such as *Goltz's syndrome* and *Rothmund-Thomson syndrome*.

Telecanthus
This is present when the inner angles of the eyes are abnormally placed giving the effect of widely spaced eyes. This may occur whether or not the distance between the two eyes is increased. It is described in a number of conditions associated with mental handicap.

Temporal lobes
The right and left temporal lobes are situated in the lower region of each side of the brain. Hearing is registered in both temporal lobes but the left lobe contains the centre for understanding language. The temporal lobes also play an important part in memory and learning.

Temporal lobe seizures / epilepsy
= *complex partial seizures*.

Teratogens
Substances which can potentially damage an unborn child through exposure of the pregnant mother. These include alcohol (*fetal alcohol syndrome*), phenytoin (*camptomelic dwarfism*) and radiation.

Terman-Merill Test
= *Stanford-Binet*.

Tetra-X syndrome
= *XXXX syndrome*.

Tetrahydrobiopterin
This is an *enzyme* found widely in the human body and has a key role in the formation of the chemical messengers (neurotransmitters) in the brain. It is particularly deficient in *phenylketonuria* and is also reduced in *Down's syndrome* and *Alzheimer's disease.*

AZIZ, A.A. et al (1982) Tetrahydrobiopterin metabolism in Down's syndrome and in non-Down's syndrome mental retardation. J. Ment. Defic. Res., 26:67–71.
BLAIR, J.A. & LEEMING, R.J. (1984) Tetrahydrobiopterin metabolism, neurological disease and mental retardation. In: Scientific Studies in Mental Retardation. Dobbing, J. et al (Eds.). London: Macmillan Press. pp. 161–171.

Tetralogy of Fallot
= *Fallot's tetralogy*.

Tetraplegia
Paralysis or weakness affecting all four limbs as may occur in *cerebral palsy*.

Thallium poisoning
This is usually caused by the swallowing of thallium-containing pesticides. Large doses are fatal but more moderate poisoning causes hair loss, unsteadiness, drowsiness, *seizures* and nerve damage. About half the survivors have persistent signs of damage to the nervous system, most commonly mental handicap and unsteadiness (*ataxia*).

CAVANAGH, J.B. et al (1974) The effects of thallium salts with particular reference to the nervous system changes. Quart. J. Med., 43:293.

Thenar area
The area of the palm between the thumb and first finger, the patterns of which can be significant in *dermatoglyphics*.

Therapeutic
A description of something which has a healing and beneficial effect.

Therapy
Treatment.

Thioridazine
A tranquillizer of the *phenothiazine* group which is used for the treatment of *schizophrenia* and other major *psychiatric illnesses*. It is also used for anxiety, agitation, restlessness, *hyperactivity*, excitement, violent behaviours and *self-injurious behaviour*. It can be used for children. Side-effects include drowsiness, dry mouth and stuffiness of the nose. Blurring of vision and constipation can also occur. Confusional states and *seizures* can occur on higher doses. Prolonged high dose treatment can cause the deposition of pigment in the *retina* of the eye and impairment of vision. It should be used with caution in people with heart disease, kidney disease, liver disease and *epilepsy*. Blood cells should be checked early in treatment. *Extrapyramidal signs* and *tardive dyskinesia* which are common with other phenothiazines occur much less often with thioridazine. Skin rashes and sensitivity to sunlight are rare. Some studies suggest that it has a beneficial effect on behaviour problems but others show an adverse effect on learning and task performance.

BREUNING, S.E. et al (1983) Effects of thioridazine on the intellectual performance of mentally retarded drug responders and non-responders. Arch. Gen. Psychiat., 40: 309–313.

HEISTAD, G.T. et al (1982) Long term usefulness of thioradazine for institutionalized mentally retarded patients. Am. J. Ment. Defic., 87:243–251.

GUALTIERI, C.T. et al (1982) Corneal and lenticular opacities in mentally retarded young adults treated with thioradazine and chlorpromazine. Am. J. Psychiat., 139: 1178–1180.

WYSOCKI, T. et al (1981) Effects of thioridazine on titrating delayed matching-to-sample performance of mentally retarded adults. Am. J. Ment. Defic., 85:539–547.

Thorax

The chest. It may be abnormal in shape in some conditions associated with mental handicap including *pectus carinatum, pectus excavatum* and *scoliosis*.

Thorazine

= *chlorpromazine*.

Thrombocytopaenia

Reduction in the number of platelets in the blood. The platelets are involved in the clotting of the blood and, if reduced, excessive bleeding and bruising can occur. This is a rare side-effect of *sodium valproate* especially when used in high doses. It also occurs in *osteopetrosis* and a few other conditions associated with mental handicap.

Thumb opposition

= *finger-thumb opposition*.

Thymus

A gland found in the chest above the heart and between the lungs. It is thought to play a part in the immunity of the body to disease. It may be underdeveloped in the *Louis-Barr syndrome, cerebro-hepato-renal syndrome, Fanconi's hypoplastic anaemia, Edward's syndrome* and *Smith-Lemli-Opitz syndrome*.

Thyroid

A gland in the front of the neck which produces thyroxine, an important hormone involved in the *metabolism* of the body. Underactivity of the gland is called *hypothyroidism* and overactivity is called *hyperthyroidism*.

Thyrotoxicosis

= *hyperthyroidism*.

Thyroxine deficiency

= *hypothyroidism*.

Time-out

A *behaviour modification* procedure in which an individual is temporarily deprived of a reward, generally attention from others, in order to reduce the frequency of an inappropriate behaviour. It is more accurately referred to as time-out from positive *reinforcement* and should immediately follow an undesirable behaviour which is positively reinforced by remaining in the situation. It may involve removal of the person or of the reinforcer (e.g. food or attention). The duration of time-out from social events should be several minutes and longer periods of time tend to be counter-productive. Most psychologists recommend starting with shorter periods and increasing if necessary. Release from time-out should preferably follow good behaviour if only for a short period. Time-out procedures are more likely to be effective when combined with *differential reinforcement of other behaviours*. Time-out procedures can easily be misused and should therefore be carefully monitored and recorded.

HOBBS, S.A. & FOREHAND, R. (1977) Important parameters in the use of time-out with children: A re-examination. J. Behav. Ther. Exp. Psychiat., 8:365–370.

KENDALL, P.L. et al (1975) Time-out duration and contrast effects: A systematic evaluation of a successive treatment design. Behav. Ther., 6:609–615.

MACDONOUGH, T.S. & FOREHAND, R.

(1973) Response contingent time-out: Important parameters in behaviour modification with children. J. Behav. Ther. Exp. Psychiat., 4:231–236.

SOLNICK, J.V. et al (1977) Some determinants of reinforcing and punishing effects of time-out. J. Appl. Behav. Anal., 10: 415–424.

WHITE, G.D. et al (1972) Time-out duration and the suppression of deviant behaviour in children. J. Appl. Behav. Anal., 5:111–120.

Tissue culture

See *fibroblast culture*.

Todd's paralysis

A temporary period of paralysis which may follow an epileptic *seizure* especially when it arises from an abnormality (focus) in a motor area of the brain. It may last from a few hours to a day or more.

Tofranil

= *imipramine*.

Toilet-training

A very important set of self-help skills which nearly all mentally handicapped people can master by adult life so long as there is no physical cause for *incontinence*. There are a number of *behaviour modification* approaches and techniques recommended to avoid incontinence including those for nocturnal *enuresis* and for *encopresis*.

AZRIN, N.H. & FOX, R.M. (1971) A rapid method of toilet training the institutionalized retarded. J. Appl. Behav. Anal., 4: 89–99.

DIXON, J. & SMITH, P.S. (1976) The use of a pants alarm in daytime toilet training. Brit. J. Ment. Subn., 42:20–25.

SMITH, P.S. (1979) A comparison of different methods of toilet training the mentally handicapped. Behav. Res. Ther., 17(1): 33–43.

SMITH, P.S. et al (1975) Problems involved in toilet training profoundly mentally handi-

capped adults. Behav. Res. Ther., 15: 301–307.

WILSON, B. (1980) Toilet training. In: Behaviour Modification for the Mentally Handicapped. Yule, W. & Carr, J. (Eds.) London: Croom Helm; Baltimore: University Park Press. pp. 133–150.

Tokens / token economy

Tokens are used in *behaviour modification* programmes as a generalized *reinforcer*. They may be points, stars, coins, etc. They can be used immediately to reinforce a wide variety of behaviours while the reward earned by the tokens may be given later. They are suitable for those mentally handicapped people who can understand the idea of earning tokens and exchanging them later.

AYLLON, J. & AZRIN, N.H. (1968) The Token Economy: A Motivational System for Therapy and Rehabilitation. New York: Appleton-Century-Crofts.

FERNANDEZ, J. (1978) Token economics and other token programmes in the United States. Behav. Psychotherapy, 6:56–69.

GATHERCOLE, C. & CARR, J. (1980) The use of tokens with individuals and groups. In: Behaviour Modification for the Mentally Handicapped. Yule, W. & Carr, J. (Eds.). London: Croom Helm; Baltimore: University Park Press. pp. 48–68.

KAZDIN, A.E. (1977) The Token Economy: A Review and Evaluation. New York: Plenum Press.

KAZDIN, A.E. (1982) The Token Economy: A decade later. J. Appl. Behav. Anal., 15:431–445.

WINKLER, R.C. (1971) The relevance of economic theory and technology of token reinforced systems. Behav. Res. Ther., 9: 81–88.

Tomography

= *CT scan*.

Tone

A term which can be used to refer to the degree of tension and firmness in muscles which is regulated by the brain. It is important in the maintenance of a given position. Change in tone permits movement. When tone is increased (hypertonic), as in the spastic type of *cerebral palsy*, the muscles become tight and relax with difficulty. Lax muscles are described as *hypotonic*.

Tongue thrust

A problem for some people with *cerebral palsy*. When food is placed on the tongue there is a reflex pushing out of the tongue and food. This can be reduced by placing the food in alternate sides of the mouth.

THOMPSON, G.A. (1979) Operant control of pathological tongue thrust in spastic cerebral palsy. J. Appl. Behav. Anal., 12: 325–333.

Tonic neck reflex

A reflex normally seen in young babies between 1 and 6 months of age. If the head is turned to one side, the arm on that side stretches and the other arm bends. If this reflex persists after 6 months of age it is suggestive of the diagnosis of severe *cerebral palsy* and while it persists walking is never likely to be achieved.

CROTHERS, B. & PAINE, R.S. (1959) The Natural History of Cerebral Palsy. Cambridge, Mass.: Harvard University Press.

Tonic seizure

A generalized *seizure* in which the muscles tighten and become stiff. Consciousness is generally lost. It is a type of *myoclonic epilepsy*.

Tonic spasm

See *spasm*.

Tonic stage of seizure

See *grand-mal convulsion*.

Tonic-clonic seizure

= *grand-mal convulsion*.

Topographic brain mapping

The use of computerized analysis of electro-encephalographic activity to produce a map instead of the usual *electroencephalogram* recording. Multiple scalp electrodes are required.

DUFFY, F.H. et al (1979) Brain electrical activity mapping (BEAM). A method for extending the clinical utility of EEG and evoked potential data. Ann. Neurol., 5: 309–321.

METALIS, S.A. (1986) Introduction to topographic brain mapping. Physicians and Computers, 3:12. April.

PETSCHE, H. (1976) Topography of the EEG: Survey and prospects. Clin. Neurol. Neurosurg., 79:15–28.

TORCH

An acronym for the micro-organisms which most commonly infect the fetus in the womb. It stands for *TOxoplasma, Rubella, Cytomegalovirus* and *Herpes simplex*. A TORCH screen is a blood test designed to detect high antibody levels to any of these organisms, which would indicate a recent infection.

Torticollis

Tightness of one or more of the neck muscles causing the head to be held in an abnormal position. The contraction of the muscles may occur as an *extrapyramidal* side-effect of certain drugs.

Total communication

An approach to *communication* which was developed for deaf people. It consists of a combination of amplification (*hearing aid*), spoken language, lip reading and a suitable *sign language*. This approach is recommended even with people of quite limited ability. It provides the maximum opportunity for keeping in touch with the environment.

KOFCHICK, G. & LLOYD, L. (1976) Total communication programming for the severely language impaired: a twenty four hour approach. In: Communication Assessment and Intervention Strategies. Lloyd, L.

(Ed.). Baltimore: University Park Press.
SCHAEFFER, B. et al (1980) Total Communication: A Signed Speech Program for Non-verbal Children. Champaign, Illin.: Research Press.

Touraine's syndrome

= *nail-patella syndrome*.

Tower skull

= *acrocephaly*.

Toxaemia

A complication of pregnancy in which the blood pressure is raised and abnormal fluid retention and swelling occur. Prolonged toxaemia may cause the fetus to be small or to be still-born. It can cause haemorrhage behind the placenta which may damage the fetus and premature labour may occur. The mother may start to convulse (eclampsia) which may further damage the fetus. This disorder therefore puts the baby at risk of death or brain damage.

Toxoplasmosis

Infection with an organism known as toxoplasma gondii which is a common parasite of birds and mammals. Raw meat and cat faeces are common sources of infection. In an adult it causes a very mild infection but if it occurs during the last seven months of pregnancy it can be transmitted to the fetus. A severe infection may be apparent at birth or develop within a few days or weeks. *Seizures*, anaemia and inflammation of the lining of the eye (*choroido-retinitis*) are the usual signs. There may be extensive brain damage, areas of *cerebral calcification* and *hydrocephalus* may develop. The liver and spleen may be enlarged for a few weeks and a skin rash or *jaundice* may be early signs. Mental handicap occurs in 90% and *epilepsy* and *spasticity* are also usual. Impaired sight, deafness and a small head are common. The diagnosis can be made by the use of antibody tests such as the Sabin-Feldman dye test. Levels are high within two weeks of the infection and decline between 2 and 5 years of age. The calcifications seen on the skull X-ray are suggestive of the diagnosis. Treatment with sulphonamides, pyrimethamine and folinic acid should be started as soon as possible and continue for 6 months. Treatment within one month of birth is likely to give a better outcome.

BEATIE, C.P. (1984) Congenital toxoplasmosis. Brit. J. Obstet. Gynaecol. 91: 417–418.
COUVRIER, J. & DESMONTS, G. (1962) Congenital and maternal toxoplasmosis. A review of 300 congenital cases. Dev. Med. Child Neurology, 4:519–530.
FELDMAN, H.A. (1968) Toxoplasmosis. New Engl. J. Med., 279:1370–75, 1431–1437.
WILSON, C.B. et al (1980) Development of adverse sequelae in children born with subclinical congenital toxoplasma infection. Pediatrics, 66:767–774.

Toy libraries

In the U.K. there is an association of Toy Libraries which is registered as a charity. The aims are to assist the development of handicapped children with the best possible toys; to foster the understanding of the *play* needs of handicapped children; to give guidance on the selection of toys and play materials and to work with other interested organizations and professionals. Toy libraries also exist in many other countries.

JONES, E. (1979) Play, toy libraries and adventure playgrounds. In: Modern Management of Mental Handicap. Simon, G.B. (Ed.). Lancaster: MTP Press. pp. 241–247.
WROE, B. (1979) Organizing a Toy Library. A Description of the IMS Toy Library Service. Kidderminster: British Institute of Mental Handicap.

Further information:
Play Matters / Toy Libraries Association, 68 Church Way, London NW1 1LT.

Training centres

= *adult training centres*.

Tranquillizers

Drugs used to calm without making the person drowsy. These are mainly used in the treatment of *psychiatric illnesses* and for severe *behaviour disorders* in people with a mental handicap. The major tranquillizers include the *phenothiazines* and *butyrophenones* and the minor tranquillizers include the *benzodiazepines*.

BREUNING, S.E. & POLING, A.D. (1982) Drugs and Mental Retardation. Illinois: Charles C. Thomas.

Translocation carrier

See *chromosome translocation*.

Translocation of chromosomes

= *chromosome translocation*.

Transverse palmar crease

See *palmar crease*.

Treacher-Collins syndrome

People with this condition have a characteristic facial appearance which is evident at birth. The eyes slant downward from the nose and there is underdevelopment of the cheek bones and lower jaw. The mouth may be large, the corners downturned and the roof high and sometimes cleft (*cleft palate*). In 75% of cases there is a notch in the outer third of the lower eyelid and more rarely a defect (*coloboma*) of the *iris* or *choroid*. Small and abnormal ears are usual and hearing is often impaired. Abnormalities of the heart and of bones have been described. Mental handicap occurs in less than 5% of people with this condition. This condition is inherited from one parent (*dominant inheritance*) and some people are only very mildly affected.

FAZEN, L.E. et al (1967) Mandibulo-facial dysostosis (Treacher-Collins syndrome). Am. J. Dis. Child., 113:405–410.
ROGERS, B.O. (1964) Berry-Treacher Collins syndrome: a review of 200 cases. Brit. J. Plast. Surg., 17:109–137.

Tremor

A shaking, trembling or jerking of muscles. It is often evident in the hands. A tremor may be coarse or fine or may only occur in certain situations e.g. an intention tremor which occurs when attempting a voluntary movement. Tremor may occur as a result of abnormality in the brain as in *parkinsonism* and damage to the *cerebellum*.

Treponema pallidum

The organism which causes *syphilis*.

Trichopoliodystrophy

= *Menkes' syndrome*.

Trichorrhexis nodosa

A condition in which there are swellings along the length of hairs which fracture readily. The hair shows loss of pigment, is dry and grows irregularly. The ends of hairs are frayed and the hair has a tufted appearance. It is found in several disorders but particularly in *argininosuccinic aciduria* and *Pollett's syndrome*.

Tricyclic / tetracyclic antidepressants

A group of drugs, including *amitriptyline*, *imipramine* and *doxepin*, which are used in the treatment of *depression*.

Tridione

= *troxidone*.

Trifluoperazine

A drug mainly used in the treatment of *psychiatric illnesses* such as anxiety and *schizophrenia*. It is a tranquillizer of the *phenothiazine* group of drugs. Side-effects are similar to those of *chlorpromazine*.

Trigeminal cerebral angiomatosis

= *Sturge-Weber syndrome*.

Trigonocephaly

An abnormal skull shape with indentations of the bones on each side of the forehead and a vertical bony ridge which may be seen or felt in the midline of the forehead. The head, when seen from above, appears triangular or egg-shaped and is abnormally wide. It is due to *craniostenosis*. It may be associated with an underdeveloped nose and the eyes may slant upward. Brain defects commonly occur, as may many other *congenital* abnormalities. Mental handicap is usual and varies from mild to profound. Partial *deletion* of the long arm of chromosome 11 and other rare *chromosome* abnormalities have trigonocephaly associated with them.

CASSIDY, S.B. et al (1977) Trigonocephaly and 11q-syndrome. Ann. Genet., 20:67.
CURRARINO, G. & SILVERMAN, F.N. (1960) Orbital hypotelorism, arhinencephaly and trigonocephaly. Radiology, 74:206.
RIEMENSCHNEIDER, P.A. (1957) Trigonocephaly. Radiology, 68:863.

Trimethadione
= *troxidone*.

Triple X syndrome
= *XXX syndrome*.

Trisomy
The presence of an additional *chromosome* to a pair making three as in *Down's syndrome*, *Edward's syndrome* and *Patau's syndrome*. This makes the total chromosome count 47. It is also possible to have *partial trisomies*.

Trisomy 13
= *Patau's syndrome*.

Trisomy 18
= *Edward's syndrome*.

Trisomy 21
= *Down's syndrome*.

Trophoblast culture
The trophoblasts are the cells obtained by *chorion biopsy*. These cells can then be cultured so that tests can be carried out in order to diagnose any suspected abnormalities.

Troxidone
An *anticonvulsant* drug used in the treatment of *absence seizures*. It is liable to serious side-effects including interference with the manufacture of blood cells in the bone marrow. It may also affect the kidneys and the liver. It should be used under strict medical supervision and is not generally available. If a mother takes trimethadione during pregnancy it can damage the developing fetus causing growth deficiency, prominent forehead, short upturned nose with broad, low bridge, eyebrows meeting in the middle, squint, drooping eyelids, *cleft lip /palate*, small jaw, ear defects, abnormalities of the genitals and mental handicap. This is known as fetal trimethadione syndrome.

ZACKAI, E.H. et al (1975) The fetal trimethadione syndrome. J. Paediatr., 87:280.

Tryptizol
= *amitriptyline*.

Tryptophanaemia / tryptophanuria
A very rare condition which is similar to *Hartnup disease*. The level of the *amino acid* tryptophan is high in the blood and urine. Growth is slow and a skin rash develops by 6 months of age. The skin is thickened and excessively pigmented. Unsteadiness and *spasticity* occur. The degree of mental handicap is severe. The nature of the *enzyme* defect and the mode of *inheritance* is not known and there is no known treatment.

Tuberculous meningitis
Meningitis caused by the tubercle organism usually has a very gradual onset. By the time the diagnosis is made considerable brain damage may have taken place leaving 20% of survivors with mental handicap.

Tuberose sclerosis / tuberous sclerosis
A condition in which there is a characteristic skin condition usually in association with mental handicap, *tumours* in body organs and *epilepsy*. The symptoms vary greatly

with respect to age of onset, severity and rate of progression. The degree of mental handicap varies widely and is often associated with *autism* or autistic features. About 30% of people with this condition are of normal intelligence. Sometimes there is normal development for the first few years of life with signs of intellectual deterioration between 8 and 14 years of age. *Seizures* are the most common presenting problem and *infantile spasms* are common during infancy. Later the other forms of epilepsy may occur. The earlier the onset of seizures the greater the likelihood of mental handicap. The severity of the seizures and the response to *anticonvulsants* is unpredictable but there is generally an improvement with age. The characteristic skin rash is known as *adenoma sebaceum*. Areas of depigmentation known as *ash-leaf marks* are also common. Areas of fibrous thickening (fibromata) may occur on the trunk, gums, under the nails and along the hair-line or eyebrows. The *shagreen patch* is another type of skin thickening. *Café-au-lait spots* may also be seen. The tumours are found throughout the body and may be seen on the *retina*. Malignancy may develop in the brain or a tumour may cause an obstruction to give signs of raised *intracranial pressure*. Tumours in the heart may cause heart failure in infancy but are usually harmless. A *CT scan* confirms the diagnosis by showing many scattered calcium deposits especially in the walls of the *cerebral ventricles*. It is usually inherited from one parent who is very mildly affected (*dominant inheritance*) or it arises spontaneously. Treatment is directed to control of the seizures and removal of any troublesome skin or internal tumours.

GOMEZ, M.R. (1979) Tuberous Sclerosis. New York: Raven Press.

KAPP, J.P. et al (1967) Brain tumors with tuberous sclerosis. J. Neurosurg., 26:191.

MAKI, Y. et al (1979) Computed tomography in tuberous sclerosis. Brain Dev., 1:38.

PAMPIGLIONE, G. & MAYNAHAN, E.J. (1976) The tuberous sclerosis syndrome: clinical and EEG studies in 100 children. J. Neurol. Neurosurg. Psychiat., 39:666–673.

ROTH, J.C. & EPSTEIN, C.J. (1971) Infantile spasms and hypopigmented macules: Early manifestations of tuberous sclerosis Arch. Neurol., 25:547.

WARKANY, J. (1981) Tuberous sclerosis. In: Mental Retardation and Congenital Malformations of the Central Nervous System. Chicago: Year Book Medical Publishers. pp. 325–337.

Further information:
Tuberous Sclerosis Association of Great Britain, Secretary Mrs. J. Medcalf, Little Barnsly Farm, Milton Rd., Catshill, Bromsgrove, Worcs. B61 0N9.

Turner's syndrome

A condition caused by the absence of one of the sex *chromosomes* in a girl leaving a single X chromosome. The result is short stature, sexual underdevelopment, a *webbed neck*, right/left disorientation and a defect in perceptual organization leading to underachievement on performance items, such as spatial perception and mathematics, on the standard *intelligence tests*. It is no longer thought to be associated with mental handicap.

WABER, D.P. (1979) Neuropsychological aspects of Turner's syndrome. Dev. Med. Child Neurology, 21:58.

Turrenicephaly / turricephaly
= *acrocephaly*.

Tyrosinosis / tyrosinaemia

Several disorders are characterized by an increase in tyrosine (an *amino acid*) and its derivatives in the blood and urine. It may occur transiently at birth or in infants fed high protein milks when it is probably harmless. Hereditary tyrosinaemia (tyrosinosis, tyrosinaemia Type I) is caused by deficiencies of *enzymes* involved in breaking down tyrosine. The liver, kidneys and growth are affected but there is no damage to the brain or nervous system. There is a rare form of hypertyrosinaemia (tyrosinaemia Type II) in which there is a deficiency of the enzyme tyrosine aminotransferase. This causes mental handicap, small head, clouding of the *cornea* of the eye and thickening of the skin. A diet low in phenylalanine and tyrosine appears to improve the eyes and skin.

ANDERSSON, S. et al (1984) Persistent tyrosinaemia associated with low activity of tyrosine amino-transferase. Paediatr. Res., 18:675.

GOLDSMITH, L.A. (1983) Tyrosinaemia and related disorders. In: The Metabolic Basis of Inherited Disease (5th edit.). Stanbury, J.B. et al (Eds.). New York: McGraw-Hill, p. 87.

U

Ulegyria

A type of brain damage caused by a sudden fall in blood pressure, lack of oxygen and/or swelling of the brain as may occur following a difficult birth in a full-term infant. The damage is often restricted to areas of the brain which are less well supplied with blood vessels and which are particularly active at birth. It is a common abnormality and accounts for about one-third of brain damage caused by disorders of the blood circulation immediately after birth. There is more damage in the inner parts of the folds of the brain (gyri) than on the surface and this can be easily seen at a microscopic level.

FREYTAG, E. & LINDENBURG, R. (1967) Neuropathological findings in patients of a hospital for the mentally deficient: A survey of 359 cases. Johns Hopkins Med. J., 121: 379.
TAKASHIMA, S. et al (1978) Subcortical leukomalacia, relationship to development of the central sulcus and its vascular supply. Arch. Neurol., 35:470.
TOWBIN, A. (1969) Cerebral hypoxic damage in fetus and newborn. Arch. Neurol., 20:35.

Ullrich's disease

A type of *muscular dystrophy* which is associated with normal intelligence.

Ullrich's syndrome

= *Noonan's syndrome*.

Ulna

The larger of the two bones of the forearm. It may be deformed in a few conditions associated with mental handicap including *Rothmund-Thomson syndrome* and *XXX syndrome*.

Ultrasound scanning / ultrasonography

A method of investigation which uses high frequency, low intensity, ultrasonic waves to produce a picture on a television monitor. Tissues and organs vary in the way they transmit and reflect ultrasound and it is this that gives contrast to the images. It can be used to examine the fetus in the pregnant uterus in order to detect anatomical abnormalities or to monitor growth. It can show *meningomyelocoele, anencephaly* and an increasing number of other defects in time for termination of pregnancy (*abortion*). It can also be used to examine the head and brain of an infant up to 6 months of age and, although it does not produce such detailed pictures as a *CT scan*, it is safe, rapid and can be carried out at the bedside. It is particularly useful to show an abnormal collection of fluid or blood in the brain (echoencephalogram).

CAMPBELL, S. & PEARCE, J.M. (1983) Ultrasound visualization of congenital malformations. Brit. Med. Bull., 39:322–331.
LEVENE, M.I. (1984) Paediatric ultrasound. Intracranial scanning in the newborn. Hospital Update, 10(5):417–426.
SAUERBREI, E.E. & COOPERBERG, P.L. (1981) Neonatal brain sonography of congenital anomalies. Am. J. Neonatol. R., 2:125.
SHIELDS, D. & MANGER, M. (1983) Ultrasound evaluation in neonatal intraventricular haemorrhage. Perinat. Neonatol., 7:19.

Umbilical hernia

A protrusion of abdominal contents, usually fat or bowel, through the navel. If it is not covered in skin it is known as *exomphalos*. It occurs in *Beckwith syndrome, Hurler's syndrome, Hunter's syndrome, Patau's syndrome, Edward's*

329

syndrome and *Down's syndrome* all of which are associated with mental handicap.

Unbalanced translocation
See *chromosome translocation*.

Unfit to plead
See *fitness to plead*.

Unilateral
On one side only. A few conditions associated with mental handicap affect only one side of the body.

United Cerebral Palsy Associations
See *cerebral palsy*.

United Nations Declaration on the Rights of Mentally Retarded Persons
This was adopted in 1971 and is based on the principle of *normalization*. In the General Assembly it was totally supported and member states pledged to promote *integration* as far as possible in normal life and in the life of the community. It called for proper legal safeguards against every form of restriction of rights, abuse, exploitation and degrading treatment.

Unverricht's myoclonus epilepsy
A disorder characterized by progressive intellectual deterioration and *myoclonic epilepsy*. The disease usually becomes apparent between 7 and 14 years of age with the onset of *epilepsy* (myoclonic and *grand-mal convulsions*). Myoclonic *seizures* are often triggered by stimulation with light or by concentration on co-ordinated movements. The *electroencephalogram* is usually abnormal. As the disease progresses the myoclonus and intellectual deterioration become more severe and grand-mal convulsions become less frequent. *Spasticity* of limbs develops and death usually occurs within 10 years of diagnosis. The diagnosis is confirmed by finding characteristic abnormal substances (polyglucosans) in biopsies of muscle, sweat glands or liver. Such substances are also deposited in the brain. This disorder is

inherited from both parents who are carriers (*recessive inheritance*).

CARPENTER, S. et al (1981) Sweat gland duct cells in Lafora disease: Diagnosis by skin biopsy. Neurology, 31:1564.
HARRIMAN, D.G.F. & MILLAR, J.H.D. (1955) Progressive familial myoclonic epilepsy in three families: Its clinical features and pathological basis. Brain, 78:325.
JANEWAY, R. et al (1967) Progressive myoclonus epilepsy with Lafora inclusion bodies. Arch. Neurol., 16:565–582.

Urinary
To do with the urine. The urinary tract includes the passages and organs through which urine passes (kidneys, ureters, bladder and urethra). Abnormalities of the urinary tract occur in a few conditions associated with mental handicap.

Urinary amino acid
= *amino aciduria*.

Usher's syndrome
A condition in which deafness is present from birth due to an abnormality of the tissues of the inner ear (*sensori-neural deafness*). Balance is also affected. Deterioration of vision is caused by deposition of pigment in the *retina* of the eye (*retinitis pigmentosa*). About 25% of people with this condition are mentally handicapped. It is inherited from both parents who are carriers (*recessive inheritance*).

HALLGREN, B. (1959) Retinitis pigmentosa combined with congenital deafness, with vestibulo-cerebellar ataxia and mental abnormality. Acta Psychiat. Scand. (Suppl.), 138:1.

Uvea
The area of the eye which includes the *iris* and *choroid*. Inflammation of this area is known as uveitis and may occur in *Bloch-Sulzberger syndrome*.

Uzgiris-Hunt scales

These measure the *sensori-motor* skills of children according to the level of development of concepts. They are based on Piaget's theories of concept development. They cover the range of development from 2 months to 24 months. The seven independent sets of scales are: visual pursuit and permanence of objects, means-ends relationships, vocal imitation, gestural imitation, construction of objects in space, causality and behaviours relating to objects.

ULREY, G. (1982) Assessment of cognitive development during infancy. In: Psychological Assessment of Handicapped Infants and Young Children. Ulrey, G. & Rogers, S.J. (Eds.). New York: Thieme-Stratton.
UZGIRIS, I.C. & HUNT, J.M. (1975) Assessment in Infancy: Ordinal Scales of Psychological Development. Urbana, Illin.: University of Illinois Press.

V

Vaccine

Administration of infectious material which has been rendered harmless in order to stimulate the resistance of the body to that disease.

Vaccine damage / vaccine encephalitis

This usually refers to the inflammation of the brain which can follow vaccination against pertussis (whooping cough). The incidence of this complication is about one in 168,000 vaccinations. The symptoms may occur within minutes or as long as 3 days after vaccination. A generalized convulsion and impairment of consciousness are the usual presentation sometimes with weakness of one side of the body. There is no association with the onset of *infantile spasms*. Most children survive but are left with mental handicap and/or physical handicap and/or *epilepsy*. It is recommended that children who have a history or family history of *seizures* should not have the vaccine and revaccination of children who have reacted badly should be avoided. In the U.K. compensation for a severe disability as a result of vaccination is paid under the vaccine damage payments scheme introduced following the Vaccine Damage Payments Act (1979). It is a one-off, tax-free payment.

BELLMAN, M.H. et al (1983) Infantile spasms and pertussis immunization. Lancet, 1:1031.
MILLER, D.L. et al (1982) Pertussis immunization and serious acute neurological illness in children. Brit. Med. J., 282:1595.
MURPHY, J.V. et al (1984) Recurrent seizures after diphtheria, tetanus and pertussis vaccine immunization. Am. J. Dis. Child., 138:908.
POLLOCK, T.M. et al (1984) Symptoms after primary immunization with DTP and with DT vaccine. Lancet, 2:146.
ROBINSON, R.J. (1981) The whooping-cough immunization controversy. Arch. Dis. Childh., 56:577.

Further information:
Association of Parents of Vaccine Damaged Children, 2 Church St., Shipston-on-Stour, Warwickshire, CV36 4AP.
Leaflet HB3. Payment for people severely disabled by vaccine. From local Social Security Offices or from Vaccine Damage Payment Unit, DHSS, Norcross, Blackpool FY5 3TA.

Vaccine Damage Payments Act (1979)

See *vaccine damage*.

Valgus

Turning outward of part of the body as in talipes valgus which is one type of *club foot*.

Valium

= *diazepam*.

Valproic acid

= *sodium valproate*.

Van Bogaert's disease

= *cerebrotendinous xanthomatosis*.

Varicella

If a woman has chickenpox the infection of the fetus with this virus in the first 19 weeks of pregnancy can cause mental handicap, abnormalities of the eye, *epilepsy*, restricted growth and underdevelopment of limbs, fingers and/or toes.

An *encephalitis* may occur following infection and this can rarely cause permanent brain damage.

JOHNSON, R. & MILBOURN, P.E. (1970) Central nervous system manifestations of chickenpox. Canad. Med. Ass. J., 102:831.
McKENDRY, J.B. & BAILEY, J.D. (1973) Congenital varicella associated with multiple defects. Can. Med. Assoc. J., 108:66.

Varus
Turning inward of part of the body as in talipes varus which is one type of *club foot*.

Ventricle
A small cavity in an organ of the body, such as the ventricles of the heart and the *cerebral ventricles* of the brain.

Ventricular septal defect
A type of *congenital heart disease* in which there is a hole in the heart due to a defect in the wall between the two *ventricles*. This reduces the efficiency of the heart which has to work harder and is under strain. This may lead to heart failure and other complications. Small defects may close spontaneously but most require operative interventions which may involve high risk. This type of congenital heart defect is quite common in *Down's syndrome* and in many other conditions associated with mental handicap.

Venticulogram / venticulography
= *air encephalogram*.

VER
= *visually evoked response*.

Verbal intelligence
Some *intelligence tests* measure verbal intelligence separately from non-verbal *performance skills*. Verbal intelligence depends on the person's ability to understand and use spoken language and, sometimes, written language as well. It is measured as a verbal *intelligence quotient*.

Verbalisms
The use of words without any real understanding of their meaning. Mentally handicapped people may use verbalisms especially if they are also *autistic* or have a severe visual handicap.

Vertebra
A bone of the spine. Deformities of the bones of the spine may occur in a few conditions associated with mental handicap including *atlanto-axial instability* in *Down's syndrome*.

Vibration
Many mentally handicapped people who are profoundly or multiply disabled find vibration very pleasurable. This is particularly noticeable in blind/deaf people. This has led to the use of vibratory pads to deliver *reinforcement* in *behaviour modification* programmes. It may also be used to relax people including those with severe *cerebral palsy*.

Village communities
A type of care for mentally handicapped people which involves *segregation* into large communities which aim to be as self-sufficient as possible and which often have an ideological basis to the way in which they operate. Such communities have been established in the UK by the *Camphill* organization and the *Home Farm Trust*.

Vineland Social Maturity Scale
A scale which assesses the person's ability to look after his or her own practical needs and social achievements. It covers an age range from less than 1 month to more than 25 years. The areas covered are general self-help, eating, dressing, locomotion, occupation, communication, self-direction and socialization. A rating is made on each item using information from a person who knows the client well. A booklet gives, for each item, a series of examples of behaviour that should be present if the skill is to be rated as having been achieved. An overall score can be given as a social age and *social quotient* but

it is generally more useful to look at the pattern of scores so that strengths and weaknesses can be identified. Many of the items depend on understanding and use of language and for this reason some people will score lower on this test than on *intelligence tests* which have more non-language items. Nevertheless, it is a useful way of assessing a person's ability to cope in the real world.

DOLL, E.A. (1953) The Measurement of Social Competence: A Manual for the Vineland Social Maturity Scale. Washington: Educational Test Bureau.
DOLL, E.A. (1965) The Vineland Scale of Social Maturity: Condensed Manual of Directions. Minnesota: American Guidance Service.

Virchow-Seckel Dwarf
= *bird-headed dwarfism.*

Visual acuity
The clarity with which the environment is seen.

Visual defect / visual impairment
Any abnormality of the eyes, nerves from the eyes and/or brain which impairs *visual acuity*. Such problems are quite common in conditions associated with mental handicap. See *blindness.*

Visually evoked response / visually evoked potential
A way of assessing the presence of vision. It is derived by computer analysis of the electrical response of the back of the brain (*occipital lobe*) to a visual stimulus. The use of this technique involves very specific technical skills and experience and it is not, therefore, widely available.

Visuo-motor skills
Skills which involve the use of information from the eyes when carrying out movements. *Hand-eye co-ordination* is one example.

Vitamin B6
= *pryidoxine.*

Vitamin therapy
Treatment with high doses of vitamins has been recommended for people with *Down's syndrome* on the theoretical basis of poor absorption of these vitamins from the foods in which they naturally occur. Other dietary supplements, especially minerals, are often recommended. The evidence for the value of this approach is inconclusive.

BENNETT, F.C. et al (1983) Vitamin and mineral supplementation in Down's syndrome. Pediatrics, 72(5):707–713.
ELLMAN, G. et al (1984) Vitamin-mineral supplement fails to improve I.Q. of mentally retarded young adults. Am. J. Ment. Defic., 88:688–91.
ROLLAND, C.P. & SPIKER, D. (1985) Nutritional treatment for children. In: Current Approaches to Down's Syndrome. Lane, D. & Stratford, B. (Eds.) London: Holt, Rinehart & Winston. pp. 120–130.
WEATHERS, C. (1983) Effects of nutritional supplementation on I.Q. and other variables associated with Down's syndrome. Am. J. Ment. Defic., 88 (2):214–217.

Vocational training
Training organized to prepare people for *employment.* It usually includes skill training, work experience, career education and the relevant social skills.

WEHMAN, P. & McLAUGHLIN, P.J. (1980) Vocational Curriculum for Developmentally Disabled Persons. Baltimore: University Park Press.

Vogt cephalosyndactyly
See *Apert's syndrome.*

Vogt-Spielmeyer disease
= *Batten-Vogt disease.*

Voluntary organizations
Voluntary organizations in the U.K. such as *The Royal Society for Mentally Handicapped*

Children and Adults, National Association for Mental Health and *Spastics Society* are playing an increasingly important role in advocating for mentally handicapped people and in providing services.

RUSSELL, P. (1985) The role of the voluntary organizations. In: Mental Handicap. Craft, M. et al (Eds.). London: Baillière Tindall. pp. 365–372.

Vomiting

Chronic vomiting and *regurgitation* in severely mentally handicapped people may be a psychological problem requiring *behaviour modification*. It may also be due to reflux from the stomach and if investigations show this is the cause then surgery may be indicated.

BYRNE, W.J. et al (1982) Gastro-oesophageal reflux in the severely retarded who vomit: criteria for and results of surgical intervention in 22 patients. Surgery, 91:95–98.

Von Recklinghausen's disease

A condition in which many tumours arise in the body especially in the nerves and under the skin. Pigmentation of the skin (*café-au-lait patches*) or depigmented patches may be evident. Abnormalities of bones, eyes and hearing may be caused by such tumours as may *epilepsy* and/or mental handicap. *CT scans* are recommended at regular intervals to exclude tumours of the brain which may require operative intervention. There is a slight tendency for the tumours to become *malignant* but this is very unusual in childhood. This condition is either inherited from one parent, who may be only very mildly affected (*dominant inheritance*), or it arises spontaneously.

CROWE, F. et al (1956) Clinical, Pathological and Genetic Study of Multiple Neurofibromatosis. Springfield: Charles C. Thomas.

MAKI, Y. et al (1981) Computed tomography in Von Recklinghausen's disease. Child's Brain, 8:452.

RICCARDI, V.M. (1982) The multiple forms of childhood neurofibromatosis. Paediatr. Rev., 3:293.

VSD

= *ventricular septal defect.*

Vulpe Assessment Battery

A comprehensive method of assessing the behaviours of the child, the environment and the relationship of the care givers with the child. It attempts to identify the many aspects of the child's interaction with the world. It covers the development range from birth to 5 years and is designed for 'atypically developing children'. The subscales relating to the child include basic senses and functions, gross and fine motor skills, expressive and receptive language skills, cognitive processes and specific concepts and organizational behaviours. It can be reliably administered by child-care staff to children with various disabilities.

VULPE, S.G. (1977) Vulpe Assessment Battery. Toronto: National Institute on Mental Retardation. Canada.

W

WAIS
= *Weschler Adult Intelligence Scale.*

Walking reflex
A primitive reflex seen in newborn babies which sometimes persists in children with delayed development or brain damage. When the baby is held with the soles of the feet on something solid, the legs bend at the knees and then straighten. It is normally lost by the end of the first month.

Warfarin embryopathy
Warfarin is a drug which is given to stop the blood clotting in someone who is prone to thrombosis. Treatment of a mother with this drug during pregnancy can damage the fetus. Features of the baby may include lack of development of the nose, shortened fingers, underdeveloped nails, deformities of bones, *congenital heart disease, optic atrophy* and severe mental handicap.

KERBER, I.J. et al (1968) Pregnancy in a patient with a prosthetic mitral valve associated with a fetal anomaly attributed to warfarin sodium. J. Am. Med. Ass. 203: 223–25.

Warnock Committee Report (1978) (The Committee of Enquiry into the Education of Handicapped Children and Young People)
In the U.K. this preceded the *Education Act (1981)* which follows the broad framework of the report. The report recommended that the planning of services should be based on the assumption that one in five children at some time in their school career will require some form of special educational provision. *Special education* should be provided in response to *special educational needs* rather than to defined categories of handicap. It was recommended that the term 'learning disabilities' should be used instead of mental handicap. It also recommended a system for recording the needs of children as assessed by a multidisciplinary team and of meeting these needs as much as possible in ordinary schools. There is considerable emphasis on parental involvement. This is now embodied in the procedure of making a Statement of Special Needs under the 1981 Act.

WARNOCK COMMITTEE (1978) Special Educational Needs: Report of the Committee of Enquiry into the Education of Handicapped Children and Young People. Cmnd. 7212. London: HMSO.

Water on the brain
= *hydrocephalus.*

Webbed fingers and/or toes
= *syndactyly.*

Webbed neck
= *neck webbing.*

Werner's syndrome
A condition in which there is premature ageing with *cataracts*, thickening of the arteries and shrinkage and wrinkling of the skin. There is an increased incidence of *diabetes mellitus* and *malignancy*. Half the people with this condition are mentally handicapped. The onset is in the second decade of life and life expectancy is reduced. It is inherited from both parents who are carriers (*recessive inheritance*).

BLAU, J.N. (1962) Werner's syndrome. Proc. Roy. Soc. Med., 55:328.
EPSTEIN, C.J. et al (1966) Werner's syndrome. Medicine, 45:177.

Weschler Adult Intelligence Scale

This *intelligence test* is widely used and has both verbal and performance scales. It has been standardized on a large population of people between 16 and 60 years of age. There are 10 subtests in each part of the scale and reliable *intelligence quotients* can be given overall and separately for verbal and performance skills. The subtests include: information, comprehension, arithmetical reasoning, memory span for digits, similarities, picture arrangement, picture completion, block design, digit symbols, and object assembly. The vocabulary test can be used as an alternative test. The complete battery of tests may be given or, if time is short, the first five. Tables are provided to enable the actual score of each individual test to be changed to be comparable with the scores on the other subtests. From the total 'weighted' score the I.Q. can be read from the tables for the appropriate age group. With this scale it is not possible to give an intelligence quotient of less than 40 and it is less reliable in the lower range. It does not therefore differentiate between the the more severe degrees of mental handicap.

WESCHLER, D. (1955) Weschler Adult Intelligence Scale. New York: The Psychological Corporation.

Weschler Intelligence Scale for Children

This *intelligence test* for children covers an age range from 5 to 15 years 11 months. The types of subtests, the scoring system and the limitations are the same as for the *Weschler Adult Intelligence Scale* except that vocabulary and mazes subtests are included. It was revised in 1974 (known as WISC-R version). It has also been standardized for children with a hearing impairment.

WESCHLER, D. (1974) The Weschler Intelligence Scale for Children – Revised. New York: The Psychological Corporation.

Weschler Pre-School and Primary Scale of Intelligence

This *intelligence test* for children covers an age range from 4 to 6 and a half years. It has been standardized on a British sample of children. The types of subtests, scoring system and limitations are similar to *Weschler Intelligence Scale for Children*.

WESCHLER, D. (1967) Weschler Pre-School and Primary Scale of Intelligence. New York: The Psychological Corporation.
YULE, W. et al (1969) The WPPSI. An empirical evaluation with a British sample. Brit. J. Educ. Psychol., 39:1–13.

Wessex register

A widely used case register format for mentally handicapped clients. The form is designed by the Health Care Evaluation Team, is quick and easy to use but there have been criticisms of low reliability.

KUSHLICK, A. et al (1973) A method of rating behavioural characteristics for use in large scale surveys of mental handicap. Psycholog. Med. 3:466–478.
MAY, A.E. et al (1982) The inter-rater reliability of the Wessex Mental Handicap Register. J. Ment. Defic. Res., 26:121–122.

Western equine encephalitis

This condition is caused by an organism known as Group A arbovirus which occurs in western parts of the U.S.A. It is carried by mosquitoes. Most people have mild infections but babies under 1 year of age may have a high temperature and *seizures*. It is sometimes fatal. Full recovery may occur but some infants are left with *epilepsy*, mental handicap and/or *spasticity*. The younger the child at the time of the infection, the more likely it is that the consequences will be serious.

FINLEY, K.H. et al (1967) Western encephalitis and cerebral ontogenesis. Arch. Neurol., 16:140.
HERZON, H. et al (1957) Sequelae of western equine and other arthropod-borne encephalitides. Neurology, 7:535.

West's syndrome
= *infantile spasms*.

White matter
The white matter of the brain is the part of the brain which is white to the naked eye and which lies beneath the grey surface layer of the *cortex of the brain*. It consists of nerve fibres which inter-connect the various parts of the brain to each other and to the rest of the nervous system.

White Paper – Better Services for the Mentally Handicapped (1971)
This paper recommended a move from hospital-based care to *community care* for mentally handicapped people in the U.K. At that time, half of the severely mentally handicapped population were living in hospital, the majority being adults. It gave indications of the numbers of people involved and the increase in community resources, especially *adult training centre* places, which would be required. It also recommended *phased care* and parent support groups. It represented the start of very different attitudes and approaches toward mentally handicapped people and their care.

DEPARTMENT OF HEALTH AND SOCIAL SECURITY (1971) Better Services for Mentally Handicapped People. Cmnd. 4683. London: HMSO.
DEPARTMENT OF HEALTH AND SOCIAL SECURITY (1980) Review of Better Services: Mental Handicap: Progress, Problems and Priorities. London: HMSO.

Whooping cough
A common infection in childhood which can be very unpleasant but rarely life-threatening in small infants. It can cause *encephalitis*. Vaccination against whooping cough may very rarely cause brain damage. See *vaccine damage*.

LITVAK, A.M. et al (1948) Cerebral complications in pertussis. J. Paediatr., 32:357.

Whooping cough vaccine encephalitis
See *vaccine damage*.

Whorls
A type of pattern of palm prints which can be significant in *dermatoglyphics*.

Wide Range Achievement Test
This is a test of academic skills which is widely used in the U.S.A. It has subtests for reading, spelling and arithmetic. Each subtest has two levels, one for children between 5 and 12 years of age and another from 12 years to adulthood. It can be administered within half an hour.

JASTAK, J.F. & JASTAK, S.R. (1965) The Wide Range Achievement Test (Revised edit.). Wilmington: Guidance Associates of Delaware.

Wildervanck's syndrome
A condition in which a short neck, due to abnormal neck bones (as in *Klippel-Feil syndrome*), is associated with *sensori-neural deafness*, paralysis of one of the nerves to the eye muscles (causing retraction of the eyeball) and absence or delay in the development of speech. Intelligence may vary from normal to severe mental handicap. It is probably inherited from the mother and is lethal to males, being passed on only to females (*sex-linked inheritance*). Life span is normal.

EVERBERG, G. et al (1963) Wildervanck's syndrome, Klippel-Feil syndrome associated with deafness and retraction of the eyeball. Brit. J. Radiol., 36:562.
FRASER, W.I. & MACGILLIVRAY, R.C. (1968) Cervico-oculo-acoustic dysplasia. J. Ment. Defic. Res. 12:322.

William's syndrome
= *infantile hypercalcaemia*.

Wilm's tumour
A *malignant* tumour of the kidneys which is present before birth but not evident until

later. It may occur in the *Beckwith syndrome* and *aniridia-Wilm's tumour syndrome* both of which are associated with mental handicap.

Wilson's disease

A progressive condition caused by an *enzyme* deficiency in the body which interferes with the normal process of dealing with copper absorbed from the diet. As a result there is an abnormally high level of copper in the body, notably in the blood, liver, brain and forming a ring in the iris of the eye (*Kayser-Fleisher ring*). The condition usually becomes evident when *jaundice* or other signs of liver abnormalities develop. Abnormalities of body tone, tremor, indistinct speech, difficulty in swallowing, *extrapyramidal signs* and minor intellectual impairment may develop later. It can become evident in late childhood or in adult life. It is treated by reducing copper in the diet and giving a drug which removes excessive amounts of copper. The earlier the start of treatment the better the outlook. It is inherited from both parents who are carriers (*recessive inheritance*).

ARIMA, M. et al (1977) Prognosis of Wilson's disease in childhood. Eur. J. Pediatr., 126:147.
SCHEINBERG, I.H. & STERNLIEB, I. (1984) Wilson's Disease. Philadelphia: W.B. Saunders.
WALSHE, J.M. (1962) Wilson's disease. Arch. Dis. Childh., 37:253.
WALSHE, J.M. (1983) Hudson Memorial Lecture: Wilson's disease: genetics and biochemistry – their relevance to therapy. J. Inherited Metab. Dis., 6, Suppl. 1:51–58.

WISC / WISC-R

= *Weschler Intelligence Scale for Children.*

Withdrawal dyskinesia

The same as *tardive dyskinesia* but it occurs when a drug is withdrawn and usually disappears within twelve to sixteen weeks of discontinuation.

BREUNING, S.E. & POLING, A.D. (Eds.) (1982) Drugs and Mental Retardation. Illinois: Charles C. Thomas.
BREUNING, S.E. et al (1982) Effects of thioridazine and withdrawal dyskinesias on workshop performance of mentally retarded young adults. Am. J. Psychiat., 139: 1447–1454.

Wolf's syndrome / Wolf-Hirschhorn syndrome

This condition is caused by the absence of part of one of the short arms of the fourth pair of chromosomes. It is associated with severe mental handicap, *seizures* and a characteristic facial appearance. The eyes are set widely apart, there are marked *epicanthic folds*, a squint is usual and the nose is rather broad and beaked in shape. The corners of the mouth turn downward, the upper lip is short, the jaw is small and *cleft palate / lip* often occurs. The ears are low-set and simple in shape. Growth is slow, stature small and the limbs floppy. Several other abnormalities have been described throughout the body. Death in infancy or childhood is usual.

CENTERWALL, W.B. et al (1975) Translocation 4p syndrome. A general review. Am. J. Dis. Child., 129:136.
GUTHRIE, R.D. et al (1971) The 4p syndrome. A clinically recognisable chromosomal deletion syndrome. Am. J. Dis. Child., 122:421.
MILLER, O.J. (1970) Partial deletion of the short arm of chromosome No 4 (4p-): Clinical studies in five unrelated patients. J. Paediatr., 77:792.
WILSON, M.G. et al (1981) Genetic and clinical studies in 13 patients with the Wolf-Hirschhorn syndrome. Hum. Genet., 59: 297–307.

Wolman's disease

This condition manifests itself in a way which is similar to *Niemann-Pick disease*. The person has mental handicap and enlargement of the liver and spleen. Abnormal yellow materials (sudanophilic granules) are stored especially in the nervous system and there is an excess of certain fats (lipids) in the liver, spleen, adrenal glands, intestine and lymph nodes. This is due to deficiency of an *enzyme* (acid lipase). It is inherited from both parents who are carriers (*recessive inheritance*). It can be detected during pregnancy following *amniocentesis*.

ETO, Y. & KITAGAWA, T. (1970) Wolman's disease with hypolipoproteinaemia and acanthocytosis: Clinical and biochemical observations. J. Pediatr., 77:862.
WOLMAN, M. (1968) Involvement of nervous tissue in primary familial xanthomatosis with adrenal calcification. Pathol. Eur., 3:259.

Wood's lamp
A lamp used for examination of the skin under ultraviolet light. This makes it possible to see defects of pigmentation as may occur in *tuberose sclerosis*.

Word blindness
= *dyslexia*.

Work
= *employment*.

Workshops
A practical and structured way of teaching skills. Parent workshops are often used to establish a partnership between parents and professionals and to help parents develop and maintain the skills necessary to teach their child and to facilitate his or her development. See also *sheltered workshops*.

ATTWOOD, T. (1978) Priory Parents Workshop. Parent's Voice, 28(1): 12–15.
CUNNINGHAM, C. & JEFFREE, D.M. (1975) The organization and structure of workshops for parents of mentally handicapped children. Bull. Brit. Psychol. Soc., 28: 405–411.
FIRTH, H. (1982) The effectiveness of parent workshops in a mental handicap service. Child: Care, Health & Development, 8:77–91.
PUGH, G. (1981) Parents as Partners. London: National Children's Bureau.

Work stations
A means of training mentally handicapped people using the actual work setting as the training area. Once trained the person is then employed but still monitored and supported by the trainer. Several employees may be supervised by one person.

WEHMAN, P. (1981) Competitive Employment: New Horizons for Severely Disabled Individuals. Baltimore: Paul H. Brookes.
WEHMAN, P. et al (1982) Job placement and follow-up of moderately and severely handicapped individuals after three years. J. Assoc. Severely Handicapped, 7:5–16.

World Health Organization Classification of Mental Handicap
See *mental retardation*.

WPSSI
= *Weschler Pre-School and Primary Scale of Intelligence*.

Wyburn-Mason syndrome
A condition in which there are abnormalities of blood vessels in the brain, on the face and on the *retina* of the eye. Symptoms may develop from early childhood to adolescence and may be quite sudden in onset. There may be blindness or other abnormalities of the eye and vision and paralysis of one side of the body. A birthmark or small webs of blood vessels may be evident on the face and mental handicap is common.

WYBURN-MASON, R. (1943) Arteriovenous aneurysm of mid-brain and retina, facial naevi and mental changes. Brain, 66:163.

X

X chromosome
See *chromosomes*.

X-linked disorders
= *sex-linked inheritance*.

X-linked hydrocephalus / X-linked aqueductal stenosis
A form of *hydrocephalus* caused by narrowing or absence of the opening from the *cerebral ventricles* to the outside of the brain. It is inherited from the mother by a *sex-linked inheritance* transmitted on the X-chromosome and only affecting males. Head enlargement is often present at birth. Abnormally bent thumbs have been described. Treatment is with use of a *shunt* to relieve the pressure but if already severe at birth the outcome is likely to be poor. Other abnormalities of the brain are often present. *Spasticity* is common and is most marked in the lower limbs. Abnormalities of the kidneys have also been described. Most affected infants are stillborn and if treatment is unsuccessful severe mental handicap and reduced life expectancy is usual.

EDWARDS, J.H. (1961) The syndrome of sex-linked hydrocephalus. Arch. Dis. Childh., 36:486.
EDWARDS, J.H. et al (1961) Sex-linked hydrocephalus: report of a family with 15 affected members. Arch. Dis. Childh., 36: 481–485.
SOVIK, O. et al (1977) X-linked aqueductal stenosis. Clin. Genet., 11:416.
WARREN, M. et al (1963) Sex-linked hydrocephalus with aqueductal stenosis. J. Pediatr., 63:1104–1110.

X-linked ichthyosis
In this condition there is mental handicap, thickening and scaliness of the skin (*ichthy-osis*) and underdeveloped testes. This has only been described in men and it is therefore assumed that this syndrome is inherited from the mother as a *sex-linked* recessive condition.

HOLMES, L.B. et al (1972) Mental Retardation. New York: Macmillan. pp. 378–379.

X-linked inheritance
= *sex-linked inheritance*.

X-linked non-specific mental retardation
= *fragile-X syndrome*.

Xanthoma / xanthelasma
Flat areas of yellow pigmentation on the skin as may occur in *Niemann-Pick disease* and *cerebrotendinous xanthomatosis*.

Xeroderma pigmentosum
A condition in which exposure of the skin to light causes redness, pigmentation and thinning with some thickened areas. Premature ageing of the skin and the development of *malignant* tumours of the skin also occurs. The person experiences discomfort of the eyes in bright light and later may develop inflammation of the *retina* and ulceration of the *cornea* of the eye. The skin is normal at birth but redness of areas exposed to sunlight becomes evident before the second or third year. It is followed by dryness, scaling and freckling of the exposed skin. Death usually occurs by the third decade from malignancy or from susceptibility to infections. Xeroderma pigmentosum is sometimes associated with mental handicap, *restricted growth*, underdevelopment of the testes or ovaries, *sensorineural deafness*, *spasticity*, *seizures* and a small head. This is known as the De Sanctis-

Cacchione syndrome. Most forms are inherited from both parents who are carriers (*recessive inheritance*) but there is a very mild form which may have a different mode of inheritance. Treatment is by avoidance of sunlight and surgery or radiotherapy for malignancies.

REED, W.B. et al (1965) Xeroderma pigmentosum with neurological complications. Am. Med. Ass. Arch. Dermatol. (Chicago), 91:224–226.

REED, W.B. et al (1969) Xeroderma pigmentosum. Clinical and laboratory investigation of its basic defect. J. Am. Med. Ass., 207:2073–2079.

REGAN, J.D. et al (1971) Xeroderma pigmentosum: a rapid sensitive method for prenatal diagnosis. Science 174:147–150.

XO syndrome

= *Turner's syndrome.*

XXX syndrome

Women with one extra X *chromosome* are usually of normal appearance, may be of normal intelligence or only mildly mentally handicapped and are likely to be fertile. They may have some of the characteristics described in the *XXXX syndrome.*

BARR, M.L. et al (1969) The triplo-X female. Canad. Med. Assoc. J., 101:247.

PENNINGTON, B. et al (1980) Language and cognitive development in 47 XXX females followed since birth. Behav. Genet., 10:31.

XXXX syndrome / 48,XXXX

Women with two extra X *chromosomes* are usually mildly mentally handicapped and may have a slightly unusual facial appearance with wide-set eyes (*hypertelorism*) or with some similarities to *Down's syndrome*. Fusion of the bones in the forearm, *congenital dislocation of the hips*, incurving of the fifth finger and several other congenital abnormalities have been reported in women with this condition. *Menstruation* may be irregular or normal and fertility has been described.

BERG, J.M. et al (1988) Twenty-six years later: a woman with tetra-X chromosomes. J. Ment. Defic. Res., 32:67–74.

DICAGNO, L. & FRANCESCHINI, P. (1968) Feeblemindedness and XXXX karyotype. J. Ment. Defic. Res., 12:226–236.

LEONARD, M.F. et al (1974) Early development of children with abnormalities of the sex chromosomes: A prospective study. Pediatrics, 54:208.

XXXXX syndrome / 49,XXXXX

The presence of three extra X *chromosomes* in a woman is very rare. It causes severe mental handicap and a characteristic facial appearance with widely spaced eyes (*hypertelorism*), upward slant to the eyes and folds of skin at the inner angle of the eye (*epicanthic folds*). Abnormalities of bones including *club foot*, short neck, *scoliosis* and overlapping toes are common and *congenital heart disease* has been described. Sexual development and fertility are reduced.

BRODY, J. et al (1967) A female child with five X chromosomes. J. Pediatr., 70: 105–109.

YAMADA, Y. & NERIISHI, S. (1971) Penta X chromosome constitution: a case report. Jap. J. Hum. Genet., 16:15–21.

XXXXY syndrome / 49,XXXXY

In this condition there are three extra X *chromosomes* and affected men are usually severely mentally handicapped and *epileptic*. The head may be small and/or an usual shape and the eyes are widely spaced and slant upward. *Epicanthic folds* and a squint are often present. The nose is broad and flat and the lower jaw may protrude a little. The ears are low-set. A short, broad neck and spinal curvature are common. The genitals are underdeveloped and infertility is usual. Abnormalities of bones are common and height is below average. In infancy the baby is very floppy and feeding problems and slow weight gain are common. Survival into adult life is usual.

SCHERZ, R.G. & ROECKEL, I.E. (1963) The

XXXXY syndrome. A report of a case and review of the literature. J. Pediatr., 63: 1093–1098.

SHAPIRO, L.R. et al (1971) Deceleration of intellectual development in a XXXXY child. Am. J. Dis. Child., 122:163–164.

XXXY syndrome / 48,XXXY

Men with this condition have two extra X *chromosomes* and have similar features to the *XXXXY syndrome* but are usually more mildly affected. Height is in the normal range and mental handicap is generally mild. Mild breast enlargement is common after puberty.

FERGUSON-SMITH, M.A. et al (1960) Primary amentia and micro-orchidism associated with an XXXY sex chromosome constitution. Lancet, 2:184–187.

MCGANN, B.R. et al (1970) XXXY chromosomal abnormality in a child. Calif. Med., 112:30–32.

XXY syndrome

= *Klinefelter's syndrome.*

XXYY syndrome / 48,XXYY

Men with this condition have an extra X- and an extra Y-*chromosome* and are usually mildly to severely mentally handicapped. *Neck webbing*, breast enlargement and reduced facial hair is usual. The testes are small. There is a tendency to have varicose veins. Many men with this condition are excessively tall and a few have been reported to have had aggressive or bizarre behaviour.

BORGAONKAR, D.S. et al (1970) Do the 48,XXYY males have a characteristic phenotype? Clin. Genet., 1:272–293.

PARKER, C.E. et al (1970) The 48,XXYY syndrome. Am. J. Med., 48:777–781.

XYY syndrome

This is a common *chromosome* abnormality in which there is an extra Y chromosome. It has been associated with unusually tall stature and dull normal intelligence with delayed speech and some learning problems. Minor abnormalities of the nervous system have also been detected on neurological examination. The idea that it was associated with criminal behaviour derived from its high rate of detection in surveys of prisons and secure hospitals before the rate in the general population was known. This became very controversial but more recent studies have confirmed a tendency to impulsive behaviours, temper outbursts and problems in dealing with aggression. Any association with mental handicap is slight.

CLARKE, D.F. & JOHNSTON, A.W. (1974) XYY individuals in a special school. Brit. J. Psychiat., 125:390–396.

DALY, R.F. (1969) Neurological abnormalities in XYY males. Nature, 221:472.

HOOK, E.B. (1973) Behavioural implications of the XYY genotype. Science, 179:139–350.

MONEY, J. et al (1974) Cytogenetics, hormones and behaviour disability: Comparison of XYY syndromes. Clin. Genet., 6:370.

NOEL, B. et al (1974) The XYY syndrome: reality or myth? Clin. Genet., 5:387–394.

XYYY syndrome

This condition is similar to the *XYY syndrome* but with a stronger association with mild mental handicap.

TOWNES, P.L. et al (1965) A patient with 48 chromosomes (XYYY). Lancet, 1:1041.

Y

Y chromosome

See *chromosome*.

Y chromosome enlargement

It is thought that enlargement of the Y *chromosome* in men may be associated with some, or all, of the traits found in *XYY syndrome*.

Z

Zarontin
= *ethosuximide*.

Zellweger's syndrome
= *cerebro-hepato-renal syndrome*.

Zinsser-Engman-Cole syndrome
A very rare condition in which the skin becomes thickened and pigmented and the nails are shed some time after 5 years of age. The skin may also be reddened and small areas of fine blood vessels (*telangiectasia*) may appear. The hair is sparse and the teeth irregular. White patches and ulceration of the tongue and lining of the mouth may lead to *malignancy*. The eyes may become affected. The bone marrow frequently reduces or stops producing blood cells and this (or malignancy) leads to death in childhood or early adult life. It is sometimes associated with mental handicap and delays in physical development including shrinkage of the testes. It nearly always occurs in males and is therefore thought to be caused by sex-linked inheritance.

BRYAN, H.G. & NIXON, R.K. (1965) Dyskeratosis congenita and familial pancytopenia. J. Am. Med. Ass., 192:203.
HOLMES, L.B. et al (1972) Mental Retardation. New York. Macmillan, p. 228.

Zuclopenthixol
One of the phenothiazine group of drugs. It can be given by mouth or by long-acting injection (*clopenthixol decanoate*). It is used in the treatment of *schizophrenia*. It is also used in the management of aggressive and disruptive behaviour in mentally handicapped people. It is reported to have a calming effect. Side-effects are the same as those reported for other *phenothiazines*.

MLELE, T.J.J. & WILEY, Y.U. (1986) Clopenthixol decanoate in the management of aggressive mentally handicapped patients. Brit. J. Psychiat., 149:373–376.

Zygodactyly
Webbing of two fingers or toes, usually the third and fourth. This may rarely be seen in those conditions associated with *syndactyly*.